SPIRIT AND ART

SPIRIT AND ART

PICTURES OF THE TRANSFORMATION OF CONSCIOUSNESS

by Van James

ANTHROPOSOPHIC PRESS

Published by Anthroposophic Press

Library of Congress
Cataloging-in-Publication Data

James, Van, 1949–.
Spirit and art: pictures of the transformation of consciousness /
by
Van James.
p. cm.
ISBN 0-88010-497-X
1. Art and religion. 2. Consciousness in art. 3. Art. I. Title.
N72.R4 J36 2001
704.9'48'09—dc21

2001002111
Printed in the United States of America

Design: Martin Moskof
10 9 8 7 6 5 4 3 2

TABLE OF CONTENTS

PART TWO

To my teachers:

John Davy, William Mann, and Gerard Wagner

Acknowledgments

I wish to thank the following people for their help and support with various stages of this book's production: David Adams, Christopher Bamford, Judy Blatchford, Deborah Brandow, Caroline Chanter, Michael Dobson, Phyl Dwyer, Gitta Gerhold, Paul Gierlach, Ursula Held, Janet Hicks, Kathee Hoover, Michael Howard, Tom Jacobs, Ilja Karenovics, Horst Kornberger, Michael Lipson, Robert Littman, Hans-Joachim Mattke, Cindy A. Pavlinac, Metta Pratt-Bosley, Duane Preble, Michael Preston, Joseph Proskauer, Uta Raschke, Penny Roberts, Melisande Rodenacker, Genie Sakaguchi, William Scherer, Mary Settegast, Richard Smoley, Barbara Stephan, Patrick Stolfo, Thorwald Thiersch, Heidi Violand, Elizabeth Wagner, Fumiko Wellington, and Arthur Zajonc.

Thanks to the Artists Rights Society, Art Resouce, The Chagall Estate, Verlag am Goetheanum, Rudolf Steiner Nachverlassenverwaltung, National Gallery of Art (Washington, D.C.), Honolulu Academy of Arts, Musée Guimet, and the National Gallery of Canada for permission for the use of images. (Every effort has been made to secure rights for images used in this book. Please pardon any omissions.)

I would also like to acknowledge the Future Value Fund for their financial support during the writing of the manuscript as well as the faculty of the Honolulu Waldorf High School for its patience with me during the years of assembling materials.

I especially wish to thank M.E. James and George and Dorothy Mason for their generous support, which has made possible the inclusion of color plates.

Most of all I wish to acknowledge my wife, Bonnie Ozaki-James, for her unending encouragement and advice, without which this work would not have been possible.

INTRODUCTION

The Spiritual in Art

Art does not represent the visible, it makes visible.
—Paul Klee

As an art student in the late 1960s, I recall how painfully dry and intellectual my art history classes were. I thought, or rather *felt*: "There must be something more than this, something deeper than the lifeless mechanics of a picture and the leaden concepts of a detached, onlooker consciousness." Most art history books seemed to be content with the strictly "surface" aspects of art—names, dates, and styles—and sidestepped any deeper meanings or spiritual significance to art. However, the works themselves spoke a language that I did not always understand but nevertheless heard as a gentle whisper. It is this language I wish to address here—what I now understand to be the language of the spirit in art.

We all have a notion of what the spiritual is, but it is rather difficult to articulate without seeming academic and formal on the one hand or sentimental and wishy-washy on the other. Roger Lipsey, in *An Art of Our Own: The Spiritual in Twentieth Century Art,* suggests that the spiritual is a "transient experience of intensity, of a larger world and larger self."[1] Without fixing too rigid a definition or leaving the question entirely unanswered, I propose one starting point for understanding the spiritual in relation to art to be the creative impulse from which artworks are born. It is this active principle in the human being—the artist—that kindles an image, form, word, sound, or gesture in order that something new may come into being. To this way of thinking, the arts are a bridge between our perception of the visible and our experience of the invisible. Paul Brunton says of the visual arts, "When they fulfill their highest mission, painting and sculpture try to make visible the invisible, unimaginable mystery of pure Spirit."[2]

Spirit in art is most apparent in sacred or religious art. Historically, the establishment of religion is the first indication of a falling away from direct spiritual revelation or what Owen Barfield calls "original participation," for it is an acknowledgment or remembrance of the divine from outside. This remembering, this religion, in all its marvelous and unusual manifestations is represented and made visible by means of art—songs, chants, dances, dramas, costumes, gestures, images, and buildings—all of which unite as sense impressions and raise one to an experience beyond the purely sensible. This is the magic of art and the power of the spiritual. As Mircea Eliade noted, "Sacred art seeks to represent the invisible by means of the visible."[3]

Sacred arts, when not carried out by the individual shaman, are usually utilized by initiates at sacred sites called mystery centers. Among the most notable mystery places are those of ancient Greece. Celebrations took place at such sites as Delphi, Eleusis, and Samothrace, where ritual proceedings occurred in close connection with the rhythms of nature and the movements of the stars and planets. Mystery places sought to awaken the human being to an experience of the spirit in the cosmos and to develop faculties of soul lying dormant within the individual. Most early civilizations appear to have had such mysteries—ritual services, sacred enactments, and various forms of cultus designed to confront men and women with the spiritual reality of their being and the universal processes of life, death, and transformation.4 According to mystery traditions, the training of initiates was necessary so that human beings, by example and by degree, might gradually find their true potential as co-creators of the universe. An initiate is one who "begins," or has initiative for spiritual practice, spiritual creativity.

Fragments of these mysteries are discussed to some extent in ancient manuscripts, and aspects of them still exist within the ritual practices of indigenous peoples today. However, these rites have always been guarded from

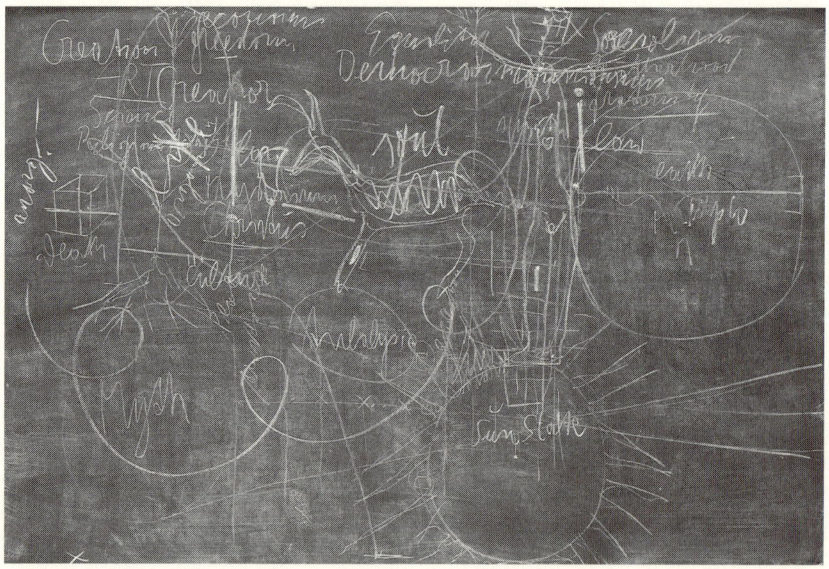

Fig. 1. Blackboard drawing by Joseph Beuys, *The Sun State,* 1974, chalk on slate. (Museum of Modern Art, New York.)

the uninitiated, often under pain of death, and are therefore sketchy at best. What is more, our present-day orientation toward external issues generally helps us avoid entertaining the idea of mysteries, initiates, and spiritual realities. Some scholars dispute the very existence of the mysteries, while others acknowledge only their late manifestation. In some circles, the term "spiritual" is frowned upon even in connection with the arts. Nevertheless physical evidence of esoteric practices can be found in ancient architecture, archaic sculpture, and prehistoric painting, as well as in other art forms throughout the ages and across the globe. In fact the history of art is nothing less than a description of the spiritual development of humanity in the form of a pictorial record. Walter Otto points out: "The many and different creations which we call the arts were formerly much closer to *cultus,* in fact, belonged to its own particular province. . . . From the arts, we can still observe how they freed themselves [over the course of history] from their connection with *cultus* and [eventually] became secular. They were [in earlier times] unquestionably called into life by a more powerful, a more deeply experienced afflatus of the miraculous, whose presence is attested to by the emotions of ecstasy and grace even today when the arts seem to have a completely independent existence."[5]

What is this rich tableau of human culture that we call the history of art? Is it not a picture of the transformation of humanity, the family album of the evolution of human consciousness?

What follows is an attempt to explore not only the spiritual continuity of art throughout history but also how it mirrors developments in human consciousness. This story does not begin where most art histories start—at the so-called beginning—but it starts where we are and remembers, step by step, how we arrived at this place we are now.

While pains have been taken to ensure accuracy in the present work, it is best taken as an artistic exploration of images and ideas rather than as a strictly scholarly study. Although short, quick brushstrokes are often used to describe long periods of time and vast distances of space, an impression is all that is intended here—as in a charcoal sketch or watercolor study. The reader is encouraged to view the sometimes foreign and perhaps unusual ideas presented in the following pages as one might view a painting or a sculpture. In looking at an installation by Joseph Beuys (fig. 1)[6] an altar painting by Hieronymus Bosch (fig. 2),[7] or a cave drawing by a Paleolithic artist (fig. 3), one quite naturally suspends disbelief in the unfamiliar and often bizarre images in order to let the artistic message be felt. Here too the reader is invited to withhold immediate judgment and to look upon this work with active openness of mind in order that perhaps in some small way the spiritual language of art, in its wonder and mystery, might whisper from these pages. As

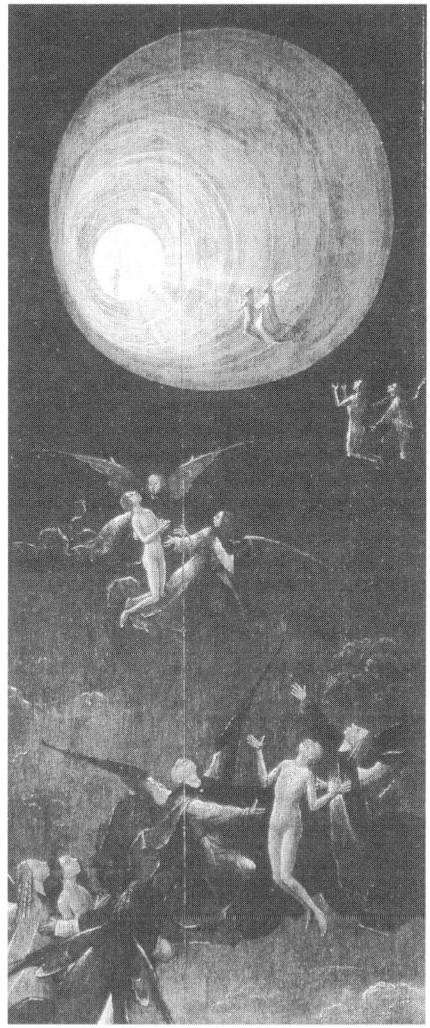

Fig. 2. Hieronymus Bosch depicts the passage of the human soul across the threshold, through the tunnel of death, and toward the light, in the *Ascent to the Empyrean,* part of the Venice Afterworld panel.

Albert Einstein once remarked: "The most beautiful thing we can experience is the mysterious. It is the source of all true art and science."

In discussing the nature of spirit in art, I have attempted to cite from numerous and varied recognized sources from Campbell, Eliade, and Jung to the artists themselves. However, it will become noticeable that I have repeatedly drawn upon the work of the Austrian philosopher and visionary Rudolf Steiner and given it an entire subchapter and appendix. This was not intended at the outset of this work but only gradually became necessary as the theme of spirit in art and the transformation of humanity found its form as a book. Even though the reader may be unfamiliar with this historic figure, it is hoped that his prominence within these pages will be seen as entirely appropriate to the subject at hand.

Notes

1. Lipsey, R. *An Art of Our Own: The Spiritual in Twentieth Century Art,* p.16.
2. Brunton, Paul. *The Notebooks: Human Experience, the Arts in Culture,* p.21.
3. Eliade, M. "Divinities: Art and the Divine," *Symbolism, the Sacred, and the Arts,* p.55.
4. "All actions which flow from and are determined by religious experiences are to be regarded as practiced expressions of cultus. In a narrower sense, however, we call cultus the act or acts of the homo religiosus: worship." J. Wach, *Sociology of Religion.* Cited in Otto, W. *Dionysus: Myth and Cult,* p. 4.
5. Otto, W. p. 26–27.
6. Joseph Beuys (1921–1986) was a controversial professor of sculpture and German *avant-garde* performance artist, influenced by the ideas of Rudolf Steiner's Anthroposophy.
7. Hieronymus Bosch (c. 1453–1516), also known as Jeroen van Aeken, a Dutch allegorical painter from the village of Hertogenbosch, Holland. He was a member of the Christian brotherhood known as the Brethren of the Common Life. Recent research has linked him with the Cathar and Manichean movement, and his paintings were admired by the twentieth-century Surrealist movement.

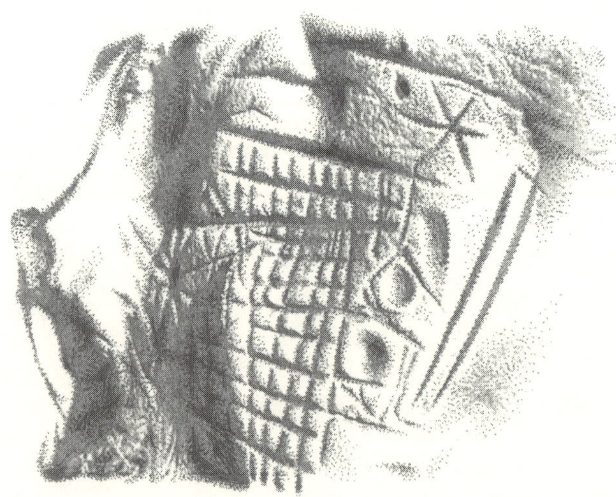

Fig. 3. Prehistoric markings from a cave site in France depict a visual language of form and pattern that we have long since forgotten how to read.

PART ONE

FROM WEST TO EAST

The history of art is structurally parallel with the developmental history of individual human beings like you and me.

—ARTHUR C. DANTO

Let there be fired from the East
What through the West is formed.

—RUDOLF STEINER

We form not only the object of our activity, but also ourselves.

—HERBERT WITZENMANN

I. ECHOES OF ANCIENT MYSTERIES

Methinks hereafter in some later spring
Echo will bear to men the songs we sing
—Sappho

The artist's first visit to America was a performance piece, an *aktion.* He arrived at Kennedy Airport in New York City, was wrapped in felt, laid on a stretcher, and transported by ambulance to the René Block Gallery in Manhattan. He stayed for the next three days in a caged section of the gallery with a coyote. While symbolically wearing brown gloves, carrying a flashlight, and walking with a cane, he arranged strips of felt and stacked copies of the latest issue of *The Wall Street Journal* into two piles. This was all by way of developing a relationship with the coyote. The artist wrapped himself in felt, a material that had saved his life as a young pilot following a plane crash during World War II, and talked to the coyote, encouraging it to tear the felt. The coyote eventually curled up on the felt and the artist lay down on the coyote's straw. The artist occasionally struck a triangle that he wore suspended around his neck and recorded sounds of turbines played in the background. On the third day the artist and coyote were used to each other. The artist gently embraced the coyote, said goodbye, and scattered straw throughout the gallery. Once again he was wrapped in felt, put on a stretcher, and delivered back to the airport by ambulance. The artist left New York having seen nothing of America apart from the enclosed gallery space with the coyote.

The artist is sculptor Joseph Beuys, and the piece, performed in 1974, is *I Like America and America Likes Me* (fig. 4). Beuys, who is often described in such terms as urban shaman, artistic medicine man, modern alchemist and avant-garde guru, used the coyote as the central figure in his portrayal of the "American trauma with the Indian, the Red Man."[1] This animal, which modern society considers a cunning pest, was once a divine figure, an angel, according to Beuys. In the Pueblo Indian tradition, the coyote is the archetypal Trickster, the creative spark or initiator for many of the significant world events and happenings. Coyote causes mischief that results in

Fig. 4. Facing page: *I Like America and America Likes Me,* 1974, is an *aktion* or performance piece by Joseph Beuys, for which he spent three days and nights caged with a coyote at the René Block Gallery in New York City. (After Beuys.)

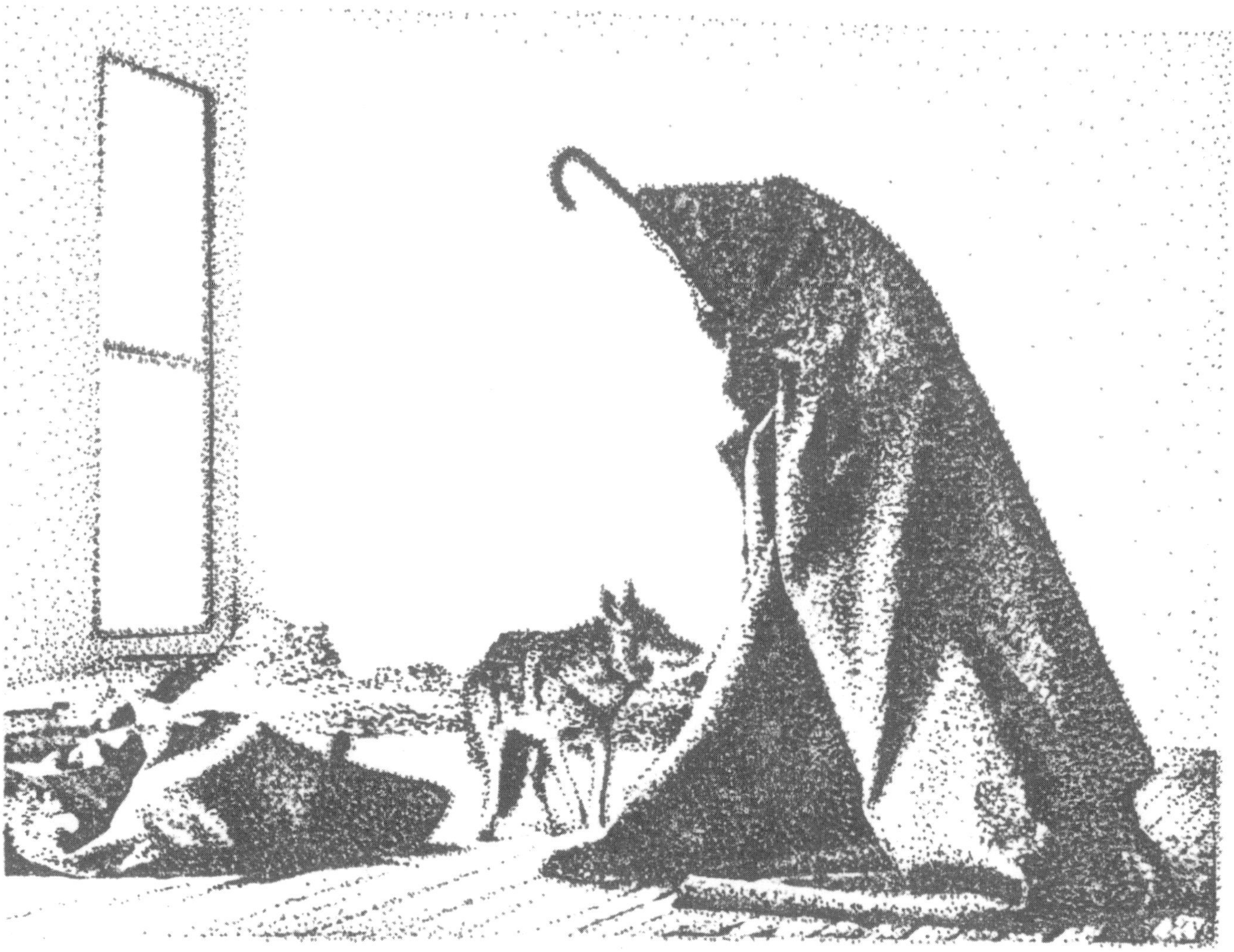

Fig. 5. Fat on a Chair, 1964, by Joseph Beuys, is the result of a performance piece in which fat was placed on a wooden chair. Hessisches Landesmuseum, Darmstadt. (After Beuys.)

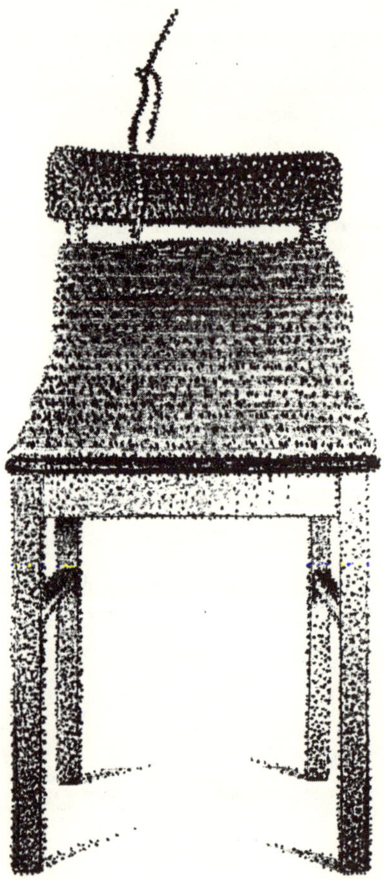

things getting done. Beuys wants to acknowledge the Trickster spirit as a provocative force for awakening knowledge. He says, "I was trying to show people that there is a realm that exists below the human realm and which is a precursor to human evolution, an autonomous animal realm. I took a creature out of this realm and brought it into contact with human beings, and people felt provoked—in the end it provoked them to asking themselves whether there might not be other realms that exist 'above' the human realm. We really ought to reconsider our sense organs and what they're capable of, you know, because they can penetrate far into other realms, realms we have lost touch with."[2] For this reason many of Beuys' actions had to do with animal themes. One animal that will be considered later in the context of traditional imagery is the stag. Beuys created a number of works focused on this creature, with titles such as *Wounded Stag, Bleeding Stag, Dead Giant Stag, Dead Stag and Moon, Dead Man on Stag Skeleton.*

Whether the substance was an animal or a lump of inanimate material, Beuys was interested in the transformation of substance rather than the "traditional aesthetic understanding of beautiful appearance." *Fat on a Chair* (fig. 5) is a perfect example of Beuys' artistic agenda. A large slab of animal fat sits on a chair—it is a foul material that feels greasy, smells putrid, and tastes rancid. Beuys was fond of using fat in his sculptures because it "is objectionable to several of the senses simultaneously." It also has a psychological impact that suggests unhealthiness and obesity, "repulsive human characteristics." It is because of this aspect of Beuys' work that he is viewed as a kind of art alchemist, searching for something beyond the usual, searching for audience reaction, searching for something more than the given. Rudolf Steiner, in whose ideas Beuys took a deep interest, said: "All genuine art seeks the spirit. Even when art wishes to represent the ugly, the disagreeable, it is concerned, not with the sensory-disagreeable as such, but with the spiritual, which proclaims its nature in the midst of unpleasantness. If the spiritual shines through the ugly, even the ugly becomes beautiful. In art it is upon a relation to the spiritual that beauty depends."[3]

Beuys' approach, which developed parallel to the American neo-Dadaist movement of the early 1960s called Fluxus, is essentially "social, not aesthetic." Beuys often referred to his work as "social sculpture" and looked at it as a kind of social therapy, which reunites art, science, and religion through ritual, pseudoscientific imagemaking—in shamanic fashion: "While shamanism marks a point in the past, it also indicates the possibility for historical development. . . . So when I appear as a kind of shamanic figure, or allude to it, I do it to stress my belief in other priorities [than those of late industrial society] and the need to come up with a completely different plan for working with substances. For instance, in places like universities, where everyone speaks so rationally, it is necessary for a kind of enchanter to appear."[4] With the help of his social sculpture, Beuys played a significant role in the political scene of Germany in the late 1960s and the 1970s.

A striking contrast to the politicized shamanic showmanship recognized by market-driven art may be seen in the work of contemporary artists such as the British sculptor John Wilkes. After years of studying the organic forms of nature, with special focus on the shapes of bones, he asked himself the questions: "What is the form that water wishes to take? What sort of shapes will the fluid element feel most at home in?"

For more than three decades, Wilkes experimented with what he calls flow forms, sculpted vessels, water tables, and fountains, shaped in such a way as to encourage and enhance the innate qualities that are natural to water and its fluid movement (fig. 6). This artistic research has led to a number of interesting discoveries, not the least of which is that certain forms through which water passes help to oxygenate and revitalize it. This purifying process regenerates the water's properties by way of rhythmic movement and is activated by the specific forms through which the water flows. And as in Beuys' work, a transformation of substance occurs.

Wilkes asked a selfless question: "What forms are natural and true to this element of water?" And he opened a door to the spiritual language of

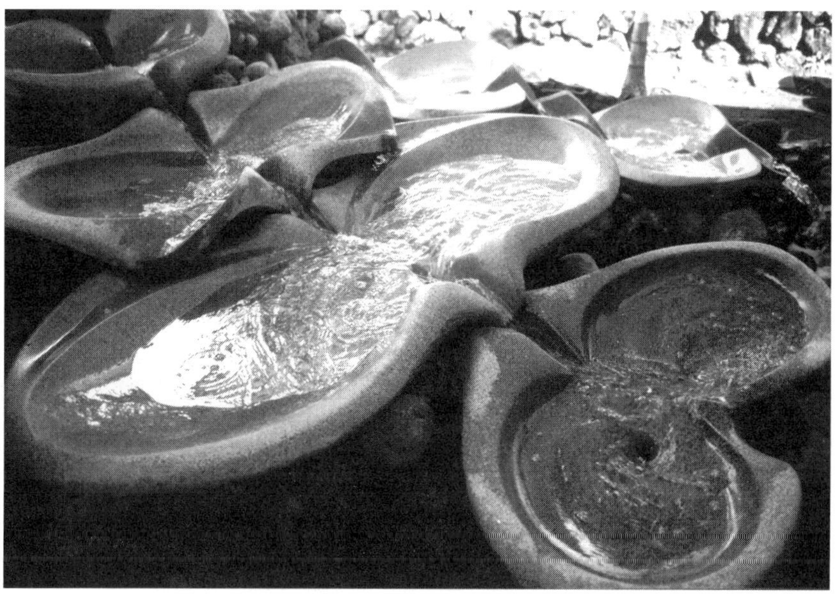

Fig. 6. Flow forms were developed by British artist John Wilkes to enhance the natural movements of water. Various series may be found at hundreds of sites throughout the world, such as this one at Castle Medical Center, Kailua, Hawaii.

art, to "the secret laws of nature," as Goethe calls them. He could have asked, "How can I create a unique, personalized form, a humorous form, or a socially and politically relevant form?" Questions of self-expression and social relevance have tremendous value at a certain level, yet the sacrificial (that is, "that which makes sacred") question that is offered up selflessly leads to a threshold where profound truths reside. As in former times such a path draws one towards the mysteries of creation.

Today's art has a unique character; it is unlike the art of any other time in history. Yet echoes from a distant primal source find meaningful resonance in our contemporary creations, and they carry us toward the very discovery of our future potential. (See Appendix 1.)

I.1 The Spiritual in Modern Art

Those to whom nature begins to disclose her open mystery feel an irresistible longing for her worthiest interpreter, Art.
—Johann Wolfgang von Goethe

The shamanic aspect, as seen in the work of Joseph Beuys, is found throughout modern and postmodern art. Michael Tucker, in *Dreaming with Open Eyes: The Shamanic Spirit in Twentieth Century Art and Culture,* suggests that contemporary art is, at its best and its worst, the imagery of our primal being crying out for acknowledgment. "No less than the shamans of old, modern artists have developed a 'suggestive magic' of redeeming potential. Viewed in the light of shamanic wisdom, much of what too many have taken to be a 'heap of broken images' in twentieth-century art can reveal its true identity, as a rich and variegated mosaic, inspiring dreams as ancient as they are new."[5] In the reemergence of shamanism and other traditional disciplines from alchemy to Zen Buddhism, their connection to art has become apparent, and they have received increased attention in recent years for providing a model "for guiding the Western mind back to its estranged primal roots."[6] Spirit in art continually struggles to the surface even in the materialistic climate of postindustrial society. One need only look at this "heap of broken images" of modern and contemporary art to see that it is the result of a material world colliding with a spiritual world. The chaotic images of today's art forms let only a small, personalized shaft of light, darkness, and color shine into the gap between these two worlds, and we seem to have only our own tiny vantage point from which to assess them. Thus the traditional wisdom of earlier ages can be a tremendous aid when we attempt to embrace the spiritual dimensions of artistic creation and human expression. From shamanic ritual in action painting to sacred geometry in abstraction, art of the twentieth century can be viewed from a fresh perspective that transcends the formalism of our recent past. Influences such as alchemy, anthroposophy, hermeticism, mysticism, Rosicrucianism, spiritualism, Taoism, theosophy, and Zen on twentieth-century art are now rich avenues of exploration for artists and scholars.

Wassily Kandinsky, a Russian painter working in Germany during the

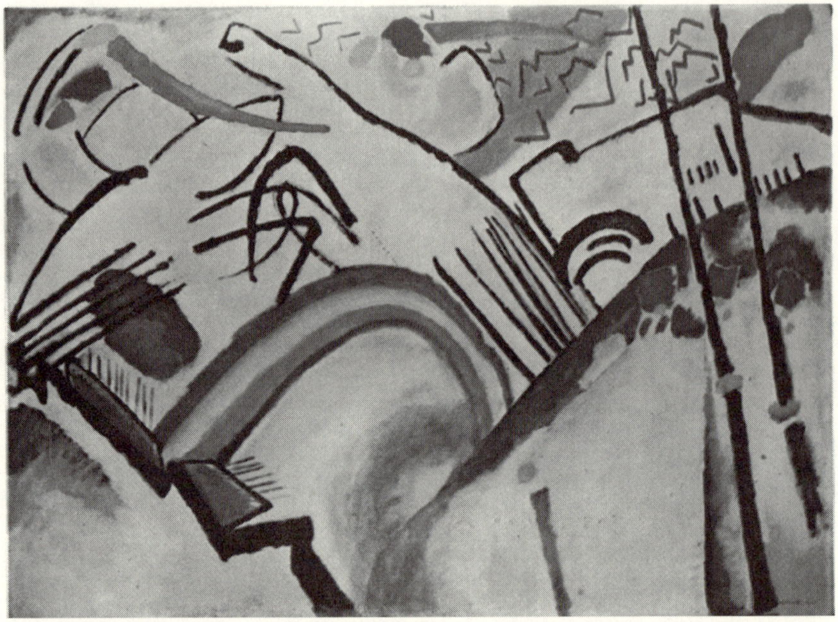

Fig. 7. Wassily Kandinsky is regarded as one of the first twentieth-century artists to paint nonobjective, abstract pictures. *Cossacks,* 1910, shows his transition from figurative painting into a pure language of color and form. (Tate Gallery, London.)

early twentieth century, was one of the first artists to create a non-objective, abstract painting (fig. 7). Around 1910, when science was just beginning to visualize matter in terms of atomic structure and quantum theory, Kandinsky declared that: "Abstract forms (lines, planes, dots, etc.) are not important in themselves, but only their inner sound, their life.... The world sounds. It is a cosmos of spiritually active beings. Even dead matter is living spirit."[7] And further, "Behind Matter, within Matter, the creative Spirit is concealed."[8] Piet Mondrian, the Dutch painter, who, like Kandinsky, was involved with theosophy and anthroposophy, sought the primal elements that underlie the visible world. "In this manner [of abstraction] one approaches Spirit, or purity itself. It follows from this, that Spirit is more easily approached by means of [abstract] form which is closer to Spirit—and indeed least of all by the physical [naturalistic] form."[9] For many artists, spirit was the justification for abstraction in art (fig. 8). Their experience was that an objective spiritual world stood behind and penetrated the world of appearance.

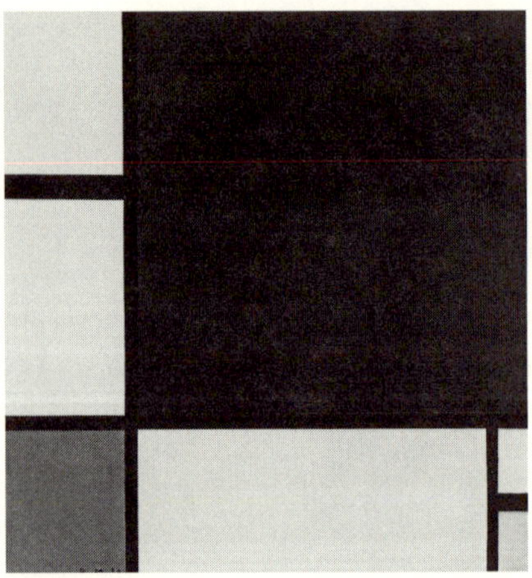

Fig. 8. Piet Mondrian's work with rectangles, vertical and horizontal lines, primary colors, and black and white demonstrates an early form of minimalism. By reducing form and color to what was for him its most essential elements, he pursued his path to the spirit in art. *Composition with Red, Blue, and Yellow,* 1930. (Bartos Collection, New York.)

Those twentieth-century artists who did not pursue this particular path to the spiritual found answers to their questions in other realms, such as the unconscious or subconscious and the intellect. These three realms—the spirit, the unconscious, and the intellect—all have to do with our experience of an inner life in an outer world. And it is as contemporary human beings that we seek to explain and come to terms with the dualism of inner and outer life.

André Breton, speaking of Surrealism as a "tiny footbridge over the abyss," argued for the exploration of the unconscious and of dreams. In his manifesto of

1924 he states: "Surrealism aims quite simply at the total recovery of our psychic force by a means which is nothing other than the dizzying descent into ourselves, the systematic illumination of hidden places and the progressive darkening of other places, the perpetual excursion into the midst of forbidden territory, and that there is no real danger of its activities coming to an end so long as man still manages to distinguish an animal from a flame or a stone."[10]

Surrealist painters construct their "tiny footbridge over the abyss" by combining realistic images in unrealistic situations, as dream sequences that explore the unconscious. In this way the inner and outer worlds meet in the creation of a schizophrenic world where the recognition of animal, flame, and stone remains intact but their usual context disappears. Animals are on fire, stones hover in thin air, and the world is a delightful, unreal dream or a frightfully unnerving nightmare (fig. 9).

The French artist Marcel Duchamp said, "I am interested in the intellectual side, although I don't like the word 'intellect.' For me 'intellect' is too dry a word, too inexpressive. I like the word 'belief.' I think in general that when people say 'I know,' they don't know, they believe. I believe that art is the only form of activity in which man as man shows himself to be a true individual. Only in art is he capable of going beyond the animal state, because art is an outlet toward regions which are ruled by time and space."[11] Duchamp's own artistic production culminated in the definitively unfinished piece called *The Bride Stripped Bare by her Bachelors, Even* (1915–23), which features the "bachelor machine" below and the bride's "Milky Way" above (fig. 10). The entire assemblage is set between two panes of glass incorporating shatter patterns that occurred by accident. Duchamp said of this work, also called *The Large Glass*, that it is a "wedding of mental and visual elements" but "the ideas . . . are more important than the actual visual realization."[12] In this way he articulates the groundwork for conceptual art. In further explaining his work, he describes it thus: "Something as nonsensical as possible. It's not easy to be nonsensical, because nonsensical things so often turn out to make sense."[13] Duchamp's emphasis on the power of intellectualizing suggests that his work has esoteric depth in the sense of authentic spirituality. In fact it more often expresses a complex convolution of ideas which, according to Lipsey, is the practice of "'pataphysics," where "meanings shift and change, and the ruling spirit is an ironic wit and mock seriousness that doesn't drive toward truth so much as toward an obsessive intricacy."[14] As in the case of Beuys, the question may arise, are we dealing with an alchemist or a charlatan?

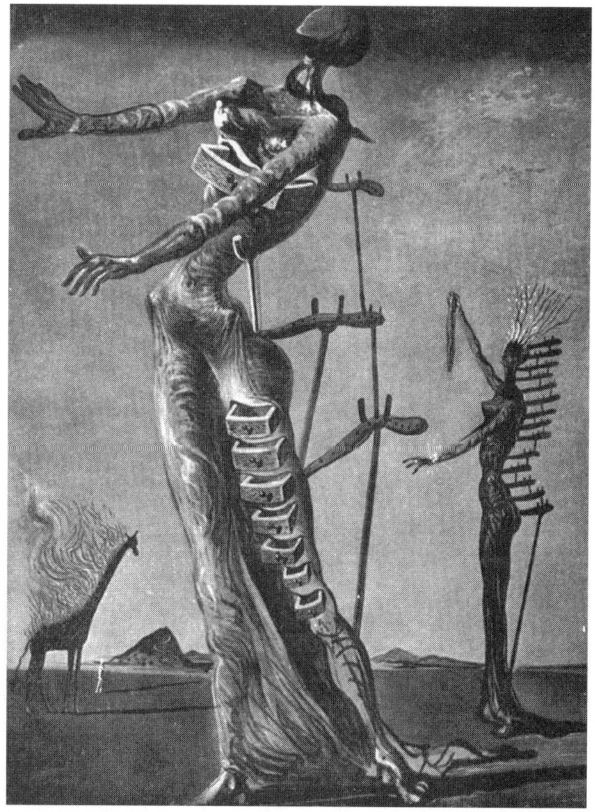

Fig. 9. Spanish surrealist Salvador Dali created lucid dreamscapes of the unconscious. *Burning Giraffe* is just such an example. (Kunstmuseum, Basel, Switzerland.)

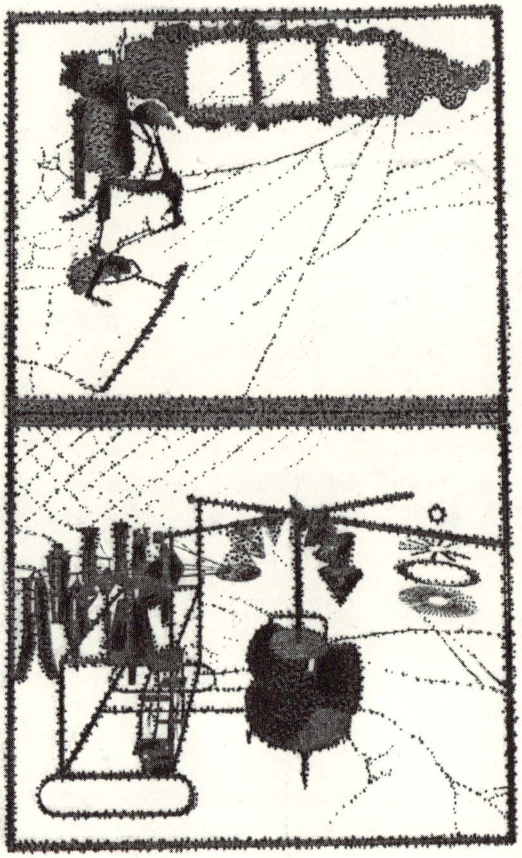

Fig. 10. The Bride Stripped Bare by Her Bachelors, Even (1915–23), also known as *The Large Glass*, by Marcel Duchamp, was one of the artist's many explorations into intellectual symbolism. (After Duchamp.)

Such questions of sincerity and significance versus superficiality and show point to why the modern art movement does not sit well with everyone. The psychologist Carl Jung, whose work often focused on the mystery of the unconscious, questioned: "What is wrong with our art, that most delicate of instruments for reflecting the psyche? How are we to explain the blatantly pathological element in modern painting? . . . Most of it is alien to me from the human point of view and too disagreeably reminiscent of what I have seen in my medical practice."[15] And yet the "blatantly pathological element" in modern art often seems to be naïvely accepted, erroneously elevated and acclaimed, as well as aggressively exploited. Rudolf Steiner likewise felt something to be amiss with the art of the twentieth century when he stated: "The chief characteristic in the development of modern art is that it has lost the inner impulse that should drive it to place before the world what is felt by humanity as a pressing need."[16] More recently, artist and writer Suzi Gablik, whose accomplished research has inquired into the values and goals of modern art, asks if in fact modernism has failed: "Our culture expects us to be manic—to overproduce, to overconsume, and to waste—but in all this, something vital is missing: the knowledge that life can be transformed by a sacramental experience."[17]

One of the exceptions to this unfulfilling tendency of modernism is seen in the work of Marc Chagall (1887–1985), who, although feeling the strong influence of "the geometric tunnels" of cubism, consciously turned away from destroying the traditions of the great masters and refrained from demolishing the "natural cosmos." Chagall, whose work creates a mystic, dreamlike world of color and form, says: "The art of the nineteenth and twentieth centuries appears as a feeble reflection of scientific discoveries. Whereas, up to and including the epoch of the Renaissance, art reflected the religious spirit, or at least illustrated the intense religious feeling of the times."[18] He recognizes "a moral crisis" in modern art and states that "it is a crisis of color, of matter, of blood and its parts, of words and sounds, and all the rest of the elements with which one constructs a work of art as well as a life."[19]

Fig. 11. Facing page: *Artist with His Model*, 1948, is a recurrent theme for Marc Chagall. As an angel perches on his canvas and a sun-cock oversees the scene, the artist takes in his model as she sits upon an animal form below. (National Gallery of Canada, Ottawa.)

In his own life and work, Chagall sought the spiritual component—that which cannot be weighed, measured, or quantified. His paintings, which may at times remind us of out-of-body, shamanic visions, are more like the fairy-tale pictures of childhood, filled with wonder, imagination, and love. He shows human beings communing intimately with plants and animals, with angels and with each other. He transports us through his vision to a realm where spirit and matter are unified in the life of the soul, for his search goes beyond the "art which exists only

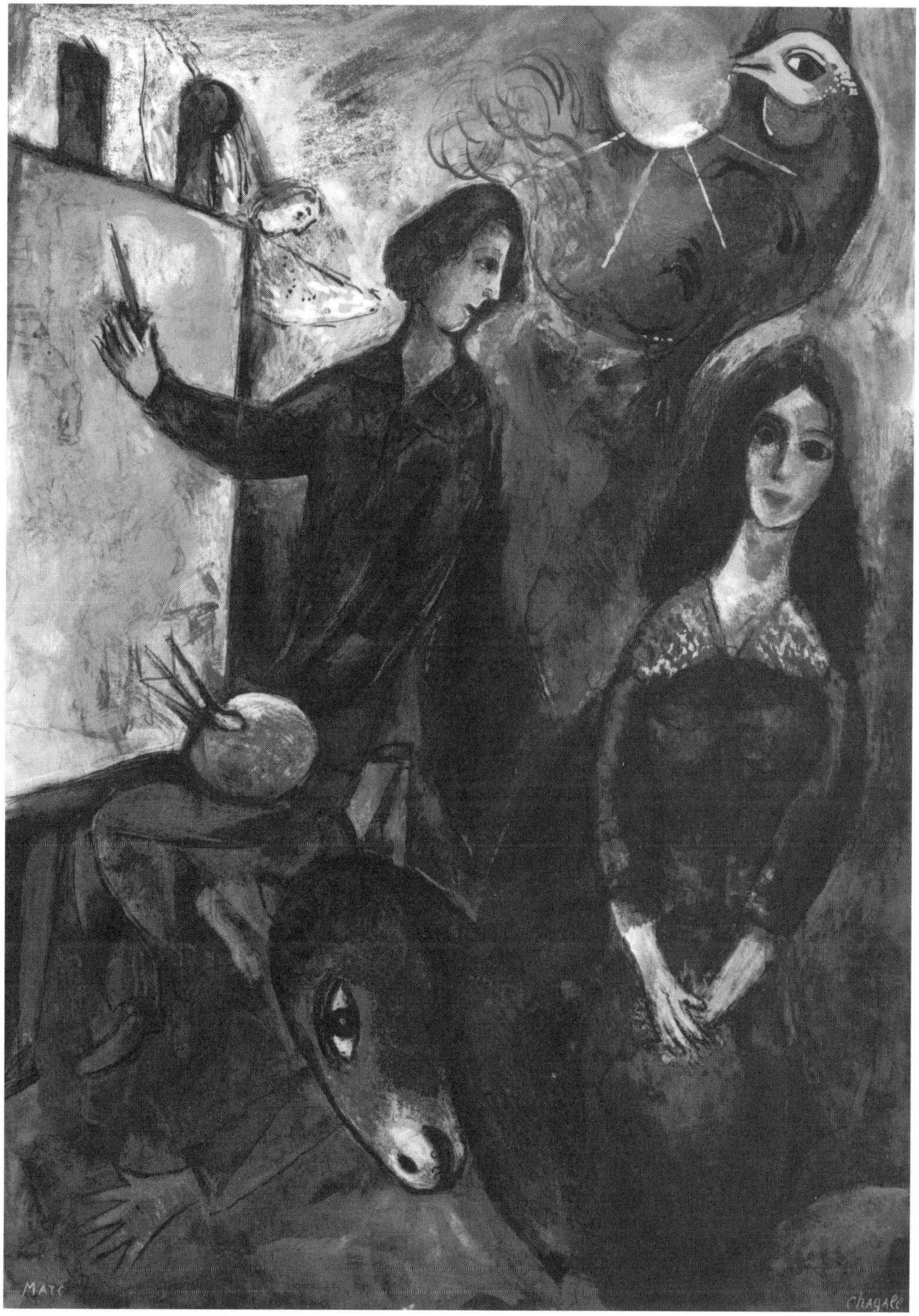
MARC
Chagall

to please" or "that pitiless art whose purpose is to shock us."[20]

In *Artist with a Dove* (front cover), Chagall depicts a scene that he painted many times throughout his life, the artist at his easel, inspired by his love and his vision. Here his feminine inspiration, his muse, reaches out to an animal's head that rises up from the bottom of the painting. Shining above the artist's head is a tableau of childhood memory pictures, which act as a backdrop to the painter's vision and arise directly from his heart in the form of a dove. His vision and inner self are given wings. Sometimes an actual angel appears, as in *Artist with His Model* (fig. 11). The bouquet of flowers in the artist's painting comes alive as male and female counterparts embrace. Color both divides and unites the composition.

The renowned anthropologist Mircea Eliade stated: "The Nature created by Chagall is primeval and maternal—a place where man, the animal, and the angel live together peacefully under the eye of God, or beneath a great moon such as appeared when the world was first created." Eliade likewise noted that "Chagall takes his place among the very few [modern] artists who have recovered the holiness that is present in the world and in human life."[21] And Chagall's granddaughter, Bella Meyer, recalled, "Paintings were more to him than art; they were a sort of celebration of a mission, which was to find meaning and one's own inner path."[22]

One's own inner path!

Chagall observed that in the atomic age, "We shrink back on the edge of the precipice of universal destruction." And the challenge at hand is "to transform the human being."[23]

1.2 A Modern Master

Art is the revelation of secret laws of nature, which, without it, would remain forever hidden.
—Goethe

Let's imagine a broad, snow-covered expanse spread out in front of us, dotted with frozen rivers and lakes. Most of the nearby beach is also covered with ice, and massive blocks of ice are floating in the ocean. Here and there, low trees and thickets are totally covered with icicles and masses of snow. It is evening. The sun has already gone down, leaving behind the golden glow of sunset.

There are two female figures in view. Then, out of the sunset a messenger is born—sent forth, we might say, from higher worlds. He stands before the two women and listens intently to what they say about their innermost feelings and experiences.

One of the women stands there pressing her arms close to her body. Holding herself aloof, she speaks the words, "I'm freezing!" The other woman gazes out over the snow-covered expanse, the icy waters, and the trees covered with icicles. The words spill from her lips, "How wonderfully beautiful this countryside is!" She completely forgets her own feelings and is oblivious to the sensations of cold caused by the outer physical landscape. We feel warmth streaming into her heart, for she forgets everything that the physical influence of the cold could make her feel. She is overwhelmed by the incredible beauty of this very frosty landscape.

The sun sinks still lower, the glow of the sunset fades, and the two female figures fall into a deep sleep. The one who had felt the cold so strongly in her own bodily Self sinks into a sleep that could easily become the sleep of death; the other sinks into a sleep in which we see that the aftereffects of the sensation expressed in the words, "Oh, how beautiful!" are still resonating, thoroughly warming and revitalizing her limbs, even in sleep. And this female figure hears the youth who was born out of sunset's glow say to her, "You are Art!" And she falls asleep, taking with her into her slumber all the results of the impressions she had of the landscape that has been described.[24]

So begins the lecture entitled "The Spiritual Being of Art," given by Rudolf Steiner in Berlin in 1909. It goes on to describe how one after another, spiritual beings approach the woman referred to as Art, and according to her dream, she sees they are in need and she asks them what she can do for them. Then by uniting her soul with each being, the various arts—dance, drama, sculpture, architecture, painting, music, and poetry—arise. This was Steiner's attempt, in story form, to present his ideas on art.

In accompaniment to his lectures, of which he gave over three thousand, Steiner often did diagrammatic blackboard drawings to help illustrate his ideas (fig. 12). He was well aware that words only go so far in expressing ideas.

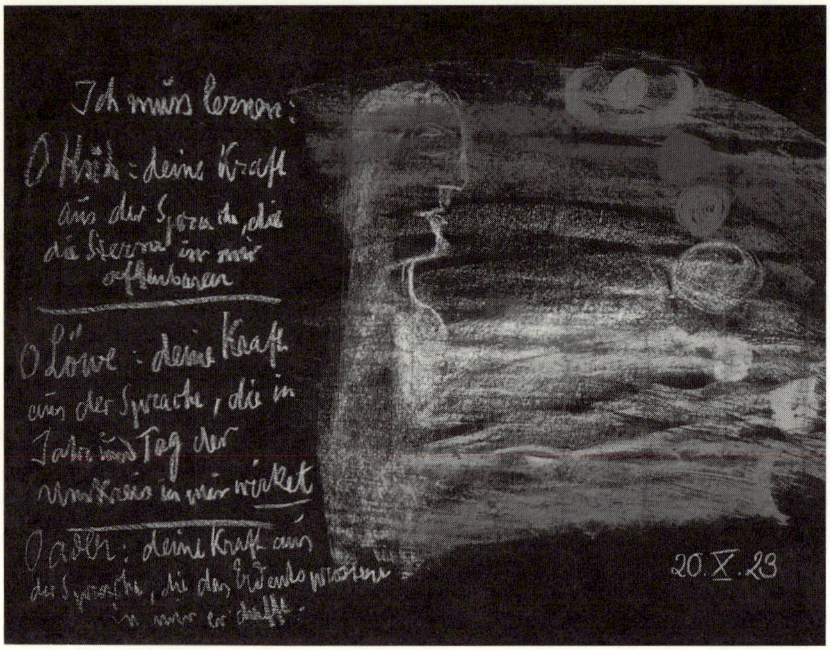

Fig. 12. Rudolf Steiner's blackboard drawings, done over three-quarters of a century ago, have only recently been "discovered." Here Steiner depicts the human being influenced by the planets (right) and describes in the text on the left how "I must learn" from the cosmic forces that work in the world as Cow, Lion, and Eagle. (Copyright © Rudolf Steiner Nachlassverwaltung.)

Often a visual image, a few sketched lines or a stroke of color, can help a concept to be grasped in deeper layers of the soul and can help to bring about a greater level of comprehension. The special strength of the black background with its light chalk markings produces a visual metaphor for the dark cosmos with its celestial characters spelling out the mysterious message of creative origins of light within darkness. Steiner spoke of the color black as "the spiritual image of the lifeless," and white as "the soul's image of the spirit."[25] So it follows that for the spirit, black is the color of death, and for the soul, white is the color—in the form of an image or symbol—of spirit. By way of this powerful juxtaposition of black and white, death and spirit, the blackboard with its chalk drawings becomes an icon for the creative realm in which ideas enter into existence and depart again from it.

Joseph Beuys was also aware in his own way of this power of the blackboard as a medium, and he was the first to be recognized for using it as an art form in his action pieces of the 1970s and '80s (fig, 1). The connection between Beuys' and Steiner's blackboard drawings has recently prompted the showing of Steiner's chalk drawings as art. Steiner's chalk drawings were yet another point of influence for Beuys, since the German artist had studied much of Steiner's written work (especially ideas on the spiritual hierarchies, Christology, the nature of substance, and the social question). Beuys had even become a member of the Anthroposophical Society, which was founded by Steiner early in the twentieth century. Oddly enough, Beuys never fully took up Steiner's artistic impulse, an aesthetic program that encompassed literally all the arts. (See Appendix 2.)

In recent years Rudolf Steiner's blackboard drawings have been exhibited internationally with great acclaim. Yet Steiner would have likely scoffed at the exhibition of his drawings as fine art in museum settings disassociated from their original context. Ironically, it appears as though this is the art form that he is now most known for today. And although there is a fascinating quality and primal power to his chalk drawings, Steiner's real contribution to twentieth-century art is for the most part overlooked or considered by critics as insignificant.

At the very time when cubism was shattering and rearranging the visible world in search of its own primal imagery, when abstraction was dissolving the material world in search of spirit in art, when Dada in reaction to the madness of World War I set about demonstrating that all things are contrved nonsense—at this auspicious time, the first quarter of the twentieth century, Rudolf Steiner brought into being the much-discussed ideal of European artistic striving—the total work of art (*Gesamtkunstwerk*). As artists dreamed of creating "the new cathedral," where all the arts would come together, Steiner succeeded—even as the cannon fire of the Great War could be heard sounding across European borders.

The German architect Bruno Taut, working quite independently of Steiner, declared in 1918, "There will be no boundaries between the crafts, sculpture, and painting; all will be one: Architecture. A building is the direct carrier of spiritual values, shaper of the sensibilities of the general public who slumbers today but will awaken tomorrow. Only a total revolution in the realm of the spiritual can create this building; yet this revolution, this building, does not happen by itself. Both have to be sought—today's architects must prepare the way for this edifice."[26] Many architects shared this view and sought through their own work for what Peter Behrens, the teacher of Mies van de Rohe, Walter Gropius, and Le Corbusier, describes as "the sense of a higher purpose,

Fig. 13. Right: The design of the first Goetheanum, 1913–1922, was based on the relationship of two interlocking domes of different sizes.

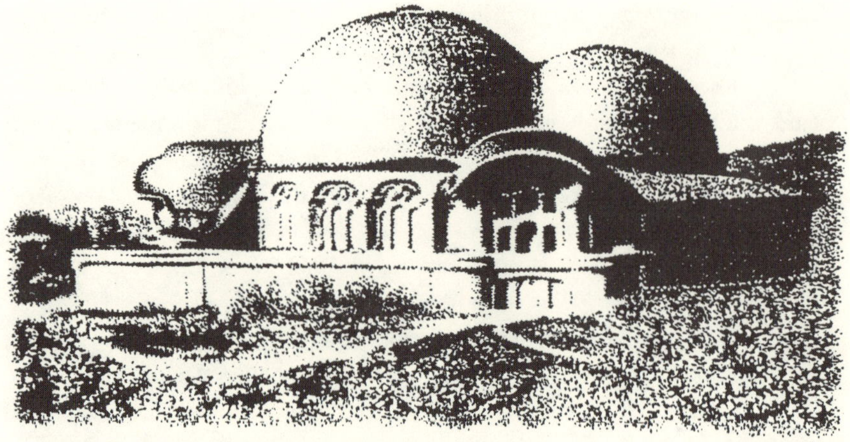

a purpose that was merely translated into material terms, a spiritual need, the gratification of our transcendental nature."[27]

As the Allies and the Central Powers battled one another, artists from seventeen different countries worked in neutral Switzerland on a building named for the poet Johann Wolfgang von Goethe. The Goetheanum was a unique structure, an integrated work of art, which wove all the arts together in such a way that it could be linked to the great temple and sacred architectural traditions of Europe, Greece, and Egypt (fig. 13). However, the Goetheanum was a theater, a spiritual-cultural center, not a spiritual-religious center.

It was not until the early 1920s that the Goetheanum building neared completion. It was a unique structure in that it combined the two basic principles of architectural form: the central axis and the longitudinal axis. If one enters a circular building such as the Pantheon in Rome, one experiences a sense of peace and security, for wherever one stands in a central axis structure one feels at rest, as though one is always embraced by the roundness of the form. There is no motivation or urge to move onward, for harmony emanates from this perfect shape. When Steiner combined a smaller interlocking dome for a stage area with a larger circular auditorium (fig. 14), he in effect brought about an invisible axial experience. A longitudinal axis, such as one finds in Greek temples and Gothic cathedrals, evokes a sense of movement lengthwise through the space. The remarkable thing about the Goetheanum was that the visitor could freely determine which of these two experiences, the central (rest) or longitudinal axis (movement), would take precedence. This freedom provided by the architectural setting had never before occurred in a modern building. As Hagen Biesantz points out concerning the first Goetheanum: "The

Fig. 14. Below: The ground plan of the first Goetheanum demonstrates a unique geometrical design. (After Carl Kemper.)

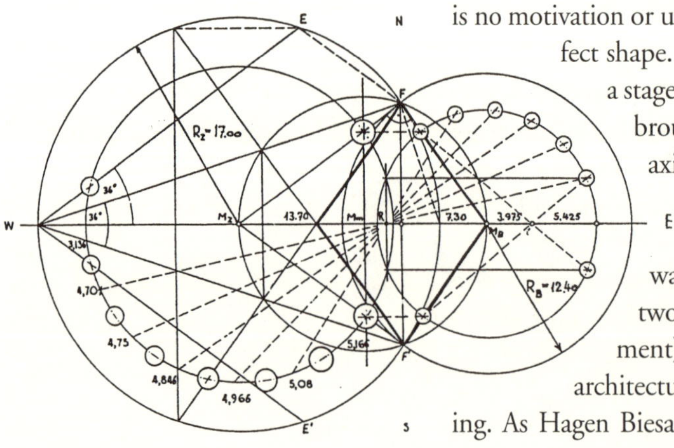

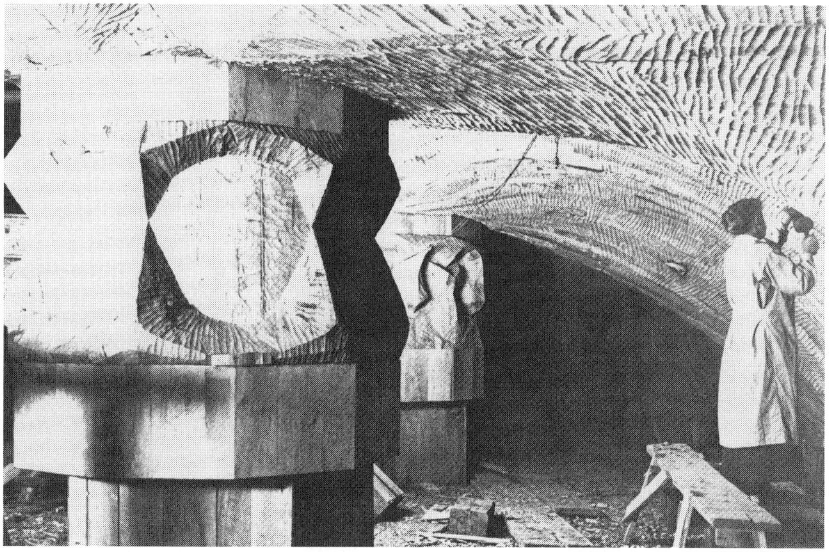

Fig. 15. Left: The entire interior of the first Goetheanum was hand-carved following Rudolf Steiner's design. Each capital was made from a different wood, and each expressed through its forms a particular stage of development—as in the transformation from seed to sprout, to leaf, blossom, and fruit. Steiner intended the metamorphoses of the capital forms to artistically express the developmental phases of human evolution. (Copyright © Verlag am Goetheanum.)

double-domed building conveys the spatial experience of the human being awakened to individual freedom."[28] The building did not impose the authority of one directional experience or the other upon the visitor, thus providing a place of true freedom.

The columns in the Goetheanum also promoted this end in that each hand-carved base and capital, as well as the architrave above, was shaped in artistic forms that were unique in design and yet related one to another. In an aisled building, columns that are all the same form encourage the eye to move rapidly towards the opposite end of the space, toward the altar in the case of a temple or church. When colonnades feature different capital motifs, the movement is halted and an appreciation of the uniqueness of each motif is possible, as in Romanesque sculpted capitals. In the Goetheanum the capital forms were each unique, thus promoting a visual rest at each one; however, as they were alllinked to one another through an underlying principle of metamorphosis, they stimulated visual flow and movement at the same time (fig. 15). Here again a choice based on individual freedom was provided to the observer.

Other integral artistic aspects in Steiner's Goetheanum were carved, colored glass windows depicting the seeker's path of inner development (fig. 16) and the ceiling murals with images portraying the greater spiritual evolution of humanity (fig. 17). All of this iconography culminated in the carved wooden statue at the back of the stage area, called *The Representative of Humanity* (fig. 18).

The Goetheanum burned down, at the hands of an arsonist, on New Year's Eve 1922/23, and Steiner began designing the second Goetheanum almost immediately. Like the first Goetheanum, the second would incorporate the subtlest

Fig. 16. Below: Nine large colored-glass windows were featured in the first Goetheanum. Each shows a scene on the path of esoteric development. This rendering after the north green window depicts a human being on the summit of a mountain (*axis mundi*) confronted by a winged serpentlike being, whose body contains the planets. The same motifs are used in the windows of the second Goetheanum. (After Assia Turgenev.)

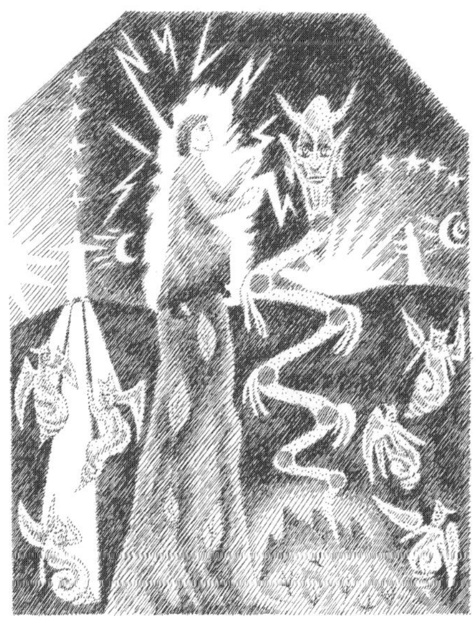

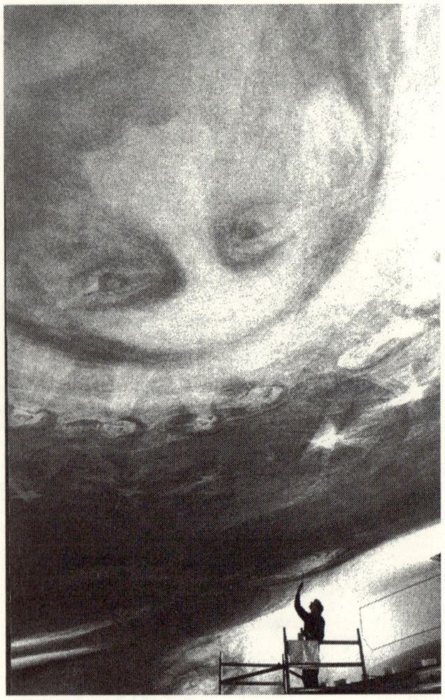

Fig. 17. Above: The ceiling of the second Goetheanum was completed in 1998 by an international team of artists working with plant color pigments developed by Rudolf Steiner. The ceiling murals depict the spiritual evolution of humanity. (Copyright © Jürg Buess.)

Fig. 18. Right: *The Representative of Humanity* is a twenty-seven-foot-tall elmwood sculpture depicting the human being between the contrasting forces that either tear one away from earth (above right) or drag one down (below left). Carved by Rudolf Steiner with the help of several assistants, it was not yet in place and was therefore spared when the first Goetheanum burned down in 1923. It had been intended as the culminating motif of the building's artistic design.

aspects of sacred geometry, but this time, combined with the most advanced building techniques, stretching its engineering possibilities and materials to their limit. The second Goetheanum is recognized to this day by architects and historians as one of the outstanding works of architecture of the early twentieth century and as an unsurpassed example of spirit in art (color plate 2).

Steiner's commitment to the arts was so far-reaching and in advance of his time that at the beginning of the twentieth century he could say: "However much study may be given to the elimination of crime and wrong-doing from the world, true redemption, the turning of evil into good, will in future depend upon whether true art is able to pour a spiritual substance into the hearts and souls of men. . . . Edifices and buildings will begin to speak and in a language of which people today have hardly an inkling.

"Peace and harmony, and humanity's rightful situation can only be established when the gods speak to us. . . . Art is the creation of organs through which the gods are able to speak to humanity."[29]

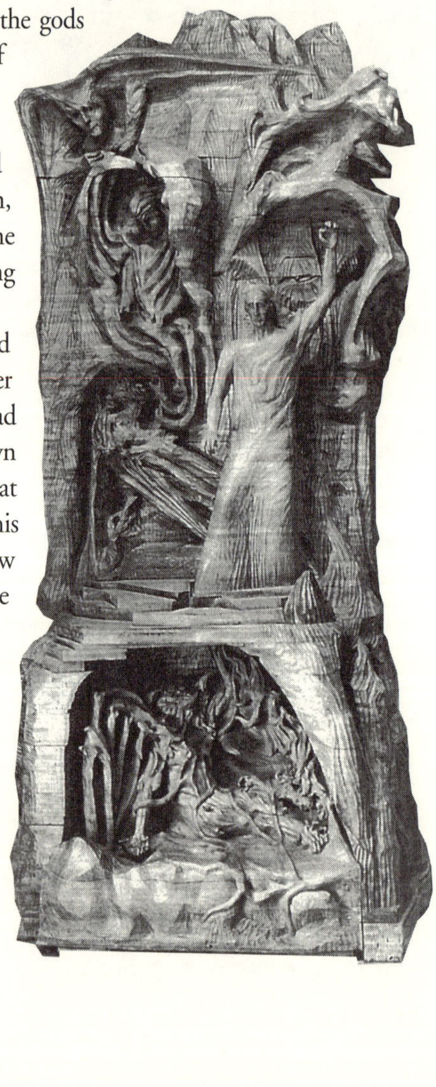

After describing the origin and nature of the arts in legendary fashion, Steiner concludes his 1909 lecture "The Spiritual Being of Art" in the following way:

"Once again she looked toward the sunrise, and the sunrise became for her a symbol of the state from which she had awakened and also a symbol of her own imaginations. And she understood what the poet had said out of the wisdom of his divining. What she heard out of a new spirit resounded toward her from the whole Earth: Only through beauty's dawning shall you approach the land of knowledge!"[30]

I.3 The Road to Modernism

O Sun, the face of truth is veiled by thy golden disc. Withdraw it, that I, a seeker after truth, may behold truth's splendor.
—Isha Upanishad

One misty morning in 1851, as the English artist J.M.W. Turner lay on his deathbed, the rising dawn light shone through his window and as the warming rays of the sun touched his aged face he declared, "The sun is God!" He died shortly after.

The motif of the sun as an image of God has been recurrent throughout history. Artists and entire civilizations have honored the sun as the physical symbol of that which is most spiritual in the universe, the source of light and life. It is indeed interesting that the father of the modern movement, Paul Cézanne, who painted so often out in nature, spoke of all living things as the stored-up "remembrance of the sun." He said: "Perhaps the moral force distributed over all the world is only man's striving to become sun again."[31]

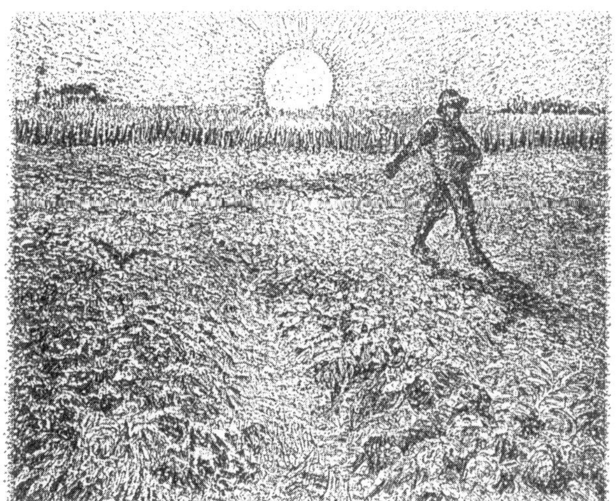

Fig. 19. As J.M.W. Turner did before him, van Gogh placed the sun on a high horizon in the center of his picture. The sun radiates like the earth's own halo in *The Sower,* 1888. (After van Gogh.)

This principle seems to be abundantly clear in the work of Vincent van Gogh. His late landscapes are so sun-drenched that it is as if a solar radiance has entered into the stuff of earth in order to illuminate all matter (fig. 19). Everything is bursting with life and light, "palpable substance becomes flame-like energy."[32]

In a free rendering of Rembrandt's *Raising of Lazarus,* van Gogh does not include the figure of Christ calling forth the four-day-dead brother of Martha and Mary Magdalene. In his place van Gogh adds a prominent golden sun to the upper center of the composition as if this were the spiritual agent that brings about the miracle of resurrection (fig. 20).

Turner is another artist who did not shrink from placing the sun directly in the center of his paintings (fig. 21). Even when the sun is not visible in his pictures, something of the moral force of the sun—its light and

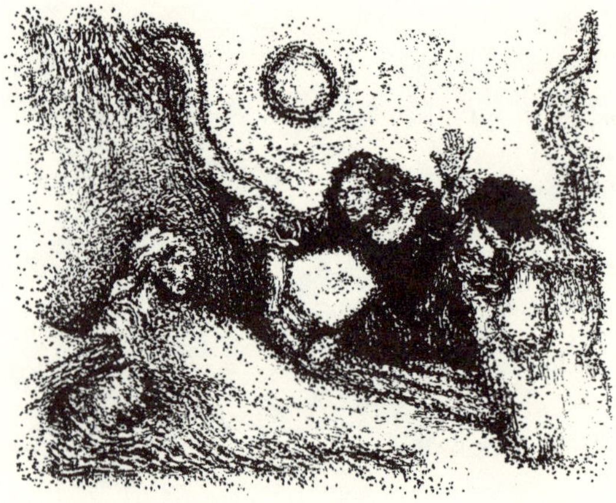

Fig. 20. Above: Van Gogh's free rendering of *Raising of Lazarus,* 1890, from a Rembrandt print, substitutes a radiant sun for the figure of Christ. (After van Gogh.)

color—is a dramatic, shining presence. Only after thoroughly mastering perspective did Turner go beyond the realism of topography to capture his own unique perception of the living landscape. He prepared the way for French Impressionism, transforming nature from an academic backdrop into a vital focus where the revelations of light, darkness, and color can occur. For the first time in European painting, form becomes secondary to light and color; drawing (line), the basis of academic art training, becomes subordinate to painting (color). As Rembrandt penetrated the spiritual dimensions of light and darkness, Turner expressed the very soul of light and color. His "paintings are of states of consciousness," according to William Anderson, "of moments of absorption and unity, when the division of inner and outer is abolished, and the light of the world is one with the light of the mind. It is as though he is telling us: 'This is what my true nature is and in this dissolution of dream and waking, of inner and outer, is where you too will find the truth of your existence.'"[33]

As Goethe and Cézanne both pointed out, the eye sees neither lines nor linear forms but only fields of light, darkness, and color. This light, darkness, and color constitute our most immediate visual experience. Without our noticing it, the eye traces perceived areas of color, light, and darkness, making us aware of shape and form—straightness, curvature, and depth. This comprehension of form culminates in our recognition of actual things—trees and hills—by means of a conceptual activity, all in a split second. Our sense of sight, our pure visual perception grasps only the experience of the light-dark scale and color values, not form.

Fig. 21. Right: *Mortlake Terrace,* 1827, demonstrates Turner's fearless placement of the sun in the center of the composition. Note the embankment wall dissolved by glare from the sunlight, a metaphor for the spirit overcoming matter. (National Gallery, Washington, D.C.)

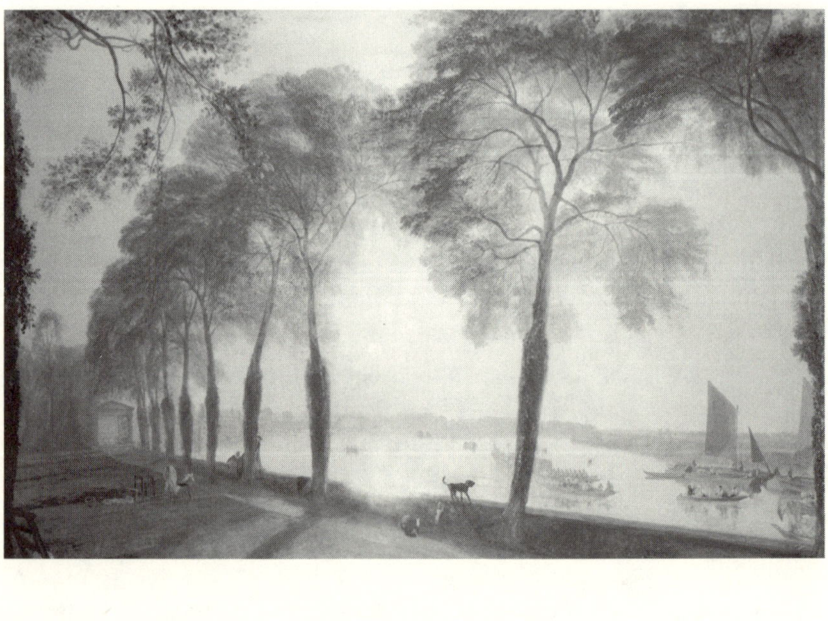

This is demonstrated by experience. Experiencing color that is free of fixed forms is an intermediary step between perceiving physical, material objects and recognizing the creative forces behind them. Thus the biblical declaration: "I do set my bow [spectrum of colors] in the cloud, and it shall be for a token of a covenant between me [spirit] and the earth [matter]" (Gen. 9:13).

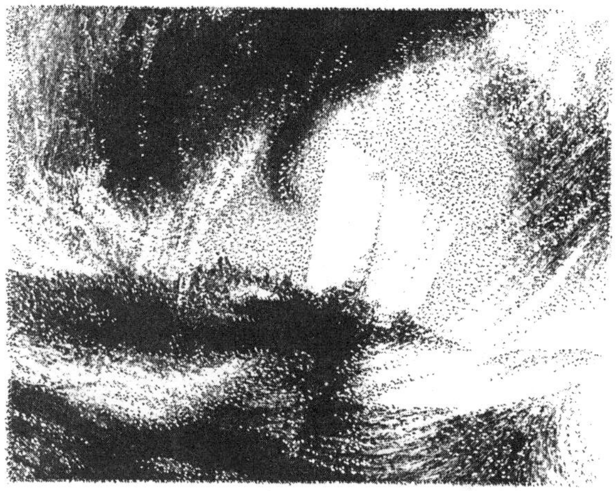

Fig. 22. Above: Turner's *Snowstorm at Sea* is a dynamic preparation for later Impressionism and Expressionism. (After Turner.)

By introducing such visual directness particularly in his later paintings, Turner, directly influenced by Goethe's Theory of Color, promotes the cultivation of pure perception as well as the enhanced faculties of imagination and intuition. In such pictures as *Snowstorm at Sea* (fig. 22), where he had himself lashed to the mast of a ship during a gale, Turner lays the groundwork not only for Impressionism but also for the action painting of Abstract Expressionism.

William Blake is another master of spirit and art, who, utilizing Renaissance drawing combined with transparent watercolor washes, elaborates his own spiritual vision and prophetic experiences (fig. 23). In a sense, here is a master similar to Rudolf Steiner, an artist-seer, who saw the essential nature of humanity as artist and co-creator with God. Therefore, Blake declared, "A Poet, a Painter, a Musician, and Architect: The Man or Woman who is not one of these is not a Christian." For Blake, art was a way of life, a spiritual discipline and path of devotional necessity. His concern was with the development and

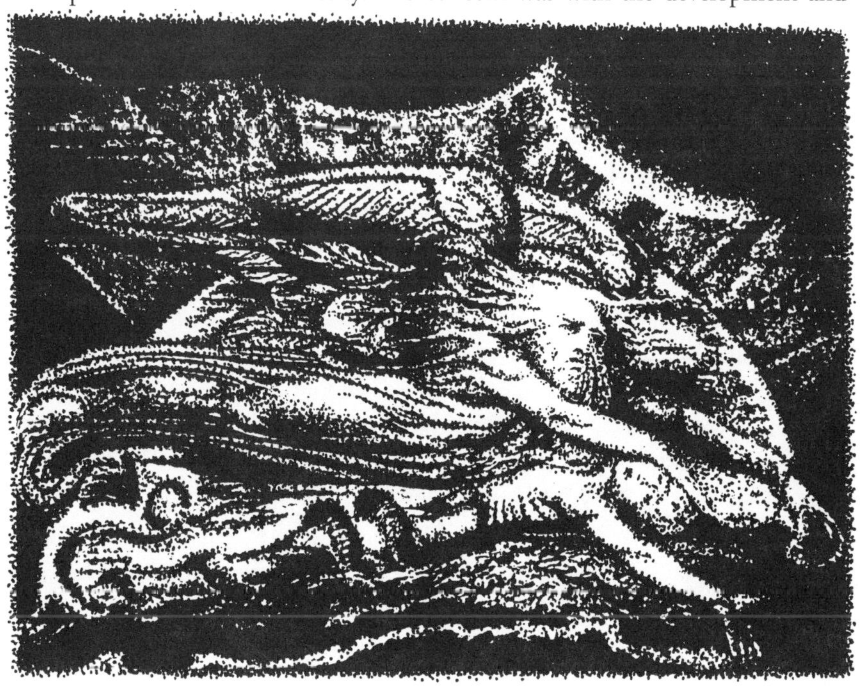

Fig. 23. Left: William Blake's vision of the *Elohim Creating Adam,* 1795, shows the intense inner concentration of God in the act of creation and the great anguish of Adam in being born into existence. The serpent entwining Adam indicates that the First Man is now mortally bound to the material world. (After Blake.)

redemption of humanity's higher potential, its true universal condition. His writings, illustrations, and paintings of spiritual events are a reminder to the Age of Reason that there are other modes of perception besides those that produce the prevailing materialistic outlook. Blake could already see the destructive and inhuman (i.e., inartistic) conditions that stem from the Industrial Revolution, and as artist-prophet and mystic-thinker he asserts:

> You Must leave Fathers & Mothers & Houses & Lands
> if they stand in the way of Art.
> Prayer is the Study of Art.
> Praise is the Practice of Art.
> Fasting &c., all relate to Art.
> The outward ceremony is antichrist.
> The Eternal Body of Man is The Imagination, that is, God Himself
> The Divine Body Jesus: We are his Members
> It manifests itself in the Works of Art (In Eternity All is Vision).[34]

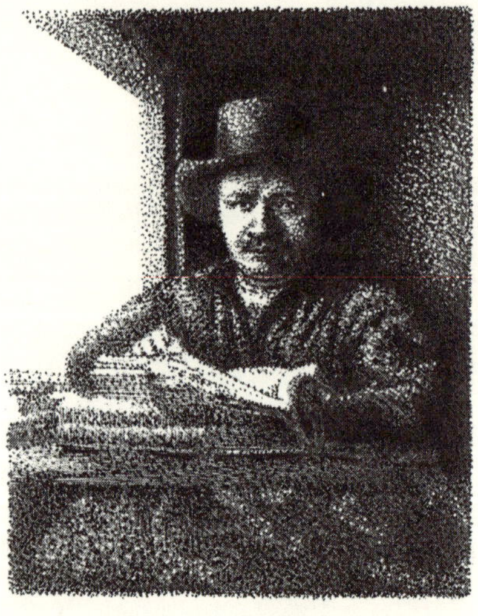

Fig. 24. Rembrandt's self-portraits are so numerous that one would think the artist self-indulgent if it were not for the penetrating self-study and skillful execution they reveal. (After Rembrandt.)

Among the post-Renaissance and pre-Romantic artists, Rembrandt can be singled out as one who was able to draw upon the spirit of his time. His deep-shadowed paintings brood with mysterious inner power that defies intellectual explanation. Uninterested in the Italian journey prescribed for artists of his time and totally engulfed in the Dutch palette of subdued earth tones, Rembrandt redeems darkness by finding the sacred measure of light within shadow (color plate 3). Rembrandt's *Evangelist Matthew* (1661) gazes into another world beyond this one while an angelic figure lightly touches and softly whispers, breathing inspiration toward the Gospel writer's illuminated face. Matthew's enlightened head translates this vision into words, while one hand touches his throat for confirmation and his other hand writes the words on pages reflecting the light of the original inspiration. Rembrandt perseveres in the struggle of light with darkness and captures the moral dimension of his theme in the dynamic tension between the spiritual qualities of light and shade. The unequaled number of self-portraits he produces speak not of self-interest but of a path of inner self-questioning and individual striving (fig. 24). His work penetrates the depths of what the visual language of line, light and darkness, and subtle coloration can achieve, and seems to flow directly from the very depths of his being in the tradition of a Michelangelo.

1.4 The Dance of Death

It is not now as it hath been of yore:
Turn wheresoe'er I may,
By night or day,
The things which I have seen I now can see
no more. . . .
Whither is fled the visionary gleam?
Whither is now, the glory and the dream?
—William Wordsworth

Perhaps best known through the series of forty-one woodcuts by Hans Holbein the Younger, the Dance of Death depicts, in stark black and white, a skeletal figure triumphantly accompanying people in their daily occupations. Beginning with a scene of Death awaiting Adam and Eve as they are cast out of Paradise (fig. 25), the series shows the grim reaper with individuals of every possible profession from the rich man to the plowman. Even the abbot is shown in the struggle of being taken away by the figure of Death. The reality of death overshadowed human beings who could no longer directly experience spirituality in the same way as their forefathers. Nor could they justify it with their newly dawning scientific outlook. Death was the ultimate end for a thinking that could only perceive the physical, material world.

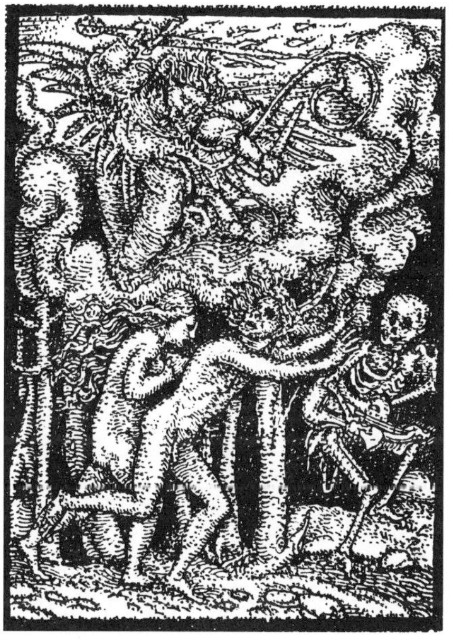

Fig. 25. In the *Dance of Death* series of forty-one woodblock prints, Hans Holbein depicts Adam and Eve as the first people to encounter death. (After Holbein.)

Of course death was known to earlier ages—certainly ancient Egyptians were well aware of it—but to the mythic consciousness of early peoples it was not feared; the afterlife was openly anticipated. By the time of the Renaissance, the "bone man" of mechanistic thinking was waking up in humanity and with it the conception that the universe is a finely tuned clock, entirely machinelike, dead and lifeless.

The skull became the symbol of mortality. As the former dwelling place of the human spirit, it was now to be the casket for dead intellectual thoughts and brain-bound materialistic reasoning. Dürer's *Saint Jerome* (fig. 26), like Shakespeare's Hamlet, contemplates this "mysterious vessel" (as Goethe calls it in his poem "Reflections on Contemplating the Skull of Schiller") and asks in a glance if we know the riddle of death.

Holbein, in one of his most enigmatic pictures, *The Ambassadors,* paints an optically distorted skull across the floor on which two French gentlemen stand (fig. 27). On the left is Jean de Dinteville, French ambassador to the

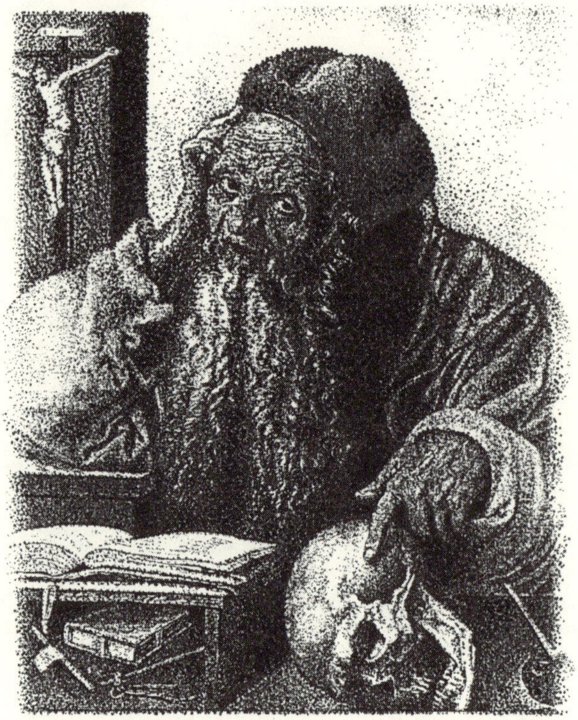

Fig. 26. Albrecht Dürer's *Saint Jerome,* 1521, contemplating a skull, points not so much to the hollow bone as to the question, "What has dwelt within the physical vessel and was once alive?" (After Dürer.)

court of Henry VIII, with his friend George de Selve, the Bishop of Lavaur, who visited his countryman in London in 1533. The exact date and time is recorded by instruments on the shelf. The upper shelf holds objects that deal with the celestial world, and the lower shelf has to do with the terrestrial world. The two men demonstrate contrasting temperaments and lifestyles through their gestures and dress, one clearly a man of the world, the other, one who follows inner pursuits. The pavement in the picture is a copy of the floor design found in the sanctuary of Westminster Abbey, and above it hovers a curiously foreshortened skull. When viewed from the lower right side of the painting, the skull comes into proper perspective; however, from a frontal vantage point it is distorted beyond recognition. Besides the skull, a broken string on the lute, and a crucifix in profile, almost invisible behind the right shoulder of de Dinteville, are further symbols of mortality. Holbein and the ambassadors he painted were in the midst of the court intrigues of an English king whose personal destiny led to momentous historic changes for Christianity. One of the most realistic painters of his day, Holbein depicts the poignant drama of humanity facing the mysterious realities of life and death.

Although we usually think of the great art of the Renaissance, it was actually scientific thinking that was coming to birth with the help of the representational arts. It was, after all, the artists of the Renaissance who were some of the first scientists, experimenting and probing into the material world of appearance. This scientific consciousness was the manifestation of a newly awakening self-awareness. And this developing individuality brought undeniably self-centered and destructive impulses leading to many of the crises we see around us today. However, it also brought about tremendous gifts, not the least of which was personal choice and individual freedom. Such blessings and curses are reflected in the mirror of art, for art is a picture of this unfolding struggle of human development. The many shades of egotism as well as self-sacrifice are vividly expressed in all the arts.

Fig. 27. Facing page: *The Ambassadors,* 1533, by Hans Holbein the Younger, is a portrait of two colleagues, Jean de Dinteville and George de Selve, who viewed the intrigues of Henry VIII's court each from his own perspective. In the foreground appears the distorted specter of death in the form of an optically distorted skull. (National Gallery, London.)

This change in consciousness, characterized by analytical, scientific reasoning, was experienced by Renaissance man as a death process. As Richard Tarnas reflects, "Here is the painful separation from the timeless all-encompassing womb of nature, the development of self-consciousness, the loss of connection with the matrix of being, the expulsion from the Garden, the entrance into

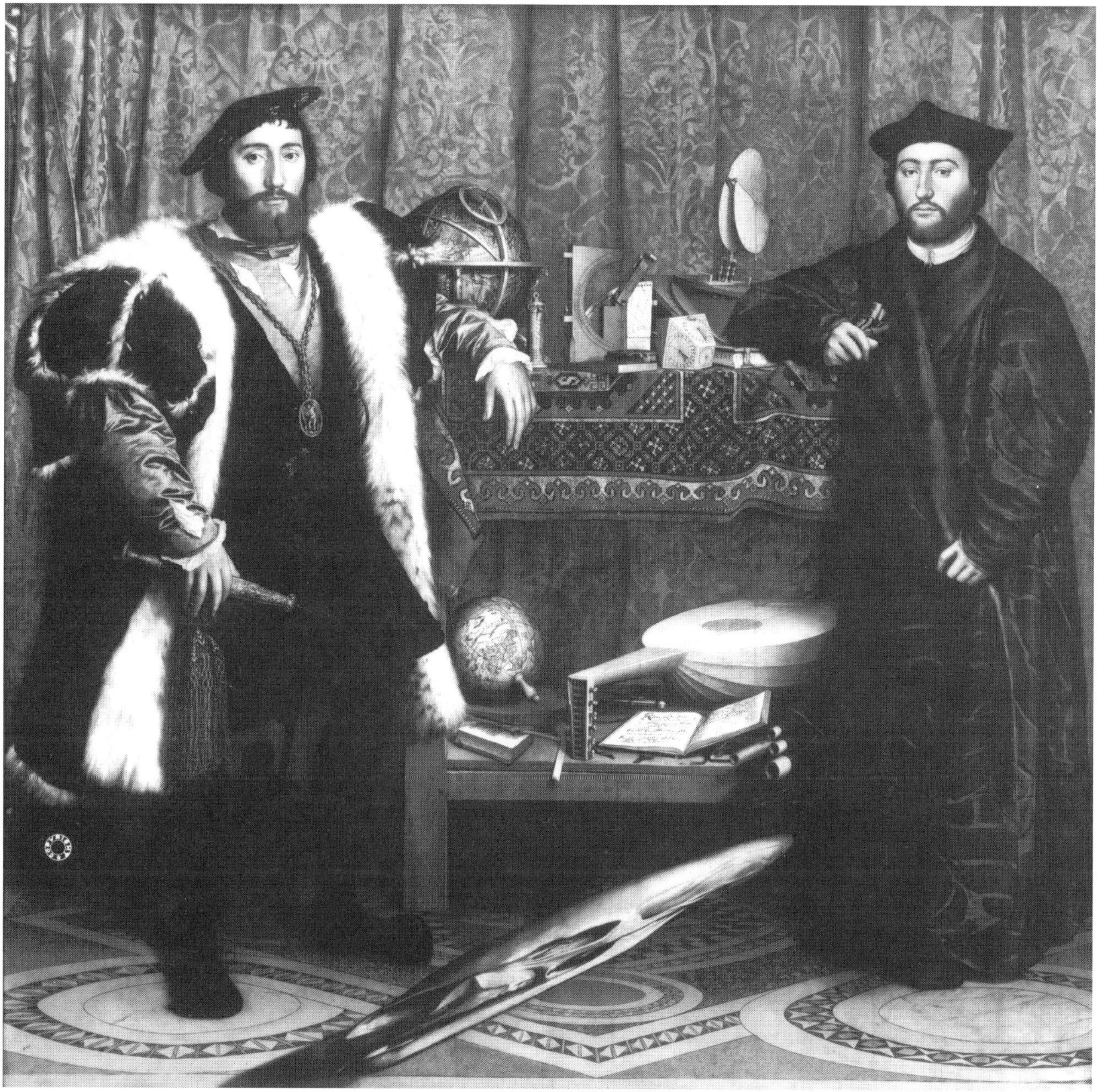

time and history and materiality, the disenchantment of the cosmos, the sense of total immersion in an antithetical world of impersonal forces. . . . Here is the primal fear of losing control and dominance, rooted in the all-consuming awareness and fear of death."[35] This Dance of Death, from which there was no escape, was a popular theme. It is human fate to dance this dance, and although it meant a loss of an earlier spiritual condition, it was nevertheless a feverishly engaging dance that aroused everyone in Europe and swept throughout the Western world. As the year 1500 came and went, plagues wiped out entire populations in Europe and the end of the world was anticipated in the form of great natural catastrophes. The foundations of scientific thinking were being laid down in art by one-point perspective, the study of anatomy, and emphasis on realism married to mechanistic and mathematical thinking. It was an important turning point in history, the age of instinctive knowing was fading, and destiny found a responsive, if somewhat disturbing, partner in the Dance of Death.

1.5 Renaissance and Realism

My eyes, which are in love with beauty, and my soul, which is in love with salvation, can only ascend to heaven by the contemplation of all the beauty surrounding me.
—Michelangelo Buonarotti

A story told about Giotto, the initiator of realism in Renaissance painting, is that as a boy he was discovered scratching the image of a sheep on a rock as he watched over his father's grazing flock. The Florentine artist Cimabue, traveling in the region, was so impressed by the shepherd boy's study from nature that he convinced Giotto's father to let the boy apprentice with him back in Florence. After a very short time Giotto had not only mastered Cimabue's style but showed himself so capable at drawing from life that he made a decisive break from the dominant Byzantine style of the day and set the course for a renaissance in the art of painting.

As a young apprentice in Cimabue's workshop, Giotto painted a fly on the nose of a figure his master had executed. The fly was so lifelike that when Cimabue returned to continue his work he tried several times to brush it away before realizing it was only painted. Giotto surpassed his master by bringing weight and volume to renderings of human figures as well as a realistic quality hardly seen before in painting. The figures he depicted began almost to look like individual people rather than variations of the same person. He was the first artist of his era to replace the traditional gold background (depicting the immediacy of the spiritual world) with a blue sky (fig. 28). He was in this way the founder of realism, which would dominate Western art for the next five hundred years.

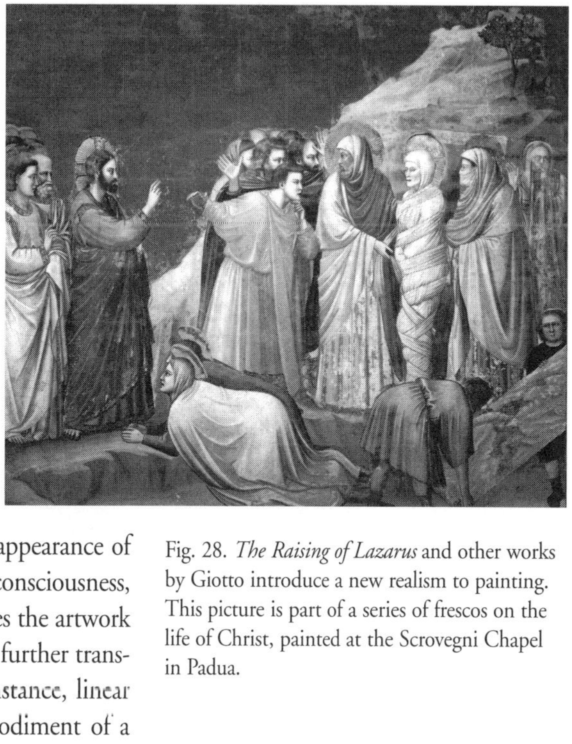

Fig. 28. *The Raising of Lazarus* and other works by Giotto introduce a new realism to painting. This picture is part of a series of frescos on the life of Christ, painted at the Scrovegni Chapel in Padua.

With the Renaissance a new fascination with capturing the appearance of the objective physical world begins. This is concurrent with a shift in consciousness, for when the inner life of humanity undergoes a transformation, so does the artwork that is produced. And when artistic expressions change they promote a further transformation of consciousness as they work back upon humanity. For instance, linear one-point perspective emerges in the fifteenth century. It is the embodiment of a

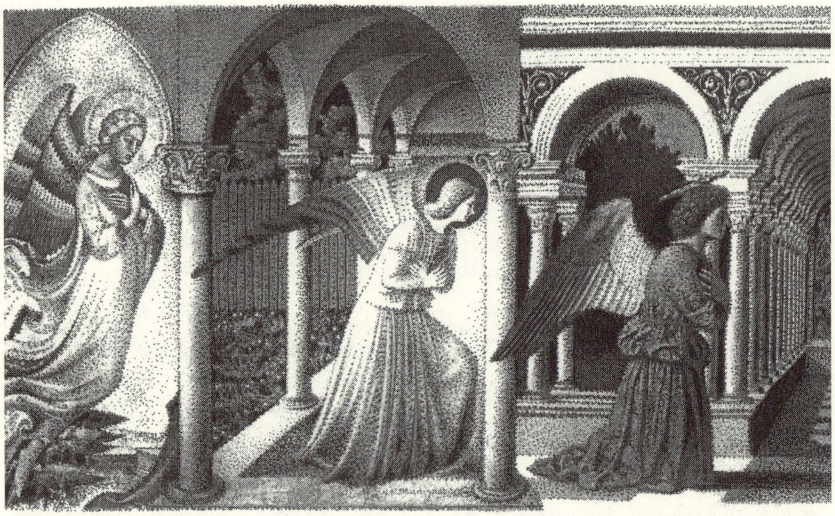

Fig. 29. The Annunciation, after paintings by (from left to right) Lorenzo Monaco, 1420, Fra Angelico, 1432, and Piero della Francesca, 1455, depict the Archangel Gabriel as increasingly earthly and three-dimensional, and less angelic and heavenly, over the course of one generation. During the Renaissance, gold backgrounds and halos disappear while figures gain volume, weight, and shadows.

rationalistic, mechanistic point of view. Jose Argüelles sees it as a standardizing of perception at a visual-sensory level and rightly states that "the grid system employed by one-point perspective is the forerunner of refined cartography and of the Cartesian system of coordinates, the source of all later scientific systems using graphs. Essentially, the one-point perspective is just that—a graph applied to the eye for the purpose of mechanizing vision, and thus mind."[36] Unlike the perspective of other cultures such as the Chinese or the earlier European medieval system, one-point linear perspective arises from and promotes independent, onlooker consciousness with a single vantage point on reality. The more this perspective prevails in the visual arts, the more one-sided and mechanistic is the outlook it engenders.[37]

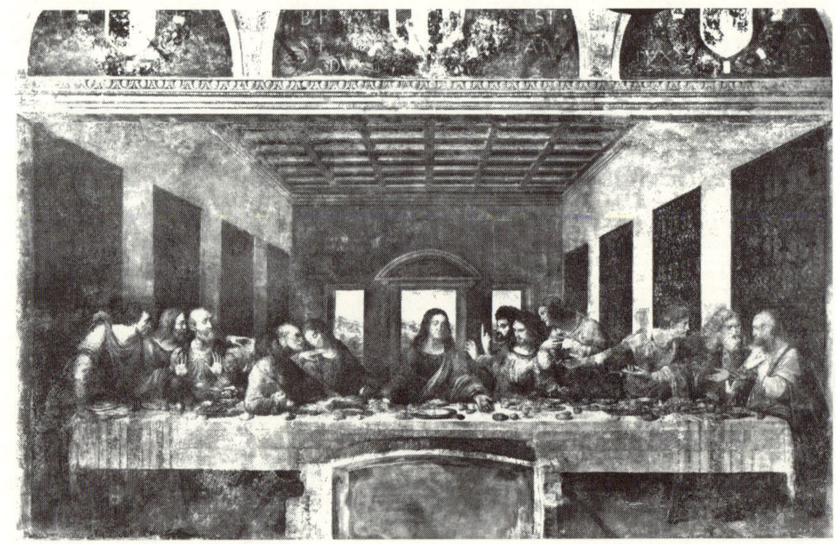

Fig. 30. Right: *The Last Supper* by Leonardo da Vinci is considered the first high Renaissance painting because of its ideal use of symmetry and single-point perspective. It is the first painting to depict Christ without a halo. (Santa Maria delle Grazie, Milan.)

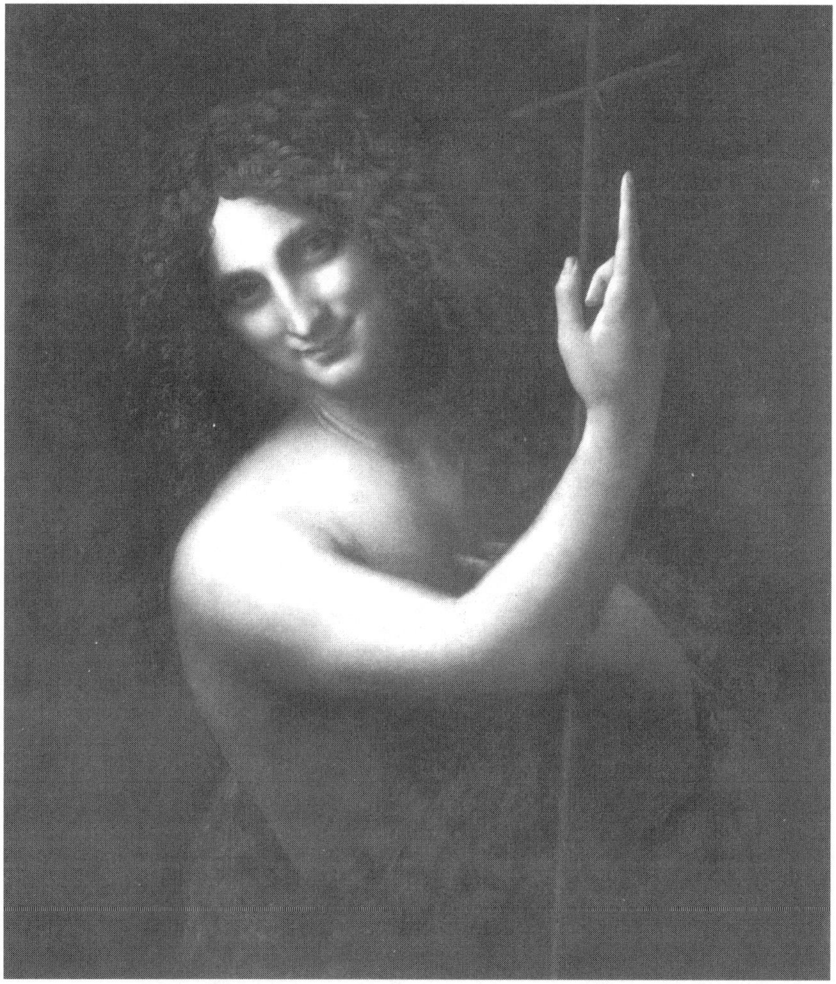

Fig. 31. St. John is an example of Leonardo da Vinci's later work, where he avoids linear perspective and, using his sfumato technique of softening edges, creates a glowing atmosphere that enhances the mysterious spirit of his theme. (Louvre, Paris.)

This embracing of realism occurs over a very brief span of time (fig. 29). Within a generation, the incarnation of perspective (the illusion of depth and volume and the reflection of light and shadow) is complete. Painted in 1420, Lorenzo Monaco's Archangel Gabriel luminously floats against the golden background of a spiritual world. The figure is light and ethereal, with decorative two-dimensional wings. Twelve years later Fra Angelico paints Gabriel with more substantiality, but has him touching the earth only lightly. The surroundings include perspective and delicate shading, but give the impression of a stage set that only intimates the real world. By 1455 this situation is completely transformed as Piero della Francesca turns Gabriel into a being of flesh and blood. The inner illumination of Monaco's angel is now replaced by strongly contrasting light and shadow on the solid, kneeling figure. The wings are no longer flat and stylized, but look like real bird wings.

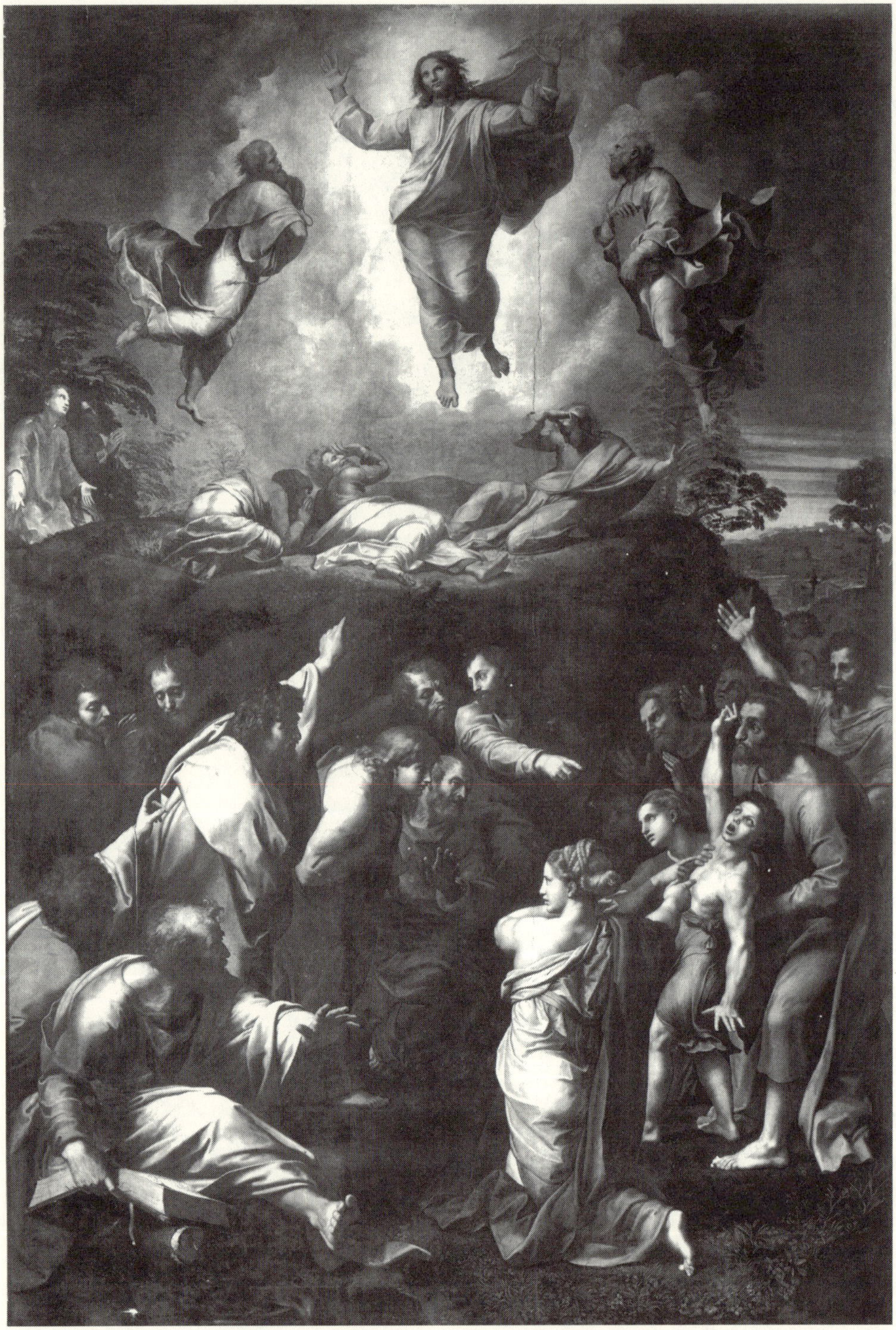

The halo is not a two-dimensional radiance around the angel, but a platelike object balanced precariously on the head. Piero's focus is on the way light falls on a three-dimensional figure in a particular spatial setting, not on the spiritual aspects of the theme. We see how a materialization, an incarnation process in painting as well as in the evolutionary development of consciousness, becomes visible through art. A descent from the spiritual results in an awakening to the physical surroundings.

Artists have always managed to adapt and to overcome obstacles that confound the spirit in art, as Leonardo so ably demonstrates. He set the tone for high Renaissance art in his grand one-point perspective painting of the Last Supper (fig. 30). In it he dropped the use of halos not only from the heads of all the apostles but from Jesus as well, but nevertheless he embodies the work with a powerful spirit. Later in life, Leonardo abandoned linear perspective entirely for a more atmospheric approach to painting with his *sfumato* technique—a cloudy, soft-edge treatment of form. In his late paintings of *Bacchus* and *St. John the Baptist* (fig. 31), Leonardo creates an enigmatic figure, mysteriously pointing within a misty realm. The romantic handling of these late pictures leaves the intellect unable to grasp their full meaning and intent. Kenneth Clark says of the St. John that he is not human but a symbol of "force and mystery," a messenger "from a world which Leonardo da Vinci, the disciple of experience, has not explored, though he has earned the right to proclaim its existence."[38] This world of force and mystery is the place of spirit and art.

Raphael too, in one of his last paintings—still on its easel at the time of his death—ignores perspective at the same time as he demonstrates his proficiency in it. *The Transfiguration,* which depicts Christ on Mt. Tabor with three of his disciples, James, Peter, and John, while his other disciples are confronted by a woman with a possessed child, shows a foreground of great movement and turmoil (fig. 32). Below, none of the disciples knows how to heal the boy; their gestures and postures show a receding composition, yet in the distance Christ appears larger than many of the figures in the foreground. Does Christ hover above the apostles in the foreground or is he far in the distance? He seems to be everywhere. The prostrate disciples on the summit of Tabor are dwarfed just as they are blinded by Christ's spiritual glory. The perspective is entirely unrealistic, and, like Egyptian painting, is founded to some extent on the figures' order of importance. Moses and Elijah appear in spirit on either side of Christ, and the vision of simultaneous events and levels of revelation is dramatic. Christ appears as a symbolic image of his own transfigured spirit being, raising his arms in the orant gesture of life and light.

Michelangelo cared very little for perspective, and in his paintings it is rarely suggested. This is due in part to his avoidance of landscape and his exclusive focus on the human body. This was his world in both painting and sculpture, the microcosm, Man (fig. 33).

Fig. 32. Facing page: Raphael was still working on the *Transfiguration* at the time of his death in 1519. It depicts Christ rising above Mt. Tabor in an aura of light between Moses and Elijah. Peter, James, and John are overcome by the brilliance of the transfigured Christ, and below them, a possessed boy is brought to be cured. The upper scene is symmetrical and solemn, while the lower scene is wild and full of drama. Unusual perspective and a striking contrast of light and darkness are used to their utmost effect. (Vatican, Rome.)

Leonardo, Raphael, and Michelangelo are like the head, heart, and limbs of the Italian Renaissance, and express through their work the very heights of creative thinking (Leonardo), the breadth of human feeling (Raphael), and the depth and power of will (Michelangelo). Together they set a new mark of excellence for which artists would strive for the next half-millennium.

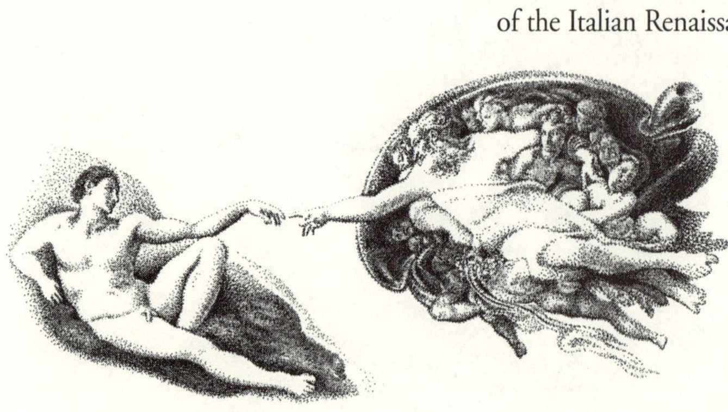

Fig. 33. Above: *God Creating Adam,* from the Sistine Chapel ceiling by Michelangelo, is one of the artist's most powerful images of the human being. (After Michelangelo.)

This proclamation of the spirit and art, exploding in a blaze of Classical form and style, was often best effected at this time through the use of allegory. "For Nature herself is allegorical. Yet nowhere does she impose her allegories on us, or show them to us outwardly."[39] One example of the use of allegory is in Sandro Botticelli's *Primavera* (color plate 4), which serves as a poetic example of how naturalistic figures, freely rendered with little adherence to anatomical rules or linear perspective, can reveal the primal language and inner meaning of art.

Fig. 34. Below: Detail from Sandro Botticelli's *Primavera.*

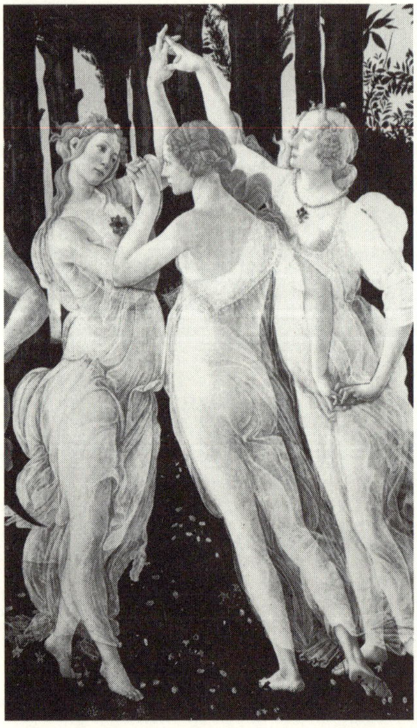

Read from right to left, a blue-grey Zephyr, with puffing cheeks, pursues the fleeing earth-nymph, Chloris. Frightened by the cold winter wind rushing through the trees, she tries to escape Zephyr's embrace, but as he breathes on her, flowers spew from her mouth to decorate Flora, the victorious beauty of Spring. In the center of the garden, with her eyes upon us, is Venus directing the dance of the three Graces. Above her is the blindfolded Cupid aiming his flaming arrow at the central Grace, Castitas (chastity). Like all the female figures in Botticelli's painting, she is full-bellied, as though pregnant. Her movement to the left is countered by Voluptas (passion), the only figure in the picture moving opposite to the processional flow. The third Grace, Pulchritudo (beauty), clasps the hands of the other two in a gesture that surrounds Castitas (fig. 34). Edgar Wind describes the visual poetry of the Graces thus: "That this gesture is made to hover like a crown above the head of Castitas defines the theme of the dance as her initiation. Castitas [juvenescence] is the neophyte, initiated into Love by the ministrations of Voluptas and Pulchritudo. Protected by Venus and assailed by Cupid, she adopts some of the traits that she resists. Her garment has fallen from her left shoulder, this being the side on which she is joined by Voluptas [abundant pleasure]; and in deference to Pulchritudo [splendor], on her right, a rich flowing tress escapes from the knot of her hair. Yet as she acts the part of the 'enraptured' Grace who unites the opposites in her person, the whole dance becomes imbued with her own spirit of chastity which she imparts to her two companions. In this she appears to have the sanction of Venus; for however recklessly Cupid may shoot his fire, Venus tempers the dance and keeps its movements within a melodious restraint."[40] Castitas, as the central Grace, is the only figure who turns her back to us and looks toward the youthful Mercury, "messenger of the gods" and "guide of souls." Mercury, in his traditional garb, plays with a patch of clouds that hover above the golden apples of Venus. As Virgil writes of Mercury in the *Aeneid,* "With his staff, he drives the wind and skims the turbid clouds."[41] Mercury, with his magical staff, is the hierophant and mediator between mortals and gods. He is the messenger of secret, "hermetic" knowledge, the one who parts the veil and "reveals the mysteries." He directs our attention above and beyond the painting, back to the beginning of the procession, to his counterpart, the complementary force of Zephyr.

In the first grouping, Zephyr, as Passion, transforms fleeing Chloris as Chastity into Flora or Beauty. Marsilio Ficino, the Neoplatonist philosopher and teacher of Michelangelo, called this a "productive triad," because of its forward, descending movement. It is a process that descends into the physical. The Graces, overseen by Venus and Cupid, transform the theme through their giving, receiving and returning into what Ficino regards as a "converting triad," a transformative circling and recycling dance. The third phase of the composition is reascension in the figure of Mercury with his orientation towards the spiritual worlds. Mercury directs us past the visible images of the picture to the forces active behind them. Even though we have a painting of sensual beauty and loveliness before us, it is to the invisible, supersensory world that Botticelli's *Primavera* ultimately directs our attention. It is the spiritual nature of springtime and Love that is ultimately portrayed here. As Charles Dempsey describes the picture: "It is a hymn to the abundance and liberality of the earth, and to the inseminating wind that flies over it, and it is especially a hymn to the regenerative spirit of life in nature, a spirit summarized in Venus Physica."[42] And: "The painting in its wholeness is the portrait of love."[43]

Eventually the use of allegory leads from a spiritually meaningful, moral content to a rigid moralizing in the form of fixed ideas and images. And as realism becomes the dominant vehicle of post-Renaissance visual representation, we observe that the Christian legend becomes less and less the central theme in European art. Both these developments have an overwhelming influence on the formative arts and on human consciousness. Just as faculties of human cognition shape the arts of this time, so are they shaped by the arts.

> *What greater gain in life can man ere know*
> *Than when God-Nature has to him revealed*
> *How matter's form to spirit it lets flow*
> *And the spirit-quickened in matter's form be sealed.*
> *—Goethe*[44]

1.6 Cathedral

Let the churches be filled with paintings that they who do not know their letters may be able to read on the walls what they cannot read in the manuscripts.
—Pope Gregory III

Imagine you live in medieval Europe. You have not yet learned the Dance of Death; you do not engage in abstract, logical thinking. You live in tune with nature and her rhythms and you have an unshakable faith in the creative spirit working through the world. Your faith and your devotional life have led you to take a pilgrimage to one of Europe's great cathedrals. A journey of this kind requires preparation, separation, transformation, and return. Such a journey can be a substitute for traditional initiation rites. As you approach your goal, perhaps after weeks of expectant travel on foot, you see the spires of the cathedral from afar, stretching heavenward, like clasped hands in prayer, piercing the sky. Across the meadows and farmland, it is the tallest structure, a sacred focal point, presiding over the entire town. As the church comes clearly into view, the architectural forms reveal elaborate stone tracery and sculpted stone figures in niches upon the facade. In the carved images you recognize Old and New Testament figures as well as fantastic creatures in the form of gargoyles (fig. 35). These latter figures, which often serve as rainspouts ("gargoyle" comes from the French word *gargouille,* also the root of "gargle"), carry runoff from storms, directing the flow of water and fury of the elements away from the holy house. These striking images are intended to draw evil forces into their stone forms, thus diverting negative influences away from the church itself. Cathedrals were intended to serve as unassailable bulwarks against demonic forces and to turn these forces to stone.

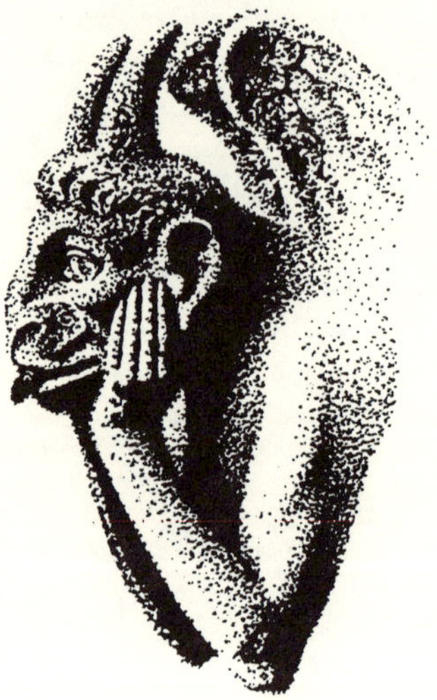

Fig. 35. Gargoyles guarded the House of God by redirecting mischievous and malevolent elements away from the cathedral. (Chartres Cathedral, France.)

As you approach the great west portal, you learn about heaven and earth by relief sculptures of saints and prophets, spiritual beings, and symbols of cosmic powers. The image of Christ within the tympanum suggests the words from the Gospel of Saint John, "I am the way, and the truth, and the life; no one comes to the Father but by me" (fig. 36).[45] As you enter the royal portal you leave behind the outer world of nature for an otherworldly, inner space unlike anything you have ever beheld before. Entering the narthex, you first experience a compression of space, then you move into the vast nave of the church (fig. 37). "The root of the word 'nave' is the same as *navy*, with its overtones of the ark, and of protection from the boundless fears of the deep."[46] This is why the church is often referred to as a ship. Reverence for this sacred space overwhelms you and you drop to your knees and cross yourself. Holy water is provided for the act of purification. As you collect yourself, you notice the harmony of the interior architecture: distances between pillars and the length of the nave, transept, and choir were sometimes based on the divine proportion or Golden Section. But more often the architects stressed the vertical direction through progressively elongated proportions so that one feels drawn out of oneself. Three entrances appear at each of the four directions, twelve gates in all, referring to the New Jerusalem (Rev. 22:12–13). In the east, behind the altar, toward Paradise, the gateway is not physical, but spiritual.

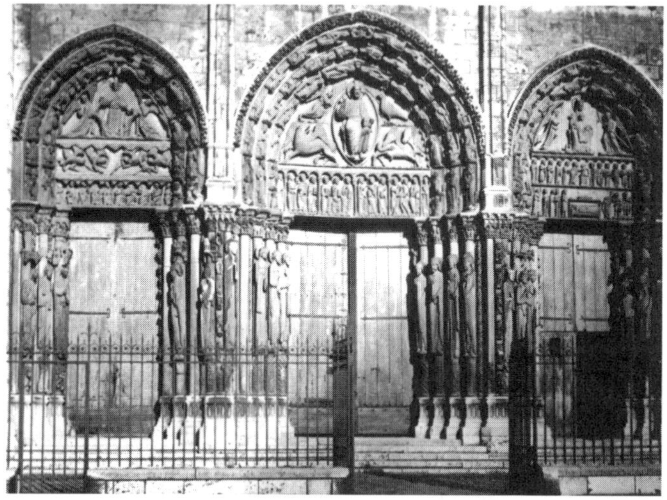

Fig. 36. The royal portal with its tympanum displayed images appropriate to the threshold of a sacred place and the House of God. (Chartres Cathedral.)

Fig. 37. Chartres Cathedral's ground plan shows it to be one of the few cathedrals oriented to other than a strict east-west axis. This allows for seasonal light effects to occur within the structure.

Fresco paintings on walls and tempera paintings on wood panels become visible as your eyes adjust to the diffuse, interior light; their forms and colors are framed and accented with the glitter of gold leaf. Finely crafted woodcarvings are illuminated by atmospheric colored light streaming in from gem-like stained glass windows along the aisles. The window pictures tell of genealogies, ancestral deeds, and great spiritual destinies, as the medium of outer sunlight, by penetrating translucent glass, is transformed into a colorful radiance. A metaphor was thus given in the art of stained glass for the virgin birth, the birth of colored light into the world out of the clear, divine light of the heavens.

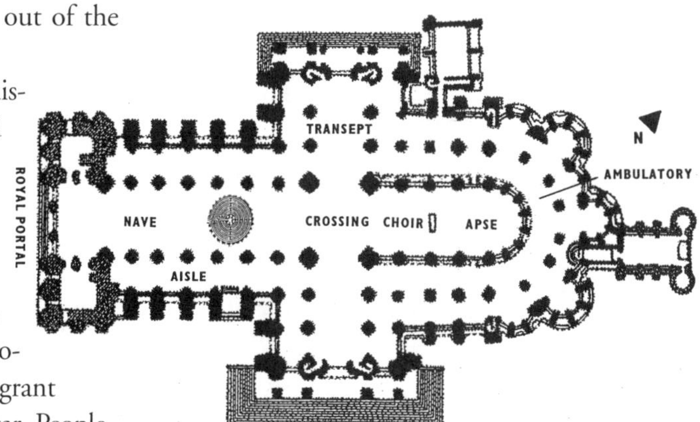

All the visual arts work together in order to dissolve the walls in a diaphanous experience of color and light. Music resounds through the interior spaces of the cathedral. "Then the voices rebound to become musically what the vault is architecturally," as the sculptor Auguste Rodin observed. "Music and architecture meet, cross one another, and unite in elegant melodies."[47] The art of the chanted and spoken word reverberates as chromatic displays of light catch the rising columns of fragrant smoky incense. A ritual procession moves toward the altar. People in regal, flowing garments, holding candles and sacred objects, carry out a religious choreography as the sacred drama of High Mass is celebrated. All the

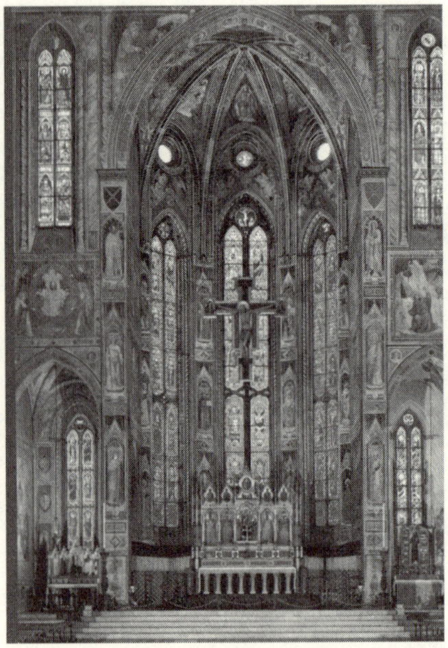

Fig. 38. Above: Santa Croce, in Florence, displays an impressive sacred space with powerful religious imagery, including frescos by Giotto.

Fig. 39. Below: Chartres Cathedral's labyrinth is a central feature of the nave and part of a pilgrim's sacred journey. (Copyright © Cindy A. Pavlinac/Sacred Land Photography.)

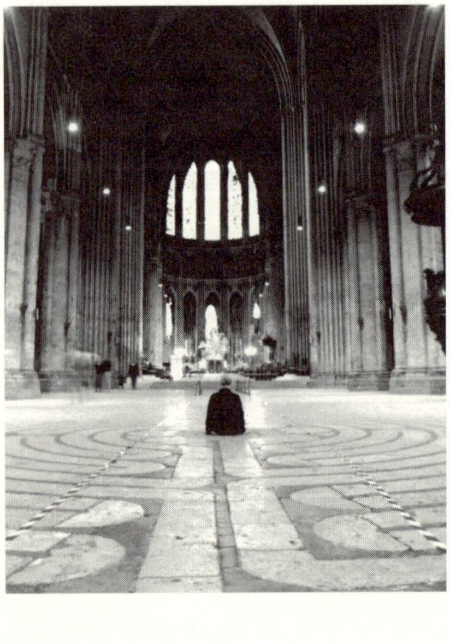

arts come together in a festive, yet sacred display of the spiritual (fig. 38). As Otto von Simpson writes of the Gothic cathedral, "Within its walls God himself was mysteriously present. The medieval sanctuary was the image of heaven."[48]

Perhaps the cathedral has a tile labyrinth on its floor, as does Chartres in France, of which Emile Male says, "Other cathedrals of the Christian world have not known how to say so many things, nor how to say them in such a splendid order. . . . Chartres is the very spirit of the Middle Ages made manifest."[49] The labyrinth is the largest decorative element at Chartres (fig. 39). Other cathedrals with ritual labyrinths include Amiens, Reims, and Saint Quentin.

Again you fall to your knees, this time remaining on them as you proceed, rosary in hand, in solemn prayer, along the path of the labyrinth. This final stage of your pilgrimage, before you reach the altar, finds you moving in straight lines, in gently curving arcs, and in rounded 180-degree turns, coming close to the heart of the labyrinth then moving further away from it. Finally, after spiraling through eleven giant rings, you enter the six-petaled center of the labyrinthine design, the twelfth rung. You have traced a 660-foot-long pattern on the floor of the cathedral, an image of the inner path of the soul on its journey to its source, a recreation of the pilgrimage to Jerusalem, the way to God. You see a brass plaque at the center of the Chartres labyrinth (no longer there) depicting Theseus, Ariadne, and the Minotaur, an allegorical depiction of overcoming the devil with the help of the Virgin Lady. (The labyrinth is not only a symbol for Christ's descent into hell for redemption and resurrection but it is also a picture of the complexity within cosmic order, and an image of humanity as microcosm.) You look up from your prayerful journey towards the sanctuary at the eastern end of the church to find that all these movements and all these sense impressions have brought you to the threshold of a mystic experience, the ecstasy of spiritual revelation.

The cathedral is based on the plan of a cross and the human form. One enters at the foot of the cross, from the base level of the earth, and gradually approaches the heart of the church at the crossing and the head at the ambulatory and sanctuary. Enlightenment is sought between head and heart at the altar by receiving the host in the form of bread and wine, as the body and blood of the Creative Word.

This supersensory experience, kindled by ritual arts and inner faith, is described by Argüelles thus: "The Gothic cathedral provides an example of an aesthetic process whose end is achieved when a participant is able to experience a state of psychosensorial interfusion. The effect of different sensory agents acting upon the participant simultaneously transfuses and uplifts the whole being, evoking a transcendent experience. With the onset of the Renaissance this total experience became much more the exception than the rule."[50] This "transcendent experience," based on a "state of psychosensorial interfusion" occurs even far less today and is seen as a pathological condition when it does occur. However, such a state is akin to the shaman's trance condition and the seer's visionary experience in that it provides a momentary "crossing of the threshold," or transcendence of the barrier between the spiritual and sensorial worlds. The arts work upon the senses in such a way that the senses themselves are transcended and, rather than the exception to the rule, this was likely the predisposition of early humanity.

Wherever a cathedral was being constructed, the townspeople, as well as those of the surrounding countryside, would be involved in the building, usually for generations. It was the building of a community as much as it was the construction of a church. This is what many artists and architects of the twentieth century dreamed of when they spoke of building the "Cathedral of the Future" and the "Crown of the City." They felt a spontaneous urge would take hold of people to erect a "Peoples' House" and form a new community of brothers and sisters.[51] Such buildings would in turn shape and mold the individual within his or her community. As Winston Churchill remarked, "We shape our dwellings, and our dwellings shape us." In medieval times every stone was set in place by an individual who took pride in his or her work. Every door handle and hinge was singularly handcrafted by someone who poured his thinking, feelings, and will into the work (fig. 40). This work affected and

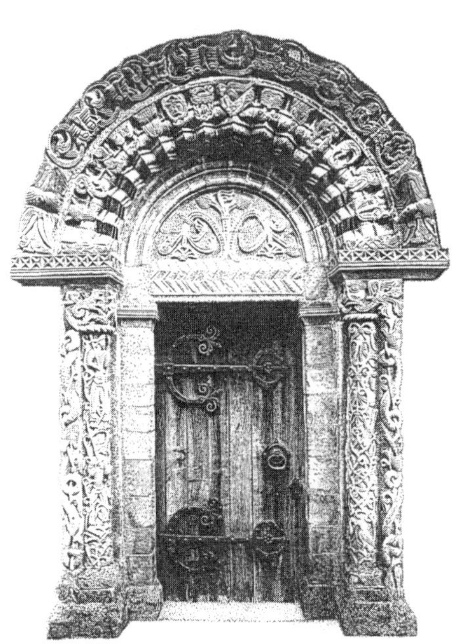

Fig. 40. Above: Medieval entrances were often designed to lift the soul of the visitor toward a mood appropriate for religious services. This twelfth-century church doorway at Kilpeck, England, supports such a task by way of its design patterns and figurative imagery, which includes signs of the zodiac and mythical beasts. The grapevine in the tympanum symbolizes Christ, "the true vine."

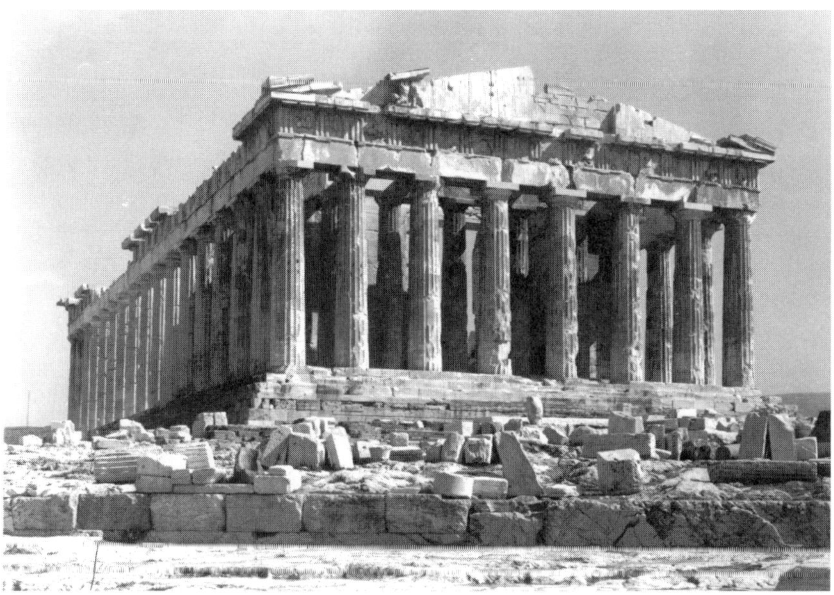

Fig. 41. Left: Greek temple architecture, such as that seen in the Parthenon in Athens, expresses balance and harmony between heaven and earth. The Parthenon, dedicated to Athena, goddess of wisdom, incorporates slight "imperfections" that help create visual balance and harmony: end columns are closer to their neighbors, column shafts swell slightly to allow for a more harmonious perspective from the ground, and the floor rises at its middle by as much as four inches.

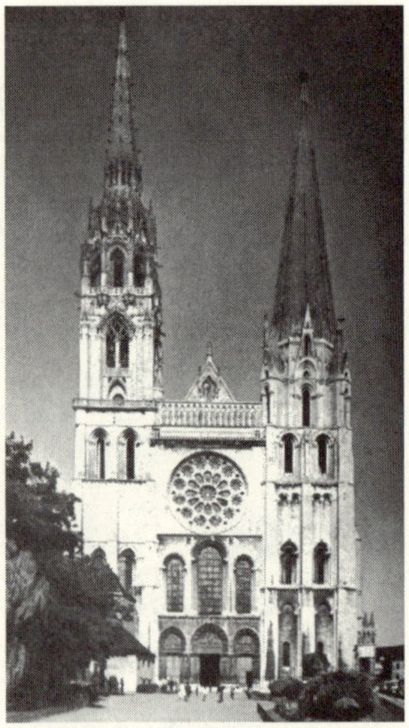

Fig. 42. Above: The cathedral exterior demonstrates a striving to the heights, rather than a balance of lightness and weight. The difference in the spires of the cathedral at Chartres (above) resulted from successive building phases.

Fig. 43. Flying buttresses, like these at Chartres cathedral (below), form a skeletonlike-structure that carries weight away from the walls, allowing them to be thin and light and to rise to great heights.

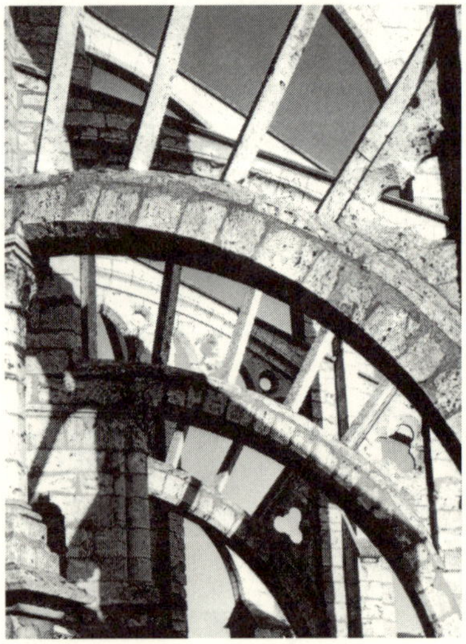

influenced everyone who came into contact with it and became part of the inner life of the townspeople. A moral-aesthetic impulse was passed on in this way. Secret societies like the Masons were well aware of this power of the arts, and the builders of the cathedrals, in the ancient temple-building tradition, put the spiritual language of form to profound use.[52] Rodin could say out of his artistic sensibility, "If we could but understand Gothic Art we would be irresistibly led back to Truth."[53]

The Gothic cathedral is a total work of art. In it all the arts come together in the service of the sacred. The Greek temple was intended only for the god; no people were admitted into the interior apart from the priests. The Christian church was a dwelling not only for God but for the entire congregation. The faithful were allowed entry into the house of God. They needed to enter his house because they were fast losing the experience of God in nature. The Greek temple stood like an altar in the landscape (fig. 41), expressive of human beings living on the earth in communion with the spiritual worlds. The Christian church presents a duality in its striving beyond the landscape, attempting to rise above nature (fig. 42). Christians had to leave nature, leave their land and the outer affairs of daily life, in order to seek the spirit within the cathedral. Even within the cathedral there was a division between congregation and priest, between nave and sacristy.

A curious structural aspect of the Gothic cathedral is the piers and buttresses that form a bonelike framework on which the walls and windows are placed like a thin skin (fig. 43). This skeleton of the cathedral prefigures the structural design of the modern skyscraper, and prepares medieval men and women for the discovery of their own skeletons, their own dances with death. The essential spirituality of the cathedral, in the temple-building tradition of the ancients, is achieved by way of exemplifying the mysteries of the human body, at the same time as providing a picture of upward striving toward God. The forms of the Gothic cathedral lead out into the great beyond.

Baptistries and mausoleums are often built adjacent to cathedrals and basilicas. In contrast to the axial layout of the church, which invokes movement and directional flow towards the altar, the baptistry and mausoleum have round or octagonal central floor plans, which elicit rest. Whereas the baptistry and mausoleum are places for approaching the thresholds of birth and death, respectively—entrances and exits of life—the cathedral is where one encounters the threshold of the spirit while in the midst of life's journey. The architectural forms are in each case suited to the purpose of the building in the way they encourage peace or movement.

Imagine entering an eighth-century baptistry for your conversion and baptism into the Christian faith. You step into the waist-deep water of the

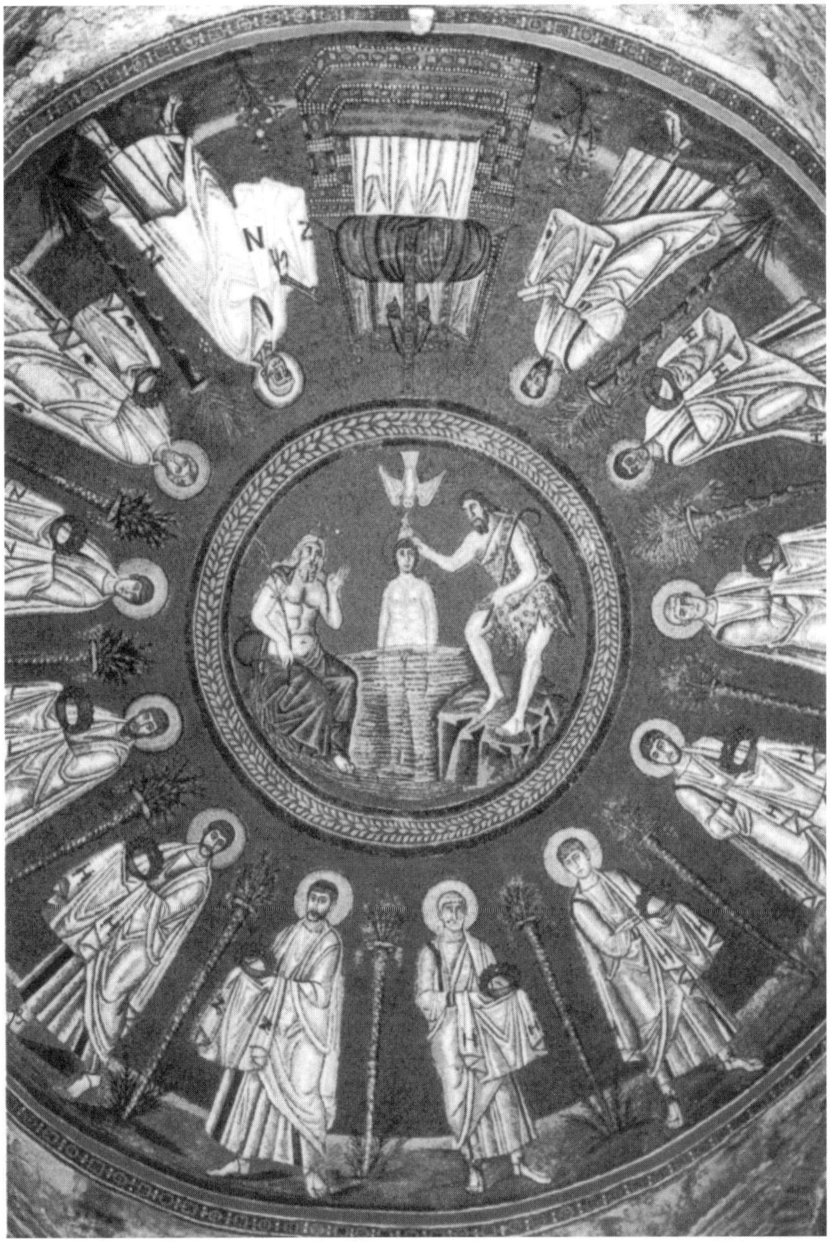

Fig. 44. The cupola mosaics in Ravenna's Arian Baptistry, from the late fifth century A.D., portray the beardless Christ-Apollo and acknowledge the river god, Jordana.

sacred font with the officiating priest and he bends you backwards, immersing you completely in the blessed water. It may only be a few moments, but the simple dunking is a "trial by water," inducing a near-drowning experience where your entire life flashes before you in a great panorama of pictures. You are quickly raised up out of the water gasping for breath and the first thing you see on the ceiling is the mandala-like mosaic image of the Twelve Apostles surrounding Jesus at his baptism, which represents the constellations of the zodiac surrounding the sun.

In this vast ceiling mosaic, Jesus stands in the river Jordan with the river god on one side, representing the beings of nature, and John the Baptist on the other. John is the Hebrew prophet who "makes way" for the one who will "baptize with fire," the one "who must increase." Above, the hand of the Father God releases the Holy Spirit in the form of a dove, which descends via the living water into the Son. This is the moment of the birth of Christ, the Son of God, in Jesus, the Son of Man. It is also the beginning of the three and a half years that the Christ, the Highest of the Sun Sphere Beings, will live on earth in a human body. In many early depictions, Jesus is shown beardless, as the Apollo-Christ (fig. 44), whereas later representations usually show him bearded as "the man of sorrows." Jordana, god of the river, is crowned with two flaming horns, demonstrating that the chthonic gods and the elements take part in this event.

Today we look at the art and objects of the church as symbols of religious belief, but to genuine practitioners, people of premodern consciousness, they are far more than mere symbols. Polynesians would say such sacred objects are imbued with *mana* (spiritual power). Although such a relationship to the art of the church may be for the most part lost today, for early Christians religious art was imbued with divine power that could heal and save souls lost in a world of baffling temptations and desires. Painted icons, sculpted figures, stained-glass images, and architectural forms were, along with holy sites and relics of saints, experienced as a part of the sacred practice that helped form men and women into whole human beings. Francis of Assisi describes the artist's part in this practice as follows: "He who works with his hands is a laborer. He who works with his hands and his head is a craftsman. He who works with his hands, his head, and his heart is an artist."

1.7 Catacomb

O truly sacred mysteries! O pure light! In the blaze of the torches I have a vision of heaven and of God. I become holy by initiation.

—Clement of Alexandria

Jesus said, Take ye away the stone. Martha, the sister of him that was dead, saith unto him, Lord, by this time he stinketh: for he hath been dead four days. Jesus saith unto her, Said I not unto thee, that, if thou wouldest believe, thou shouldest see the glory of God?

—John 11:39–40

And when he thus had spoken, he cried with a loud voice, Lazarus, come forth. And he that was dead came forth, bound hand and foot with graveclothes: and his face was bound about with a napkin. Jesus saith unto them, Loose him, and let him go.

—John 11:43–44

Scenes such as the raising of Lazarus, Noah's ark, and Jonah and the whale are frequently depicted in catacomb art and are generally explained as parables of resurrection. However, Lazarus, Jonah, and Noah, once having undergone their crucial transformation of soul after a death or near-death experience, return to their physical bodies. Resurrection transcends the physical body for a higher form of existence in a spiritual "body." Lazarus, Jonah, and Noah are all symbols of initiation, for in each of them the soul returns to the physical body.

In catacomb art, Noah's ark is often pictured as a square box, a coffin on four legs, bearing a striking resemblance to a sarcophagus in which the neophyte of the mysteries undergoes the "temple sleep," or mystical death. A boat is not represented. Noah stands erect, arms in the triumphant orant gesture, a gesture significant of prayer and uplifting, body-free experience. Sometimes Noah appears with wings and other times a dove flies above him with an olive sprig in its beak (fig. 45)—a picture of the soul reaching beyond the coffin of the body into the realm of spirit, where it finds solid ground after drifting on the waters of the deep.

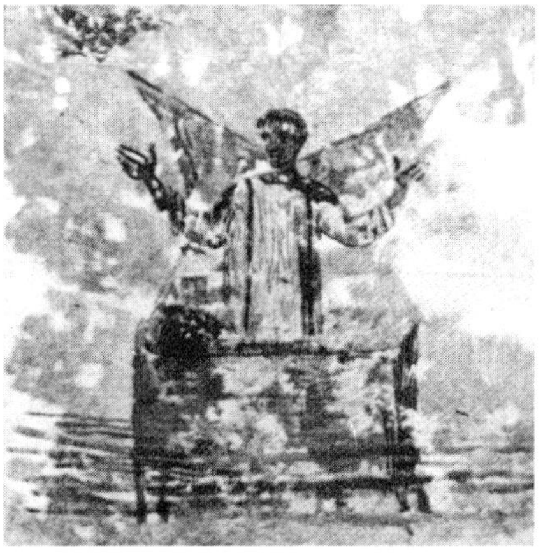

Fig. 45. Above: Noah, shown with wings, gives the orant gesture from an "ark" as a dove bearing an olive sprig hovers above. (Domitilla Catacomb, Rome.)

Jonah is frequently depicted in catacomb art in three successive scenes:

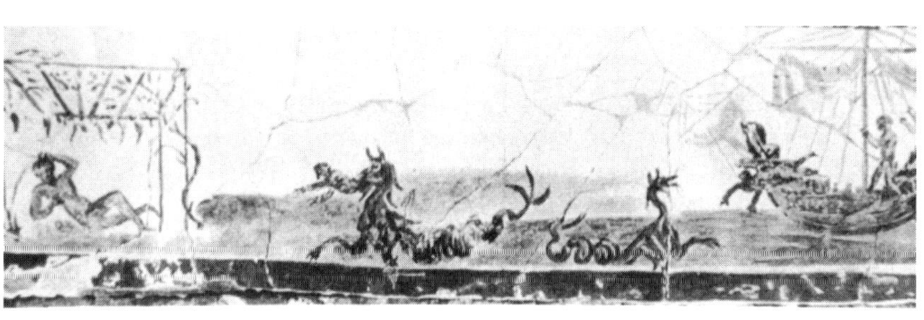

Fig. 46. Left: Three images, moving from right to left, describe the story of Jonah: he is thrown overboard to quell God's wrath; is spat out of the mouth of a "great fish"; and reclines in the arbor. (Callistus Catacomb, Rome.)

being tossed into the stormy sea for trying to flee from God, and being swallowed by the "great fish" or whale; being spewed out onto dry land after "three days and three nights," and finally, in the arbor (fig. 46). The first scene depicts the trial by water, where the soul becomes one with the elements of nature. As expressed in the Bible: "The waters encompassed me about, even to the soul; the depth closed me round about, the weeds were wrapped about my head. I went down to the bottoms of the mountains; the earth with her bars was about me for ever" (Jon. 2:5–6). The second scene illustrates the three-day mystical death, in which the soul departs from the body and sojourns in the spiritual world. The final scene points to a further level of development, a new awareness and relationship to the spiritual worlds.

In *The Raising of Lazarus,* Christ stands before a tomb with the wand of a hierophant, poised to initiate his beloved pupil (fig. 47). The figure of Lazarus, who was dead for several days, is bound like an Egyptian mummy in grave wrappings. The raising of Lazarus can be viewed as the first Christian initiation, linking it to the ancient mystery traditions and the three-day temple sleep. To carry out a rite of initiation in public was against the traditions of occult brotherhoods, and it was from this moment on that the Pharisees and Hebrew initiates sought the death of Jesus. His pupil, Lazarus, raised from the dead, takes on his initiation name, John, becoming "the disciple that Jesus loved"—the only apostle able to witness the crucifixion and death of Jesus on Golgotha, the "place of the skull." Golgotha is traditionally linked with the locale where Adam was laid to rest. The skull depicted in medieval pictures beneath the cross is that of the First Man.

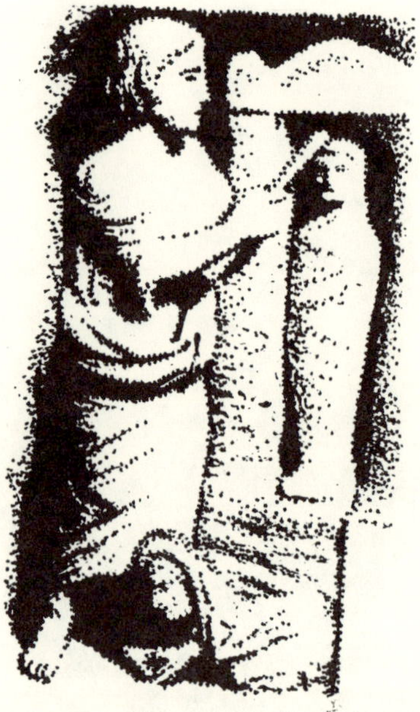

Fig. 47. The Raising of Lazarus (above) shows Jesus with the wand of the hierophant performing the first Christian initiation. (After a sarcophagus relief sculpture from the Lateran Museum, Rome.)

Fig. 48. A passage in the Catacomb of Alexander (below) shows empty niches in which the dead were buried. The niches were sealed with stone slabs, which were often decorated with carved symbols and painted images.

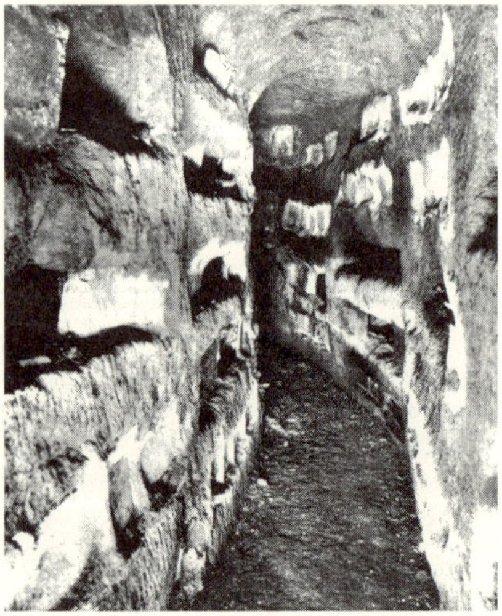

It was not uncommon during the Roman era to bury the dead below the foundations of living quarters. Family plots often became extensive cemeteries, and included not only relatives but also friends of like religious persuasion. Early Christian Romans continued the practice of burying their dead beneath their homes and many such underground cemeteries are now referred to as catacombs. *Ad catacumbas* refers to a particular Roman subterranean cemetery (now known as St. Sebastian's) and might be translated as "sunken valley," or "by the caves." Found throughout Italy, Sicily, Malta, France, Greece, and the Near East, catacombs appear in their greatest concentration in and around Rome.[54]

Catacombs were usually constructed by digging an underground stairway that led to horizontal tunnels, six to eight feet high and three to five feet wide, that ran in various directions below the property of well-to-do early Christians. The passageways had bunk-style niches dug into their walls in which the dead were laid to rest and the corridors connected to chambers used as sanctuaries and chapels (fig. 48). When all of the underground area had been dug with intersecting passageways and galleries, another stairway was dug deeper and another level of corridors and chambers was constructed. Some catacombs have as many as six levels, and their passageways are so extensive and mazelike that it is possible to get lost in them.

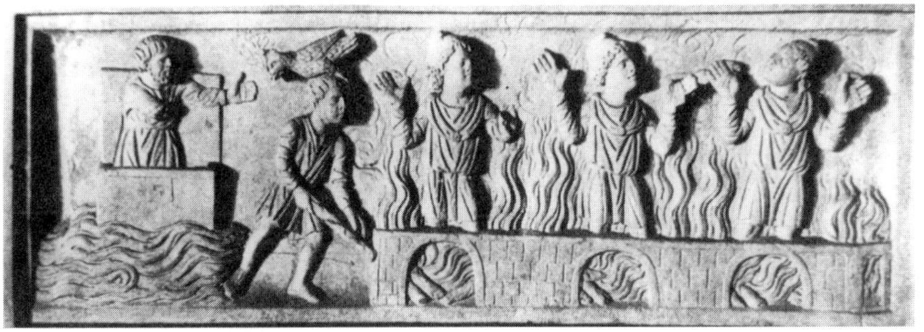

Fig. 49. Left: Scenes from the stories of Noah and of the young men in the fiery furnace are depicted on the side of this sarcophagus in the Lateran Museum in Rome. The trials by water and fire are clearly indicated.

Fig. 50. Below: A sarcophagus relief of Daniel in the Lion's Den shows the prophet standing in the orant gesture above the lions which flank him on either side. (Ravenna, Italy.)

It is curious that later Christian churches often had labyrinthine designs placed on their floors, reminiscent of these first Christian sanctuaries that were, in fact, underground labyrinths.

Tomb niches for the dead were sealed with marble slabs or ceramic tiles, on which inscriptions or paintings were often fashioned. Paintings were mostly done in red ochre colors and extended into larger chambers as full-scale fresco murals. Catacomb painting, most prevalent in the second and third centuries A.D., dealt with themes well beyond Old and New Testament subjects. Often pagan mythology was featured in catacomb art. However, the themes always pointed to the significance of spiritual transformation and moral development. All catacomb paintings, hidden as they were from the outer gaze of imperial Rome, were rendered in the service of the sacred mystery described in Christian scripture as "the Word (Logos) made flesh." In the catacombs *mysterion* (Greek) became *sacramentum* (Latin).[55]

The trials of initiation and the stages of the soul's purification are well illustrated in sculptural relief carved on sarcophagi of this period. Before Constantine became emperor, numerous reliefs appeared in catacomb burial chambers. Once Christianity became the state religion and basilicas were built above ground, sarcophagi were placed below the altar (the altar itself is a sarcophagus) in subterranean crypts, the transformed catacomb. Sculptural scenes from the fourth and fifth centuries capture the spiritual vision of the early Christian Mysteries. Daniel in the lions' den is a theme that juxtaposes the animal and the human being (fig. 49). A simple and perfect pyramidal symmetry is used in one striking composition where Daniel poses in the orant gesture and lions heel to prophetic authority. The lion throne, where a pair of lions flank the Great Goddess or Egyptian pharaoh, is echoed here with Daniel radiating the strength drawn from these sun creatures. Daniel wears the Persian-style Phrygian cap of the initiate, or wise man, and stands with a triumphant bearing indicative of one who has overcome the animal nature with lionlike courage. We can easily understand the power such an image must have had for early Christians who, for a time, were persecuted by imperial Rome, and thrown to their deaths before wild lions.

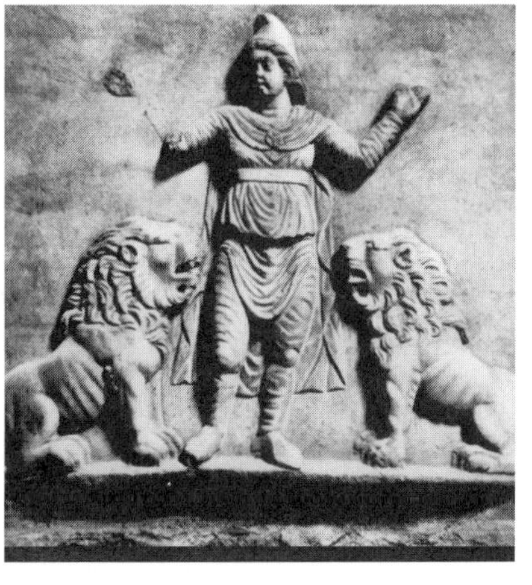

Another beautifully carved sarcophagus relief renders Noah in his

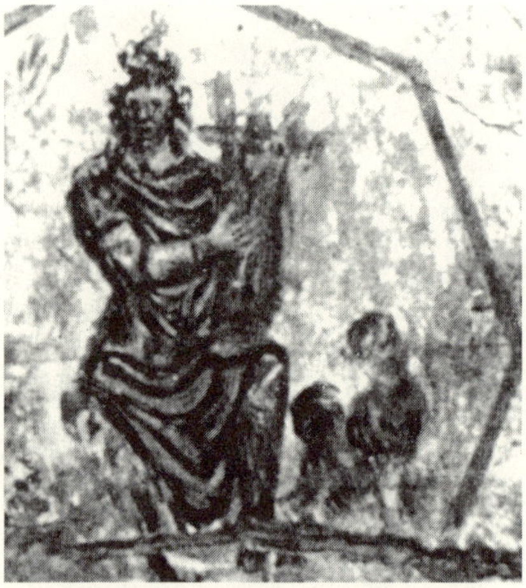

Fig. 51. Above: Orpheus with his lyre, an allusion to Christ, appears at Callistus Catacomb, Rome.

Fig. 52. Below: The killing of the Hydra, one of the twelve Labors of Heracles, depicts a trial of the soul. (Via Latina Catacomb, Rome.)

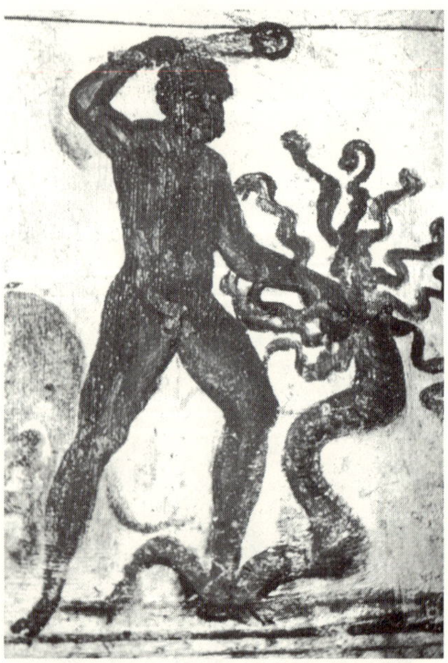

ark-casket upon the flood waters (fig. 50). He reaches out to receive the olive branch carried by a dove indicating that dry land is near. Beside this scene a man stokes the fiery furnace in which Shadrach, Mishach, and Abednego have been sent to die. However, the three young men are unhurt. In fact, they seem to be radiant as they stand in the orant gesture of life, rejoicing and praising God. Wearing Phrygian caps, they prove themselves to be possessors of initiate knowledge. These two scenes indicate a successful negotiation of the trial by water and the trial by fire. Noah is the initiate that can survive in a body-free spiritual condition where reliance on the physical body—solid ground—is no longer necessary. It is a state of being in which one is set adrift upon the Cosmic Sea. The trial by fire is the realm of burning desires. Here the three soul forces (thinking, feeling, willing), represented by the three Children of Israel, are purged of their earthly passions and longings, their doubt, hatred, and fear, to bring about true humanity through purity of soul.

Greek and Roman mythology frequently appears in early Christian catacomb art in themes such as Eros and Psyche, an image of Christ's transformative influence on the human soul; the Good Shepherd, a position held by Hermes in Egypt and Greece; and Orpheus with his lyre and magic power of music, who anticipates the Logos (fig. 51). In the early Christian era, Eusebius of Caesarea said: "Orpheus made wild beasts tame by playing the lyre, and by the magic of his song he even induced oak trees to follow him. Still more sublime was the deed of God's all-wise Word. In order to heal the corruption of men, He took upon Himself the nature of Man, that instrument fashioned by His own wisdom, and He played on this instrument a magical music that changed the customs of Greek and Barbarians in that He healed the wild animal instincts of their spirits with the medicine of divine teaching."[56] When Eusebius speaks of Christ healing "the wild animal instincts of their spirits," we cannot help thinking of the special role played by animal imagery in art.

Zoomorphic images are used in early Christian art as in the theme of the Labors of Heracles (fig. 52). This Greek hero, known to the Romans as Hercules, was blessed with unearthly strength by the goddess Hera, wife of Zeus. He is depicted in catacomb art carrying out twelve great labors. Almost all of these labors involve overcoming a beast for the sake of the departed soul of Alcestis: a lion, hydra, boar, birds, a hind, cattle, the Cretan Bull, horses, a dragon, monsters, and Death itself. The trials end with a descent into the nether world and a battle with Hades, prophetically anticipating Christ's descent into hell for the salvation of the human soul. These twelve stages of initiation into the mysteries of death and the redemption of the soul, which Heracles undertakes, emphasize the taming and overcoming of the spirit animal powers that arise and overwhelm the human soul as drives, instincts, passions, and desires.

By the time of the Renaissance, when the Dance of Death is taken up in Christian art, this theme of trial and transformation is dealt with in pictures such as *The Temptation of St. Anthony* (fig. 53), where the holy man Anthony is brutally attacked by animal-like creatures. This realm where the battle for the soul takes place is described in esoteric tradition as the astral world. Here the novice, when seeking insight into the spiritual without sufficient preparation, will find him-or-herself confronted by an enigmatic picture in the soul. Desires and passions arise as animal-like or, more rarely, humanlike forms. The animal forms from this realm are never quite the same as those of the physical world, yet they possess an obvious resemblance that cannot be mistaken. Steiner describes this ensuing inner battle for the soul in the following way: "Passions residing in the lower part of human nature can assume animal forms or similar shapes that hurl themselves against the individual. In reality, these passions are headed outward; they seek satisfaction in the outer world, but this striving outward appears in mirrored reflection as an attack on the individual from whom they proceed."[57] This is why esoteric training advises that before attaining insight into spiritual realms, the student should learn by hard and sincere self-observation to realize the qualities and defects of his or her own character. In this way, at the moment when the inner self is confronted at the threshold, the student will find strength and courage to conduct him- or herself in the appropriate manner. Individuals who fail to test themselves in this way and are insufficiently acquainted with their "shadow" sides will not recognize themselves in their own vision and will discount it as an illusion or a foreign reality. Alarm over such visions can lead to instability of soul and insanity. Through their accurate portrayal of the spiritual realities encountered along the inner path, artistic images prepare the soul for what it is to meet on the other side of the threshold. The temptation of St. Anthony is such a powerful theme in Christian art because it represents an "exact imagination" of spiritual events.

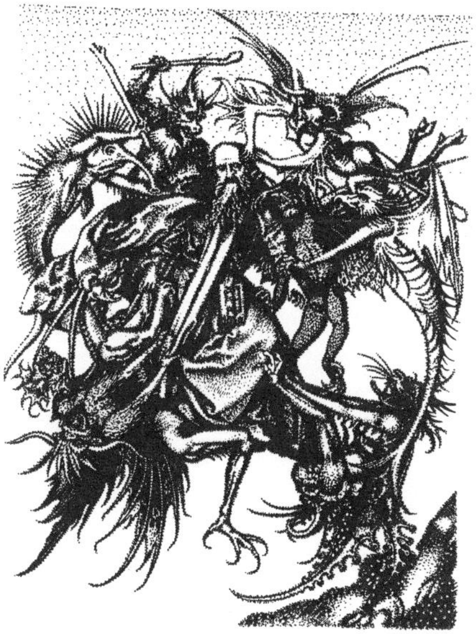

Fig. 53. The Temptation of St. Anthony by Martin Schongauer illustrates the inner struggles that may be experienced as the soul strives to overcome baser elements on its path to the spirit. (After Schongauer.)

Depicting double meanings was a frequent practice in catacomb art. It served as a rich teaching tool, as it did in later church art, but it also concealed the mystery teachings which were necessarily forbidden to those uninitiated.

Catacomb art is generally divided into two schools of interpretation: the historic and the symbolic. The historic school regards the art of the catacombs simply as illustrations of biblical and mythological stories, expressing no deeper or hidden meaning. The symbolic interpretation sees this early Christian art as allegorical, and symbolic of fundamental concepts and moral precepts such as resurrection and life after death. However, a third interpretation is also possible. What if early Christian communities actually shared in a direct relationship with a world of spirit? Could catacomb mural paintings and sculptural reliefs be the result of a consciousness that still participated in spiritual events and realities? Alfred Heidenreich proposes that "it was these first-hand spiritual experiences which the Christians of the

Catacombs wanted to express, and for this purpose a special type of biblical and pagan stories offered the best medium, stories in which their own experience was implicit."[58]

It seems obvious that the early Christian Mysteries were still inspired by the same spirit that moved the Gospel writers. In the New Testament, visionary pictures revealed spiritual truths that the church only later translated into moral allegories. The spiritual revelations expressed in catacomb art became mere moral theology as church doctrine took hold of the new religion in later centuries. As early Christianity left its cavelike sanctuaries and entered into the outer light of historic consciousness, the subtle inner light of these Christian Mysteries gradually dimmed. The esoteric thread of Christianity, the deeper mystery character, remained "underground" as exoteric Christianity rose to a position of world power and glory. It is this underground or esoteric aspect of art—the spiritual in art—that continues from civilization to civilization, from culture to culture, as a living impulse that transforms yet remains ever creative in its fashioning of imagery appropriate to further stages of human development. This is the ever-resounding echo of ancient mysteries, the creative spirit at work in the world, at work in art.

Notes

1. Tisdall, C. *Joseph Beuys,* 1979, p. 228, cited in Tucker, M. *Dreaming with Open Eyes,* p. 290.
2. Bastian, C. and J. Simmen, *Joseph Beuys: Drawings,* 1979, p. 97, cited in Tucker, p. 291–92.
3. Steiner, cited in Fitzgerald, A., *An Artist's Book of Inspiration,* p. 114.
4. Tisdall, p. 23, cited in Tucker, p. 289.
5. Tucker, M. *Dreaming with Open Eyes,* p. 75.
6. Cited in Tucker, p. 60.
7. Lipsey, R. *An Art of Our Own,* p. 42.
8. Bovi, A. *Kandinsky,* p. 8.
9. Welsh, R. and J.M. Joosten. *Two Mondrian Sketchbooks,* p. 36.
10. Choucha, N. *Surrealism and the Occult,* p. 66.
11. Lipsey, R. *An Art of Our Own,* p. 115.
12. Tomkins, C. T*he Bride and the Bachelors,* pp. 55–56.
13. Ibid, p. 39.
14. Lipsey, R. p. 113.
15. Tucker, p. 56.
16. Steiner, R. *The Social Future,* p. 77.
17. Gablik, S. *Has Modernism Failed?,* p. 128.
18. Chagall, M. "Why Have We Become So Anxious?" cited in Eliade, *Symbolism, the Sacred, and the Arts,* p. 89.
19. Ibid. p. 88.
20. Ibid, p. 89.
21. Eliade, M. "Beauty and Faith," S*ymbolism, the Sacred, and the Arts,* p. 92.
22. Cited in L. Attias, "Spreading Chagall's Message," *ARTnews,* Feb. 2000, p. 153.
23. See note 14, p. 91.
24. Steiner, R. "The Spiritual Being of Art," cited in Howard, *Art as Spiritual Activity,* pp. 135–36.
25. Steiner, *Color,* p. 21. "If you use black on a white surface you introduce spirit into it; the effect of a black stroke . . . is to spiritualize the white." Max Lüscher, in *The Lüscher Color Test* (New York: Random House, p. 69), describes black as representing "the absolute boundary beyond which life ceases, and so expresses the idea of nothingness, of extinction."
26. Taut, B. *Ein Architecture-Program.* 1918.
27. Cited in a lecture by Mann, W. "The Spiritual

History of Art," Emerson College, 1979.
28. Biesantz, H. *The Goetheanum: Rudolf Steiner's Architectural Impulse,* p. 19.
29. Steiner, R. *Ways to a New Style in Architecture,* June 17.
30. Steiner, R. "The Spiritual Being of Art," p. 153.
31. Cited in Richter, G., p. 251. Rudolf Steiner speaks of the sun in the following way: "When the soul begins to comprehend the wondrous nature of what cosmic wisdom has built up, when it attains to clearness (to light) about this, then the sun may appear to it as the most glorious symbol for expressing this inner awakening." (Steiner, lecture of Dec. 4, 1907, cited in Wagner, p. 43).
32. Rosenblum, R. *Modern Painting and the Northern Romantic Tradition: Friedrich to Rothko,* p. 96.
33. Anderson, W. *The Face of Glory: Creativity, Consciousness and Civilization,* p. 312.
34. Cited in Argüelles, J., pp. 91–92.
35. Tarnas, R. *The Passion of the Western Mind,* p. 430–31.
36. Arguelles, J. *The Transformative Vision,* p. 25.
37. "It is only when space itself has become an idol—when it has become simply the absence of phenomena, conceived in the phenomenal mode—that perspective takes the place of participation." Barfield, O. *Saving the Appearances,* p. 149.
38. Clark, K. *Leonardo da Vinci,* p. 160.
39. Steiner, R. *The History of Art,* Lecture 1, p. 40.
40. Wind, E. *Pagan Mysteries of the Renaissance,* p. 119.
41. Virgil cited in Wind, E., p. 122.
42. Dempsey, C. *The Portrayal of Love,* p. 49.
43. Ibid., p. 157.
44. Goethe, "Contemplating Schiller's Skull" (Excerpt).
45. Tympanum comes from the Greek word *tympanon,* meaning kettledrum. The drum is a traditional percussion instrument used esoterically to help induce the shamanic trance state and exoterically to call one to action, to stir the will by means of beat. Barrie suggests that the drum's taut skin stretched on a frame expresses the tension of "the opposing forces present at any spiritual decision." Barrie, T., p. 225.
46. James, J. *Chartres: The Masons Who Built a Legend,* p. 85.
47. Rodin, A. *Cathedrals of France,* p. 264.
48. von Otto, O. *The Gothic Cathedral,* p. vii.
49. Emile Male cited in James, J. *Chartres: The Masons Who Built a Legend,* p. 12.
50. Argüelles, J., p. 49.
51. Biesantz, H. *The Goetheanum,* pp. 94–95.
52. Schmidt-Brabant, M. "Architecture and Community: Age-Old Impulses in Temple Architecture." *News from the Goetheanum,* vol. 19, no. 4, 1998, p. 1. "The social element emancipated itself from art as the Roman idea of a state based on purely juristic principles came into influence. Although the connection between religious life and Roman and Gothic church architecture continued for a long time still, right up until the end of the Middle Ages, their one source was recognized only by a few in whom the wisdom of the ancient mysteries still flowed in an esoteric form of Christianity. Such teaching continued for a long time, especially in the building communities of the cathedrals in the Middle Ages."
53. Rodin, p. 10.
54. Somewhere between 750,000 and a million people are believed to have been buried in Roman catacombs. Various relics and sometimes the eucharistic food of consecrated bread and wine were buried with the dead. Heidenreich, p. 15.
55. Roman law stipulated that where the dead were buried a sacred place was established that could not be violated. Because of this, the catacombs were protected right up to the second half of the third century when the emperors Decius and Diocletian attempted a wholesale purge of Christianity, at which time the sacrilege of trespassing hallowed ground under arms occurred. Nevertheless it was in these subterranean cemeteries that the ancient practice of the mysteries was transformed into the new religion of Christianity.
56. Cited in A. Heidenreich, *The Catacombs,* p. 32.
57. Steiner, R. *Knowledge of the Higher Worlds and Its Attainment,* p. 179.
58. Heidenreich, A. p. 10. Joseph Wilpert, 1903, *Die Malereien der Katakomben,* Freiberg, was the first historic interpreter; Paul Styger, 1933, *Die römischen Katakomben,* Berlin, was the major proponent of the symbolic theory; and Emil Bock and Robert Goebel, 1931, *Die Katakomben: Bilder von den Mysterien des Urchristentums,* Stuttgart, represent the third school of thought.

II. ANCIENT ART OF THE GRECO-ROMAN ERA

Roman rule is the great Twilight of the Gods: an eclipse of the spiritual sun that encompasses the whole history of the world. For the fact that at that time more temples were built, more idols were erected, more sacrifices made and more cultic rites performed than ever before is a clear sign that men were no longer filled with the power of the older, simpler gods.
—Gottfried Richter

One night, Mars, the god of war, lay with the virgin daughter of the King of Alba. The result was the birth of twins—Romulus and Remus. The baby boys were placed in a reed basket and set adrift on the Tiber River. Eventually they washed ashore beside a grotto, where they were suckled by a she-wolf (fig. 54). The infants were later brought up by a shepherd and his wife, in whose care they grew strong and knowledgeable in the ways of nature. Deciding to found a city, the twins carefully studied the flight of birds and noticed twelve vultures in the part of the sky that the augur's wand had assigned to Romulus, but only six in Remus' part of the sky. With a white bull and cow harnessed to a plow, Romulus proceeded to cut a furrow in the ground that would mark the boundary of the new city. Defying his brother, Remus jumped over the shallow furrow and Romulus killed him. Thus Rome was founded by Romulus on the blood of his brother.

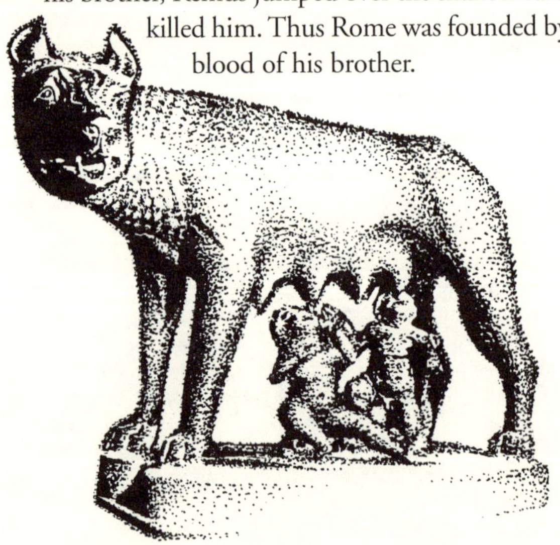

Fig. 54. The image of the Capitoline she-wolf dates to the fifth century B.C. Romulus and Remus, the legendary founders of Rome, here shown as children being suckled by the wolf, were added by Antonio Pollaiuolo in the fifteenth century A.D. (Rome, Italy.)

II.1 Power and Glory

The Romans had the best foresight in those matters which the Greeks took but little account of, such as the construction of roads and aqueducts, and of sewers that could wash out the filth of the city.
—Strabo

The Romans were not the originators of the arch or the discoverers of concrete, but they exploited to the maximum the usefulness of both in their bridges and aqueducts, as well as in their buildings (fig. 55). The arch, vault, and dome were taken to their heights by Roman architects, as can be seen in the Pantheon, built by Marcus Agrippa in 27 B.C. and reconstructed under Hadrian (fig. 56). It might be said that the arch and the dome were architectural metaphors of the vault of the heavens brought down to earth, a reflection, too, of the dome of the human head projected into outer nature. It is between the dome of the sky and the dome of the head that architecture presents the dome that honors the meeting of macrocosm and microcosm. The keystone, which closes the arch at its top and helps to distribute weight, is like the closing of the fontanel at the crown of the skull. The use of the keystone and the arch in Roman architecture is a metaphor for the closing off of contact with the heavens above—the Twilight of the Gods. The triumphal arch, heavy and massive, and symbolic of this cutting off of the earthly from the spiritual, is a picture of humanity no longer in direct interaction with the divine.[1]

Fig. 55. Aqueducts such as this one at Le Pont du Gard, Nîmes, France, dated at A.D. 15, show the remarkable engineering skills of the Romans.

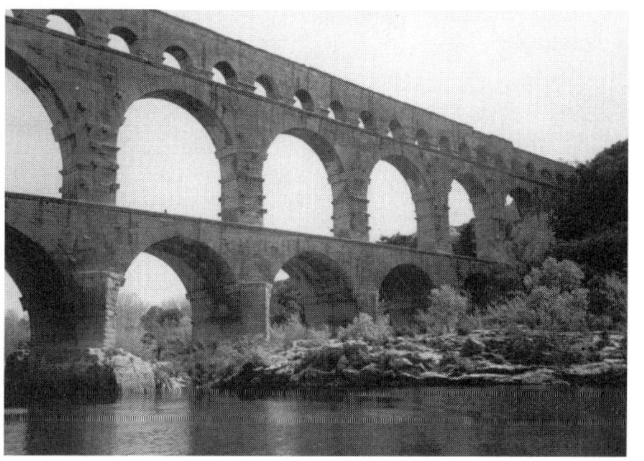

It is as if these triumphal arches were the result of an unrelenting will for earthly power and glory, a determination to challenge eternity. They were in fact erected to show that the emperor had entered the city as conqueror of a new land for the empire. However, the triumphal arch was more a monument to this entrance of the god-king, the Caesar, than to a military campaign or conquest. Gerhard Richter suggests that the triumphal arch is a "dark counterimage" of the spiritual "entrance" of the human individuality or "I" principle that occurs at this time.[2] One thing is clear: the emperor was no more a true god-king in the primal sense than the triumphal arch was a true gate, for the latter stood isolated, spanning a street or plaza, unattached to any walls. In contrast to other Roman

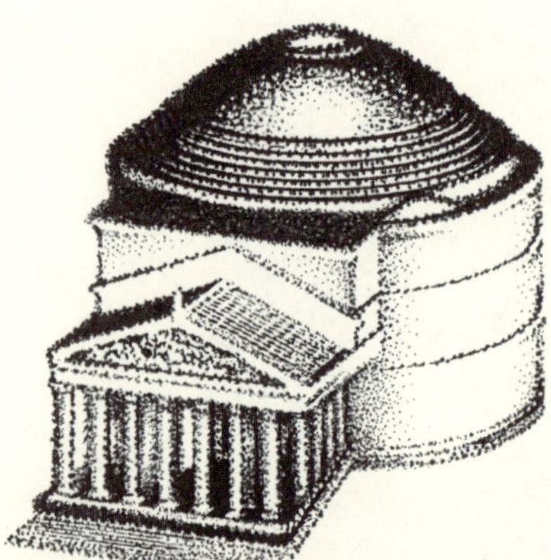

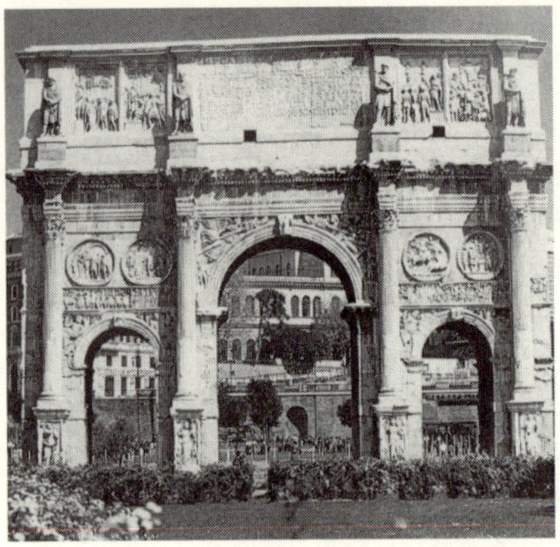

structures, the triumphal arch (of which there are some 150 still standing today) was not functional. It was strictly political, and in this regard marked the introduction of decoration as superfluous adornment (fig. 57).

The triumphal arches, which are the most significant architectural expressions of the Roman spirit, first appeared in the second century B.C. and were eventually covered with ornamental relief, decorative columns, blind windows, false doors, and inscriptions. Fake columns gave no support to the overall structure of the arches and false windows provided no views. These ornamental devices were grand features but were unable to achieve any high aesthetic levels in the hands of the Romans. The arch stood separated and alone, cut off from any significant relationship with its surroundings other than to declare its power and domination of space. This was the spiritual significance of the triumphal arch: that it served as a doorway to a new era in art and human consciousness, one in which art becomes decorative, political, and disconnected from meaning.

The term "triumphal arch" is also used to describe the western crossing arch above the apse in Christian basilicas, because of the placing of an image of Christ in Majesty on the uppermost part of the arch (fig. 58). So the arch becomes an expression not only of political power but also of spiritual authority. The apse of the basilica is seen as the doorway to the spirit through which the Host descends to the altar and prayers ascend to the Godhead. The architectural plan of the basilica was itself borrowed from the Roman forum.

Consider also the Roman circus, an elaboration of the Greek stadium and the amphitheater. Whereas Greek athletics and drama dealt with the idealized

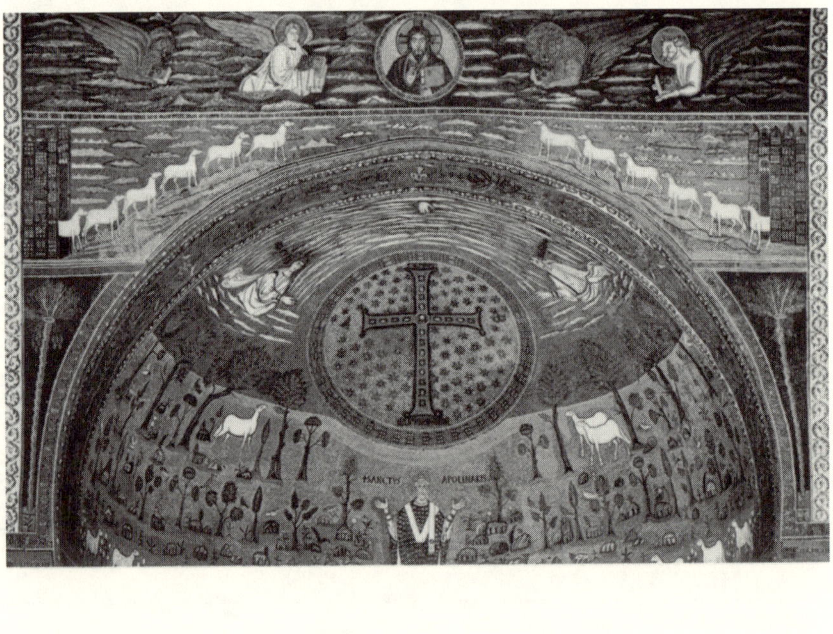

Fig. 56. Top: The Pantheon in Rome, constructed by Marcus Agrippa in 27 B.C., was renovated by Hadrian in 125 A.D. Its form is based on the circle, the triangle, and the square.

Fig. 57. Above: The Triumphal Arch of Constantine in Rome is one of 150 such arches built by Roman emperors and still existent today.

Fig. 58. Right: The triumphal arch in a Christian church is where Christ is portrayed in glory above the apse. (Saint Apollinare in Classe, Ravenna, Italy.)

strivings of the human soul to transform itself through meaningful struggle, Roman spectacle often demoralized and retarded the soul through meaningless violence, brutality, and death. The circus did not attempt to serve the higher longings of the human being as much as it set itself in the service of man's baser nature. Similarly, the forum was a combination of the Greek agora and sacred temple space, dedicated no longer strictly to the gods but to the power of the Roman state.

Roman sculpture too is more decorative than it is artistically outstanding. The Romans developed no new styles or techniques, and their highest achievements were technically perfect copies and imitations of Greek originals. The Greeks did not work from models but relied on an innate sense of their own formative life forces. The Romans clearly worked from models, perfecting their skills as imitators while their passion for collecting and copying also contributed to a divorce of art from any sacred setting. The use of stock models and interchangeable features led to an extensive art industry verging on mass production. This would eventually result, on the one hand, in the study of art history, the practice of conservation, preservation, and the establishment of museums, and on the other, to an ornamental, decorative art that functioned more on the level of fashion than fine art. Art became a commodity and a luxury item, and in this way its spiritual significance was compromised—not unlike the situation in today's art market.

Roman sculpture popularizes the individual portrait in the form of the bust—the head detached from the body (fig. 59). The disconnected head becomes a picture of the spiritual condition of the historic human being at this time. For historic man, thinking is independent of feeling and impulses of will. Thus, the head becomes the all-important center of power and authority. Portraits of individuals are carved and placed on generic bodies of statesmen, matrons, and centurions, or simply placed without torso and limbs upon a pedestal. The importance of the thinking head over other members of the human being is made clear in Roman art.

Portrait statuary develops in two directions at this time: towards idealism and towards realism. Side by side, and in alternation, depending on the taste of the reigning emperor, the two streams continue until technical ability begins to deteriorate in the third century A.D. The one style is idealized to the point of vanity, the other demonstrates the absoluteness and authoritative power of strict realism. André Malraux points out, "Her portraiture, on which Rome set such store, was that of faces separated from the universe....Even when Rome managed to give them life, she put no soul into them; for she had none."[3] This may seem an unreasonably severe critique of such a great civilization, but the mission of Rome appears elsewhere than in creative artistic genius.

The polarities of idealism and realism, glory and power, in art had to some extent been held in check by the harmony and balance in Greek art.

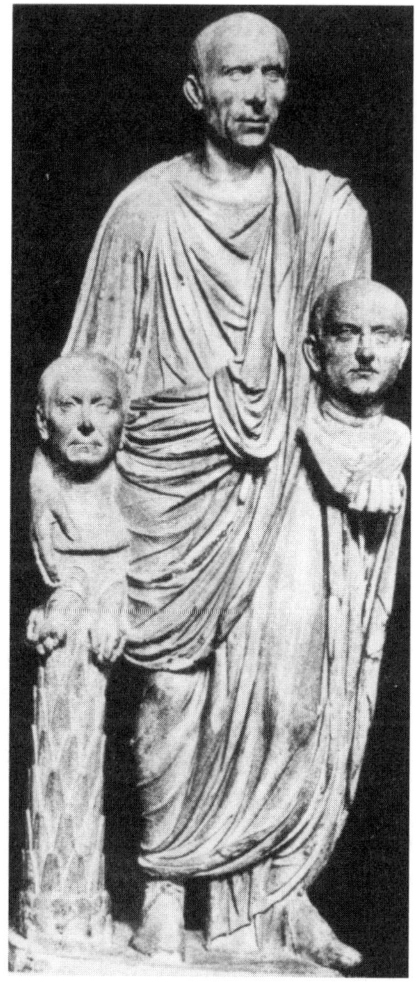

Fig. 59. A Roman patrician with busts of his ancestors, c. 30 B.C., shows the importance placed on preserving the image of the head. (Capitoline Museum, Rome.)

However, Roman art did not arise as the result of an inner seeking for "all things in moderation," but was the pursuit of extremes. The conflict of opposites is already evident in Rome's primal beginnings in the picture of Romulus slaying his brother. The fratricide on which Rome is founded seems to be a metaphor that works on throughout the whole of Roman history, providing a model for what might be described as pathological competitiveness.

The best of Roman art, its underlying primal power and spiritual glory, is often found in the imagery of its many mystery religions. One such example is the masterful mural painting known from the Villa of the Mysteries in Pompeii (color plate 5). Executed between 31 B.C. and 14 A.D. in the private home of a women's Orphic cult that celebrated the mysteries of Dionysus, these fresco paintings are powerful symbols of the path of initiation and transformation. To describe them in any detail is not possible here, but a brief explanation will be helpful: A narrow entrance into the consecrated rectangular chamber is the first stage of the path. One slips into the room and is confronted by a tableau of ten scenes painted in shallow stage perspective on a brilliant vermilion red background. In walking around the chamber from one mystery scene to another, one performs a circumambulation that continually unfolds as it reveals new meaning. By submitting oneself to the sacred cult images, the participant experiences a kind of "divine transformation" toward individuation. Linda Fierz-David describes this process in the following way: "As long as the old myths were alive for mankind, participation in a mystery cult could be an original experience for each individual; that is, through a cult, the participant could be directly touched through archetypal images, could be deeply affected by them, and thus could be rescued from the animal, collective psyche."[4]

In scene seven is a sacred mystery image hidden from view by a cloth covering. Before it kneels an initiate, poised and ready to lift the covering (fig. 60). On her shoulder is a long torch, symbol of divine illumination, used in the nocturnal processions of the mysteries. Earlier scenes picture the Dionysian element as water, but gradually this is transformed into the image of fire—expressed here by the torch. Opposite the kneeling woman is one of the most impressive figures of the entire Villa of the Mysteries cycle. It is a winged angel that suddenly appears as the sacred image is about to be revealed by the initiate. That the angel is descending from the heavens is indicated by her billowing garments and lifting hair, and she raises her left hand in warning to the kneeling woman. The angel, in full action, clasps a whipping switch in her other hand, which is raised above her head ready to deliver a strong blow. This flagellation and chastisement is inflicted upon the one who profanes the mystery, pictured as the female figure with her back exposed to the angel on the adjacent wall in scene eight. The mystery must remain concealed to those who are unprepared, and so the guardian angel is severe at this threshold. Fierz-David says: "The spirit of Dionysus swoops down upon the initiate as feminine pneuma [breath, wind, spirit]—a dark angel—in order to bear witness to her true humanity. As feminine pneuma we might describe the angel also as Sophia; this is surely the 'startling light of self-learned wisdom' of which Philo speaks, that strikes the initiate unawares, accusing, ruling and mediating. What the angel mediates, above all, is the spiritual feeling of modesty as a gift of grace of the Holy Ghost."[5]

Such Roman mystery centers as this one in Pompeii relied on artistic images to carry the soul of the participant to a threshold of inner experience that could not be approached solely with the help of verbal instructions. Such pictures were truly mystery images in their capacity to transform the souls of women and men alike, leading them beyond the limitations of normal waking consciousness.

Fig. 60. Scene 7 in Pompeii's Villa of the Mysteries (detail) depicts the moment in initiation when the neophyte awakens to the spirit.

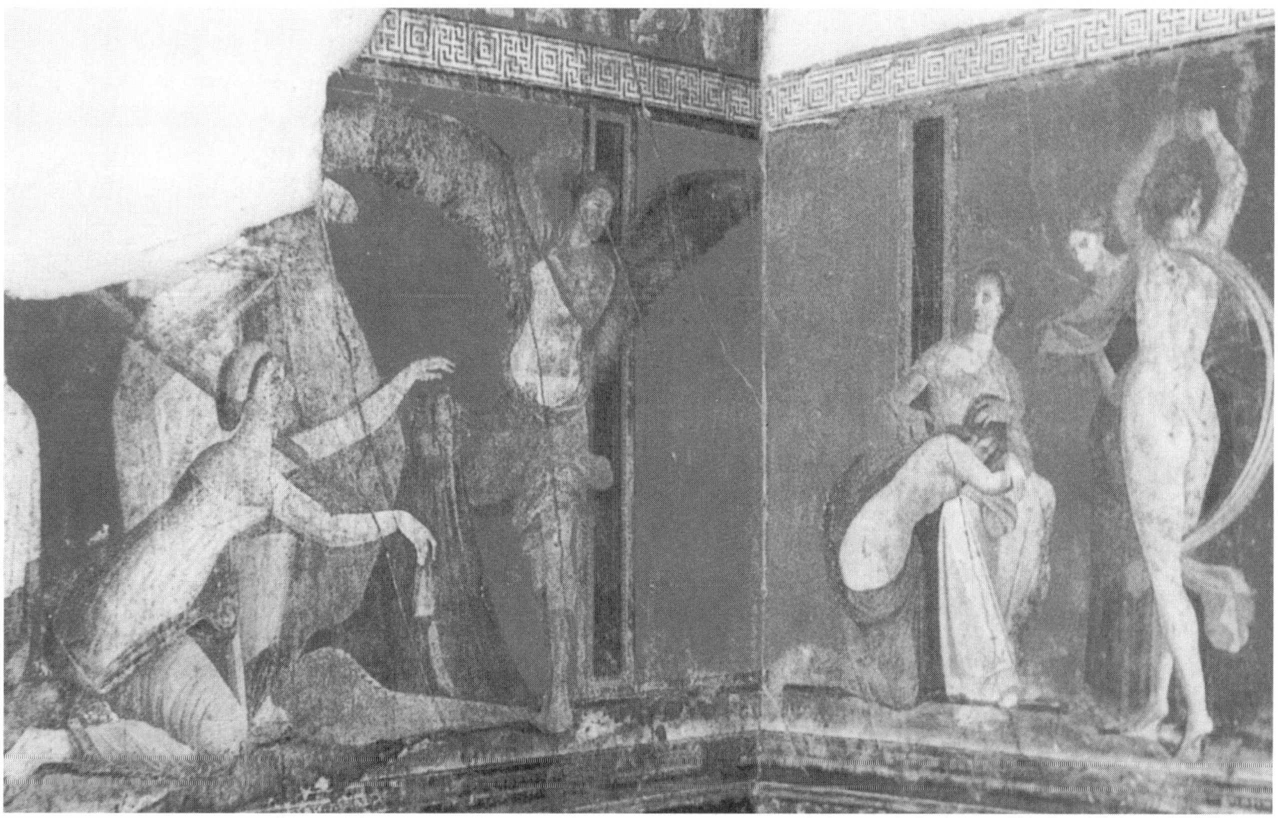

II.2 The Mithraic Mysteries

Mithraic iconography was a cosmological code created by a circle of religious-minded philosophers and scientists to symbolize their possession of secret knowledge: namely, the knowledge of a newly discovered god so powerful that the entire cosmos was completely under his control.
—David Ulansey

He was born on December 25, and his birth was witnessed by shepherds. He lived a remarkable life of miracles, often traveling with twelve companions. He died in the spring and was resurrected from the dead. Members of the religion that was established around this revered avatar were baptized and partook of a eucharistic meal of bread and wine. The name of this solar deity, whose ritual celebration spread throughout the Roman Empire, was Mithras.

Of all the mystery religions that appear in ancient Rome, perhaps the most fascinating are the Mithraic Mysteries. Centered around the worship of a sun hero known as Mitra in India, Mithra in Iran, and Mithras throughout the ancient Roman Empire, this is one of the oldest surviving deities in the world, still worshipped in Bangladesh. Mithraic Mysteries were widespread in ancient times, with sanctuaries from North Africa to Scotland and all across Europe to the region of the Black Sea. Over a hundred Mithraic temples have been discovered in and around Rome.

Fig. 61. This Mithraeum in Rome is a barrel-vaulted structure meant to simulate the cave in which the Sun-Hero Mithras was born.

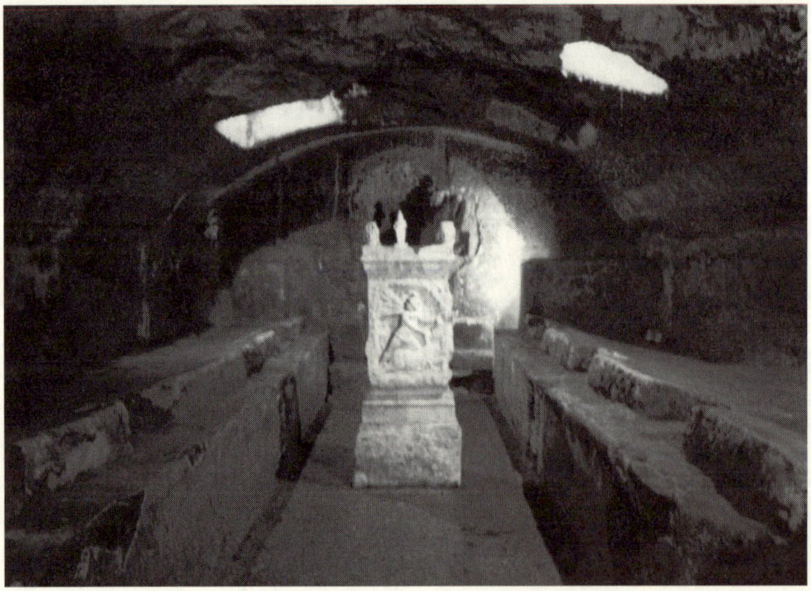

Mithraea, subterranean temples, were imagined to be the birth cave of Mithras and a model of the universe (fig. 61). Often decorated with stars on the ceilings, these painted chambers represent the celestial vault of the heavens and suggest a resemblance to the initiation caves of the Paleolithic era.[6]

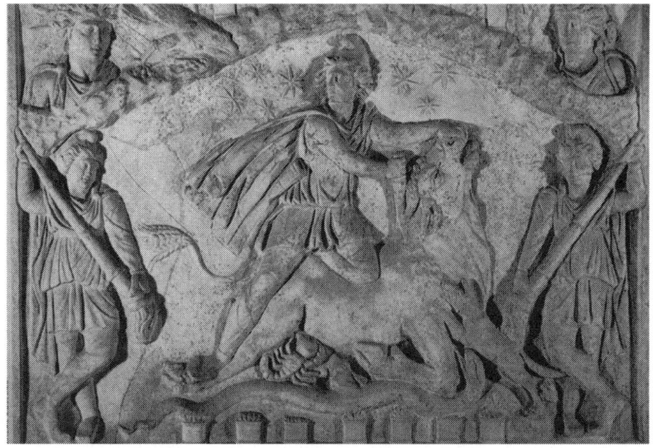

Fig. 62. Mithras slaying the bull is a central motif in the Mithraic Mysteries. The scene is flanked by figures representing universal polarities and the fourfold nature of the cosmos.

At the back of the Mithraea, which were sometimes natural grottoes, sometimes underground barrel-vaulted chambers, stood the carved stone cult image of Mithras slaying the cosmic bull. In a way similar to the atoning sacrifice of Christ, the sacrifice of the divine bull bestowed everlasting life on the followers of Mithras.

Mithras is recognized for his slaying of the divine bull after chasing it down, seizing it by the horns, and riding it to submission. After carrying it back to his cave, he dispatches the bull with his dagger and wheat sprouts from its wound. In some depictions, a shaft of grain grows from the bull's tail and the wound is licked by a dog and a snake as a scorpion attaches itself to the bull's genitals (fig. 62). Mithras listens to the inspirational call of a raven above him and is shown wearing a Phrygian cap, indicating he possesses the capacities of an initiate.[7] Images of this ritual scene are associated with ancient star wisdom concerning the constellations of the Bull, Taurus; the Dog, Canis Minor; the Snake, Hydra; the Raven, Corvus; and the Scorpion, Scorpius.[8] The pronounced astrological symbolism throughout this and other cults indicates hints of a spiritual vision that flowed from intuitive knowledge of the universe. The slaying of the bull by Mithras may indicate a knowledge of the precession of the equinoxes, a movement of the vernal equinox from the constellation of Taurus the Bull into the next solar age of Aries the Ram.[9] However, the bull forces are also a picture of the instincts and will-power in human nature. In this regard Alfred Schutze notes: "When a man comes to the stage of consciously experiencing for the first time his own inner being, he sees that this 'I,' or Ego, stands over against everything that does not belong to it and so [that which does not belong to the 'I'] can therefore be called the 'not-I.' He discovers that the 'not-I' comprises not only other people, the external world and so on, but also his own bodily makeup, his dispositions, capacities, weaknesses, the whole complex of his desires, inclinations and temperament. With all this he is certainly connected, but it is not himself. To all of it he can say 'I have it,' not 'I am it.' All this 'Not-I' was known to ancient Mystery-wisdom as 'the Bull.' . . . Through his individual activity man must set himself the goal of transmuting in a spiritual sense the 'not-I,' the purely natural, in himself. He will then be himself a 'Mithras,' who overcomes the bull."[10]

Sometimes surrounding the bull-slaying scene are other figures such as the sun and the moon, the signs of the zodiac, and the four winds. Also standing nearby are the figures of Cautes, holding a torch upwards, and

Cautopates, with an upside-down torch. Dressed like little Mithras figures, they are associated with the rising and setting sun, the summer and winter solstices, and the incarnation and disincarnation of light and life. Other scenes illustrate Helios bowing to the superior power of Mithras or Mithras riding in the sun chariot of Helios as the two solar beings descend to the earth.

Mithraism was in evidence amongst pirates of the southeastern Mediterranean during the first century b.c., and, as a strictly male cult, was spread widely throughout the empire by Roman soldiers, sailors, and officers.[11] It recognized no class distinctions, and even slaves could become initiated.

According to the Zoroastrian *Avesta* of old Persia, the figure of Mithra—god of light, truth, and justice—fought on behalf of the all-wise Ahura Mazdao against the dark falsehood of Ahriman. However, apart from the slaying of a bull by the evil Ahriman, little historical connection can be found between the old Iranian Mithra and the Mithraic hero of the Roman era. Nevertheless, according to legend, Mithras was born in a cave on December 25, marking the time following the winter solstice and connecting him with the Sol Invictus, the Unconquered Sun. Parallels between the life of Mithras and that of Jesus Christ are, to say the least, striking.

Initiation into the Mithraic Mysteries involved advancement to ever higher stages along a path of seven degrees. The initiate climbed a ladder of inner development whose rungs were associated with the seven gates of heaven, each gate linked to a planet, a metal, and a day of the week.[12] Initiation led to "insight into the secrets of the forces operating in the universe."[13]

By the time Christianity was declared the official state religion of the Roman Empire, Mithraism was at its peak as a mystery religion. Although having much in common with early Christianity, Mithraism was eventually declared heretical and gradually disappeared from Europe. Many Mithraea were destroyed or simply taken over and rebuilt as Christian churches. St. Peter's in Rome, the center of Catholicism, was built upon a Mithraic sanctuary.

Roman arts set traditions that were reproduced for centuries. But Roman art was itself inspired by the creativity of a culture that had an altogether different grasp of the spiritual: this culture was ancient Greece. The Roman aptitude for law, politics, engineering, and militarism was preceded by the development of Greek philosophy, literature, education, and art. The underlying Greek influence on Rome can be seen from the Roman poet Horace's comment concerning the overthrow of Greece by Rome: "The Greeks, captured, took the victors captive."

II.3 The Art of Balance

The aim of art is to represent not the outward appearance of things, but their inward significance.
—Aristotle

The Graces are generally considered children of the father-god, Zeus. However, it is also said they were the daughters of Helios, perhaps because of their personification of the sun's rays and their delight in the sunshine. Their names and even their numbers changed constantly throughout history, but Aglaia, Thalia, and Euphrosyne were their most common names in antiquity. Aglaia means "the brilliant"; Thalia is "she who brings flowers"; and Euphrosyne, "she who rejoices the heart." They mingle with the nymphs every spring, joyously dancing in groups and presiding over the budding plant life and ripening fruit. For this reason, Pindar says of these nature goddesses, "With you all becomes sweetness and charm." Aphrodite cherished them as her companions, and they attended the goddess of beauty whenever she wished to adorn herself in all her loveliness. The Graces were closely connected to Apollo as well, and formed a part of his retinue. From the end of the fourth century b.c. the Graces appear as three nude women holding each other's hands or shoulders as they dance. As we have seen already, the Neoplatonists of the Italian Renaissance saw the Graces as beauty, chastity, and passion, and named them accordingly, linking them with the driving forces of the soul (color plate 4). Their three-part nature was understood as the archetypal working of divine law. This triune order of the Graces is demonstrated throughout Greek art.

For instance, the styles of Greek columns, known collectively as the Greek Order, appear in threes beginning with the Doric. The Doric capital lightly curves as it meets the weight of the architrave above and provides a rounded cushion between the architrave and the column's shaft (fig. 63). The Ionic capital pushes with greater force and curls back upon itself much like an unfurling fern or the horns of a ram. The Corinthian capital thrusts upwards in a bouquetlike excess of lifting energy. All three styles are true to the inner nature and function of the capital as the mediator between thrust and load. The three styles show the dynamic pressure point where support engages weight and levity encounters gravity. These basic architectural principles of support and load

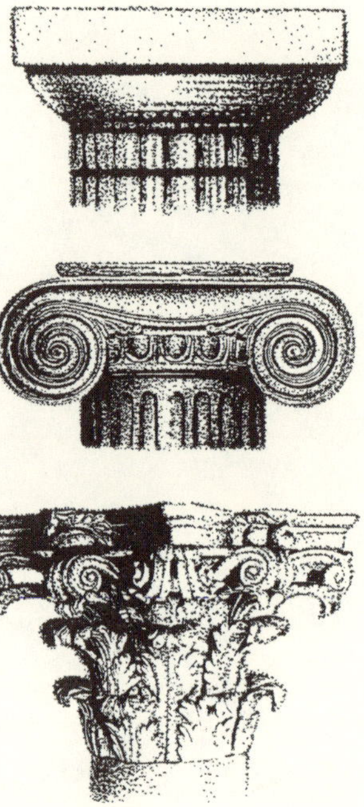

Fig. 63. Above, from top: The Doric capital is the oldest and simplest of the three Greek orders; the Ionic capital has rounded volutes that emphasize support meeting load; and the Corinthian capital, developed by Callimachus, is a picture of the up-building forces that give plant forms their distinctive gesture.

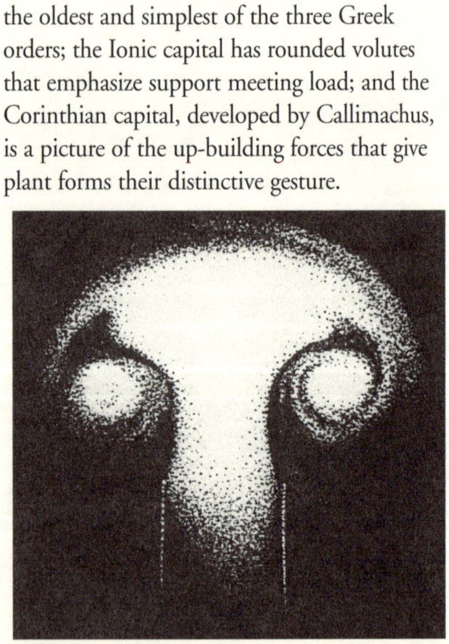

Fig. 64. Experiments with water demonstrate that when one fluid is injected into a standing fluid, the resulting forms reveal the same dynamics as are expressed in the Greek Ionic capital. (After Schwenk.)

are often lost to the eye in modern buildings, but Greek architecture emphasized the art of balance.

From the Doric to the Ionic and finally to the Corinthian capital, a fundamental principle of formative, sculptural-architectonic forces is made visible. Compare the volute or scroll form of the Ionic capital to the spiral forms created when a fluid dye is injected into an inert liquid under controlled laboratory conditions (fig. 64). We can see from this experiment how the same forces that create organic forms in nature are also the inspirations behind many ancient art forms. The Greeks perceived the forces at work in nature and they incorporated these living laws into their architecture, thereby creating not simply a beautiful shape, but also a true artistic form. By constructing such "force-forms" the Greeks created a structure into which a particular spiritual quality could enter. Steiner suggests that the ancient Greeks "did not think out these forms, but they perceived the forces streaming through space, and filled them with stone; that which was already there [spiritually] they filled with substance. Hence the Greek temple is a material presentation of actual forces working in space; a Greek temple is crystallized space-thought in the purest sense. . . . The result of this was very important; by giving material expression to force-forms in space the Greeks gave divine spiritual beings the opportunity of using these material forms."[14] Steiner insists that it is not merely a metaphor but a spiritual reality that gods dwelt in Greek temples. "The Greek temple is the 'dwelling place of the spirit.' A Zeus or Jupiter temple is shaped in such a way that it forms a worthy abode for what the guardians of the Zeus or Jupiter initiations perceived with their spiritual eyes."[15]

David Fideler expresses the same idea when he says, "Based on the idea of 'like attracts like,' the temples of antiquity . . . were designed to reflect, and hence enshrine, the living spirit of harmony which underlies the universe. . . . That this act of invocation was not merely theoretical, but a living reality is one of the most difficult things for the modern mind, hypnotized by the dogmas of materialism, to understand. The spirit of harmony is not just a pretty notion, or an ideal formulation of the ultimate nature of things, but is capable of expressing itself in quite tangible ways, if carefully and properly invoked."[16] This fundamental principle of harmony is at the root of ancient art, and is essential to the appreciation of the spiritual significance of Greek culture. As Spiro Kostof puts it, "[the temple] was the meeting ground between the human and the divine. At the same time that humans were lifted up by the proud soaring of the columns, deities came down to the level of human visibility."[17]

Vitruvius, the Roman architect, tells us that the Corinthian capital was first conceived when the Greek architect Callimachus observed an acanthus plant growing around a basket placed on the grave of a deceased girl from

Corinth. Steiner suggests that the story indicates Callimachus had a vision of the departing life forces of the deceased maiden and the architect saw above the grave forms striving upward like leafing plants. Roman decorative capitals usually use the acanthus leaf as a model for this capital, but the forms that Callimachus intended for the Corinthian capital, according to Steiner, are inspired by the actual formative life forces that underlie the creation of the acanthus forms. As Plotinus points out in the third century, "the arts do not simply imitate what they see but reascend to those principles from which Nature herself is derived."[18]

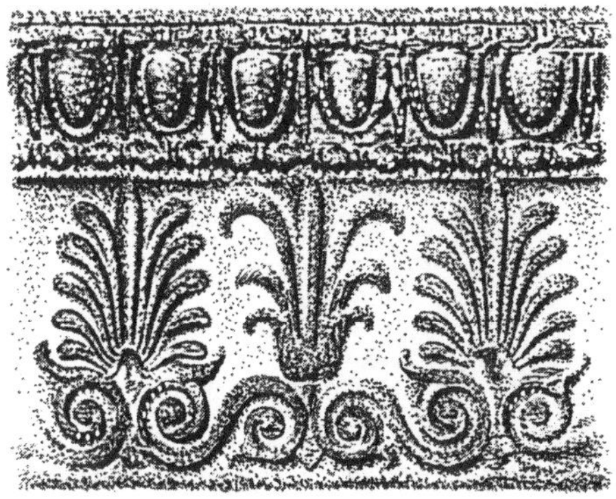

Fig. 65. Above: The Greek palm motif indicates sun and earth forces in alternating rhythms of expansion and contraction. This motif suggests contrasting triangles, one with its base below (earth) and one with its base above (sun). The egg-and-dart motif is another design feature that expresses the rhythms of expansion and contraction.

Beneath the capitals of many Doric columns and at other strategic places on the temples were "palm" motifs depicting the theme of earth and sun. This motif, which had its origin in very ancient times and was used in processional movements, represented cosmic forces by means of an upward pointing triangle (earth) and a downward pointing triangle (sun; fig. 65).

The development of the Greek capital comes to a remarkable culmination in the Erechtheum (fig. 66) adjacent to the Parthenon on the Acropolis. Here the upright principle of the column reveals itself as a human figure, or, one might say, the human form becomes visible as the column. Poised between heaven and earth, the human being supports the load that has been placed upon it by the gods from above, while standing firmly in relation to the ground beneath. The human being is thus portrayed by the caryatid, as the column in the temple of creation, ideally achieving the art of balance between heaven and earth, spirit and matter.

Fig. 66. Below: In the Erechtheum, on the Acropolis in Athens, the shaft of the column in its supporting role between load and foundation is equated with the human being in its carrying role between heaven and earth. Such columns, which use the human figure as a model, are called caryatids.

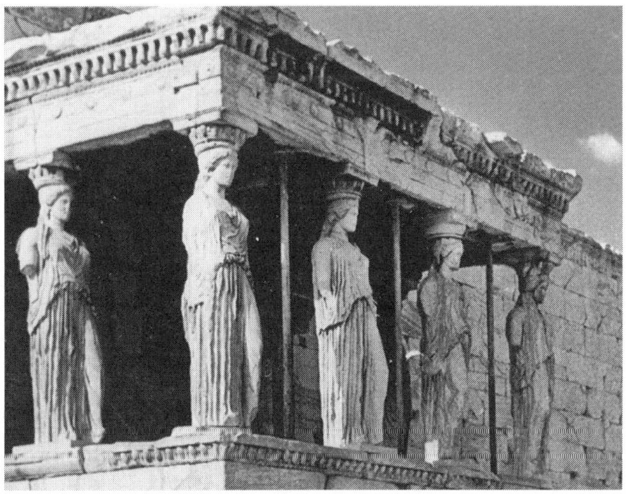

The tripartite rhythm seen over time in the Greek order also occurs in space throughout the entire structure of the temple. Looking more closely at foundation, support, and load, we notice that the temple stairs and base, the columns and walls, as well as the pediment and roof are triads. The stairs number at least three, including the stereobate and stylobate; the columns with their bases, shafts, and capitals have a general three-part character; and the pediment together with the architrave and its triglyph and frieze, as well as the entablature suggests a triad arrangement. Groupings of three often hold sway down to details like the three vertical lines of the triglyph featured above the temple columns in the architrave. This triform aspect of the temple relates directly to the human form with its limbs, trunk, and head. Just as the three major parts of the body contain further divisions of three (limbs—foot, shin, thigh; trunk—solar plexus, breast, shoulders; head—chin, cheeks, brow) so too does the Greek temple unfold in triads. Although there are exceptions to this general

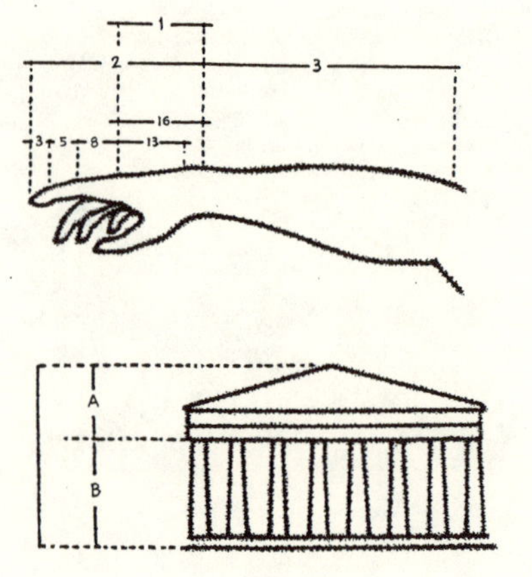

Fig. 67. Because the proportions of the Golden Mean are visible in the form of the human being, Greek artists and architects incorporated these ratios into both temple architecture and sculpture. (After Mitchell.)

observation, nevertheless an order and harmony is found here that corresponds to the Greeks' view of the cosmos, in which "man is the measure of all things."

The order represented in both man and temple is often due to the proportion known as the Golden Mean, magic section, or divine proportion, which proposes that AB is to BC as BC is to AC. Growth curves, patterns found in shells and flowers, are generally governed by this mathematical formula of 1.618. Greek sculpture is often fashioned according to it as the work of Phidias demonstrates. In fact, the Golden Mean proportion is called phi by mathematicians after the initial of Phidias, who also used the ratio in his design for the Parthenon (fig. 67). As Walter Wili states, "Significantly, the basic proportions both of statue and of temple are the same as those of man."[19] This divine proportion is found in Hindu, Egyptian, and Greek temples, and occasionally in the Gothic cathedral. A Hindu architectural sutra states, "The Universal Being is present in the temple by means of proportion."[20]

Although the Greek temple retains columns within the walls of the cella or sanctuary, it also places columns outside the temple walls in a gesture of conversant openness with the surrounding environment. Egyptian pillars stand inside the temple walls, thus a closing and cutting-off from the outer world is observable in the impassable walls. The Greek temple (fig. 68a) is light and open, radiating a harmonious, palacelike nobility, an approachable residence from which the god oversees the creations of the world. The Egyptian temple (fig. 68b), as we will see, is heavy and fortresslike, a place from which the gods rule with superhuman authority. The Egyptian temples create an interior focus while the Greek temple, expressive of a newly won human freedom and clarity of vision, stresses the outer space through its architecture. The Greek temple likewise embodies a sense of balance and equilibrium. The Gothic cathedral endeavors to escape the static balance of lintel and column by means of its striving piers and arches. Gothic architecture tends upwards towards a point, while Greco-Roman temples maintain a perfect equipoise.

Observing the columns of the Parthenon, we see they are closer together on the ends of the building (fig. 41). Foundation and steps are gently bowed to be higher in the middle of the structure and lower on the ends. Columns have a slight tapering about a third of the way up from the base, called the entasis, enhancing the gesture of uprightness and the feeling of thrust in the columns, giving a sense of vitality. All this is in order to better hold the weight of the structure from a visual point of view. What often seems to be a right angle or parallel line in the Greek temple is actually a feature that has been adjusted ever so slightly in order to appear more harmonious to the eye of the viewer. An example of visual harmony in architecture, the temple's façade is laid out in accordance with the Golden Mean. To quote Fideler again on the nature of sacred architecture: "The temple, in its highest manifestation, was seen as constituting a microcosm, an image of the entire universe, and was laid out accordingly. The temple was seen as an organism, possessing a body and a living spirit. This spirit was attracted through the temple's underlying geometry and proportions . . . thus reflecting the harmony of the universe and those principles which underlie the genesis of life."[21]

For ritual services an altar was placed in front of the Greek temple, underlining its gesture of openness and compatibility with the surrounding nature. However, the interior of the temple was the dwelling place of the god, accessible only to the priesthood. The temple stood as a focal point of harmony within outer nature and expressed the essence and ideal of Greek culture: unity of art, science, and religion.

Aristotle said, "Virtue is the human capacity or skill guided by reason and insight, which, as regards man, holds the balance between the too-much and the too-little."[22] This was the philosopher's intuitive yet reasoned way of restating the wisdom of the Greek mysteries—that the human being, in order to be free, needs to stand like the fulcrum of a scale, always between two possible extremes. Thus human freedom and virtue are only possible in terms of realizing a triad of forces, as in the case of infatuation—love—hate, or foolhardiness—bravery—cowardice (not the polarized dualism between love and hate, bravery and cowardice). This threefold point of view, in effect a balancing of opposites, is at the basis of Greek art. Upon the temple at Delphi were written the words, "Thou art. All things in moderation. Know thyself." Thus, between the states of being (thou art) and knowing (know thyself) lies the condition of balance (all things in moderation). To the ancient Greeks, moderation was not a restriction, as it might be considered today, for they felt that the freedom to engage in "all things" was not limiting. Greek temple art embodies the very ideals of moderation, creating a harmonious and balanced dance—a dance like that of the three Graces.

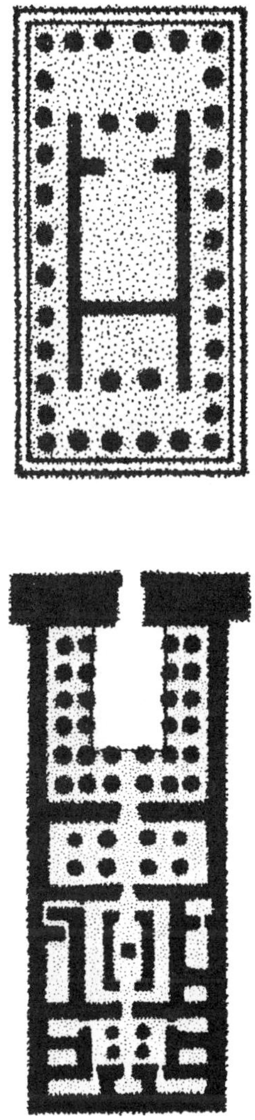

a

b

Fig. 68. The Greek temple walls (a) stand inside the colonnades whereas the Egyptian walls (b) lie outside the colonnades. What had been directed inward in Egyptian temple architecture is now, in the Greek temple, directed outward.

II.4 Free Form

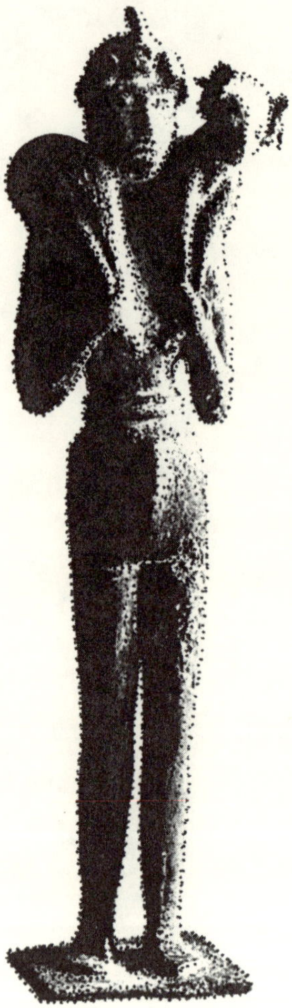

Imagination made them, and she is a better artist than imitation; for where the one carves only what she has seen, the other carves what she has not seen.
—Philostratus

The art of ancient Greece has long been regarded as the height of aesthetic expression and the ideal form of artistic beauty in the Western world. Its development and transformation is so organic and natural that it can be compared to the growth of a plant, with a germination period, a sprouting phase, a blossoming, and finally, a fruiting stage. Many historical periods of art show similar phased development, but nowhere does such a pattern appear so clearly and distinctly as in Greek art.

The early Greek Geometric period runs from about 1100 B.C.. to the first recorded Olympic games in 776 B.C.[23] This is a phase of rudimentary temple architecture, early vase painting, miniature terracotta and bronze figurines. Both painted and sculpted human figures from this period are small, simple and sticklike (fig. 69). However, most characteristic of this period are the geometric designs (*ars lineandi*) and linear figures found on pottery (fig. 70). An example is the Greek key or meander (fig. 141), which often denotes a specific numerical ratio in linear form and in some cases can be expressive of musical meter and measure. Isadora Duncan choreographed some of her Greek-inspired dances on the basis of rhythmic patterns and figure gestures from Greek pottery. These and other geometric patterns delineate a pure language of form, holding within them the germinal secrets of rhythm and movement as the potential for growth is held within the seed. The Geometric period might be described as the seed stage of Greek art.

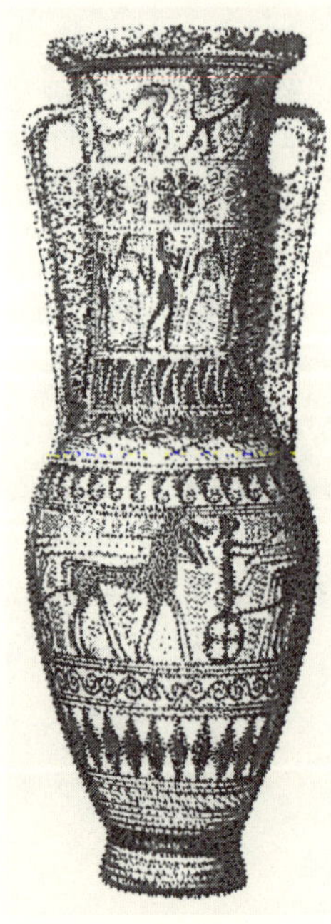

Fig. 69. Above: Figurines from the Geometric period are simple and small. This one above shows the "good shepherd" theme. Before the Christian era the good shepherd was regarded as a personification of Hermes or Mercury, "messenger of the gods."

Fig. 70. Right: The geometric linear patterns found on pottery of the early Greek era gave the period its name. Patterns may demonstrate musical rhythm and meter, or themes of expansion and contraction, and waxing and waning.

The Archaic period begins in the eighth century B.C., when pottery painting flourishes and the

Doric style of stone architecture develops. It is also at this time that full-size sculpture appears in the form of the youthful *kouroi* and *korai* (meaning literally "youths" and "maidens," respectively). Also called Apollo figures, the *kouroi* are free-standing statues, unlike their Egyptian predecessors, which were usually connected to a backstone and showed no hollow spaces (fig. 71). Nevertheless, Archaic figures like the Apollo of Tenea (fig. 72) display the frontal symmetry, forward-stepping left foot, clenched fists, and shoulder-length hair supporting the head and neck like a headdress, all typical features of standing Egyptian figures. Also characteristic of sculpture from this period are the subtle Archaic smile and the large eyes. Unlike the serious countenance of Egyptian sculpture, the Archaic Greek face suggests an inner stirring for the joy of life. It is as if the *kouros* smiles out of the knowledge that he is beginning to free himself from the severe authority of the gods. These figures radiate such a sunlike quality that it is only right they be referred to Apollo, a sun being.

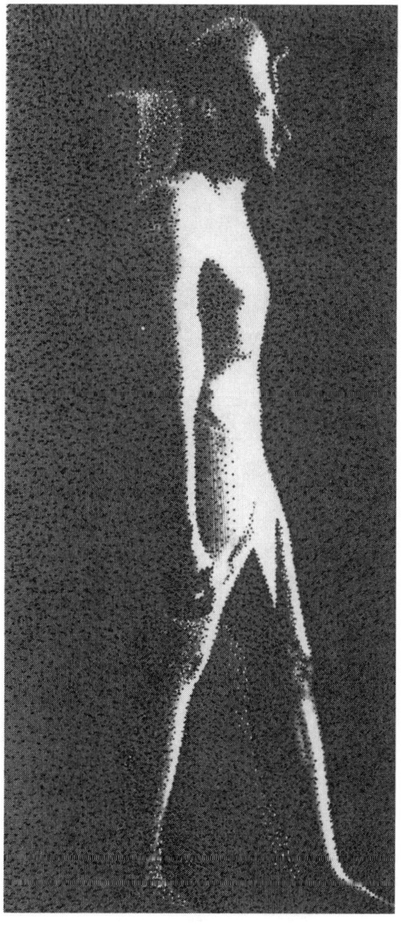

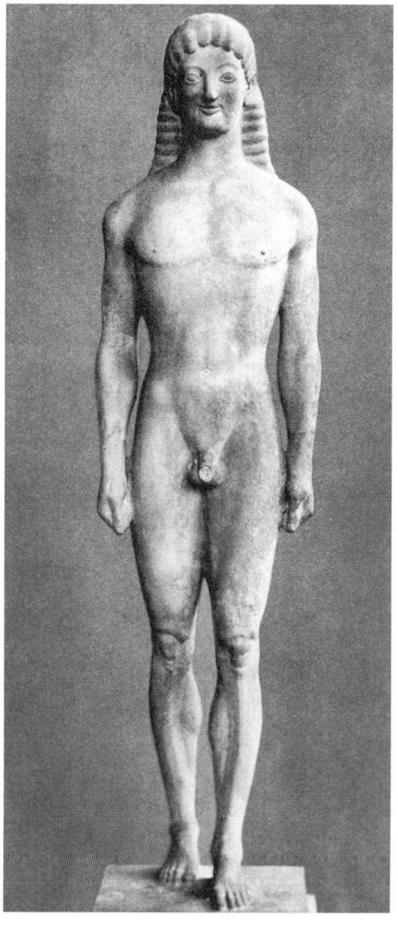

Fig. 71. Far left: This image of Tutmosis III shows how most Egyptian sculpted figures are connected to solid stone backing and appear to emerge from a bas relief.

Fig. 72. Left: The Apollo of Tenea is an example of Archaic free-standing sculpture. Like Egyptian sculpture, it stands on its right leg and steps with its left, yet weight remains evenly distributed on both legs.

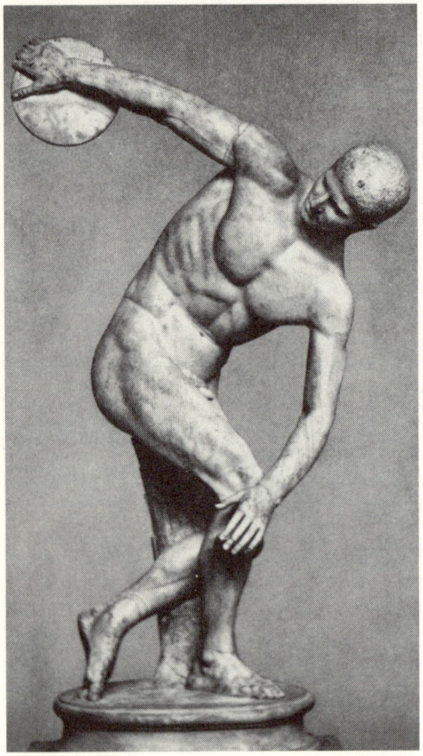

Eliade comments that "perfect serenity, a mysterious smile, and wide-open eyes, all serve to indicate that one is dealing with personages who transcend human modes of being."[24] In their glowing exuberance they give the impression of thriving, energetically sprouting, plants.

The end of the Archaic and the beginning of the Classical period is usually marked by the Persian Wars, specifically the sack of Athens in 480 B.C. This is the era when the Doric style of architecture reaches its height and the Ionic style begins its development with the rebuilding of Athens. During the Classical period, sculpture achieves a solemn and serene majesty unequaled in technical sophistication and quiet beauty. The Greek ideal now finds its highest expression in the human form. Even the gods appear in human form. If one looks back to the time of the Paleolithic caves, where divinity appeared in the form of animals, and to Egypt where gods were composite man-animals, it is remarkable to see how, in the Greek Classical period, the gods have been transformed. They are now human in form. This transformation represents a powerful shift in consciousness. That which is most sublime and spiritual is exemplified through the human figure, no longer through the animal powers.

The Classical figure is thoughtful and restrained, revealing a grandeur and naturalism never realized in art before. An earlier emphasis on the frontal view is now displaced by the importance of the entire figure in space. Although still designed to be viewed from one position only, Classical sculpture provides a more complete perspective of the human figure as a spatial being. Myron's *Discus Thrower* (fig. 73), c. 450 B.C., is an example of this Classic view of the human figure in action. Along with sculptures like Phidias's lost *Athena Parthenos,* 438 B.C. (fig. 74), known only by Roman copies, these works create the Greek *typos* or ideal.

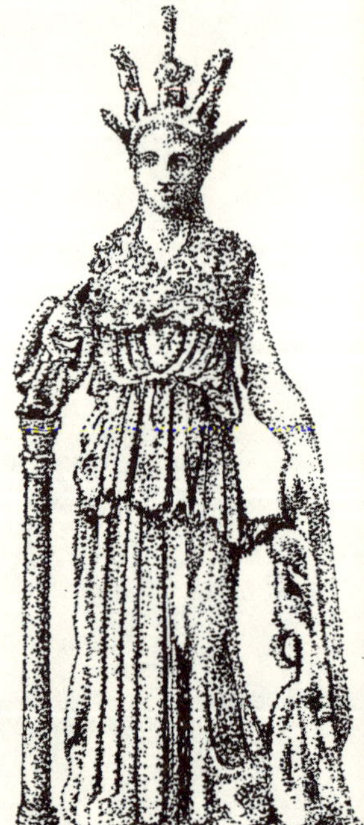

What is perhaps most significant in Classical sculpture is that a shift occurs from two weight-bearing or standing legs in Archaic sculpture to one standing and one relaxed leg. This is in fact what creates the escape from frontal symmetry, for only when weight is released from one leg can full movement be expressed. This weight shift makes true freedom of movement possible in three-dimensional sculpture (fig. 75). It is remarkable that this occurs at the same time as the birth of philosophy. As the fifth-century Greek philosophers explore the newfound realm of logical, critically weighed, reflective thinking that can develop

Fig. 73. Above: *The Discus Thrower,* c. 450 B.C., by Myron, is an example of the newfound freedom of movement in space revealed by Classical sculpture. The statue pictured is a copy made in antiquity.

Fig. 74. Athena Parthenos (right), 438 B.C., was created by Phidias with gold and ivory embellishments, for the Parthenon in Athens. When opponents of the artist accused him of embezzling gold allocated for the statue, he melted it all down to show he had used every ounce and then reconstructed the statue.

concepts such as democracy and the idea of politically free individuals, artists explore the free movement of the human form in three-dimensional space. Early Greek thinkers, Thales of Miletus (c. 636–c. 546), Pythagoras of Samos (c. 582–c. 507), and Heraclitus of Ephesus (c. 535–c. 475) are unlike the Egyptian initiates, Hebrew prophets, and other ancient spiritual leaders in that these Greeks begin to withdraw from the cults, oracles, and mysteries in order to conduct independent intellectual research. They prepare the way for Empedocles of Acragas (c. 495–c. 435), Protagoras of Abdera (c. 485–c. 411), Socrates (469–399), and Plato (c. 428–c. 347), contemporaries of the Classic sculptors Phidias (c. 490–c. 417), Myron (c. 480–c. 445), and Polyclitus (c. 450–405).

Compare an Archaic Greek sculpture to a Classical figure (fig. 76). One observes that even with the Archaic smile the facial features of the earlier sculpture do not express any real emotion. If anything, the earlier figures possess a kind of vacant expression behind their smiles. With the Classical figures a thoughtful, contemplative, inwardly active being appears. Earlier sculpture is content in itself, simply existing, plantlike in character. It is waiting to move, waiting to think. Powerful reserve is present. But Classic sculpture appears to have an inner life and seems to be thinking. It is remarkable that the freeing of the sculpted human figure, through the introduction of the relaxed leg, should occur at precisely the same time that analytical thinking arrives as a newly won human faculty. But that this same sculpture also captures the very appearance of this independent thinking is an artistic revelation. This is the greatness of Greek sculpture, that it mirrors the unfolding consciousness of the time and pictures the working of the Time Spirit.

By the end of the Classical period Socrates, Plato, and Aristotle had paved the way for independent thinking, which brought with it an ever-shrinking dependence on the gods and on instinctual cognition. Logic, natural science, and metaphysics were the transformed mystery wisdom of primal consciousness. With long preparation the Classical Greek philosophers led humanity into a new era where individual intellect could function as the art of thinking, the love of wisdom, philosophy. For the Classical Greek philosophers the new form of initiation was through thinking.[25] Richard Tarnas says of Classical Greek thought and its achievements: "Reflecting the archaic mythological consciousness from which it emerged, informed by the artistic masterworks that preceded and accompanied it, influenced by the mystery religions with which it was contemporaneous; forged through a

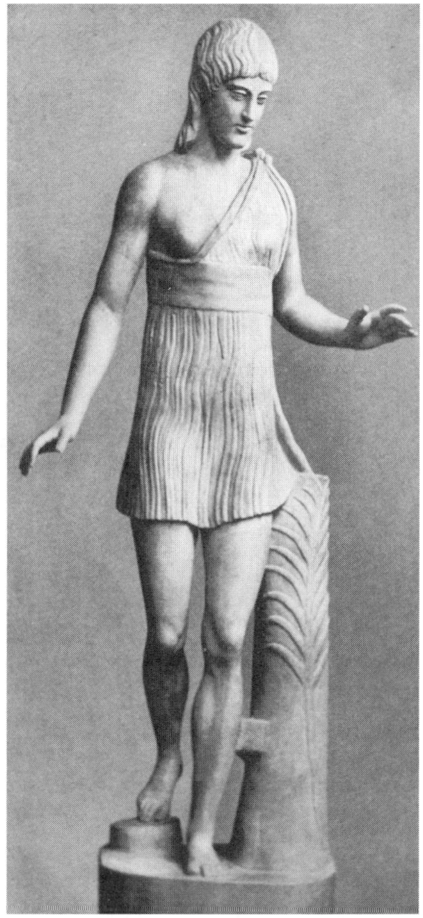

Fig. 75. Above: This figure of a female runner demonstrates the weight-shift occurring around the fifth century B.C., when Greek sculptors depicted a new relationship to space. This artistic innovation occurs simultaneously with the beginnings of philosophy.

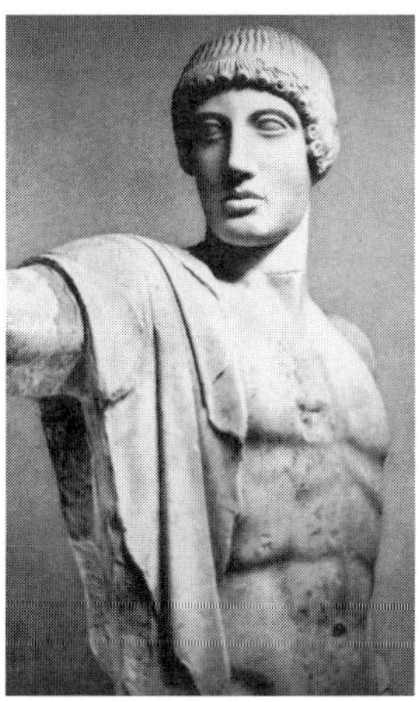

Fig. 76. Left: Classical sculpture reveals an inner life of thought and contemplation not visible in the Archaic-era figures, even though the latter are characterized by their Archaic smiles. This Apollo figure from the Zeus temple at Olympia is a powerful example of the expression of the inner life of the Classical period.

dialectic with skepticism, naturalism, and secular humanism; and in its commitment to reason, empiricism, and mathematics conducive to the development of science in succeeding centuries—the thought of the great Greek philosophers was an intellectual consummation of all the major cultural expressions of the Hellenic era. It was a global metaphysical perspective, intent on encompassing both the whole of reality and the multiple sides of the human sensibility."[26]

This Classical period marks the height and crowning glory of Greek art and culture. In sculpture, Praxiteles begins to move from modeling the ideal *typos* to tentatively suggesting individual characteristics. *Hermes with the Infant Dionysus,* c. 350 B.C. (fig. 77), is an example of tendencies that will unfold more fully in the Hellenistic period. Hermes' relaxed stance shows a casualness and ease that would be impossible in ancient Egypt. The Classical period of Greece might be compared to the blossoming or flowering phase of a plant.

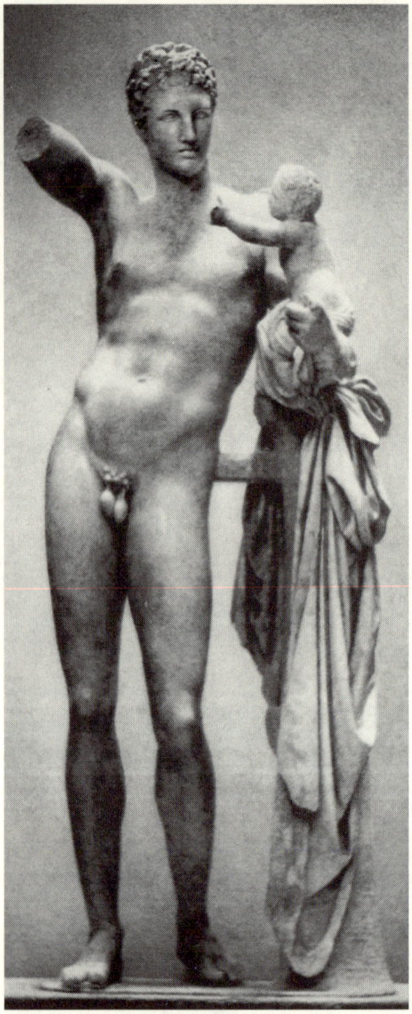

Fig. 77. Hermes with the Infant Dionysus, c. 350 B.C., by Praxiteles, intimates a new tendency in Greek sculpture: its relaxed stance and slight facial expression suggest greater individuation than is seen in earlier figures.

During the Hellenistic period the Ionic architectural style reaches its climax and the Corinthian style makes its appearance. In sculpture the human figure becomes even freer and more relaxed. Greater movement and emotion is expressed, and individual portraits leave universal characterizations behind. Nude female figures appear and sculptors work statues to a highly polished finish. The Classical model is gradually replaced by more dramatic and emotional effects, pomp, and novel ideas. Private wealth and patronage become a major factor in the growth of collecting and copying art. Hellenistic art reveals many stylistic trends existing side by side; because of its overflowing exuberance, like the last stages of a flowering plant going to seed, it is sometimes called Hellenistic-Baroque.

The Laocoön group (c. 150 B.C.; fig. 78) is an example from this period. It was lost for centuries, but was well known in the Renaissance through ancient literary sources. It was discovered in Michelangelo's lifetime—he witnessed its excavation—and it strongly influenced his work. It depicts the moment of death for the Trojan priest Laocoön and his two sons. A large wooden horse is left before the gates of Troy. Laocoön sees through the hoax. He knows the Greeks left the horse, but the ancient serpent forces that he serves turn on him in order that a new era of consciousness may be ushered in: an age of intellect represented symbolically by the horse. The Laocoön group thematically demonstrates the departure of life from the figures, "where life is passing into death."[27] At the same time it illustrates stylistically the departure and final breath of the Greek ideal in sculptural art. The expression-filled faces, taut muscles, extreme gestures, and differentiation of body parts, which so inspired Michelangelo, all characterize this late Greek period.

The *Apollo Belvedere* (fig. 79) exemplifies the Hellenistic-Baroque in Greek art. Compare the Apollo figure from the west pediment of the Zeus temple at Olympia (fig. 76) with the *Apollo Belvedere.* They are both heroic in entirely different ways. *Apollo Belvedere* displays an outer glory, which streams through his elegant gestures with self-righteous demeanor, and replaces with a kind of vanity the inward poise and composure that is found in the Classical figure. This Apollo gives up the Classical spirit of inner strength for outer show, flair, and glamour. The *Apollo Belvedere* illustrates a substitution of inner thoughtfulness for outer display. The lightness and levity of this piece will soon be replaced in its turn by the weighty display of Roman power and authoritative self-possession, as exemplified in the statue of Caesar Augustus (fig. 80). Caesar's bearing typifies the mood of soul that seeks dominion over nature, over self, over humanity, and over the gods.

From the decline of the Greek system of independent city-states until the rise

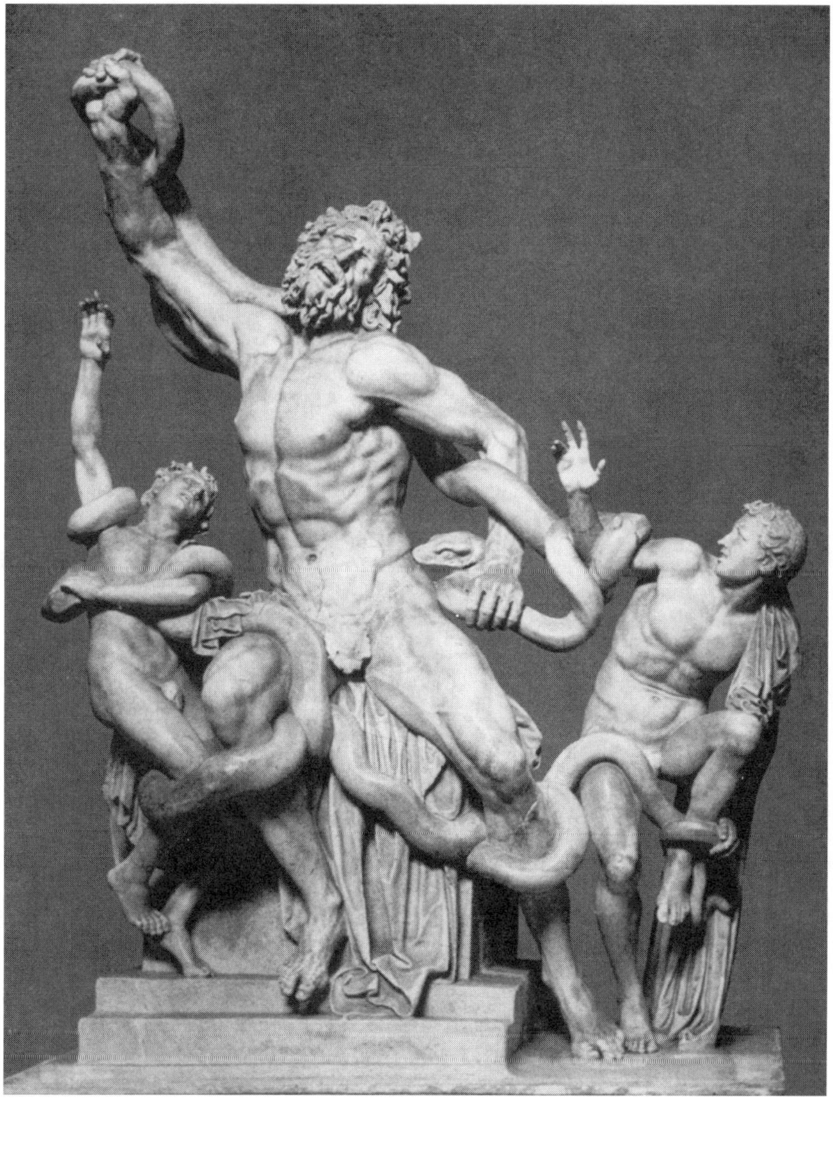

Fig. 78. The *Laocoön* group, c. 150 B.C., demonstrates the emotional expressiveness of the Hellenistic style. The three Trojan priests, Laocoön (center) and his two sons, entangled in the serpent's coil dramatically symbolize the progressive stages from life to the moment before death.

of the Roman empire, Greek art and culture burst into a kind of fruiting stage; in some cases, what might be seen as an overripeness becomes visible. However, seeds for a future unfolding of Greek aesthetics lie dormant within this final phase of Hellenistic art. It is in fact this Hellenistic style that will spark and fire imaginations, and lay the groundwork for the Renaissance ideal of beauty a millennium and a half later.

Plotinus maintains that the work of the great Greek sculptors such as Phidias is not fashioned from models but is entirely the result of the artists' own inner creative forces: "Phidias wrought the Zeus upon no model among things of sense but by apprehending what form Zeus must take if he chose to become manifest to sight."[28] By the time of the Renaissance, this approach to the human figure gives way to working from a model and the "things of sense."

Completing its life cycle in the course of a little more than a millennium, Greek civilization leaves behind the fruits of its art and culture ripe and full upon the earth.

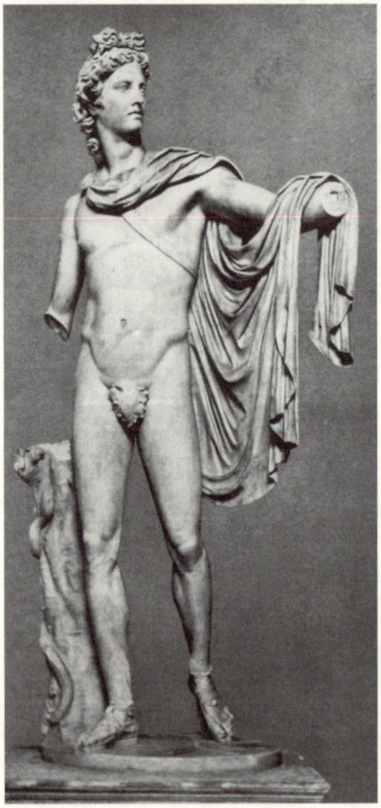

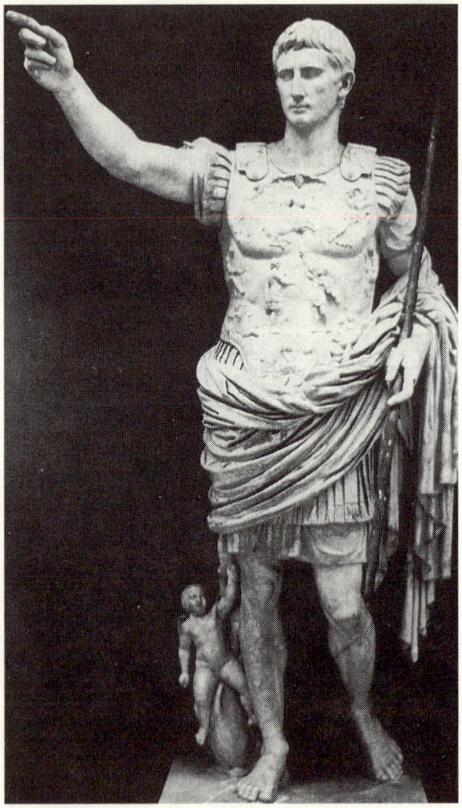

Fig. 79. Apollo Belvedere (right) exemplifies what is sometimes called Hellenistic-Baroque because of its proud, flamboyant style. Note the emphasis on drapery and outer gesture.

Fig. 80. The power and authority (far right) of the Roman emperor Caesar Augustus is depicted in this sculpture through its gravity of bearing. Generally speaking, external rather than internal power characterizes Roman art.

II.5 The Oracles and the Mysteries

Happy is he among men upon earth who has seen these mysteries; but he who is uninitiated and who has no part in them never has lot of like good things once he is dead, down in the darkness and gloom.
—Hymn to Demeter

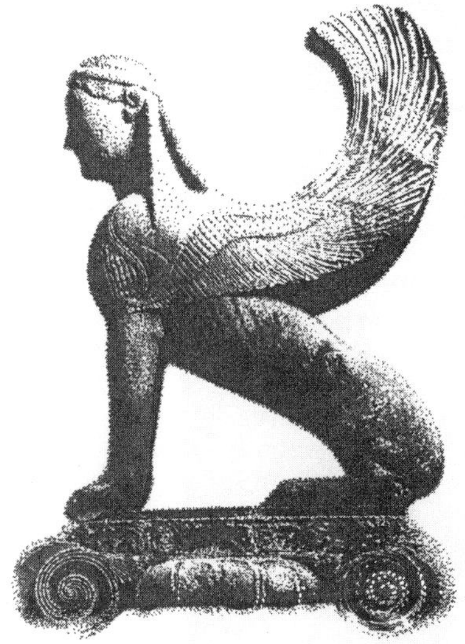

Fig. 81. The sphinx at the entrance of Delphi's sacred precinct (above) is part human (head), part lion (body), and part bird (wings). The sphinx is traditionally a cosmic being who confronts the human being with questions concerning the nature of humanity.

Fig. 82. The *omphalos* or Navel Stone (below) at Delphi was considered to be the seat of Apollo and the center of the world. Its location was determined by Zeus, who sent two eagles flying in opposite directions; their flights ended when they met at Delphi.

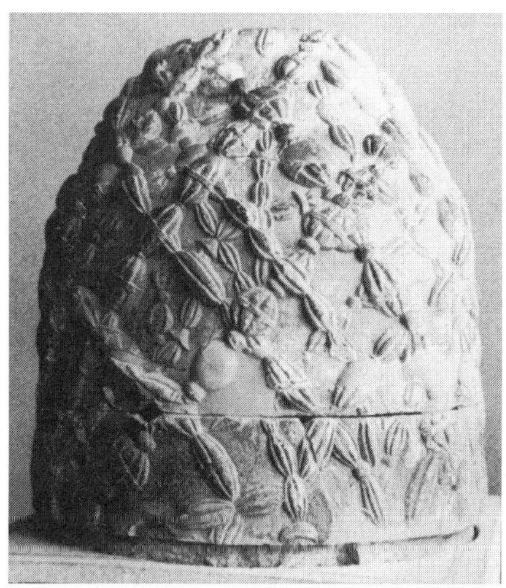

At the conclusion of a long overland journey, the pilgrim finally approaches the foot of Mt. Parnassus and the entrance to the sacred precinct at Delphi. The traveler has brought a burning question to the oracle that Apollo may be able to answer. Reverently he climbs the pathway until he can see the sacred buildings among the cypress and olive trees. A winged sphinx poised atop a single column warns the stranger that this is holy ground requiring the utmost respect (fig. 81). Passing small marble structures, the pilgrim comes to a shrine built by his own city-state in honor of the god and the holy oracle. It is a treasury holding the offerings that pilgrims bring to honor Apollo. He presents his gift and goes to the sacred Castalian spring where he cleanses himself for presentation at the temple. Other travelers have gathered here to put their questions to the god and take part in the famous Pythian games, where the chariot races are most renowned. The pilgrim, after proper inner preparation, makes his way to the temple of Apollo. In front of the temple, a priest meets him, takes a fee, and oversees the pilgrim's sacrifice of an unblemished kid. First, cold water is thrown on the animal, and if it shivers it is a sign that the god is at home. At the same time, the Pythia, a virgin seeress, descends to a secluded subterranean chamber beneath the nave of the temple, while the priest and the pilgrim wait in another small enclosure. The Pythia drinks water from the spring Cassotis, which flows through the underground shrine, and chews laurel leaves as she mounts a tripod placed over a fissure in the ground. The gap releases powerful fumes that put the maiden into a trance as she touches the nearby omphalos, or Navel Stone, seat of the god (fig. 82).[29] The pilgrim reads his question, and in an unearthly speech, the Pythia replies with the voice of Apollo. The priest writes down the cryptic answer, translating it into the rhythmical hexameter verse, "the metre which harmonises the pulse of the blood with the flow of the breath."[30] The answer, in the form of a riddle, is finally given to the pilgrim.

Before the dawn of philosophy, both the oracles and the mysteries played a significant role in the spiritual life of ancient Greece. The oracles interpreted the revelations of the upper gods of the cosmos by means of clairvoyant and clairaudient perception of natural forces through a dimming of consciousness; the oracle's seer or seeress became a medium for receiving the communications of the gods. The mysteries, on the other hand, inspired the pupil through tests and trials to enhance his or her own spiritual organs of perception. By repeated exercises in inner self-discipline, the initiate of the mysteries was able to approach and commune with the spirit. The oracles involved no spiritual experience on the part of the seeker, for oracles were primarily concerned with giving answers or directions to specific questions. Directions that arose out of the mysteries were usually concerned with spiritual experience and initiation.

Plato described two classes of oracles, the "sane" and the "insane." The one involved a conscious examination of observable natural events, while the other was based on conditions of trance or ecstasy. The sane oracles took on many forms, for when all earthly events were seen as reflections of cosmic happenings it was natural to conceive of the macrocosmic impulses as working through the elements. Hence wind and rain, thunder and lightning, shooting stars and the flights of birds were all prophetic voices. The oracle at Dodona relied on the sound of the wind blowing through the leaves of oak trees, or of the tones produced from aeolian harps hung on the branches. The priestesses of Dodona claimed to hear the voice of Zeus in such sounds.

One of the earliest Greek oracles was located at Olympia and was dedicated to Cronus (Saturn), the father of Zeus. Epidaurus was the site of a healing oracle, where, after due preparation, the sick would sleep in the temple precinct, be possessed by the god, and dream the remedy appropriate to their illness. However, the most famous and frequented oracle in the ancient world was at Delphi, nestled below the legendary Mt. Parnassus, where Apollo slew the great Python of the Earth Goddess. This deed of Apollo was seen as the archetypal picture of the higher spiritual element cleansing the soul of its lower, baser, atavistic nature. Apollo's special relation to prophecy comes from his being a god of light—spiritual or unmanifested light, not the physical sun and visible light. (Helios was god of the sunlight and drove his sun chariot across the sky. There is a clear distinction between Apollo and Helios.) As mentioned above, the Pythia,[31] in trance beside the omphalos,[32] recited cryptic words from the god, which a priest framed into intelligible verse. These divine messages, often ambiguous riddles, were thought-provoking. King Croesus consulted the oracle at Delphi during his war with Cyrus of Persia. The Pythia pronounced a seemingly clear answer to his question about the war's outcome by saying, "If Croesus crosses the river Aly, he will destroy a great kingdom."[33] The kingdom Croesus destroyed was his own. During the Persian Wars the Athenians were told that "safety would be within wooden walls." Themistocles correctly interpreted this to mean the Athenians should take to their ships, and although Athens was destroyed, the Athenians defeated the Persians at sea. The oracle had a way of revealing yet concealing the truth, challenging the questioner to consider the answer carefully and thoughtfully, before acting upon it. The importance of the oracles was not so much their accuracy in predictions but in the impulse they gave to thinking in connection with human action. The oracles were concerned with thinking as a reflective activity and with the will, inasmuch as the future reveals itself through will. In later medieval Europe the church was concerned with controlling the will impulses of humanity, whereas the Delphic oracle inspired them.

The oracles were closely connected with the arts; at Delphi, Apollo with his lyre and retinue of nine muses bestowed the gift of music and lyric poetry, while at Dodona contributions to the development of epic poetry were made. At Olympia, where the oldest example of Greek temple architecture is found, Phidias created his most adored work—a sitting statue of Zeus. Now lost, this work is known to us only through antique coins and written descriptions telling of pilgrims from the Greek frontiers who paid homage to this great sculpture of the Greek father-god (fig. 83). According to Pausanias, when Phidias completed the statue, he prayed to Zeus for a sign that the work was accepted, and immediately a flash of lightning struck the ground. Besides the fine arts, the art of gymnastics was also a feature of the Olympian oracle. The oracle's games demonstrated the knowledge that "originated from an insight into the vital or rhythmical forces of the body."[34]

A beautiful example of the vital forces in this connection is the Classical statue of a female runner (fig. 75). This sculpture depicts an athlete in possession of such buoyancy and lightness that the ability to "hover," a high athletic pursuit in the Olympic running events, becomes visible. The desired outcome of a running event was not simply to finish first, but to run so lightly upon the ground, with such grace and ease, that the feet barely imprinted the earth. This piece conveys the qualities of the life forces in all their lightness and vitality, right down to the plant form at the foot of the figure.

While the oracles aroused devotion, piety, and awe toward the many gods of the upper world, the mysteries impelled one to an experience of the divine within oneself. The pupil of the mysteries strove to strengthen faculties of soul, avoiding the trance state. The initiate of the mysteries sought the highest goal possible and ignored the song of the poet Pindar, "O man, seek not to become a god."

Samothrace, an island mystery center in the north Aegean Sea, cherished knowledge of agriculture, medicine, writing, and speech. It was here that the cult of the Cabiri was celebrated. Represented by three sculpted jars linked to Apollo, Ares, and Hermes (fig. 85), the Cabiri were said to produce imaginative pictures in the smoke that rose from burning

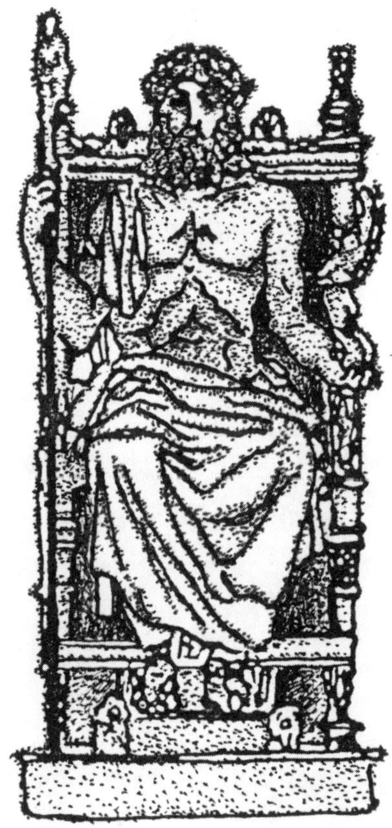

Fig. 83. This seated figure of Zeus is based on the renowned statue created by Phidias for the temple at Olympia. Now lost, this statue is known only through its appearance on antique coins and in written descriptions.

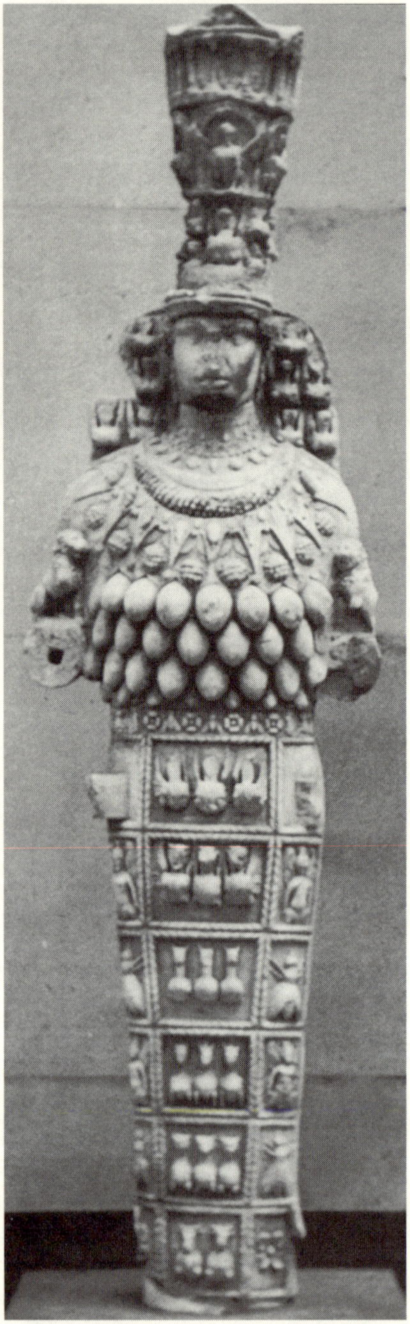

Fig. 84. The goddess Artemis is depicted with many breasts, which symbolize abundance, nurturing, and fertility. (Ephesus, Turkey.)

certain substances. These pictures were then interpreted as prophetic messages from the gods. A canon of proportions based on the human body was also influenced by these mysteries at Samothrace and laid down by the sculptor Polyclitus. Through sculpture and architecture the esoteric principles behind the Golden Mean found their way eventually into exoteric life.

Ephesus, on the western coast of present-day Turkey, was home to the mysteries of Artemis (fig. 84). She is depicted as a multibreasted nurturing goddess of abundance and fertility. We will see later how Artemis bears a special relationship to the Paleolithic "Venus" figurine (fig. 86). Artemis, sister of Apollo, was connected with the moon, just as her divine brother was linked to the sun. According to tradition, the gaze of the initiate envisioned the goddess with three heads: Selene or Luna, the moon in the heavens; Artemis, the huntress on earth; and pale Hecate, of the lower world. In this way the mystery of the human soul forces—thinking, feeling, and willing—was contemplated. Here too is the birthplace of philosophy. Heraclitus, a priest of Artemis, wrote his philosophy of the Logos at Ephesus. Later St. John the Evangelist established a Christian community at Ephesus and connected the old mysteries with the Christ Mystery by writing, "In the beginning was the Logos, and the Logos was with the god and the Logos was a god" (John 1:1–3).

Eleusis was the site of chthonic mysteries, whose rites were concerned with both the paternal principle of Greek cosmogony (Zeus and Dionysus) and the maternal secrets of nature and the earth (Demeter and Persephone). These mysteries had to do with the descent of the human soul (Persephone), its imprisonment within matter, and its longing to return to the upper world. This aching inner question concerning death, transformation, and rebirth was always present in Hellenic thought, and it appeared most urgently in the nocturnal rites of Eleusis.[35] The Eleusinian Mysteries made it clear that the paternal and maternal principles were not separate but deeply intertwined. Here the neophyte might experience some of what Apuleius did during initiation:

I descended to the confines of Death,
I entered Persephone's threshold,
I drove through all the elements
And came back.
I saw the sun at midnight
Glittering in dazzling light.
The nether gods and higher gods
I freely approached and I worshipped them
In heartfelt nearness![36]

Through such an experience the soul "came in contact with the secret power of the Sun, with solar impulses irradiating the Earth, with the forces of the Moon . . . streaming into the Earth, with the . . . stellar impulses and the impulses of the individual elemental forces—the warmth, air and fire forces and so on. The external elements streamed through man's soul (which had been withdrawn from the body) and in this encounter with the external forces he attained self-knowledge."[37]

Delphi, though an important oracle of Apollo, was at the same time a place of the Dionysian Mysteries. As an oracle, Delphi was an exoteric center open to everyone who wished to participate. Here Apollo radiated the light of the sun (human reason) around which the Muses (arts and sciences) orbited. The oracle was given on the seventh day of each month, except the three winter months when Apollo, according to tradition, left Delphi and went to the Hyperboreans in the north. During these months Delphi was given over to the worship of Dionysus, celebrated not only with feasting but also with esoteric ceremonies closed to all but neophytes and initiates. As the reigning god of this mystery center, Dionysus stood for the inner world of visions and dreams. He annihilated "the spell of individuation" and opened "the path to the maternal womb of being."[38] He played the flute and, with his satyrs, inspired the arts of dance and drama. Dionysus worked through the breath and blood, Apollo with his lyre worked in the nerves and senses. At Delphi, the distinctly different streams of the brothers Apollo and Dionysus came together as oracle met mystery. Clairvoyance led to initiation and polytheism to monotheism, as tribal blood ties gave way to individuality. At Delphi the fundamental polarities of these two sons of Zeus were reconciled.

By A.D. 360, the oracle at Delphi and the cult of Apollo were all but at an end.[39] The Roman emperor Julian, later known as Julian the Apostate, attempted to revive the ancient mystery center, but his envoy took away the following answer from an aged Pythia: "Tell the King, the fair-wrought hall has fallen to the ground, no longer has Phoebus [Apollo] a hut, nor a prophetic laurel, nor a spring that speaks. The water of speech even is quenched."[40] The faithful were already flocking to a new sun god and the new mystery religion of Christianity. A new spirit in art was taking shape.

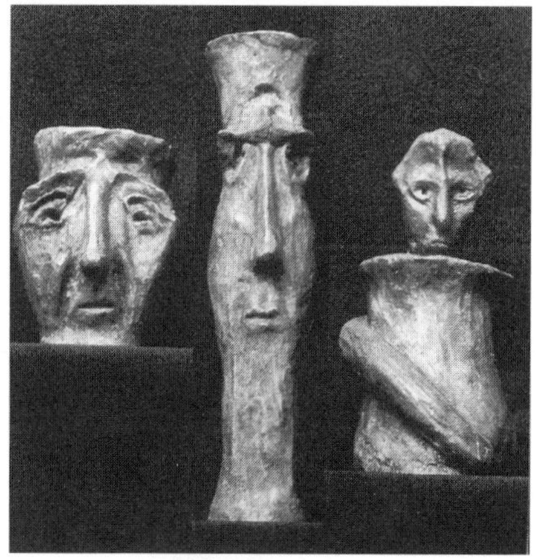

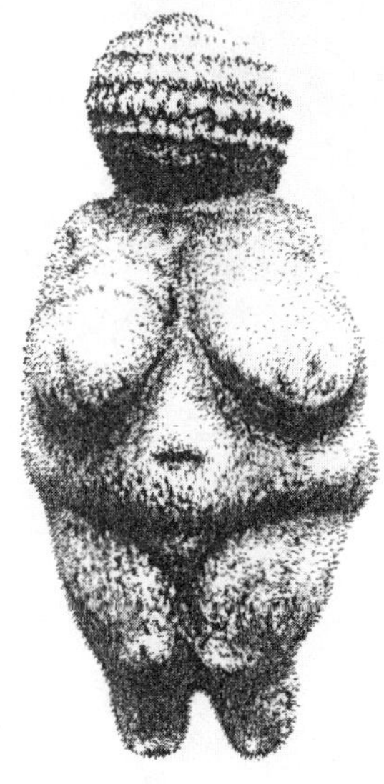

Fig. 85. Top: Connected to the mysteries of Samothrace, the Cabiri are associated with Apollo, Ares, and Hermes, and are represented by three vessels with sculpted faces. The original Greek vessels have never been found, but Rudolf Steiner sketched and sculpted his interpretations of them. (Copyright © Rudolf Steiner Nachlasseverwaltung.)

Fig. 86. Above: "Venus" figurines of the Paleolithic era might be considered the ancient ancestors of the goddess Artemis.

II.6 The Labyrinth and the Bull

We must speak also of the labyrinths, the most astonishing work of human riches, but not, as one might think, fictitious.
—Pliny the Elder

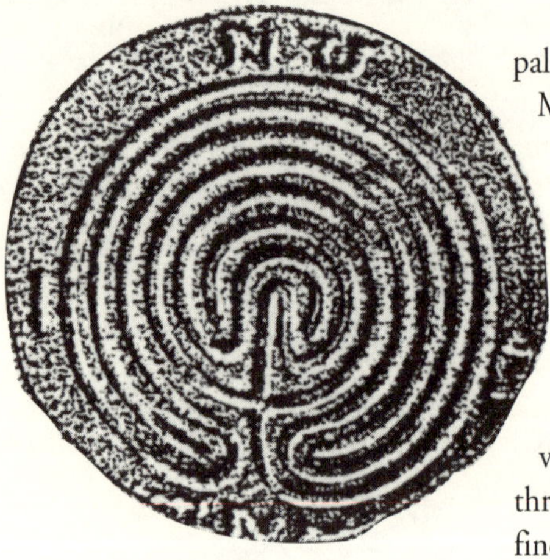

Fig. 87. The Cretan unicursal labyrinth is found on early Hellenistic coins. It has seven circular pathways (planets) concluding at a niche in the center.

Hidden deep within the intricate palace complex, built by the master architect Daedalus at the request of King Minos, was the half-human son of Queen Pasiphaë. The god Poseidon, angry with Minos, inspired the queen with a monstrous lust for a great white bull and the hideous offspring from this union was the Minotaur, a creature with the body of a man and the head of a bull. The Minotaur, with a taste for Athenian blood, annually demanded the lives of seven maidens and seven youths as sacrifice. Theseus, a Greek prince, voluntarily entered the palace maze as one of the victims and slew the Minotaur, escaping with the help of Minos' daughter, Ariadne, who provided him with a ball of yarn and a sword. The thread of yarn, unwound through the complex passages of the maze, was the only way Theseus could find his way out of the confounding corridors after he had slain the Cretan bull-man.

The unicursal or single-path labyrinth—as opposed to the multicursal, numerous-path maze—is shown on early Hellenistic coins (fig. 87), linking it with the Minoan culture which built its capital at Knossos, on the island of Crete.[41] The traditional two-dimensional, unicursal labyrinths have seven pathways that lead to an eighth (octave) alcove at the center. The inward path mysteriously leads one at first very near to the center and then further and further away before returning slowly to the goal at the middle. The design, based on the circle or square, has a cross form within the heart of the contracting concentric channels (fig. 88). It is a mystery image of the cosmic cross, a pre-Christian picture of the macrocosmic spirit (circle-spiral) within which is formed the microcosmic glyph of humanity (cross). It can be seen as a representation of the convolutions of the brain, through which the line of thought threads its way, like the yarn of Ariadne given to Theseus in

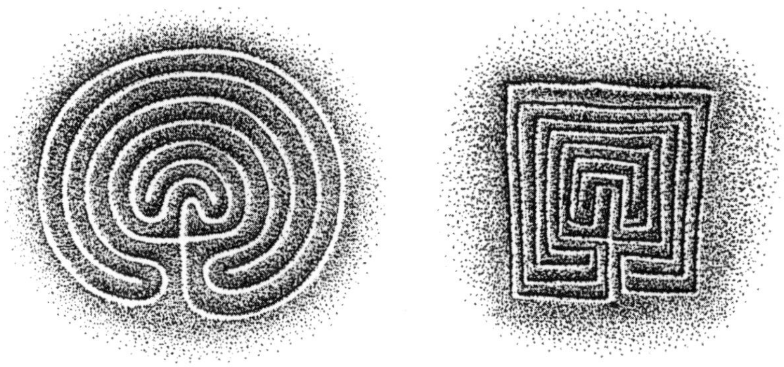

Fig. 88. Left: The ancient unicursal (single-pathway) labyrinth, found throughout the world, appears both in circular and square forms. (After Schuster and Carpenter.)

Fig. 89. Below: Pilgrims entering many medieval cathedrals passed through labyrinth designs such as this one from Chartres Cathedral.

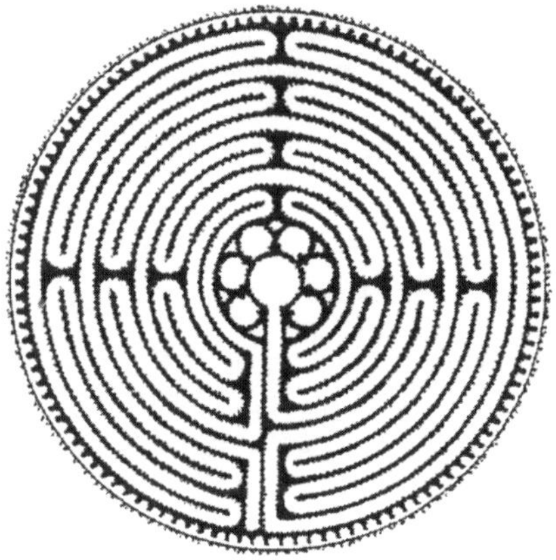

Cretan mythology. Or, turned upside-down, it can be a picture of the metabolic system (digestive tract and reproductive organs), with which the bull is associated. In both cases the labyrinth is a place of trial and transformation where courage, continuous attention, and thoughtfulness are crucial. It is a form that signifies initiation in that one must find the innermost chamber of the labyrinth, the Holy of Holies, the Self, and return, changed, to the outer world. It is a place of order or chaos, depending on one's perspective, and it is clearly analogous to other images such as the crossroads, the forest, the sea, the cave, the braid and knot, the meander, and the interlaced pattern. The entire process of creating the labyrinth, then entering it, represents the human quest for self-knowledge and the path to spiritual enlightenment.

In medieval times, as we have seen, elaborate labyrinth forms were inlaid into the floors of a number of French cathedrals, such as Chartres, Amiens, and St. Etienne, for the devout to follow in prayer as part of their holy pilgrimage (fig. 89). Church labyrinths can also be found in England, where gardens too incorporate enigmatic labyrinth and maze forms with landscaped paths and manicured hedgerows. In fact, throughout the world in recent years an incredible resurgence of interest in constructing and walking labyrinths and mazes has taken place, both for reasons of entertainment and spirituality. However, the mystery of their original purpose still lies hidden from our present-day knowledge.

Herodotus, the Greek historian, noted the earliest documented labyrinth to be in Egypt in the nineteenth century B.C. Pliny states that this temple, dedicated to the sun-god, with precincts for other Egyptian gods, must have cost a fortune in time and gold to build. The earliest verified date for a labyrinth pattern is 1200 B.C., in Pilos, Greece, and it is etched on the reverse side of a Linear B tablet. It has been suggested that Linear B tablets "were shorthand notes given to the dead to take with them into the hereafter."[42] A labyrinth is considered symbolic of death as it may have been a kind of map of the Underworld to be used by the departing soul.

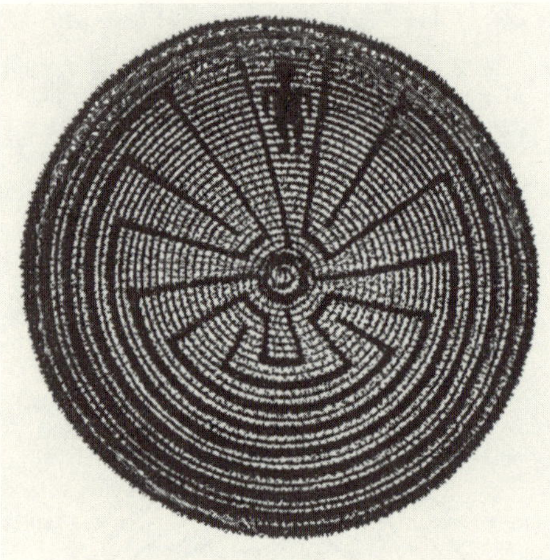

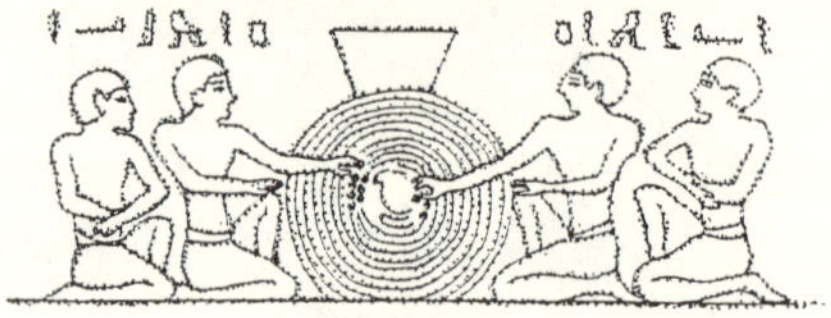

Fig. 90. Woven into a Pima Native American basket, the unicursal labyrinth (top) is seen as a symbol of the place of emergence and of Mother Earth.

Fig. 91. Finger labyrinths (bottom) were in use as early as Egypt's New Kingdom and may have been used in ritual practices that led to games of skill. (After Schuster and Carpenter.)

The Cretan labyrinth pattern is found in many other parts of the world beyond the Mediterranean. A wonderful open-air stone-lined labyrinth can be walked in a field on the island of Gotland, off the eastern coast of Sweden, and other walkable labyrinths exist on the Finnish island of Wier, in Iceland, and Kandalakscha in Russia. These field labyrinths and many turf mazes have been dated to the Neolithic period, when participants traveled the labyrinth pathways with a three-step dance. Labyrinth dances are linked to fertility and rebirth because of the spring rituals involving the rescue of a girl from the center of the form. Such labyrinths were called Virgin Dances in Finland, where the event is depicted in a fifteenth-century wall painting at Sibbo Church. Similar practices are known in India.

Before they went on a quest, King Arthur's knights were said to go to the double labyrinth petroglyph carved on a rock wall near Tintagel, England, that is dated to c. 1800–1400 B.C. Such small relief labyrinths could be traced with one's finger. The Anasazi, Hopi, and Pima Native Americans called this form Tapu'at, symbol of Mother Earth, and carved it, sometimes upside-down or in reverse, beside their ancient cliff dwellings, as at Casa Grande in Arizona. They also wove its design into their basketry. Rina Swentzall, a Tewa Native American of the Santa Clara Pueblo, says of the woven labyrinth which pictures a human figure walking the pathway (fig. 90): "This basket [design] is about the complications of life coming out of the center. The center represents the origin point in the earth, and the human figure is coming and going from it. Everything is coming and going out of this center, emergent place."[43]

Labyrinth drawings were often laid out and traced by means of continuous lines, without lifting the hand. Such ritual-artistic form drawing was practiced in ancient Egypt (fig. 91), and then the forms were used for games with moveable playing pieces. String figures such as the cat's cradle are distant relatives of the labyrinth, in that their linear patterns are built up through a process which brings about a pictorial transformation which could be interpreted on various levels: as fairy tales for children, as moral fables for adults, and as esoteric wisdom for initiates.

Although found in almost every quarter of the earth, this image of the labyrinth is profoundly linked with Crete and the Minoan civilization. A relatively small but powerful seafaring nation, Crete extended its influence throughout the Mediterranean region just before the Greek Geometric Period and during the Egyptian New Kingdom. After but a few brief centuries, the Minoan civilization came suddenly to an end following a series of destructive earthquakes around 1400 B.C. However, the Minoans left a wealth of artistic treasures that declare an important transition stage in human development.

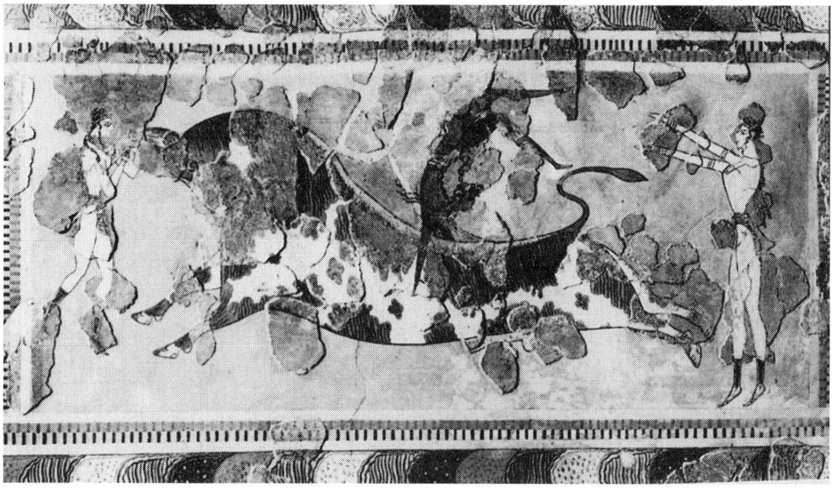

A striking example of the Minoan artistic style is the graceful Bull Dancers (fig. 92). Controlled fluidity seems to pervade the entire picture as if the action could be taking place in an aquarium, under water. The dancers or acrobats, who catch the bull by the horns and somersault over its back in order to land upright once again, have a lightness and a buoyancy that Egyptian figures, as we shall see, do not exhibit. In fact the bull and the dancers do not touch ground. There is no earth in the picture, and in this regard it bears a certain resemblance to Paleolithic art. All the figures live in a world filled with life and levity, where gravity and weight are insignificant. Lightness overcomes heaviness and even the stiff limbs appear to be weightless and floating. Figures have a fluid quality, yet are nevertheless held and firm. Perhaps it is only natural that Minoan art is pervaded by the water element, for this island culture was itself entirely surrounded by the forceful life energy of the sea.

Just as Crete lies geographically between Greece and Egypt, so too did the ancient Minoans lie culturally between the two dominant civilizations to their north and south. This "in-between" position can be seen in the way Minoan art anticipates certain qualities that will appear in Greek art and also has much in common with its Egyptian predecessors. Minoan art demonstrates a unique intermediary style between the earlier and later cultures, for in the art of ancient Crete, the static quality, stillness, and restraint of Egyptian art as well as the lightness and freedom of Greek art blend together in a harmonious way.

Minoan depictions of the bull are a religious and artistic expression of the vital life quality. To take the bull by the horns might be life-threatening, but the exhilaration of living life to its fullest, by literally grasping the

Fig. 92. The Bull Dancers, a mural painting found at Knossos in Crete, shows three acrobats, a male and two females, grabbing the horns of a bull and somersaulting over its back. The mural demonstrates a stylistic transition between Egyptian and Greek two-dimensional visual arts.

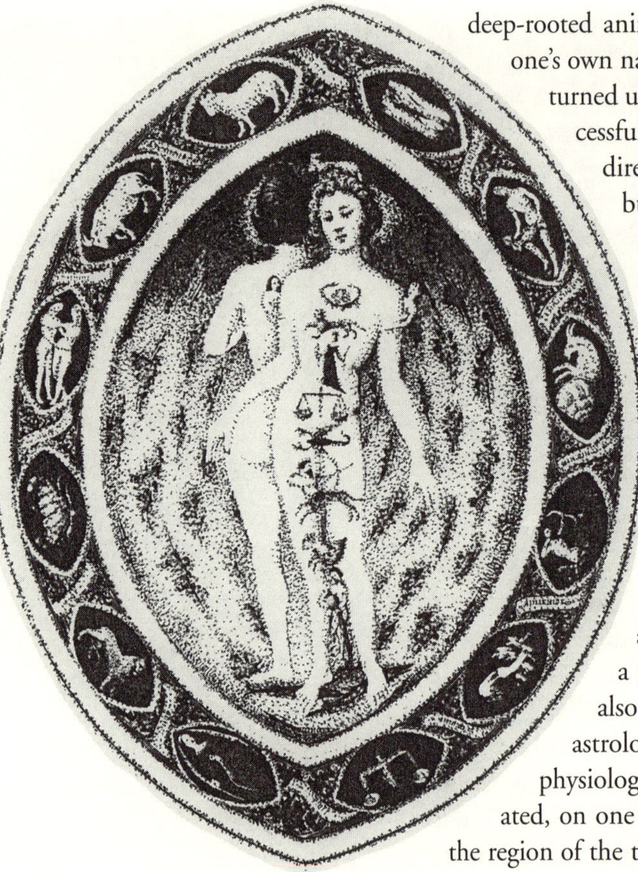

Fig. 93. The medieval conception of the human being still retained a zodiacal connection and associated the various parts of the human organism to specific constellations, as this manuscript illumination of the Duc de Berry's *Book of Hours* by the Limbourg Brothers demonstrates. Such cosmic pictures of the human being have their origin in Egyptian esoteric tradition and even older world mythologies. (After the Limbourg Brothers.)

deep-rooted animal passions and powerful unconscious will forces within one's own nature, was a picture of the inner trials of initiation. One was turned upside down in the process of meeting these forces, but a successful encounter meant arriving back on one's feet with a new direction in life. In ancient Crete and in early Greece the sacred bull dance was a deed of cosmic significance. Theseus, who successfully trod the labyrinth and overcame the old bull nature, was a representative of the dawning new consciousness in which intellectual thinking would ultimately replace instinctive primal consciousness. Both the slaying of the legendary Minotaur by Theseus and the sacrifice of the sacred bull by Mithras point to the end of one cosmic era and the beginning of a new stage of human development. At the end of the Egyptian age and the beginning of the Greek, the sun moves out of the constellation of Taurus (the bull), and enters into the next zodiacal region, that of Aries (the ram). According to ancient tradition, the constellation of Taurus not only holds a position within certain starry realms of the heavens but it also influences specific parts of the human organism. The old astrological sciences connected the zodiacal influences with human physiology and human development (fig. 93). Besides being associated, on one level, with the metabolic system, Taurus also presides over the region of the throat or larynx and the faculty of speech. The constellation of Aries, on the other hand, is linked with the head organization and thinking. The development of language arts, including written alphabets, occurs mostly during the era of Taurus, while the birth of philosophy and logical thinking develops under the sign of Aries. Mystery imagery such as the labyrinth, the bull, and the ram are pictures from traditional esoteric sources that become visible by means of art. They show us how the ancients experienced their world.

Homer tells us that the deceased Achilles, mourning his situation in the underworld, declares to Odysseus that it is "better to be a beggar on earth than a king in the Land of the Shades." The lowest condition in life is for him better than the highest station in death, for life well lived is all-important to the Greek, and this is equally true for the Minoan. The realm of the dead has become, in the Greek era, an ominous and undesirable place. As we shall see, the Egyptian, on the other hand, while bound by the severity of physical life, finds joyful release in the afterlife. In the desert civilization of Egypt, one's life is a preparation for death. Death is revered as the homeland of the spirit and dwelling place of the great gods.

Notes

1. Mann, A.W. Lecture given at Emerson College, Dec. 6, 1973.
2. Richter, G., p. 110. "If one assumes that the Mystery of Golgotha [the deed of Christ] was an event of cosmic proportions, it at least makes sense to see in these triumphal arches of the Caesars something like a dark counter-image of that other 'entrance.' Naturally, this was not a conscious plan. It simply happened—on the one hand, in such a way that the whole earth trembled in the dreaming depths of the human soul from the might of this event: His entrance and, on the other hand, that of the Caesars, whose own forcible initiations into the mysteries made them experienced in the use of magic, also forced a distortion of that experience up out of the depths, seating themselves in the place that was meant for someone else." Richter, G. *Art and Human Consciousness,* p. 113.
3. Malraux, A. *Voices of Silence,* p. 193.
4. Fierz-David, L. *Women's Dionysian Initiation: The Villa of the Mysteries in Pompeii,* p. 17.
5. Ibid., pp. 100–101.
6. Settegast, M. P*lato Prehistorian: 10,000 to 5,000 B.C. in Myth and Archaeology,* p. 113, and Fideler, D. *Jesus Christ, Sun of God: Ancient Cosmology and Early Christian Symbolism,* p. 143.
7. The form of the Phrygian cap—a sweeping gesture from the back of the head, curving upwards and forwards, ending in a rounded knob—appears in many cultures as a sign of high rank, overseeing authority, spiritual vision, and power.
8. Fideler, D. p. 147.
9. Ibid., p. 151.
10. Schutze, A. *Mithras-Mysterium und Urchristentum,* pp. 52–53. We recognize the bull as one of the four creatures that make up the archetypal Sphinx and later symbolically portray the four Evangelists (the bull—Luke, the lion—Mark, the eagle—John, the man—Matthew). These four figures, significant to pagan and Christian spirituality alike, were seen as representing the essential forces that stream in from the universe and which, when harmoniously working together, can create the earthly human being.
11. Generally, women joined the mysteries of Cybele, where initiates were drenched in the blood of a sacrificial bull. Exclusively female, the cult of Bona Dea was also popular at this time. Godwin, J. *Mystery Religions in the Ancient World,* p. 98.
12. The grades of initiation from novice to highest initiate were: (1) Raven—Mercury, quicksilver, Wednesday; (2) Occultist—Venus, copper, Friday; (3) Warrior—Mars, iron, Tuesday; (4) Lion—Jupiter, tin, Thursday; (5) Persian or National Folk—Moon, silver, Monday; (6) Sun Hero or Solar Messenger—Sun, gold, Sunday; (7) Father—Saturn, lead, Saturday. The designation of planet, metal, and day of the week vary according to different traditions. In many cases the highest level of initiation, the Father, is recorded as corresponding to the Sun. Fideler, p. 144.
13. Steiner, R. *Building Stones for the Understanding of the Mystery of Golgotha,* p. 165.
14. Steiner, R. *Universe, Earth, and Man,* p. 19.
15. Steiner, R. *Occult Science: An Outline,* p. 242.
16. Fideler, D. *Jesus Christ, Sun of God.* pp. 197–198.
17. Kostof, S. *A History of Architecture: Settings and Rituals,* p. 127.
18. Plotinus, cited in Barfield, p. 128.
19. Wili, W. "The Orphic Mysteries and the Greek Spirit," *The Mysteries: Papers from the Eranos Yearbooks,*. p. 65.
20. Cited in Lawlor, R. *Homage to Pythagoras,* p. 86.
21. Fideler, D. *Jesus Christ, Sun of God,* pp. 197–198.
22. Aristotle, cited in Steiner, R. *The Spiritual Foundation of Morality,* p. 58.
23. Other dates that might be equally appropriate for marking the end of the Geometric period are c. 800 B.C., when the blind seer Homer was writing, or 747 B.C., the beginning of the Greco-Roman cultural epoch when, according to Steiner, the sun moved from the constellation of Taurus (Bull) and entered into that of Aries (Ram).
24. Eliade, M. Divinities: Art and the Divine, *Symbolism, the Sacred, and the Arts,* p. 61.
25. It should be noted that Aristotle, who represents the end of reliance on mystery religions, was deeply influenced by the mysteries. Hiebel

points out: "Aristotle showed a profound knowledge of the ancient mysteries; he wrote a survey summarizing all ancient wisdom including that of India, Persia, the teachings of the Magi, Zarathustra, Egypt, Orpheus, Pythagoras, Delphi, and the seven sages . . . and it was under the shadow of the mysteries of the Cabiri of Samothrace that Aristotle wrote about the meaning of initiation: 'Those who are being initiated are not required to grasp anything with the understanding *(mathein)* but to have a certain experience *(pathein)* and so to be put into a particular frame of mind, presuming that they are capable of this frame of mind in the first place.'" Hiebel, F. *Gospel of Hellas,* p. 238. Kerenyi says: "The Mysteria took the initiate back to the very beginning of life, its natural genesis, and not to any philosophical 'principle.'" Kerenyi, C. *The Mysteries of the Kabeiroi,* p. 39.

26. Tarnas, R. *The Passion of the Western Mind,* p. 69.

27. Steiner, R. *Kunstgeschichte als Abbild innerer geistiger Impulse, IX.* The *Laocoön* group, rediscovered during Michelangelo's time, has received a good deal of comment from aestheticians and historians beginning with Lessing.

28. Plotinius, *Enneads,* V.8,1, p. 411.

29. An actual cleft at Delphi has never been located. It has been suggested that the prophetic Pythia relies entirely upon the spiritual, not physical, forces of the depths.

30. Harwood, A.C. "Oracles." *The Golden Blade,* 1969, p. 38.

31. The name *Pythia* was derived from the mythic python that inhabited the area and was the focus of a pre-Hellenic serpent or Earth Mother worship. Apollo slew the divine snake, for which he later had to make atonement. The Pythia was usually a young maiden, but in later antiquity she was more often an older woman.

32. According to legend, Zeus let fly two eagles from opposite ends of the earth. They met at the center of the world—at Delphi. Here, the *omphalos* stone was kept in the temple of Apollo as the god's seat, and is depicted on coins, reliefs, and vase paintings. A replica of the stone was placed in front of the temple for open services.

33. Petracos, B. *Delphi,* p. 8.

34. Hiebel, F. p. 94.

35. Hiebel, F. p. 111. The Eleusinian Mysteries were divided into two parts. During the Lesser Mysteries, celebrated in February at Agrae, the drama of Persephone was performed. The Lesser Mysteries prepared the soul, and those who participated were called *mystai.* The Greater Mysteries, those of Dionysus, took place in archaic times only every fifth year, in September, and lasted nine days. Those who participated in the Greater Mysteries were called *epoptai,* meaning clairvoyant seers or initiates. Purification and catharsis were achieved through the drama of Persephone in the Lesser Mysteries. Initiation was gained through Dionysus in the Greater Mysteries.

36. Apuleius, *Metamorphoses.* Cited in Hiebel, *Gospel of Hellas,* p. 92.

37. Steiner, R. *Building Stones for an Understanding of the Mystery of Golgotha,* p.167-168.

38. Nietzsche, F. quoting Schopenhauer, *The Birth of Tragedy,* cited in Ryan, p. 188.

39. The word *Delphi* is connected with *Delphus,* meaning "womb,"and with *Delphinos,* the dolphin, for Apollo came to Greece in the form of a great dolphin that leapt on to the land "like a star at midday."

40. Petracos, B. *Delphi,* p. 6.

41. Doob, P. *The Idea of the Labyrinth,* p. 19, "The myth of the many-pathed ('multicursal') Cretan labyrinth [maze] existed in some form as early as Homer. . . . The labyrinth design in the visual arts—a square or circular diagram in which a single unbranched ('unicursal') circuitous route leads inevitably, if at great length, to the center—is older still, dating back to prehistoric times."

42. Schuster, C. and E. Carpenter, *Patterns That Connect,* p. 313.

43. Rina Seventzall. Tewa, Santa Clara Pueblo. From a display caption at the Native American Museum of Art, New York.

III. THE ART AND MYSTERIES OF ANCIENT EGYPT

Blind Soul! Arm thyself with the torch of the Mysteries, and in the night of earth shalt thou uncover thy luminous Double, thy celestial Soul. Follow this divine guide and let him be thy Genius, for he holds the key to thy lives, both past and to come.
—The Egyptian Book of the Dead

It is the height of Egypt's greatness; the temples and royal palaces are a wonder to behold. The massive stone facades sculpted in relief and painted in brilliant colors, hung with festive banners, are visited by grand processions, announced by sounding trumpets and beating drums. But all this outer show of pomp and flair is not what interests the one who seeks to penetrate the secret knowledge of Egypt's mystery centers.

Before being allowed to enter into the temple mysteries, the neophyte undergoes a searching examination by the hierophant. If he passes this fateful interview, he is brought in the strictest silence before a statue of Isis, goddess of wisdom. She is seated in meditation, her face is veiled, and a closed scroll is upon her lap. "No mortal has lifted my veil," are the words upon her mute lips.

Flanking the portal of the sanctuary stand two columns, one red, one black. The red column signifies the ascending spirit on its quest toward the light of Osiris, the black one represents its bondage in matter. Once the neophyte passes between these pillars there is no turning back. Madness or death awaits the untruthful soul.

The neophyte who braves this journey passes into a humid corridor that leads to a narrow vault crackling with fire and glowing with red-hot coals. If the novice is properly prepared he can walk coolly across this room, passing through the trial by fire. He next comes to a dark chamber with a cold, black pool of stagnant water that he must cross through and overcome his fear at the loss of solid ground. If he successfully completes the trials of fire and water, he is dried by servants, clothed in fine linen, and requested to await the hierophant in a dimly lit grotto. After a time, soothing music begins to play in the distance and the scent of perfume dances in the air. Suddenly, a sensuous woman of great beauty, clothed in transparent purple gauze, appears before him. From the goblet she carries, she offers a drink—a draft of happiness, a promise of oblivion to pain and sorrow. If the novice is tempted and he drinks from the cup of pleasure, he falls into a stupor and upon awakening is told he has succumbed to the temptation of the senses. Although he had triumphed over the trials of fire and water, he has not conquered himself and must, therefore, under penalty of death, remain a slave in the temple.

However, if the candidate dashes the goblet to the ground and resists the advances of the temptress, he is brought before the hierophant and amidst the assembled priesthood swears an oath of silence and loyalty. He then begins his training with studies of the minerals and plants, medicine, and geometry, the history of the earth and of humankind. Architecture, astronomy, and sacred music are learned, as is the secret language of hieroglyphs. If all proceeds well for the neophyte, esoteric techniques are given to him by the hierophant and these help to overcome the inner trials of fire and water that are far more burning and far more suffocating than the mock tests undergone at the start of his training.

The hierophant observes the progress of his pupil over the course of many years. Finally, it is clear the pupil is ready for initiation into the sacred mysteries. The candidate is brought into a cryptlike chamber and instructed to lie down in a cold stone sarcophagus. Twelve priests circle the coffin and the neophyte is put into a deathlike "temple sleep." His life passes before him in successive scenes in backward order as he feels his earthly consciousness drifting away. Scarcely visible in the darkness, a distant shining light appears. This starlight becomes a sun as the ecstatic soul of the novice pursues its radiance. Out of the light a shape takes form. It is the figure of Isis, the spiritual self, divine wisdom. She speaks to the seeking soul in words of comfort and love: "I am thy invisible sister, thy divine soul, and this is the book of thy life. Some of the pages are filled with records of thy past existences, the blank pages are for thy future lives. Some day, I will unroll them all before thee. Thou knowest me now, call me and I will come!"[1] When the vision begins to fade, a terrible rending occurs and the pupil is drawn back into his body as into a corpse. He is in a state of lethargy and a frightful weight takes hold of him. He awakens to find the brotherhood of hierophants warmly welcoming him back as a newly initiated fellow priest of the Egyptian Mysteries.

III.1 The Art and Craft of the Mysteries

Saith Horus the son of Isis: I have come to thee. . . . I have brought to thee Osiris. . . . His heart is right coming forth from the balance, not sinned hath it against any god or goddess. Thoth hath weighed it according to the decree uttered by the cycle of the gods. . . . May he be like the followers of Horus for ever!
—*The Egyptian Book of the Dead*

What were the Egyptian Mysteries? Herodotus, the Greek historian, claims to have been initiated into these mysteries but tells us little about them.[2] Pythagoras trained for some seventeen to twenty-two years in the Egyptian temple wisdom before starting his school of mathematics.[3] Many of the Roman emperors forced their way into Egyptian temple initiations during the decline of these mysteries.[4] However, little documentary evidence of the inner procedures of the mystery centers actually exists because of the absolute secrecy demanded under penalty of death. Nevertheless it is in ancient Egypt, more than any other place or period in history, where clear physical evidence of the presence, and to some extent the procedures, of mystery activities can be found. These activities, though inseparable in practice, can be arranged into three main categories:

1. Ancestor worship, the cult of the dead, and knowledge of the afterlife.
2. Spiritual beings (gods) and the spiritual world (cosmology).
3. Initiation, the path of esoteric development, and the human relationship to spiritual worlds.

We know something about all three of these areas from the artifacts of Egyptian culture, particularly from the arts of painting, sculpture, and architecture, as well as hieroglyphic texts.

Ancestor worship, practiced by many prehistoric cultures, is basically a living connection with the dead, a communication with or vivid remembrance of the departed. In some cases the dead would be called upon to assist the living. In ancient Egypt this relationship was developed into an elaborate cult of the departed. In fact most of Egypt west of the Nile River belonged to the dead. Therefore one can read a third-millennium B.C. tomb inscription that states: "The span of earthly things is as a dream; but a fair welcome is given him who has reached the West."[5] Souls of the dead traveled westward with the setting sun.

Monumental art and architecture, literature and festivals were all part of

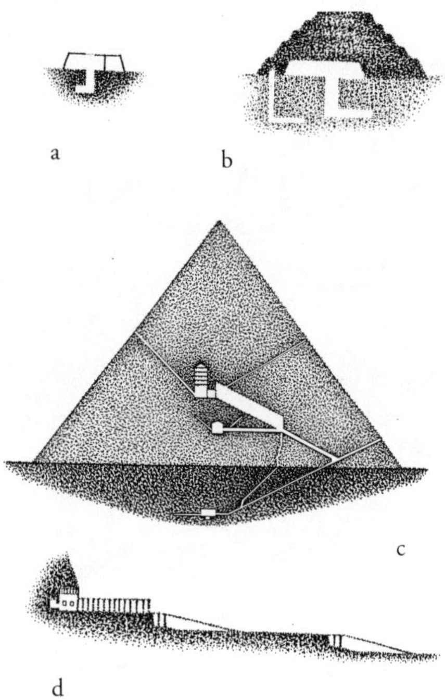

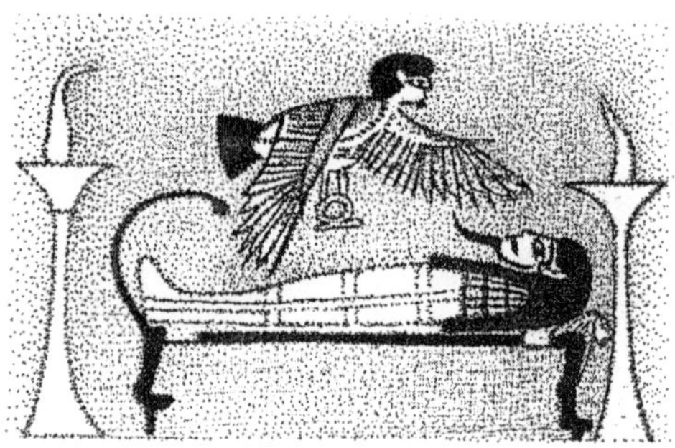

Fig. 94. Top: A monumental architecture in service to the cult of the dead evolved in Egypt. Surviving examples range from (a) simple open-pit burials and mud-brick mastabas, to (c) cut-stone pyramids and (b and d) rock-cut temple tombs.

Fig. 95. Bottom: This papyrus painting shows the departing soul as it lingers above the corpse after death. The soul or *ba* is depicted as a human head on the body of a bird. After death the *ba* hovers about the *khat* or physical body and then takes flight for the Otherworld or afterlife.

the ritual activities for the deceased. According to their art, the early Egyptians still had direct perception and knowledge of the departed soul in the afterlife, and the initiate-priests, even after thousands of years of Egyptian culture, seem to have maintained this bond through cultic activities.

What are some of the characteristic procedures used in the Egyptian cult of the dead? Burial is the most obvious; from the early open-pit burial, and simple mud brick mastaba structures, to the monumental cut-stone architecture of the pyramids, and the rock-cut temple tombs, a colossal architecture developed for the purpose of serving the dead during their passage between the realm of the living and that of the gods (fig. 94). No dwellings have survived from dynastic Egypt, only buildings constructed to serve the gods or the dead—temples and tombs.

A highly technical and complex ritual of embalming was developed to preserve the physical body after death. Even the architectural form of the pyramid helped to further this preservation. It is generally believed that mummification was a device used for the purpose of continuing life after death, an attempt at immortality through preserving the body. However, the ancient Egyptians had a firm knowledge of life after death and therefore had little need for notions of immortality or salvation. Rather it seems they needed to turn greater attention to earthly life. From a spiritual standpoint, ritual embalming appears to have had the effect of encouraging the departed soul to linger after death and to associate for a longer time with the preserved physical body, as may be seen in some paintings (fig. 95). In this way the soul could bond with the corpse, strengthening an interest in the physical, material nature of earthly life—an interest that was likely to have been weaker in earlier times.[6] It would be more consistent with Egyptian wisdom to think that preserving the physical body, a "creation of the gods," was not simply an attempt to continue the soul's life after death—for the Egyptians lived their entire lives with the expectation and longing for that certainty—but to maintain and build a stronger connection between the departed soul and the physical world for a future life on earth.

The burial of food and funeral objects would in this sense serve as offerings for the journey after death. Obviously the Egyptians did not believe the dead would eat the food offerings, but rather that the spiritual substance, as well as the life forces in the food and attached to objects, would nourish the soul and bind it more closely to the physical world after death. It is likely that through this close contact with the dead, the living could be assured of a mediator with the gods and the departed soul could be encouraged to return to the earth for later incarnations.

Accompanying the dead were tomb paintings and scrolls depicting what the departed soul could expect to encounter after death. An illustrated papyrus scroll would be wrapped in cloth strips and laid between the legs of the mummy, or the illustrations were painted on the inner walls of the tomb. These pictures, with their accompanying hieroglyphic text, constitute the *Egyptian Book of the Dead*.[7] This "book" was in fact a

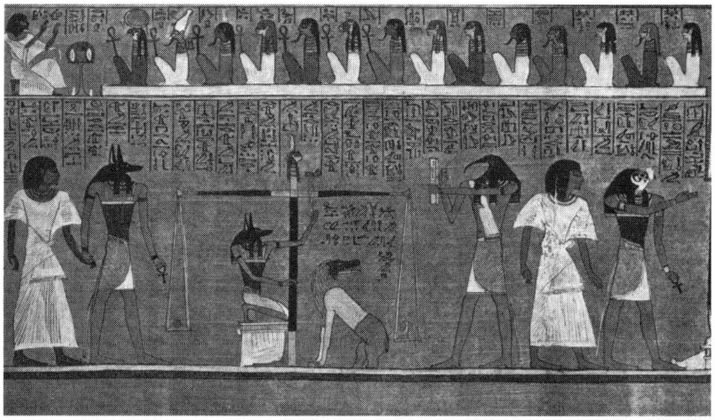

guide or manual for the soul's journey in the afterlife. *The Book of the Dead* varies in content according to region and period, but usually depicts the stages of transformation after death, gives a picture of the hierarchical structure of the spiritual worlds, and illustrates the spiritual makeup of the human being.

For example, the *ba,* or soul, is pictured as a bird's body, often that of a falcon, with a human head. For the Egyptian, the soul was "winged," like a bird. This image of the departed soul prefigures the image of the angel, or spirit being, as a winged entity, and is related in nature to the shaman's spirit flight. We often see in later art the incarnating and excarnating soul depicted with wings, or guided by a winged being (fig. 2).

Other illustrations from *The Book of the Dead* depict the passage after death with scenes such as the weighing of the heart against the goddess Maat's "Feather of Truth"; the crossing of the threshold with the beast that devours the unworthy heart; the recording of events by Thoth, the god of scribes; the meeting with Horus and gaining of an audience with the Lord of the Afterlife, Osiris (fig. 96). Such works suggest firsthand knowledge of the spiritual occurrences that meet the soul in the realms of spirit. This knowledge can only be gained through initiation and supersensory perception, for the ancient Egyptians had no word for "belief," only one for knowledge.[8]

Tradition tells us that admittance into the Egyptian Mysteries is no easy undertaking. Many tests, including the trials by water and fire, are to be met and overcome. In the trial by water, all firm ground in the sense of a familiar earthly reality is washed away. One is set adrift in soul and spirit. The trial by fire burns away all that clings to the soul in the life of desires and passions—a purgatory experience. Then after years of training, upon reaching a certain maturity, the pupil undergoes the temple sleep. Under the direction of initiate-priests, the neophyte is laid in an open sarcophagus and put into a trancelike sleep, a clinical death, for three and one-half days. During this time of separation from the body, the soul and spirit enter into realms normally experienced only after death. Here the would-be initiate meets the Divine Isis, the wisdom of the human soul, and Osiris, Lord of the Afterlife. The Sun at Midnight is beheld. The Harmony of the Spheres sounds as the gods themselves instruct the pupil in the mysteries of the cosmos and the secrets of creation. The initiate-priest now sees into the past and into the future. Returning to the body as a Son of Horus and a priest of the Egyptian Temple Mysteries, the new initiate brings fresh experiences from the spiritual worlds to share with fellow priests.[9] We are told that such awareness of the divine will is considered to be the only appropriate background and training for one who stands as pharaoh or as spiritual advisor to the people of ancient Egypt.

Fig. 96. The Papyrus of Ani, one example of *The Book of the Dead,* shows Ani, the deceased, in white, accompanied by the god Anubis. They stand in front of the scale that weighs Ani's heart against the "Feather of Truth," symbol of the goddess Maat. If the heart contains the lightness of truth it will not be heavier than the feather and will not be devoured by the composite creature from the abyss. Thoth records the weighing and Horus, the falcon-headed god, leads Ani to the ultimate goal (not shown here), a meeting with Osiris, Lord of the Afterlife.

III.2 Egyptian Theosophy

He counts his bones. He assembles his members. He turns his face toward Amentet, the beautiful West. He comes renewed, reborn every day, for this is his image, a body of gold carrying the light of Light.
—The Egyptian Book of the Dead

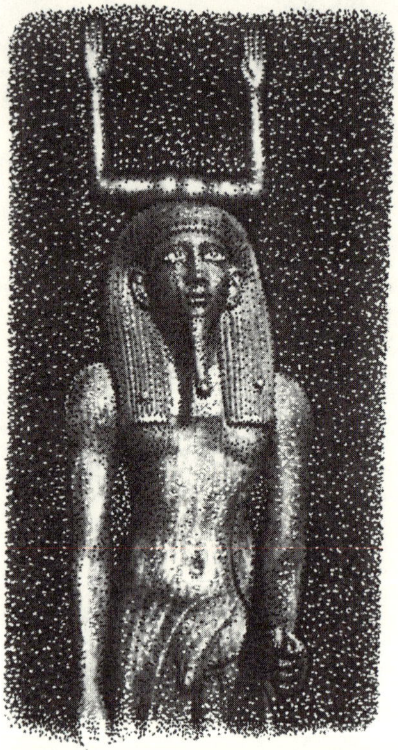

Fig. 97. The *ka,* represented by two arms in a U-shaped gesture, is synonymous with the life forces or vital energy, which sustains the physical body of a person. The *ka,* as symbol of life power, may appear in place of food offerings to show the importance of the life force as the real nourishment. Hor Auibre, a Thirteenth-Dynasty pharaoh, wears the *ka* as the crowning vital element on his head, similar to the shaman's horns. The *ka* indicates that which gives lightness and life to the material body.

From their art and sacred texts we know that the Egyptians saw the human being as having several members or sheaths, the most substantial being the *khat* or physical body. The *khat* was built up and maintained by a living system of vital energy or invisible formative forces called the *ka.* While the *khat* was seen as a body of matter, subject to the laws of gravity and decomposition, the *ka* was perceived as a living field of energy—*chi* in Chinese—characterized by lightness and working as a continual building, regenerative power. The *ka* was represented in Egyptian art and hieroglyphic writing as two arms stretched upward in a parallel, U-shaped gesture. As the symbol for life power, the *ka* often appears in different kinds of settings, even in place of food offerings. The *ka* crowning the head of Hor Auibre, a pharaoh of the Thirteenth Dynasty, is worn like the shaman's horns and represents the monarch's luminous double (fig. 97). We have seen this feature in another context as the orant gesture in Christian art (figs. 32, 45, 49, 50).

The soul or emotional life of the human being is known as the *ba* and, as mentioned earlier, is usually depicted in Egyptian art as a bird with a human head. The *ba* or soul of the departed is often shown hovering over the mummified *khat* in its sarcophagus (fig. 95). With wings outstretched the *ba* clasps the upper portion of the ankh of life in its talons. The ankh is a symbol of the incarnate living spirit—the cosmic circle joined to the earthly Dao cross (fig. 98). The lower part of the ankh is broken off to show that life (*ka*) is no longer bound to the physical body or *khat.* The *khat,* meant to stand upright like the vertical shaft of the ankh, at death lies horizontally, in the form of the mummy, separated from its spiritual principle.

Khu is a higher aspect of the human being synonymous with the psyche or spirit. Other finer members of the human being are described, bringing the total number of sheaths to nine. At death these members are shed just as at birth they are taken on and incorporated. These members of the human being are represented in the burial practices, for example in the nine successive layers in which the famed boy-king Tutankhamen was interred: mummy, three coffins, sarcophagus, and four golden shrines. In this way the spiritual members or sheaths of the deceased are expressed in concrete artistic forms.

The priesthood of ancient Egypt possessed a theosophy, or "wisdom of the gods," that revealed the esoteric nature of the human organization in its relationship with the universe. It is said that the highly trained priesthood could affect the separate members of a person's organization in such a way as to overcome and cure bodily illness, stimulate fearlessness in battle, communicate a desired image for artistic rendering, and increase physical strength for the purpose of moving heavy weights.[10] It is in this direction we might look for possible answers to the question of how the pyramids and other megalithic structures were built. Egyptian theosophy provides a model of the human shared by numerous cultures throughout history that acknowledge spirit reality and make it visible in art.

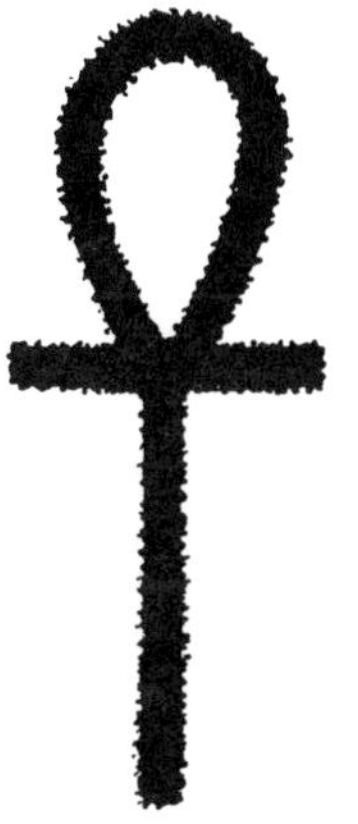

Fig. 98. The ankh is the Egyptian symbol for incarnate life-spirit. The vertical stem represents the physical body, the horizontal element expresses the widths of space, and the circle or oval pictures the eternal element of divine unity.

III.3 Immortal Images

The single unifying theme which is invariably found in Egyptian art is its symbolic message.
—Richard Wilkinson

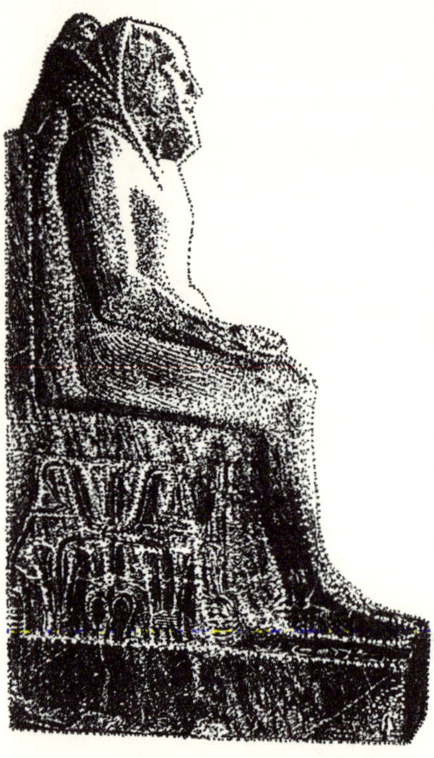

Fig. 99. This green diorite statue of the Fourth-Dynasty pharaoh Kephren sits rigidly in observance of divine law. Slightly smaller than life-size, fourteen of these statues lined the pink granite hall of the Valley Temple at Giza.

Fourteen stone sculptures, seven on either side of the pink granite hall of the Valley Temple at Giza, sit in concentrated alertness (fig. 99). These green diorite statues, all of the Fourth-Dynasty pharaoh Kephren, "see" into a realm beyond the finite world and "listen" to the eternal sounding of worlds beyond the threshold of sense experience. That Kephren sees in this visionary, godlike way is made clear by the falcon-headed god Horus, perched behind the pharaoh's head as his genius and guardian (fig. 100). The winged god inspires the pharaoh from the other world, describing what can be seen there and directing the initiate-king accordingly. The pharaoh's distant gaze suggests a form of consciousness different from our own. The gaze is "parallel"—as though the path of sight never focuses on a point in this world. It is peripheral and all-seeing, as though the pharaoh is in a visionary state.

Ancient Egyptian sculpture normally portrays the human figure as static and held, stiff sometimes to the point of paralysis. Gestures are locked in place and unmoving, severe and controlled, holding the subtle mysteries of life hidden from superficial gaze. Egyptian figures appear bound and unable to act out of self-determined motives. It is as if the gods still guide and bind them to their divine will of "unquestioning obedience to a higher law."[11] Similarly, the animal appears obedient to the laws beyond its own choosing, utterly bound to instinctive behavior. This connection to the animal runs deep in ancient Egypt, as well as in other primal cultures, particularly in the case of zoomorphic portrayal of the gods. Egyptian art confirms that early humanity perceived animal powers as a direct link to the realm of the gods. As we have seen, in Greece the gods appear in human form; in Egypt they are often animal-like in form.

Egyptian painting likewise depicts the human figure as still and fixed in space. Gestures are often stiff and suspended on the two-dimensional plane, entirely lacking freedom of movement, yet wonderfully expressive of how life is the limited stage upon which a larger drama is orchestrated. The held gestures emphasize the timelessnes of the moment. Human heads and limbs are seen characteristically in profile, while the eye, shoulders, and chest are represented full-on. Entirely two-dimensional, with little interest in foreshortening or perspective, Egyptian painting and bas relief illustrate the way in which early humanity experienced the physical body in relation to the outer world. The flat, hard-edged simplicity of Egyptian pictorial representation is a window through which the essence of this era's spiritual life can be seen.

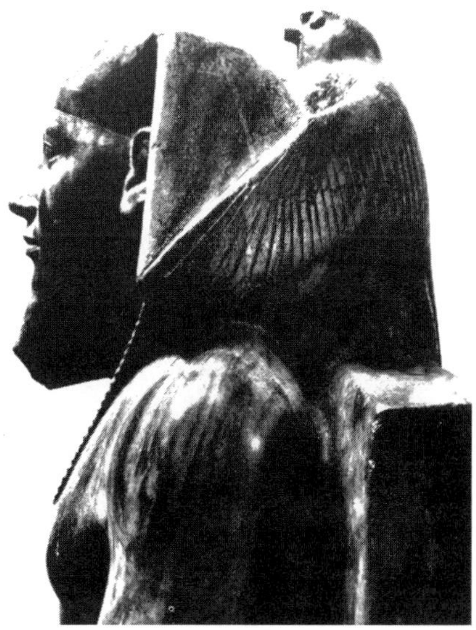

Paintings on parchment and on tomb walls depicted not only spiritual beings but also events from everyday life, such as performing musicians and dancers, shipbuilders, and farmers at work (fig. 101). Still, these pictures were not trivial scenes intended to entertain the living. These works were to be reviewed by the soul of the departed as memory pictures from the collective experiences of the life just lived. These paintings were sealed into tombs as part of burial practices and were not decoration to be enjoyed by the eyes of mortals. Scenes that illustrate the daily life of an important vizier or advisor to the pharaoh may recall the cowherder or shipbuilder overseen on his daily rounds and for whom he was responsible. However, such pictures may have been aids to the soul as it went through its life review after death. According to esoteric traditions, experiencing a detailed tableau of events from one's life is a common stage in the post-death process, and these painted scenes of daily life might be viewed as a kind of prologue to the Book of the Dead intended to help the departed soul on its journey in the afterlife.[12] Besides being an aid to the departed soul, the paintings were to acknowledge and honor the work of the gods.

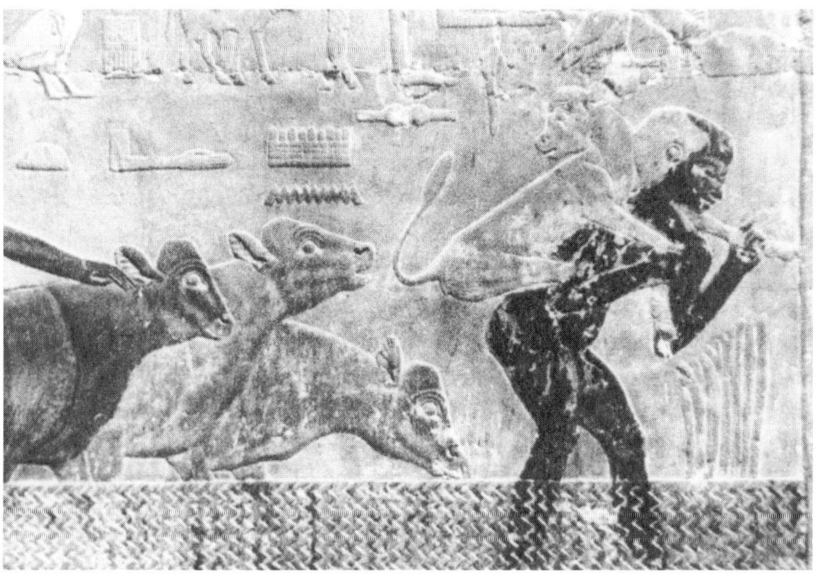

Fig. 100. Above: Horus, the hawk-headed son of Osiris and god of the rising sun, inspires Kephren from the spirit world.

Fig. 101. Left: Egyptian painting and sculpture both depict a restrained yet deliberate human archetype: profile face, full-on eye, profile limbs, and full-on shoulders, with no foreshortening or shading. Egyptian art shows many scenes from daily life, such as cattle herding. These pictures on the walls of tombs are presented, not merely to record daily life, but to show the departed person's memories. The vizier for whom this picture was painted supervised such scenes during his life in his role as advisor to the pharaoh. After death the vizier's soul reviews its earthly deeds.

III.4 Art of the Riddle

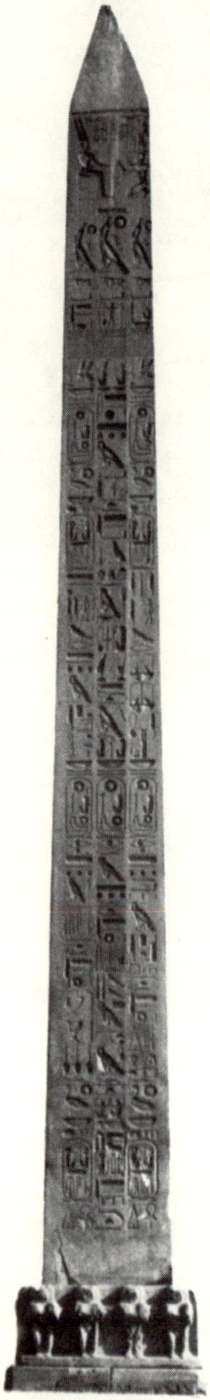

Fig. 102. The obelisk, carved from a single block of granite and adorned with hieroglyphic writing in honor of the gods, is a monument to the miracle of uprightness and striving. (Luxor, Egypt.)

The recognition that a temple can be both a reflection of the perfect order of the cosmos and also symbolic of the individual is a theme throughout history.
—A.T. Mann

According to ancient lore there was a time when the human constitution was not yet upright in stature but was horizontal and fluid in its condition. Egyptian initiates gazed back into this primordial period, called Zep Tepi, the First Time, and perceived the spiritual powers responsible for the gift of uprightness. The obelisk was then fashioned as a monument dedicated to the sun god who made this erect stature possible (fig. 102). Its influence is both esoteric and exoteric, for inwardly the obelisk stands for the divine impulse that permits every human being to stand upright, and outwardly it simply is this uprightness.

More than a mere memorial, the obelisk appeared as an active presence to the ancient Egyptian people and represented the sun's divine connection to upright posture. An image of Horus, the hawk-headed solar deity, or a winged solar disc was often carved at the pinnacle of the obelisk, where it caught the first and last rays of the sun's light. This New Kingdom architectural feature was carved from a single piece of granite, sometimes more than one hundred feet long.

It is also part of tradition that long before the Egyptian epoch, human speech was in danger of falling into the expression of mere subjective sounds, only slightly more articulate than animal noises. The ability to speak in an objective manner to articulate more than just personal desires and urges was due once again to the intervention of the same deity who had enabled humanity to take on an upright stature. The Egyptian initiate-priests perceived this development in speech as being a deed of their sun god together with other great gods of the cosmos, and they fashioned the mysterious image of the sphinx in reference to this mystery (fig. 103).[13]

The Egyptian sphinx can be seen as a descendent of earlier zoomorphic figures of the Paleolithic era. In Egypt, Greece, and the Near East, the sphinx is not a simple decorative element but an essential feature of sacred architecture (fig. 104).

Avenues of sphinxes focus the attention, while directing the path, of the approaching pilgrim, and present an intimidating challenge. The sphinx is a reminder to humanity of what it receives from the cosmos and the gods, for the sphinx is a picture of the entire celestial zodiac (which literally means "animal circle"). At Giza, the Great Sphinx has the head of a man emerging erect from the reclining body of a lion. However, the archetypal sphinx reveals, in addition, the hindquarters of a bull and the wings of an eagle, thus pointing to the four fixed points of the zodiac—Aquarius (waterman), Leo (lion), Taurus (bull), and Scorpio (eagle).[14] These four cosmic aspects of the sphinx are later embraced by early Christian art and become symbols for the Four Gospels (fig. 105). United in the sphinx, this "circle of animals" challenges the human being to "know thyself!" Thus the sphinx is a mystery image of primal forces, which stand behind and work through the origins and development of the human being.

A Greek legend tells of the sphinx confronting Oedipus with the riddle,

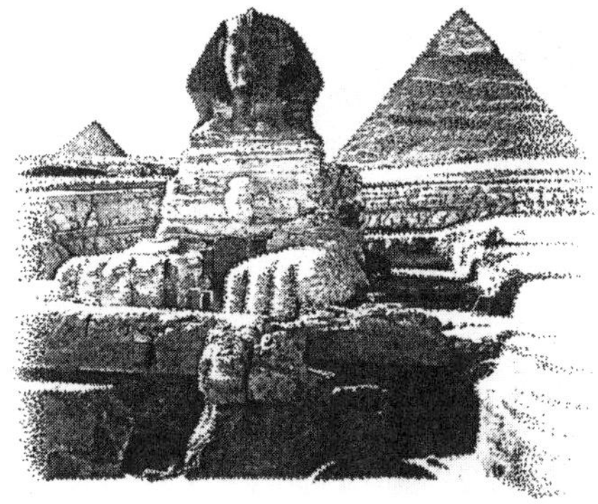

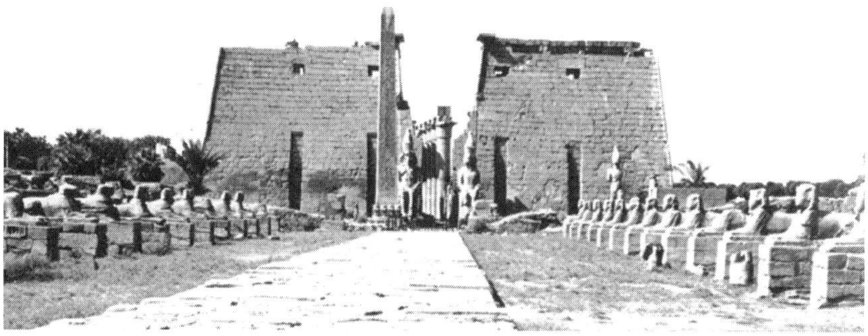

Fig. 103. Above: The sphinx was associated with the development of speech in the human being and was seen as an embodiment of the cosmic word, the questioning voice of the gods, and the instreaming celestial forces.

Fig. 104. Left: Avenues of sphinxes were essential architectural-sculptural elements in many cultures, especially in Egyptian temple architecture, where their presence along the sacred way helped prepare the pilgrim for entrance to the temple.

Fig. 105. Below: The eagle, lion, bull, and man-angel together form a picture of the four fixed points of the zodiac. They eventually became associated with the four Christian gospels. This example is from the Irish *Book of Kells.*

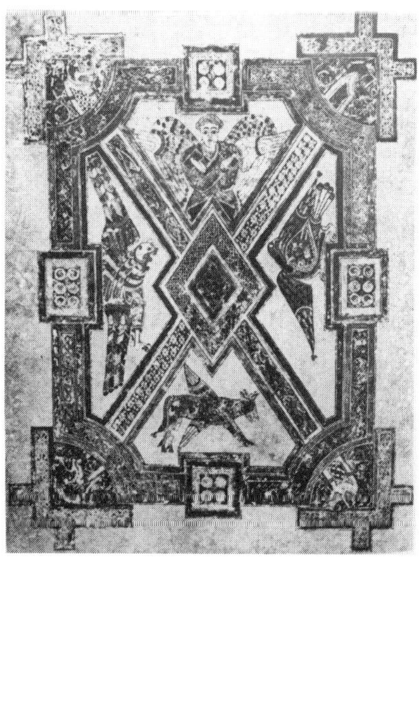

"What walks on four legs in the morning, on two legs in the afternoon, and on three legs in the evening?" The answer indicates three stages in the life of the human being: the child crawls on all fours, the adult stands on two feet, and the elderly person walks with a staff or cane. "Behold, Man!" is essentially the secret of the sphinx, for the human being, to the Egyptian, is the microcosm within the macrocosm.

The Great Sphinx and the Great Pyramids at Giza are usually dated to about 3000 B.C., although recent research suggests the Sphinx might be as old as 10,500 B.C.[15] Legends tell of when the Sphinx actually "spoke." When the first rays of the morning sun struck its cold limestone form, an awesome sound, perhaps due to expansion of the stones after the cold desert night, was emitted toward the rising sun in the east. This is only a superficial aspect that has connected the sphinx with speech.

Egyptian initiates gazed not only upon past events, but looked intuitively to a future time when the beginnings of a conceptual, reflective thinking would appear. This tremendous change in human consciousness would also be brought about by the god, who was seen descending ever closer to earth with greater and greater influence on the life of humanity.[16] Inspired by this divine

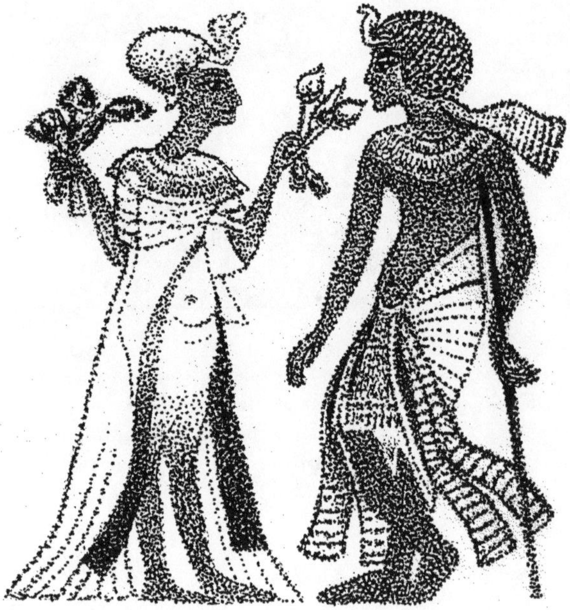

being, Akhenaten, pharaoh of upper and lower Egypt, declared that Aten, the sun's solar disc, was the supreme god of the universe. Defying tradition and the established priesthood, Akhenaten challenged the Egyptian Folk Spirit to look toward the time when independent, conceptual thinking would be achieved by each individual. The art carried out under his reign reveals a more relaxed posture, with far less severity than is seen in the earlier dynasties of Egypt (fig. 106). A new spirit glimmers for a time under the reign of Akhenaten and then disappears following his death, when the old political-religious order resumes and earlier artistic canons return.

However, long before Akhenaten, the builders of the Pyramids placed before the ancient world an architecture of formal harmony and perfection, a monument to cosmic wisdom. A marvel of mathematics and geometry, the pyramid, though resting on the earth, points to a world and order above (fig. 107).[17] Like the obelisk, the pyramid is one of the first earthly objects to be illuminated by the rays of the rising sun each day. Starting at the capstone or pyramidion (fig. 108), light descends along the polished white limestone surfaces of the pyramid's form until it reaches the earth. Receiving the radiant morning light from infinite space, the pyramid conveys it into the earthly realm.

Just as the sun's light descends to earth from the gods, so the Egyptian felt that thoughts poured into human beings, and in the third millennium B.C., the pyramid arose as mystery architecture—a picture of the cosmic head receiving "light" from above. But thoughts expressing the wisdom of the cosmos would one day arise from within the human head. Thoughts would no longer be direct insight received as gifts from the gods, but would originate independently, brain-bound, conceived of as the property of the individual thinker. This capacity for independent thinking would begin to emerge in the fifth and sixth centuries B.C. with the Greek philosophers, when the Egyptian civilization was already in decline. In this sense, pyramids were built in order to place into the world a picture of the thinking potential for the human head.

The obelisk, sphinx, and pyramid are, in Hegel's words, "art of the riddle."[18] They express in primal artistic form images of uprightness, speech, and thinking for early humanity. Standing upright, speaking, and thinking are achieved in rudimentary form by every healthy human being in the early years of life.[19] These attributes, which make the human being something other than an animal, are spiritual faculties. They form the basis for all moral development as well as the capacities we call freedom, love, and understanding.

Schiller said that architecture is frozen music, tone come to rest in matter. Following the poet's lead, we might say that architectural and sculptural forms are

Fig. 106. The art under Akhenaten's reign shows a more relaxed posture and attitude than that of previous centuries. This rendering of Akhenaten's daughter with her husband shows the young prince anticipating the freedom of the individual by way of this stance: one standing leg and one relaxed leg.

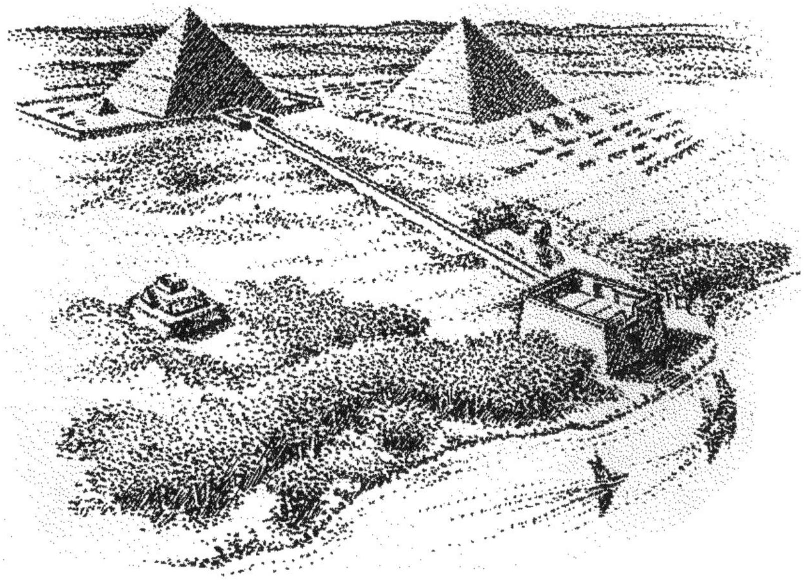

Fig. 107. Left: The Pyramids of Egypt are remarkable monuments to order and lawfulness in the universe.

Fig. 108. Below: The pyramidion is a small black stone believed to have been covered in gold leaf and set as the capstone on a pyramid.

congealed sound-gestures or stilled primal vibration.[20] Esoteric tradition has long spoken of a "sounding cosmos," sometimes called the Harmony of the Spheres or the Logos or Word, as the creative primal force that calls substance into form. This formative impulse ringing throughout creation was, we are told, visible to Egyptian initiates in the "sacred script" of the heavens and was translated into artistic forms by those initiates familiar with star wisdom.[21] Therefore, sacred dance movements and body gestures, angles, color and shapes of religious objects and buildings, as well as specific musical and chanted tones reinforced and resonated with the movements and conjunctions of the stars. The French Egyptologist R.A. Schwaller de Lubicz describes this phenomenon in the following way: "Every construction, no matter how simple it may be, has a soul because it has volume. Volume is the indefinable substance—Spirit arrested in Space. It is alive, it is specific, it is Number, therefore Music."[22] For the ancient Egyptian, art was a living language expressing the mystery of the universe and the revelation of the spirit. (See Appendix 4.)

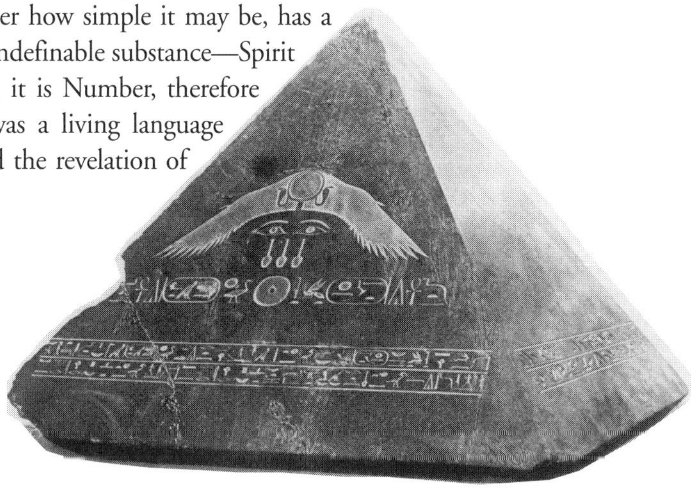

III.5 The Royal Art

At the moment of death the soul experiences the same impressions as those who are initiated into the great Mysteries.
—Plutarch

In A.D. 820, Abdullah Al Mamun and his men broke into the Great Pyramid of Khufu (Cheops), only to find an empty sarcophagus—a granite coffin of feldspar, quartz, and mica—in the so-called King's Chamber. This stark, undecorated chamber was not full of precious objects and was not adorned with fine works of art, as was customary in Egyptian royal tombs. Al Mamun had to put together a treasure of his own to reward his men for all the work they had done in forcing their way into the pyramid.

When we think of the pyramids, we think of mummies and the burials of Egyptian pharaohs. However, mummies have not always been found in the major pyramids. Perhaps this is because they were robbed early on. But it also might indicate that burial was not their exclusive purpose. According to numerous researchers, the Great Pyramid was used as a place of initiation.[23] It was here that the three-day temple sleep is believed to have been carried out amidst a circle of initiate priests watching over the neophyte as he or she crossed the threshold of death into a realm of sense-free spiritual experience. This crossing, experienced by everyone at the moment of death, brings the soul-spirit being of the pupil into a communion with the gods. Upon returning, the pupil is recognized as a full initiate in the mysteries. The meaning of the word "pyramid" in Egyptian has to do with "going out of the temple of the body to Heaven."[24] Other aspects of the Great Pyramid— its perfect north-south alignment, its orientation to certain stars and constellations, its geometry and underlying mathematics—suggest a building that functions as more than just an elaborate tomb. Air shafts, which are not necessary in a tomb for the dead, appear in the Great Pyramid and are aligned to Thuban, the "north star" of the Old Kingdom, and to Orion's Belt. "Orion stood for

Osiris and the great cycle of birth, life, death, and resurrection," according to astronomer E.C. Krupp (fig. 109).[25]

In ancient Egypt initiation was known as "the royal art," the noblest of all creative deeds—the art of self-transformation and recreation. [26] It is likely that the King's Chamber of the Great Pyramid served the early Egyptian priesthood as a place where the spiritual worlds were entered not just at the time of death but during ritual initiations as well.

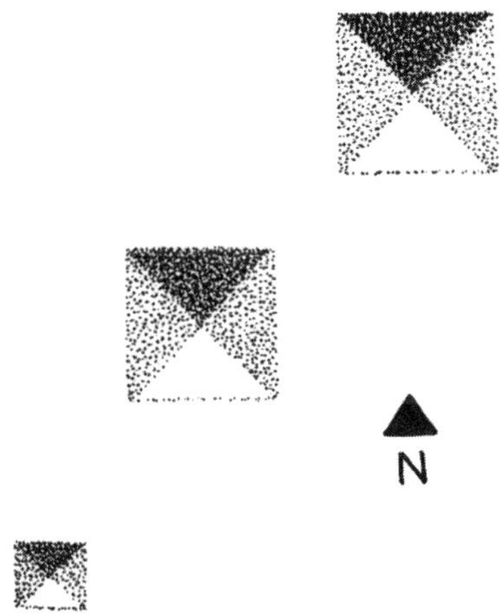

Fig. 109. According to some researchers, pyramids on the Giza plateau are aligned like the belt stars of the constellation of Orion. (After Hancock.)

III.6 The Temple Is Man

The Temple tells, in stone, in its proportions and harmonies, its art and sculpture, the story of the creation of man; it signals his development, stage by stage, and it recreates in artistic form man's relationship to the universe.
—John Anthony West

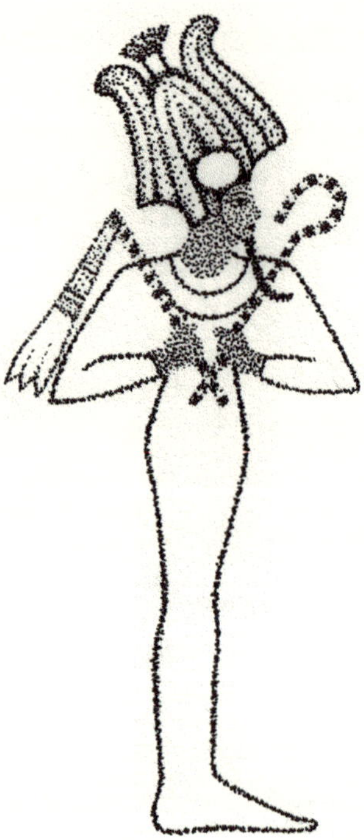

Fig. 110. The flail and the crook are symbols of the pharaoh's dominion over his enemies and rulership over his people as a shepherd. They also suggest power over the plant and animal kingdoms. Osiris, who is said to have introduced agriculture and animal husbandry to Egypt, is often depicted bearing both of these symbols.

Coming face to face with the pharaoh on his throne is like approaching the temple façade in living human form. The initiated pharaoh wears a headdress that frames the face in the same way that the pylon frames the temple. The face of the pharaoh becomes a threshold for those who gaze upon it, his countenance a doorway to the gods. The cobra and uraeus snake on the headdress are symbols of how the wisdom of the cosmos springs from the god-king's forehead. The serpents are a picture of the human spinal column and central nervous system, emerging from the head above the point of the pineal gland or brow chakra ("third eye"), and are a vivid representation of pharaoh's visionary powers.[27] As colors are used to decorate the temple façade, so too is makeup utilized to outline the eyes as windows of the soul, and accent the blush of life that pulses through the pharaoh's living body of flesh and blood. Even when the pharaoh is a woman, she wears the ceremonial beard that shows divine authority has been given to rule over the land with the will of the gods. The flail and the crook held by the pharaonic ruler are symbols of power over the plant and animal kingdoms, indicating mastery in the realms of agriculture and animal husbandry (fig. 110). However, symbolism goes beyond control of the food supply, to the very rulership over the realms of life forces (plant) and sentient being (animal). The pharaoh's position as god-king is affirmed through these implements.

Just as the pharaoh embodies spiritual authority in human form, the temple exemplifies spiritual authority in architectural form. Temple architecture is based upon the ideal proportions of the human being because the ideal human being is seen as a temple of microcosmic dimensions.

The Egyptian pylon temple is related to the early mastaba form—a simple mud-brick tomb—a truncated pyramid, raised and flattened into a façade (fig. 111). A notch called the *achet* (horizon), at the middle top edge of the pylon above the entrance, serves as an opening for the sun. Just as the sun's light appears to dissolve or melt the horizon's edge as it begins to rise or set (see fig. 21), so the pylon temple provides a picture in the form of the achet of the sun's power to overcome matter as it emerges from or disappears into the Underworld. Between the achet and the entrance portal, there sometimes appears a relief of the winged solar disc, which serves as a reminder that the temple is sacred to the sun god.

The achet is also created when a pair of lions, set back to back, form a notch between their heads. Sometimes the sun is borne upon the creatures' backs, held within the achet hieroglyph. In this context the lions are known as "yesterday" and "tomorrow," and *The Papyrus of Ani* describes them in the following way: "To me belongs yesterday and I know tomorrow. . . . Yesterday is Osiris, Tomorrow is Re."[28] Between the two is where the present moment of human existence lives.

An avenue of sphinxes lining the approach to the temple seems to repeatedly pose the question "Who art thou, humanity?" Passing between the crouching sphinxes and the upward-pointing obelisks, one confronts the overwhelming mass of the temple pylon with its painted reliefs of hero-kings and anthropomorphic god-men (fig. 205). Ritual processions and applicants to the mysteries pass through these avenues and make their way into the high vertical doorway beneath the achet. Finally, crossing the entrance threshold, through the dauntingly monumental portal with its godly proportions, one enters an expansive open courtyard surrounded by colonnades. Confronting this complex of architectural forms must have been a powerful experience for the ancient Egyptian. As Richter puts it: "These temples must have been a tremendous education toward self-awareness, guiding man into new and almost unbearable inner movements and experiences. The closer a man came to it, the more this wall [the temple pylon] pushed its way

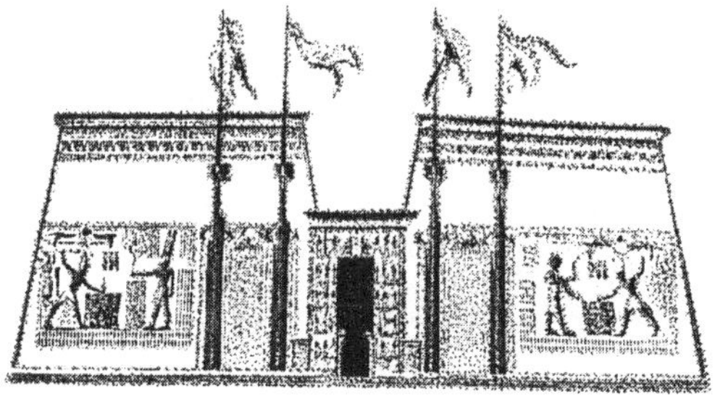

Fig. 111. Above: The pylon temple façade is directly related to the shape of the mastaba, a mud brick tomb of Egypt's Old and Middle Kingdoms. The pylon temple included features such as a sphinx-lined avenue, obelisks, painted bas-reliefs and colored banners.

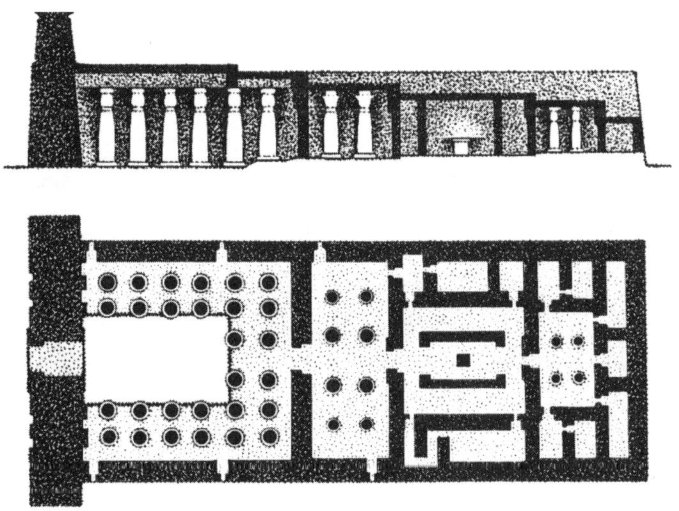

Fig. 112. Left: The enclosed spaces of the temple become smaller and more compact as one approaches the inner sanctuary or "Holy of Holies." (After Teichmann.)

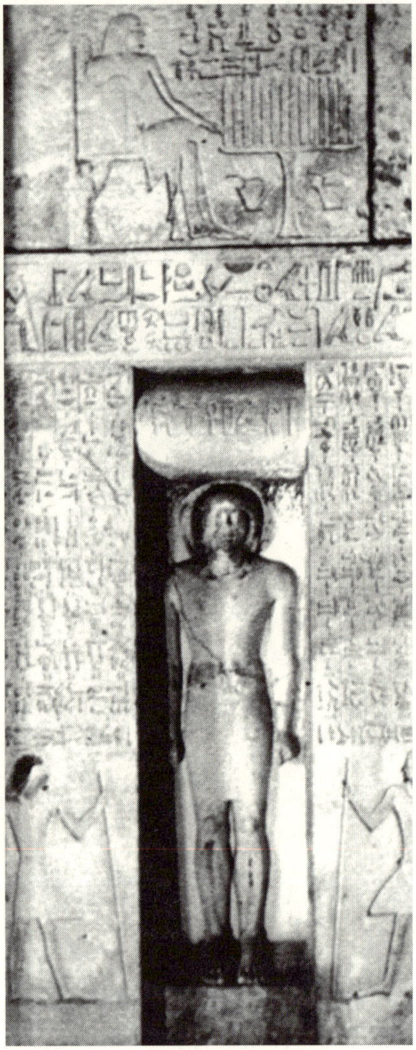

Fig. 113. False doors indicate passageways to the Otherworld. They were featured in temples and tombs and often depicted a figure standing at the threshold of the spirit world.

into him. Its gesture forced him deeper and deeper into his own physical body."[29]

The Egyptian temple, built to endure, set itself apart from the outside world. Within the fortresslike walls, in the open compound, sacrifices were offered at a large altar and smoke rose toward the heavens along with supplications of a spiritual kind. Commoners were allowed only as far as this courtyard. For the priests and pupils of the temple the sacred way continued to further thresholds. Columns were set in rows inside the temple walls, like bones within a body. As one proceeded into the covered section of the temple, one passed through narrower and lower corridors (fig. 112). Smaller and more contracted interior spaces affected the consciousness of the supplicant as he or she experienced being tightly pressed into the physical body. The repeated contraction into ever smaller and tighter spaces culminated in the "Holy of Holies," the innermost chamber of the temple. As the highest level of the temple, it served as the *axis mundi,* the primordial mound, the First Place of Egyptian mythology. This inner sanctuary, as in many Old Kingdom tombs, had false doors indicating a further portal that led beyond physical space (fig. 113). The only way through these false doors was into oneself.[30] For the ancient Egyptian, the journey led to a spirit awakening within the microcosmic human soul. Both the temple and the human body were in this way doorways or thresholds into the spiritual world.

The word for temple in Egyptian means "house of utterance," and this has to do with the resounding speech of Re, the Living Word. This divine being is represented in hieroglyphic form by a mouth.

Robert Lawlor describes the temple in the following way: "It becomes apparent from the study of Temple Architecture, that the Sages who created the structures were well aware that with the attainment of symbolic language—'the gift of the word'—especially the language of architecture, the responsibility for human evolution had shifted to a large degree to humanity itself. The Temple for them was a center of the learning and dissemination of the psycho-physical and spiritual science whose purpose was to reveal and develop symbolic, intellectual, and physical techniques which might effect perceptual, behavioral, and physiological changes in the human organism—a science having the purpose of gradually leading towards humanity's highest conceivable evolutionary potential, towards the appearance . . . of a Divine . . . being who had mastered the contingencies and dualities of mortal existence."[31]

This was the purpose of temple architecture and the visual arts used by the ancient Egyptians: to present concrete pictures of the cosmic dimensions of the human being.

III.7 In Praise of the Sun

Beautiful is thine arising
Thou living Sun,
Beside whom there is none else;
Who strengthenest the eyes with thy rays,
Who hast created all that exists.
—Akhenaten

Around 1378 B.C., in the Eighteenth Dynasty of the New Kingdom, Amenhotep IV ascended to the throne of Upper and Lower Egypt. In the fourth year of his reign he adopted the religion of Aten, the sun's solar disc, and changed his name to Akhenaten. He then moved the Egyptian capital from Thebes to Tell el Amarna and dedicated his life to the service of this god, who was represented by the hieroglyph for light. Akhenaten built palaces and temples, wrote hymns of praise and stimulated a new impulse in Egyptian culture and visual arts—all to honor the one god, Aten.[32] Akhenaten has been referred to as "the world's first individual," and Sigmund Freud even suggested that he instructed Moses in the principles of monotheism.[33]

Fig. 114. An intimate family portrait of Akhenaten and Nefertiti with their three daughters is one of the period pieces that indicate a shift from the austere artistic style of the earlier era to that of a somewhat freer time.

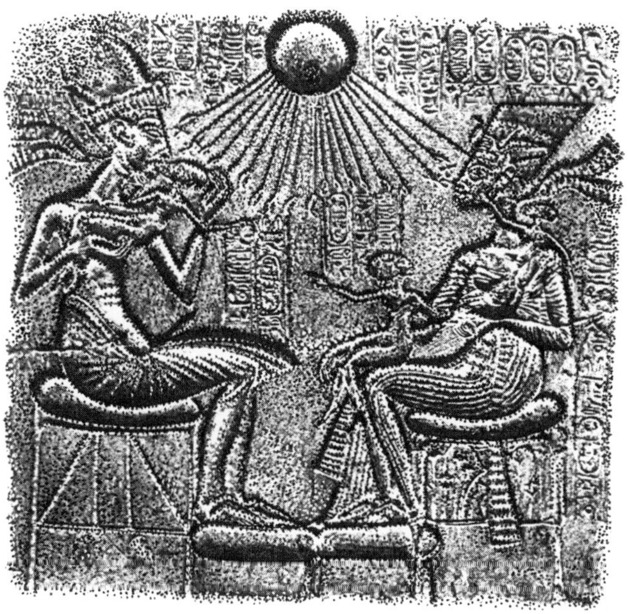

As a result of his reforms many of the former priesthoods were shut down, particularly that of Amon in Thebes, and much of Egypt outside the capital fell into neglect. However, a tremendous cultural and artistic revolution took place, as can be seen in works such as the relief sculpture of Akhenaten with his queen, Nefertiti, and their three daughters (fig. 114). This delightfully intimate and casual family scene in which the pharaoh kisses one of his daughters, while all bask in the lifegiving rays of the sun, reveals a new sense of realism and a break from many of the traditional formulas in Egyptian art. This change may well indicate a shift from an earlier mode of consciousness to one that is the basis of greater personal freedom and individual expression. The figures of Akhenaten and his family are elongated and extended beyond the earlier strict dynastic canon of proportions. The rays of sunlight hold the ankh of life with tiny hands of blessing. Steiner says of the sun ray: "In every sunbeam there streams down on all the inhabitants of the earth the force of those higher beings who live on the sun, and in the light of the sun there descends the force of love, which here on earth streams from person to person, from heart to heart . . . the warmest, most ardent, feeling of love is invisibly present in the sunlight."[34] Something of this quality is captured in the depiction of Akhenaten and his family.

Another example of the freedom of expression during this period can be seen in the painting of one of Akhenaten's daughters—here grown and married—standing next to her husband (fig. 106). The husband, leaning upon a staff, shows one relaxed leg and one firmly-standing leg, an unusual posture for ancient Egypt. Although awkward in its gesture, this painting prefigures the weight-shift that will accompany fifth-century Greek sculpture (see Chapter II). This sudden cultural transformation that created a freed-up artistic style lasted only during Akhenaten's lifetime. Just as suddenly, the old polytheistic order was restored at the end of the sun pharaoh's reign. However, as the French Egyptologist Eduard de Rouge points out: "The Egyptian religion is a pure monotheism, which manifested itself externally by a symbolic polytheism."[35]

Within a generation after Akhenaten, a priest of Osiris by the name of Osarsiph declared his belief in a different kind of monotheism.[36] He spoke of one God, the "I am that I am," and his spiritual power shook the Egyptian mystery traditions to their very foundation. The initiate Osarsiph was known in Hebrew tradition as Moses, and as he led the Jewish people out of Egypt, he took with him the "gold and silver vessels from the temple," meaning the wisdom of both the sun and moon mysteries into which he had been initiated.[37] One might say that the Egyptian era reached its outer culmination with Akhenaten, but with Moses-Osarsiph it met its inner, spiritual resolution and eventual dissolution. Moses-Osarsiph took the fire of Egypt's spiritual life with him when he departed into the wilderness for a forty-year testing of the "chosen people," as described in the Old Testament. In the meantime, the Egyptian mystery centers fell into greater and greater decadence as fewer priests were able to attain former spiritual insights through initiation. Those that did approach "Isis, the infinite, mysterious Mother of Worlds" found she had become a widow in the deepest sense.[38] The primal spirituality of early Egypt was now lost and nearly forgotten. Historic consciousness was about to be born. Foreign conquerors forced their way into the rites of initiation, and the guiding spirit of the age that had brought Egypt such greatness as a civilization seemed to pass its light on to another folk and another Time Spirit (*Zeitgeist*). The gifts of the Egyptian mysteries were given over to other mystery streams that would take human development further in a new form in the next cultural epoch, the Greco-Roman era.

Egyptian culture, with its impressive rock monuments, produced a sacred art and architecture of finely cut stonework vastly different from the coarse and unfinished rock structures of contemporaneous megalithic cultures. Egyptian temples were built, fortresslike, with carefully worked and dressed stone walls in order, in part, to withstand the harsh environment of the Sahara Desert. The Egyptian sought the eternal within the innermost sanctuary of the temple and within the depths of the human soul. The rough-hewn stones of megalithic temples were intended to stand in communion with their natural setting, open to cosmic and elemental forces, in a rugged and unrefined manner. They were intimately connected with their environment, where the "mystery of the eternal" was sought not in the human soul, but in the wide expanses of universal space. The one path led to the infinite within and the other to the infinite without. This contrast of an inner orientation in the Mysteries of ancient Egypt and an outer emphasis in the Megalithic Mysteries is a picture of the complementary gestures of each culture, its spirit and its art.

Notes

1. Schuré, E. *The Great Initiates,* p. 194.
2. Herodotus. *The History of Herodotus: Book Two — Euterpe.* See Nagel, G. "The 'Mysteries' of Osiris in Ancient Egypt," Bollingen Series xxx, 2, p. 132.
3. E. Schuré states that Pythagoras trained under the pontificate of Sonchis for twenty-two years. *The Great Initiates,* p. 21.
4. Richter, G. *Art and Human Consciousness,* p. 69.
5. Cited in Casson, L. *Ancient Egypt,* p. 35.
6. Mann, A. W. "Egyptian Art," lecture given at Emerson College, England. November 20, 1979.
7. *The New Kingdom Book of the Dead* is a collection of verses and spells from the Old Kingdom *Pyramid Texts* and *Coffin Texts. The Book of Caverns, Book of Gates,* and *The Book of That Which Is in the Underworld* are similar to *The Book of the Dead* in that they are intended to aid the soul on its journey into the life after death.
8. Teichmann, F. *Der Mensch und Sein Tempel: Ägyptem.* p. 43.
9. Schuré, E. *The Great Initiates,* 1928, p. 195.
10. Just as altered states of consciousness, such as mental illness, can bring about a condition of increased strength far beyond one's ordinary capability, so too, with an induced alteration of consciousness, the Egyptian worker could take on many times the normal workload.
11. Richter, G. *Art and Human Consciousness,* p. 25.
12. Moody, R. *Life After Life,* p. 64.
13. Steiner, R. "The Pre-Earthly Deeds of Christ," March 7, 1914.
14. The sign of Scorpio has traditionally been represented by three figures: the scorpion, the eagle, and the phoenix, denoting its lower, common, and higher aspects resectively.
15. Recent geological surveys based on erosion testing have raised questions about earlier dating and suggested the Sphinx may be three to seven thousand years older than previously thought. See John Anthony West, *Serpent in the Sky;* Graham Hancock, *Fingerprints of the Gods,* 1995; and Hancock and Bauval, *The Message of the Sphinx,* 1996.
16. According to Steiner, this being descended from the sun sphere and was only later called the Christ by Gnostic Christians.
17. Stecchini suggests that the Great Pyramid demonstrates the principles of both pi and theta. See John Michell, *New View over Atlantis,* pp. 137–38, 144. In *The Search of the New Isis: The Divine Sophia,* Mercury Press, New York, 1983 (lecture 2), p. 18, Steiner says: "The Egyptians not only wrote down in their own particular writing what they knew as a solution to the great cosmic secrets, they also expressed it in their architectural constructions. They built one of these pyramids with such mathematical precision, that its shadow disappeared in the spring equinox owing to the position of the sun—the shadow disappeared into the base of the pyramid and only reappeared in the autumn equinox. The Egyptians tried to express in this pyramid that the forces which used to shine down are now buried in the earth and stimulate the forces of the earth, so that the earth may produce the fruit which mankind needs."
18. Hegel, G. W. F. *Vorlesungen über Aesthetik,* Part 2, Chapter 1, Paragraph 1.
19. Steiner, R. *The Kingdom of Childhood,* p. 25.
20. According to esoteric tradition, the form of the obelisk embodies the directed acoustic gesture of the long "E" sound, a straight, clear tonal stream. The form of the pyramid angling down to the earth from its apex, and from its apex opening upward in an invisible mirror image gesture of its physical

mass, produces a gesture of openness, expressed in the sound "Ah," an open, yet receiving gesture. "O" is the sound-gesture of encircling, embracing and surrounding. The sphinx is the image of the great "circle of animals," the zodiac, the all-embracing twelve. The sphinx is the picture of the forming power of "O." Falk, K. "Cosmic Archetypes," Lecture given at Tobias School of Art, England, October 7, 1980. See also R. Steiner, *Speech Eurythmy.*

21. Steiner, R. *Aspects of Human Evolution,* p. 38. During the Egyptian cultural epoch, as a part of normal human evolution, the old spiritual perception faded as sense perception became stronger. Because the stars were now seen clearly, a "star cult" developed. Earlier, during the fourth and fifth millennia B.C., the spiritual worlds were experienced directly "through imagination and the music of the spheres," therefore no star cults were necessary at that time.

22. Schwaller de Lubicz, R.A., *Le Temple de l'Homme,* Vol. III, cited in West, *Serpent in the Sky,* p. 59.

23. Besides Rudolf Steiner, *Discussions with Teachers* and *The Temple Is—Man!,* many other writers including H.P. Blavatsky, *The Secret Doctrine* and *Isis Unveiled;* Manly P. Hall, *The Secret Teachings of All Ages;* Tons Brunes, *The Secrets of Ancient Geometry;* William Kingsland, *The Great Pyramid in Fact and in Theory,* speak of the Great Pyramid as a place of initiation. Other alleged functions besides "an ancient initiation temple" are "an astronomical observatory; a telescope; a standard for systems of weight and measures; a surveying instrument . . . ; a geodetic marker for the geometric centre of the known world; and the most powerful and perplexing example of sacred geometry of the Ancients." Mann, A.T., *Sacred Architecture,* p. 112.

24. Merry, E. *The Flaming Door,* p. 172.

25. Krupp, E.C. *Echoes of the Ancient Skies,* p. 101.

26. "The Royal Art" is a term still used in Masonic circles for initiation and inner development by degrees. It is also associated with the building arts and sacred architecture in the tradition of Solomon's temple.

27. The serpent springs forth as clairvoyance, spirit vision. (It might be noted here that the brain was regarded as useless by the Egyptians. At death many of the internal organs were removed from the body and preserved along with the corpse, but the brain was removed through the nose and discarded. A brain-bound, reflective thinking was not yet possible in ancient Egypt. See Appendix 3.)

28. The Great Sphinx of Giza associated with solar imagery was called "Horus in the Horizon." The achet appears carved on the "Sphinx Stele" that is set between the front paws of the Great Sphinx. In this carved relief scene, Thutmosis IV is shown making offerings to a pair of back-to-back sphinxes which represent dual aspects of the same god. "Because these sphinxes are placed back to back with the winged sun disk above and between them, this whole composition can be seen to be a complex elaboration of the 'horizon hieroglyph.'" Wilkinson, R. *Reading Egyptian Art,* p. 135. See also Lawlor, R. "Ancient Temple Architecture," *Homage to Pythagoras,* p. 57.

29. "In his architecture the Egyptian shaped in stone what he experienced when in the morning he would come back from the world of night into the 'enclosure' of his body. This is where man breaks through the wall; he steps out of the heavenly expanses of the cosmos and crosses the threshold into the narrow, disquieting house of his body. Man's experience in ancient Egypt was to wake up to his own earthly body." Richter, G. *Art and Human Consciousness,* p. 15.

30. "Modern interpreters occasionally maintain that these false doors were built in order to deceive would-be tomb robbers. But this primitive explanation contradicts many of the facts, ignoring the most essential ones in the process. Works of art and religion are never concerned originally with some outward purpose but rather with the struggle to express inner experiences, to create a world in which inner and outer experiences are intimately and exactly interwoven." Richter, p. 17.

31. Lawlor, R. "Ancient Temple Architecture," *Homage to Pythagoras,* p. 57.

32. It is known that while Akhenaten worshipped Horus, Re, and other gods in addition to Aten, he nevertheless created a monotheistic religion that was counter to earlier Egyptian tradition.

33. Allen, J. "The Ugly Egyptian," *Artnews,* Dec. 1998, p. 125.

34. Steiner, R. *Egyptian Myths and Mysteries,* pp. 52–53.

35. de Rouge, E. cited in Budge, p. xcii.

36. Schuré, E. *The Great Initiates,* p. 227. "Osarsiph was Menephtah's cousin, the son of the princess royal, sister of Rameses II. Whether he was an adopted or a natural son has never been known." pp. 228–29: "Manetho, the Egyptian priest, to whom we are indebted for the most authentic information regarding the dynasties of the Pharaohs, information now confirmed by the inscriptions on the monuments, affirms that Moses was a priest of Osiris. Strabo . . . also bears witness to this fact."

37. Richter points out the essence of the sun and moon mysteries in the following passage: "But just as the sunlight is not seen directly but reflected from the Moon, so did Moses see the Christ in reflection. And as we call the sunlight 'moonlight' when we see it reflected from the Moon, Christ was called at that time, Jahveh or Jehovah. Jahveh or Jehovah is the reflection of the Christ before He Himself appeared on Earth," p. 71. See also Steiner, R. *The Gospel of Saint Luke,* p. 134.

38. Richter, G. p. 68.

IV. MEGALITHIC CULTURE AND ART

For an archaic culture, one that is really still close to nature, every form, however abstract it may be, has as a matter of course a purpose and a name . . . and for that reason there is no actual representation of nature but only images which express the cosmic event in its entirety and with a regard to its eternal foundation.
—Titus Burckhardt

Egypt is flourishing! It constructs monumental buildings with precisely cut and dressed stones. It seeks the mystery of the eternal within the inmost depths of the human soul and within the inner sanctuary of the temple, according to the traditions of the Southern Mysteries (see Appendix 4). At the same time, in Western Europe, the Hibernian, pre-Celtic civilization is also flourishing. Like the Egyptians, the Hibernians use large stones, and their culture therefore is known as Europe's megalithic ("great stone") culture. In contrast to the enclosed sanctuaries of the Egyptians, these megalithic structures are of rough, natural stone, openly arranged within the environment. Megalithic temples stand in communion with the natural setting, open to cosmic and elemental forces in a rugged and unrefined manner, so that the eternal might be sought in the expansiveness of the cosmos.

IV.1 Hibernian Mysteries

The principle that observes was called Ceridwen—the soul. And that which came to meet the soul was called Hu, the spiritual world. The initiate experienced the union between Hu and Ceridwen. . . . When we are told today that the ancients paid homage to a God Hu and a Goddess Ceridwen this is simply another way of describing initiation. And with this the true myths are always concerned.
—Rudolf Steiner

You are a pupil of the great Hibernian Mysteries, which have their center in Ireland. You undergo a rigorous training, which eventually brings you before two large statues. One is a male figure made of an elastic material that, when pressed upon, springs back to its original shape. A sun symbol is above this statue. The other statue, a female figure, is of soft material that loses its form when touched. A moon symbol is above this effigy. Through long preparation and repeated visits before these two contrasting figures, inner images and experiences begin to arise and threaten to overwhelm you. Before the male statue inner coldness and visions of winter landscapes arise. Thoughts of prebirth and early phases of earthly and cosmic development are experienced. A word comparable to "science" appears in place of the statue and you hear the statement: "I am Knowledge but I lack Being." Before the female statue, inner warmth and summer scenes become visible. Pictures arise as from the depths of your will, and these pictures are of a future time after death and beyond present earthly conditions. A word equivalent to "art" appears in place of the female figure and the words sound forth: "I am Imagination, but I lack Truth." Because of these two powerful experiences an inner crisis occurs in your soul. A struggle arises between Being and Truth, Imagination and Knowledge. No solution seems possible. Finally, a spiritual presence makes itself felt to you and a harmony without negation of the two opposite positions is realized. This presence that oversees your initiation into the great Hibernian Mysteries is identified as the highest of spirit beings.[1]

These two statues, described in esoteric tradition, have never been recovered, yet they nevertheless give us a background with which to ponder the significance of artistic images and ritual symbols of the Megalithic culture that have survived over the millennia. Like the Laocoön sculpture (see fig. 78), which was described in literature centuries before it was rediscovered, perhaps one day physical evidence will surface to support many of the still unconfirmed traditions of the past, traditions of spirit and art.

IV.2 Druidism

The inferences, as I read the facts, seem to be that Druidism in its essential features was imposed upon the imaginative and sensitive nature of the Celts . . . by the earlier population of Western Europe, among the Megalithic People.
—Thomas Rolleston

At the time of the Indo-European invasions, around 1500 B.C., a people referred to as the Celts (*keltoi,* meaning "those who wear coats or clothes") moved from the region around the Black Sea into Western Europe and mixed with the indigenous people, who had already established a Megalithic culture.[2] The impressionable Celts took up many of the religious and cultural practices of these Megalithic peoples of Western Europe, who drew their spiritual guidance from the great Hibernian Mysteries. The Celts were, in this way, practitioners of the lesser Hibernian Mysteries through their connection to cultic practices handed down from the earlier Megalithic culture. The shaman-priests of the Celts who passed on this sacred wisdom have come to be known as druids. According to Pliny, druid means "great, or deep, knowledge" as well as "knowledge of the oak."[3] "Far-seeing," "deep-seeing ones," and "very learned" are other descriptions for these Celtic initiates. There is much debate concerning the origins of druidism and its relationship to Megalithic and Celtic peoples, but the term "druid" is used in the following pages to denote those who engaged in primal forms of shamanism or loosely organized mystery practices in prehistoric Europe. These practices included healing techniques, weather-changing rites, animal mastery, prediction, vision quests, out-of-body journeys, and other forms of practical magic.

By most accounts, the druids practiced a nature religion that connected them through supersensory perception to the working of the elements and the subtle cosmic influences that penetrate the earth from the depths of space. The druids' spiritual capacity to attune to these elemental forces is indicated in such pictures as that of the *cernunnos,* lord of the Underworld, depicted on the Gundestrup Cauldron (fig. 115). On this finely-crafted silver vessel we see a druid-shaman or *cernunnos* in meditation, sitting with legs folded beneath him in Eastern fashion and eyes closed or in a trancelike stare, a placid expression on his face. He wears a neckband like the one held in his right hand—a Celtic design executed in precious metal and symbolic of kingly status. In his left hand the *cernunnos* holds a snake. Animals, some in pairs, energetically move about

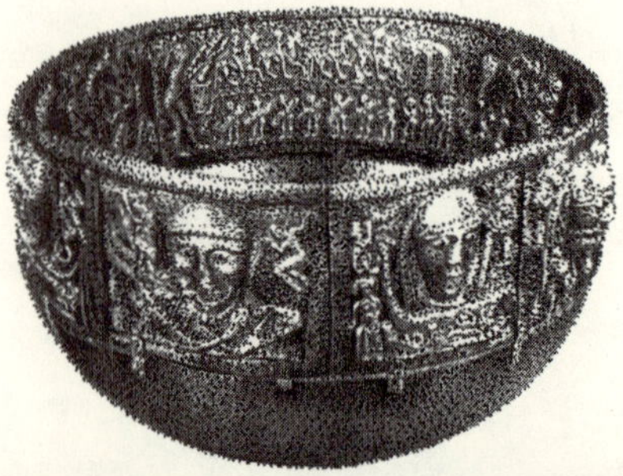

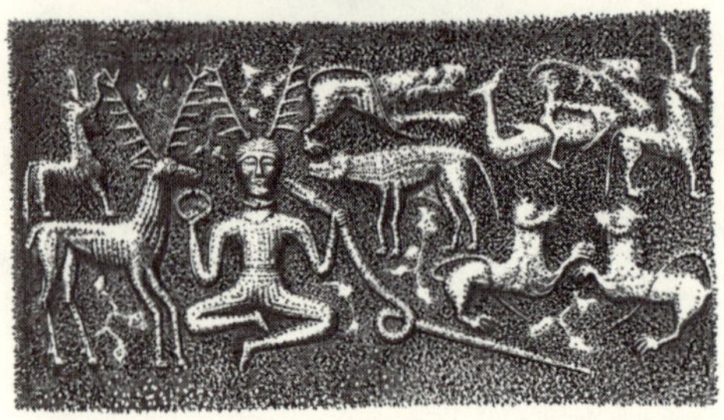

Fig. 115. The Gundestrup Cauldron, 200 B.C., a Celtic silver bowl found in Denmark, depicts numerous scenes including this one of a *cernunnos,* or druid-shaman, surrounded by various power animals. (National Museum of Denmark.)

in a weightless background. On the druid's right, the still side of the scene, a deer approaches with antlers that echo those worn by the central figure. Blossoming or leafing plants appear with textured surroundings as though emitting a field of life energy. The scene appears as an imaginative soul picture of the inner journey taken by the initiate priest-king. The ritual stag antlers appear as an expression of the visionary capacities possessed by the shaman and are a mystery image common among ancient peoples. On the Gundestrup Cauldron they are also suggestive of the tree of knowledge to which the *cernunnos* has access. Ritual masks with antlers or horns may have been worn to enhance or recall the earlier visionary faculties of primal humanity when such capacities began to fade. Many communities had an individual who retained these spiritual faculties, for the good of the clan, and the stag antlers were a part of this person's regalia.

According to Rudolf Grosse, the crescent shape and silver material of the Gundestrup Cauldron identify it as a ritual implement associated with lunar mysteries. Beyond this, however, he suggests that, as the Greek Cabiri emitted readable forms in the columns of smoke that rose from them, the water forms held within the Gundestrup chalice permitted a loosening of normal earthly consciousness and initiated a "moon" clairvoyance in the practitioner[4]

The cauldron or cup is a spiritually significant symbol in many world mythologies as the container and form giver for the living substance of creation. It holds within itself the secret potential and unknown elixir of the gods. It also denotes the quest through the elemental kingdoms or the Underworld—the realm hidden within the physically visible world of nature—in order that one may gain initiation into higher knowledge. Chinese ritual bronze vessels held ceremonial wine and grain for tomb burials and were often elaborately decorated as the symbolic bodily sheath containing vital life substance as well as spiritual nourishment. Vessel symbolism is equally important in the pottery used in Native American rituals, in which a sacred pot, once having fulfilled its purpose, is "killed" by punching a hole in it, releasing the spirit of the vessel and making it no longer functional as a container. The most sacred Christian vessel is the Holy Grail, the chalice into which the blood of Christ Jesus flowed during his crucifixion. The vessel imagery represents the human capacity to take in the living substance of the spirit.

There were three distinct grades of training for the Celtic shaman, the most elementary of which was the bard.[5] At this stage of schooling the would-be druid traveled from tribe to tribe, and later from court to court, as a storyteller and minstrel—first as an apprentice, then as a master singer—sustaining the mythology and oral traditions of the folk. Some senior bards in early Christian times could recite hundreds of stories, drawn mostly from a traditional Celtic repertoire.[6] However, classical material such as the *Iliad,* the *Odyssey,* and epics of Alexander the Great were also told, even as far north as Ireland. To these were later added stories from the Old and New Testaments. Such stories could often take months to tell and it was through these sagas and songs that the conscience of the people could be roused and indirect advice could be given to tribal chiefs and clan leaders. In early times, the poet-bards set the tone at banquets and feasts by instilling courage and enthusiasm for the common good while mocking weakness and evil. As Alwyn and Brynley Rees indicate, "There is evidence from the Celtic countries and from India that the poets were also the official historians and the royal genealogists. The poet's praises confirmed and sustained the king in his kingship, while his satire could blast both the king and his kingdom. . . . Such priestly functions as divination and prophecy also came within the province of these early . . . poets who, it may be added, wore cloaks of bright feathers as do the shamans of Siberia when, through ritual and trance, they conduct their audiences on journeys to another world. It was initiates with their power and authority who had the custody of the original tales, and they recited them on auspicious occasions, even as the priests of other religions recite the scriptures."[7] The bard thus worked on the moral life and spiritual development of the listeners while the full druid performed a similar task through shaping the content of religious festivals and sacred rites.[8]

The second degree of druidism was that of the vates or filid, who were known as judges in Ireland and possessed prophetic abilities. However, it was the full druid who stood behind all high-level government decisions and was always the first to speak in assemblies, even before the king. These were the healers familiar with suggestive magic and natural medicine. They were also the keepers of the mystery centers and as such oversaw communication with and entry into the spiritual worlds. "All rites of initiation were a means of revealing to the pupil that death is only one of the many processes in life. . . . . In the Druidic Mysteries (Druid means an initiate of the third degree) the neophyte was put into a condition resembling death, so that his senses could not function as organs of perception . . . yet the neophyte is [nevertheless] able to experience and observe."[9] In this way, the druid priest was hierophant and initiator, as well as spiritual leader.

According to tradition, the Celtic druid, as the representative of the lesser Hibernian Mysteries, was heir to the greater mysteries that reached still further back to the mystery centers of primeval Hyperborea.[10] Initiation into these older mysteries was long and difficult, requiring extensive trials and self-transformation. The monumental stone structures that still stand in parts of Ireland, Britain, and France were places consecrated to these early mysteries and passed on to the Celts of later centuries.

IV.3 Three Faces of Megalithic Man

As it was, As it is,
As it shall be, Evermore,
O Thou Triune of Grace!
With the ebb
With the flow,
O Thou Triune of Grace!
With the ebb
With the flow.
—Traditional Celtic saying

In art the portrait has always been a way of reflecting on the human condition; the self-portrait, a searching for self-knowledge. And if God said, "Let us make man in our image, after our likeness" (Gen. 1:26), then it would follow that portraiture is a longing for the divine, a looking for that

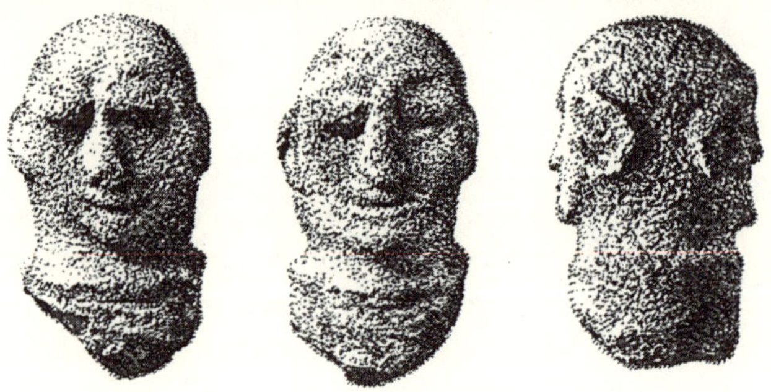

Fig. 116. Numerous double-faced heads in the tradition of the Roman god Janus have been found throughout Europe. (Leichlingen, Rhein-Wupper.)

godly image that is suggested in our own earthly visage. In any case, the portrait can tell us something about who a subject is, his or her relationship, or lack of relationship, to self and world.

Numerous prehistoric stone busts have been uncovered in the British Isles and Western Europe, some having a single countenance while others show a forward-and-backward-looking, double-faced Janus head (fig. 116). Very rare are three-faced sculptures like the 4000-year-old stone "idol" recovered in Woodlands, County Donegal, Ireland. Why multiple faces on a single head?

The Janus figures, so named for the Roman god who could look in two directions at once, and whom we honor with the month of January, expresses the strength that lies in duality. To look forward into the future and also backwards into the past is a godlike ability that gives one a more complete viewpoint from which to operate in the present. This aspect, in combination with the polar qualities of male and female, youth and age, provides a picture of the inner dynamic or spiritual tension that might exist in a two-faced being. In the positive sense given to the Janus theme by the Renaissance artist Raphael, it can represent the virtue of Prudence looking in two directions (fig. 117).

Fig. 117. Below: The Janus theme, a figure looking forward and backward, is portrayed by Raphael in the library of Pope Julius II at the Vatican in Rome. Prudence is depicted as a female figure looking into a mirror, with an older man gazing from the back of her head towards the sky. (After Raphael.)

But what of the three faces? The most striking thing about the Woodlands three-faced stone head is how different the three faces are from each other (fig. 118, a, b, c). Figure 118a is a well-proportioned head, with ample hair framing a protruding brow and bulging eyes. This face appears to be very intense and concentrated. It is filled with light and its consciousness is one of full wakefulness. In Figure 118b we are struck by the very lyrical and musical quality of the narrow, sweeping face. Lifted up on the side where it meets Figure a and drooping noticeably where it is connected to Figure c, this curved face lives as if in a dream. Figure 118c has an unusually large, flat face, in which the smallish features are almost lost. The expression is dull, dense, and heavy. What seems most important about all three of these portraits taken together is the distinct levels of consciousness that they suggest—waking, dreaming, and sleeping. It appears in Figure a that we have a fully conscious thinking being; an awake intellect, or perhaps one that "sees clearly" (clairvoyant). Figure b is only semiconscious, as though dozing off, in a dreamy reverie—not really awake, not fully asleep. Figure c, though open-eyed, appears somehow dim in his awareness. This third face appears to live not in conscious thoughts or even in dreamy feelings but in the dark forces of the unconscious. Perhaps these three faces can be seen not only in terms of stages of consciousness—wakefulness, dreaming, and sleeping—but also as the three soul forces, thinking, feeling, and willing? It seems plausible that the artist-craftsman of this piece was depicting the very nature of man—a portrait that reveals a penetrating knowledge of human nature.

In addition, if we consider the social order among the early Celts, we might wonder if this three-faced figure is at the same time a portrait of the druid-priest, the minstrel-bard, and the warrior-king, all on the same head. Could Figure a be the countenance of the prophetic druid-seer in a visionary state? Is Figure b the poet-bard chanting his musical verse? And perhaps the will power of the warrior-king is expressed in the rather bold visage of Figure c. Tom Cowan posits that the use of three faces goes beyond vision into two different worlds—spiritual and physical—as depicted by the Janus heads, and illustrates "the resulting composite vision, the shamanic vision of a person-between-the-worlds."[11]

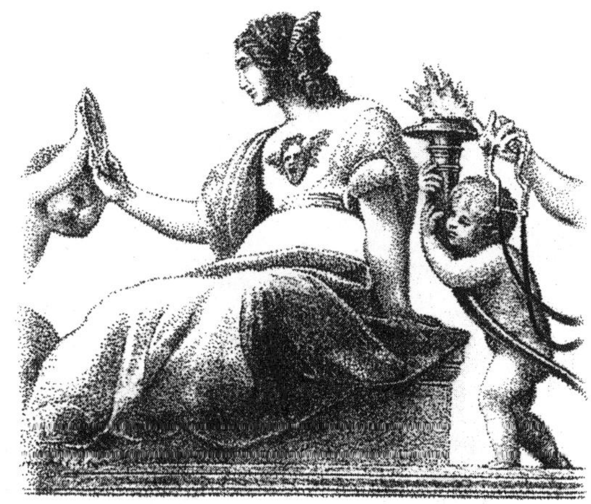

The triple condition is very apparent in Celtic mythology, where many deities, both male and female, reveal a threefold nature, though it is most apparent among the goddesses who have several different names. Morrigna, for instance, is the singular equivalent of Morrigan, Badh, and Nemain. There are also three Brigits and three Macha, indicating the threefold goddess who contains aspects of the Virgin (innocence and purity), Mother (nurturing and creativity), and Crone (transformation and maturation). Amongst the male deities there are the Three Gods of Skill, personified in Gobniu, Credne, and Luchta. Even the principal gods Lug and Dagda show some evidence of a triune aspect. T. G. E. Powell sees such triads not as "a tendency to trinitarian concepts, or of the union of three distinct supernatural beings. It is, in fact, an expression of the extreme potency of any one deity. It may be likened 'to the power of three,' and this number was sacred, and auspicious, far beyond the Celtic world."[12] Triads also appear in the Celtic social structure. Julius Caesar wrote of the "threefold division of Gaulish society into druids, *equites* [knights], and plebs."[13] As mentioned earlier, the three stages of schooling for a druid were bard, vates, and druid, and one of the divisions of Celtic society (over and above the commoners) was the druid-priests, bards, and warrior-kings. The early Celtic world view with its triads seems to encompass many aspects of human nature, society, spirituality, and art. It forms a strong image in which, as the Old Testament suggests, "a threefold cord is not easily broken" (Eccl. 4:12).

a b c

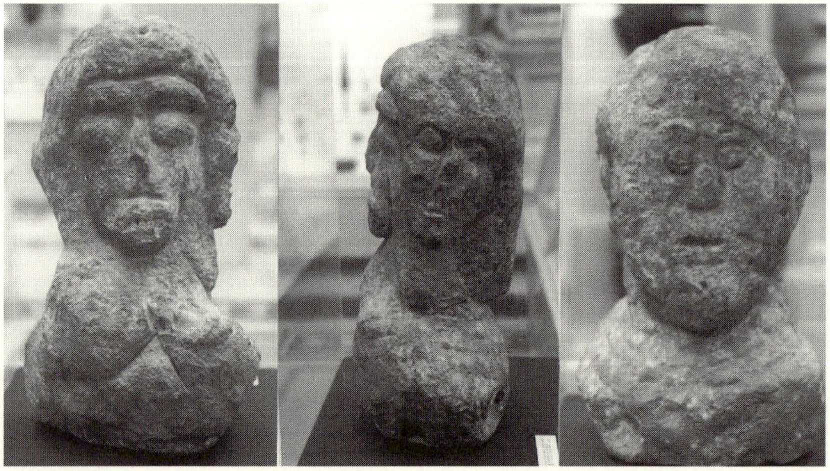

Fig. 118. Known as the Woodlands three-faced stone head, this figure shows a triad of distinctly different carved visages: (a) one, well-proportioned with bulging eyes and protruding brow, (b) another with a fluid diagonal gesture, and (c) a third with a full, broad, flat face. (National Museum, Ireland.)

IV.4 Megalithic Monuments

A feeling of infinite isolation and loneliness overcomes us in these places. The air seems to us to be thin, empty and silent. . . . But then the greatness and the customs of a distant, forgotten time begins to speak. In the cromlechs and avenues we can trace as though in a skeleton the hieroglyphs of a life that once had meaning and significance.
—Werner Schupback

The megalithic monuments of prehistoric Europe fall into several distinct categories: standing stones or menhirs, alignments or avenues, stone tables or dolmens, stone circles or cromlechs, and passage mounds or tumuli. They are a direct expression of the culture's mystery religion and spirituality, and as art and architecture are related to each other from the simplest construction to the more complex. From the menhir to the tumulus a development can be observed similar to the geometric progression from the point to the circle.

Sacred Center

The standing stone (menhir) gives off a mysterious psychic vibration. To this day humans and animals are drawn to menhir by their magical powers, people touch them or go three times around them in order to be cured of illness; sick livestock are brought to rub against them.
—Marija Gimbutas

The menhirs or "long stones" are simple unworked, upright stones set within the natural environment (fig. 119). These standing stones, often gigantic but sometimes small and modest, are stations of worship and offering, and although human remains are sometimes found at their bases, these rock monuments are not intended merely as gravestones.[14] They are sacred places where early peoples might commune with the spiritual worlds, aided by ancestral spirits whose ashes have been deposited there. In this sense menhirs are focal points or channeling posts for communication between the worlds below and those above—sacred centers of spiritual import.

Contemporary artist Marko Pogacnik refers to standing stones as "lithoacupuncture," as they may be placed, as he does in his sculptural work, at certain meridian points in the earth's energy flow and may thereby harmonize the elemental forces within a given landscape.[15]

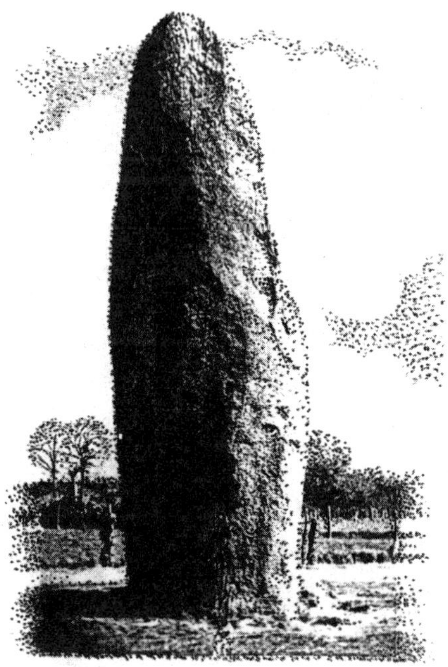

Fig. 119. Menhirs or standing stones are large upright stones set perpendicular to the earth to indicate a sacred place or *axis mundi.*

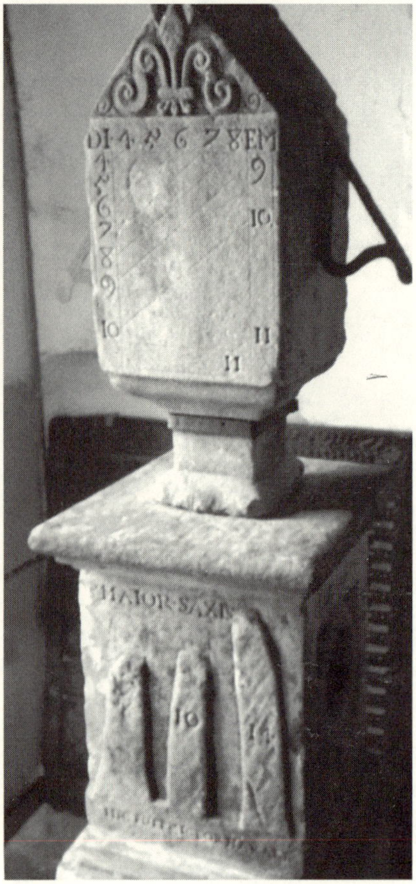

In prehistory, ritual sites were sometimes marked with wooden posts or designated by an oak tree. As late as the eighth century A.D., Germanic tribes called these upright markers Irminsäule or "pillars of the world," indicating the connection and support they provided between human beings and the gods.[16] The "World Tree," the *axis mundi,* can be linked in this way to the menhir. Curative powers are often attributed to such sites and many standing stones are remembered to this day as places of healing.

A further aspect of the standing stone is that it was also used as a marker to recall an event that took place at a particular locale. In this sense the menhir was like a forerunner to the memorial. It stimulated "localized memory" or recollection connected with the place. The memory was outside, identified with the location and only awakened when the stone marker was seen. (See chapter VI.1.)

Like the Egyptian obelisk, these standing stone monuments are a picture of human uprightness—depicting the same life force that also causes the plant to grow toward the sun and directs the spiritual striving of the human being—within time and space. Standing stones served as a metaphor for and a vehicle of the spirit. Because the shape of the Great Spirit was unknown, the stone was not carved but left in its natural form. Menhirs were an indication to outsiders that the sacred art of the mysteries was practiced in the area and that a genius loci or "spirit of the place" was marked by the stone.

Sacred Way

Not a single ancient religious rite can be found without dancing.
—Lucian

Alignments are the placement of two or more standing stones in relation to each other. Many of these alignments are oriented to the terrestrial environment or have a relationship to celestial phenomena, in particular the sun. One such example is Harold's Stones in southwestern Wales: three standing stones in a row (fig. 120). A seventeenth-century sundial in the nearby church of Trellech depicts the stones with numbers on them, an indication that the ancient stones, much older than the eleventh-century King Harold, who fought a battle at the site, may have been used for marking time by the passage of the sun (fig. 121).

Fig. 120. Harold's Stones (right) in southwestern Wales is an alignment of three upright granite stones containing flecks of white quartz.

Fig. 121. Above: A sundial in the local Trellech village church depicts Harold's Stones and indicates an early association of these megaliths with the sun and with marking the passage of time.

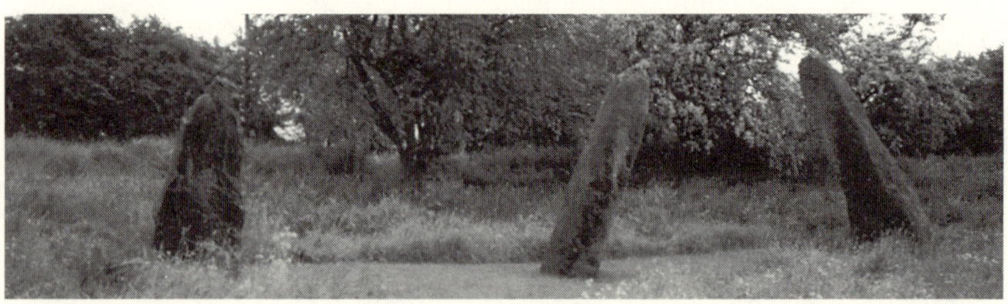

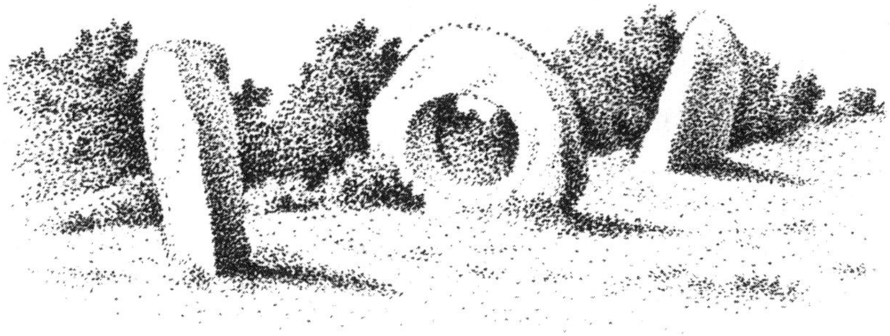

Fig. 122. Left: Men-a-tol, in Cornwall, England, is a holed stone aligned with an upright on either side. To this day it is associated with healing.

Other alignments are associated with healing, as the Men-a-tol, in Cornwall, England, where to this day children and adults crawl through a hole in one of the stones, hoping for good health. Literally meaning "hole in stone," the Men-a-tol alignment has two upright monoliths opposite each other and a ring stone between them (fig. 122). Local tradition claims that children with ailments such as rickets can be healed by passing through the central Crick Stone nine times in the same direction.

The larger alignments or stone avenues evidently include both astronomical and healing aspects. However, the central use of the stone avenues in Menec, an open-air temple near Carnac, France, appears to be for high ritual celebration. One of the important features of this alignment, which includes 1,169 megaliths believed to have been erected before 3000 B.C., is that every other stone subtly points to the earth while the in-between stones point toward the heavens (fig. 123). These alternating gestures of the stones, arranged in parallel multi-avenues, most likely express the downward streaming gifts of the cosmos (sunlight, rain, snow) and the upward rising response (plant growth, smoke, fire). Gifts of the heavens are answered by offerings and prayers that men and women give up to the gods. This rhythmic alternation in the stones is not unlike the Greek architectural motif of the egg-dart and palm, which is an expression of the great pulse beat of the cosmos, the dynamic breathing of contraction and expansion. The stones at this site gradually become larger the further one follows them to the west, and the avenues curve together and close in a semicircle around a large horizontal altar stone, the culmination point for ritual processions and the place for sacred high offerings. Festive processions and ritual dances were a major part of ancient religions and could have been an enactment of the cosmic movements of the stars and the planets through

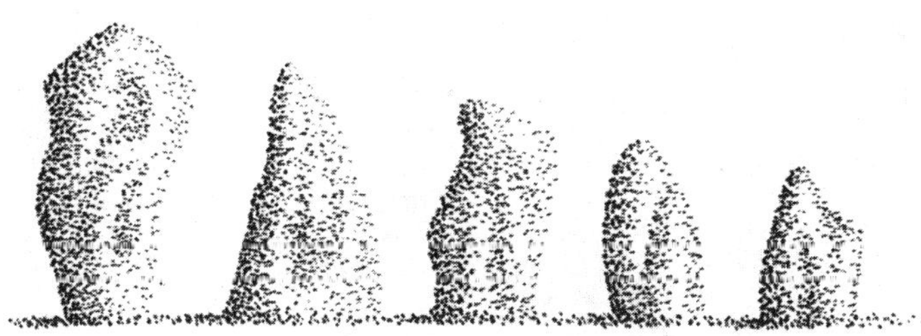

Fig. 123. Left: Some megalithic alignments alternate stones in a rhythmic pattern that points toward the earth and then toward the heavens.

whose influence life is ordered upon the earth. The ritual dance would proceed along the sacred way, through the stone avenues, artistically portraying the planetary movements and reenacting the holy mystery drama of the universe.

Sacred Doorway

In the two vertical stones of the Druid trilithons, united by the horizontal covering stone, we have something like a picture of the horns of the celestial bull—which represented two great cosmic forces—separated, but united by the universal power of the Sun, or of the spiritual world.

—Eleanor Merry

Dolmens, or quoits, are a close grouping of two or more standing stones with a lintel stone resting horizontally on top of the others (fig. 124). The term *dolmen* comes from the Breton word meaning "stone table." In Wales, dolmens are referred to as "druids' altars," and in Denmark as "giants' beds." Their simple structure creates a crude shelter, often appearing like a stone doorframe or gateway.

Steiner suggested that the dolmen was a special place for the druid-priest to come into communion with nature through meditation on the elements. The roofed space created by the dolmen aided the druid in "reading" the phenomena of nature by blocking out the physical light of the sun so that the druid could "see" the spiritual qualities of the sun as revealed in the shadows of the enclosed space. By reading the inner qualities of the sun's light and how it worked upon the earth, the priest could direct the community accordingly, as far as agriculture, healing, and other matters were concerned. Subtle nuances of warm or cool-colored shadows indicated seasonal changes; from such estimations the druid knew when the planting of crops should begin or what measures should be taken to ensure the health of the tribe.[17]

As with the menhirs, dolmens were sometimes consecrated with the ashes or skeletal remains of deceased ancestors. However, as mentioned earlier, this does not mean that these megalithic structures were simple gravestones or mausoleums in the contemporary sense.[18] In historic times the dolmen became strictly a tomb for the dead, but in earlier periods they seem also to have marked active stations for communion with the spirit world mediated by the souls of the dead. In this sense the dolmen was a doorway through which the druid could come and go on his or her spirit journey into other worlds.

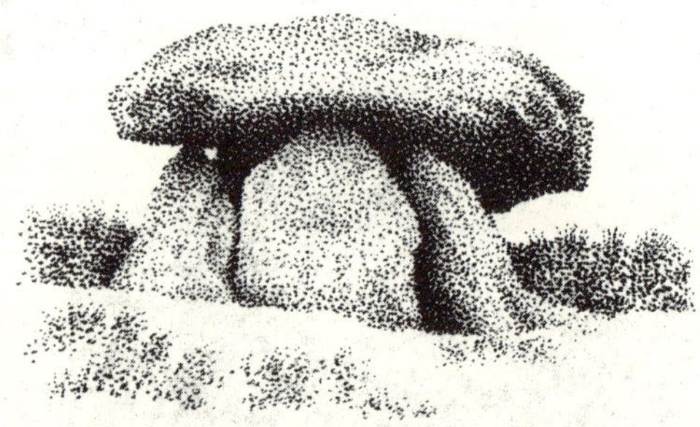

Fig. 124. The dolmen or quoit, also called a stone table, is composed of several upright stones holding a horizontal "roof" stone on top. Such sites are thought to be doorways or thresholds between worlds.

Sacred Circles

We can deduce that the builders of tombs, rings, henges, and avenues developed a considerable body of astronomical knowledge for what were, ultimately, ritual purposes. There was an undeniable interest in the winter solstice, and in particular in marking the position of the moon at that point. This suggests the practice of winter rituals when the sun is at its weakest and seen as dying. . . . The purpose of such rituals essentially is the regeneration of life powers, made possible through energetic ring dances combined with the powers of stones standing in a circle. The stone circles are not fully activated unless the calendrical events are accompanied by human rituals and dance.

—Marija Gimbutas

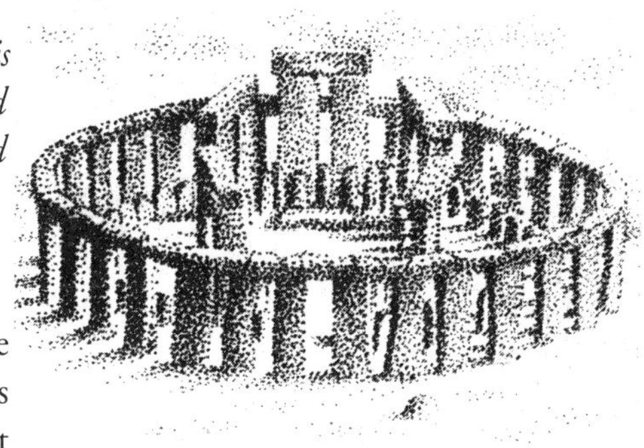

Of all the megalithic monuments, the cromlechs, meaning "round place," are perhaps the most impressive. These stone circles, of which there may be as many as a thousand in the British Isles, are circular arrangements of upright stones aligned to solar and lunar movements, placed in special connection to natural features such as valleys, hills, mountains, and bodies of water. The more elaborate cromlechs include trilithons (a horizontal lintel stone carried by two upright monoliths), curb stones, an altar stone, petroglyphs, trenches, and burial mounds.

Fig. 125. Above: Stonehenge, or Cathoir Gall ("Hall of the Giants' Dance"), is perhaps the most renowned stone circle or cromlech in Britain. Eight annual moonrises and four sunrises at the solstices and equinoxes are confirmed alignments at this megalithic site.

Fig. 126. Below: Avebury (viewed from above) was a high ceremonial megalithic site. The largest stone circle in Britain, it is not far from Stonehenge in southern England.

Stonehenge, on which much has been written, is just such a complex (fig. 125). The Gaelic name for Stonehenge is Cathoir Gall, which means "Hall of the Giants' Dance," and here, as at other cromlechs, sacred processions, circumambulations, and the ritual "round dance" were likely performed. The altar stone at Stonehenge is set just off center to allow the presiding druid to stand in the exact center of the circle during ceremonies, and the entire circular arrangement of stones suggests a symbolic picture of the cosmos. Although no connection with planetary movements has been fully established as yet, a special relationship to sun and moon has been observed through the ages. Eight annual moonrises and four sunrises, at solstices and equinoxes, are confirmed alignments, as are stones that foretell lunar eclipses. Stonehenge's complicated astronomical alignments are only possible at its precise location on the Salisbury Plain in southern England. If it were moved a few miles away from its present latitude, its astronomical alignments would fail to be accurate in the same way. Krupp has pointed out that "we can no longer doubt whether Stonehenge had astronomical significance. Instead, we might marvel that it had so much significance."[19] Stonehenge was constructed in three successive stages before reaching its impressive culmination Three thousand years ago. Its large blue stones were said to have been magically moved to their location by the legendary wizard Merlin. The stones are known to have originated in the Preseli Mountains of Wales.

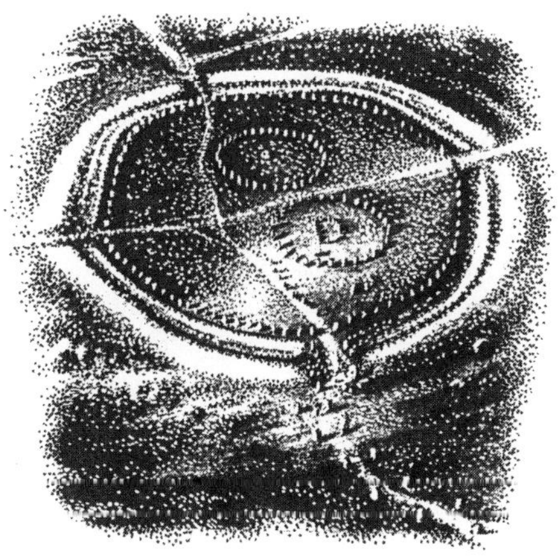

Many of the religious functions carried out at menhirs, alignments, and dolmens took place at cromlechs as well. However, the larger cromlechs, such as Stonehenge and Avebury (fig. 126), were clearly places of seasonal festivals and high ritual ceremonies intended for the benefit of a larger community. Perhaps Diodorus Siculus, a historian of the first century B.C., describes

Stonehenge when he writes of Britain: "It is inhabited by Hyperboreans . . . [and] there are stories that Apollo is honored there above all other gods. On this island there is also a magnificent temple precinct consecrated to the sun god . . . a temple of the God which is circular."[20]

Sacred Sun Cave

While the megaliths were indeed connected with beliefs about the sun and moon, it is clear that these were only aspects of a complicated mass of ideas and practices involving the afterlife, ancestral spirits, and the fertility of beasts and humans.

—Evan Hadingham

The passage mound, or tumulus, is a further development of the alignment, dolmen, and cromlech. It is a dolmenlike structure, often with an entrance corridor, roofed over with lintel stones and covered with smaller stones and earth to create an underground chamber. It is a constructed cave. Ancestors whose remains were placed in the tumulus were honored with stones, often brought long distances to be added to the mound. These gift rocks gradually built up the mound into a stone hill or cairn of some size. Hans Hartmann notes, "There are graves of important persons of prehistoric times which are still being honored with gifts of stone today."[21]

However, like the great pyramids of Egypt, the passage mounds of Western Europe were not exclusively burial places or tombs. They were also places of initiation and induction into the mysteries of life, death, and rebirth. As Mircea Eliade notes, "it is in caves that aspirants have their dreams and meet their helping spirits."[22] Just as the Egyptian initiate sought Osiris, in the dark realm of "the sun at midnight," so the Celtic druid entered the passage mound in order to find the spiritual light in the absence of the physical sun—the inner "light of the world."

Newgrange, just north of Dublin, is a restored passage mound said in Irish legends to be the abode of Aengus, son of Dagda, the Celtic sun god (fig. 127). On the shortest day of the year, December 21, just before 9 A.M., the disc of the sun appears above the southeastern horizon and a shaft of light enters the passage

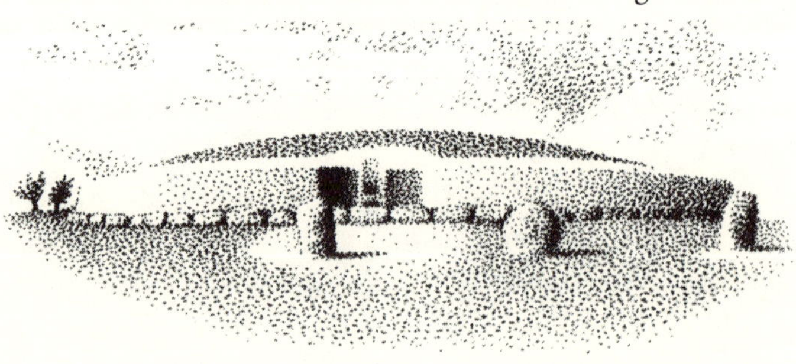

Fig. 127. Newgrange is a restored passage mound in Ireland said to be the legendary home of Aengus, son of Dagda, the Celtic sun god. The site is aligned to the winter solstice sunrise.

mound through a small window opening above the entrance and threshold stone.[23] The beam of sunlight travels the length of a cross-shaped corridor until it strikes the back wall of the passage, painting a luminous wedge-shaped blade of morning light on the backing stone within. Three large stone bowls in the side chambers contain ancestral ashes, and a triple spiral is carved into the interior rock wall near the back of the passage mound (fig. 128). The most striking aspect of the passage mound's alignment to the winter solstice is that its cruciform floor plan creates a cross of sunlight within the circular earth mound. A sun cross is formed, symbolizing the incarnation of the Sun Spirit as revitalizer of the dark mineralized Earth.[24] At Newgrange the passage mound renders a microcosmic picture of a macrocosmic, spiritual event (fig. 129).

Research is being conducted at many megalithic monuments on what have been called energy fields, ley lines, or power points. Such research, often viewed as outside the accepted limits of established science, raises the question of what sort of energy, measurable or otherwise, is made manifest and may have been utilized in megalithic structures. Studies indicate that megalithic monuments were often built on or near magnetic fields, water currents, unusual geological formations, and other possible energy sources. Many megaliths were constructed with a combination of minerals, such as limestone and granite. At Newgrange, white quartz is featured. The convergence of these dynamics at Megalithic sites has led many to speculate on the possible beneficial use of the resulting influences for the health and prosperity of communities connected to such sites.[25]

Megalithic structures were clearly an important art form expressive of the Hibernian Mysteries. However, they are also an architectural expression that is found throughout the entire world. Connected with burial practices, ancestor worship, and initiation, megalithic monuments are lasting evidence of the spiritual language of art and architecture (see Appendix 5, "World Megaliths").

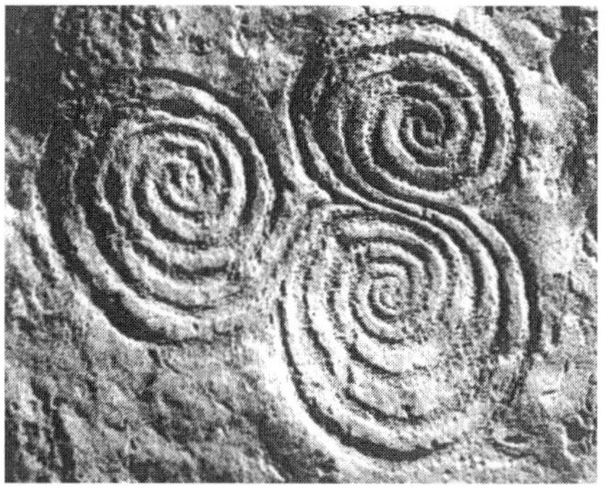

Fig. 128. Above: At the back of Newgrange passage mound is a triple spiral petroglyph. Spirals are also carved on the threshold stone at the passage entrance.

Fig. 129. Below: The plan of Newgrange is in the form of a cross. At the winter solstice sunrise the cruciform passageway is illuminated by morning light.

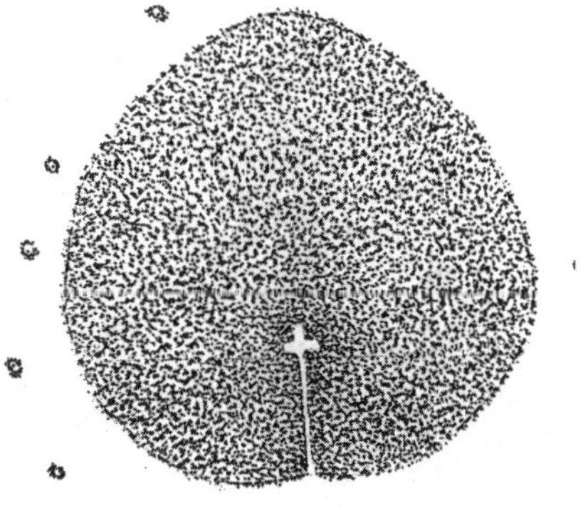

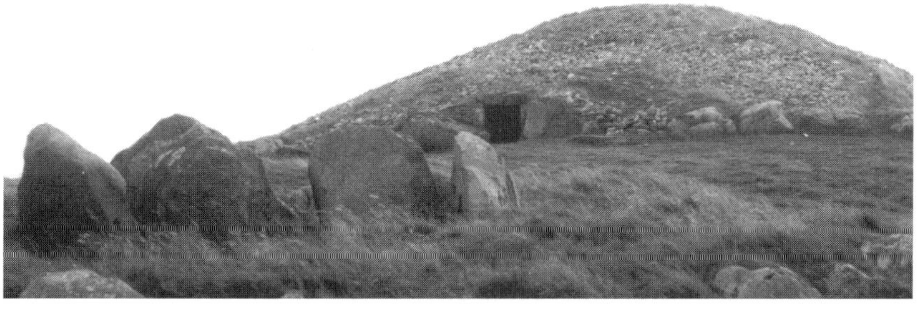

Fig. 130. Left: Slieve na Cailighe, or Cairn T passage mound, is set dramatically on a hilltop in the Loughcrew mountains within sight of Tara, Ireland's ancient capital.

IV.5 Cosmic Script

As the mind explores the symbol, it is led to ideas that lie beyond the grasp of reason. The wheel may lead our thoughts toward the concept of a "divine" sun, but at this point reason must admit its incompetence; man is unable to define a "divine" being. . . . This is one reason why all religions employ symbolic language or images.
—Carl Jung

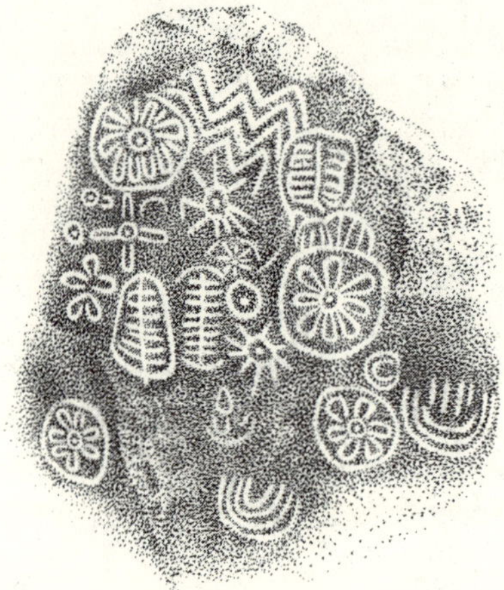

Fig. 131. Petroglyphs (above) inside Slieve na Cailighe passage mound are illuminated by the sun's rays at the spring equinox sunrise. The petroglyphs, of stacked concentric crescents, are reminiscent of vessels being filled and emptied, just as the moon "fills up" with the reflected light of the sun and "empties out" during its various phases. The ladder motif is associated with the Tree of Life, the shaft of grain, and the human spinal cord. Numerous sun symbols also appear.

Fig. 132. In megalithic cultures throughout the world, the sun motif (below) is a dominant image. It appears in a range of forms from dynamic sunwheel patterns to symmetrical sun-cross designs.

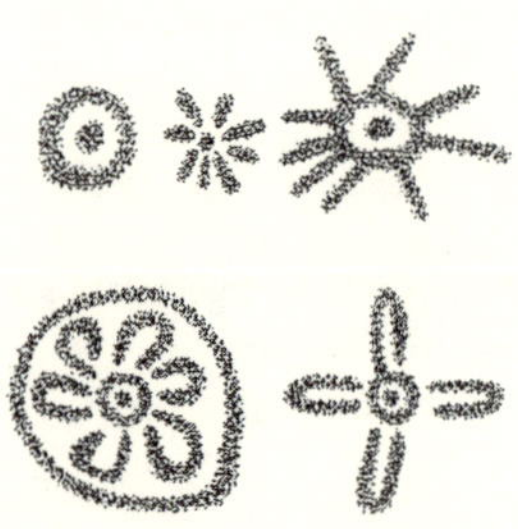

Petroglyphs of a simple linear and geometric character can be found carved into many of the stone surfaces at passage mounds and other megalithic sites. On curb and threshold stones outside of mounds, as well as on interior passage walls deep within tumuli, pure linear designs depict the forces of nature and action of the cosmos. Dots, circles, spirals, crosses, zigzags, triangles, and diamond shapes portray in elemental fashion the dynamic energy of the universe. Many of the carved images are strategically placed, some in order that they may be illuminated and traversed by the sun's light at certain turning-points of the year. Such a site is Slieve na Cailighe, "Hill of the Sorceress," also known as Cairn T, an exceptional passage mound in the Loughcrew hills of central Ireland (fig. 130). Here at dawn on the spring equinox, the sun's rays move slowly across petroglyphs of circles, crescents, zigzags, and ladder designs (fig. 131).

Circles and floral patterns often indicate the radiant energy of the sun and are employed as the most common image throughout the world. Many variations appear, from elaborate sunflower patterns to symmetrical sun cross designs (fig. 132). These are all transformations of the simple point within a circle, still recognized today as the international symbol for the light source and center of our solar system—the sun. Other petroglyphs, such as the diamond shape and the double spiral, illustrate the sun's passage through space and time. The diamond or lozenge points to the sun's relationship to the directions of space and the seasons of the year. The double spiral suggests a movement from winter at its lowest and weakest point, in the center of one spiral, to the journey of the sun through spring to summer, where it comes to its highest and most expanded station before going back through autumn to winter in the center of the second spiral, a continuous cycle of fading and becoming, waning and waxing. A rather remarkable illustration of this journey of the sun is the engraved Tully Stone (fig. 133). The greater rings on top represent the summer sun at its highest and fullest, the middle rings show the sun at the autumn equinox, and the small, lower rings are the sun at midwinter. The middle rings are also the spring equinox taking the sun back to its highest station at summer. We see once more the importance of three in the artistic rendering of natural events. Such artistic motifs might also provide

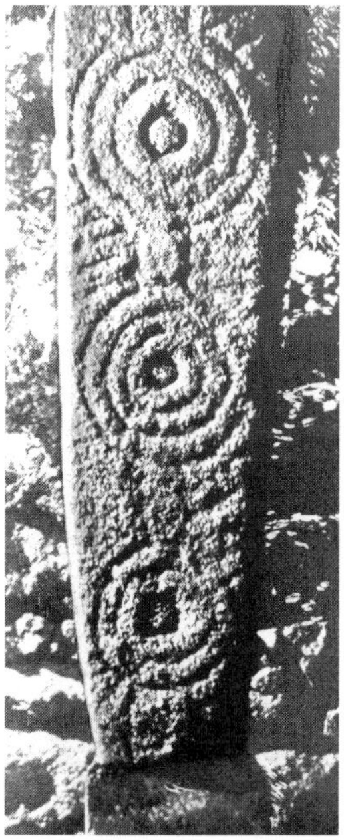

a symbolic language for expressing in picture form the Celtic idea of repeated earth lives.[26] The triune Celtic spiral comes to mind, for the mystery image of the spiral has long been associated with the process of incarnating and excarnating. Many petroglyphs are purely abstract elements such as stacked concentric arcs, rhythmically repeated one after another (fig. 134). Megalithic sites in Ireland, Brittany, Spain, and Malta have minutely engraved patterns reminiscent of expanding water ripples, tree rings, or radiating magnetic fields. These piled-up lines and rhythmic patterns suggest the inexhaustible generative forces of the formative life realm.[27] Such vibrant images give the impression of a huge fingerprint, as though some primeval giant or mythic god had left an imprint on the stones while moving them into place. Such forms are directly related to the ladder motif and the Tree of Life, the shaft of wheat or corn, and the spinal cord. Sometimes, as at Cairn T, these stacked concentric arches look like bowl forms or vessels (fig. 131). Their crescent shape is suggestive of the moon that fills up with and then empties out the reflected light of the sun as it passes through its cyclical phases. Surely these forms receive and return a special spiritual power through the winter solstice sunlight shining across them year after year.

Upon entering the passage mound known as Fourknocks, not far from Newgrange in County Meath, Ireland, one is immediately confronted with two carvings on the northwestern and northeastern lintel stones (fig. 135). On one stone round, curvilinear forms and concentric circles appear. On the other stone four zigzag lines can be seen—jagged, angular, and repetitive. Might this be a presentation, in a simpler visual language, of the two statues described earlier? Could we have here the soft, lunar, feminine qualities juxtaposed with the elastic, solar, male characteristics? Is something of summer seasons, future premonitions, and artistic creativity contrasted with winter moods, past recollections, and scientific experimentation? Is "imagination without truth" set beside "knowledge without being"?

Many of the primal images carved in stone at megalithic sites appear to speak about the journeys of stars and planets, the rhythms of nature, the pulse of life itself, and the passage of spirit through time and space. The stone engravings are an imaginative sign and symbol language, predating written language, in some cases, by millennia. Petroglyphs are a kind of cosmic script telling us in picture form about the origins of humanity and the development of the natural world. They are a visual language of spirit and art, pictures of the transformation of humanity.

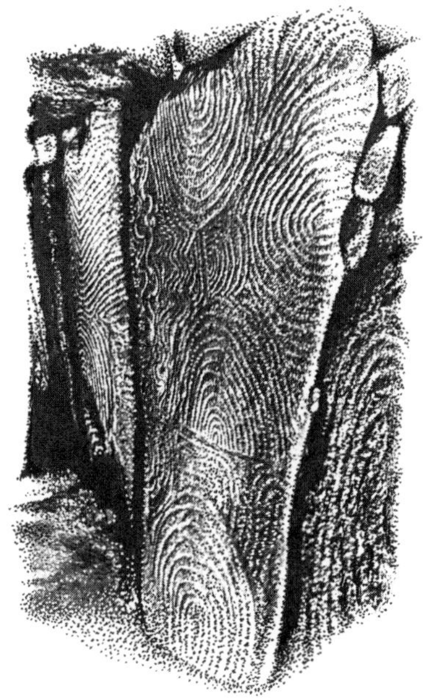

Fig. 133. The Tully Stone (left) indicates the passage of the sun through the four seasons by means of a threefold image of stacked concentric circles: summer above in the highest station, autumn in the middle, winter at the lowest position, and spring again in the middle.

Fig. 134. The stacked concentric arcs found at many megalithic sites, such as Gavrinas in France (above), are often linked to pulsating water ripples, rhythmic tree-ring growth patterns, and radiating magnetic force fields.

Fig. 135. Within the passage mound at Fourknocks in Ireland, a striking pair of contrasting engraved forms can be seen (below). One stone has curvilinear forms and concentric circles while the other has only straight, jagged, zigzag lines. The contrasting engravings suggest polar opposite forces.

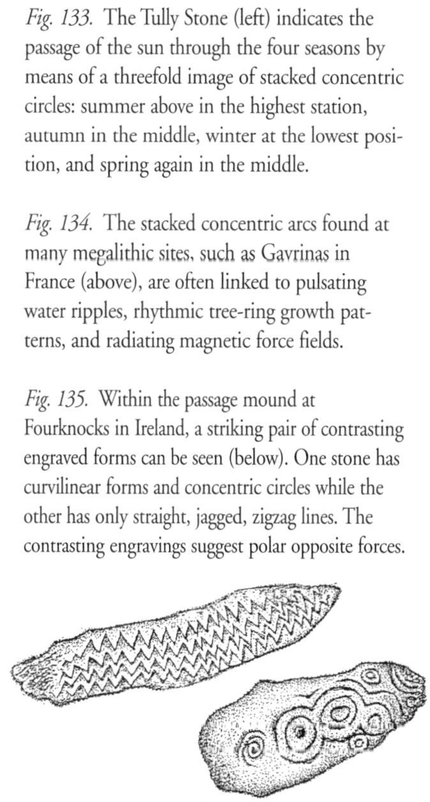

IV.6 Sun and Cross

Raise the stone and there thou shalt find me.
—The Gospel of Thomas

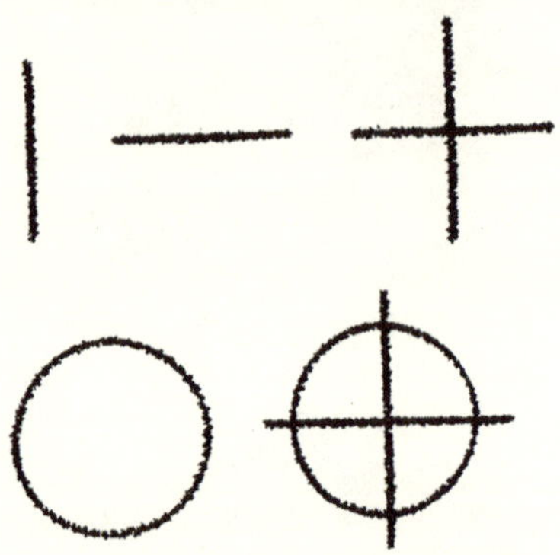

Fig. 136. The vertical line declares an independent striving in its upright gesture while the horizontal line reaches dreamily into the widths of space. When the plant-like vertical intersects the sentient horizontal, the cross of humanity is formed. The masculine cross of consciousness, pain, and death contrasts with the feminine circle of wholeness, inclusion, and harmony. Only when the circle and cross are united do we have the unity of spirit in matter, God in humanity.

The circle is a single, continually curving line that has no beginning and no end, and forms a perfect, angleless, geometric form. It is enclosed, at rest, and complete in itself. Primal peoples recognize the circle as a powerful image of wholeness, a picture of the universe in its all-encompassing nature. In this sense the circle is the unity of God, or more often, the oneness of the Goddess (the Eternal Feminine), Nature, and life itself.

The vertical straight line is the antithesis of the circle. It is separated off from the whole, it declares itself independent where it sinks to the depths (feminine) and rises to the heights (masculine). It is upright, alert, and active in its directional striving. It forever goes in opposite directions and is never fulfilled or at rest. It is active in time, with an aggressive character.

The horizontal line stretches out into its surroundings and ranges within the widths of space as a dreamlike, sentient, or feeling gesture. As the vertical has to do with timely growth forces and the plant kingdom, the horizontal is associated with movement through space and the animal.

When the vertical and horizontal combine, the cross of humanity is formed (fig. 136). This intersection of the directional streams—up and down, left and right—creates a focusing of energy into a single crossing point. Time and space meet. Every point is the center of an invisible circle. However, the cross in itself is only straight lines and right angles. The intersecting elements of the cross create a form in which wakened consciousness, pain, and death come about. The cross declares itself broken and fragmented as it divides and conquers space. To the Egyptians the hieroglyphic symbol of the cross meant destruction and revenge.[28] Yet it is also a symbol for the human being with outstretched arms taking a stand within the four directions.[29]

This powerful, masculine form of the cross is united with the feminine principle of the circle in the images of many primal and prehistoric cultures throughout the world (see Chapter V). It reappears in the Christian era as the Celtic high cross or the Irish sun cross (fig. 137). The circle and cross form is more than a convenient symbol for Celtic Christianity, as it speaks in the living language of mystery imagery of the unity of matter and spirit within the four kingdoms of nature. It depicts the incarnation and sacrifice of consciousness, the Logos, within the being of the universe. Graphically related to the Egyptian ankh, the sign of incarnated life, the sun cross is for the Celtic Christian a picture of the sun being, Christ, incarnating into earthly substance for the redemption of matter.

The sun-cross (fig. 138) is set upright in a meadow like the menhirs of the old religion. The horizontal crossbeam shows that the spiritual striving of the vertical is weighed down by earthly gravity and the cross it forms leads to man's inevitable fate—death. However, the crossing point or sun center symbolizes individual passage through death, surrounded by the solar ring of cosmic life.

One of the most striking aspects of the sun-cross is that it has carved on its surface braided linear designs and interwoven patterns. Though such forms are also found in other cultures in other eras, this meticulous interlacing of line and form reaches a particularly high degree of articulation in the stone high crosses and the illuminated manuscripts of Celtic Christianity (fig. 105). They signify the vital, streaming breath of life, the creative spirit power that weaves together the entire fabric of the universe. It turns the dead image of the cross into the thriving picture of the Tree of Life, from which spiritual rejuvenation flows. The sun cross in Celtic art does not depict the crucifixion, a theme that appears only after 600 A.D., but it represents the resurrection, the triumph of life and spirit over death and matter. It is a continuation of the *axis mundi* of the pre-Christian era brought into a new age.

Braided pattern has a pre-Christian origin, but its introduction to high crosses required a refinement in stone-carving technique. By the eighth century the carved patterns reached a high degree of articulation and then gradually declined into decorative motifs, losing their mythic significance as the potency of early Christian spiritual experience faded and church doctrine gained ground. Streit indicates four basic pattern types consistent with the four realms of nature (fig. 139):

1. Mineral: geometric forms;
2. Plant: stem, leaf, and blossom shapes;
3. Animal: snake, dragon, wolf, and bird forms;
4. Human: bodies and heads[30]

It is not uncommon to find all four categories on one cross.

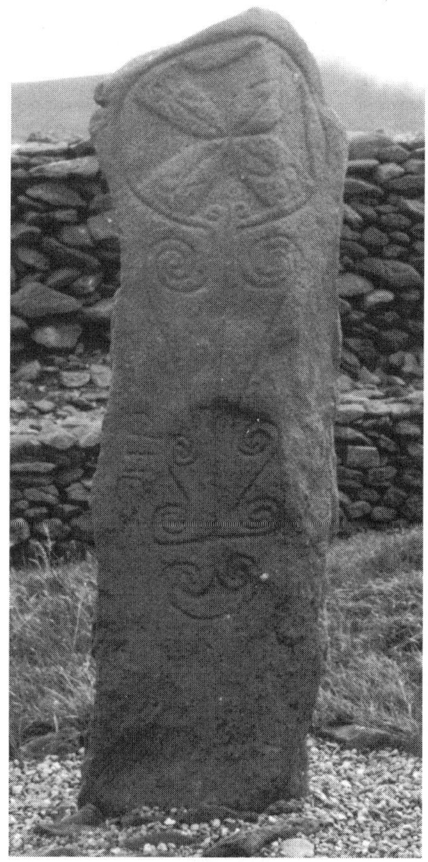

Fig. 137. The Irish sun cross is a picture of the unity of the universe and the incarnation of the macrocosmic principle within the microcosmic. The sun cross appears as a transformation of the menhir, as in this sunflower cross at Reask, Dingle Peninsula, Ireland.

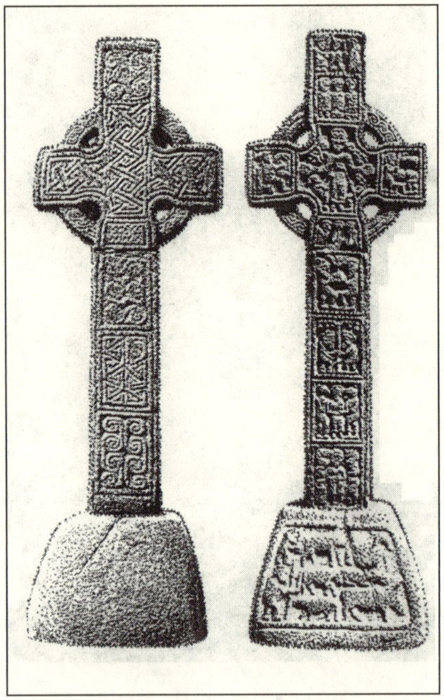

Fig. 138. The resurrection and the Tree of Life themes are central to the Celtic sun cross, but the crucifixion does not appear in art until the second half of the first millennium A.D. The South Cross of Casteldermat, c. 800 A.D., has a distinctive alternating pattern of angular and curvilinear forms on its eastern face (above left). Carvings on its western face (above right) depict representations of Old and New Testament stories, including Adam and Eve, St. Anthony and St. Paul in the wilderness, St. Anthony's temptation, the three Israelites in the fiery furnace, Abraham and Isaac, David playing the harp, the adoration of the Magi, and the massacre of the innocents. The resurrected Christ, as opposed to the crucified Christ, appears in the center of the cross.

One of the exceptional high crosses of County Kildare, Ireland, is the South Cross of Casteldermot that dates to about 800 A.D. On its east face are alternating angular and curvilinear patterns within rectangular partitions. The field of woven pattern transforms the cross of death into a living, flowing Staff of Life. On its west face are figurative representations from the Old and New Testaments (fig. 138). Adam and Eve succumbing to the temptation of the Tree of Knowledge are depicted at the center of the cross's shaft. Immediately above and below are scenes of Anthony and Paul receiving food from the raven, and St. Anthony's Temptation, respectively. Above and below these pictures are Old Testament trial scenes of the three men in the furnace and Daniel in the lion's den. In the center of the cross, surrounded by the sun's aureole, is the risen Christ, with Abraham about to sacrifice Isaac, on his left—images of New and Old Testament sacrifice. On his right, David plays the harp and sings hymns of creation. Above the head of Christ are the three magi from the east who visited the birth of Jesus, and above them is a scene of the massacre of the innocent children by order of Herod—the first Christian sacrifice. The Castledermot high cross rests on a base that is carved only on its west face. It illustrates a hunting scene where two men with weapons pursue six different animals. Notice how the central figure of Christ, although on the cross, is not the dead "crucified one," but the living "resurrected one."

Pictorial scenes such as these eventually replaced the earlier braided designs on high crosses. The scenes were used in connection with instructing the people in the mysteries of Christianity, and in this way the cross was a teaching tool for converting the Celtic peoples to the new religion. In Ireland, Christianity spread without bloodshed due in no small part to the effective working of spirit and art (see Appendix 3).

We believe and worship the true sun, Christ, who will never set.
—Confessions of Patrick

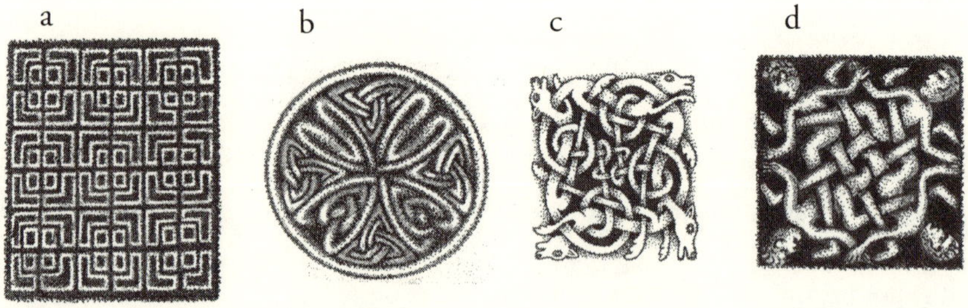

Fig. 139. The four pattern types used on Irish stone crosses, represent the four kingdoms of nature: (a) mineral, (b) plant, (c) animal, and (d) human.

Notes

1. Steiner, R. *Mystery Centers,* p. 72.
2. Ibid., pp. 67–73.
3. The oak was considered sacred to the Celts. Pliny describes in some detail a druid ceremony that centers on "observing the growth of mistletoe on an oak tree. . . . The time chosen for the subsequent rite was the sixth day of the moon, and preparations were made for a feast and a sacrifice of two white bulls." Piggott, S. *The Druids,* p. 110.
4. Grosse, R. *Ein Rätsel keltischer Kunst,* pp. 41, 70.
5. Streit cites the poet Strabo: "Among the Gallic peoples, generally speaking, there are three sets of men who are held in exceptional honor: the Bards, the Vates, and the Druids." Strabo, *Geographica,* Bk. IV, Vol. 4.
6. Greatly impressed by the Celts, Julius Caesar wrote: "Report says that in the schools of the Druids they learn by heart a great number of verses, and therefore some persons remain twenty years under training"; *De Bello Gallico,* VI, 14. Cited in Streit, p. 26.
7. Rees, A. & B. *Celtic Heritage.* The earliest fragments of Irish law, written down in the sixth century, are in verse form. It is noteworthy that the musical arts of rhyme and rhythmic repetition were an essential form of communication in prehistoric Ireland.
8. The bards were a distinct order unto themselves and they had three aims: the reform of morals and customs, the maintenance of peace, and the glorification of all good and beautiful things. The bards had tremendous authority and power over the entire country. According to Eugen Kolisko, the bards possessed a complete wisdom of their own which was communicated through wise sayings concerning various domains of life. This bardic wisdom, always having three aspects, was called "Triads." For instance, there were three branches of knowledge—wisdom concerning God, wisdom concerning one's fellowmen, and wisdom concerning oneself. There were three main features of wisdom—love, truth, and courage; three signs of the upright individual—silent lips, open eyes, and fearless bearing. Three principle things to be observed in poetic descriptions were imagery, awakening of sympathy, and sharp characterization, and the three principle parts of goodness were wisdom, strength, and love. "When we observe their content we realize how they have arisen from a deep understanding of human nature as body, as soul, and as spirit. On the one hand they are truly artistic, scientific, and penetrating views of the human being in its threefold nature and, on the other hand, harmonious triads of musical poetic art, the basis for deep religious experience." Kolisko, E. "Music and the Art of Healing Among the Druids and Bards," *The Present Age,* Vol. 1, No. 7, June 1936.
9. Steiner, R. *Anthroposophy,* Vol. 4, No. 3. Cited in Merry, E. *The Flaming Door,* pp. 136–37.
10. Hyperborea was an important early mystery center. It was also the name of a mythical region in the north where, according to the Greeks, Apollo retired each year during the winter season. Kutzli, R. *Langobardische Kunst,* p. 60–61. See also Lievegoed, B., *Mystery Streams in Europe and the New Mysteries,* p. 39.
11. Cowan, T. *Fire in the Head,* p. 67.
12. Powell, T.G.E., *The Celts,* pp. 154–55. Gimbutas also points out, "In the grand megalithic tomb-shrine of Newgrange, Ireland, the repetition of threes is striking; three-sided cells; three stone basins; engravings of triple snake spirals . . . and three cartouches (an oblong figure enclosing symbols) each with three cup marks. . . , James Mellaart remarks on the frequency with which objects are found in groups of three in the shrines at Çatal Hüyük. For example, there were three bull's heads . . . three horn cores on a bench . . . and three rows of triangles . . . [in shrines]. The importance of the number three is also visible in Maltese temples, the earliest of which were trefoil in shape. . . .Triple shrines and triple columns are common in Minoan culture." Gimbutas, M. *Language of the Goddess,* p. 97. Eleanor Merry says, "Working out of the prevalent idea of a threefold structure and life of the world, the Druids distinguished the opposition in plant life, of the hardening and 'salt' processes in the roots, as against the sublimation or burning—the 'sulphur' processes—in the blossoms; and the 'mercurial' element—that is, a rhythmic upbuilding of substance, the flowing of saps, in the balanced structure of stem and leaves." Merry, E. *The Flaming Door,* p. 180.
13. Powell, T.G.E. *The Celts,* p. 86.
14. Cooke, I. *Journey to the Stones,* p. 11.
15. Pogacnik, M. *Nature Spirits and Elemental Beings,* p. 9.
16. Streit, J. *Sun and Cross,* p. 13. "This symbol of a Mountain, a Tree or a Column situated at the Center of the World is extremely widely distributed." Eliade, M., *Images and Symbols: Studies in Religious Symbolism,* p. 42. John Matthews observes that the standing stone or the "pillar at the center of the world . . . the great trees which upheld the sky; these are all common factors in the cosmological myths of the Celts. They would have been very much part of the shaman's stock, the universal maps which enabled him to describe the indescribable and to find his way to the unreachable realms to hold

converse with the spirits." Matthews, J. *Taliesin: Shamanism and the Bardic Mysteries in Britain and Ireland,* p. 246.

17. Steiner, R. *The Sun-Initiation of the Druid Priest and His Moon-Science,* p. 68.

18. Devereux, P. *Places of Power, Secret Energies at Ancient Sites: A Guide to Observed or Measured Phenomena,* p. 150.

19. Krupp, E. *In Search of Ancient Astronomies.* "Stonehenge was apparently used for a number of purposes simultaneously—as a sacred ceremonial centre, a priestly observatory, a measuring device for the calculation of accurate calendars, a burial monument, and as a container or transmitter of powerful earth energies. The purposes attributed to it vary according to the bias of those who have studied it, but it seems clear that these many purposes were integral to its functioning." Mann, A.T. *Sacred Architecture,* p. 66.

20. Cited in Streit, p. 23.

21. Hartmann, H. *Der Totenkult in Irland,* p. 136.

22. Eliade, M. *Shamanism: Archaic Techniques of Ecstasy,* p. 52.

23. Brennan, M. *The Stars and the Stones: Ancient Art and Astronomy in Ireland,* p. 73.

24. Cowan muses about the purpose of these sun chambers or Hollowed Hills in regard to folk traditions about elemental beings. He suggests that, as faery mounds, "they are places where humans could meet the faery folk and taste the riches of the immortal worlds that lie beneath the landscape of ordinary consciousness." Cowan, T. *Fire in the Head,* p. 122. "Now, when the Druid-priest entered this burying place—like other old cult sanctuaries, the cromlechs [tumuli] were mostly erected over graves—he set up this arrangement which in a certain way was impervious to the physical sun-rays; but the spiritual activities of the sun penetrated it, and the Druid-priests were specially trained to perceive this. So he looked through these stones—they were always specially selected—into the chamber where the spiritual activity of the sun penetrated, but from which the physical effect was excluded. His vision had been finely schooled, for what can be seen in a primitive darkroom of that sort varies according to the date, whether February, July, August, or December. In July it is lightly tinged with yellow; in December it radiates a faintly bluish shade from within. And one capable of observing this beholds the whole cycle of the seasons in the psycho-spiritual activity of the sun's radiance." Steiner, R., *Michaelmas and the Soul Forces of Man,* p. 41.

25. "Individual megalithic sites were placed over a point where the main lines of energy flowed through the earth and to where these 'currents' converged before flowing out again. This energy is the vital fertilizing force which flows through the ground and is closely associated with water courses and magnetic activity beneath the surface. It affects the nerve cells of animals and humans as well as the germination and growth of plants. . . . The whole purpose of this system [of megalithic monuments]—the art of living in harmony with nature and of being 'in the right place at the right time'—was to harness the basic natural forces for the maximum benefit to society so that the tribe might continue a healthy, satisfied life into the next generation and beyond." Cooke, I. *Journey to the Stones,* p. 130. "Dolmens included quartz in their mineral composition. Quartz is a hard, crystalline, vitreous mineral composed of silicon dioxide. It is found worldwide in sandstone, granite, flint, opal, chert, and rock crystal. In electronic circuits, quartz is a commonly used frequency-control, due to the fact that its dimensions determine the frequency to which it responds." Zink, D. *The Ancient Stones Speak,* p. 180.

26. Diodorus Siculus, in the first century B.C, wrote that "the Celts hold the doctrine of Pythagoras that the souls of men are immortal and that after a predetermined number of years the soul returns again to life, and enters another body." Streit, *Sun and Cross,* p. 60. "That the druids had views on the nature of an afterlife is nothing remarkable in face of the great weight of archaeological evidence, from Celtic graves, showing the solicitude for a continued existence in providing weapons, ornaments and food, for the journey, if not for the feast at the other end." Powell, T.G.E., p. 184.

27. "The piled-up signs seem to say that the creativity of the Goddess is inexhaustible and comes from the cosmic deep . . . a symbol of rising generative force." Gimbutas, *Language of the Goddess,* p. 225. "The human being still experienced the stream of formative life forces in the body and how they resounded together with cosmic forces, and they formed these inner experiences with full living breath and tonality into stone carvings such as on the dolmens at Gavrinis." Roggenkamp, W. and H. Gerbert, *Bewegung und Form in der Graphik Rudolf Steiners,* pp. 14–15.

28. Verstockt, M. *The Genesis of Form,* p. 71.

29. Steiner, R. *Ancient Myths,* p. 30.

30. Streit, J. *Sun and Cross,* pp. 125–26.

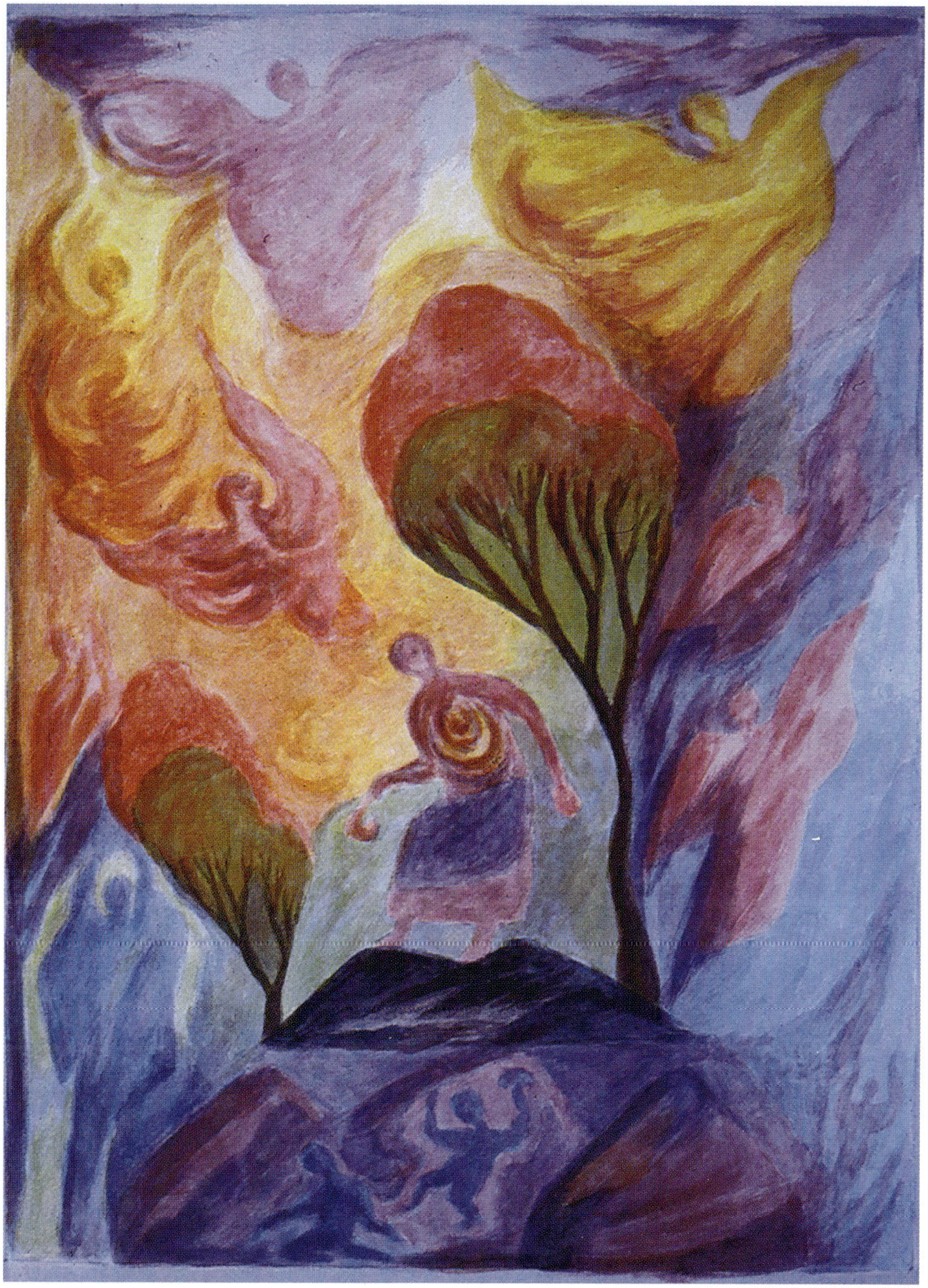

Color Plate 1. The Gardener by Gerard Wagner (1996) demonstrates that even "after the death of art" painting continues to live.

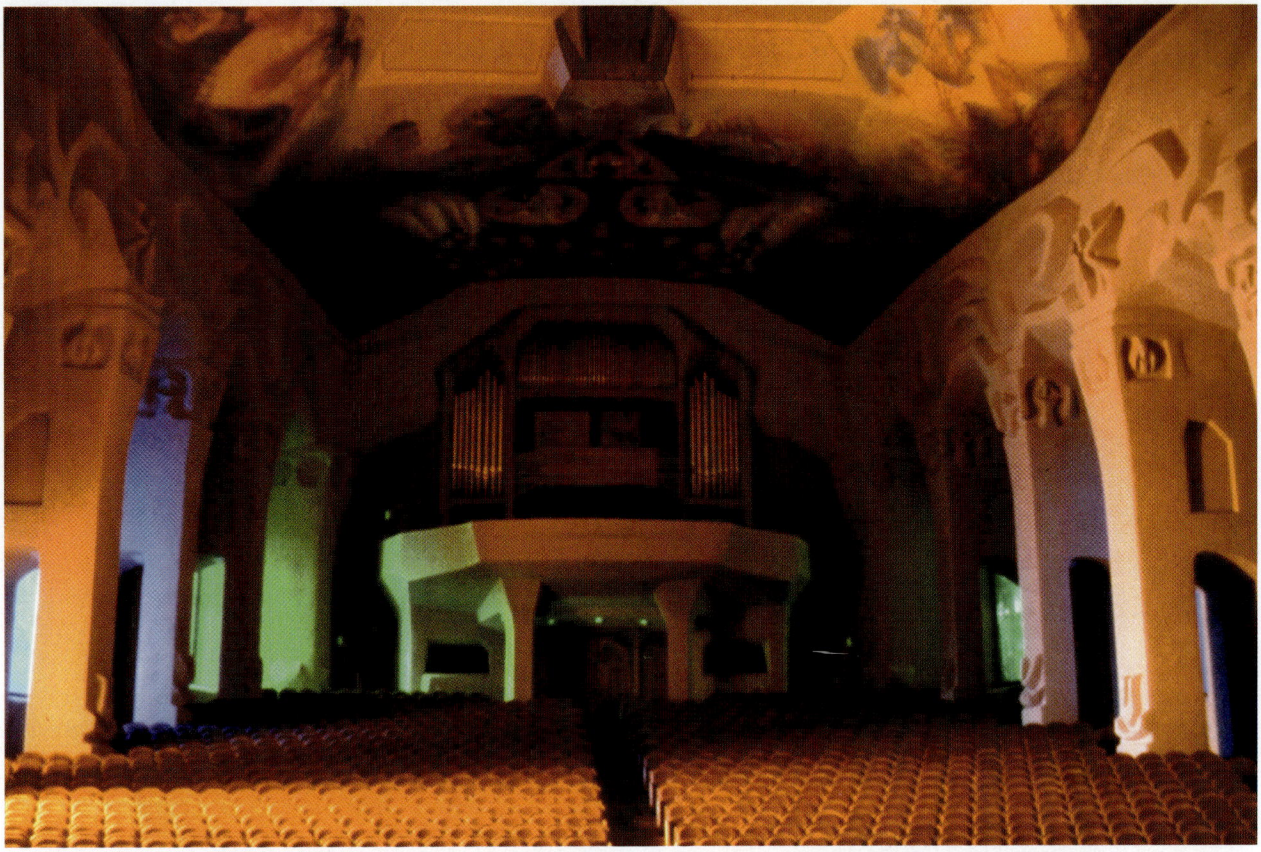

Color Plate 2. The interior of the second Goetheanum includes an auditorium that was completed in 1998. Viewing the Great Hall from the stage area, one observes sculpted concrete columns with carved architrave, vividly painted ceiling murals, and engraved, colored-glass windows, all in tribute to the Spirit of the Time. (Copyright © Thorwald Thiersch.)

Color Plate 3. Rembrandt's *Evangelist Matthew,* 1661, demonstrates the artist's brilliant use of light and darkness, from the subtle touch of light upon the evangelist's shoulder to the radiance of inner sight on Matthew's face and the reflected illumination on the pages of his holy book. (Photo copyright © Ursula Held.)

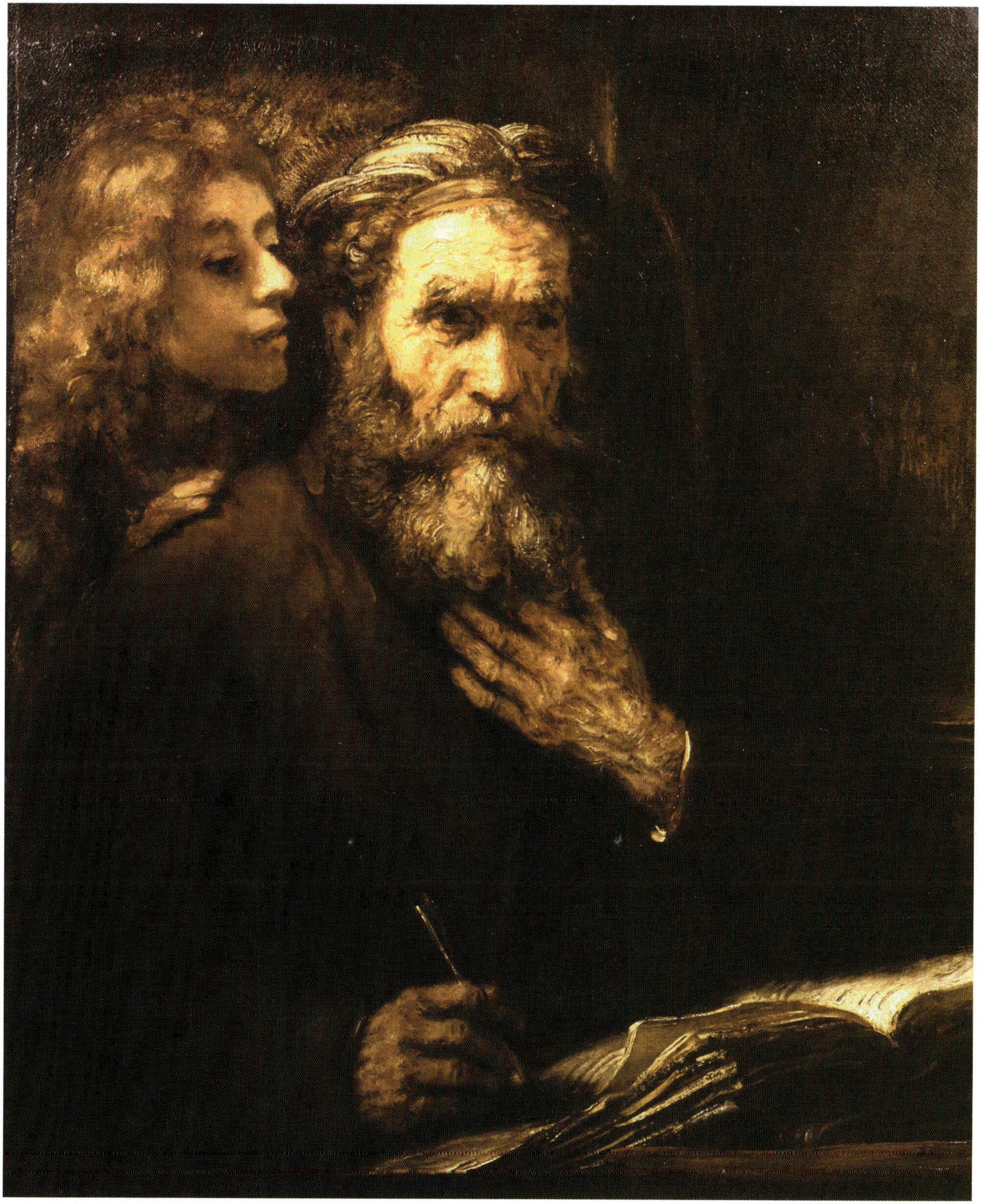

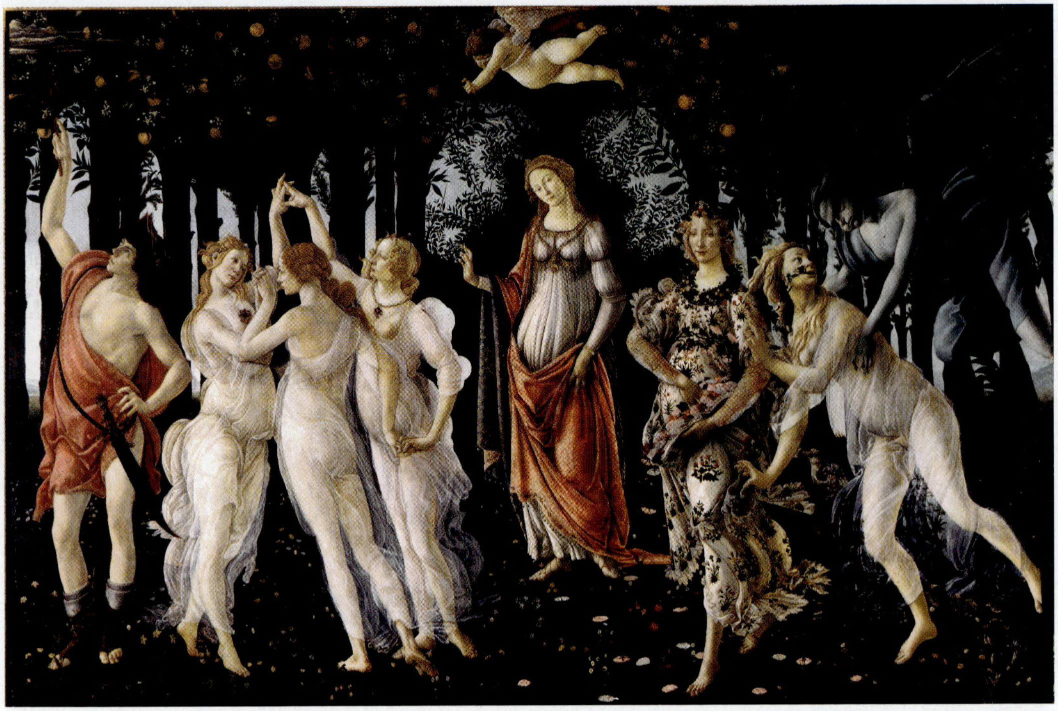

Color Plate 4. The Primavera by Sandro Botticelli is an allegory, not only of spring, but of life, love, and human transformation. (Uffizi, Florence.)

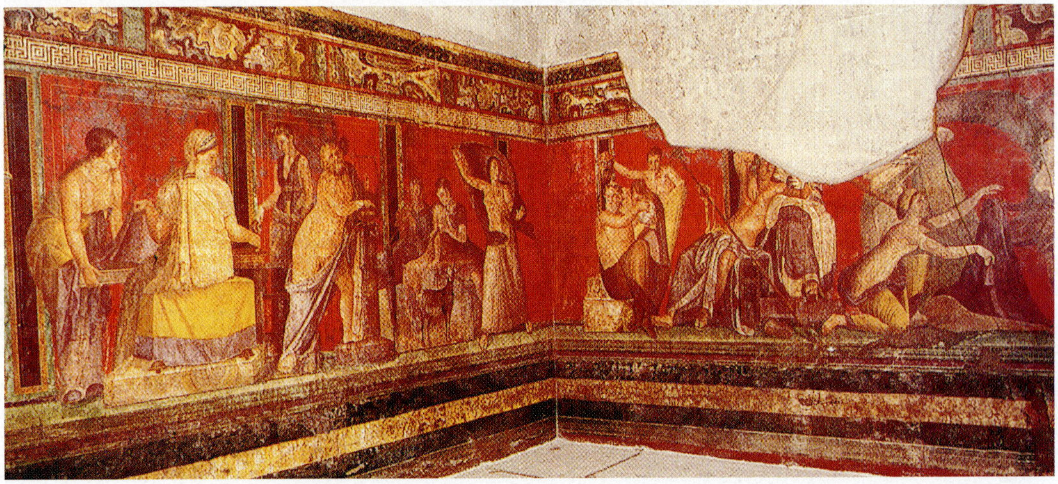

Color plate 5. The Villa of the Mysteries in Pompeii houses a series of fresco paintings depicting scenes believed to be associated with initiation into a women's Orphic mystery cult.

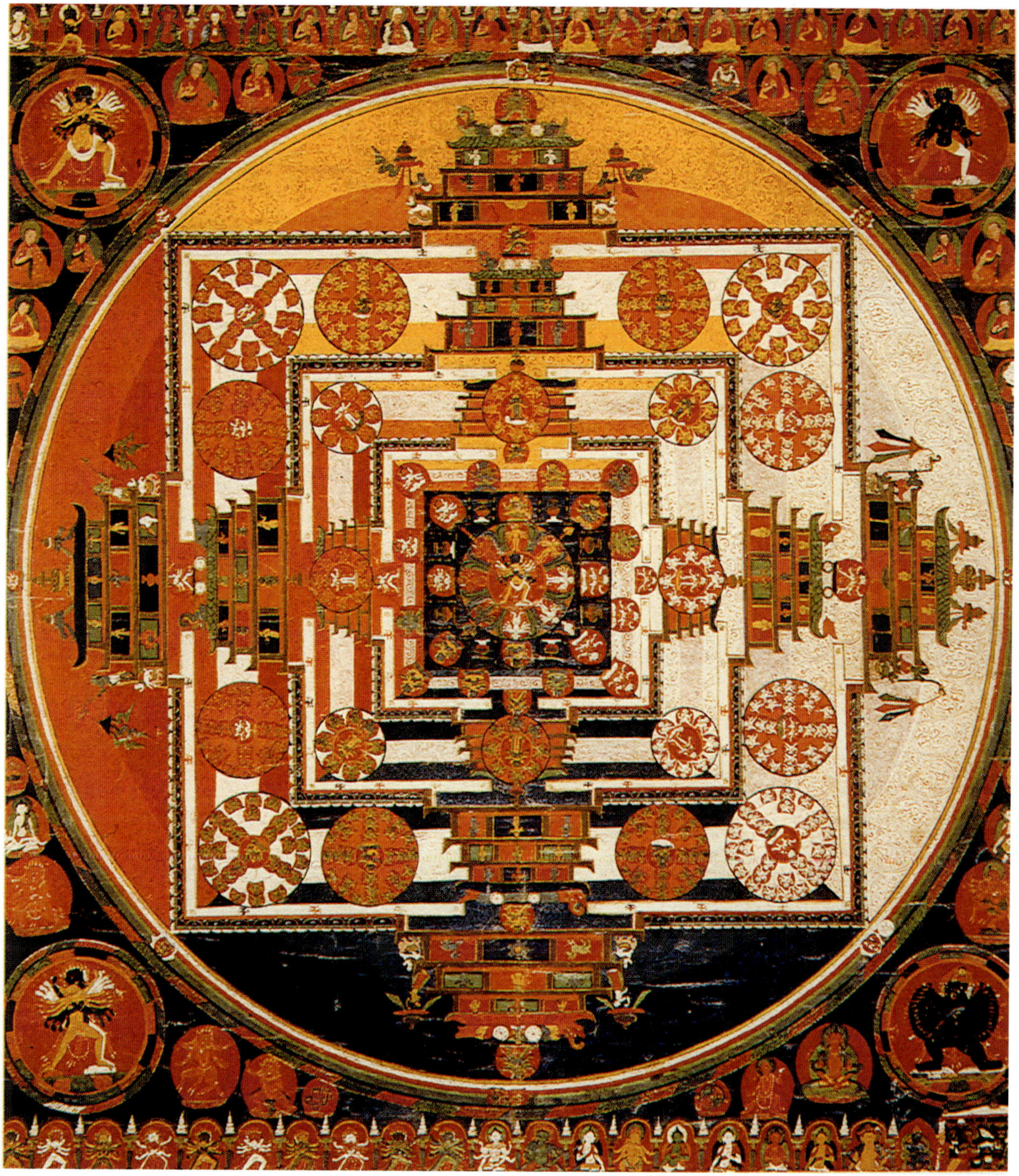

Color plate 6. Kalachakra Mandala

PART TWO

FROM EAST TO WEST

Approach a great painting as thou wouldst approach a great prince.
—Kobori Enshiu

Inspiration and aspiration are not exclusive alternatives, but one and the same; because the spirit to which both words refer cannot work in the man except to the extent that he is "in the spirit."
—Ananda K. Coomaraswamy

The subtlest of subtleties, this is the gateway to all mysteries.
—Lao Tzu

V. MYSTERY IMAGES

The lines and forms are visible signs of divine gestures. Learn to understand them and you will comprehend how God created the universe.
—Filippo Brunelleschi

Giorgio Vasari, painter and biographer of Italian Renaissance artists, describes how, at the beginning of the fourteenth century, Pope Benedict IX sent one of his courtiers to Tuscany in search of the most talented artist of the day. The courtier solicited drawings for the Pope's consideration from the finest artists in Siena and Florence, including the Florentine artist Giotto. The commission for mural paintings in Rome was explained to Giotto and he was asked for a sample of his work. At this the artist took a sheet of paper and a brush dipped in red paint, pressed his arm against his side, and with a turn of his hand drew in one stroke a perfect circle. Then, with a smile, he said to the Pope's representative, "There is your drawing." The courtier, expecting a more finished illustration exclaimed, "Is this the only drawing I'm to have?" Giotto warmly replied, "It is more than enough. Send it along with the others and you'll see whether it is understood or not." The Pope's messenger, convinced he was being made a fool of, returned to the Vatican with his collection of pictures. When Benedict IX was reviewing the artwork, his eye fell upon Giotto's drawing and it was explained how, without the use of a compass, the artist precisely drew the circle. The Pope, realizing that this was the sign of a master, awarded Giotto the commission to paint five scenes from the life of Christ in the apse of the old St. Peter's in Rome.[1]

Giotto's circle is more than an entertaining story, for it points to the important connection between the spirit and art. Similar stories concerning the drawing of a circle as a sign of genius and perfect simplicity are attributed to Leonardo da Vinci and Albrecht Dürer. These tales can lead us to ask the question: what is this visual language we call art and what is the spiritual significance of image and symbol?

V.1 Image and Symbol

The symbol points back to the world of form-making forces, out of which the earth has arisen; out of the world of pre-birth, from which the human being incarnates on to the earth.
—Hildegard Gerbert

Some of the earliest artistic records are the abstract, purely geometric symbols and signs carved in rock (fig. 3), etched in clay, and painted on stone and pottery. In the Paleolithic painted caves, symbols are three times more numerous than animal and human depictions. Such images were reserved for use by those who understood their esoteric meaning and purpose. In prehistoric cultures, it was the initiates—priests, shamans, healers, tribal chiefs, artists, and expert craftsmen—who were the custodians of sacred forms within society. They carried out the cultic display of these signs.[2]

For early humanity these signs and symbols, together with most art and images, had spiritual meaning and significance and at the same time expressed incredibly precise details. Eliade describes how in certain traditional cultures a jade bracelet made of a specific number of specially shaped and particularly colored stones "indicates that the girl wearing it belongs to a family that came from the North, that her father is an administrator, that she has three sisters, that she will be engaged in March, that she likes a certain genre of poetry."[3] But beyond the quantitative information provided, every sign, every picture, every gesture was filled with mana or spiritual power. To primal consciousness, value-free phenomena were rare. Decoration for the sake of mere ornamentation appears only later, usually as a manifestation of decadence. In prehistoric times art was a vital and living expression of the pulsing universal energy brought into form and substance, slowed down and made visible. The underlying forces and growth patterns of all living things; the dynamic forces active within the elemental kingdoms of earth (solid), water (liquid), air (gaseous), and fire (warmth and light); the immediate gestures and ongoing deeds of supersensory beings—all these creative, formative qualities that primal humanity experienced as living spirit were seen as the progenitors of material objects and forms. It is these primal forces that early artists recognized and pictured in image and symbol. Symbols preceded the actual depiction of figurative gods, but as depictions evolved, the symbols remained to represent the attributes of those gods (e.g., lightning, sun, and moon, the lotus, the bull, the stag; fig. 140).[4]

Proclus, a Neoplatonic philosopher of the fifth century A.D., describes what he experiences when contemplating *ars lineandi* ("art of the line"), the rhythmic linear designs such as Greek meander forms and braided patterns: "*Ars lineandi* is the recaptured memory of the invisible ideas of the soul, and this is its achievement: it gives life to its own cognition, awakens the spirit, purifies understanding, and brings the formative element, which is part of our being, to light. It eliminates the baseness and ignorance that clings to us from birth, and liberates us from the bondage of unreason. It rouses the soul from sleep and impels it toward the spirit. It makes us a true human being, allows us to behold the spirit and guides us towards the gods" (fig. 141).[5] If Proclus in his time could experience such linear forms as empowering one to become "a true human being," then one might imagine the spiritual power such line art had on prehistoric peoples who were far more open and impressionable.

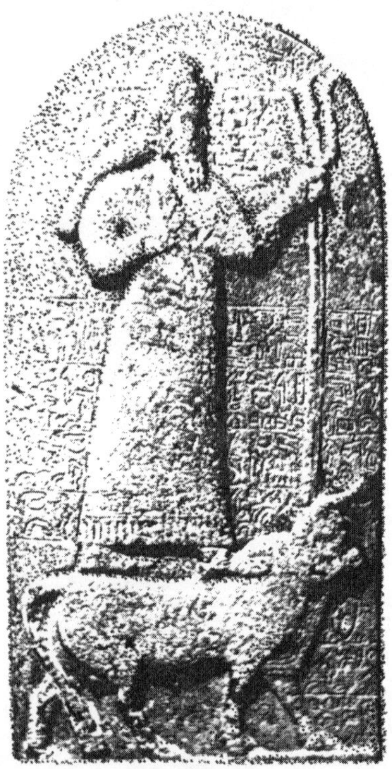

Fig. 140. Surrounded by his representative symbols and holding his trident and dagger, the Babylonian lightning god stands on a bull.

Images and symbols of this kind are some of the most powerful tools of cultic practice and mystery religions. They appear before the use of letter signs and written words, as they precede abstract concepts and formal ideas. It is likely that in earlier times the meaning of the symbol was not grasped by intellect, but through instinctual cognition and direct spiritual perception. The Greek word *symbolon* means "to join what is separated, to join together." The symbol, though often meaningless to the uninitiated, unites a sensory phenomenon with its corresponding supersensory reality by means of a picture. Mystery images and ritual symbols are important because of the cultic function they served in linking the sense world with the spirit world. It is quite clear today that the signs and symbols of prehistory are not meaningless scribbles but the most complex features of early artistic iconography.[6] As John Ruskin noted in the nineteenth century, "Form is a diagram of forces." At the same time these diagrams express a spirit-filled content. "One might even say that wisdom flows through the meaningfully guided line," says Rudolf Kutzli.[7]

In this sense, primal imagery is a key ingredient of ritual practice, esoteric instruction, and the procedures of initiation. It is presumably the first form of notation, the first setting down of what the adept calls the "cosmic script" or "sign language of the gods," comprehensible only to those initiated into the mysteries. As Hugo Rahner contends: "It lies in the very nature of the symbolic word [the symbolic image], and the symbolic action that a spiritual meaning can never be fully and exhaustively expressed in sensuous terms. The symbol always retains its mysterious background; it is a garment that reveals and at the same time masks the form. . . . Indeed, this quality of the symbol is needed to conceal the radiance of the transcendent and divulge it only to those who have eyes for it."[8] This kind of artistic activity is a threshold experience, an initiatory revelation that opens a doorway into the secret realm of creation, into the spirit.

Images and symbols are a fundamental expression of the spiritual in early art and they continue to play a significant role in the language of visual art today. They have the power to form our very future. Suzi Gablik maintains that "symbols are evocative; they are transformers and conductors of psychic energies; they have an integrating value and can evoke positive feelings. . . . We will determine which future we create by the views and images we hold now. If art has a social function, it is, perhaps, to show humanity its optimal parameters."[9]

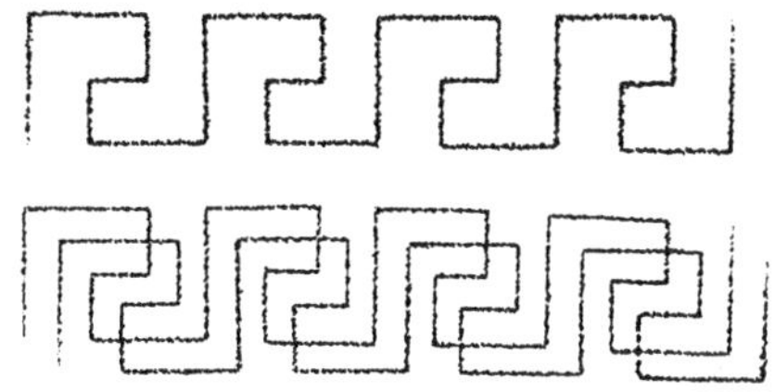

Fig. 141. The Greek meander, or Greek key, and similar rhythmic patterns were described by the Neoplatonic philosopher Proclus as "the invisible ideas of the soul."

V.2 Asian Art

Asiatic art is ideal in the mathematical sense: like Nature, not in appearance, but in operation.
—Ananda K. Coomaraswamy

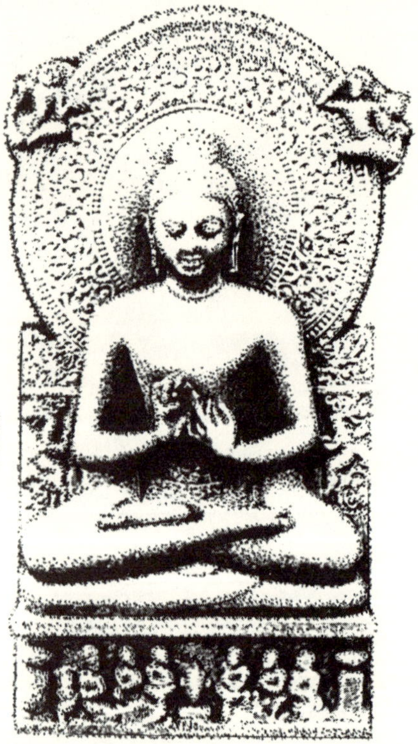

Fig. 142. This rendering of a fifth-century A.D. sandstone stele from Samath, India, depicts Buddha in the Dharmachakra-mudra, or teaching position.

It was prophesied that Gautama Siddhartha, born in the foothills of the Himalayas, was one of the great Bodhisattvas and would attain enlightenment in this, his final earthly incarnation. His father, wishing his son to remain with the world, protected him from all but the princely pleasures of palace life. Nevertheless signs appeared to the sensitive and highly intuitive young man. The first came when he beheld an aged man. The second occurred when he saw a sick person, the third when he encountered a corpse, and the final sign when he met a sage who had renounced the world as an ascetic. It became clear to the prince through these four mysteries of life that he must change his own life, pursue knowledge of higher worlds, and fulfill his own destiny. He left the luxury of the palace, as well as his wife and child, to wander in self-denial and poverty for six years, at the end of which he realized that a path of self-chastisement would not of itself lead to truth. He then sat in meditation under the sacred bo or bodhi tree, determined not to move until he had attained enlightenment. He dispelled the three temptations of the demon Mara, freeing himself from all earthly desire and thereby finding enlightenment. It was in this way that Buddha established the Middle Way: the avoidance of both extreme self-denial and uncontrolled satisfaction of desires. This and the Eightfold Path were the basis of Buddha's teaching of *dharma,* "saving the truth." The Eightfold Path consists of right thought, right judgment, right word, right action, right standpoint, right practice, right memory, and right examination. This Buddha taught with compassion by means of his resolve, his speech, and his actions, gaining many followers. When he died at age eighty, it was no longer necessary for him to be reborn in an earthly body. He was now free to work upon humanity from the spiritual world without need for further earthly lives.

The image of Buddha in meditation or in the teaching position of the yogi is an archetypal image of the East. It is a familiar image even to Westerners. We see the Buddha in a posture of repose and withdrawal, of gathering in and focusing energy. It is a picture that possesses both strength and compassion; it is inwardly alert, yet entirely at peace (fig. 142). The legs are crossed and folded together with the soles of the feet turned upwards, directed to the heavens, cut off from the earth. When the right foot is shown in front of and resting on the left thigh, it usually indicates the image belongs to an esoteric sect. When the left foot is shown in front of and on the right thigh it usually indicates a nonesoteric sect. Eyelids are often half-closed, suggesting deep introspection and inner vision. Outer action is stilled as inner activity shines through the radiant features of the enlightened one's face. The overall form-gesture is rounded, yet upright, buoyant, and stable; a triangular composition is formed.

Like that of the yogi, his body is well-disciplined through sacred exercises and perfect breathing. "Buddha light" radiates around the head and body, symbolic of great wisdom. Such aureoles or halos, which indicate the subtle fields or spiritual members, show rays and flamelike forms. The circular representation of halos seems to occur spontaneously at about the same time in the art of India, Iran, and Greece, most notably in depictions of Buddha, Mithras, and Helios. However, early Hindu depictions of the *naga* serpent show a hoodlike aura that is also suggestive of the aureole (fig. 302).

Buddhist scriptures indicate thirty-two major signs of the Buddha and eighty minor signs. Only a few of these can appear in any given image, and some have become standardized with time (fig. 143). The head of Buddha displays some of these features—long earlobes, distended from wearing heavy jewelry. This is an Indian mark of nobility and an esoteric sign of powerful will. The topknot, so characteristic of the Buddha image, is also a sign of princely stature. It is seen as a receptacle of supersensible power and wisdom, and in Thailand can sometimes be seen as a lotus bud or flame. Buddha's short locks are depicted in "snail-shell" spirals, curling to the right. The *urna,* which appears between the eyes of Buddha, is a white curl of hair or a small crystal symbolizing wisdom. It was viewed as different from Shiva's "third eye" until later Tantric Buddhism assimilated the latter. Another of the thirty-two favorable marks of the Buddha is a gold-colored body. According to the *Sutra of Cause and Effect, Past and Present,* "The Buddha's golden hue is marvelous, ethereal."

Buddha displays hand gestures or mudras specific to the nature of his task. The Dhyana-mudra of folded or overlapping hands, palms upward on the lap, shows yogic meditative concentration (fig. 144). The Bhumisparsha-mudra shows Gautama as he reaches Buddhahood and touches the ground with the fingertips of his right hand as a call for the earth's acknowledgment of the deed. The Dharmachakra-mudra is shown by the thumb and forefinger of both hands each forming a circle in imitation of the motion of a wheel. This is a gesture used

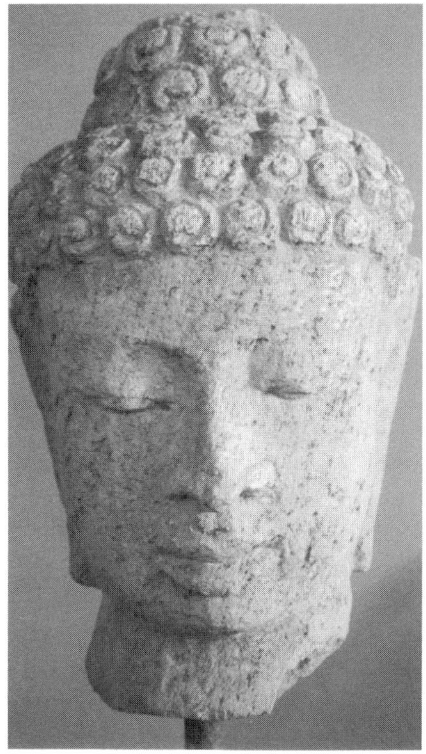

Fig. 143. Any given image of the Buddha shows only a few of the thirty-two "favorable marks." The topknot and the peaceful eyes are two such marks.

when Buddha teaches the Dharma, "turning the Wheel of the Law." His hands are held at the level of the heart with the two circles formed by the thumbs and forefingers touching each other. The Namaskara-mudra is indicated when both hands are clasped together, fingers upward. This is a gesture of blessing, welcoming, and homage. The right hand raised with palm outward and the left hand held with the palm upward is the Abhaya-mudra of protection and assurance. In Thailand, sometimes both hands are raised. These mudras and others are connected with the Buddha image but find their origin in ancient Hindu tradition.

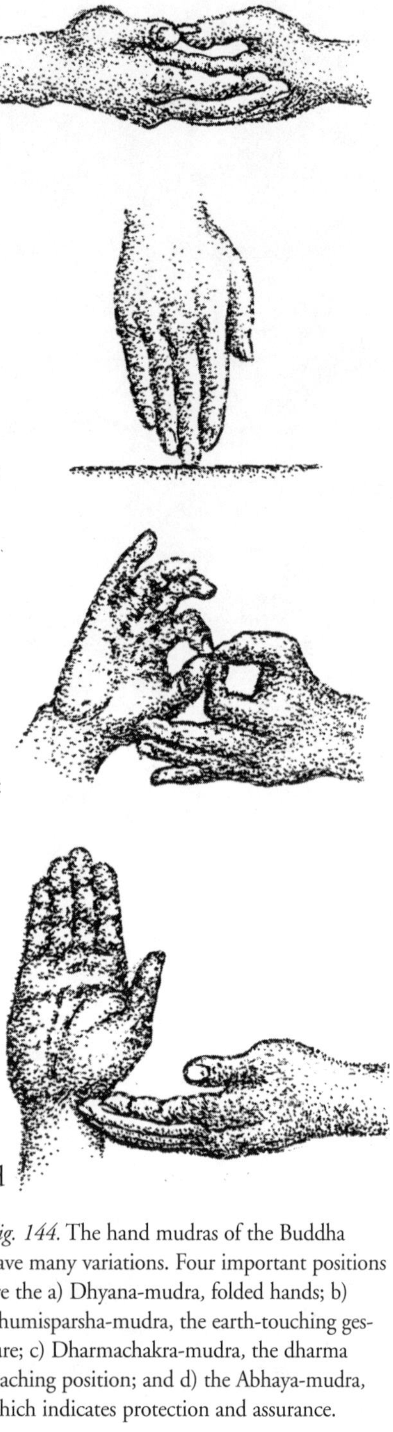

a b c d

Fig. 144. The hand mudras of the Buddha have many variations. Four important positions are the a) Dhyana-mudra, folded hands; b) Bhumisparsha-mudra, the earth-touching gesture; c) Dharmachakra-mudra, the dharma teaching position; and d) the Abhaya-mudra, which indicates protection and assurance.

Southeast Asia

> *Toward it [the image] the devotee has the most intense attachment, for he rit ually touches with his gaze the part of the image on which he concentrates, affecting a magic transfer of his living self, whereby he is one with the deity. Man becomes what he worships.*
>
> —Stella Kramrisch

The sitting posture that is singularly identified with Buddha is frequently seen in early Asian art and predates Buddhism. Hinduism, one of the oldest religions in the world, often portrayed its gods in the cross-legged or lotus sitting position. One figure in particular that assumes this gesture is the goddess Lotus herself, the ageless Mother Earth, personification of procreative energy and good fortune on the physical plane. Over many centuries she is transformed from the Hindu goddess into Prajna-Paramita, the most divine feminine figure in Mahayana Buddhism. She might be seen as the equivalent of the Christian Sophia, for her name means "the culmination of Enlightening Wisdom." According to Heinrich Zimmer, "The wisdom (*prajna*) that leads to Nirvana is the highest virtue (*paramita*): it is the very essence of the Buddhas, the wholly enlightened ones, and the Buddha-in-the-making, the Bodhisattva. . . . Under the influence of mature Buddhist and late Hindu conceptions, the maternal goddess of earthly goods and happiness, of fertility and earthbound life, the wife-consort and embodied energy of the cosmic sleeper—Vishnu, dreamer of the world—has become the highest representative of world-transcending wakefulness, the most spiritual feminine symbol in all the iconographies of the East."[10]

A splendid sculptural image from thirteenth-century Java in Indonesia, shows Prajna-Paramita, as in most Indian renderings, in less than life-size statuary (fig. 145). Behind her ornate, flamelike crown, a plain oval halo expresses purity of spirit while the background is framed with flames, "radiating the spiritual energy of enlightenment."[11] Holding a lotus in her right hand, as another grows along her right arm, she presides as queen of wisdom in a spiritual realm attained only through enlightenment. The lotus pedestal, upon which she sits, was originally the special feature of her predecessor, the Hindu goddess Lotus. Over millennia the lotus becomes a familiar image associated with many supersensible deities in the Asian pantheon of gods and goddesses, but especially with Buddha and his female counterpart, Prajna-Paramita.

The lotus, like the lily—a monocot with flower petals in multiples of three —is a symbol of the harmony of creation and divine birth. In Tantrism, it is a symbol of the feminine principle, and the Satapatha Brahmana depicts the lotus leaf as a picture of the womb. According to Tajima Ryojun, "in esoteric Buddhism, the heart of the beings is like an unopened lotus; when the virtues of the Buddha develop therein, the lotus blossoms; this is why the Buddha sits on a lotus bloom."[12]

The threefold lotus motif is implicit in the Indian Sri Yantra mandala, a geometric design used in the support of meditation (fig. 146). A yantra is any device that "encompasses the doctrine." This one has a square outer form, made up of straight lines broken in a regular framework to express a sanctuary with four doors opening out to the four quarters. Landings stand before each entrance with low ramps or flights of steps leading to the raised platform and the circular inner sanctuary that contains an arrangement of concentric circles and stylized lotus petals. Enclosed within the center are nine interpenetrating triangles, four pointing upward and five pointing down. Those pointing downward are the female yoni or shakti principle and those pointing upward are the male lingam or "fire" principle, indicating the grander cosmic dualities that stand behind sexual division. The center of the yantra is the bindu, or essental drop, which is both the heart of the devotee and the seat of divinity. Through concentrated visualization on such a mandala form, the juxtaposition of opposing forces and the "logic-shattering paradox of eternity and time" are confronted.[13] It is a pattern for evoking the inner presence of god, an instrument for focusing one's spiritual experience. One assimilates the doctrine through meditative practice with such forms. As Robert Thurman points out: "The mandala idea originated long before historical Buddhism. In the earliest level of Indian or even Indo-European religion, in the Rig Veda and its associated literature, mandala is the term for a chapter, a collection of mantras or verse hymns chanted in Vedic ceremonies, perhaps coming from the sense of round, as in a round of songs. That the universe was believed to originate from the mantra hymns, whose sacred sounds contained the genetic patterns of beings and things, already shows a clear sense of mandala as world-model."[14]

In Sanskrit, *mandala* means any circle or round form, and can refer to the sun or moon. In early Vedic texts, *mandala* signifies a sacred enclosure, a place for the performance of certain rituals, and a point that contains an essence.

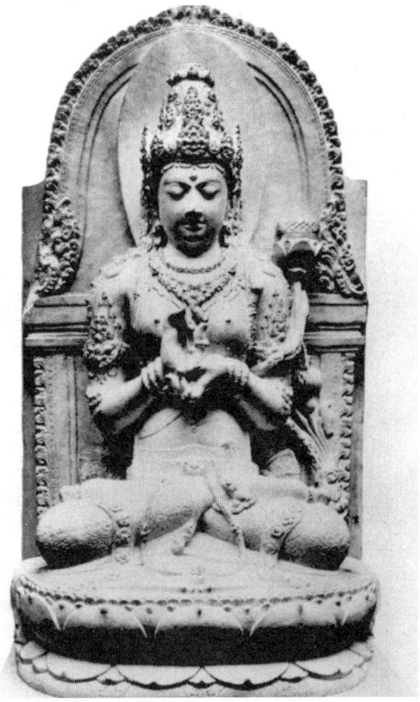

Fig. 145. Above: This thirteenth-century A.D. Javanese stele of Prajna-Paramita, "the Culmination of the Virtue of Enlightening Transcendental Wisdom," may be seen as the Asian equivalent of the divine Sophia.

Fig. 146. Below: The Sri Yantra mandala is a traditional sacred image used in connection with meditative practices and focused visualization. The square, circle, and triangle are its fundamental elements.

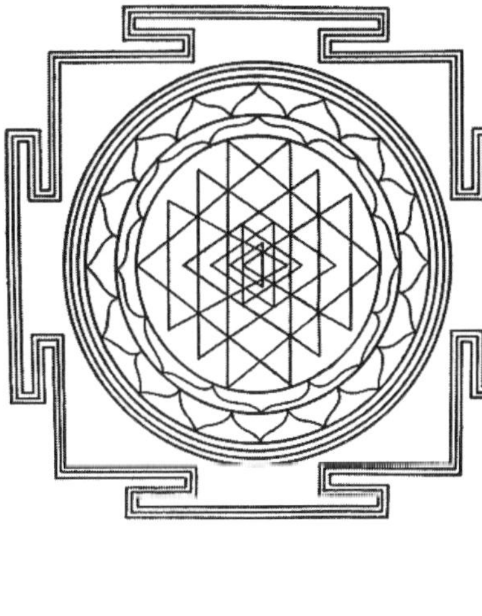

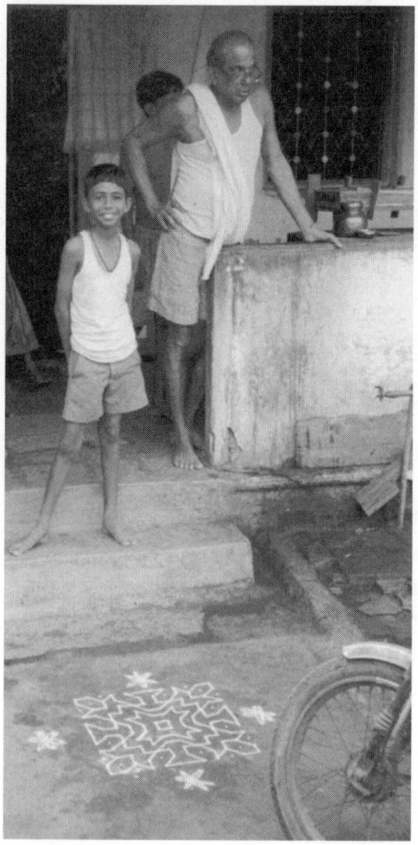

However broadly defined the mandala is a geometric design intended to symbolize the universe. Widely used in present-day India as *rangoli, kolam,* or *osa,* these ritual diagrams are used to invoke beneficial deities, expel evil spirits, and reconcile wandering souls (fig. 147). One finds them in Hindu and Buddhist tradition painted on fabric with pigments or fashioned on the earth with colored sand, rice paste, ground gems, metal, wood, or even butter. Interestingly, the mandala is conceived as three-dimensional architecture. The mandala assumes a tiered palace or temple plan with revered deities placed at various stations within the sacred form. In this sense it is the celestial city, the equivalent of the heavenly Jerusalem mentioned in Revelation, or Golonooza, William Blake's city of art. The royal city of Angkor Wat in Cambodia (fig. 148) and Kum Bum Chapel at the Gyangtse Monastery in Tibet are based on the mandala plan.

One of the most breathtaking examples of an architectural mandala is Borobudur in central Java (fig. 149). Described by noted researchers as nothing less than a symbolic representation of the universe, it was constructed under the Shailendra dynasty around A.D. 800 and is the largest Buddhist temple in the world, measuring over four hundred feet on each side, standing more than one hundred feet high. Its mandala pattern of earthly squares and heavenly circles, arranged in rising terraces, is a microcosmic picture of the Sacred Mountain and it is oriented to the four directions. Intended for circumambulation by pilgrims, following the sun's course, Borobudur consists of six square terraces, a "level of transfer," and three round terraces on top; ten levels in all, conforming to the stages of development in a Bodhisattva's path to becoming a Buddha.[15] (The ten levels of initiation are [1] joy; [2] freedom from defilement; [3] brightness; [4] enthusiasm; [5] invincibility; [6] showing one's face; [7] going far away; [8]

Fig. 147. Above: *Rangoli* is a linear art form practiced today in India to invoke good spirits and expel the bad. Drawn in sticky rice paste at the doorstep by the women of the household, *rangoli* is practiced by people of various religious persuasions.

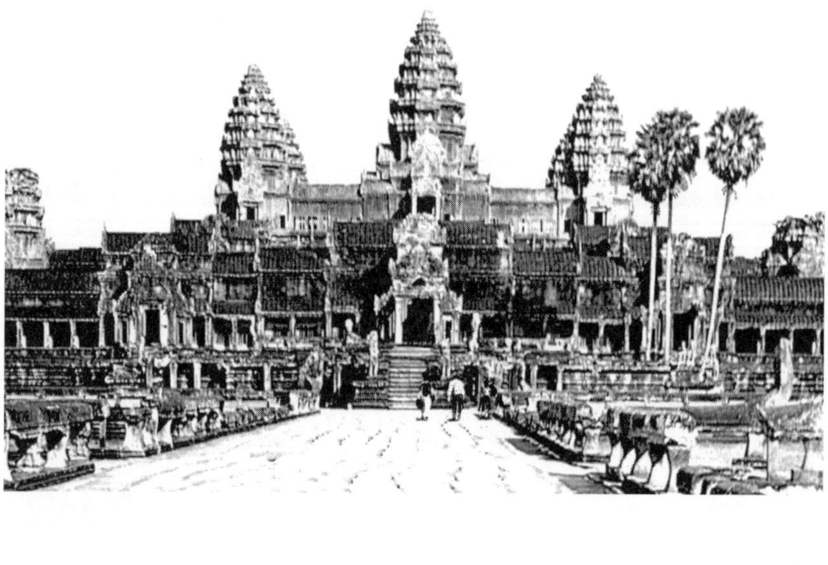

Fig. 148. Right: The ancient Khmer city of Angkor Wat in Cambodia is based on a mandala plan.

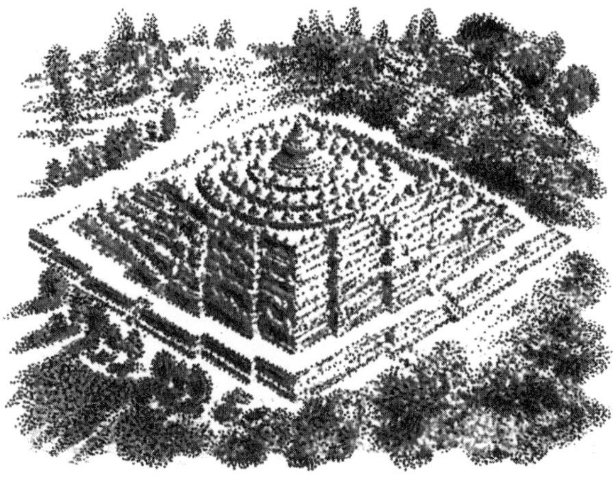

strength; [9] good intelligence; and [10] clouds of dharma.) The ten terraces are grouped according to Mahayana theology into three levels: the lowest level, in which earthly desires and base impulses hold sway in man; the middle level, where one has control over negative impulses and uses one's good impulses but is nevertheless tied to human nature; the highest level, in which humanity is no longer dictated by physical, earthly desires. The first two terraces feature galleries of bas-reliefs depicting the former lives of Buddha and his final incarnation as Gautama Siddhartha. Further levels represent the stories of Prince Sudhana, who encounters the various Bodhisattvas on his own path to enlightenment. The directional Dhyani Buddhas regularly appear as sculpture in niches on these levels, with the Vairocana Buddhas appearing on the summit.

Three upper circular levels at Borobudur represent the pure Buddha-nature and the reality of Absolute Truth expressed by the sculptures of seventy-two meditating Buddhas enclosed in stupas of bell-shaped, latticed stone (fig. 150). The ordered doctrine of Mahayana Buddhism with its *trikaya*, or "three body," system is laid out as a path ascending from the world of earthly appearances and desires to the apprehension of the inner journey and ultimate achievement of enlightenment. The Buddhist doctrine of birth, striving, reincarnation, and karma is explicitly depicted for the pilgrim, who, through circumambulation of the three-dimensional mandala, is reminded of past lives and told of future incarnations. According to Thomas Barrie, Borobudur "provides a setting

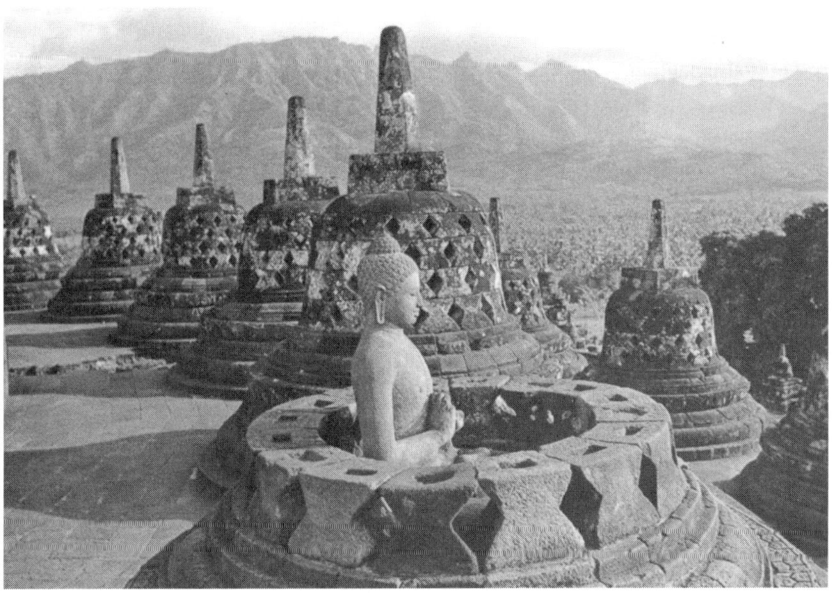

Fig. 149. Above: Borobudur, in central Java, ninth century A.D., is the largest Buddhist temple in the world and is a three-dimensional mandala created for circumambulation. Pilgrims to this monument encounter over twelve miles of relief sculpture on its terraced walls.

Fig. 150. Left: A Buddha statue (without its lattice stupa surround) on the top level of Borobudur is one of hundreds of Buddha images at the site.

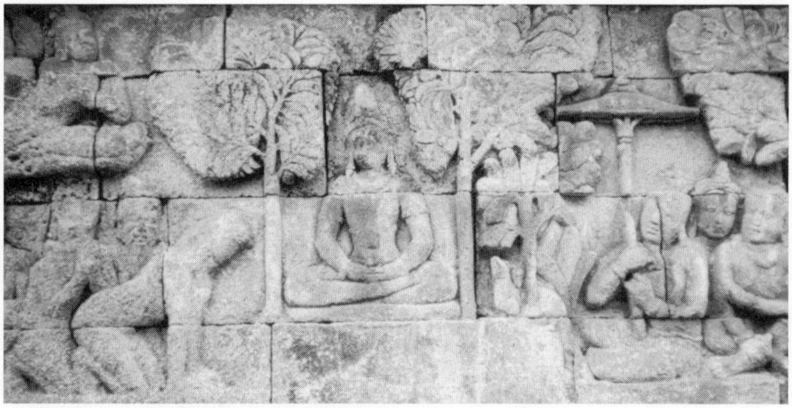

Fig. 151. Above: Twelve miles of relief sculpture are viewed by the pilgrim progressing through the several terrace levels of Borobudur Temple. With each level or story, the pilgrim rises nearer the goal of enlightenment.

Fig. 152. Below: The Great Stupa of Sanci is believed to originate during the time of Asoka, in the third century B.C., and has gone through numerous building phases. It has four, beautifully carved, stone gateways leading to a hemispherical dome or "sacred mountain," which is fifty-four feet high and 105 feet in diameter. It too is a three-dimensional mandala.

for the appearance of deities, and creates the setting for an initiatory experience of passing through the various realms of enlightenment. It is not a place to venerate the Buddha but to actively participate in the journey of becoming enlightened oneself, to become a bodhisattva."[16] There are over twelve miles of relief sculpture and more than a thousand Buddhas appearing at Borobudur making it an enormous mandala of initiation into Buddhist spirituality (fig. 151). The narrative content of the sculptural work at this site is far richer than its Indian influences and already intimates the later Javanese folk art style with its dramatic caricatures. The architecture and sculpture of Borobudur creates a sacred space in which the pilgrim is raised by mystery images beyond the pictorial imagery itself. The artwork as sense-world phenomena opens up faculties for seeing beyond the realm of mere appearance or maya, in order that the seeker may experience his or her own karma. Eliade says, "Only the initiate who goes through all the galleries discovers gradually the planes of supersensible reality, the grades of meditation expressed iconographically."[17]

Steiner emphasizes that imaginative picture content is essential to inner esoteric development: "Everything of the nature of cult and ritual, not the external rites only but comprehension of the world expressed in imagery and pictures, leads man towards his innermost being. As long as he strives for self-knowledge with abstract ideas and concepts, nothing is achieved. But when he penetrates into his inmost being with pictures that give concrete definition to experiences of soul, then he achieves his aim. . . . man must meditate in pictures, in images."[18] The inward-turned gaze is held firm, formed and fashioned by ritual imagery such as mandalas and mantras. On the other hand, in gazing out into the world of nature, human perception is bounded by sacred architecture, by architectonic forms. Between these two domains of inner self-knowledge deepened through pictures and symbols, and outer sense perceptions of significant architectonic forms such as those in sacred architecture, is an intermediate realm of experience that, if nurtured, may lead to direct knowledge of reincarnation. "By cultivating that domain that lies between the experience of true architectonic form and the experience of true, symbolic imagery along the path inwards, a man becomes sensitive to the strokes of destiny. He feels that what befalls him comes from earlier lives on earth."[19]

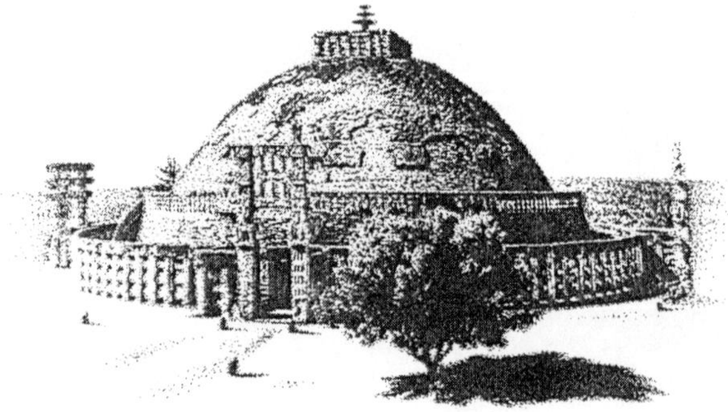

Borobudur's architectural plan is based on the archetypal Indian stupa form, that is likewise the inspiration behind the Tibetan *chorten,* and Far Eastern pagodas. Stupas are derived from pre-Buddhist tradition where they display solid hemispherical domes, such as are seen in the Great Stupa at Sanci, India, of the third century B.C. (fig.152). The stupa is thought to originate from the earlier tumulus or burial mound, and one can observe the similarities between the stupa and the megalithic tumulus of other parts of the world. The dome imitates the infinite expanse of the vaulted heavens, which includes all creation and destruction, birth and death. Over time the hemisphere stretches vertically into a bell shape. The altarlike *harmika,* which sits atop the dome, is the sanctuary above the world, beyond cause and effect, birth and death. Here were enshrined the ashes of the Holy One. A pole runs from top to bottom, through the center of the stupa, connecting the umbrellas above with relics (hypothetically belonging to the Buddha) below. This pole, which forms the spire, can be understood as the *axis mundi* or World Tree of related traditions, and its placement on the stupa recalls earlier practices that celebrated the sacred tree. The revered Bodhi tree is the most closely related to local tradition—it is the holiest place in the world, for beneath this tree the Buddha achieved enlightenment.

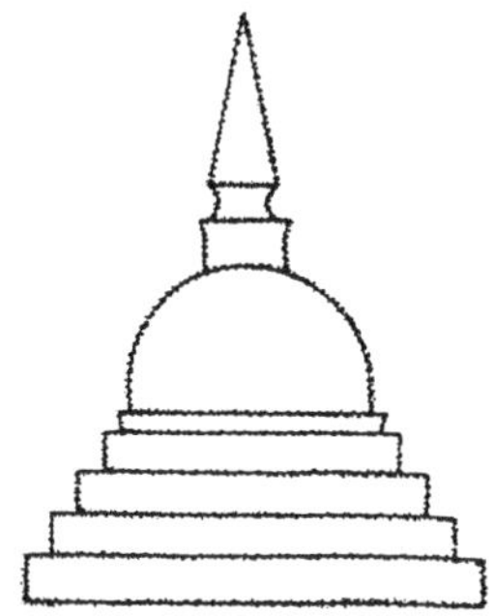

Fig. 153. The ideal stupa had a threefold structure corresponding to the Hindu principles of Brahma, Shiva, Vishnu, and to the Buddhist principles of the Buddha, Dharma, and Sangha. This three-part structure is related to the human features of head, torso, and limbs.

Lama Anagarika Govinda says, "It is explained in later scriptures that the different strata of the cone (separated by horizontal notches) correspond to certain psychic faculties or stages of consciousness on the way to enlightenment and to their respective world-planes."[20] The cone-shaped spire shows the gradual reduction of the universe into the point of complete perfection, metaphysical emptiness, the greatest sacrifice—that of self, in the Buddhist sense.

It is worth noting that human dwellings in northern Asia, every house, every tent, every yurt, "is conceived as being situated in the Center of the World; the central pole or smoke-hole signifies the *axis mundi.* We can then say that archaic man endeavored to live continuously in a consecrated space, in a Universe kept 'open' by the communications between the cosmic levels. From a certain stage of culture, the human dwelling imitates the divine dwelling."[21] Cosmos, house, and human body are in fact related images.

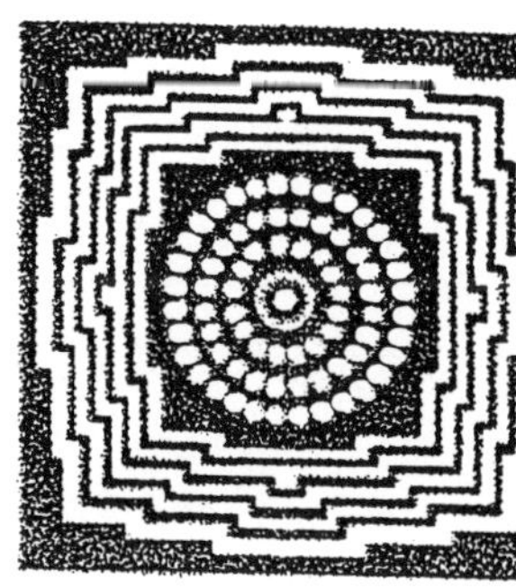

Fig. 154. The sixty elements of spiritual development or stages of the meditator, according to Indian (Pali) scripture, coincide exactly with the ground plan of Borobudur. The pilgrim places himself at each of sixty corresponding positions around Borobudur, the final one being enlightenment at the summit.

The threefold structure of the stupa is traditionally seen as symbolizing Brahma, Shiva, and Vishnu, the great Hindu trinity of gods (fig. 153). Buddhists transfer the three-part significance to the Buddha, Dharma, and Sangha. Further symbolism is allocated to the square-stepped base of the stupa: the first step corresponding to the four foundations of mindfulness (mindfulness to the body, sensation, mind, and phenomena). The second step corresponds to the four efforts (effort to destroy the evil which exists, effort to prevent the evil which does not yet exist, effort to produce the good which does not yet exist, and effort to cultivate the good which does exist). The third step has to do with the four

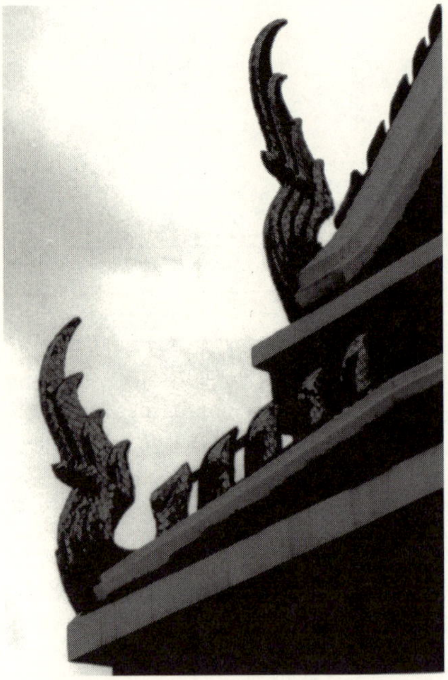

Fig. 155. The "sky lord" or "sky hook" is a traditional Southeast Asian cornice motif. It is derived from the naga serpent, a beneficial supernatural being that protects the building to which it is attached and leads the soul and spirit to the heavens.

psychic powers (desire to act, energy, thought, investigation); the fourth step and the circular base of the dome correspond to the five faculties (faith, energy, mindfulness, concentration, and the faculty of reason). The cupola itself represents the seven factors of enlightenment (mindfulness, discerning the truth, energy, rapture, serenity, concentration, and equanimity). The *harmika* has to do with the Eightfold Path, and the spire or tree of life corresponds to the tenfold knowledge (knowledge of the law, of other persons' thoughts, of relations; empirical knowledge; knowledge of suffering, of the cause of suffering, of the annihilation of suffering; knowledge of the way that leads to the annihilation of suffering; knowledge of things connected with despair; and knowledge of the nonproduction of things). The spire is also symbolic of the mystical powers of the Buddha.

There are many subtler associations connected with the three-part structure of the stupa. For instance, according to tradition, within the three worlds or levels of consciousness represented by the stupa, there are sixty elements corresponding to spiritual development. Lama Govinda states that "these sixty elements constitute a continuous way ascending through the three worlds and its different states of existence in the form of a spiral, spiritual circumambulatory path."[22] Perfectly demonstrated in the great stupa of Borobudur (fig. 154), it is described as a book of stone "offered for meditation, not for ordinary reading."[23] The ground plan of this terraced monument coincides exactly with the spiritual pathway indicated by orthodox Buddhist symbolism and can be seen in relation to the spiral path of the labyrinth.

According to Buddhist tradition stupas represent the Buddha's mind, just as scripture stands for his speech, and painted or sculpted images are an expression of his body. They are intended to make visible the Law (Dharma) and can be seen as memorial mandalas to the Buddha; reminders concerning the inner path to enlightenment. Stupas symbolize spiritual development and illumination, as Werner Speiser proclaims: "Memorials though they unquestionably are, in the final analysis it is not their physical presence but their dominantly spiritual quality that counts."[24]

Barrie says of temple architecture in general that it is "didactic, inculcating spiritual lessons to those who walked its paths and entered its sanctuaries. In this way sacred architecture performed the role of a hierophant; it revealed the mysterious unknown and guided the spiritual pilgrim toward enlightenment."[25]

An important architectural feature found on many temples in Thailand is the flamelike cornice called a "sky lord" or "sky hook" (fig. 155). Placed on the corners and peaks of roofs, the sky lord is a stylized representation of the sacred naga serpent, a beneficent snakelike deity of high spiritual import. Tasks of the sky hook, similar to those of the Christian gargoyle, include protecting the temple from malevolent spirits as well as guiding the soul rightly to the heavens. Eliade notes that there are "widespread beliefs of Europe and Asia that the soul of the deceased leaves by the smoke-hole or through the roof, and notably through that part of the roof which is found above the 'sacred angle.'"[26] Steiner too points to the spiritual significance of building arts when he says, "Architecture unfolds out of the principle of the soul's escape from the body after passing through the portal of death."[27] It is for the sake of the dead that the first forms of architecture arise, not for utilitarian purposes of shelter. It is likewise striking that in many ancient cultures it is only the tombs and temples that remain, the dwellings of the ancestors and the gods, not those of the living. Lama Govinda states: "While the habitations of the living were of the most primitive and impermanent character, the dwellings of the dead were built for eternity. One would think that man would have tried to satisfy his material needs first, before bothering about spiritual things. But the history of humanity shows just the contrary. The practical attitude of man is a later achievement."[28]

Tibet

> *Though different forms are perceived, they are in essence empty; yet in the emptiness one perceives forms.*
> *Though different sounds are heard, they are empty; yet in the emptiness one perceives sounds.*
> *Also different thoughts arise; they are empty, yet in the emptiness one perceives thoughts.*
> —Dudjom Rinpoche

In ancient Tibet, as throughout prehistoric Asia, guardian spirits and powerful demons were honored in trance rituals through shamanic practices. When Buddhism was introduced in the seventh century A.D. with Indian Tantric ceremonies, the demons were reputedly brought under control by mantric spells and ritual magic, which turned them into protectors of nation and religion. From that time Tibetan Buddhism has employed powerful colors and often brutal imagery in its visual arts as a stirring contrast to what we will see in the art of Japanese Zen Buddhism, with its understated, austere, and nearly monochromatic iconography.

Tibetan monastery walls are covered with colorful murals and hung with cloth thangkas, painted with a distemper medium, similar to watercolor, but applied in opaque layers, producing a striking intensity. Tibetan painting is executed in a wide range of formats from miniature manuscripts to colossal, sixty-foot-high wall hangings and banners, representing "the most varied and creative medium of expression in the world's religious art."[29] Of the varied types of painting, it is the mandala—a sacred icon in the elaborate mystery imagery of Tibetan esoteric Buddhism—that most pursues the Buddhist idea of "liberation through sight." It is said that the Buddha himself made the first mandala.

One of the most widely known Tibetan mandala paintings is the Kalachakra (Time Wheel) mandala (color plate 6). Kalachakra tantra is considered especially important in yogic or lama practice and this particular image is a favorite of the current Dalai Lama. The design is a two-dimensional representation of a five-story palace for the deity Kalachakra Buddha, and it is often fashioned as a sand painting over several days. Specially prepared colored sand is carefully placed on prepared ground by a monk-artist who builds the forms gradually outward. As it gets larger, other monks join in the work on each of the four quadrants. All aspects of the mandala are exactly based on scripture, and, as in Byzantine and Russian icons, no individual expression is desired beyond the perfecting of skill.

The central image of the father-mother couple, Kalachakra and Vishvamata (All-Mother) are in embrace on an eight-petalled lotus-throne, surrounded by eight shakis, and make up the Great Bliss Mandala (the inner square portion of the mandala). Kalachakra is the expression of compassion, and Vishvamata is the embodiment of wisdom. The square terraces are the Mind Mandala Palace, the Speech Mandala Palace, and the outermost Body Mandala Palace of the Buddhist *trikaya* or "three-body" system. Inside the large square enclosure appear twelve animals representing the twelve months of the year and the twelve cosmic forces. They carry thirty deities each, a token of the three hundred days of the Kalachakra year. The outermost circle surrounding the square palaces represents the six elements of earth, water, fire, wind, space, and wisdom. It is called the Great Protective Circle. The symbolic color scheme, related to the four directions, uses yellow, white, indigo, and red as primary hues. Gurus and lamas of the Kalachakra lineage from between the seventh and the eleventh centuries sometimes are portrayed around the mandala. This sacred image is believed to have originated around the time of the great fifth Dalai Lama. Seven hundred twenty-two deities are customarily depicted within the mandala as a whole.

Tibetan mandalas provide a ground plan or blueprint of the cosmos for invoking deities that might aid in the pupil's inner development. They are also used in connection with temple liturgy, especially in the case of sand paintings; they confer powers not only on the novice but on the master or lama as well. Denise Leidy characterizes the diverse functions of the mandala as follows: "In Tibetan life, mandalas are used to decorate and sanctify temples and homes, in initiation rites for monks and rulers, as the focus of visualization by the clergy and of worship by lay followers, as well as in such specified roles as a support for the corpse in cremation."[30] Ngakpa Chogyam quite simply describes the mandala and its symbols as the "windows through which we can view the essential nature of our being."

Such images are considered the first of the three "supports" for meditation and ritual. This support work of mandalas (and all two-dimensional visual arts) is connected with the activity of prostration and circumambulation and is referred to as "body work." The second support has to do with written words and spoken mantras derived from Buddha and other masters and is known as "speech work." The third support is linked to the *chorten* or *stupa* (temple) architecture, symbolizing the enlightened mind and called "mind work." These three supports for body, speech, and mind are directly related to the devotee's appeal to the "three bodies" or *trikaya* of the Buddha: Nirmanakaya (Body of Manifestation or body of human incarnation), Sambhogakaya (Body of Bliss or body of transcendence), Dharmakaya (Body of Law or body of truth). One might draw a parallel between these bodies and the spiritual capacities of imagination (body—clairvoyant seeing in pictures), inspiration (speech—clairaudiant hearing in words), and intuition (mind—direct spiritual knowing).

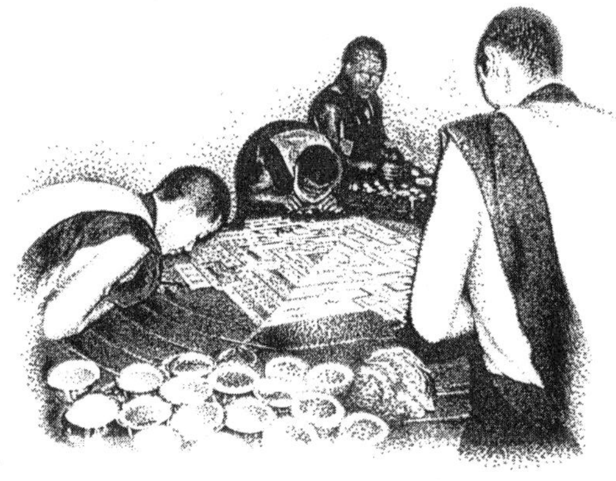

Fig. 156. Above: Monks construct the Kalachakra mandala as an outer meditative practice, an artistic, spiritual activity.

As the pupil visualizes his or her way into the mandala architecture—builds, and rebuilds, again and again, through visualization of the mystery image—the subtle inner spiritual organs or chakras ("wheels") begin to turn, to "open up" in response to the exercises. The very proportions and dimensions of the mandala seem to aid in this sensitizing process. Robert Thurman describes the work of the mandala in the following way: "Our insight into the mandala principle allows us to see that this is not only a matter of vague cultural imagery contributing to a vague personal sense of things, but is rather a matter of imaginal world-patterning directly affecting inner structuring of physical and mental senses through actual brain organization."[31] Thurman rightly maintains that the ritual art of the mandala, like most sacred art, instills spiritual capacities in the human being as it fashions the physical basis in the organism for such development to occur.

Construction of a Kalachakra sand mandala can take five days; dismantling occurs on the twelfth and last day of initiation (fig. 156). When the mandala is dismantled, prayers request that all deities invoked by the mandala return swiftly to the spirit world. As the Kalachakra mantra is recited, the colored sand of each of the 722 deities is carefully removed and placed in a specially prepared urn. Starting on the eastern side and moving clockwise, all the quadrants are cut through in order to terminate the energy of the mandala. Dismantling of the mandala is carried out from the perimeter to the center, in reverse order to how it was made, and the sand is swept to the center and placed in an urn. The sand is taken by monks to a nearby river or lake, where the protective

Fig. 157. Below: Eyes painted on the Nepalese Saladhola stupa (below) near Kathmandu are suggestive of the meditative glance of the Buddha resting on all things in the universe.

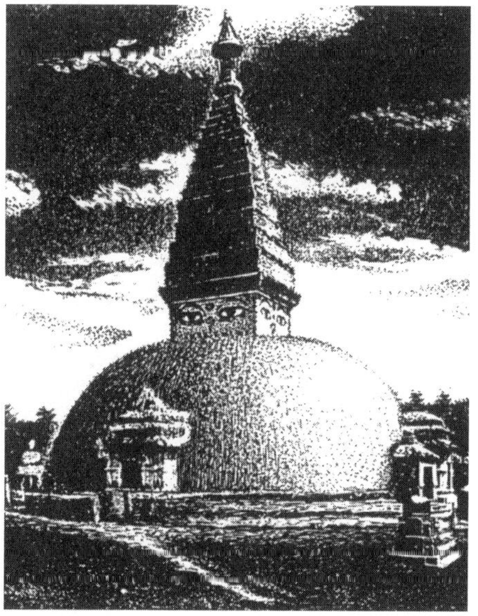

spirits of the water are called upon to receive the consecrated sand for the benefit of all beings. The sand is poured into the water where the mandala is "preserved" in the most effective way possible—spiritually.

"The dismantling of the sand mandala may be interpreted as a lesson in non-attachment, a letting-go of the 'self-mind.' The ceremony reflects the Buddhists' recognition of the impermanence and transitory nature of all aspects of life."[32] The dismantling of the sand mandala in reverse order can also be a powerful esoteric exercise linked to the process undergone by the soul after death in kamaloka — reviewing in backward succession the life just lived.

The *chorten,* Tibet's version of the stupa, is the purest Buddhist element in Tibetan architecture. Like the mandala, it is a representation of the sacred World Mountain, the Cosmic Pillar, and the Tree of Life and is to be circumambulated in worship as the Center of the Universe. Some *chorten* include interior chapels or small reliquaries with wall paintings. Nepalese stupas display stylized human eyes painted on the *harmika,* suggesting a human figure, such as the Buddha, in meditation: the crossed legs as the base, the torso as the hemisphere, and the head as the altarlike *harmika,* crowned by the spire (fig. 157). The different parts of the stupa are also identified with the elements: earth (base), water (hemisphere), fire (*harmika*) and air (spire). And the trinity of Hindu gods, Brahma, Shiva, and Vishnu, reign over the foundation, middle and upper portions, respectively.

Generally speaking, the progressive geographical development of Asian temple architecture tends from the rounded, more horizontal gesture of the stupa in India, to the squared, vertical form of the pagoda in China and Japan, with the Tibetan *chorten* representing an intermediary stage. Over time the stupa shows a steady transformation into the vertical (fig. 158).

Steiner claims that: "our feelings have no relation to the three space-dimensions; only our will. By their very nature, feelings are bound within two dimensions. That is why they are best represented by two-dimensional painting."[33] If this is so, then the mandala and *thangka* as two-dimensional images are accessed through the feeling-life of the practitioner, thereby awakening the will, whereas the *chorten,* through circumambulation, is encountered by means of the will, thus kindling the feelings. Here are two different artistic approaches for engaging the spiritual life of humanity.

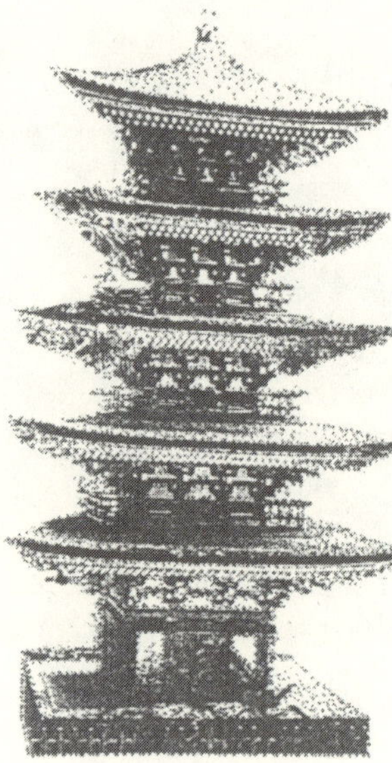

a

Fig. 158. The progressive development of Asian temple architecture tends from the rounded, more horizontal gesture of the stupa, to the squared, vertical form of the pagoda (a), with the chorten (b), representing an intermediary stage.

b

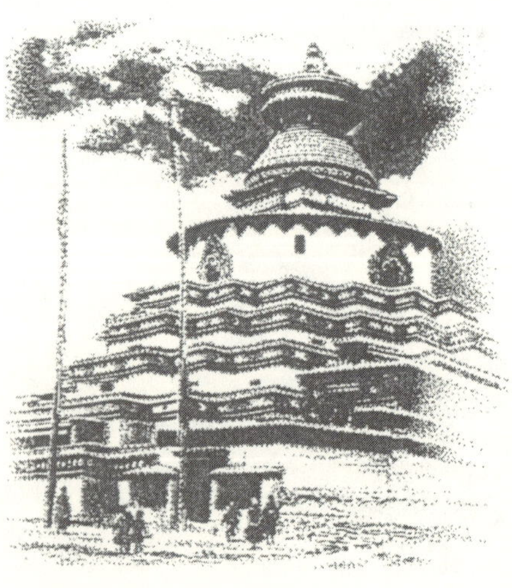

China

Mold clay into a vessel; from its not-being [that is, the vessel's hollow] arises the utility of the vessel. Cut out doors and windows in the [walls of the] house, from their not-being [their empty space] arises the utility of the house. Therefore by the existence of things we profit. And by the nonexistence of things we are served.
—Lao-Tzu

The legendary Huang-ti or "Yellow Emperor," whose reign, according to the old Chinese lunar calendar, began in 2698 B.C.,[34] controlled most of the Asian central plain and areas to the west and north. After forcing most of his enemies to flee, Huang-ti was confronted by his foremost adversary, the horned Ch'ih-yu, inventor of weapons. Using magic powers, Ch'ih-yu enveloped the Yellow Emperor's army in a dense fog, blinding and confounding them. However, a chariot bearing a figure that unswervingly pointed south led the Yellow Emperor out of the fog to safety. Eventually, Ch'ih-yu was defeated and Huang-ti gained dominance over the entire Yellow River Valley. Huang-ti is credited with inventing the compass and the carriage, developing writing, weaving, and the raising of silkworms, and designing innovative clothing, boats, and dwellings.

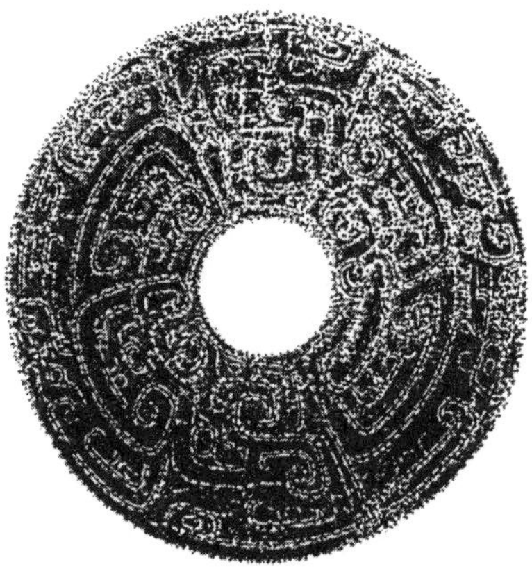

According to Rudolf Steiner, an exalted spiritual leader who appeared at about this time in China and became a great teacher of humanity initiated a cultural stream that would last for thousands of years as it spread westward. This exceptional being, who grew up in the precincts of an East Asian mystery center, became the first to "grasp through the faculty of human intellect what had formerly come into the mysteries through revelation."[35] It was through this remarkable figure that Eastern mystery wisdom flowed to the West on the wings of newly born human intelligence and inspired cultures such as that of ancient Greece, with its high art and philosophy. It was this particular influence which, as Gnostic spirituality, lasted up into the fourth century A.D. before fading from human comprehension. It was, says Steiner, this pagan wisdom that made it possible for early Christians to grasp the spiritual significance of the Christ event. The auspicious Chinese figure behind this spiritual stream ironically became known in later esoteric tradition as Lucifer, "the Light Bringer." One wonders if Steiner is describing the same being as the Yellow Emperor.

Some significant images of prehistoric China are the *pi* (*bi*) disc and the *ts'ung* (*cong*) column, the archetypal circle and the rectangle. The *pi* is a symbol of the sun, also of heaven, and was often carved in jade, with a hole about a third of the total size of the disc, representing the path of transcendence or the Absolute (*t'ai-chi*) and the eternally fixed Pole Star (fig. 159). Some discs were placed in the mouth of the dead to ensure vitality and prevent the body's decay. Zhou (Chou) period records also mention the disc as being placed under the corpse, but in both

Fig. 159. The *pi* (*bi*) disc is a prehistoric Chinese sun emblem, also symbolic of heaven. Buried with the dead to ensure spiritual life after death, it may have been used in connection with sunrise sacrifices.

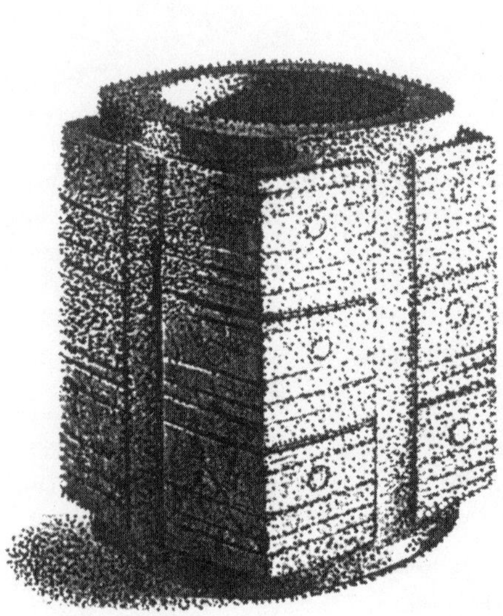

Fig. 160. The *ts'ung* column is an earth symbol used in Shang and Zhou (Chou) dynasty burial practices.

Fig. 161. The whorl motif is a solar emblem; a *pi* symbol set in motion.

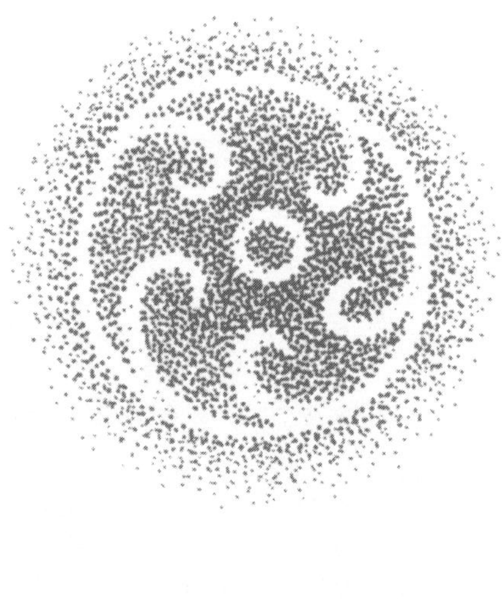

cases it was seen as a vehicle for guiding the spirit of the deceased heavenward. It was the highest emblem of noble status and the most important funerary object for assisting communication with the ancestors and gods. However, it is likely that in earlier periods it was used in connection with daily sunrise sacrifices offered to the Supreme Being of Heaven, Shang Ti.

The word "ritual" in Chinese originally meant "to serve the gods with jade." And the written character for "shaman" depicts two overlapping tools, demonstrating who had the technology and the exclusive power to produce the *pi* disc and to present sacrifices with it.

The *ts'ung* is a rectangular container with a cylindrical hollow and is often found among Shang and Zhou period grave offerings (fig. 160). By the Zhou period, the *ts'ung* was placed on the abdomen of the deceased and signified the earth as the *pi* did heaven. However, as Hugo Munsterberg points out, "this explanation is very late and may no longer express the meaning that these motifs had in Shang times."[36] Nevertheless the designation of *pi* as sun and later as heaven, and *ts'ung* as earth, are approximations of meaning that point us in the direction of the spiritual significance of these images.

The whorl motif is closely related to the *pi* as a solar emblem (fig. 161). Often found on Shang period bronzes, it consists of two concentric circles separated by several curling lines, reminiscent of the swastika. The whorls are likely pictoralizations of the Chinese glyph for brightness and fire, and are also connected with the sun. In contrast to Western symbols abstracted into letters, Chinese writing developed first as pictures that evolved later into glyphs. In Chinese it is said that one "writes" a picture. Both painting and writing are done with brush and ink; painting is usually monochrome and often includes writing. Thus it is easy to understand that "a picture tells a thousand stories." The Chinese sensitivity for brushwork and its spiritual significance is matter-of-factly expressed by the fifth-century master Wang Wei: "People who discuss painting merely concentrate on the outward aspects and structural effects. . . . Alas! . . . painting cannot be achieved by the physical movements of the fingers and the hand, but only by the spirit entering into them. This is the nature of painting."[37]

Chiang Yee, in *The Chinese Eye: An Interpretation of Chinese Painting*, points out that "no definite religious system has ever been evolved in China,"[38] for Taoism and Confucianism are philosophical rather than religious. Tao, (the Way) has to do with the eternal, natural order and the harmonious sense of wholeness for humanity's relationship with Nature and cosmos. It underlies the I Ching, a twelfth-century B.C. practice of divination that uses a sign system for determining changes in the universe resulting from the polar opposite forces, yin and yang. According to the Tao, the dynamics of the cosmos are made up of two complementary forces that express themselves through polarities such as father and mother, light and dark, sky and earth, dry and wet, mountain and valley, straight and curved. Yang is the male principle and yin is the female in this sense. They are graphically brought together in the t'ai-chi t'u image that was used by Taoists and Confucianists alike as a symbol of the Supreme Power of the Universe (fig. 162). The symbol is later taken up by Buddhism. "It could decorate everyday objects, gates, ritual objects for exorcism, the robes of a Taoist priest and even the wrap for babies in the belief that the design would be a protective charm against demons."[39]

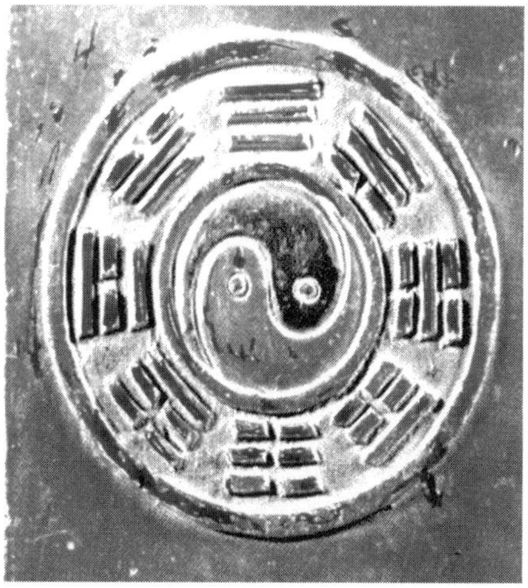

Fig. 162. The Taoist yin-yang symbol, called *t'ai-chi t'u,* is later incorporated into Buddhist iconography. It represents the great dynamic polarities at work in the universe.

The constant creative interplay of these yin and yang forces is expressed in the two droplike forms moving together in a reciprocal curving gesture, forming a rounded twofold swastika with a dot of the opposite's nature, like an eye, in the head of each form. Eight trigrams surround the central form with groups of three solid *(yang),* broken *(yin),* or solid and broken lines. Set in the eight directions, these trigrams are associated with heaven and earth, wind and thunder, fire and water, mountain and lake. They were used for oracular consultation as well as for philosophical interpretation and are still used to this day.

Tao serves as a basis for Feng Shui, a form of applied geomancy that deals with the reading and harmonizing of *ch'i* within natural and built environments. Literally meaning "wind" and "water," the two elements that are intermediaries between heaven and earth, Feng Shui acknowledges the lines of force that manifest as gently flowing life force. *Ch'i* is often depicted by undulating, curvilinear designs on vessels and as freely meandering forms between naturalistic images in Chinese artworks of various media (fig. 159). *Ch'i* is considered the cosmic breath and manifests through the changing seasons, weather, movements of the heavens, seas, human emotions, and thoughts. It has three phases: *sheng,* which is a moving upward or waxing and has to do with a bright, fresh environment; *si,* which means dying or waning, and is characterized by a depleted and depressed situation; and *sha,* which is harmful, dangerous, negative energy, appearing as malevolent jabbing forces or "secret arrows."

Ch'i has five "moods" or elements: water, wood, fire, earth, and metal. Water, which is wavelike and flows, curves, carries, and cleans, has to do with wisdom and intelligence. But water is also associated with fear. It is the element of the cold north, and its colors are black and dark blue, its season is winter, and its part of the body is the kidney. Wood is an element that is characteristically strong yet flexible. Considered a kind and friendly element, its negative side is anger. It is upright, narrow, and rectangular, its colors are green and light blue, its position easterly, and its weather condition is rainy, its season spring, and its part of the body is the liver. Fire shines, is hot and dry, courageous and joyful. It is also hyperactive and rash. Its shape is jagged, its colors purple and red, its position is southerly, its season summer, its organ the heart. Earth supports because it is solid and displays

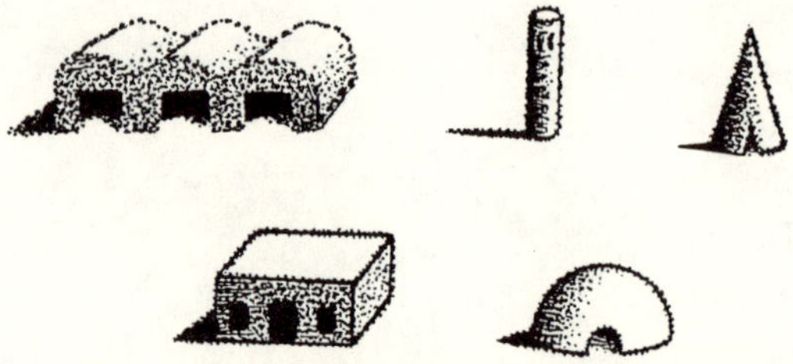

Fig. 163. According to Feng Shui principles, each of the five elements is characterized by a particular shape. Architectural forms thus convey a certain elemental signature.

equanimity and patience, but also worry. Its shape is square and flat. Its color is orange and yellow, its position is in the middle. Earth weather is cloudy and windy, summery as well as autumnal. The stomach is an earth organ. Metal reinforces, and is the perfection of earth. It represents morality and justice, but also inflexibility. Its form is round, its color white, gray, or silver, its direction is west, its weather is clear, pleasant, and autumnal. The lungs are seen as related to the element of metal. According to Feng Shui, the shape of a building classifies it as belonging to one or more of these five elements. A low, flat roof connects a building with the earth element; an irregular roof, with the water element; a tall, narrow construction fits the wood element; domes are associated with the metal element; and sharp, pointed roofs belong to the fire element (fig. 163). Thus, according to Feng Shui practitioners, a fire form would not be appropriately placed within the surroundings of water forms, for it would not flourish.

The five elements must be considered in relation to four directions and their geographic animal characteristics, such as the summer Red Phoenix, who rules over the South and brings invigorating forces and good fortune. The White Tiger dominates the West, is unpredictable and disruptive as an autumn power. In the East, bringing protection and wisdom is the Green Dragon of spring. And to the North is the sleepy and mysterious Black Tortoise, who brings nurturing in the winter season. These four earthly animal powers stand in striking contrast to the twelve cosmic animal powers as indicated in the Chinese calendar.

The position of a dwelling in relation to the four directions, to mountains, rivers, and the prevailing wind is of major concern in Feng Shui. The positioning of doors and windows, mirrors, artworks, furniture, vegetation, and pathways are all crucial in the directing of *ch'i* and displacement of *sha* in the environment. Royal palaces were always carefully aligned; before office buildings and homes are built in China today, a Feng Shui master is usually consulted.

Artworks and images are important to Feng Shui planning, as the form and character of a particular object is just as important as its placement. A rounded or squared form, a human or animal image, creates completely different spiritual environments for the patron. Although Feng Shui principles were only written down in the centuries A.D., it can be assumed that such doctrines were based on earlier undocumented traditions of a similar nature. However, what we know of Feng Shui today is only a shadow of its earlier form.

Feng Shui, concerned as it is with forces at work upon the earth, finds its complement in the sophisticated science of Chinese astronomical astrology. The Chinese were very intent on following the movement of the stars and the emperor, as Sun King, had to live every day and every hour of his life in accordance with the celestial choreography. He was the earthly representative of Shang Ti and the great family of ancestors and was therefore obliged to demonstrate the actions of the entire heavenly system. Sudden, unforeseen stellar events such as comets were the cause of great anxiety as they foreshadowed change and upheaval. Emperors had to demonstrate great wisdom and control at such times in order to maintain their position and power.

The Chinese, unlike the Indians, did not develop clairvoyance based on a perception of their own organism. Instead, by instinctively projecting themselves into their environment, they gained exceptional understanding of the outer world. What they knew of the human being arose from their adept penetration of the sense world, whereas the Indians knew the world by means of perceiving their own organism. In other words, the Chinese cultivated intuition and the Indians fostered imagination.[40] This capacity in the Chinese accounts not only for the sciences of Feng Shui, astronomy, acupuncture, and martial arts but also for .the inventiveness and the capacity for making so many practical discoveries such as silk production, gunpowder, and writing. It also explains, in part, the general lack of very early anthropomorphic deities and human images.

One of the rare exceptions to this absence of deities is an image found in prehistoric northwestern China of a horned shaman featured on the lid of a clay pot (fig. 164). Painted with zigzags and straight lines, the bearded shaman has a slithering snake form modeled on the back of his head, reminding us of the sacred serpent on the headdress of Egyptian pharaohs as the symbol for inner vision and seership. On the front of the star-shaped lid twelve serpentlike lines are painted between straight, bold lines. The two hollow horns may have been used to dispense seed from the cultic vessel at planting times. As we have seen, the shaman is the spiritual advisor in most early communities and China is no exception. *Discourses of the States,* a narrative history of the fourth century B.C., describes the importance of these spiritual leaders in early Chinese civilization: "The possessors of such power were, if men, called *xi* [shamans], and if women, *wu* [shamanesses]. It is they who supervised the positions of the spirits at the ceremonies, sacrificed to them, and otherwise handled religious matters."[41] Shamanism was the earliest form of Chinese inner discipline. As A.C. Graham describes it, "the meditation practiced privately and recommended to rulers as an arcanum of government descends directly from the trance of the professional shaman."[42] The shamanic theme is one that pervades all of Asia and persists to this day in isolated areas.

Another naturalistic image, this one from the time of the Discourses, is that of a cast-bronze Mongolian youth (or maiden) with two ceremonial wands in hand (fig. 165). A carved jade bird sits atop each of his ritual staves—a picture of the spirit-messenger upon the sacred tree. This shamanic bird imagery, indicative of spirit flight, is apparent in images throughout the world and over the course of time, as we shall see. The staff and bird are a meaningful mystery image seen throughout prehistory. Eliade describes its use in various parts of the world: "In the mythologies of Central Asia, Siberia, and Indonesia, the birds perched on the branches of the World

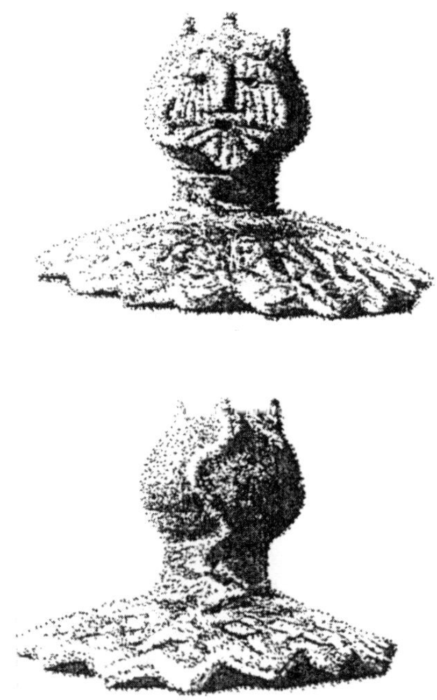

Fig. 164. One of the earliest intact prehistoric anthropomorphic images is this clay vessel top found in northwestern China. It probably represents a bearded shaman wearing two horns, with a snake slithering up the back of his head. It was possibly used in connection with ritual agricultural practices during the Neolithic period.

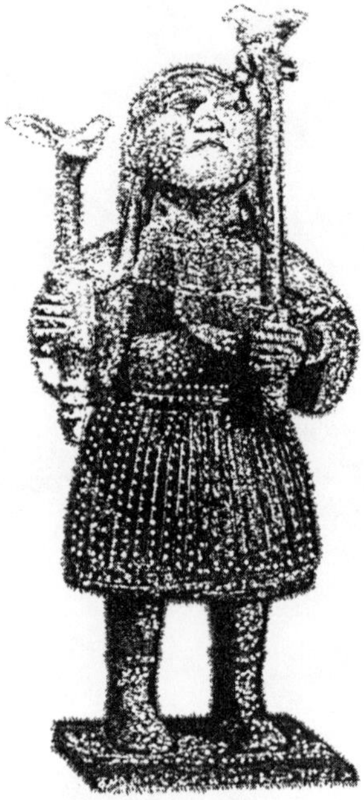

Fig. 165. Above: This fourth-century B.C. bronze figure of a shaman youth/maiden holding two sticks with sixteenth-century B.C. jade birds perched atop, was misidentified as a falconer, for the birds have hooked beaks, which make them unequipped for hunting. The bird symbolizes the shaman's spirit flight; the stick represents the World Tree.

Fig. 166. Below: The *lung* is not simply a dragon, but a zoomorphic composite creature, which, as the guardian of elemental forces, can bring good or ill fortune.

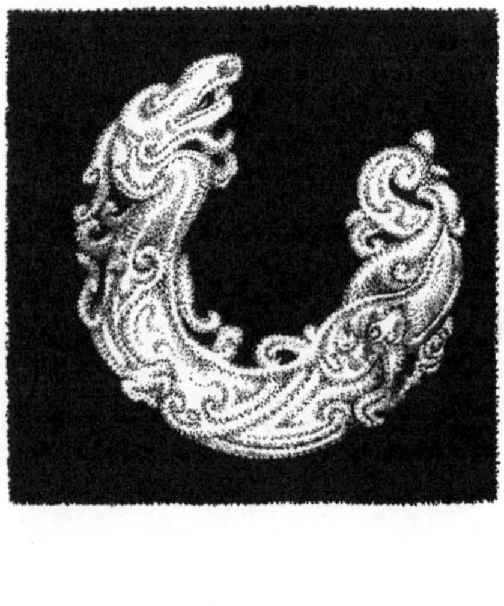

Tree represent men's souls. Because Shamans can change themselves into 'birds,' that is, because they enjoy the 'spirit' condition, they are able to fly to the World Tree to bring back soul-birds."[43] And in Siberia,"the Goldi, the Dolgan, and the Tungus [tribes] say that before birth, the souls of children perch like little birds on the branches of the Cosmic Tree and the shamans go there to find them."[44] Among the Siberian Buryat the eagle is the ancestral shaman.

However, the *lung* is the most important zoomorphic image in China even to this day. This dragonlike creature, visible only to the gods, has the jaws of a tiger, the brow of a bear, the antlers of a deer, and the body of a lizard (fig. 166). It dwells in air and water, making it a mediator between the regions above and the regions below. It provides rain and is therefore, like the serpent, a symbol of the chthonic powers associated with fertility. In India, serpents are powerful beings, regarded as guardians of the earth's treasures and possessors of all the sciences. Called *nagas*, they can appear with the head of a man. When they came to China they were known as Dragon Kings, and Buddhists may pray to them to this day for rain.

There are numerous accounts of dragons fathering great rulers or appearing in the sky at the time of royal births, and by the first dynastic period the dragon was already a symbol of sovereign power and an emblem of royalty. The emperor's throne was called the dragon throne and his face was the dragon's countenance. Unlike the snake, which is bound to the earth, the dragon has wings and feet. A royal dragon has five claws instead of four. "In contrast to the Western dragon, which is thought of as a negative force, representing evil and the devil, and which is slain by heroes . . . the Chinese dragon is considered beneficial and auspicious, bringing good fortune and abundance."[45]

The Ch'an sect of Buddhism reveres the dragon image as a mystical vision of the Buddha-nature. Legend speaks of a dragon rising out of the Yellow River and making known the circular *t'ai-chi t'u* diagram of the yin-yang symbol. Dragon images from the third millennium B.C. have been found in China, although the earliest examples known, also associated with water and fertility, are from Mesopotamia.

The *t'ao t'ieh,* meaning "glutton mask" in modern Chinese, is another zoomorphic mystery image, most often seen on vessels as a stylized masklike face (fig. 167). The face is always symmetrical and is usually accentuated by a flange or ridge that runs vertically down the forehead and nose. Different animals are recognizable in the *t'ao t'ieh,* such as the bull, deer, and tiger, but most often the face appears like that of a dragon (fig. 168).

The function of the *tao t'ieh* is believed to be that of a guardian spirit that protects the living during ritual ceremonies and drives away evil spirits from the tombs of the dead. The bronze ritual vessels of the Shang and Chou dynasties upon which the *tao t'ieh* images most often appear are containers for ceremonial use, holding wine or grain. The ritual vessel, as a container filled with nourishment for the

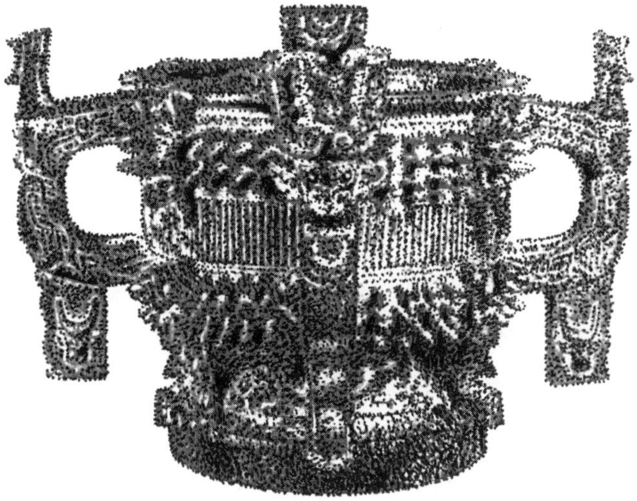

Fig. 167. Left: The *tao t'ieh,* besides appearing as the traditional *lung* mask, also appears as other animals such as the bull.

Fig. 169. Below: Human and animal guardian figures are common in both painting and sculpture, not only in China but throughout the world. They often protect entrances to shrines, temples, palaces, and homes.

ancestors, provides an image of the head as a vessel of *ch'i*-permeated thought substance offered up to the gods. The elaborate curvilinear patterns on such vessels resemble the convolutions of the brain and may represent the dynamic weaving forces of the thinking head similar to the way in which the shaman's horns and pharaoh's serpent headdress express the visionary capacities of the initiate.

The T'ang dynasty emperor Tai Zong became very ill after his invasion of Korea. None of the court physicians could relieve his agony, for he was tormented by evil spirits. Every night ghosts visited the emperor and robbed him of his sleep, severely weakening him. Two of his generals volunteered to stand guard at the emperor's door, and from then on no spirits dared to appear. The emperor soon recovered his health and strength. He released the generals from their watch and hung painted portraits of them to continue the work of keeping the evil spirits away.[46] This Chinese story is associated with the practice of placing images of martial door-gods or heroes on either side of a gate or entranceway. Pairs of tomb attendants also appear as funerary figures and are buried with the dead, in place of living attendants, as threshold guardians. Lokapala and Mahakala are the Buddhist guardian deities who stare angrily, weapons at the ready to protect the dharma. They are usually positioned at temple entrances and suggest that the power of images is equal to that of living beings. This is why throughout prehistory painted images and wood, stone, and clay figures appear as substitutes or stand-ins for actual objects or beings (fig. 169); for the image embodies spirit.

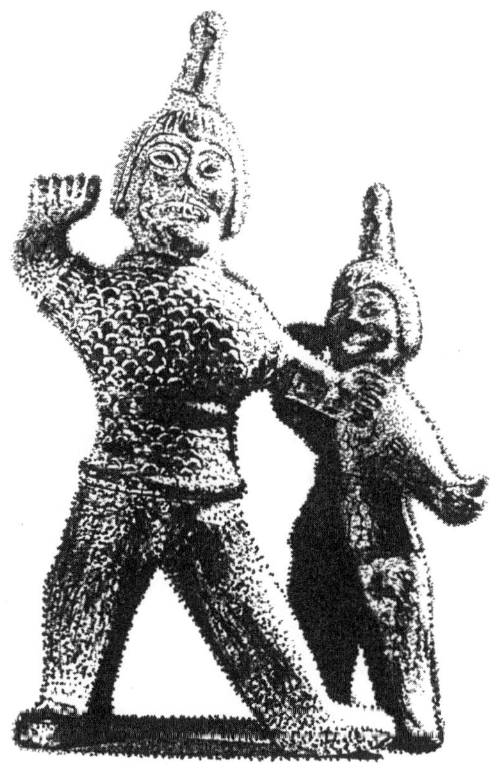

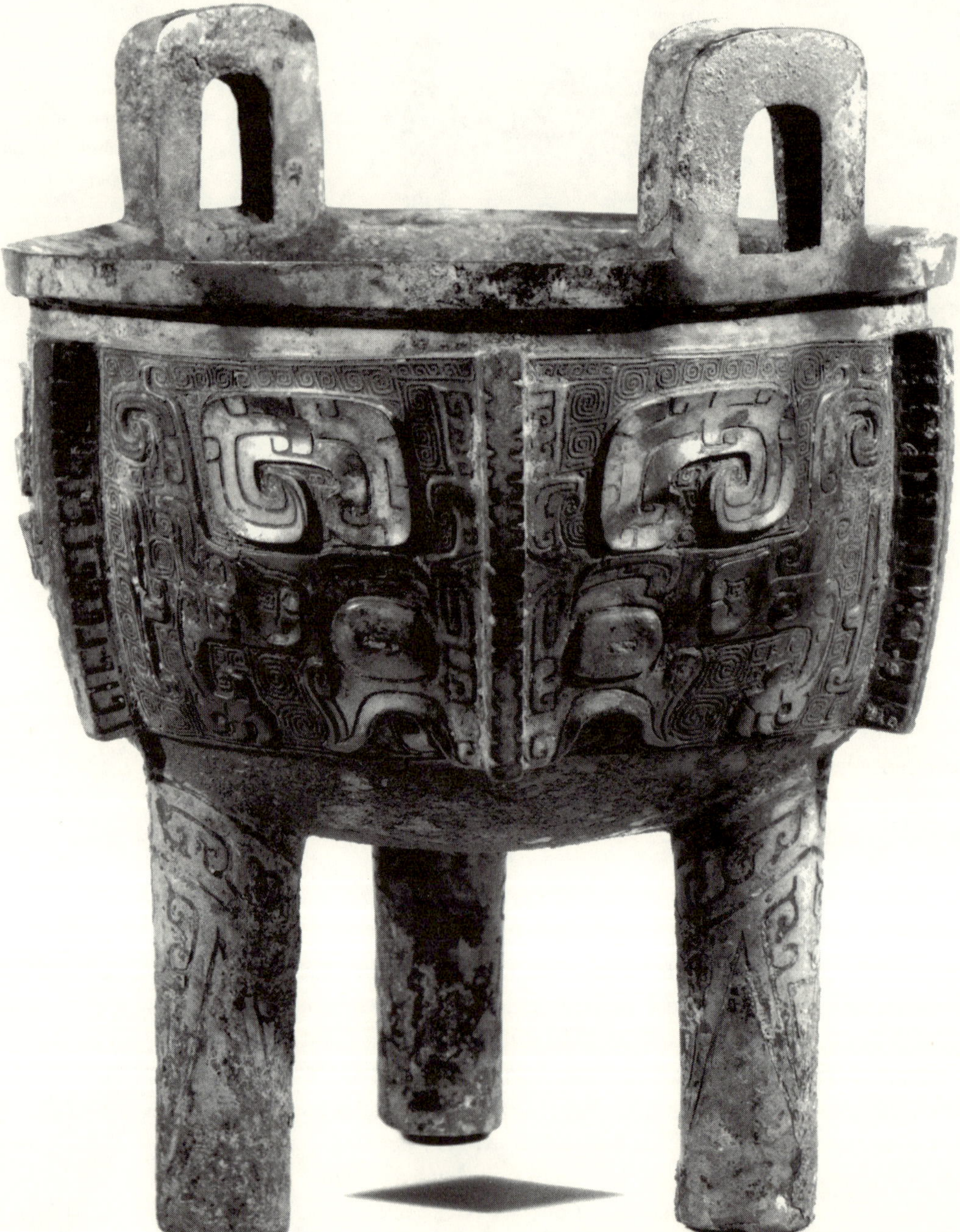

Fig. 168: T'ao t'ieh means "glutton mask" and was believed to combat greed. It may also hold an esoteric significance related to the head as a sacred vessel. The stylized *t'ao t'ieh* countenance is sometimes human, sometimes animal, but most frequently seen as a dragon or *lung* face. (Honolulu Academy of Arts).

Japan

In order to understand a masterpiece you must bow yourself low before it and await with bated breath its least utterance.
—Kakuzo Okakura

According to the Japanese creation myth, three divinities, the Kojiki, were born of themselves at the time "when the earth was young and like floating oil." Then, "moving like jellyfish," two more divinities were born, followed by seven generations of gods. The last couple were called Izanagi and Izanami, and they were directed by the gods to consolidate and fructify the earth. From all the couples' deeds and misdeeds the gods of islands, mountains, trees, winds, and rivers were born. Last to be born was the god of fire, who burned his mother so badly that she died and descended to the Underworld. Following a frightful journey to hell in a failed attempt to rescue his deceased wife, Izanagi sadly returned to earth and cleansed himself of hell's impurities. The impurities became different ills, and Izanagi then created gods to cure them. He dove into the sea, and washing his left eye gave birth to the great goddess of the Sun, Amaterasu. Washing his right eye he gave birth to the goddess of the Moon, Tsukiyomi. Then he washed his nose and brought into the world a son, Susanoo, the deity of thunder, storms, and rain.

As firstborn, Amaterasu was given a necklace of jewels and instructed to

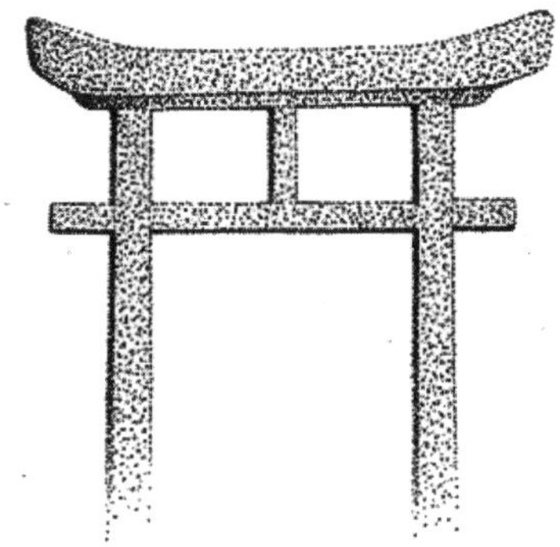

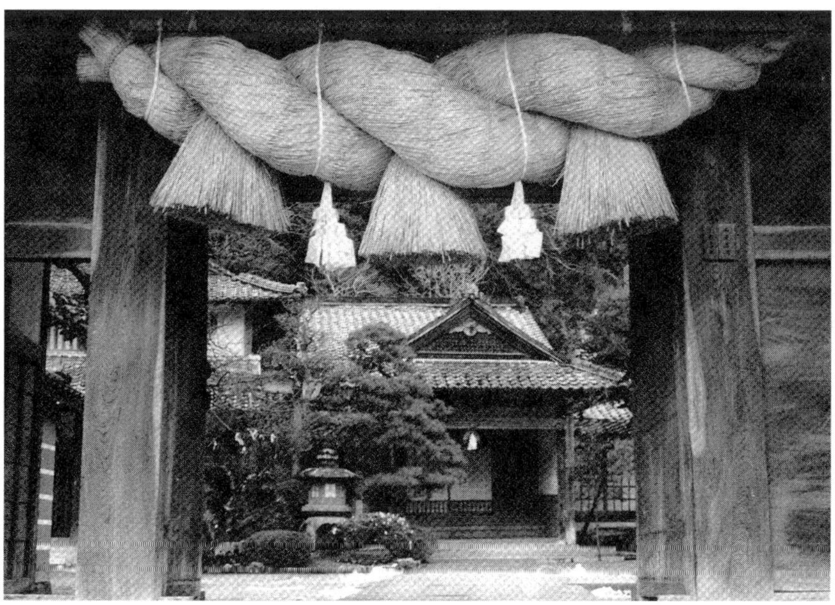

Fig. 170. Above: The Shinmai-Dorii is the gateway of the sun that honors Amaterasu, the sun goddess. Also called *torii,* and symbolic of immortality or crossing of the threshold, such structures are found at the entrances to temple precincts and sacred grounds.

Fig. 171. Left: *Shimenawa,* "sacred rope," is one of the most ancient images connected with the Japanese New Year festival. Its ritual knot (*musubi*) indicates the threshold between sacred and profane areas stressing the "tie" or "bond" between spirit and matter. (Photo copyright © Barbara Stephan.)

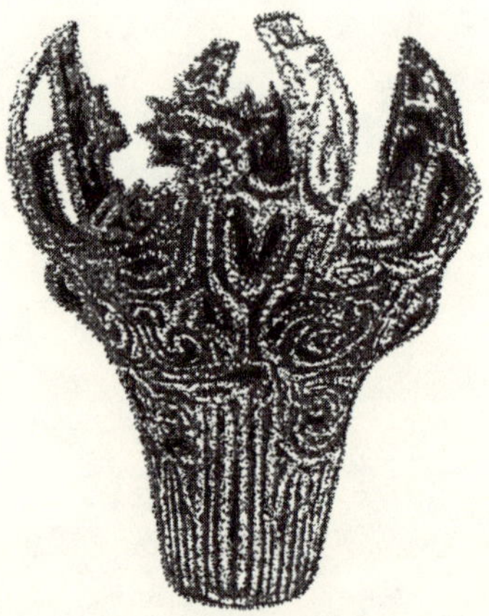

Fig. 172. Above: The Japanese Jomon ("cord") period, 3000–2000 B.C., is named for its high relief, rope-patterned pottery. Jomon pottery is organic in its form and expressive of the dynamic life forces in nature.

Fig. 173. Below: *Haniwa,* "clay circles," were fashioned into model houses, animals, female figures, and warrior guardians in armor. They were placed as offerings in royal tombs, sometimes in great numbers. Such earthenware sculpture demonstrates both simplicity of form and expertise of execution.

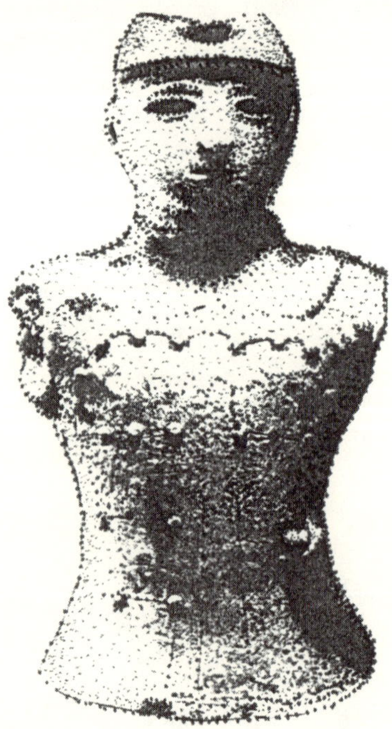

rule the plain of heaven. Tsukiyomi was entrusted with the kingdom of the night, but Susanoo wanted only to go to the underworld to be with his mother. Before saying farewell to his eldest sister, Susanoo took Amaterasu's string of jewels, crunched them between his teeth and blew out a light mist from his mouth that gave birth to five male deities. This was in response to Amaterasu, who took her brother's sword, broke it into three pieces, chewed it, and breathed a fine mist that created three goddesses. (These newly created gods and goddesses were the ancestors of the emperors and other great families of Japan.) However, Susanoo was so pleased with himself that he lost all self-control, destroyed rice fields and irrigation ditches, fouled temples, and so terrified his sun goddess sister that she retreated and hid herself in a rocky cave in heaven, thus taking her light away from the world. Susanoo, whose attribute is the serpent, was driven out of heaven and forced to reign on earth as the god of thunder.

Then the wicked gods ran wild in the darkened world and the good gods resolved to lure the sun goddess back. The gods gathered all the cocks that crow at dawn and gave orders for a large mirror, a string of jewels, and colorful cloth streamers to be hung from the branches of the Sakaki tree. They chanted ritual words and the goddess Ama no Uzume, adorned in different plants, danced ecstatically upon a wooden drum. Hearing the crowing of the cocks, the drumming, and the riotous laughter of the gods when the dancing goddess stripped off her clothes, Amaterasu, curious about the noise, poked her head out of the cave and asked what was going on. As she gazed into the mirror hanging before the cave, the gods declared that they had found a better goddess than Amaterasu and pulled her out into the open. The gods tied a rope across the opening of the cave to prevent her retreat, and once more the world was lit up by the brilliant rays of the sun.

The Shinmai-Dorii or *torii* is the gateway of the sun and a symbol of immortality (fig. 170). Through this archway, in the "Land of the Rising Sun," Amaterasu, the sun goddess, enters the visible world each morning. At a shrine in Ise dating from the first century A.D., worshippers gather at dawn before a *torii* that stands upon a rock islet connected to a smaller rock by a sacred rope. Devotees on the seashore bow and clap their hands twice in order to gain the goddess's attention, as the sun rises spreading its beneficent light throughout creation. They offer prayers until the sun is no longer red and then clap again to take their leave. As the being of the sun, Amaterasu is revered not simply for shedding light throughout the world but also for providing continuous spiritual salvation to all things and beings. The *torii,* often found at entrances to temples and sacred precincts, is a portal into the spirit realm.

The actual landscapes of the pre-Shinto cult-centers were natural areas without buildings and often contained only one sacred tree or stone. Emphasis on pure natural elements in Shinto and later Zen practices have obvious parallels with Chinese Taoist tradition. Zen temple gardens are arranged for the specific purpose of engaging and heightening the awareness of the observer. These gardens have been called "built koans" because of the demand on the viewer to participate inwardly and to experience fully the arrangement of the landscape. Rocks in particular are seen as condensation of essential earth energy, reservoirs of *ch'i*, the bones of the earth, and are often set on raked white gravel, a symbol of flowing water and purity of spirit. The grouping of uniquely shaped stones, always in odd numbers, is meant to tell a narrative which is "heard with the eyes." "The fact that the garden is not to be occupied but only viewed adds to this experience," says Barrie. "The interplay of the garden and the architecture demands mental participation. The monk sitting on the veranda, gazing at the garden, is not passive but actively engaged in the environment, exemplifying the Zen principle of mindfulness."[47]

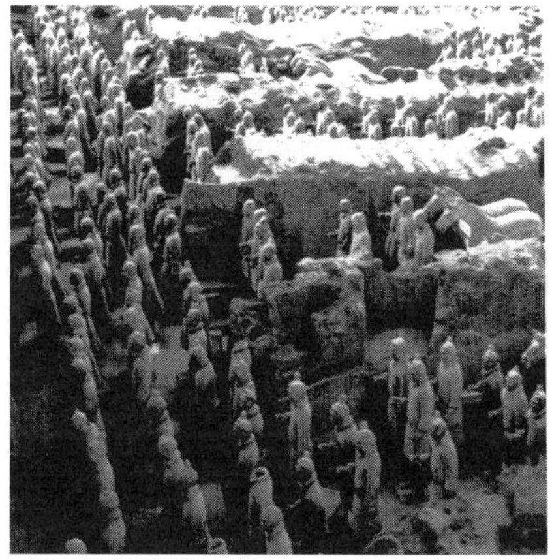

Fig. 174. Life-sized Chinese Han dynasty terra cotta figures are found in large numbers at Qin Shi Huang's Tomb, in Xi'an, Shaanxi, second century B.C. There are 7000 clay warriors, 600 horses, and 100 war chariots at this tomb. Such work was the precursor of Japanese *haniwa.*

The word Zen comes from the Chinese *ch'an,* which means *meditation.* Zen philosophy flourished in China between A.D. 700 and 900, and made its way to Japan by the twelfth century. It emphasizes living in the "here and now," striving to go beyond the limitations of intellect by way of direct experience. In Japan, the special arranging of gardens, art objects, and architecture finds its origin in spiritual, meditative practice.

Another manifestation of this Shinto-Zen aesthetic is seen in the Japanese use of ritual ropes and sacred knots. *Shimenawa* ("sacred straw rope") is probably the most ancient sacred imagery of the Japanese New Year festival and has its roots in indigenous practices (fig. 171). It indicates the threshold at the shrine or house where the realm of the profane ends and that of the sacred begins. The symbolic rope was made from rice straw grown in special fields, harvested before its grain appeared, dried in the shade, blessed under the supervision of a priest or

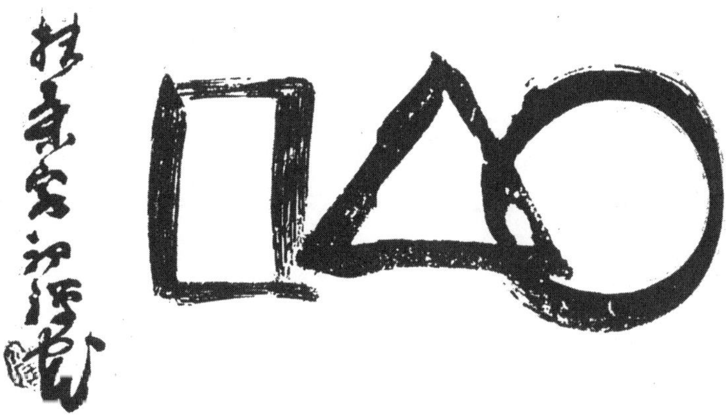

Fig. 175. Kakemono, the "Universe," also known as *Square, Triangle, and Circle,* by Gibon Sengi, A.D. 1750–1837, abbot of the Shofukuji temple at Hakata, is a description of the fundamental elements of creation in the Japanese Zen tradition. The simplicity of imagery and spontaneity of gesture is typical in Zen calligraphy. (After Sengi.)

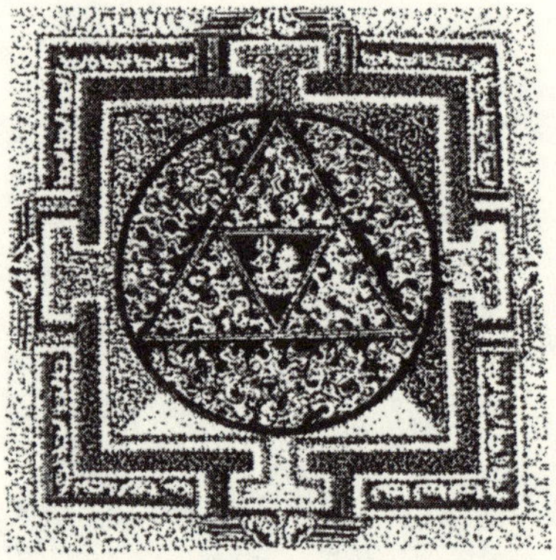

Fig. 176. The square, triangle, and circle have long been a part of the mandala tradition in Asia as this Tibetan rendered detail of the Chamunda Fierce Fire Offering Mandala demonstrates. The outer walls of the mandala mansion are made of skeleton effigies, embellished with images of intestinal garlands. The circle and triangle are filled with flames, and the innermost triangle of calm depicts in symbolic form the goddess Chamunda, consort of Yama, standing on her solar disc. This seventeenth-century mandala was used to overcome the most frightful inner enemy, insatiable egotism.

Fig. 177. In this seventeenth-century Rosicrucian illustration, the human being is placed as microcosm within the macrocosmic circle of creation. The four classical elements are represented by the square, and the three divisions of creation are shown by the triangle. The use of these three geometric forms in art is widespread.

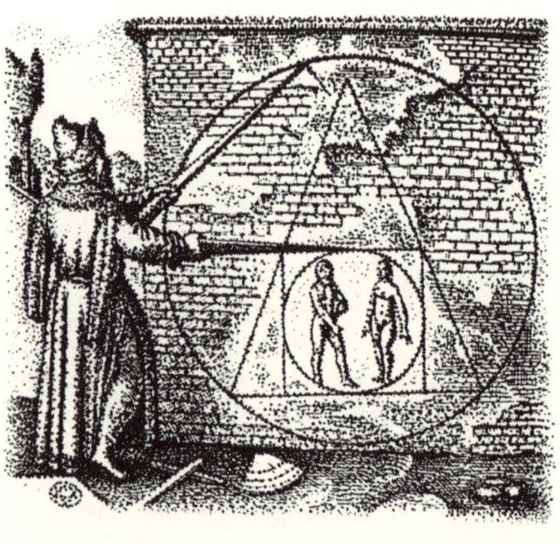

holy man, twisted to the left, and woven by the male head of the household on the last day of the year. The sacred rope was used to give protection against harmful spirits and thereby symbolized how souls are bound to Sacred Law. Yet, as in other traditions, it can indicate how the soul is fastened to the material world of desires and must free itself through inner striving. *Shimenawa* has parallels in China, Korea, Southeast Asia, Nepal, and India, where sacred rope practices are also found. The left-twisted rope is also used in the South Pacific, where it represents the threshold between the living and the dead. One observes over and over how knots (musubi) and braids possess exceptional spiritual significance. The Japanese poet Ki no Tsurayuki, in 935 A.D., muses about his home town, the imperial city of Kyoto, as he writes in his diary: "I wonder how it all looks—the straw festoons . . . at the gates of the little houses."[48]

Truly inspired imagery can be seen in the early Japanese pottery from the Jomon period, named for the cord or ropelike patterns fashioned into earthenware vessels (fig. 172). Examples bearing this high relief technique, often with fantastic plant and fire-like forms, seem to grow and flame before one's eyes. Something of the Chinese ch'i or life force comes to expression in these stylized rope patterns, which are dated between 3000 and 2000 B.C.

The Japanese *haniwa* (fig. 173), which literally means "circle of clay," is a relative of the magnificent Chinese Ch'in and Han dynasty earthenware figures (fig. 174) and was produced for the same ritual purpose—as a burial object. Warriors in armor, female figures, animals, birds, and model houses as subject matter for tomb offerings were placed in elaborate burial mounds and were intended only for the ancestors and gods. The images may in some cases be substitutes for actual people and possessions once buried with the deceased. The clay figures are constructed in simple, bold, geometrical shapes, expressing the Japanese penchant for simplicity of form. This characteristic of Japanese art holds true into more recent times where it is an obvious feature of both Zen and Shinto pictorial art.

The ink paintings of Gibon Sengi (1750–1837) are an expression of Zen's elimination of the nonessential and emphasis on basic elements in an intuitive representation of nature. In his Kakemono, Sengi very simply illustrates the fundamental forms of "the universe" in circle, triangle, and square (fig. 175), forms directly related to the mandala tradition (fig. 176). The same forms occur in a seventeenth-century Rosicrucian manuscript illustration, where the smaller circle depicts the microcosm and the dualities of the world, the square represents the earth, the triangle denotes the fixed laws of nature, and the large circle stands for eternity and the heavens (fig. 177). Although the use of these forms originates in prehistoric times, in Zen art they have come to symbolize Theravada, Mahayana, and Zen Buddhism—the three principal schools of Buddhist theology. Sengi uses the circle to represent the infinite and the triangle as the beginning of all forms. The triangle is doubled to bring about the square and this doubling process goes on infinitely to bring about the "ten thousand things," that is, the universe. The painting is carried out in the tradition of sacred writing—calligraphy or brush painting.

In Zen tradition, following meditation and concentration exercises, the master and pupil alike often engage in the art of calligraphy. Certain characters are drawn in rapid, effortless succession in order to capture the Zen state of mind. Sometimes they are not even "readable," yet their meaning is intuited. In this way the nonrepresentational nature of the glyph is seen as more than just beautiful writing. In Japan and China, calligraphy is given a high place of honor, drawn at the tops of scrolls, even above figures of the spiritual hierarchies such as Buddhas, Bodhisattvas, gods, and holy men. A language of form and gesture, born out of creative meaning, is at the source of all calligraphy. An old Chinese saying states: "Calligraphy and painting serve a single aim, the revelation of inner goodness." Even landscape painting, which was a popular subject in Japan well before an interest developed for it in Europe, is accompanied by calligraphy—signature, title, even lengthy descriptions and poetry. In his monochrome brush painting, *Hermitage by the Mountain Brook,* artist-priest Mincho depicts a Kyoto landscape with more accompanying calligraphy than painted picture (fig. 178). Mincho was so inspired by Chinese Song dynasty landscape painting that he set the standard with this work (and others since lost) for the Japanese Ashikaga school of monochrome scroll painting. A favorite theme in Zen art, the scene calls upon the viewer to make a pilgrimage to the hermit's simple refuge in its perfect natural setting, which parallels the austerity of the Zen temple gardens.

This art of landscape painting is also permeated by streams of energy, in the Chinese tradition of *ch'i,* which carry the observer along in such a way that one "reads" the picture. This is why one speaks of "writing" a picture. Japanese and Chinese landscape painting demonstrates a remarkable perception of the outer elemental world as a related whole, as a totality. Such scrolls are illustrated manuscripts, picture books.

Like the Tao, the spiritual practice of Shinto is grounded in a sense of the harmony of the universe with no fixed scripture or theology. It is more than a "nature religion," for family ancestors and folk spirits play a central part in its practices. "The multitude of Kami are not so much gods as sacred powers embodied in cosmic forces, superior men, natural objects and even abstract principles. They take up their abode in objects which symbolize their presence, such as a special stone or mirror; these are regarded as the 'divine body' (*shintai*) which is housed in the innermost sanctuary of the shrine and

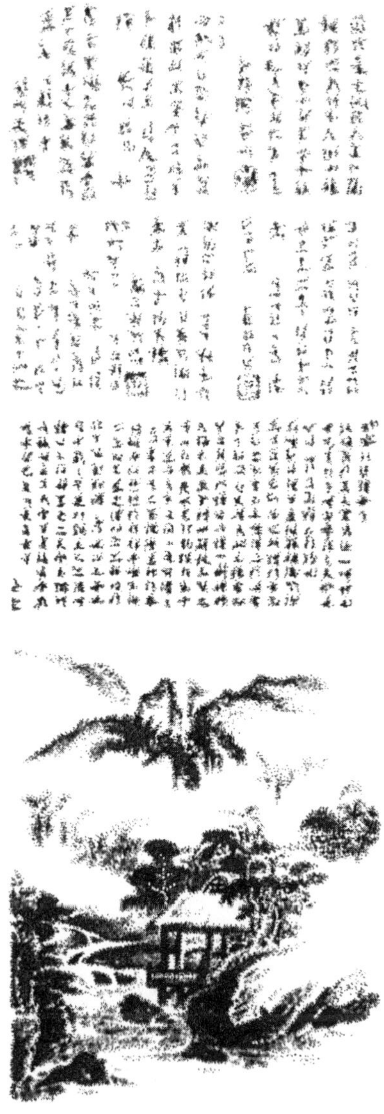

Fig. 178. Kanji or written characters have not become complete abstractions, as in the letters of Western alphabets. They still maintain something of the pictographic quality from which ancient writing arose. Here, in this rendering of a landscape painting of the Ashikaga period, attributed to Mincho, Cho-Densu, A.D. 1352–1431, the *kanji* take up more space than the picture. The priest-painter combines the two art forms into one integrated story painting or illustrated manuscript. (After Mincho.)

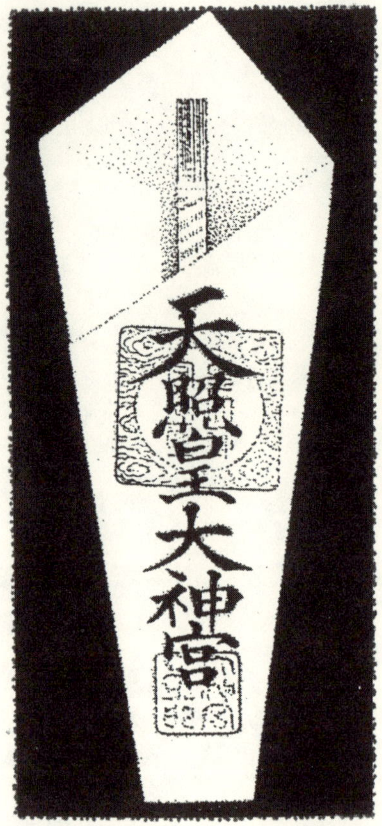

Fig. 179. It is customary in Japan to make offerings of *ofuda*, an arrangement of folded sheets of paper around a wooden stick. The sheets are marked with calligraphy honoring a particular god or goddess. This rendering is of an *ofuda* from the shrine at Ise dedicated to Amaterasu in the first century A.D., and honors her as a spiritual being, as a celestial body, and as an ancestor of the imperial family.

constitutes it as a sacred place of worship."[49] The Kami, as "beings more highly placed," are present in the sacred objects, which stand as a bond between the human and spiritual worlds. Therefore Shinto had little inclination to develop a distinctive iconography in the manner of other spiritual streams. Shinto's most characteristic symbols are the mirror (as a sun symbol), the precious stone or jewel (thunder), and the sword (moon).

The arranging of folded sheets of paper around a wooden stick, marked with calligraphy in honor of a particular god or goddess, is yet another customary practice in Japanese sacred art. Such an offering is called *ofuda*, and when it is made for the goddess Amaterasu it stands for her as a spiritual being, as a celestial body, and as an ancestor of the imperial family. This illustration is of an *ofuda* (fig. 179) from the shrine at Ise, which was dedicated to Amaterasu in the first century A.D.

India

To have lost the art of thinking in images is precisely to have lost the proper linguistic of metaphysics and to have descended to the verbal logic of "philosophy."
—Ananda K. Coomaraswamy

According to legend, Shiva visited the ten thousand heretical Rishis in order to teach them the Truth. The Rishis had nothing but hurtful curses for the god, but they had no effect. They sent a terrible tiger against Shiva, and he simply smiled and skinned the tiger with the nail of his little finger. He hung the tiger pelt over his shoulder for a cape. Immediately, a horrible serpent was sent against the benevolent god and again he defeated it and draped it around his neck as a garland. The Rishis then called up a black demon dwarf armed with a mace, but Shiva stepped onto its back and began to dance. Captivated by the dazzling rhythm and creative splendor of his dance, the heretics gazed in awe at Shiva. Suddenly the heavens opened to reveal all the gods likewise absorbed by the engaging movements of the "Lord of the Dance." The Rishis threw themselves at Shiva's feet and worshipped him as the Divine Truth.

Tenth-century bronzes depict Shiva in an idealized style with four arms and a voluminous hairpiece with grand flowing tresses and a lingamlike, upright crown (fig. 180). Shiva means "the benevolent" or "the favorable," and his dance rhythmically beats out the timeless choreography of the five cosmic functions of creation, conservation, destruction, incarnation, and liberation. A small hourglass drum appears in his upper right hand—the shamanic drum—which indicates the pulse beat of creation. A flame burns in his left palm indicating the force of will which connects Shiva to the great cosmic ring of fire around him. Fire stands for the periodic destruction and cleansing of the world. The other right hand conveys assurance as a symbol of protection, and the left hand points to the raised left leg, signifying salvation and release from further incarnations. The right foot, with pinpoint balance, tramples the demon dwarf of ignorance and forgetfulness. It is a victory dance for spiritual wisdom with Shiva as the axis and guardian of creation and destruction. Within this frenzied Dionysian dance, Shiva retains a countenance of dignified, Apollonian calm amidst the storm of activity. Like the tripartite images in which he has male and female profiles on either side of a frontal portrait, Shiva exemplifies and unifies opposites as in waxing and waning, time and eternity, mortal being and indestructible self.

In the overwhelming polytheism of Indian mythology, Shiva is linked with two other paramount gods, Brahma, the creator, and Vishnu, the preserver. This great *trimurti* or trinity—rarely represented in sculpture—reveals the subtle doctrine of Hindu unity. In the ancient Indian *Rig-Veda* is written: "God is One, but the sages give him many names." These gods have almost limitless manifestations, each with its own name, myth, and a well-defined iconography of identifying emblems, gestures, and postures. Although generally human in form, deities may have many arms and heads or animal parts, which artistically demonstrate the god or goddess's superhuman powers. Eliade remarks that "the multiplicity of members expresses by means of an artistic convention the fact that one is dealing not with a human being but with a god. Many-headedness signifies that a god is capable of looking in different directions at the same time, that he is all-seeing and consequently omniscient."[50]

An attribute of Shiva is the mystical third eye, which was created when his wife playfully covered his eyes with her loving hands while he was meditating and thereby caused the light of the world to be extinguished. However, the darkness was dispelled as a flaming eye, like the sun, opened on Shiva's forehead. Flames shot from the new eye and burned everything around. Seeing that his wife grieved at the devastation caused by the fire, Shiva, with a kindly thought restored the surroundings to robust and exuberant life. The trident is another attribute of Shiva; its three vertical lines are placed on the forehead of the devotee marking the position of the third eye or brow chakra. Shiva is sometimes depicted riding the Nandi bull, an animal god that embodies the power and virility of the lord Shiva (fig. 181). Nandi literally means "the Joyous One."

It may be that an early prototype of Shiva is pictured in the third millennium B.C. clay image of Pashupati, "Lord of the Beasts," from Mohenjo-Daro (fig. 182). This ithyphallic, horned figure, seated in yogic posture and surrounded by numerous animals, appears to be connected to fertility and asceticism—both characteristics of Shiva. The shamanlike figure has faces on both

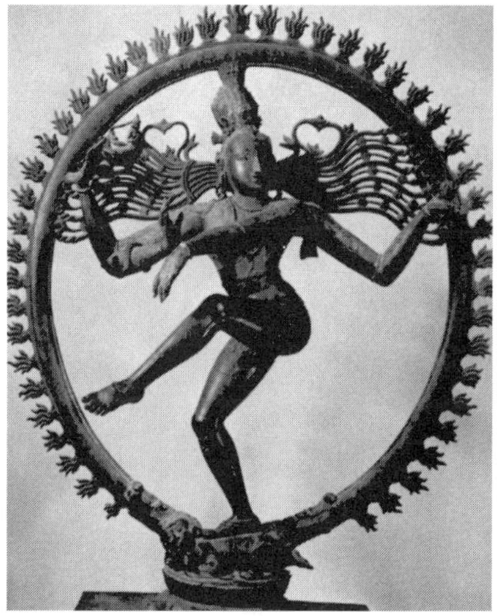

Fig. 180. Above: Shiva is depicted in this tenth-century bronze (above) as "Lord of the Dance." Within the flaming cosmic circle, Shiva dances upon the dwarf of ignorance and holds the drum that beats out the pulse of creation. He dances the creation, conservation, destruction, incarnation and liberation of worlds.

Fig. 181. Below: Nandi literally means "the Joyous One," and it is this animal god that embodies the virility and life force of Shiva. Shiva is often depicted riding on Nandi. (Ellora, India.)

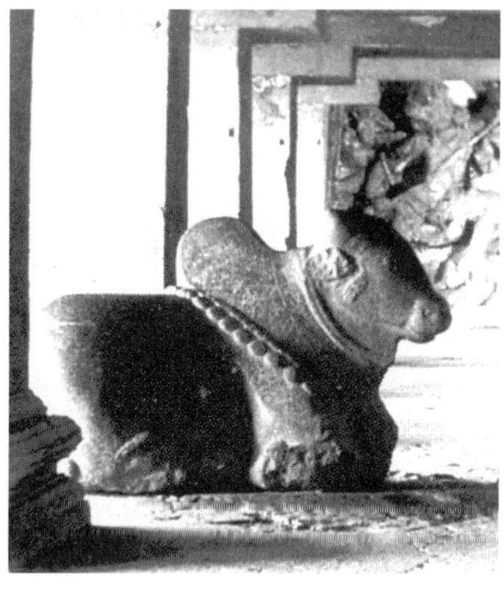

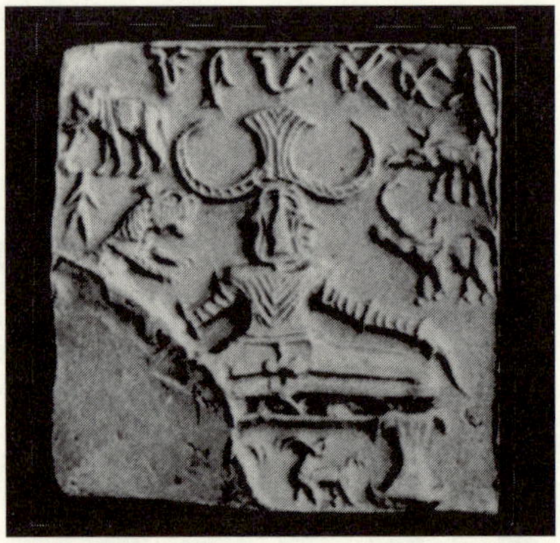

Fig. 182. Above: This third millennium clay tablet, from Mohenjo-Daro in present-day Pakistan, depicts a sitting ithyphallic figure with two faces and a horned headdress. Surrounded by animals this shamanlike Pashupati figure is a forerunner to the Hindu Shiva.

Fig. 183. Below: The *lingam,* principle of uprightness, is associated with Shiva. Devotees often bring milk with which to anoint the *lingam* stone. "The entire world has the phallus as its foundation. All is issued from the *lingam.* He who desires perfection of the soul must worship the lingam" (*Linga Purana,* 1.3.7).

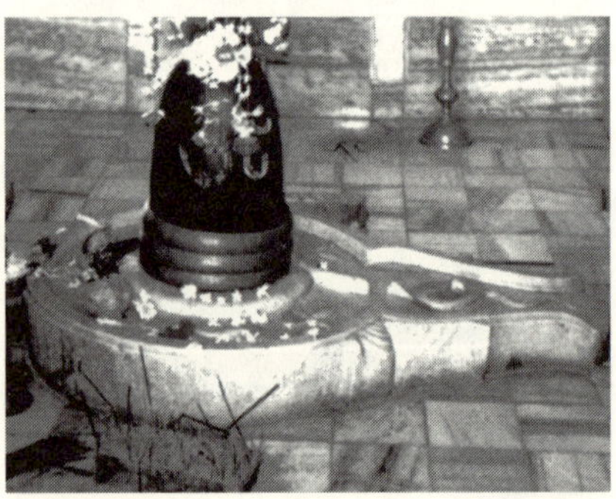

sides of its head, suggesting that it is a precursor of the three-faced Shiva of a later date. Pashupati lives in forests and groves, loves music and dance, is a nimble runner and is rarely seen. In Greece his counterpart appears as Pan—*pan* meaning "all." Like his Indian forerunner, Pan is horned, bearded, and often hairy—the god of shepherds and flocks, half god, half animal. Pan is a being who demonstrates what man is not—animal and god—and creates extremes between which man learns to discover true humanity.

As we shall see, this Pan figure has its roots in the very earliest of artistic images, and, as Alain Danielou suggests, this Shiva-like "lord of the animals is, without any doubt, the descendant of the ancient mistress of the animals of Paleolithic times, whose characteristics, props, attributes, and legends are virtually the same as those of Pashupati, the Indian lord of the animals."[51] In the ancient Indian *Linga Purana,* Shiva says, "Knowing that the things of this world are ephemeral, it is necessary to continually practice the yoga of the animals."[52]

The *lingam,* a phallic image (fig. 183), is an attribute of Shiva. Appearing often as an upright, cylindrical stone, the *lingam* usually rests upon a circular foundation that symbolizes the womb and the universal feminine principle in Nature, or *yoni.* The *yoni* is held in a base that represents Brahma, the maker. The central portion of the *lingam* represents Vishnu, the preserver, and the uppermost rounded section represents Shiva, as the "force of expansion that issues forth matter and form from its outpourings."[53]

Although the erect penis can allude to basic physical sex or ecstatic procreative energy, it more often indicates, especially when represented as a stylized lingam, the spiritual impulse that stands behind uprightness, striving and thriving—most especially, uprightness of a moral order and the principle of individuation. The *Shiva Purana* states, "It is not the phallus in itself which is revered but that for which it is the sign—the progenitor, the cosmic individual. The phallus is the emblem, the sign of the individual Shiva for whom it is the symbol."[54] As the obelisk and the standing stone harken to the spiritual principle of uprightness that has made it possible for human beings to stand erect upon the earth, so too the *lingam* is not simply a sexual image but an outer expression of the life spirit that is active as a divine force within the human individual. The Sanskrit word *lingam* means "sign."

As mentioned earlier, the ancient Indians, through deep, meditative penetration of the physical organism, developed a flexible and imaginative visual consciousness. Therefore, when picturing spiritual beings, lively and colorful anthropomorphic images were produced, often manifesting in figures with multitudinous heads, arms, and legs. Portraying the numerous aspects and positions that might be seen from a spiritual vantage point, the often extravagant Indian figures are not the result of personal expression but of primal or "unified consciousness." As William Anderson points out, according to Indian aesthetic theory, which emphasizes "quality, spirit, interior life, and gesture—not volume," the sculptor "would have seen the origins of the statue, not in his private dreams, but in a state of unified consciousness that precedes the awareness of the ego and in which the Lord of creative work, Vishvakarman, would have given him the image to be carved. He would then have worked upon it guided by his sense of discrimination and his memory of the inspiration. So much is given in that state of unified consciousness that the sculptor on completing it might have exclaimed in amazement, like the sculptor of one of the temples at Ellora: O how did I make it?"[55] (fig. 184) This way of working is also described by Shukracharya: "Let the imager establish images in temples by meditation on deities who are the objects of his devotion. For the successful achievement of this yoga the lineaments of the image are . . . dwelt upon in detail. In no other way, not even by direct and immediate vision of an actual object, is it possible to be so absorbed in contemplation, as thus in the making of images."[56]

The Buddha and Bodhisattva images of Indian artistic tradition are one side of the mystery character of India and the East—the inner contemplative path. The other side is the sensual and energetically engaging depictions of the animated physical body as in the gyrating figure of Shiva. Both aspects of Indian art are vital postures through which weaves a spiritual curriculum for Eastern humanity. (These tendencies are implied in the word *yoga,* which means both "restraint" and "union.") We have here an instruction in images. From the Sri Yantra Mandala and the meditating Buddha figures to the symbolic *lingam* and the "Lord of the Dance," Asian mystery images stimulate the unfolding of inner soul capacities, the development of moral codes of behavior, and the exercising of spiritual organs of perception. In this sense, the art of Asia is a remarkable example of the transformational potential of visual imagery and the power of spirit in art.

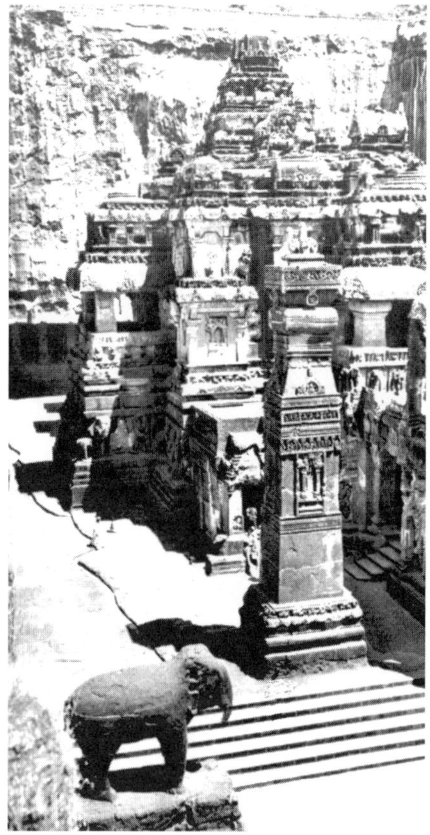

Fig. 184. Cut-rock architecture such as the Kailasa Temple at Ellora is better described as monumental sculpture as it is not built-up and put together from outside materials but it is entirely carved out of the natural mountain rock. Other monumental sculpture appears in Afghanistan, China, Egypt, Jordan, and Ethiopia. The pyramidal shape of the central tower of this temple represents the sacred mountain abode of Lord Shiva, Mount Kailasa. The various tiers are peopled with minor deities and guardian figures crowned with an eight-sided cupola.

V.3 Near Eastern Art

Art is a step in the known toward the unknown.
—Kahlil Gibran

In the great Mesopotamian city of Uruk there reigned a prince named Gilgamesh. He was "two-thirds god, one-third human" and ruled as he pleased over his people. In answer to the people's prayers, the gods conceived Enkidu, a hero strong enough to challenge the prince in his power. However, Gilgamesh and Enkidu became the best of friends and together defeated the terrible monster Khumbaba and even a furious bull sent against them in anger by the goddess Ishtar. In revenge for killing the bull, Ishtar saw to it that Enkidu fell ill and died in the arms of his friend. Gilgamesh was overcome with panic and dread at the sight of his dead friend. The fear of death made him flee, and in his flight he knew he must discover a way to escape the inevitable fate of death. It did not matter that the road might be long and dangerous, Gilgamesh would face all perils. He passed through the gates of Mount Mashu, though his face could not hide his fear and horror at the sight of the guardians whose heads reached the realm of the gods and whose chests touched the netherworld. He strode into the depths of the mountain's impenetrable darkness. Finally, light shone again and he entered a wonderful garden where the tree of the gods grew with magnificent fruit on branches of lapis lazuli. The goddess Siduri, at first frightened by the sight of the hero in this sacred place, advised him to give up his journey, but Gilgamesh refused and proceeded on his way until he reached the waters of death. Here he convinced the boatman, Urshanabi, to take him across the deadly waters to the immortal, Uta-Napishtim. But the one with everlasting life urged Gilgamesh to accept the inescapable necessity of death and, wishing to prove the force of destiny, he proposed that Gilgamesh should try to stay awake for six days and seven nights. Because sleep is the little brother of death this would be a worthy test for Gilgamesh. However, the hero was so tired from his journey that scarcely had he sat down before he fell into a deep slumber. Uta-Napishtim declared: "Behold the strong man who desired everlasting life! Sleep, like a hurricane, breaks over him."[57] Disappointed, Gilgamesh returns to Uruk, where, still haunted by the mystery of death, he invokes the shade of Enkidu, who describes to his friend the mournful state of those who are eternally imprisoned in the somber afterlife of Nergal.

Of all the Babylonian heroes, Gilgamesh is the most famous. And although his wonderous adventures end in the disappointing realization that immortality cannot be his, the epic poem of the second millennium B.C. refers to this figure as "He who discovered the source" or "He who saw all."

Excavations in northern Mesopotamia revealed an unusual temple at Tell Brak, which has many features in common with the Uruk temples in the south. Dated to about 3000 B.C. and contemporary with the Uruk period, the Tell Brak temple was cruciform in plan. The walls and altar of the shrine room were elaborately decorated with rich mosaics of semiprecious stone and copper and gold inlay. It is referred to as the Eye Temple because of the "eye" or "spectacle" motif that appears everywhere in the ornament and in thousands of votive images of black and white alabaster buried beneath the floor. Normally consisting of a flat square plate surmounted by a pair of large open eyes, the eye images also appear as amulets and stamp-seals of clay and stone at other sites such as Ur, Mari, and Lagash. Usually only a few inches in size, these small cult objects included figures with two and three pairs of eyes, arranged side-by-side as twin and triplet images or as larger and smaller, above and below, possibly as family dedications (fig. 185). A large "eye" image (fig. 186) stood upon the altar in the Tell Brak Eye Temple and may have been dedicated "to an all-seeing god who watched over the fortunes of the city."[58]

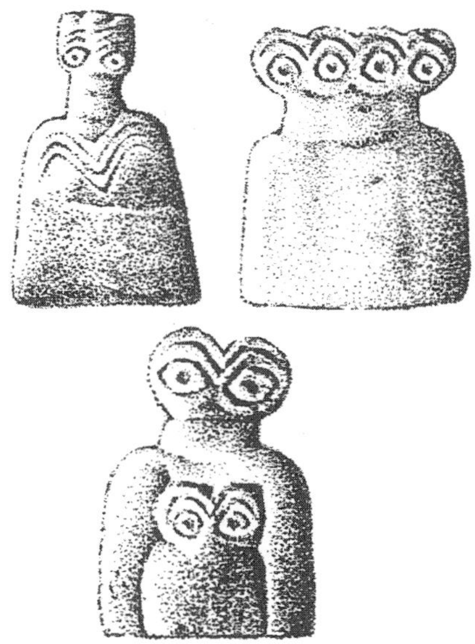

Fig. 185. Thousands of "eye" or "spectacle" images have been found in the Eye Temple of Tell Brak in northern Mesopotamia, present-day Iraq. Carved from black as well as white alabaster, the small figures with large eyes appear singly, in pairs, and in family groups of three or more.

Fig. 186. Below: A large "eye" image stood upon the altar of the Tell Brak temple. Perhaps it represents the All-Seeing God.

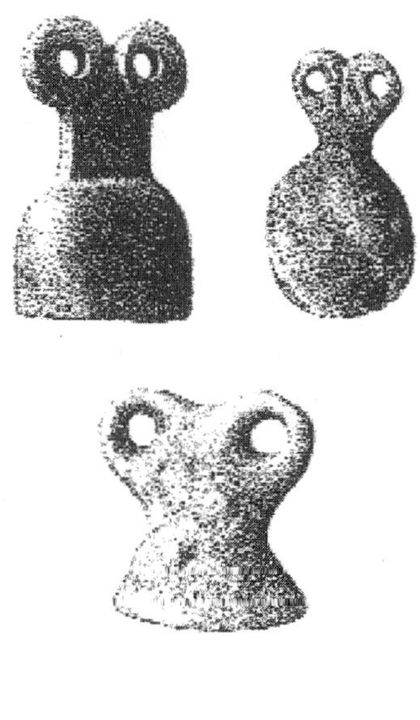

An innovative art form that developed parallel to the pictographic writing of the time is the cylinder-seal, a device used in part for recordkeeping and, more importantly, for the telling of myths and legends. It provided an opportunity both for a wide distribution of Mesopotamian mystery images as well as advancing the development of miniature relief carving. The small stones, shaped like stubby rolling pins, were delicately carved on their curved outer surface and rolled across soft clay tablets to create tiny reliefs. Recovered in great numbers from graves and house sites throughout the Near East, the cylinders and seals make their first appearance at Uruk around 3500 B.C., with fine craftsmanship from the outset. The quality of relief carving, as opposed to linear drawing, diminishes in later periods as the continuous frieze compositions are replaced by a succession of self-contained motifs. Heraldic-type designs are often symmetrically arranged in this later period. The "naked hero," sometimes identified as Gilgamesh, can be seen in various adventures upon these seals. The Bull Man, together with the hero, appears occasionally in combat with wild bulls (fig. 187). The animals are taken by

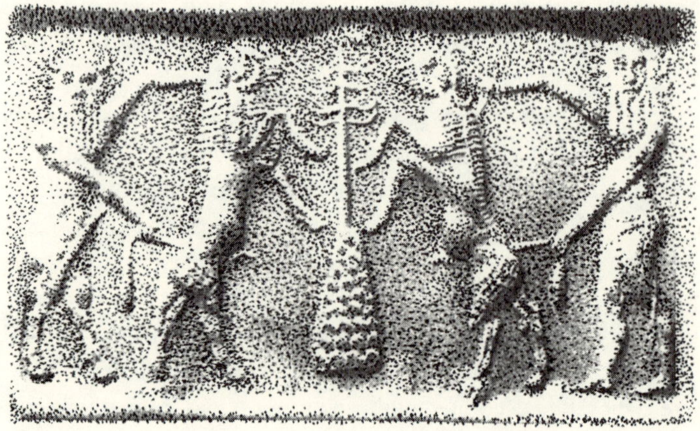

Fig. 187. The Bull Man (right) is a mythological figure appearing together with the hero (far right), sometimes referred to as Gilgamesh, in Mesopotamian seal art. A pair of bulls is being dispatched at the Tree of Life.

Fig. 188. The ziggurat has an outward gesture: stairs climb its outer surface, and there are no internal passages. This is in direct contrast to the Egyptian pyramids, which enclose interior spaces but lack outer features.

the tail and, in the case of the hero, dispatched with a knife as they stand upon the World Mountain and struggle before the Tree of Life. The mystery metaphor of overcoming the bull forces is obvious in such examples. Seals from the Abu Temple at Tell Asmar demonstrate characteristics found in Mohenjo-Daro and Harappa, establishing an early chronological link with the art of the Indus Valley civilization.

Contemporary with the Egyptian civilization, Sumerian, Assyrian, and Babylonian cultures produced remarkable art and architecture, which, unlike that of their neighbor to the west, did not place an emphasis on death and the afterlife but looked to birth and pre-earthly existence. In Mesopotamia one seeks the pathway out of the body back to the heavens. In Egypt the gesture is exactly the opposite: into the body, into the earth, into the realm of death. The Egyptian temple gate demonstrates this turning inward, and the false doors inside tombs indicate the threshold of a hidden, spiritual chamber within. The Egyptian pyramid has this inward character as it is closed on the outside, yet it conceals inaccessible corridors and chambers within its enormous mass. The Mesopotamian gate, in contrast, opens outward with guardian animals that display boundless life energy. The ziggurat too, with its stairs on the outside taking the place of interior corridors, is built for what takes place on its outer surface (fig. 188). The interior chambers of the pyramid, used for initiation through death, are transformed on the ziggurat as outside sanctuaries or "nuptial houses" for the holy meal and "marriage" ceremony to the deity. As in the case of Asian temples, the ziggurats "represent artificial mountains," according to Eliade, "because to all traditional cultures the

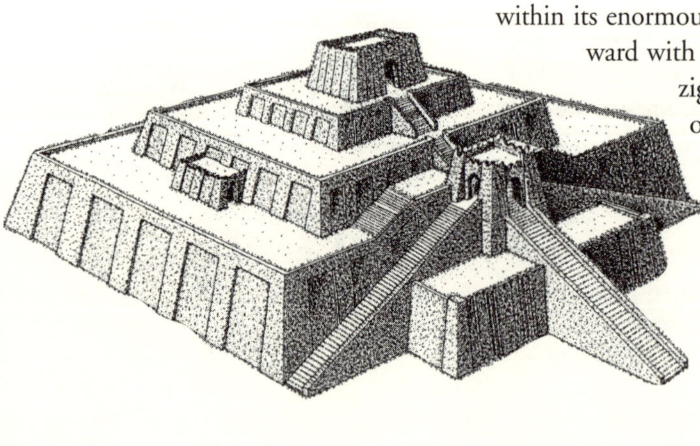

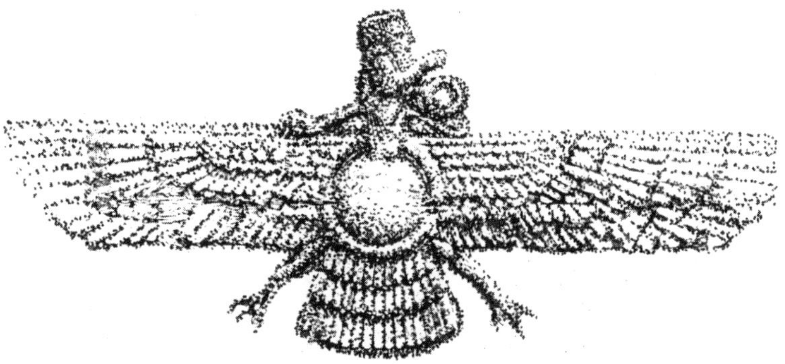

Fig. 189. The Mesopotamian gods are often pictured with large outspread wings, a metaphor for their spiritual flight. Sun God, Ahura Mazda, rides the winged solar disc (from Persepolis; left).

cosmos was interpreted as a mountain, while the highest point of the temple . . . was considered the supreme summit of the cosmic mountain."[59] It is no wonder that the gods of Mesopotamia have tremendous wingspans that enable them to descend from the heavens, bestow their blessings and gifts of fertility to humanity upon its high temple altars, and soar aloft once more, back to their own domain (fig. 189).

History credits Mesopotamia with being the cradle of civilization because of the great Sumerian, Assyrian, and Babylonian cultures that arose in its Fertile Crescent, between the Tigris and Euphrates Rivers in what is now Iraq. Mesopotamia was the gateway between East and West, Asia and Europe. It was the corridor of exchange for Indian and Persian civilizations with Egyptian and Greek cultures. In this center between East and West, between India and Egypt, four great religions arose: Zoroastrianism, Judaism, Christianity, and Islam. As a part of their religious iconography winged spirit beings, angels, begin to appear. Anderson makes an important connection in this regard: "The angel is an emblem of creative inspiration, of higher intelligence and of the highest art, which is the art of praise. The angel is also connected with important changes in the enlargement of the human capacity to think. The portrayal of winged heavenly bodies arises as a consequence of what happened in the many unconnected cultures in the fifth century B.C. when almost synchronously a new understanding dawned for the powers of the mind: in the band of Earth that stretches from China across the central plain of northern India to the Mediterranean, we find in the art . . . that was to arise from these new religions and philosophies the floating immortals of Taoism, the winged *apsaras* associated with Buddhism, the winged bulls and intelligences associated with Zoroastrianism, the seraphim and cherubim of the major Hebrew prophets, and the winged Victories and other winged beings appearing in Greek art at the same time as the wakening of Attic philosophy."[60]

Fig. 190. The divine Mother Goddess of Çatal Hüyük is depicted as a large female figure seated upon a leopard throne (below). She might be compared to the images of Artemis (fig. 84) and the Venus figurines (fig. 86).

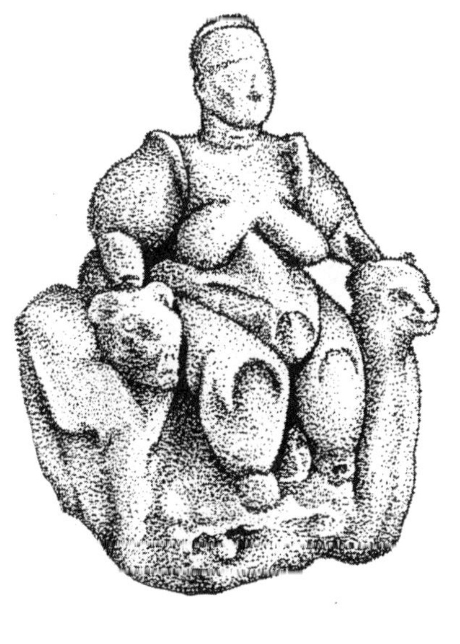

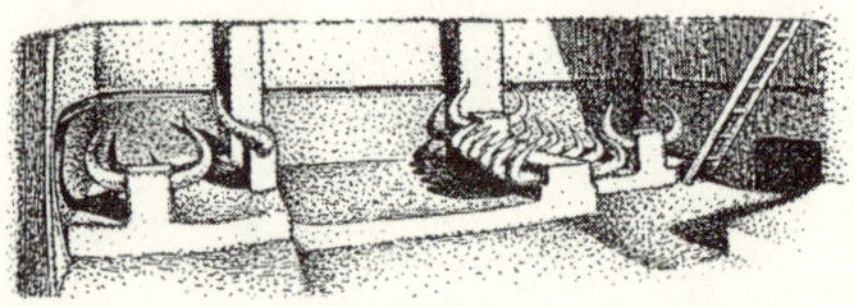

a

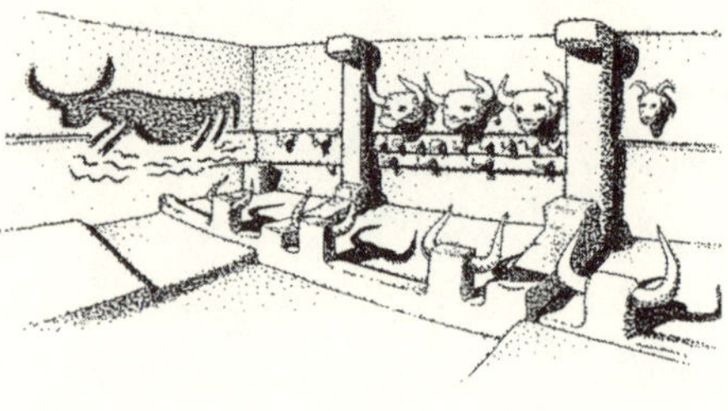

b

Fig. 191. (a) Vultures at Çatal Hüyük pick apart human figures, an indication of "sky burial" practices. Bull heads and horns, along with images of female breasts, are mounted on walls (b) and together represent the life force and principle of fertility.

Fig. 192. Below: *Lamassu,* half man, half bull, are often placed at gateways as guardian figures of the Mesopotamian culture.

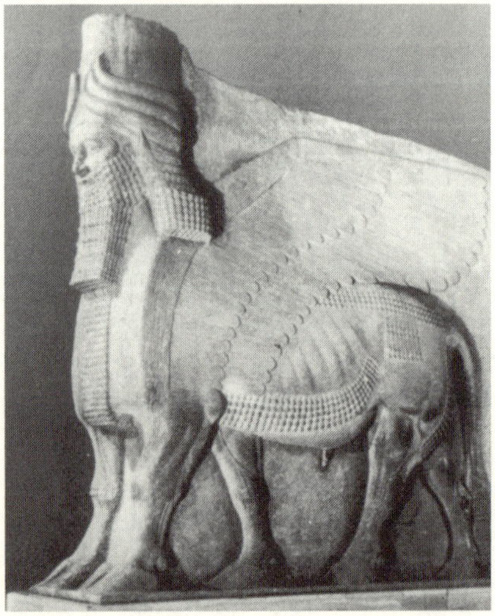

Well before the appearance of historic religions and literate civilizations, we find the remarkable early settlements of Jericho in Palestine and Çatal Hüyük in Anatolia, present-day Turkey. Referred to as "the first city" because of its extensive site, the Çatal Hüyük complex, covering some fifteen acres, has many successive building levels dating to between 6500 and 5650 B.C. Shrines and sanctuaries, distinguished by their exceptional decoration, appear in building complexes where they served every four or five apartments. Here the dead were buried below the floors of houses and shrines only after the flesh had been removed, and this most likely was done by means of vultures according to a traditional "sky burial." Such cleaning of bones is still practiced by Zoroastrians, whose early roots are traced to the Persian Near East. At Çatal Hüyük, the fleshless bones were wrapped in cloth or hides, sometimes painted with red ochre, and buried with funerary gifts such as jewelry, textiles, clay seals, wooden vessels, weapons and tools. Figurines and pottery were not part of the burial goods.

The central deity of Çatal Hüyük was a goddess depicted in three aspects: as maiden, as mother giving birth, and as old woman. She is often shown seated on her leopard throne (fig. 190) or is indicated by two leopards (her sacred animal), head to head and richly painted. She is also shown with arms and legs raised, giving birth to a bull's head. The male deity appears in two aspects, as a boy or as an older god with a beard, riding his sacred animal, the bull. The male god often appears simply in the figure of a painted or relief sculpted bull or bull's head. The shrine imagery focuses heavily on the goddess, the leopard, the bull, and the vulture. James Mellaart notes other art forms as well: "Symbols such as hands, horns, and crosses are frequently found in these paintings as befits their magical and protective function."[61] Geometric patterns of great intricacy also show up on the painted walls and suggest a prototype for traditional Anatolian textile designs. Numerous layers of paintings in red and black on white plaster walls appear in these shrines; sometimes the mural images are two meters in length. Concave and convex wall reliefs are also featured.

The shrines evidently supported the practice of a fertility cult that promoted continuity and abundance both in this life and the next. Birthing scenes on one wall contrast with scenes of death on another. Vultures are shown swooping down upon fragmented human figures as a picture of death, while bull heads and horns line benches, and together with images of women's breasts are mounted on walls as symbols of life (fig. 191).

The staggering amount of bull imagery at Çatal Hüyük is echoed in mystery images of the later high Mesopotamian civilizations. The miniature Bull Man featured on cylinder-seals and the monumental lamassu guardian figures (fig. 192) that adorn gateways and palaces of Assyrian cities speak of the bovine animal powers. The bull is revered both as an earthly and as an astral being of cosmic importance, for it is during the Assyro-Babylonian cultural period that the sun is moving through the constellation of Taurus. Kahlil Gibran recalls: "Art began when man glorified the sun with a hymn of gratitude."[62]

Islam, the most recent of the four great religions to flourish in the Near East, has three aspects to its inspirational canon: pure geometric design, arabesques, and calligraphy. The purely geometric ornamentation, crystalline and precise, suggests the infinite possibility of earthly forms to be found in the mineral kingdom, while the arabesque or *ataurique* reveals the exuberant stylized foliage of the plant kingdom (fig. 193). The paisley or *boteh* (fig. 194) is sometimes thought to be derived from a flame, a teardrop, or a cypress tree blowing in the wind. It is strikingly reminiscent of the Chinese yin-yang form, the Maori koru, and the Mayan speech scroll, and is probably an indication of the flowing life forms that also inspired the early arabesque creations. The third component of Islamic art, calligraphy, can be either geometric, built-up of straight lines and angles (fig. 195), or arabesque-like in curvilinear gestures. This uniting of polar-opposite form qualities arises directly out of the spiritual foundations of Islam. As Sayyed Hossein Nasr points out concerning the holy book of Islam: "The Qu'ran (Koran) is composed of a profusion and intertwining of plant life as seen in a forest, often combined suddenly with the geometry, symmetry and clarity of the mineral kingdom, of a crystal held before light. The key to Islamic art is in fact this combination of plant and mineral forms as inspired by the form of expression of the Qu'ran."[63] Here calligraphy is holy script and the embodiment of the sacred word of God

Islamic art is an art of decoration and is characterized by a sense of order, balance, and symmetry. Naturalism, the reproduction of the things of the outer world, is considered idolatry and is not condoned. In this way, geometric designs, arabesques, and calligraphy metaphorically provide a window into the realm of the eternal, into the spiritual.

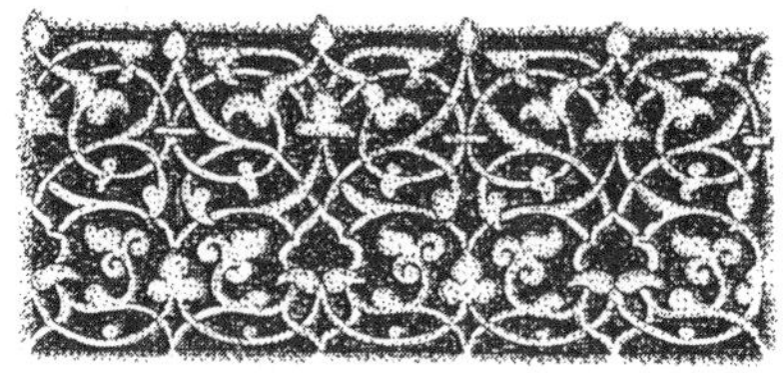

Fig. 193. Top: The arabesque or ataurique pictures the ever-unfolding forces of life as revealed in the plant kingdom and is a symbol for the eternal path of the pilgrim. This border is from the Qu'ran (Koran).

Fig. 194. Center: The paisley or *boteh*, said to be derived from the burning flame, the teardrop, or the bending cypress tree, and looking like a single cell amoeba, suggests the form of thriving life energy. This detail is from a traditional Persian carpet design.

Fig. 195. Bottom: Islamic calligraphy appears both as curvilinear, flowing script and as angular, straight print, such as this square Kufic script, which says: "There is no god but God, and Muhammad is the messenger of God."

V.4 African Art

The whole purpose of rock painting was to mark the presence of the deity in certain favored spots, places that were "on high" . . . rock shelters and caves that personified the stony womb of creation.
—Carson Ritchie

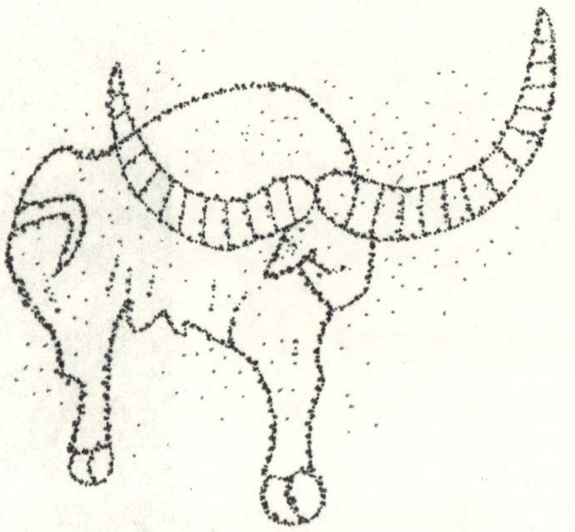

Fig. 196. Above: The Bubalus rock art style of North Africa is named for the *Bubalus antiquus* buffalo (above), which appears in many of the paintings and rock art images of this early period.

Fig. 198. Below: The ram is associated with the sun in many cultures and this North African rock art image may be a forerunner of the Egyptian sun ram of the Amon Temple at Thebes.

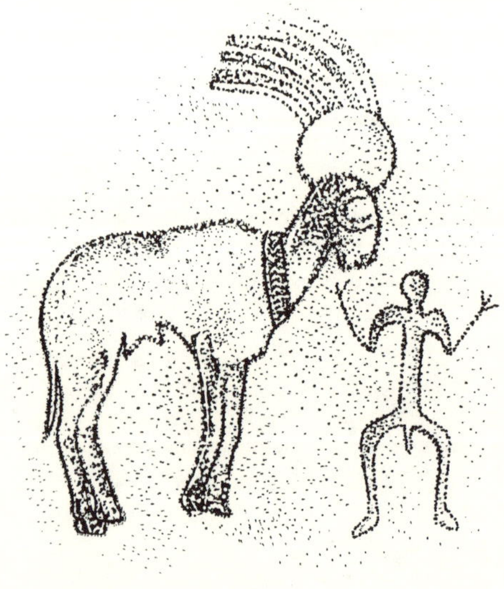

Africa, called the "Dark Continent" by nineteenth-century explorers, is home to the most diverse large land mammals in the world. Theories based on fossil evidence suggest that the origins of man are to be found here as well. According to esoteric tradition, Africa is the Heart of the Earth.

Prehistoric paintings and engravings are abundant and widely distributed throughout Africa: in caves, rock shelters, and on isolated boulders. From the Sahara region in the north to the southernmost areas of the continent, rock art paintings may date to c. 25,000 B.C., as discoveries in southwest Africa suggest.[64] According to some researchers, a relationship between early African art and the Paleolithic art of Spain is likely.

Northern Africa

The initiation societies, which often overlap traditional political boundaries, are among the principal patrons of art in Africa.
—Frank Willet

One of the earliest North African rock art styles is called the Bubalus, and is named after the large, extinct *Bubalus antiquus* buffalo, depicted in many rock engravings (fig. 196). Going back to Paleolithic times, this period is also referred to as the Large Wild Fauna phase because it depicts numerous large undomesticated animals that roamed the Sahara when this region was a far more hospitable environment than today.

The buffalo and the ram are clearly the most important animals in early North African rock art as they are illustrated more frequently than other subjects. Curiously, the buffalo often appears together with the spiral. The continuous vitality of the spiral seems intrinsically bound up with the nature of the buffalo and is sometimes drawn within the body of the bovine, perhaps as an indication of metabolic activity. Sometimes appearing outside the animal it can form the head or connect to the horns. Some examples from various locations in the Sahara are over 8000 years old (fig. 197). In contrast to the bull is the ram. In one example, two rams are crowned with solar discs, their horns projecting like rays of sunlight. Wearing a decorated neckband, the ram is revered by a simple stick-figure man (fig. 198). These solar rams may be the forerunners to the later Egyptian sun ram of the temple of Amon at Thebes.[65]

Detailed depictions of animals noticeably contrast the overly simplified human figures. It is common throughout the prehistoric period to see the importance and expertise of animal imagery while there is a lack of self-importance and self-awareness in the human form. One could say that animals have a secure place in creation, but humanity does not yet. The human being is still trying to discover what his nature and purpose is. Human figures represented during this period are often seen with bow, axe, or boomerang in hand—in pursuit of an animal, engaged in the activity of the hunt.

Another, parallel phase of Sahara art features the distinctive Round Head style generally dated to about 6000 B.C., but possibly to as early as the ninth millennium B.C.[66] Here the dominant themes are not large animals, but human figures with round featureless heads (fig. 199). Does a shift in themes indicate a shift in awareness? There appears to be an emphasis on the burgeoning, swelling outward, and rounding forces that weaken toward the

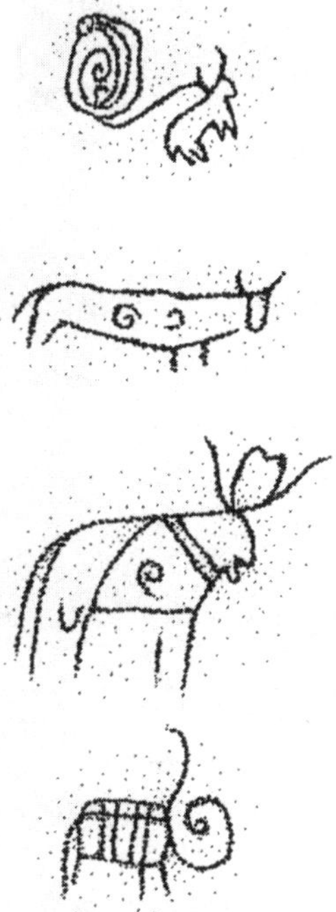

Fig. 197. In North African rock art, the depiction of the buffalo, in itself a symbol of fertility, often includes the spiral form(above), which indicates growth and increase.

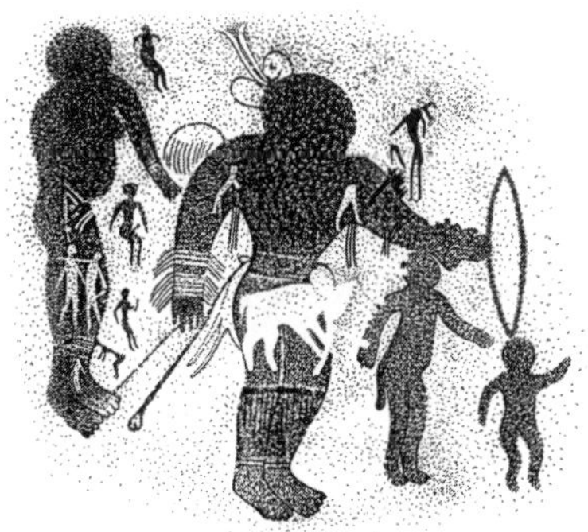

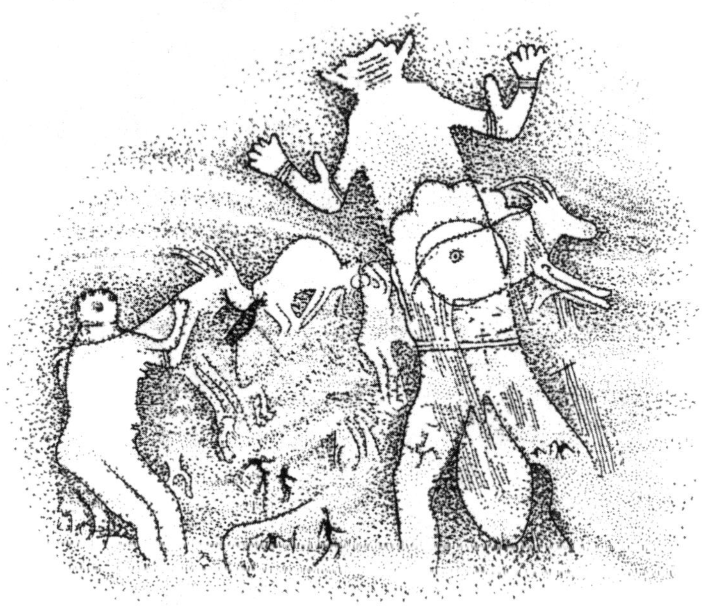

Fig. 199. Above: The Round Head style is characterized by its painted human figures with large round heads, dated from 8000 B.C. to 6000 B.C.

Fig. 200. Right: This rock painting depicts Round Head style women with a horned shaman or spirit being.

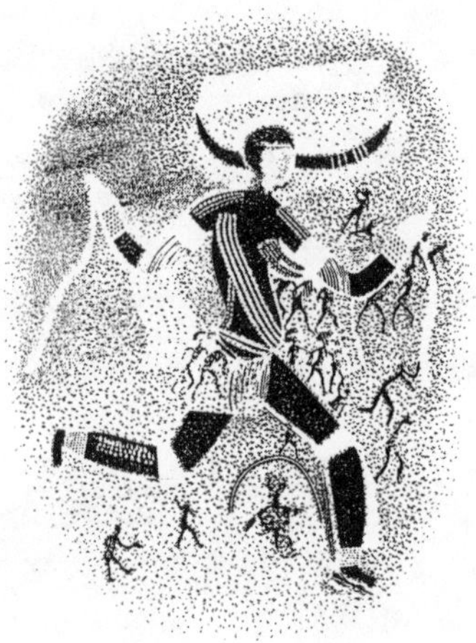

Fig. 201. Above: *The White Lady,* or *Horned Goddess of Aouanrhet,* is of the later Round Head period and may be related to the Egyptian goddess Isis, who was also crowned with cow horns.

Fig. 202. Below: Isis, Mother Goddess of ancient Egypt, was marked with cow horns by her son Horus because she let his adversary, Typhon-Set, escape with his life after slaying Osiris.

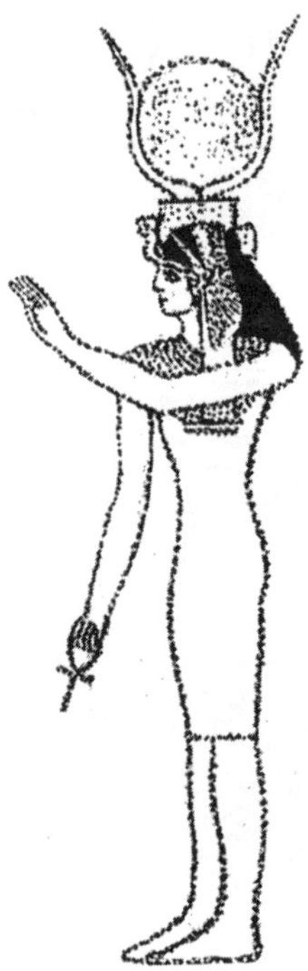

periphery (see Chapter VI.6). We might compare them to the Paleolithic "Venus" figurines, to be discussed in the next chapter (fig. 86). These Round Head figures range in size from several inches to over sixteen feet tall, the largest mural paintings known in prehistoric art. One rock art site at Sefar, Tessili n' Ajjer, depicts a procession of round-headed women with raised arms gesturing toward a gigantic horned figure, perhaps a shaman or spirit being (fig. 200). Goats and other iconography overlap the larger figures that stand as high as ten feet tall.

In its later stages, the Round Head style becomes more elegant and fluid, showing possible Egyptian influences. Exceptionally beautiful paintings like the *White Lady of Aouanrhet* are from this period (fig. 201). Also called the *Horned Goddess,* a female figure clothed with dangling fringes at her waist, arms, and hands, is shown overshadowed by what may be a cloud of grain falling from a heavenly wheat field. This shower occurs about the horned head of the figure, which likely represents a priestess or goddess. The *Horned Goddess* may also bear a connection to Isis, the Egyptian deity crowned with cow horns, whose husband, Osiris, is credited with introducing agriculture into the not so distant Nile River region (fig. 202).

Another rock painting at Aouanrhet, assigned to the period of Egyptian influence, shows a woman with elongated body and limbs floating out of, or pulling, the head of another more contracted figure (fig. 203). Two other figures crouch below, their heads overlapping the floating woman. Yet another figure, its head and hands emerging from a series of concentric circles, appears as though breaking out of an egg or snail-like shell. This picture, painted in black, white, and red ochre, may depict the birth into the spiritual world and the voyage of the dead in the afterlife, a theme common to Egyptian art. The Round Head period, lasting thousands of years, stylistically appears to be the beginning of a truly African art anticipating the imagery of later tribal art forms.

The Chariot or Equestrian period, from around 1200 B.C. to about 100 B.C., is linked to the arrival of the horse and chariot in North Africa by way of Mycenean Crete. The dynamic "flying gallop" rock paintings are the most important images from this period because of the shift in consciousness they represent (fig. 204). The theme depicts humans domesticating rather than hunting the animal. Although this period reflects an aesthetic decline the spiritual significance of the horse and charioteer motif found in Greek and Egyptian art of this same time period is noteworthy.

The horse and chariot, as carrier of the pharaoh's elite warriors, first appears in Egypt at the time of Akhenaten (fig. 205). It is not only an indication of new technology but also of a changing awareness, for the horse as a mystery image is the picture of cleverness and intelligence. In his

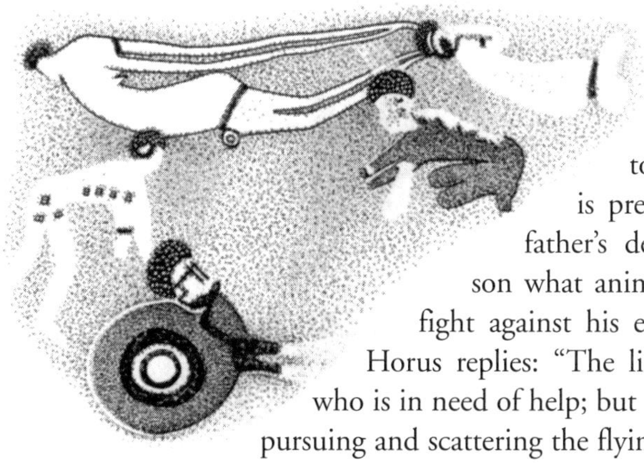

rendering of the Isis and Osiris myth, Plutarch describes how Osiris appears to his son Horus, who is preparing to avenge his father's death. Osiris asks his son what animal he will use in his fight against his enemy, Typhon (Set). Horus replies: "The lion is useful for him who is in need of help; but the horse is useful for pursuing and scattering the flying foe so that the battle may be ended utterly." The Trojan Horse, too, is a product of the Athena-inspired intelligence of Odysseus that swiftly brings the Greeks' ten-year conflict with Troy to an end, and is a vivid imaginative picture of changing human consciousness.

By the first century B.C., the Sahara has become a desert and camels are introduced from Arabia. Rock art goes into further decline as many crude rock paintings and simple engravings of camels and their riders appear at this time.

Fig. 203. Floating figures from a rock painting of the Round Head period at Aouanrhet, North Africa (left), show possible Egyptian influence. The elongated figures and dream-like imagery suggest a supersensorial scene. (After Settegart).

Fig. 204. The "flying gallop" rock (below) paintings of the Chariot or Equestrian period represent not only a change in modes of transportation but also a shift in consciousness. The domestication of the horse parallels a "reining-in" of intellectual thinking.

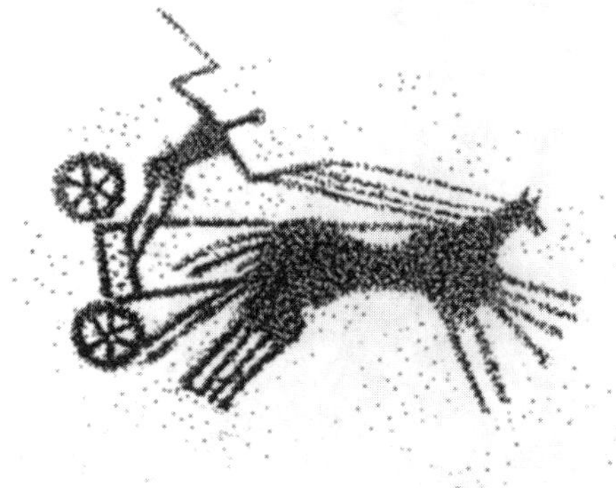

Southern Africa

[The San rock art] all recorded mythological symbols, rituals designed to overcome danger, invoke fertility and combat the threat of the supernatural. They tell of initiation and other ceremonials, for which the clans probably assembled in rock shelters. The rites centered on, and were inspired by, the art on the wall which depicted symbols known to all.
—Werner Gillon

The art of the Bushmen deals with a primal mythology centering around the eland, a large South African antelope. In one origin myth, the Bushmen tell of how the wife of the creator god Kaggen gave birth to the first eland. Kaggen attempted to kill this offspring by throwing sharpened sticks at it, but was unsuccessful. However, when his sons discovered and killed the eland, Kaggen was greatly angered. He ground together fat and blood from the animal's heart, and drops from this mixture created the first eland bulls and cows. They spread over the earth and in this way provided game for Kaggen's sons[67] In this traditional tale a child of the creator god, the eland, is sacrificed, transformed, and offered again that its siblings (humanity) may be fed. However, the eland is not a basic staple in the Bushman diet; plants and small game are. The eland has esoteric significance for

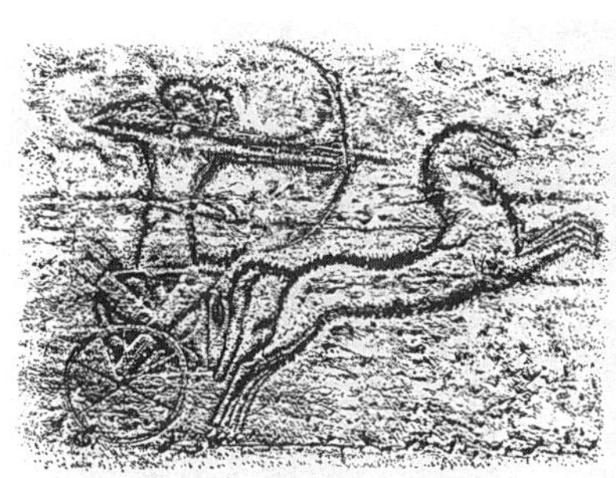

Fig. 205. The chariot appears in Egypt with Akhenaten around 1300 B.C. (above) and, as in the rest of North Africa and Greece, it indicates a clear separation of rider from animal: a transformation in consciousness to one of control over animal instincts.

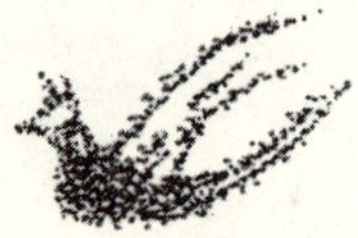

the tribe and nourishes its members in a more spiritual way. It is believed that one becomes an eland after death, and realistic rock art depictions of eland with red lines on their foreheads are said to be transformed shamans.

Rock art in South Africa often depicts the "Antelope Man," a part eland, part human, spirit being (fig. 206). With eland head and hooves, but human arms and upright stature, the Antelope Man is spirit brother of the Bushmen—he is the spirit guide and soul of the ancestors. Connected to this motif is the "Flying Buck," which represents the human soul, exalted in spirit flight (fig. 207). This image can be linked to the Bushmen's trance state when a visionary journey is undertaken. Activated through protracted dance, as women chant (no hallucinogens or solitary vision quests are taken), this out-of-body condition, experienced by the men, is brought about by a supernatural energy called *ntum,* meaning "death thing" or "fight."[68] This force rises up in the Bushman like a powerful fire, displacing ordinary consciousness. The trance dancer drops to his knees and throws his arms back in the position of "asking god for power," as one San Bushman put it.[69] Ritual trance states are not uncommon in other parts of the world, such as Bali, Nepal, and Tibet. In Mesoamerican art, Olmec depictions of shamanic "fliers" or "acrobats" may be seen as parallel images to the South African Flying Buck pictures.

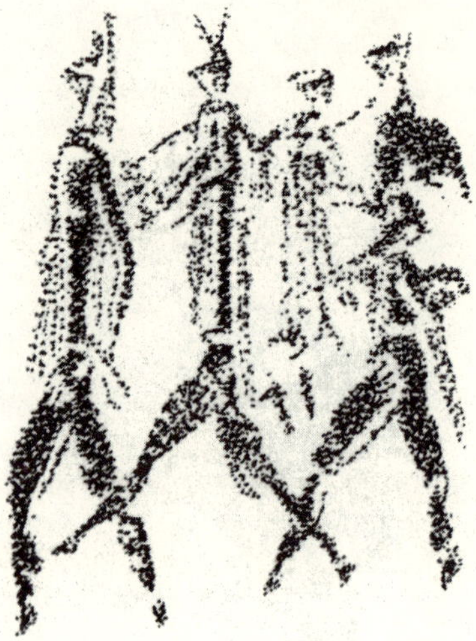

Fig. 206. Rock art of the South African Bushmen depicts the "Antelope Man" (above), an anthropomorphic figure with eland head and hooves but with upright human stature.

Fig. 207. The Flying Buck (below) is a Bushman image representing the human soul in ecstatic spirit flight.

The rock art depictions of Antelope Men and Flying Bucks are pictures that touch on the mysteries of the Bushmen's spiritual life, bridging the outer and inner worlds with the help of animal-spirit powers. Jean Clottes and J. D. Lewis-Williams, speaking of Bushman rock art, suggest: "More than simple pictures, the panels [of paintings] were gateways to the spirit world, panoramas which, in their trance experience, shamans could enter and with which their own projected mental imagery could mingle."[70] For the Bushmen, these experiences are not reserved only for shamans but are open to all eligible adult males in the tribe. Lewis-Williams and T.A. Dowson, while interviewing one of the last southern San Bushmen, recorded the following information concerning the use of pictograms: "She demonstrated how dancers seeking power turned to face the paintings on the wall

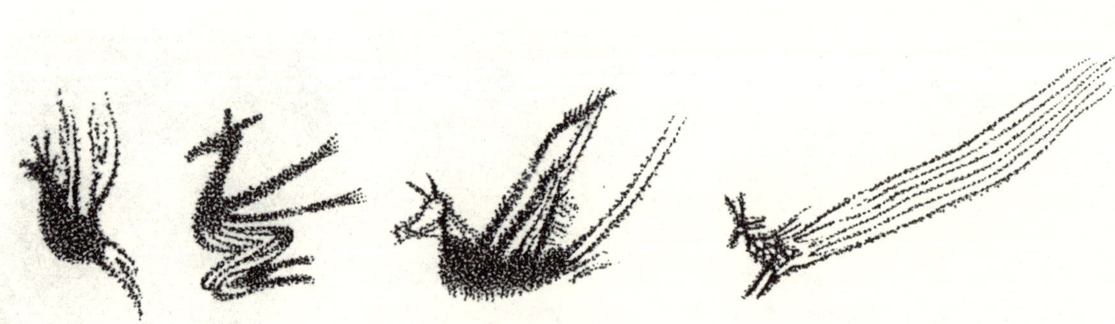

of the rock-shelter and how some people placed their hands on the paintings of the eland to gain power. The paintings, she said, had been put there by shamans and contained power."[71] This spirit potency was in part due to the eland blood and fat used as a binder in pigments (reminiscent of Kaggen's creation of the eland from drops of blood from his offspring). Blood and fat are also believed to be key ingredients used in the pigments of Paleolithic cave paintings. This art of the Bushmen has been practiced in caves and rock shelters into the last century, yet "radiocarbon-date studies indicate that some of the art can be traced back at least 10,000 years and may be more than twice as old as that."[72]

The painted rock shrines of South Africa do not fall into such easily recognizable phases as do those of North Africa. Exact dating of engravings, as well as the age of old polychrome paintings, is uncertain. In fact dates for the more recent single color paintings is also uncertain. Therefore, instead of being organized according to time periods, categories are often based on rock art techniques such as engravings, polychrome paintings in various styles, and monochrome paintings.

Petroglyphs, or etchings in stone, are probably the oldest of the three techniques, according to archaeologists (fig. 208). They appear on rock fragments and broken stone slabs as opposed to rock walls. The oldest of these petroglyphs are of single animal figures, pecked out on basalt or diorite stone with a remarkable naturalism. The polychrome paintings or pictograms, most often depicting animals, are found in the deep south as well as in Zimbabwe. Also found in Zimbabwe are the classic monochrome paintings of the distinctive "wedge style." The appearance of plants, water, and rocks in these compositions is unique in prehistoric rock art. Typical wedge period themes also include ritual killings of the king, and high-culture royal burials, which indicate that hunter-gatherers such as the Bushmen were not their creators.

Pictograms, paintings on stone, and petroglyphs in both northern and southern Africa are directly associated with many of the continent's sacred sites, which were likely places of initiation and ritual observance. In many cases rock art shrines depict local mythology as well as more far-reaching spiritual practices. These prehistoric sites are reminders of the sacred role art plays in the spiritual life of prehistoric and tribal Africa.

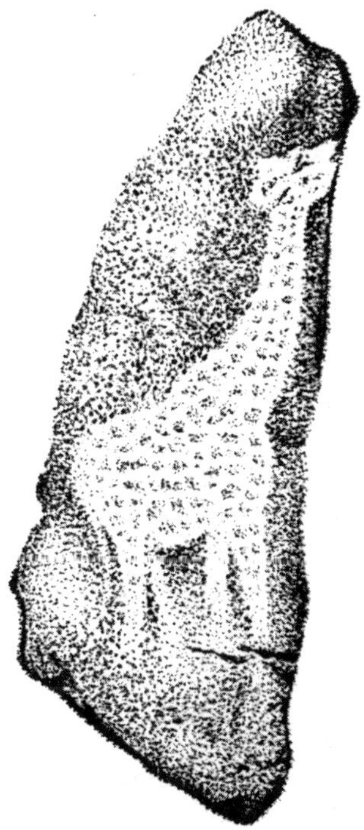

Fig. 208. Petroglyph images of animals etched on basalt and diorite stone fragments are possibly the oldest examples of South African visual art. This pecked engraving of a giraffe from the Western Transvaal is just over two feet in height.

V.5 Art of the Americas

The world before me is restored in beauty,
The world behind me is restored in beauty,
The world below me is restored in beauty,
The world above me is restored in beauty,
All things around me are restored in beauty,
My voice is restored in beauty,
It is restored in beauty,
It is restored in beauty,
It is restored in beauty.
—Native American chant

From the Arctic regions of Canada in the far north to the equally frozen landscape of Tierra del Fuego in the south, the Americas were home to a paleo-Indian spirituality that found expression in diverse shamanic practices with gods, ancestors, and animal spirits peopling the arts and crafts that were used in ritual observances. Artifacts associated with universal, local, and personal mythologies make up the largest part of these tribal arts. Relics of the finest workmanship have been found in mounds, pyramids, and ancient cities of high civilizations from the Mississippi River Valley to the Andes Mountains. Throughout the Americas, architecture, sculpture, and painting give ample evidence of the indigenous American spirit and art.

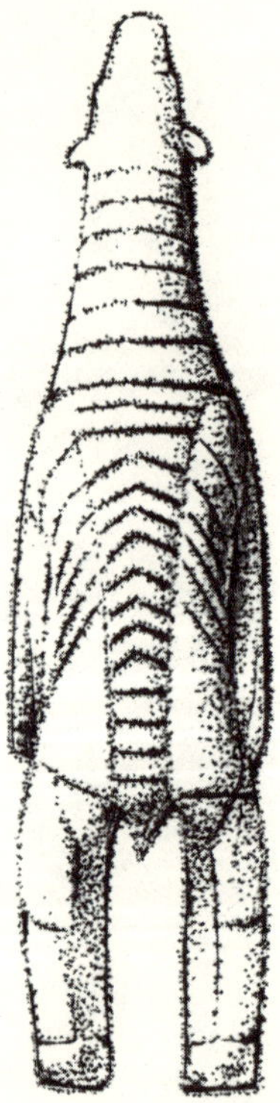

Fig. 209. Carved from walrus-tusk ivory, this polar bear figurine (above) stands upright as Bear Man and reveals its skeleton in X-ray style.

North America

And with death came also the sun, the moon, and stars; for when men die, they ascend to the sky and become brightly shining things up there.
—From a Polar Eskimo creation story

There is an extraordinary description of a shamanic initiation told by the Greenland Eskimo Antdaruta to the explorer Rasmussen in the 1920s. As a young man, Antdaruta was led by a shaman elder to a secluded cave where he watched a great polar bear first eat the old man, then spit him out. The old magician told his pupil that every time he allowed himself to be devoured alive by the bear, he acquired greater power from his spirit helpers. The young shaman apprentice tells how "sometime afterward, he took me again on a journey and this time it was so that I myself might be eaten by the bear . . . and I do not deny that I was somewhat uncomfortable at the thought of being devoured alive. I had not been lying there long before I heard the bear coming. It attacked me and crunched me up, limb by limb, joint by joint, but strangely enough it did not hurt at all. It was only when it bit me in the heart that it did hurt frightfully. From that day forth I felt that I ruled my helping spirits. After that I acquired many fresh helping spirits and no danger could any longer threaten me, as I was always protected."[73] As Antdaruta's story demonstrates, the polar bear was a powerful animal guide and initiator for the Arctic shaman. Joan Halifax too, tells us that among the Angmagsalik Eskimos of Greenland "all shamans are inevitably devoured. . . .The dismembered shaman is then reassembled and clothed with new flesh."[74]

A polar bear figurine carved in walrus-tusk ivory, probably by ancestors of the Iglulik Eskimos of the Dorset culture in northeastern Canada, shows two obvious shamanic devices (fig. 209). First, it stands upright as Bear Man, alerting us to its "higher" and "lower" natures, its human and animal aspects. Second, it is carved in X-ray style so that its skeleton is visible. The bones of the Bear Man are the densest part of its physical body; they must be penetrated in order to be overcome and transformed. The spine of Bear Man illustrates the Tree of Life, the shamanic ladder up which the spirit seeker must climb. The polar bear, the Paleolithic cave bear of Western Europe, and the grizzly bear of later North American bear clans are honored for their essential qualities of strength and endurance.

The raven is another animal figure paramount in North American shamanic tradition and lore. With a shared heritage among the Eskimos, Aleuts, and other native tribes of the Pacific Northwest Coast, the mythic raven figure can also be traced back to paleo-Siberian shamanism. Raven was both a "creator" being as Big Raven, and a "trickster" as Raven Man. As Big Raven he was an important part of ritual life and as Raven Man he was a popular personification of the actual bird—fallible, greedy, clever, and magical. This trickster aspect often appears among the native peoples of the Southwest in the figure of Coyote.

Raven is depicted on many of the ritual implements, masks, house art, and totem poles of the Pacific Northwest Coast tribes (fig. 210). Although believed to be of a relatively late date, the totem pole and its images indicate the tremendous importance animal figures have as vehicles for the ancestral spirits. The Pawnee Letokots Lasa tells us of the animals' task: "Tirawa, the One Above, did not speak directly to man. He sent certain animals to tell man that he showed himself through the beasts, and from them, and from the stars and the sun and the moon should man learn. For all things tell of Tirawa."[75]

In the story of the origins of the Kwakiutl totem pole, Chief Wakiash wakes after four days of fasting in the mountains to hear a frog telling him that he is flying around the world on the back of a large raven and must choose something that he wants to take home with him. He spies a beautiful totem pole and meeting house that he desires. There is dancing and singing in the house and when Wakiash sneaks up on the occupants, he sees they are animals without their fur, looking like men. Ashamed to be seen in this way, the animals give him the house and totem pole as well as the Echo

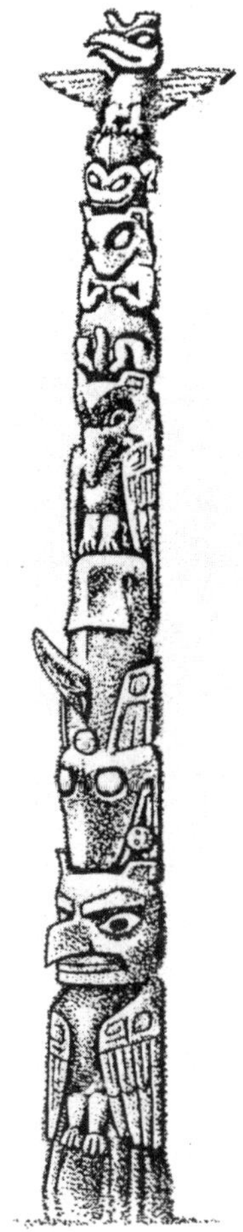

Fig. 210. Above: Raven appears in Pacific Northwest Coastal mythology and art as an important creator being and also as a legendary trickster. Totem poles have depicted Raven in both his higher and lower aspects.

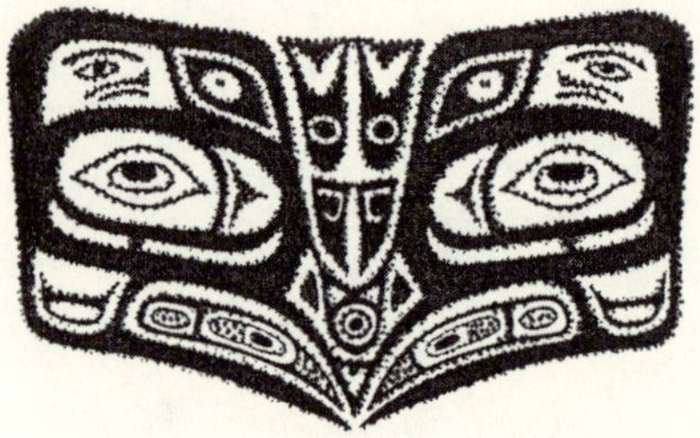

Fig. 211. Above: The powerful symmetry, and abstract hard-edged graphics, by Northwest Coast tribes are the means by which spiritual content is expressed.

mask and sacred dances, all wrapped in a small bundle, which he takes on the back of the raven to his village. What seemed like four days turns out to be four years. All of the other chiefs are humbled when they see what Wakiash brings back. The totem pole was named Kalakuyuwish, "Sky-supporting Pole," and it was the first one in the tribe's history. It stands for the center of the world and the living family tree of the spiritual ancestors. This legend indicates how the art of the totem pole was a gift connected to the animal spirit powers.[76]

The monumental cedar wood sculpture and heraldic painting of totem poles and meeting houses found today amongst the Northwest Coastal tribes indicate obvious influences from prehistory. The hard-edged graphic depictions of animals in varying degrees of abstraction, the bold forms and striking colors, as well as the weight and strength of symmetrical design, all emphasize the otherworldly, spiritual power of such images (fig. 211).

Further south, on the Western Plains of Canada and the United States, undecorated poles were erected as supports for the medicine lodges of northern Plains tribes. In the center of the lodge that was used for the celebration of the Sun Dance stood the pivotal pole, usually a freshly cut or still-living tree, representing the sun and the three worlds. At the top of the post was an eagle representing the Upper World, on the trunk was placed a buffalo skull for the middle realm of animals and humans, and tobacco and water were offered into the ground at its base for the Lower World. Twenty-eight roof beams and supporting poles radiated out from the center to form a circular structure that was then covered with buffalo hides. Entrance to the medicine lodge was made through an opening in the east. Its twenty-eight circumference poles were associated with the days in one lunar month, or one "moon" (fig. 212).

Although the medicine lodge of the Plains Indians is of a relatively late date, it appears to be directly connected with the much earlier medicine wheels along the plains and foothills of the Rocky Mountains. Also circular in form, the medicine

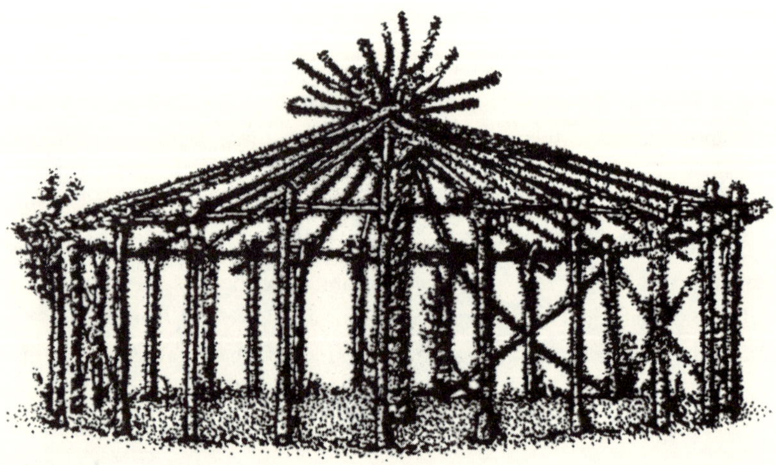

Fig. 212. The medicine lodge (right), an important ritual structure of the Northern Plains tribes, was used to celebrate the Sun Dance. The twenty-eight roof beams and supporting poles were associated with one lunar month or "moon."

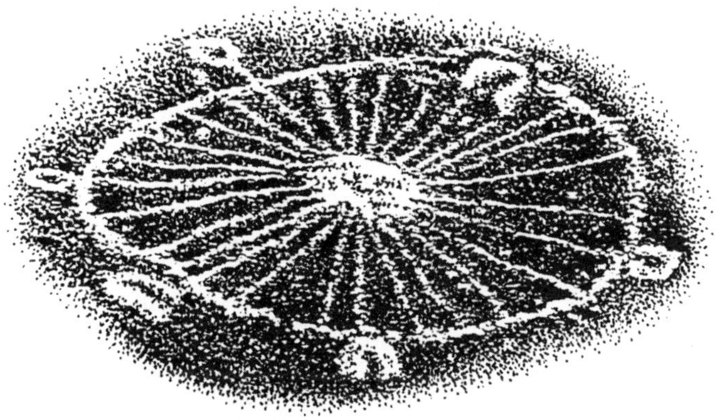

wheels have twenty-eight lines radiating from their centers laid out on the ground in stone. Evidence shows that some of the fifty "wheels" that still exist have been in "more or less continuous use from about 2500 B.C., contemporaneous with the Egyptian pyramids and the early stages of Stonehenge."[77]

Fig. 213. Medicine wheels are low-lying circular stone structures shaped like a wagon wheel. The wheels have been shown to be aligned to celestial events and may have been in use for over 4000 years. The Bighorn Medicine Wheel in Wyoming is aligned to lunar, solar, and stellar occurrences. Its 10,000-foot elevation allows for an unobstructed view of the horizon.

The Bighorn Medicine Wheel (fig. 213) near Lovell, Wyoming, coordinates lunar, solar, and stellar observations, dispelling the long-held belief that prehistoric Native American hunters could not have developed sophisticated and exacting alignments. At an altitude of just under 10,000 feet, the ancient observatory has an unobstructed view of the horizon. A Sun Dance ceremony began on June 21, the summer solstice, with sightings from two of the wheel's peripheral stones, across the rock pile in the center. The sighting fixed the points on the horizon of the midsummer sunrise and sunset. Another sighting is made from another cairn that marks the rising of Aldebaran, brightest star in the constellation of Taurus (the Bull). Twenty-eight days later Rigel, the brightest star in Orion, may be sighted and again in twenty-eight days, Sirius is in alignment with the "wheel." After this time the snows come and cover the observatory until the following June. In use only for three months of the year, this remarkable stone circle illustrates how a work of art functions as ritual technology. Although today we understand such observations in terms of "science," the ancient Medicine Wheel "observatories" are primarily sacred figures for establishing the order and harmony in Nature. They arise out of true relationships between earth and heaven, affirming the sense and meaning of a spiritual-physical universe.

Equally awe-inspiring are the earthworks of the prehistoric mound builders. Found throughout the North American Midwest, mostly along the Ohio and Mississippi River valleys, these sites are grouped according to three different culture periods: the Adena, the Hopewellian, and the Mississippian. The oldest is the Adena Culture, c. 1000 B.C.–A.D. 100, with numerous burial mounds that vary greatly in size and shape. No two mounds are the same, and they can range from a simple round or square mound to elaborate animal-shaped images such as birds and

Fig. 214. Right: Serpent Mound, in the Ohio River Valley, a 1300-foot-long earthwork of the Adena Culture, c. 1000 B.C. –100 A.D., depicts a snake figure biting an egg-shaped oval. Both serpent and egg symbolize creative energy and life force.

Fig. 215. Below: (a). The Wilmington Tablet of the Adena Culture shows an avian creature in negative relief, in a mirrored, reflex position. (b). The Gaitskill Tablet, from an Adena site in Mount Sterling, Kentucky, shows an avian figure with joint dots within a quadrated composition. These tablets were found in burial mounds.

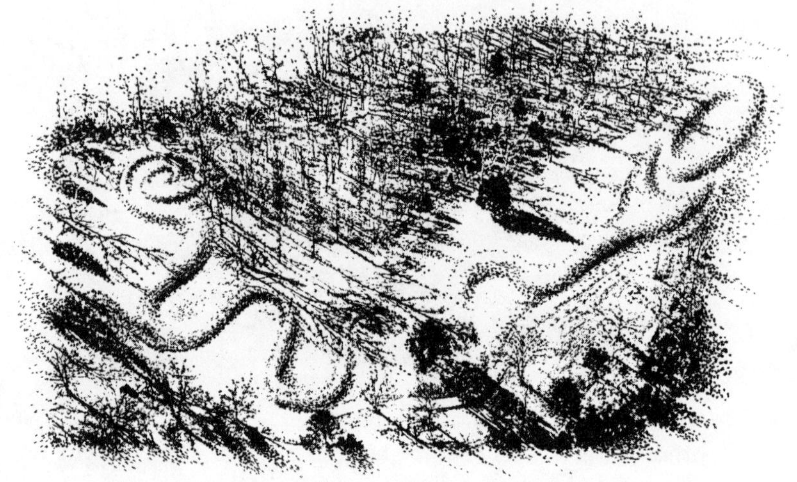

a

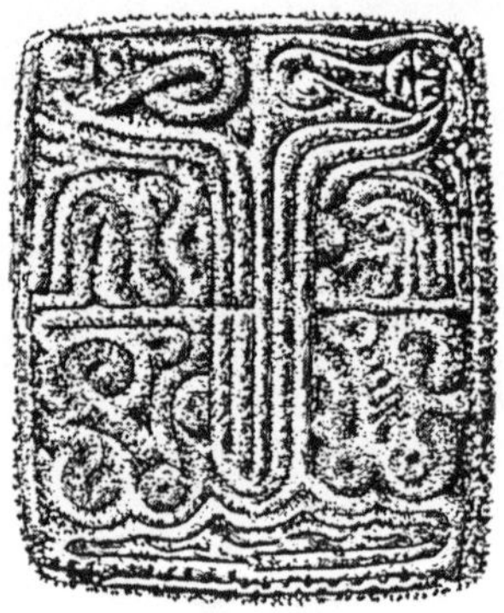

b

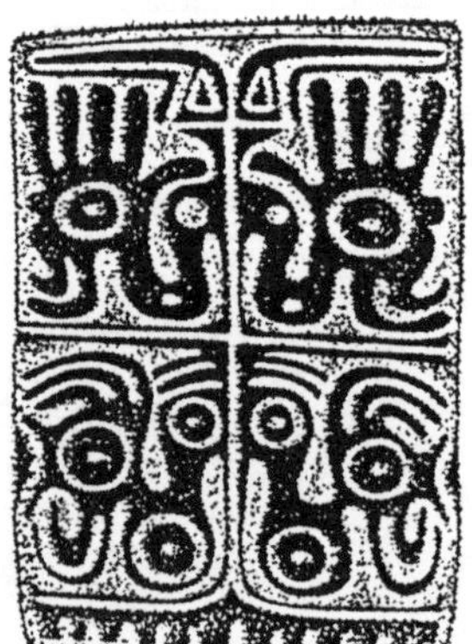

snakes. The Serpent Mound is perhaps the best-known of the Adena sites because of its three-foot-high, 1300-foot-long snake effigy (fig. 214). Near Locust Grove, Ohio, the winding serpent form seems to emerge from the adjacent river and uncoil in the direction of an oval-shaped mound, upon which the snake has its mouth. Although the exact purpose of this 1000–2000-year-old earthwork is unknown, it is likely that ritual ceremonies took place here, culminating at the oval mound, the focal point of the site. The mythologist Joseph Campbell says, "The great Serpent Mound, showing a snake bearing in its jaws an egg-like form, suggests the mythic theme (once represented in the nineteenth-century flag of the Chinese Empire) of the cosmic dragon bearing the sun in its jaws; or in India, Ananta, the serpent of the cosmic sea, bearing the universe on his head; or in India again, the Tantric image and parable of the serpent of our mortal life incubating the egg, the golden germ, of the realization of our immortality."[78] The snake appears throughout the prehistoric era as a symbol of life force, creative energy, and spirit renewal (see Appendix 6). The egg is also a picture of natural abundance, life potential, and generative spirit power, as well as being a solar symbol. No less than twelve geoastronomical alignments have been verified by archaeologists at the site, including six important lunar phase alignments and a summer solstice sunset following an eclipse transit. Serpent Mound is believed by some researchers to be an earthwork reflecting the star constellation of Draconis.[79]

Other enigmatic artifacts from the Adena culture are the engraved clay and stone tablets that depict unusual curvilinear figures. Often with strong symmetrical patterns, these relief designs depict the frontal image of a raptorial bird-creature. Such iconography is a recurrent theme in American paleoshamanic tradition. The Wilmington Tablet from Clinton County, Ohio, illustrates a birdlike creature in mirrored negative reflex, with head and wings above, feet and tail below. It is engraved on a sandstone plate, six by five inches in size. It is similar to the Gaitskill Tablet, a 4-inch by 3-inch bas-relief in clay (fig. 215). From an Adena site in Mount Sterling, Kentucky, the Gaitskill Tablet has a quadrated composition similar to the Wilmington Tablet. Above, the wings have become hands, and below, the feet have bird's talons. Dots within circles appear at joints and those in the palms are reminiscent of the mystical "eye of mercy" seen in the palms of Bodhisattvas. These palm images anticipate the "hand-eye" compositions of the later Mississippian culture (fig. 216).

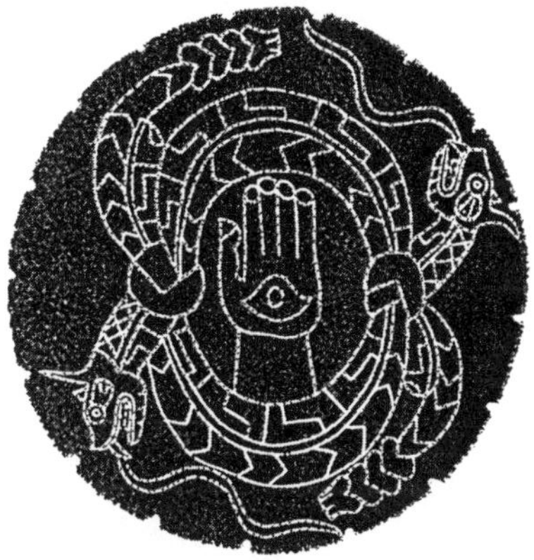

Fig. 216. The "hand-eye" motif occurs on artifacts from the Mississippian culture in North America. Two entwined rattlesnakes surround the hand-eye form. "The Eye of Mercy," an eye depicted on the palm of a Bodhisattva's hand, is a Buddhist device similar to the Mississippian motif.

Joint marks are common in the figurative art of many prehistoric cultures throughout Asia, Oceania, and the Americas. The human body was seen as an image of tribal society, with the joints symbolizing marital unions between the bones or "members" of the community. In this way the human form becomes a living kinship chart. Simple notches cut into the trunks of anthropomorphic posts, such as those of shaman graves in Siberia, are synonymous with tree knots/human joints where new branches/relatives occur. More explicit examples render spirals, eyes, faces, or skulls, to represent ancestors or relatives. Each generation is eternally joined to the entire tribe by the joint marks or cut steps on the geneological tree.[80] Shamans literally climbed on their ancestors in order to communicate with them in a trance state at the top of the ladder (fig. 217).

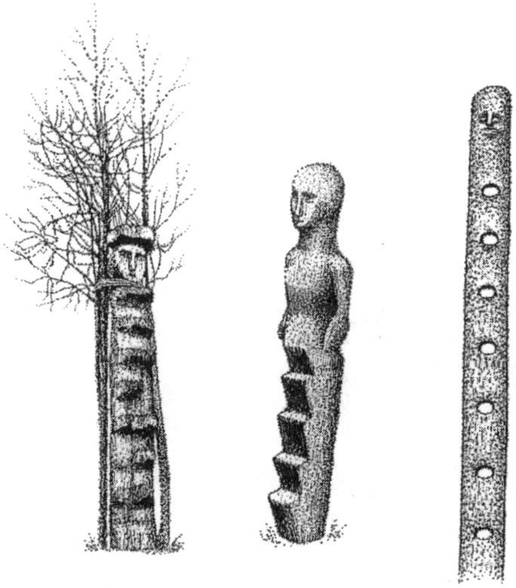

Fig. 217. Notched steps cut into anthropomorphic posts such as these indicate, as do tree knots, the joints where new relatives or branches on the family tree grow. The steps also indicate trance stages or levels in the shaman's ascent to the Otherworld. (After Schuster and Carpenter).

The exact significance of the Adena plaques is in question, but of the thirteen known tablets, many contain joint marks and all but three display serpent-bird features that link them with shamanism. All of these tablets were found in burial mounds.

The Hopewell culture, c. 100 B.C. –A.D. 300, was far more extensive, judging from its mortuary mounds and distinctive relics, spread as far south as the Gulf of Mexico and as far north as New York, Michigan, and Minnesota. Hopewellian earthworks were far more complex than the Adena sites, some covering as much as a hundred acres. Many of their art forms represented on grave artifacts carry on from their predecessors with raptorial bird themes, serpent figures, hand-eye motifs, and crosses of various kinds. Other imagery includes solar disks, swastikas, and a variety of geometric designs cut into shell, mica, and copper.

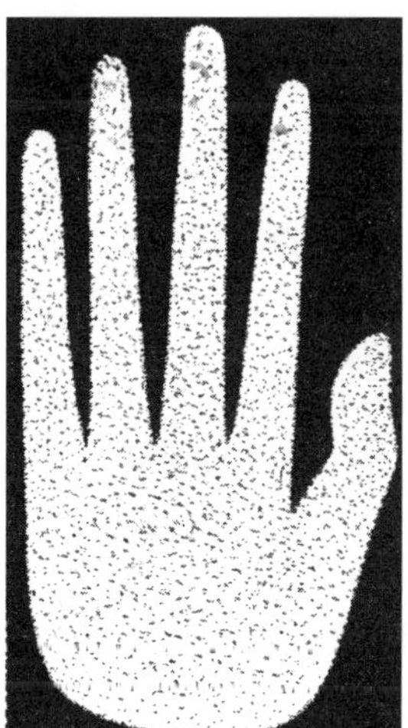

One exquisite relic is an elongated handprint cut out of sheet mica (fig. 218). In many archaic cultures, the fingers of one's hand represented family relations; therefore the handprint was

Fig. 218. The hand image, significant in Native North American art and art throughout the world, was cut into sheet mica in this fine, elongated style of the Hopewell culture (far left).

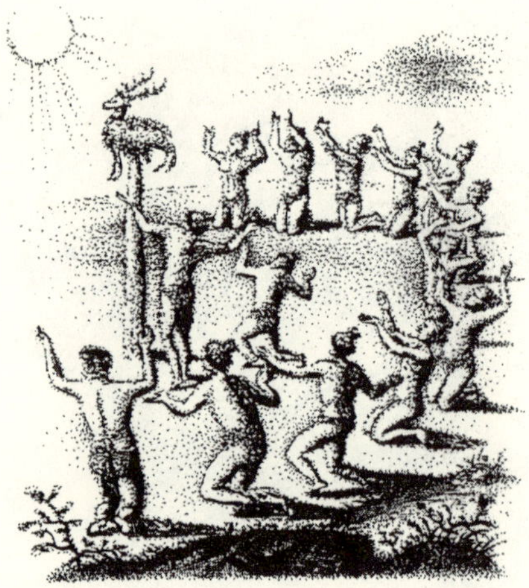

Fig. 219. Stag figures(above), associated with the sun, were placed atop posts at Native American sites connected with equinox rituals. (After an early American rendering.)

expressive of one's impressive ancestry. Fingers would sometimes be amputated as a sign of loss when relatives died. Among the Plains Indians, few designs were more highly revered than the hand motif, painted on the chest. Prehistoric cultures around the world regarded the handprint as auspicious for many reasons, not the least of which was its connection to initiation practices. (See Chapter VI.3.)

The Mississippian culture, at its height between c. 700 and 1200 A.D., developed large towns with ceremonial plazas and extensive earthen temple mounds. Although many of the Mound Societies' cultural influences are linked to northern shamanic traditions, many other characteristics, especially the large, truncated pyramid mounds, demonstrate connections with the southern high cultures of Mesoamerica. One of the most impressive sites of this period is the Cahokia Mounds, with over a hundred flat-topped and pyramidal earthen mounds within a two-by-three-mile area. Across the Mississippi River from St. Louis, Missouri, the central feature of the ceremonial complex is Monks Mound, the largest prehistoric earthen construction in the world. Approximately 1000 feet long, 700 feet wide, and 100 feet high with four levels, it covers four acres. Woodhenge, a solar observatory, composed of forty-seven postholes that anchored cedar poles 27.5 feet apart in a circle 410 feet in diameter, is aligned for equinox and solstice sightings. Henges like this were important among Native American tribes throughout the eastern U.S. for enacting seasonal festivals. Descriptions by sixteenth-century European explorers indicate that the wooden posts were sometimes topped off with anthropomorphic carvings or stag figures associated with the sun (fig. 219).

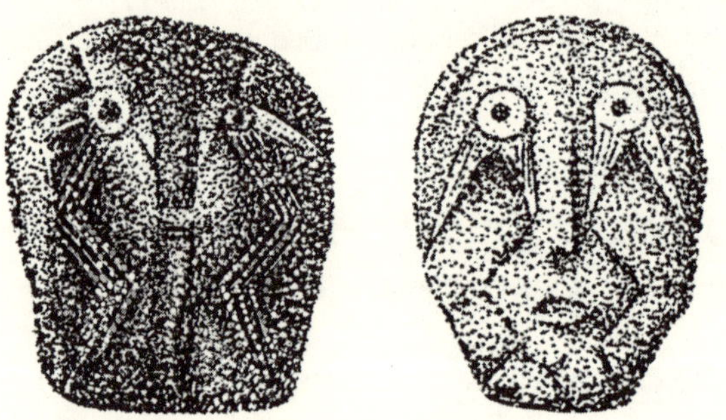

Fig. 220. The "forked-eye" or "weeping-eye" motif (right) may indicate a stream of penetrating vision or clairvoyant sight.

Two frequently occurring themes in portable shell art from the Mississippian mound builders were the "forked-eye" and the "weeping-eye" or "hail tears" motif (fig. 220). These human faces with linear patterns emanating from the eyes appear to be streams of visionary activity, rays of vital energy and power. Rather than forks or flowing tears, both themes may indicate the penetrating gaze and spiritual vision possessed by the shaman or "seer."

Fig. 221. The winged rattlesnake (below), similar to the Mesoamerican Feathered Serpent, Quetzalcoatl-Kukulcán, is seen on Mound Society artifacts such as this one: a sun-swastika formed by four figures rotating around a central cross.

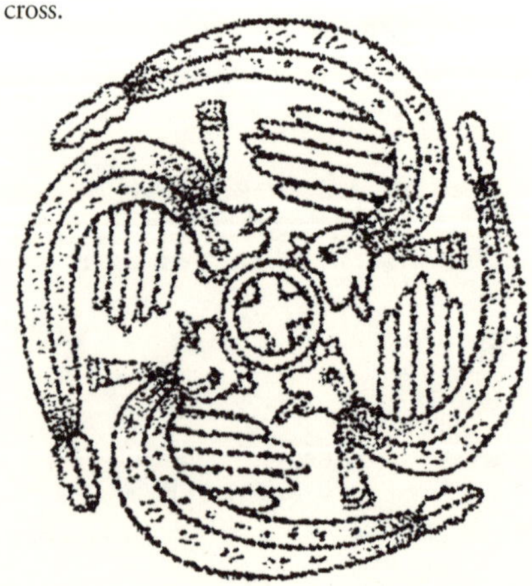

The winged rattlesnake is another important theme in classic Mound Society art that further links the American Midwest with Mesoamerica. The Feathered Serpent, Kukulcán, also known as Quetzalcoatl, was revered as a divine being by the Maya, who flourished from c. 300 to 900 A.D. Before the time of Christ, the art of Mesoamerica's Olmecs recognized the same Feathered Serpent. The winged

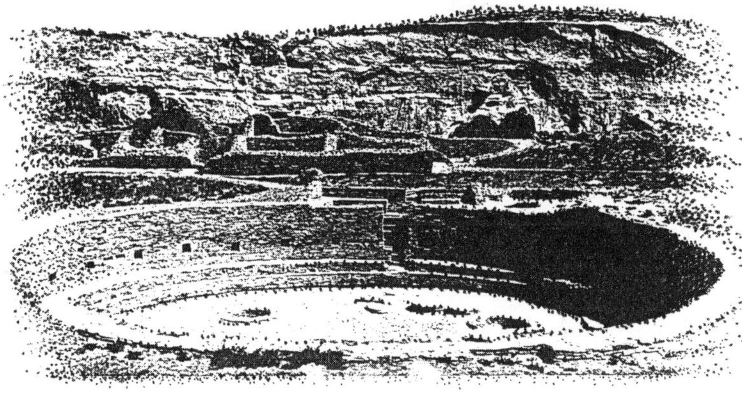

Fig. 222. The *kiva* (left) of Southwest Native American tribes is a place of emergence used by a governing society of male initiates.

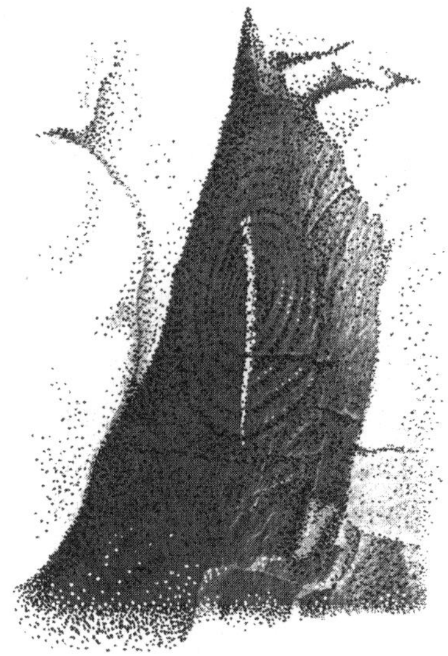

Fig. 223. On a butte in Chaco Canyon, New Mexico (above), a monolith arranged against a rock face directs a shaft of light to a spiral petroglyph, evidence of deliberate work with solar events.

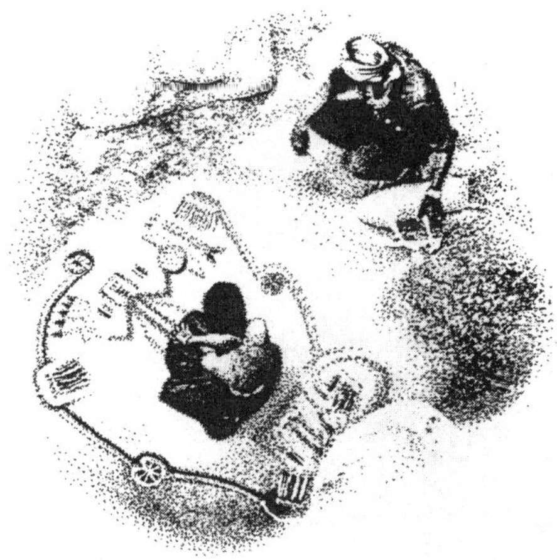

Fig. 224. Navaho sand paintings (above) were, and still are, constructed to bring about harmony and healing in a person or community. They are dismantled after use.

rattlesnake of the Mississippians appears in one example as a group of four serpents arranged in a swastika pattern surrounding a central sun cross (fig. 221). This image, found at Spiro Mound in Oklahoma, is engraved on a large marine shell not native to Oklahoma. Other plumed rattlesnake iconography occurs at Moundville, Alabama, and Etowah, Georgia.

In the prehistoric Southwest, Anasazi, Hohokam, and Mogollon cultures laid the spiritual foundations for later tribal art of that region. With origins over 2300 years ago, these cultures created unique cliff dwellings as well as underground sanctuaries called *kivas* (fig. 222). The latter were circular structures oriented to the cardinal north-south as well as to solar positions. According to the Acoma Pueblo Indians, the kiva is round because that is the shape of the horizon. The Place of Emergence, a circular shaft in the *kiva*, symbolizes the womb of the living Mother Earth. A governing society of initiates, not individual medicine men, was charged with the maintenance and celebration of appropriate rites. They descended into the dark underworld of the kiva in order to celebrate the life-giving power of the female earth and its counterpart, the "old god," fire—the sun's terrestrial ancestor. In Hopi tradition, where the *kiva* is rectangular, emergence is a central theme, for their mythology speaks of the first people as living in the Underworld, only emerging into the present, fourth world after a long migration. In terms of initiation as well, emergence is a picture of transformation. The *kiva* architecture embodies this principle of emergence, while its relation to the complex geometry of surrounding structures, sacred roadways, and even the natural features of the environment are a living association with the elements and order of space-time as well as with society and the sacred.[81]

Besides these subterranean temples, the Anasazi or "Old Ones" produced megalithic observatories, the most unusual being located on Fajada Butte, in Chaco Canyon. With three large stone slabs that funnel and focus both sunlight and moonlight, this remarkable site is an example of art, science, and the sacred inseparably united. Significant astronomical intervals are marked by a narrow sliver of sun and moon illumination that moves across spiral petroglyphs carved on the adjacent

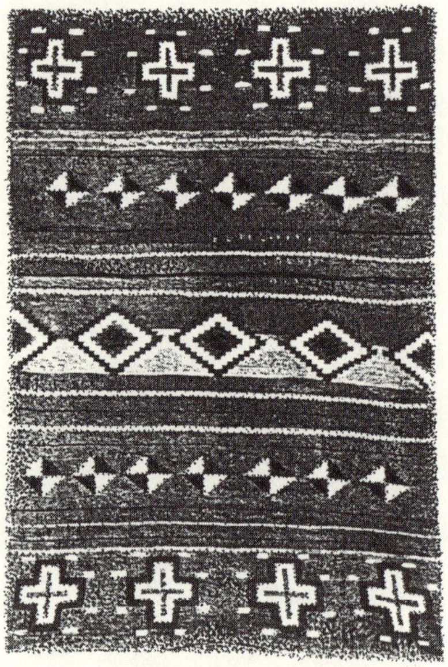

Fig. 225. This Native American blanket design (above) is an example of typical design elements used by Southwest tribal artists.

cliff face (fig. 223). Clearly, the Fajada Butte site is connected with seasonal phenomena, the speech of the universe.

Ritual sand paintings, designed for healing ceremonies, were created by Navaho medicine men of the Southwest in order that patients might journey into its sacred framework and reach the healing power of the soul's origin (fig. 224). In addition to the visual impression of the mandalalike sand painting, dance, ritual performance, and prayerful chanting of songs were enacted in order to bring the patient to identification with the god or animal spirit and thus to restoration. When activated, the sand painting becomes a portal into the Otherworld. Many of the health restoring colors and forms of sand paintings can also be found in the iconography of Native American basketry, blankets (fig. 225), and pottery. Over the centuries before our own era, designs and patterns pregnant with spiritual significance have evolved among the Native American tribal cultures.

An extraordinarily diverse range of prehistoric rock art is fashioned upon the smooth rock surfaces of isolated cliff faces, cave walls, and bluff outcroppings throughout North America. These pictograms ("picture images"—paintings) and petroglyphs ("stone writing"—engravings) feature innumerable motifs from a wide range of cultural periods. Some of the rock art themes include animals, humans, weapons, instruments, and geometric figures. Many of the ancient images relate to stellar occurrences: stars, planets, sun crosses, supernova, nebulae, starbursts, auroras, shooting stars, and comets (fig. 226). The stars were seen as the homeland of the gods, and from the various constellations and regions of the heavens different forces were experienced as radiating toward the earth, influencing nature and humanity.

A prominent Native American rock art theme is the anthropomorphic

Fig. 226. Right: Stellar phenomena, such as suns, stars, comets, shooting stars, starbursts, and supernovae, occur frequently in rock art, as these pictograms from Southern California (right) indicate.

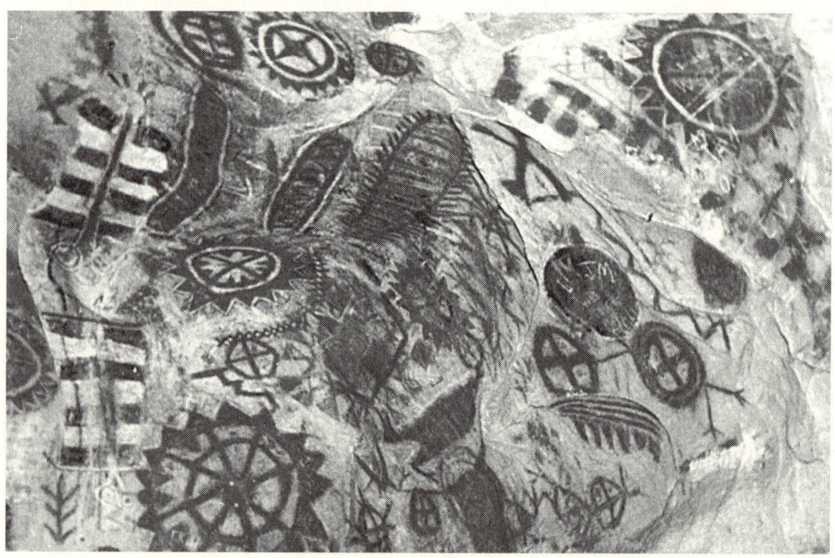

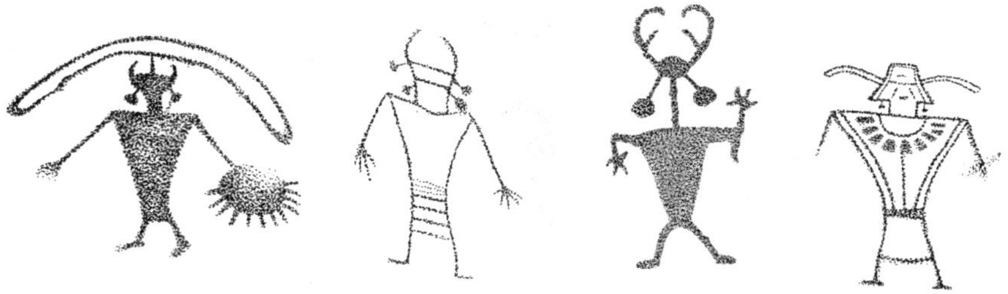

Fig. 227. Left: Southwest Native American rock art often depicts the anthropomorphic Horned Man, an upright figure crowned with horns or antlers that represents a tribal medicine man or the spirit being behind shamanic visionary experience.

Horned Man, an upright figure with two horns or antlers, often displaying large round ear ornaments (fig. 227). These images are likely depictions of tribal initiates, shamans, or medicine men. Kokopelli is a variation on this theme of the shaman (fig. 228). Mysterious and highly revered by the Anasazi, Kokopelli is a horned and hunchbacked flute player, a spirit being who is linked with abundance and known as a "rain priest" to the Zuñis. The prehistoric Hopi Kachina attribute of the flute is associated with water ceremonies. The god Pan, of Greek mythology, and the anthropomorphic figures of Europe's Paleolithic cave sanctuaries are possible distant cousins of Kokopelli. Certain similarities may be noted concerning human-animal features, gestures, and the appearance of a musical instrument or wand. The posture of these Horned Man figures suggests action is taking place, as in ritual dance movement. (See Chapter VI.6) Are the figures humans wearing ceremonial attire? Are they shamans in trance states? Are they ancestral spirits, deities, or Kachinas? Esther Pasztory points out that "it is often impossible to tell shamans, spirits, and deities apart: all partake of similar power attributes and have interchangeable iconographic traits."[82] Whatever kind of being these engravings and rock paintings represent, they are obviously significant figures indicating a rich body of spiritual experience shared and artistically expressed by the early inhabitants of North America. Such rock art sites as caves, hilltops, and secluded locations are known to be places suitable for shamans on vision quests.

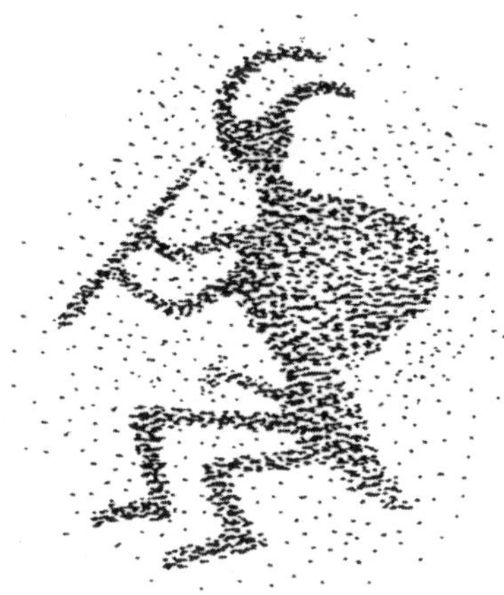

Fig. 228. Above: Kokopelli is a divine flute player, horned and hunchbacked, who was revered by the Anasazi and other Southwest Native American tribes.

Mesoamerica

Such [art] forms speak of an ancient way of perceiving divinity in the earth, the water, the sun, and the volcanic "mountains of fire," as well as in humans, who, in communion with natural and supernatural forces and phenomena, generated creative activity.

—Beatriz de la Fuente

The great art of prehistoric Mesoamerica appears suddenly with the Olmec civilization around 1500 B.C., with cosmologically planned communities, complex ritual centers, highly developed symbol systems and sophisticated artistic styles setting the standard for later Maya, Toltec, and Aztec cultures. Many themes featured in Olmec art,

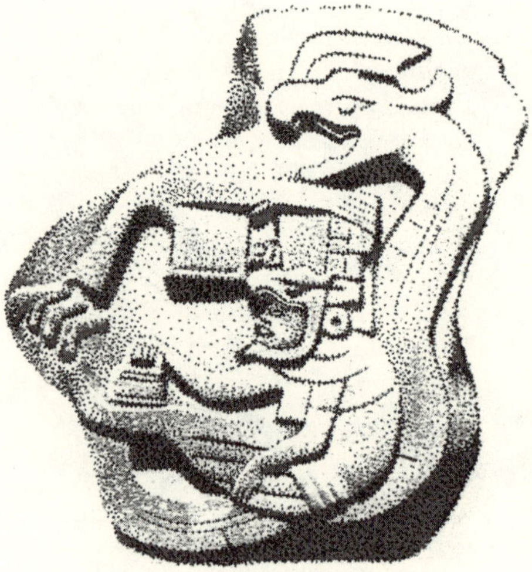

Fig. 229. Above: Monument 19 at La Venta, Tabasco, Mexico, depicts a masked shaman-chief riding in spirit flight upon an avian serpent. The shaman's jaguar headdress, with its crested brow and gaping jaw, mimics the serpent's head.

Fig. 230. The jaguar is a Mesoamerican image synonymous with shamanic spirit journeys. This figurine of gray-green jadeite (right) from Rio Pesquero, Veracruz, is dated between 900 and 600 B.C. and depicts a childlike figure with open, down-turned mouth, wide, flattened nose and snug skullcap, called the Olmec Supernatural. It rides on the back of a jaguar, clutching the animal's tail, right hand over left, in like manner to rulers grasping their ceremonial scepters. This grip of the tail shows control of the jaguar spirit, the guardian animal of shaman-chiefs. The jaguar was seen as both benevolent and antagonistic to humans, functioning as a guardian of earth, air, wind, water, rain, and the seasons, as well as an emissary of plants and animals, deities, light, and darkness. The jaguar spirit brought about the initiation of the shaman-chief.

such as the major cult of the Feathered Serpent, are perpetuated for centuries, appearing as Kukulcán of the Maya and Quetzalcoatl of the Toltec and Aztec cultures. This Avian Serpent, also seen in later ritual imagery of North America, is already apparent in Olmec culture around 800 B.C. On a stone slab known as Monument 19 at La Venta, Tabasco, Mexico (fig. 229), a carved, crested rattlesnake supports and surrounds a priestly figure who wears a shamanic animal mask and holds an offering (probably powdered copal incense) in his extended right hand, while the left hand is turned palm out in a gesture of giving. Such an openhanded gesture can be interpreted as the "boon-bestowing hand posture" of divinity. The Feathered Serpent, a composite figure of snake and bird, representing both bondage to earth and unbounded freedom of flight, carries the presumed shaman-chief in its enfolding coil, which is tipped with a large rattle. Below the serpent's head is a hieroglyph for the plumed serpent and the sky. The context of the monument's imagery may refer to seasonal rites honoring the earth, groundwater, sky, and lightning, all of which are associated with the serpent. The jaguar mask worn by the shaman mimics the serpent head and serves the wearer on his spirit journey, as jaguars were known vehicles for spirit travel into the Otherworld (fig. 230).[83]

Another example of high Olmec sculptural style is "Altar" 4, also from La Venta, c. 800 B.C. (fig. 231). A shaman-chief emerges from a niche in the rock—the primordial earth-cave. He wears a bird helmet, likely representing a harpy eagle associated with the sun and human sacrifice as well as being an obvious allusion to spirit flight. (The eagle is considered the original, ancestral shaman.) The shaman-chief holds the ends of a rope that surrounds the entire altar and is connected with lineage and kinship. Even as it demonstrates the bloodline of authority and rulership held by the figure, it binds him to his destiny and makes the shaman-chief a captive to his position and duty. At the same time the rope may point to the lifeline, which maintains the vital connection sustaining the physical body during shamanic spirit flight. Over the upper portion of the altar, a stylized jaguar mask protects the chief as the Feathered Serpent guards the figure in Monument 19. The altar would be used for offering and sacrifice as well as for a throne upon which the ruler sits as mediator between worlds. As the artistic rendering of "Altar" 4 indicates, the shaman-chief, bound to the Lower World of the elements, rises to the Upper World in spirit flight and effects changes in the human Middle World. The altar/throne is significant as a spiritual focal point

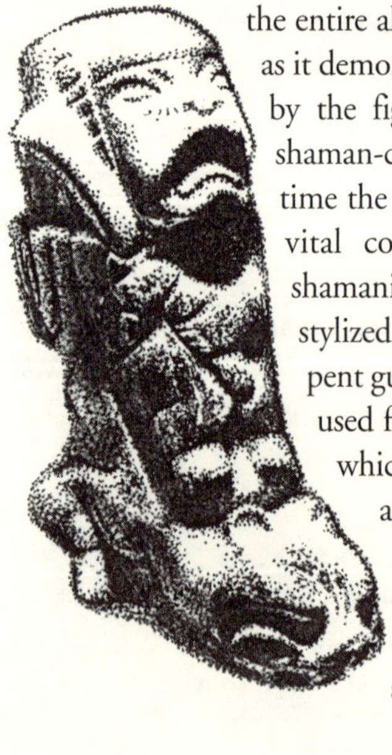

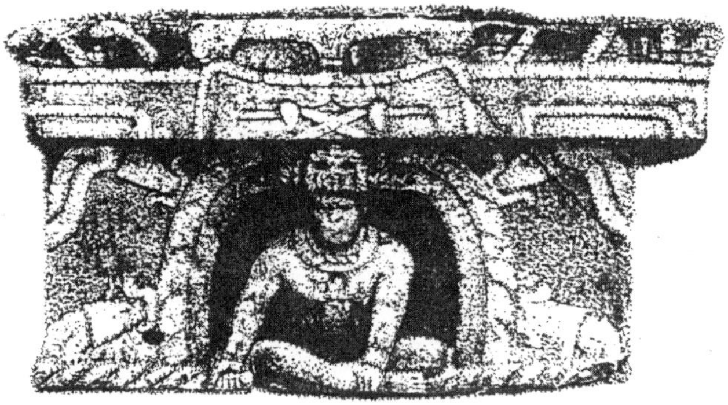

Fig. 231. "Altar" 4 (left), another example of high Olmec-style sculpture from La Venta, c. 800 B.C., depicts a life-sized human figure sitting cross-legged in a niche, as if emerging from the Lower World. He wears a headdress of the harpy eagle, a sun symbol associated with human sacrifice. He holds a rope encircling the altar, which indicates how he is bound to his destiny by his own blood ties. A stylized jaguar mask is carved on the upper altar, upon which the shaman-chief would presumably sit when it was not being used for human sacrifice. From such an altar the shaman-chief would set out upon his spirit flight.

where the three worlds come together, for, as Eliade notes, "altars and sanctuaries represent an imago mundi, a miniature cosmos—and the cosmos is the supreme example of the work of the gods."[84]

Oxtotitlan Cave, in Guerrero, Mexico, contains numerous, well-preserved polychrome murals dated c. 700 B.C. One painting, Mural 1, shows a shaman-chief in X-ray style, wearing a bird costume and mask (fig. 232). The mask, wings, feather cape, and intricate tail assemblage, along with the loincloth over a brown hide shirt, painted hand motifs with spirals, and cross bands on the chest, identify the figure as a shaman. His mask may be that of an owl, the nocturnal messenger between worlds. He sits on a throne that shows the face of an Olmec sky dragon and is poised for spirit flight in the "posture of royal ease." The eleven-by-ten-foot Mural 1 may well illustrate the function of "Altar" 4 where the shaman-chief or priest-king rises out of his bondage and sits on the altar, making it a throne (as pictured in Mural 1), and from there embarks upon his vision-quest in spirit flight as shamanic leader of his people. Research has shown that Olmec shamans were also rulers, initiate-kings, as was the case in many civilizations throughout the world. F. Kent Reilly III points out that "Mesoamerica was not alone in validating political authority through shamanic authority. In the Old World, Shang Dynasty China (1726–1122 B.C.), early Yamato period Japan (ca. A.D. 50–300), and Silla Dynasty Korea (A.D. 668–935) are prime examples of state-level political authority based on shamanism."[85] Also inherited from their predecessors and confirmed by recent

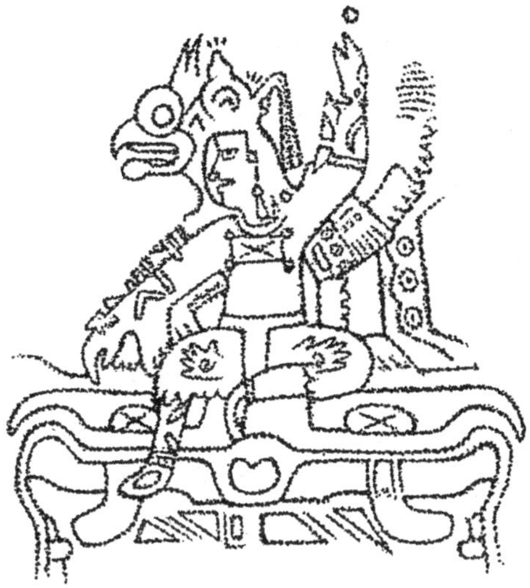

Fig. 232. Mural 1 at Oxtotitlan Cave in Guerrero, Mexico (above), is a painting dated to circa 700 B.C. Presumedly, it depicts an owl-masked shaman-chief in spirit flight sitting upon an altar similar to "Altar" 4.

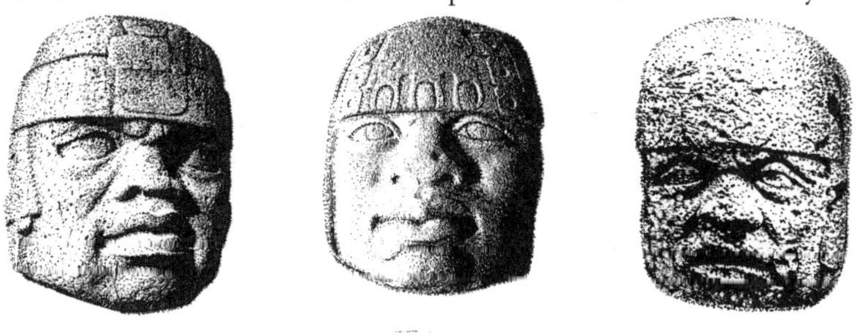

Fig. 233. The great Olmec stone heads (left), standing sometimes as high as nine feet, date to around 1200 B.C. Some believe them to be representations of an ancient race of shaman-chiefs.

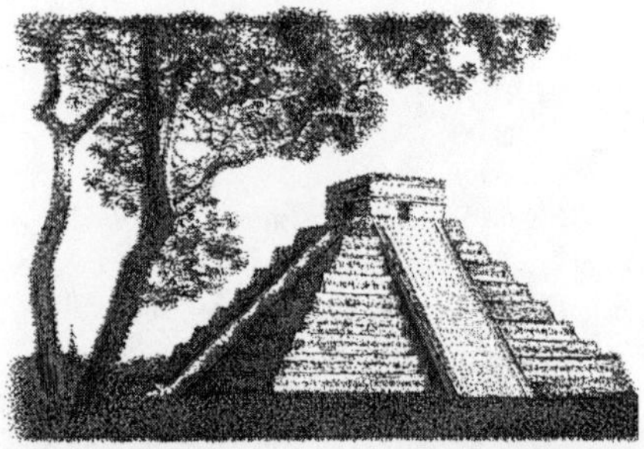

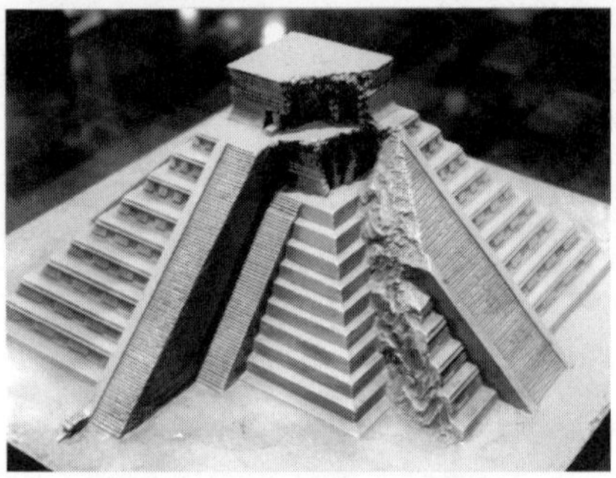

Fig. 234. One of the most outstanding structures at Chichén Itzá is the "Castle," a temple to Kuculcán in the form of a step pyramid. Built in two phases, the sacred structure demonstrates an alignment to solar equinoxes, during which the shadowy appearance and descent of the avian serpent Kuculcán is created on the structure of the staircase by the sun's movement.

Fig. 235. Below: An interior chamber of the earlier temple of Kuculcán contains a red jaguar throne with inlaid jadestone eyes. The shaman-chief validated his authority when he sat on the throne, entered into a trance state, and traveled into the Otherworld. The jaguar is connected with shamanic spirit flights.

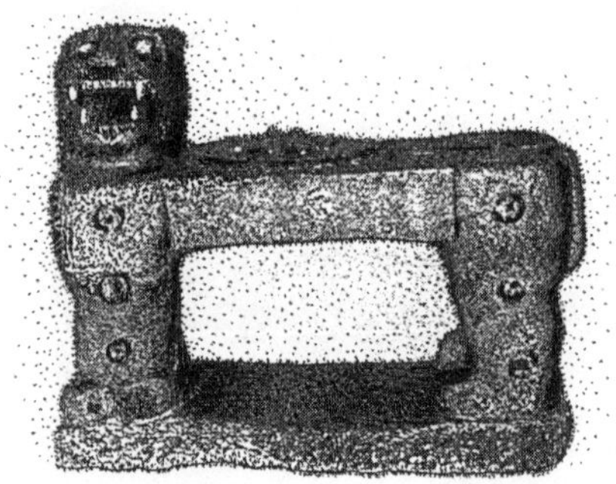

hieroglyphic discoveries is the tradition that "Maya kings validated their right to royal power by publicly proclaiming their ability to perform the shamanic trance journey and transform into power animals."[86] This ability of the shaman-chiefs is recorded in works of art to further validate their political authority and spiritual influence for posterity.

Perhaps the most enigmatic as well as the most characteristic work of the Olmecs are the large stone heads, sometimes more than nine feet tall, fashioned from basaltic rock (fig. 233). These gigantic sculpted heads weigh as much as sixty tons, are round in form, and lack bodies. It is as if the seventeen colossal sculptures found to date emphasize the sacredness of the head. De la Fuente says: "The head is a receptacle that holds the superior abilities of humanity, its creative powers; the head is the center of thought and spiritual life, of humanity's capacity to commune with those forces considered more powerful, remote, and supernatural."[87] Although one might debate the point, the head is clearly one of the major centers of human activity. All of the Olmec heads have slightly crossed eyes and express a controlled inner energy and concentration, characteristic of meditation and the visionary state. Believed to be portraits of a race of ruling shaman-chiefs or initiate-kings, they portray the traits of a ruler, who, through instinctive comprehension, can grasp the larger order of the world. The decidedly negroid facial features raise numerous questions, and debate is ongoing concerning the origin of this mysterious race of kings. Some of the stone heads have been deliberately mutilated by pitting, perhaps as part of a ritual destruction to deprive the sculpture of its mana after the death of the personage portrayed, or through vandalism by a rival cult. Such practices were not uncommon in other cultures, as in the case of Egypt, for instance. The heads have been dated to around 1200 B.C.

The rich artistic traditions and high cultural developments that follow upon the Olmec civilization stand out most remarkably in the ancient Maya city of Chichén Itzá on the Yucatán Peninsula of Mexico. Meaning "at the mouth of the well of the Water Witch," the name Chichén Itzá suggests a magical threshold of feminine life energy. Here a complex of grand stone buildings demonstrates the unique star wisdom, mathematical learning, engineering skills, and high arts of the Maya and Toltec civilizations. The Temple of Kuculcán, also known as the Castle, is one of many outstanding structures at this Mesoamerican site (fig. 234). Built in two stages, it consists of an earlier temple beneath the outer structure, with a nine-level stepped base and a single staircase on the north side. The earlier inner temple has a two-room vaulted chamber at its summit. The interior is decorated with images of walking jaguars, shields embossed with rattlesnake rattles, feathers, vertically intertwined serpents, and rosettes. A depiction of the rain god, Chac Mool, and a red-painted jaguar throne inlaid with jade eyes is also featured in this early temple (fig. 235). Human and animal sacrifices were performed as a part of the Mayan religious order, the most common forms being beheading or cutting out a victim's heart. Bloodletting was a significant part of Maya and Olmec cosmology. Although scenes of sacrificial bloodletting are more numerous in Maya art, the fact that blood was seen as a magical substance that could open the portal between worlds was already in evidence amongst the Olmec.

The second building program covered the first temple with four staircases of ninety-one steps, a total of 364. When the platform on the top is added to the steps, the total is 365, the number of days in a year. There are fifty-two levels, the number of weeks in a year and the number of years in a Maya cycle. At the spring and autumn equinoxes, sunlight striking the nine terrace levels falls across the side of the northern staircase and produces an undulating snakelike shadow that suggests the body of the serpent whose heads are sculpted at the bottom of the balustrade. The architecture provides a physical body within which the solar deity incarnates and becomes visible on earth. This step-pyramid stands over ninety feet high and was a central feature of the Kukulcán-Quetzalcoatl cult of the Maya and Toltecs. It is aligned with the sacred *cenote*, a sunken sacrificial pool that may have been the god's seasonal destination once it descended the temple and passed along a Sacred Way.

As with all natural openings in the earth, the *cenote* was conceived of by the Maya as a doorway into the Otherworld. The pyramid-temple was viewed as the sacred World Mountain, its inner chamber a consecrated cave that, like the *cenote*, leads from the Middle World of man to the Lower World of elemental forces where the ascent to the Upper World takes place. It is the World Mountain or World Tree, upon which the Feathered Serpent is represented and which unites all three realms vertically and fixes the center of existence (fig. 301). This axis or navel of the world was not located in any one physical place, but could be ritually materialized by the priest-king within the natural landscape or temple architecture. Linda Schele and David Freidel indicate it was the blood-ritual that manifested the supersensible *axis mundi*: "In the rapture of bloodletting rituals, the king brought the great World Tree into existence through the middle of the temple and opened the awesome door into the Otherworld."[88] One can only imagine the startling spectacle created at such a ceremonial site, at the height of its use. Such horrific practices can only be understood from the standpoint of a different consciousness than that of today.

It is interesting to note that Rudolf Steiner features a Feathered Serpent in his design for one of the carved glass windows of the Goetheanum building in Dornach, Switzerland (fig. 16).[89] In Steiner's twentieth-century image, the spiritual seeker ascends the World Mountain or *axis mundi* and is confronted by a great avian serpent.

Mesoamerican sacred architecture was often plastered and painted with designs and figures expressive of its function as a portal between worlds. These figurative and geometric designs are usually solid and ample in mass, stout, and powerful in their gestures and outline. Compositions are often complex and fragmented, as is evident throughout Central America.

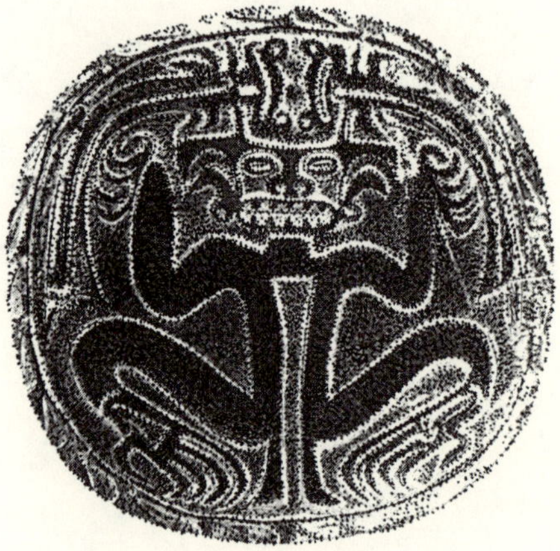

Fig. 236. This mandalalike beaten gold plaque (above) from Sitio Conte, Panama, of a crouching anthropomorphic figure, possibly a Jaguar Man, can be viewed as a picture of divine justice and order simply by way of its powerful symmetrical design. Symmetrical figures like this were often used to represent balanced judgment as expressed in the spiritual world order and karma.

Another striking Mesoamerican image found at Sitio Conte, Cocle, in Panama, is a beaten gold plaque, six-and-one-half inches in diameter, showing an anthropomorphic being in a crouching position with arms raised (fig. 236). Perhaps a Jaguar Man, the figure has lengthy claws and a spine rendered visible in X-ray style. A symmetrical headdress of matching fishlike creatures, perhaps hammerhead sharks, surmounts the squatting figure. Such figures portrayed in this strong symmetrical format express balance and often warn of impending judgment and cosmic justice. The squatting image is found throughout the world from the Americas to Polynesia, Malaysia, and China. When flanked by two animals, such squatting figures are identified in Mexico and Peru as the guardians of the sun god. When the figure is fashioned in gold, there is an additional connection with the sun, for, according to traditional wisdom, gold is the embodiment of the spiritual sun in physical matter. This indigenous view that material substance embodies spiritual powers contrasts sharply with that of the invading European culture which quickly subjugated the native peoples. Gold was valued quite differently by the invaders, for it was seen to be devoid of spirit.

South America

The imagination imitates the exemplary models—the Images—reproduces, reactualizes, and repeats them without end. To have imagination is to be able to see the world in its totality, for the power and the mission of the Images is to show all that remains refractory to the concept.

—Mircea Eliade

Fig. 237. Early Valdivian, c. 3500–1500 B.C., female figurines from coastal Ecuador (below) suggest the practice of fertility rituals and are reminiscent of the Paleolithic "Venus" figures (see fig. 86) associated with goddess worship.

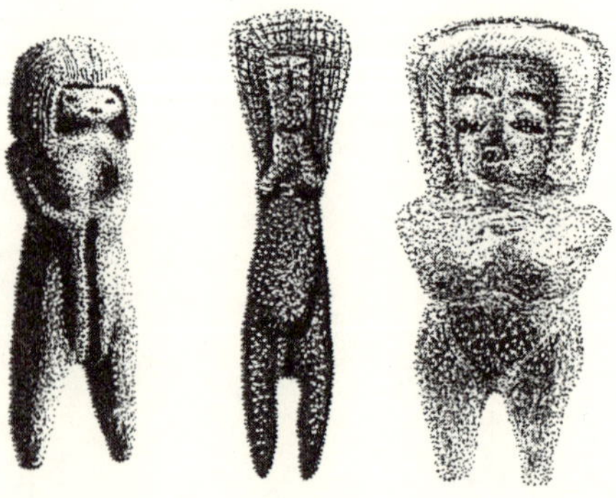

In 1532 A.D., Francisco Pizarro led fewer than 200 Spanish conquistadores into the Peruvian Andes and the heart of the Inca Empire. There he captured, baptized and executed the Inca emperor, Atawalpa, descendant of the sun god, bringing to an end the largest prehistoric civilization in the Americas. Pizarro's swift overthrow of the Incas was hastened by an elaborate and extensive road system that serviced the dry coastal regions of Peru and Chile, as well as the highland areas of Peru, Chile, Ecuador, and Bolivia. The 14,000-mile stone-paved highway system, which featured suspension bridges and tunnels cut through solid rock, is believed to have been even more extensive before the Inca inherited it from their ancient predecessors. These roads, which an early Spanish eyewitness said "excel the constructions of Egypt and the monuments of Rome," point back to the prehistoric Valdivian culture, c. 3500-1500 B.C., of coastal Ecuador.

Early Valdivian stone (fig. 237) and ceramic figures with their egglike forms and distinctive hair treatment, bear a striking resemblance to the Paleolithic "Venus" figurines of Old Europe. The prominence of these female figurines amongst the cultural deposits of early Ecuador points to the importance of the fertility and life principles amongst these agrarian peoples. Together with these images, which indicate observance of seasonal festivals and agriculturally based ceremonies, shamanic activity is persistently represented, especially that of the jaguar cult.

One of the most remarkable and mysterious images of early South American art is the Raimondi stela, c. 1000 B.C., an engraved monolith found at Chavin de Huantar in the Peruvian Andes (fig. 238). The work demonstrates a sophistication of symbolic forms unmatched elsewhere in the world at the time, with the exception of Egypt. The stone carving depicts a powerfully symmetrical standing figure that grasps elaborate staves in each of its clawlike hands. The Staff God, as the figure is known, has a square jaguar face with a fantastic headdress consisting of a succession of animal snouts with feline fangs and snakes projecting on all sides. A multiplicity of snakes dangles from the god's belt, sprouts from its head, projects from its headdress, and crowns its crest in a caduceus motif of intertwined serpents. Further snakes crowning the staves and running through the headdress bring the total count to fifty-two, the number that centuries later will be referred to in the Mayan calendar as a "Knot of Years." This may well connect the Staff God to the personification of ever-recurring, cyclical time. When this image is viewed upside-down, three zoomorphic faces become visible in addition to the two faces in the original square head and the other two jaguar faces on each staff near the figure's elbows. Although the stela would normally not be viewed upside-down, this reversed vantage point is the perspective of the gods as well as that of the shaman priest in spirit flight. The Staff God with its two staves is thought to express the unification of duality. Light and dark, male and female, good and evil, are intimated as the bipolar forces held fast and embodied in this one god.

Joseph Campbell sees in this stela an American shamanic image depicting the various spiritual centers or chakras ("circles") of the human being—at each of which the mode of the shaman's consciousness may be transformed.[90] According to ancient yogic teachings there are seven chakras, the lowest located at the base of the spinal column. As mentioned above the chakras are sometimes viewed as rungs on a ladder or branches on the World Tree—the cerebrospinal system that is ascended by the yogi or shaman. Kundalini, a specific type of yoga, engages the powerful latent energy that slumbers at the root of the spinal column. Kundalini means "that which is coiled," and the esoteric discipline of Kundalini Yoga aims at awakening the resting

Fig. 238. The Raimondi stela, c. 1000 B.C., an engraved stone slab found at Chavin de Huantar in Peru, depicts the so-called Staff God, a powerful guardian and multifaceted spiritual being. (After Campbell.)

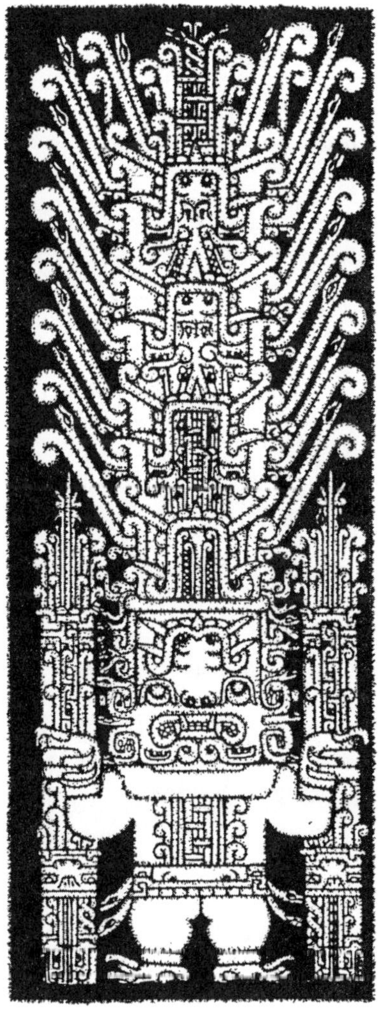

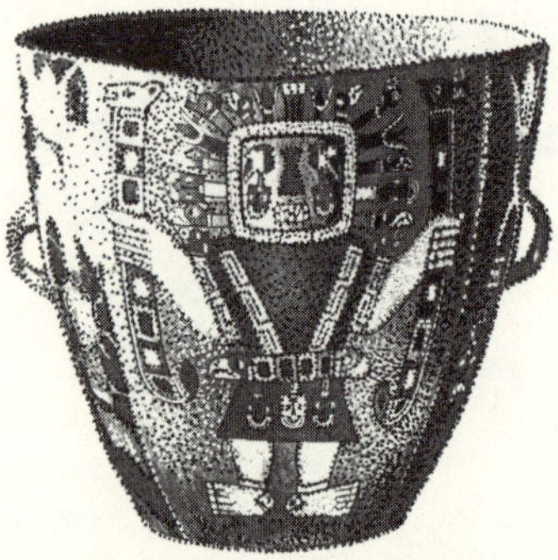

Fig. 239. Viracocha, the Andean creator god, bestowed many gifts, including agriculture, upon the people. When he left South America he was carried off, according to legend, by the "foam of the sea" (*viracocha*), an allusion to the life forces and to the generative realm of nature. Here, the Staff God, Viracocha, appears on an Inca ceramic pot, probably used for ritual purposes.

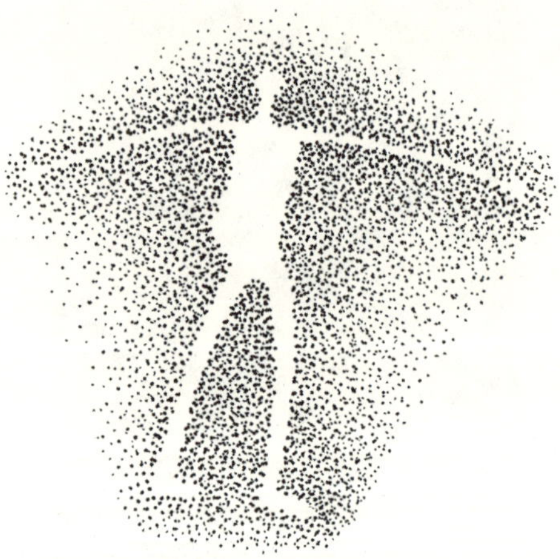

Fig. 240. Geoglyphs have been found along the dry coastal plains of both North and South America, from California to Chile. This example of a large human figure (above) is found outside of Blythe, California.

Fig. 241. Geoglyphs in Great Britain were usually formed by cutting away an upper layer of sod and grass to expose the white chalky earth below. An example in southern England is the Long Man of Wilmington (right), a 230-foot figure.

"Serpent Powers" (see Appendix 6). The chakras of Indian Yogic tradition may or may not be applicable to the Raimondi stela, but it is likely that this Andean iconography illustrates distinct levels of spiritual reality and portrays the spiritual being who is guardian of such revelations. The Guardian of the Threshold is a familiar figure in ancient mystery practices and is frequently depicted in various forms. For instance, this figure is recast as the "Gateway God," Viracocha, at Tiahuanaco in Bolivia, A.D. 600.

In Inca culture, this figure of the Staff God or Gateway God is transformed into a deity, with square jaguar face, feline fangs, and the "weeping eyes" or "hail tears" of spiritual vision (fig. 239). This Andean Father God wears a headdress of snakes, birds, and ears of corn, while bird heads gaze from his belt. Some believe this figure to be Viracocha ("Foam of the Sea"), who as the Creator God disappeared into the ocean's surf—an allusion to the living waters—after bringing great material gifts and spiritual miracles to the region. This sacred figure holds two animal-headed staves, one in each hand, an indication of his power to harmonize opposing forces. As both solar and lunar being, this Staff God indicates the unification of solar and lunar calendars, something that occurs when a culture has made a long-term commitment to agriculture. The powerful symmetry of this figure expresses the moral order and divine justice for which this being stands.

The Nazca culture of c. 200 B.C. to A.D. 600 built pyramid structures and underground canal systems unique to the Americas. Nazca textiles and ceramics were of the highest technical and artistic quality for their time. However, the most remarkable images formed by this culture are the geoglyphs, "earth writing," that appear on Peru's desert plateau at Nazca. Although such mystery images are found from Chile to California (fig. 240) and have European parallels in the large earthen figures such as the Long Man of Wilmington (fig. 241), their greatest concentration in the Americas appears to be at Nazca, where hundreds of figures and linear designs are fashioned in the rocks and sand of this arid landscape. Black volcanic pebbles were scraped away to expose linear designs of yellow desert sand and clay. However, these designs can only be appreciated from the air. Even hilltops in the region do not afford a clear view of the lines that form animals and geometric patterns. It is believed by some researchers that the geoglyphs were created to attract the atten-

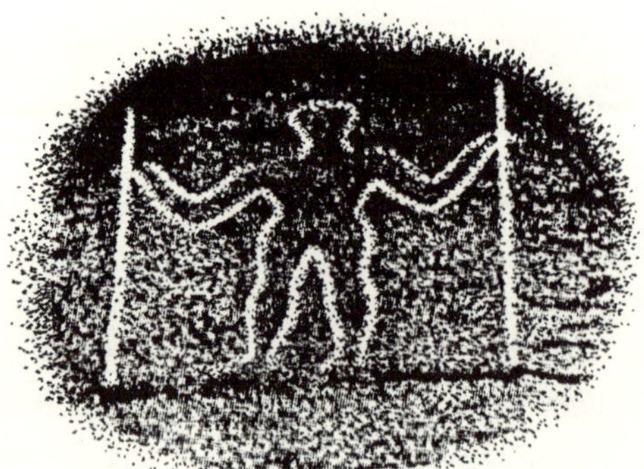

tion of mountain and weather deities. As they can only be fully observed from a great height, it would make sense that they were intended for the gods and viewed perhaps only by shamans during out-of-body spirit flights.

Many of the linear geoglyphs appear to be sacred paths used in ceremonial pilgrimages by local families and village groups over centuries. The practices of ceremonial pilgrimages continue even today, and gifts of river stones, mountain ice, and seashells are offered to particular mountain spirits. Processions follow the lines to mounds and hills with "ray centers" of converging lines, and offerings are made to the higher mountains and their spirits for water.

Regarding the animal forms, the hummingbird (fig. 242) is believed to be a manifestation of the mountain god; sea birds are linked with ocean spirits (there are eighteen bird effigies at Nazca); spiders appear before it rains (fig. 243); and monkeys are of the rain forest (fig. 244), so they are deemed beneficent creatures and like the others are associated with water. An early Spanish chronicler observed in regard to indigenous Peruvian beliefs: "For each species of animal they knew a star in the sky, and so there are many which they worshipped and they set names and assigned sacrifices."[91]

The nonfigurative linear markings at Nazca appear to have been created after the more complex figures, but it is only possible to date artifacts found beside the lines, while the lines themselves are essentially undateable. The linear patterns and straight lines have been shown in some cases to be aligned to the moon's setting and rising, to particular stars, and to some constellations. Even in the case of the animal designs, some, such as the giant spider, may be oriented toward the heavens. One researcher described the spider as "a terrestrial diagram of the giant constellation of Orion."[92] Paul Kosok has referred to the Nazca lines as "the largest astronomy-book of the world."[93] In any case the Nazca lines appear to serve a spiritual purpose as ritual pathways, spirit maps, celestial calendars, or all of the above.

An interesting contrast to the monumental works of South American cultures is the sign language of forms and patterns believed to be derived from

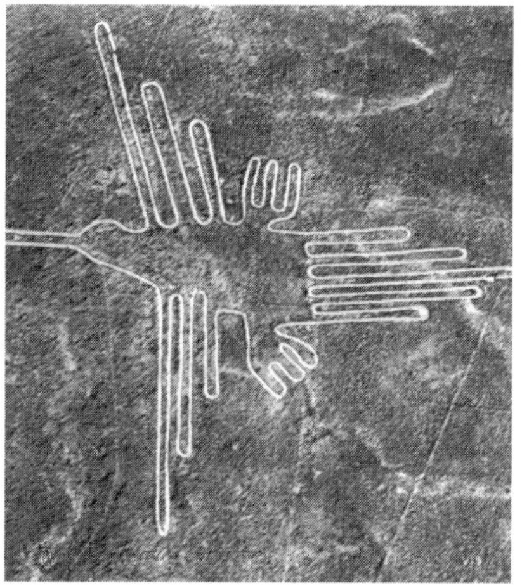

Fig. 242. There are a total of eighteen bird effigies at Nazca, including this hummingbird figure. The hummingbird, with its quick wing movement and ability to hover, is believed to be a manifestation of the mountain god. The beak of this figure ends at a group of straight lines, one of which points to the rising sun on December 21, the summer solstice in subequatorial Peru.

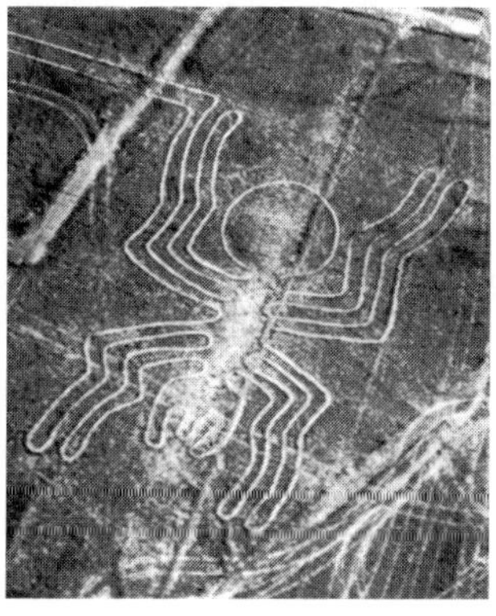

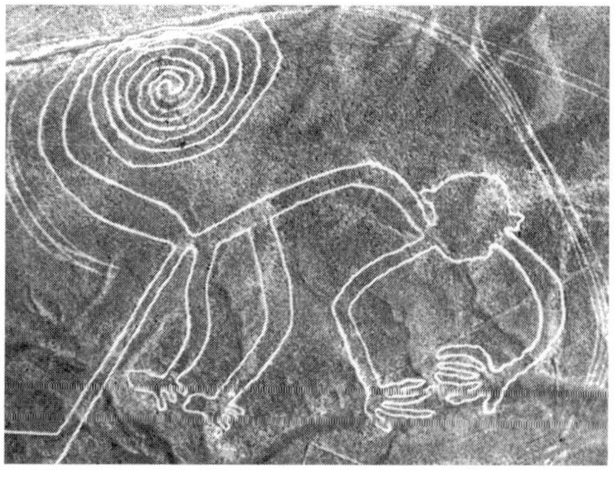

Fig. 243. Because it appears before and after rains, the spider (far left) is associated with water. Among many indigenous American peoples, such as the Hopi (Spider Woman), the Mimbre, and the Navaho, it is connected with fertility. This figure at Nazca is 150 feet long.

Fig. 244. Left: This monkey figure is made from one continuous curved line. It begins and ends below the tail, but continues outside the animal as a straight line for over a mile on one side, and becomes a wandering zigzag beneath the monkey's figure on the other end. Note the elaborate spiral tail. Monkeys do not live in this desert region but are found in the rain forests, a long journey from Nazca.

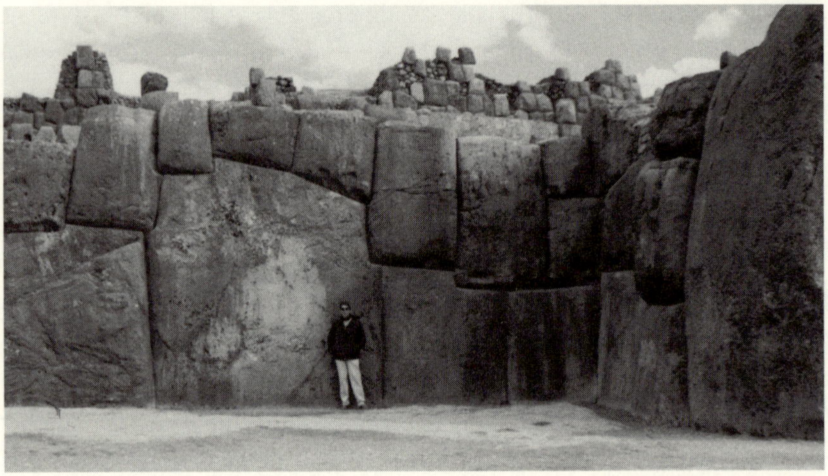

Fig. 246. With numerous angles, Inca stonework is some of the most remarkable in the world. This stone (right), at Sacsay Huaman in Peru, has nearly a dozen angles and is set in place without mortar, yet for centuries it has resisted damage from earthquakes.

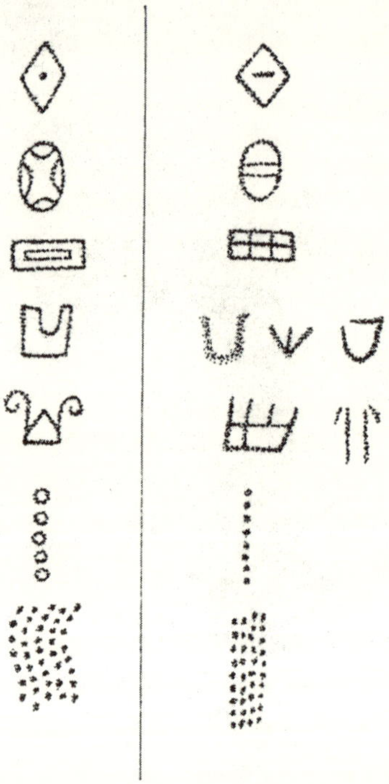

Fig. 245. Above: The designs and patterns used by the Tukano Indians of Colombia are known to be derived from the physiological images (phosphenes) that arise during the onset of shamanic trance conditions. Paleolithic symbols (left) bear a striking resemblance to Tukano designs (right), which suggests continuity between contemporary tribal practices and the oldest shamanic art forms yet known. (After Clottes and Lewis-Williams.)

the more subjective phenomenon called phosphenes. Phosphenes are fleeting physiological images produced upon the mind's eye independently of external vision. These phosphenic forms, which are common across cultures, indicate the first stages of a shamanic trance state. A sense-free condition is accompanied by the "seeing" of numerous red dots, which for the Colombian Tukano people "represents the Milky Way, the goal of shamanic flight."[94] Simple forms and patterns give way to the perception of "larger forms suggestive of animals, people, or unknown creatures."[95] Phosphenes may be induced by prolonged exposure to darkness, sensory deprivation, fatigue, rhythmic movement, flickering light, concentration, or psychoactive drugs, as has been demonstrated under controlled conditions. Contemporary Tukano people use designs and patterns in their art that are derived directly from phosphene images. When compared with Paleolithic symbols, Tukano designs demonstrate a striking similarity, which suggests continuity between the oldest shamanic art forms and those of present-day indigenous peoples (fig. 245).

By the time of the Renaissance in Europe, Andean culture in South America was experiencing a renaissance of its own. The Inca culture had developed a highly organized social order and an equally elaborate and complex ritual art. The Inca rock work in places like Cuzco and Machu Picchu, which was under construction at the same time as the Gothic cathedrals, rival the masonry of ancient Egypt in complexity and size. Some finely cut stones of Inca structures have a dozen angles that were precisely matched and fitted to their facing stones without the use of mortar (fig. 246).

Two forms that frequently appear in Inca structures are the vertical trapezoid seen as niches, windows, and doorways, and the "beak" form often incorporated into altars (fig. 247). The sides of the trapezoid forms taper upward to rest firmly on a base that lies parallel to a narrow top. Niches were used for placing offerings, and windows and doorways were obvious thresholds between inner and outer space. This trapezoid form, so characteristic of Inca architecture, does not just appear as negative space; it can also be seen as solid mass as in the supposed sundial portion of the Intiwatana, "the Hitching Post of the Sun," carved from the granite mountain (fig. 248). The beak or bow form often appears in naturally occurring rock that is slightly enhanced by carving. Most of the fourteen megalithic altars at Machu Picchu (fig. 249) reveal this form, sometimes pointing horizontally in a particular direction, sometimes pointing diagonally towards the sky.

Andean art forms are often set in solid powerful masses, ample and squat, expressive of earthly solidity and concentrated force. Here in South America, where the wheel never came into use except on small ritual models, Andean peoples never knew the ease of being carried by a wheeled cart or chariot. All movement along their extensive and well-conceived roadways was achieved on foot—by great effort and willpower. This "willfullness" is an unmistakable characteristic of prehistoric America and is clearly articulated in the old art forms of this New World.

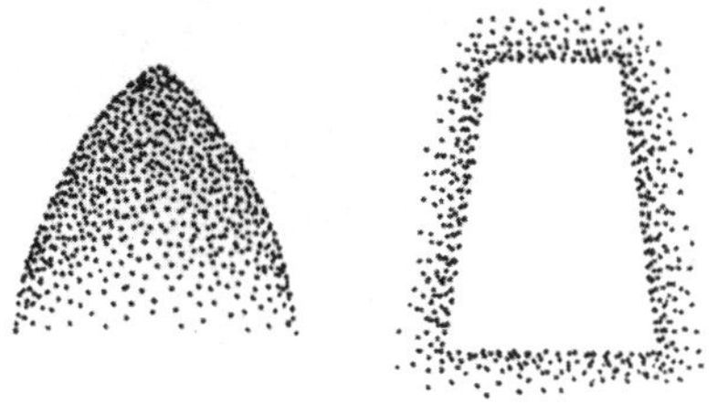

Fig. 247. Two forms used repeatedly in Inca art and architecture are the vertical trapezoid and the "beak" or "bow" form.

Fig. 248. The vertical trapezoid appears in buildings as niches, windows, and doorways. In all three cases, thresholds are created: niches provide blind portals for offerings to meet the spiritual world, while windows and doors allow visual or physical movement from one physical space to another. Intiwatana, "The Hitching Post of the Sun" (below left) is the main altar at Machu Picchu in the Peruvian Andes. Its most obvious feature, carved from the platform of the altar, is a solid vertical trapezoid. This part of the stone monument was used for solar observations.

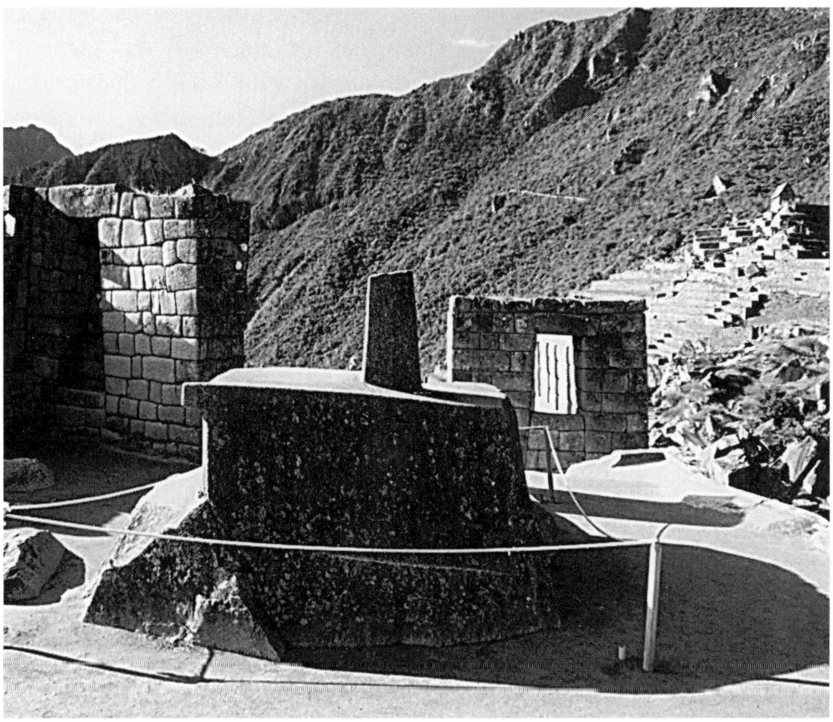

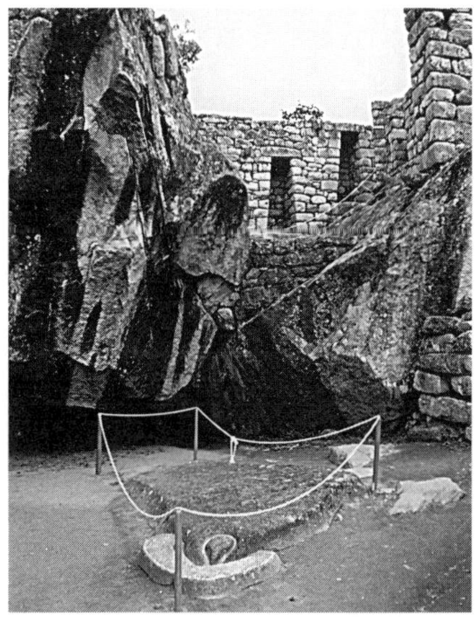

Fig. 249. Above: Most of the fourteen altars at Machu Picchu contain the "beak" or "bow" form and are carved into the naturally lying rock as monumental sculpture. The Altar of the Condor is just such a site.

V.6 The Art of Oceania

Belief that the spirit world pervaded every aspect of life and niche in the environment motivated artists to suggest its presence in articles of everyday as well as ceremonial use.
—Allen Wardwell

Just as Africa is said to be the Heart of the Earth, Oceania or the Pacific region is said to be the Womb of the World, as many traditions believe the moon was born from this part of the globe. This watery realm of tidal rhythms covers one third of the earth's surface and is dotted with the islands of Micronesia, Melanesia, and Polynesia.

There is much debate over dates of settlement in this region. Although the art and artifacts of Oceania do not appear to go back in time as far as in other parts of the world, it is clear that the late prehistoric peoples who produced this work nevertheless possessed a consciousness similar to that of prehistoric cultures elsewhere.

The art of Oceania is spiritual in nature because it is made in response to a worldview that the universe is determined by invisible forces that influence the events of life. These forces are present everywhere, creating a mystical relationship between people and elements and reflecting a sacred union.

Like other primal peoples, the tribes of Oceania generally held that the soul could leave the body and exist independently—usually during dreams, trance states, and death. At death the soul returned once more to the spirit world, but still maintained influence among the living. Complicated ceremonies with extraordinary costumes, masks, body decoration, implements, music, dance, chant, drama, painting, sculpture, and architecture were "offered" in order to win the influence of ancestor spirits and gods. This ritual art was often used to stimulate memory concerning events, traditional myths, and beliefs. If art objects had undergone the proper ritual treatments, they could serve as temporary dwellings for spirits. It was understood that these powerful spirit forces could not always be controlled, but if they were properly honored they might benefit the individual, family, and community in some way.

Unlike Africa, the Pacific Islands have no large land mammals. It is therefore noteworthy that most Oceanic art is based on the human form, although some animals and composite figures do appear. Exaggerated body parts, such as large heads, gaping mouths, hunched shoulders, flexed legs, and big feet, indicate the supersensorial at work and the presence of a spirit entity. The less naturalistically a form is depicted, the more certain that it is the embodiment of unseen spiritual forces. Entirely abstract, geometric, and linear forms represent the unrepresentable powers of nature and the supernatural world. Such artistic canons are not unique to Oceania, for the tribal art of west and central Africa reflects many of the same characteristics. But the "calculated formlessness" of Pacific island art surely has in part to do with the soul constitution of a people that live within a world of vast water forces and dynamic, flowing life currents. This is Oceania.

Polynesia

There is life in the stone.
—Ancient Hawaiian saying

The Maori of New Zealand believe that all knowledge is a gift of the great god Kane, who gave humanity three baskets containing accounts of creation, instruction in magic, and all other knowledge of the world. The arts and crafts were also spiritual in origin, being secured either from the heavens or from the underworld. Manmade arts and crafts were integrated in form and function and, like all things, had a life spirit or mana. Art objects were regarded not as lifeless but as maintaining a vital inner force that could be strengthened through appropriate rituals or drained away by improper contacts. Mana was protected by certain rules and prohibitions called *taboo* in Tongan (*tapu* in Maori, *kapu* in Hawaiian). Ceremonial art objects were imbued with great mana and were protected by severe taboos.

Throughout Oceania spiritual experiences are portrayed in artistic forms, carved in wood and sculpted in stone. Some of the themes depict anthropozoomorphic images representing ancestors, gods, and spirits—sometimes taking the shape of bird-men, pig-men, and eel and lizard beings. One of the most widespread of these images is the Birdman, an avian-human figure. Pictograms, petroglyphs, and wood carvings of Birdmen are found in New Zealand, Hawai'i, and Easter Island—the three corners of the Polynesian triangle—and are believed to be totem figures and ancestral guardians. Birds served as givers of omens, vehicles of the spirits, and guardians of the threshold between worlds. Their movements in the sky were carefully observed and their cries were listened to with the utmost attention and reverence. Their feathers were worn throughout Oceania as a sign of initiation and rank as they were in other parts of the world. The feather was a sacred symbol of the god or spirit and was often attached to a wood or stone image, symbolic of earthly humanity, with fiber cordage, expressive of the umbilical cord or spirit-line between

a
b
c
d

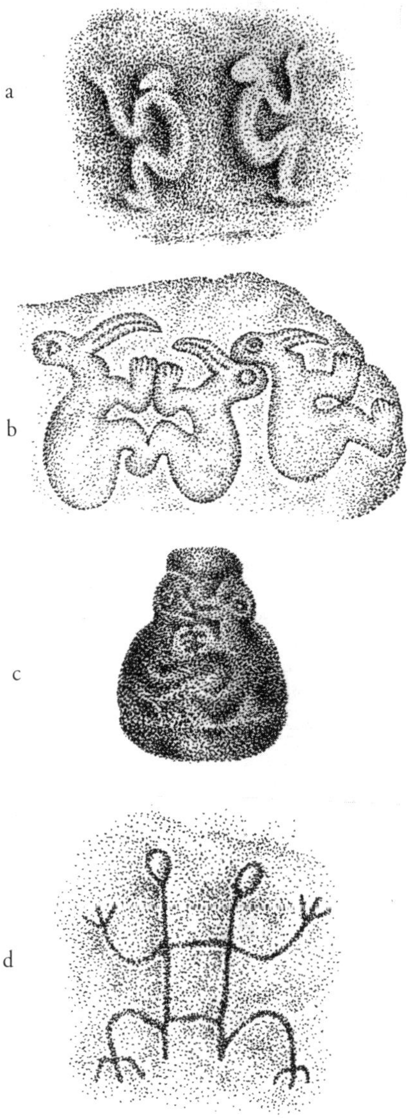

Fig. 250. (a) A Birdman petroglyph in high relief from the island of Oahu, Hawai'i, shows similarities to other Birdman images throughout the Pacific. The Birdman petroglyphs (b) at Orongo on Rapa Nui (Easter Island) are connected with the annual ceremonies celebrating the return of the migratory sooty tern. Birdmen images are found on (c) western South American islands and (d) in western Oceania as far as New Guinea.

god and man. Characteristics of the avian motif are large, round, lidless eyes, beaked mouth, flexed knees, and taloned hands and feet. Striking similarities occur in the bas-relief petroglyph found on Oahu, in the Hawaiian archipelago, and those located at Orongo, on Easter Island, where ritual ceremonies, in the form of contests, were performed around the annual migratory return of the sooty tern to offshore islets. Compare these Polynesian petroglyphs with Birdman images from the island of Puna, off the northern coast of Peru in South America (fig. 250).[96] Their back-to-back, squatting position and raised arms suggest a prayerful gesture or ritual dance movement. Eliade observes that: "certain prehistoric rock carvings seem to show supernatural beings enacting parts of their histories, now obscure to us: a magical gesture, a dance, a ritual, or some act essential for prolonging life."[97] At Easter Island, where 499 Birdman images occur, Georgia Lee and Edward Stasack say, "the petroglyphs were carved by experts who chanted and prayed for the success of the contest and who lived at the site during the competition. The designs relate to power and status, prayer and offering."[98] Birdmen do not only occur in the Pacific, for the association of the soul with the bird image is so universal that it is found in many traditional arts worldwide.

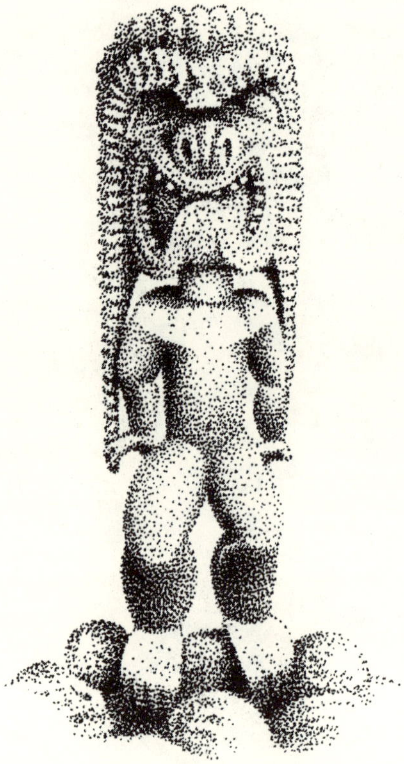

Fig. 251. Above: The tiered and crested headdresses worn by Hawaiian deities may be connected with celestial phenomena such as comets, shooting stars, and the multileveled firmament, as well as with successive generations. Ku demonstrates the bent-knee position and the tiered headdress.

The flexed-knee or bent-leg position appears throughout the prehistoric world and is one of the most common postures in prehistoric Polynesian as well as African and ancient American sculpture. The flexed-knee stance in ancient Hawaiian dance (hula) is intended to center the dancer, bringing him or her into a closer relation with the earth. This low-to-the-ground style of dance, associated with the eruptive power of vulcanism, is linked to the goddess Pele. Also a fundamental position in martial arts, it is called Hun-Yuan Kung in Chinese *tai chi*, and allows energy to sink to one's center below the navel. In Hatha Yoga the flexed-knee position is called Tadasana or the Mountain Pose and is said to help draw energy from the feet up to the head, ensuring steadiness, endurance, and contentment.[99] Such a stance is considered to carry great *mana* with it and is expressive of powerful will and potent spirit (fig. 251).

Another characteristic feature of Hawaiian temple sculpture is the elaborate tiered headdress and crested helmet found on god images. Some of these crown features, with dynamic repetitive forms, are associated with celestial phenomena such as comet tails, shooting stars, and the multileveled firmament. At the same time, they are associated with successive lineage, the lattice and ladder of ancestral genealogy. The round, crested helmet is not featured solely on the heads of deities but is worn also by chiefs as an expression of their divine origin (fig. 252). Usually fashioned in brilliant colored red, yellow, and

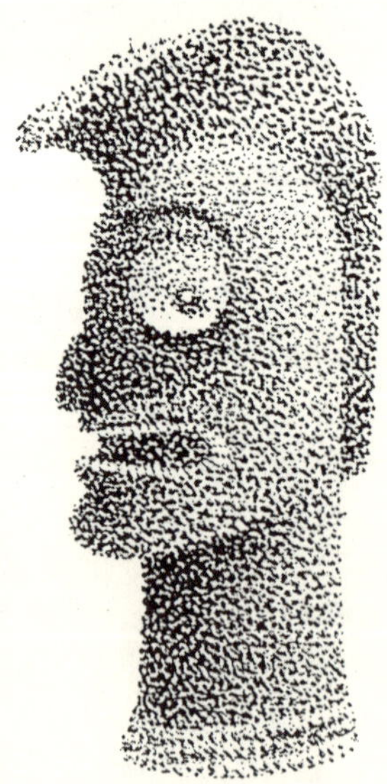

Fig. 252. Right: The crested headdress is a sign of divine nobility and indicates the visionary capacity and ancestral connections of the wearer. This rendering of a Hawaiian deity, fashioned in sennet with feathers and dog teeth, sports a crested helmet similar to that worn by Hawaiian chiefs.

black feathers on a sennet wicker frame, the crescent shape is likened to the rainbow, another symbol of divine royalty—token of the threshold between worlds. This crest form points to the visionary power and authority possessed by its wearer. These royal helmets bear a striking likeness to the sacred headgear of other cultures, such as the crested ceremonial hat of Tibet and the Phrygian cap of Persia. A related form is the Hawaiian *lei niko palaoa* (fig. 253), a hooklike ornament of whale ivory suspended from the neck by two coils of braided human hair. It is a sacred badge of rank worn only by the nobility and is an abstraction of the tongue, symbolizing the power of royalty to speak on behalf of the gods. Images of tongue, mouth, and breath are sacred forms connected with the source of life, as can be seen in the *koru,* a Maori design element with curved scroll form and a bulblike, rounded end (fig. 254). It is usually seen as an unfolding tree fern frond and is associated with plant forms. However, it is more accurate to say it has to do with growth forces and the vital energy that produces plant forms in the first place. The koru motif appears as carving on wood and stone, as tattoo designs, and painted on the rafter beams of Maori meetinghouses. It is directly related to the spiral and is found not only in Maori art but also in the works of ancient Southeast Asia and Southern China. It is also related to design elements from the opposite sides of the earth: Islamic arabesques (figs. 193, 194) and Celtic designs (fig. 138). Stone and woodcarvings, as well as manuscript illuminations (see chapter IV) demonstrate similar forms, which, like the koru, are true mystery images in the primal language of art.

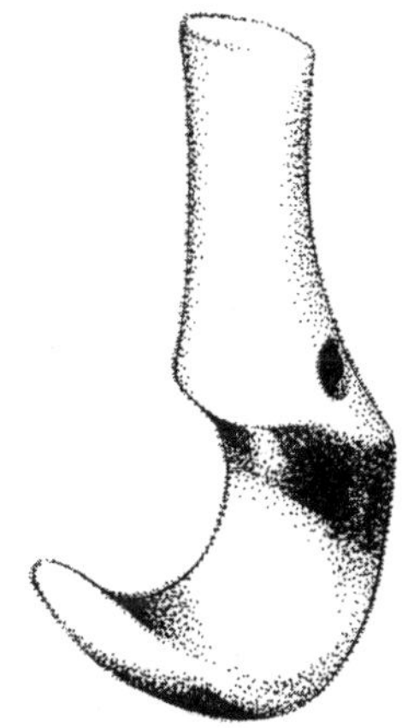

Fig. 253. The Hawaiian *lei niko palaoa,* a hooklike neck ornament carved from whale ivory, is a symbol of mana and of the divine right to speak as the official representative of the gods on earth.

Melanesia

Melanesian religions are expressed in a wide and dazzling variety of activities such as masked dances, secret societies, initiations reflecting the tension of male and female and (in remote areas) ritual cannibalism.

—Albert Moore

The arts of Papua New Guinea's Eastern Highlands are very different from those found in Polynesia. At the southwestern end of Oceania, people developed elaborate and complex rituals together with striking visual arts. For example, brightly painted *gerua* boards are worn in a spectacular ceremony associated with the feeding of ancestor spirits (fig. 255). Performed every three years at the height of the full moon, the ritual involves initiation and coming-of-age celebrations in which as many as two hundred male family leaders dance while wearing the *gerua.* The boards are strapped to the head and are spiritually activated by placing human hair at their top and attaching clan valuables to other parts. The festive dance culminates in the ritual killing of pigs and the ceremonial feeding of pork to the spirits. Some *gerua* boards

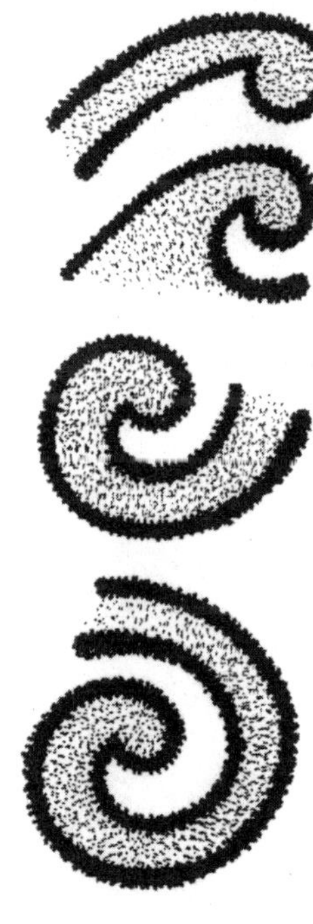

Fig. 254. The Maori *koru* is thought to have its origin in the form of the fern. However, it is more likely that the *koru* is based on the Maori perception of the formative forces that first shaped the fern.

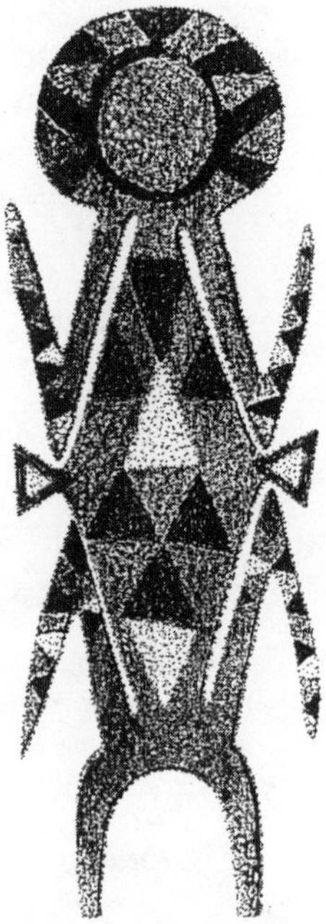

Fig. 255. Above: Gerua boards like this one are worn by male family members in connection with initiation ceremonies in which ancestor spirits are ritually fed. This six-foot gerua has a round head symbolizing the sun, a diamond-shaped body representing the moon, and angular arms and legs indicating starlike rays.

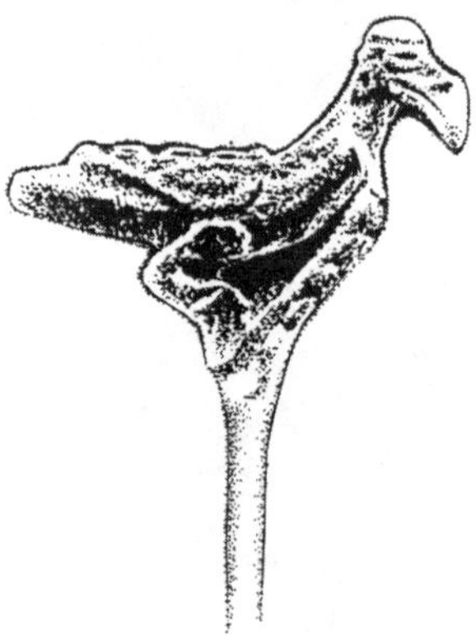

Fig. 256. Above: An artistically fashioned limestick in the form of a cassowary bird may have been used by the Iatmul people of Papua New Guinea in connection with trance and divining rituals. This limestick is made from the bone of a cassowary.

are up to six feet high and painted with patterns specific to each family. The boards are anthropomorphic in form, sometimes with a diamond-shaped body representing the moon, a round head symbolizing the sun, and angular arms and legs suggesting pathways. The image of the sun as head, moon as trunk, and limbs as starlike pathfinders is echoed in other esoteric traditions.[100] At the end of the ceremonies *geruas* are placed in bamboo groves and allowed to decay.

Throughout Oceania there is no clear distinction between ceremonial and nonceremonial art. Shields, weapons, tools, and implements are often made for ritual purposes and are decorated with abstract designs, human and animal faces, and figures of various kinds. Such an artistically rendered object is the limestick, used in conjunction with a gourd container that holds lime. (Mixed with fruit and betel nuts, lime was chewed for physical energy and to uplift the spirit.) One particular example, is a baton produced by the Iatmul people along the Sepik River in Papua New Guinea, carved from the tibia of a cassowary bird (fig. 256). The bird depicted in the carving is also a cassowary, which is an extremely important creature to the Iatmul as it is associated with initiation ceremonies and creation myths. Such batons were "probably used by shamans when going into a trance or at divining rituals before head-hunting raids."[101] The repeated appearance of the bird image in prehistoric art, its connection to the shamanic practice of spirit-flight as well as its association with the crossing into the Otherworld, is a worldwide theme.

Micronesia

Great architecture is at the very origins of humanity . . . . It is the immediate product of human instinct.

—Le Corbusier

It was once believed that complex crafts, monumental works of art, and accomplished architecture could not be achieved by early artist-builders before tools for modification of these works had been developed. However, it is now recognized that the earliest works of art and architecture were created by simply putting together materials commonly found in nature, without the help of tools. The act of placing one stone upon another was for prehistoric humanity a sacred act. As we have seen with Megalithic cultures, the erecting of a single upright stone in nature had the spiritual significance of marking the *genius loci*, or "spirit of place" (*wahi pana* in Hawaiian). Throughout Oceania, where metal was absent and stone was the strongest material—the bones of the earth—sacred sites were indicated by single stones or by massive rock monuments.

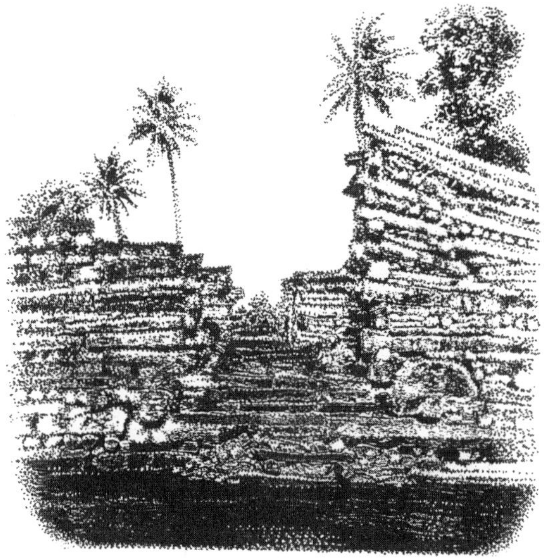

Fig. 257. Nan Madol on Pohnpei (above) is an ancient ceremonial center constructed from stacked, columnar, prismatic, basaltic stone and built along reef canals.

Throughout Oceania, on widely distributed island groups, stone platforms and rock enclosures are erected as temple sites, mortuary compounds, tribal meeting places, and royal residences. Their structural stability is often remarkable, considering the fact that the builders used no mortar to hold together the large, uncarved stones. There are many such prehistoric monuments throughout Micronesia, but most impressive are the megalithic complexes on Pohnpei and Kosrae islands.

Pohnpei (also called Pohnape) and Kosrae are located about 340 miles from each other at the eastern end of the Caroline Island group. Nan Madol on Pohnpei and Leluh on Kosrae are ceremonial urban centers for their islands, and both complexes are built with stacked columnar prismatic basalt in shallow lagoons accessed by canoes via intricate canal systems (fig. 257). Nan Madol has been described as the "Venice of the Pacific," and legends speak of an ancient underwater city offshore from Nan Madol where a dozen megalithic columns are submerged in water 50 to 90 feet deep.

Pohnpei means "upon a stone altar," and although occupation dates between 1200 and 1400 A.D. have been suggested, earlier estimates date the elaborate megalithic architecture of Nan Madol at over 2000 years old. Constructed on a magnificent complex of ninety-two artificial islets interconnected by a network of waterways, this sacred city has walls that reach a height of 25 feet at corners and entryways, and are 15 feet thick in places. Walls may curve outward and upward four feet higher and one foot thicker at their corners than in their centers. According to William Morgan, "the ancient builders seem to have understood the importance of developing adequate resistance to shear, of minimizing bending, and of eliminating tension."[102] Great seawalls and breakwaters protect the site from the relentless pounding of the ocean on exposed coastal reefs. Most of the site is believed to have been used for burials and royal residences. Some of

Fig. 258. Nandauwas, the royal mortuary complex at Nan Madol, is a monumental structure composed of four-, five-, and six-sided prismatic basalt logs.

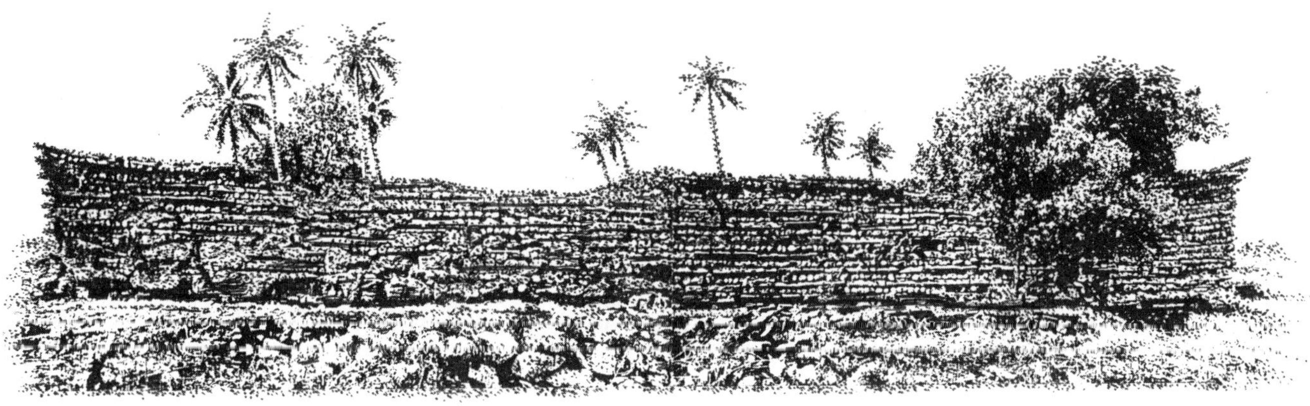

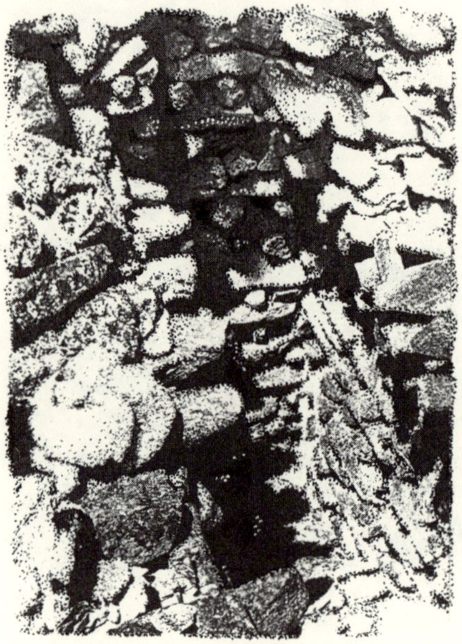

Fig. 259. The central crypt of the Inol tomb, at Leluh (above), is constructed in alternating header and stretcher courses of stacked columnar basalt.

the structures are oriented to an east-west axis, facing the rising sun and the ocean. The hexagonal stone logs have an average size of 2.5 feet thick and 17 feet long, weighing some 15 tons each. One basalt cornerstone is estimated to weigh in excess of 50 tons.

Enclosures have front entries designed to function as canoe landings. Some structures have alternate, side tunnel passageways leading into inner courtyards. The crowning architectural achievement at Nan Madol is Nandauwas, the royal mortuary compound, which contains several raised platform tombs (fig. 258). The central crypt is an enclosure covered with four, five and six-sided prismatic columnar stones.

Oral tradition says that the basaltic pillars were dislodged from quarries on the island and "floated" to the site for construction. Archaeologists believe that it is possible these prehistoric monuments were constructed with help from rafts, ropes, levers, and inclined planes. A Kosraean legend tells how the people of Tofol formed a human chain passing pieces of coral hand-to-hand across the reef in order to build an islet at Leluh. Another Kosraean legend tells that Leluh's walls were assembled by magic. When certain chants were invoked, "the stones quickly piled themselves on top of each other."[103] Such legends are common throughout Oceania when traditional histories do not attribute structures to specific prehistoric chiefs. Shamanic or kahuna practices are a deeply interwoven aspect of art and life in Oceania, and often play a significant role in the carrying-out of prehistoric building projects.

The impressive central crypt of the Inol wall tomb, at Leluh, is constructed from carefully stacked prismatic magnetized basalt of alternating header and stretcher courses (fig. 259). Most of the seventeen sacred compounds at Leluh were probably restricted to a priestly class, and contained both spirit houses and priest houses. Spirit houses, small in size, would have contained objects and offerings sacred to the gods and ancestors. It is thought that priest houses may have been used as residences only during special ceremonies and festivals, as evidence of prolonged occupation is lacking. Many additional artistic features would have been constructed of perishable materials such as wood, thatch, and twine. An idea of their character may be gleaned from study of post-contact native crafts.

The megalithic structures of Micronesia, expressions of a distinctive spiritual heritage, are another unique demonstration of the outstanding creations produced by prehistoric peoples with minimal technology at their disposal. Throughout Oceania the formative arts continually demonstrate the extensive influence of ancient mystery tradition, how the work of art is shaped by the culture and how the culture is shaped by the art.

V.7 Australian Aboriginal Art

[Our painting] . . . is like a map revealing our land, our boundaries, our sacred sites. It carries not just the history but also the spirituality of who we are.
—Banduk Marika

The Australian Aborigines may be one of the oldest peoples on earth and their images and symbols, like those of Europe's Paleolithic cave art, are often placed into two district categories—the curvilinear feminine forms and the straight, angular, masculine forms.[104] Active and passive, light and dark, warm and cold, positive and negative, acid and base, sun and moon, are but a few manifestations of the primordial dualities that are linked to masculine and feminine, straight and curved qualities.

As we have seen, all art has a sacred connection to peoples of prehistory. However, for our historic way of looking at phenomena it can be helpful to view Aboriginal art in three separate categories: personal, social, and sacred. These divisions necessarily flow together and overlap each other, but for our present considerations it will be useful to group certain types of artistic production in this manner.

Personal art among the Aborigines is often an activity performed by the women and is directly connected with storytelling. Symbols and images frequently deal with camp-making tasks, favored gathering sites, food sources, lovemaking, and fertility. Dot and line images, pulsing with patterns of energy and life, have been used to indicate radiating pathways leading from campgrounds to food gathering sites. The dot pictures have developed in recent times into elaborate abstract paintings (fig. 260). Such paintings usually depict scenes from above, as in a bird's-eye view, indicating an out-of-body vantage point, a dreamlike overview or spirit flight vision.[105] The original technique employed for these pictures was to quickly draw them in the

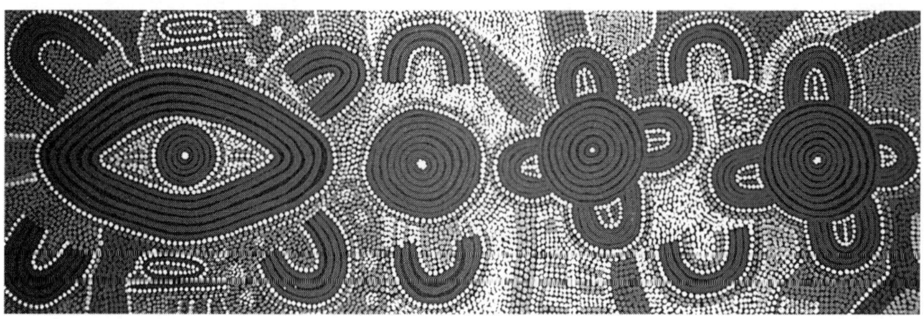

Fig. 260. Contemporary Aborigine dot paintings often incorporate the basic graphic elements of circles and straight lines. Although circles may indicate campsites or gathering places and straight lines the sacred tracks that connect them, the artist's interpretation is usually required. *Honey Ant Dreaming* is by Turkey Tolson Tjupurrula. (Orana School, Canberra, Australia.)

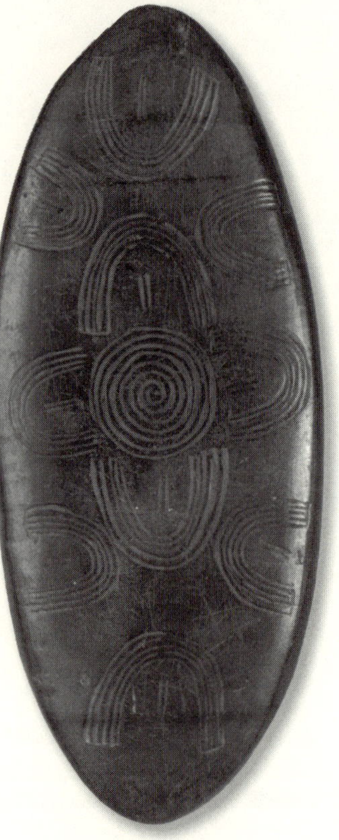

Fig. 261. The *tjuringa* is an oblong stone or wood object, carved with sacred symbols that embody the powers of ancestral spirits and divine beings, and is highly revered as a personal possession among Australian Aborigine men. (Honolulu Academy of Arts.)

sand, then erase them following the narration of a story. Many of the stories relate back to the primal era, Altjiringa, or Dreamtime of the Australian Aborigines.[106] At this time the great ancestors brought the world into being by "envisioning" stories at the first campsite. These stories were then painted, as Andreas Lommel relates: "The first beings dreamed the animals and plants; they painted the dream images on the rocks, filled them with a soul-force, and from the rock-paintings the souls of the beings represented spread over the world in physical shape."[107] The importance of the visual arts as mediators between the creative spirits and the created beings is made clear in such a description. The painted images are prototypes or "process pictures" on the way to becoming finished material forms.

Perhaps the most sacred of the personal art objects was the *tjuringa.* Every adult male possessed a tjuringa, made of stone or wood, which embodied creator beings and ancestral spirits of its owner. *Tjuringas* are usually elongated oval or stick forms with linear incisions on their surface depicting concentric circles, squares, ovals, rectangles, diamonds, arcs, spirals, zigzags, and parallel, dotted, or wavy lines (fig. 261). These designs refer to any number of beings, myths, parts of the heavens, landscapes, campsites, plants, animals, and animal tracks. Because motifs have multiple meanings, a *tjuringa* is impossible to interpret without information from its owner. The complexity of symbolism in Aboriginal two-dimensional design is not easy to summarize, as becomes clear from Frederick McCarthy's comment: "Concentric circles usually represent the principal features of the myth portrayed such as the spiritual ancestor, places where he camped, went into or came out of the ground, distributed spirit children, waged battle with an enemy or rival, and so on. On one tjuringa they represent a frog, on others, a tree, a waterhole, or other totem."[108]Tjuringas are displayed at initiations by the elders to explain legends and traditions to novices and during observances to assure adequate food supply or rain. It is clear from such uses that the tjuringas were not simply personal possessions but highly valued sacred objects. When not in use, they were safely hidden away in small storehouses.

The personal art of body painting and scarring is at the same time a social art practiced in both women's and men's ceremonies, and is connected to storytelling, song, dance, and ritual. Paul Faulstich's research into the graphic arts of the Warlpiri Aboriginal people led him to observe: "They are highly charged images expressive of kinship rules, the distribution of sacred knowledge, rights to resources, and other aspects of social organization. The process of painting is embedded in a matrix of social relations."[109] Another social art form that is an important sacred practice is the earth sculpture created by the men (fig. 262). Sometimes several acres of land are shaped into a relief sculpture of soil and rock. Blood, feathers, and other materials might also be used, and song and dance describe the underlying meaning of the various shapes and patterns as stages along a journey of transformation. Here again social art is both personal and sacred.

Whether produced for funeral services or initiation ceremonies, many art forms are destroyed after their purpose is fulfilled. Mentioned earlier, Tibetan and Native American sand paintings are examples of ritual-artistic images that are returned to the chaos (spirit world) out of which they were created. The process of manifesting that which is invisible and hidden and then returning it once again to the hidden world of beginnings is characteristic of many types of Aborigine art. This is one of the ways personal, social, and sacred art are united in the service of the spiritual life. The very essence of such art is that it is indivisible from its material, its maker, its purpose, and its ultimate meaning. Therefore its return to the nonmaterial world is only natural.

The trap appears in Aboriginal art to symbolize the ability of an image to hold fast to the fleeting spirit and essential meaning connected with an animal and its instinctual activity (fig. 263). As Robert Lawlor puts it, "The fish trap, in Aboriginal art, symbolizes the capacity of an image to trap the transformative spirit . . .to capture the fleeting, mutable ideas and meanings associated with the creatures and activities of the natural world."[110] Ancient Egyptian art depicts nets for trapping birds in a similar way. The ever-living, creative spirit is caught in the drawing or symbol of the trap as an animal might be caught in an actual trap. Many abstract, nonfigurative images found in Paleolithic caves have been interpreted as traps that likewise might aid in capturing the volatile, sentient power of the spirit-animal (fig. 264).

Characteristic of Aboriginal art is the "X-ray" style that "sees through" the external skin of an animal and reveals the normally hidden internal organs and/or skeletal features. As mentioned earlier, X-ray art also appears in American, as well as North Asian, European, African, Indian, and Indonesian traditions. The X-ray style in Aboriginal art is more than the hunter's familiarity with the insides of animals (fig. 265). As with bird's-eye perspective drawing, this is an obvious indication of experiences typical among early tribal cultures—the ability to read phenomena beyond the mere outer appearance.[111] An Aborigine description of the origins of X-ray painting goes as follows: Duruk, a dog, and Gandagidj, a wallaroo, back when they both were men, painted each other on a rock wall. Because Duruk was a seer, he painted his friend in X-ray style, showing his bones and internal organs. But they both painted each other as animals and so changed into those animals at the end of their lives when they entered into the pictures, making them Dreamings.

Aboriginal tradition holds that some work, such as X-ray art, is produced only in part by the living. It is said that the spirits of deceased ancestors as well as Dreamtime gods assist in the creation of art. Some of the older, simple line drawings found at rock art sites in Northern Australia are said to be rendered by Dreamtime "First People," called Mimi (fig. 266). Aborigine tribesmen claim the Mimi spirits blow on the rock wall and melt into the earth. It is said that the older red ochre pictures were painted by the Mimi or are imprints left behind as they passed into the solid rock

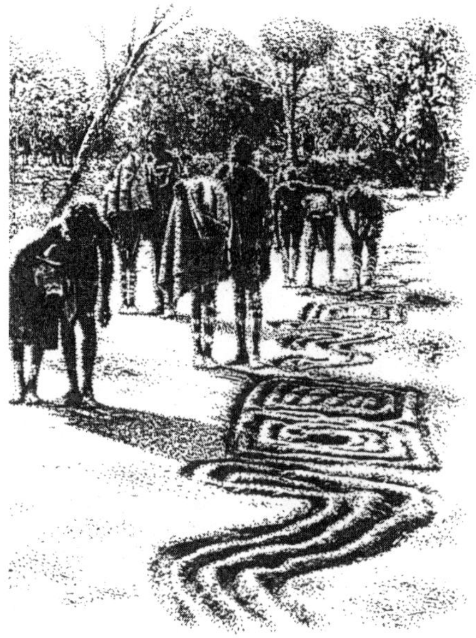

Fig. 262. As part of their initiation rites, Aborigine men created earth sculptures, sometimes shaping acres of land, moving rocks and soil, adding blood, feathers, and other material to the site where chant and dance would take place, all to create a setting for a journey of transformation from one world to another. These ritual patterns (above) were part of the journey into adult responsibility undertaken by the young men of the tribe. (Victoria, Australia.)

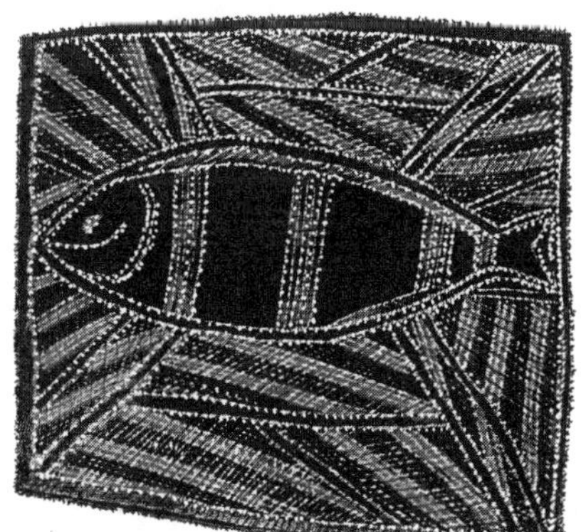

Fig. 263. Above: The trap symbolizes the ability to capture and hold fast the essential being and fleeting spirit of an animal, as in this reproduction of an Australian Aborigine bark painting of a fish trap. (After Lawlor.)

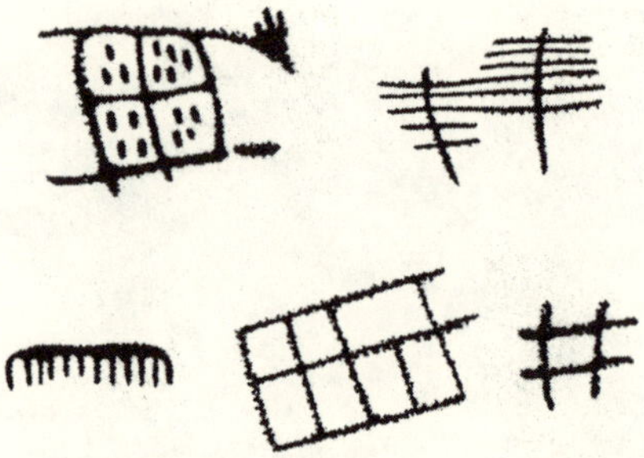

Fig. 264. Numerous abstract linear images (above), painted and engraved on Paleolithic cave walls, have been interpreted as traps or pens and may have had a purpose similar to that of Aborigine trap drawings.

Fig. 265. Right: X-ray drawing is common in Australian Aborigine art and demonstrates an attempt to make visible what is not directly apparent to outer sense perception.

and returned to the Otherworld. Some Aboriginal artists are led in their dreams by Mimi to view paintings that later, when awake, the artist reproduces. Aborigines attribute their skill in painting to Mimi. Eliade describes how "in northern Kimberley, if a rock painting is touched by a man from the proper totemic clan, rain will fall and the spirit children will become available for incarnation. Likewise, repainting the animal and vegetal images is said to increase the respective species."[112] In this way the artist and viewer both live with the Dreamtime ancestors in the artistic image, for the image acts as a body or vehicle by which the spirit-power of the ancestors is made manifest. This presence in the image works as an invisible transformative influence on the awareness of the viewer. Perhaps the story of Mimi blowing on the rocks and passing into the earth is connected with the ritual art of handprints—still practiced by Aborigines today (fig. 270). The blowing of pigment over the hand and onto a rock surface is an initiation art that was apparently practiced in the Paleolithic caves of Western Europe, and raises the question: Is this sacred art form of the Aborigines practiced in the same way it was 40,000 or more years ago?

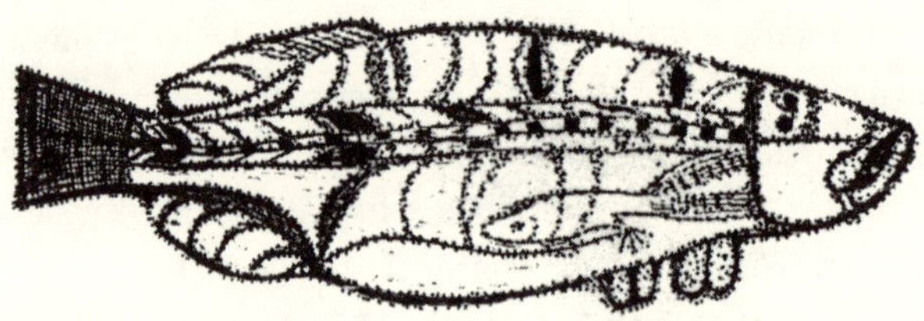

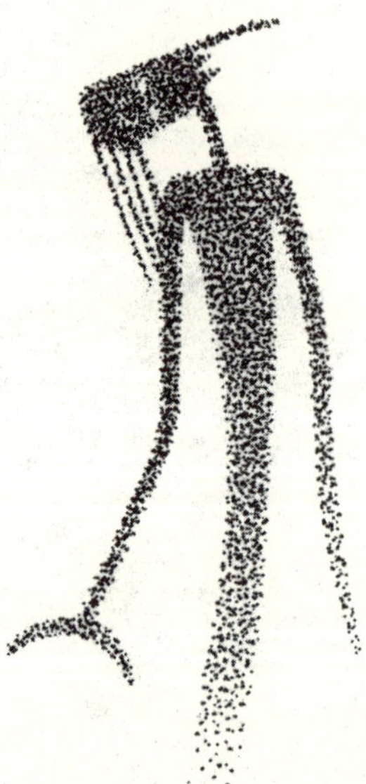

Fig. 266. Above: The older, simpler drawings of Australian Aborigines are sometimes called Mimi spirit beings. These spirits are said to have left their images on rock surfaces as they went into the Other World.

Dating of Aborigine rock art is difficult, especially since some images have been repainted in recent times. Nevertheless some paintings are of great antiquity. Boomerangs have not been used in Arnhem Land for centuries and the Thylacine or Tasmanian Tiger has been extinct on the Australian mainland for 11,000 years, surviving only in Tasmania until the nineteenth century, yet rock paintings depict these subjects, suggesting the art is of considerable age.

Although Australian Aboriginal art has been greatly influenced by Western contact for more than two centuries, it is likely that many elements in the art and culture of the Aborigine have not altered very much for millennia. Just how much one can compare present-day artistic practices to those of the Paleolithic era remains open to question. However, comparisons are valuable as we assess the extent to which the spiritual in art reveals itself from era to era.

According to traditional knowledge and tribal law, Australian Aborigines practice the visual arts as a commitment to look after the life of the earth, to care for the creatures of the land, and to revere the spirit ancestors and supernatural beings that dwell within creation. As Lawlor points out, "The Dreamtime creation myths of the Aborigines guided them to see the physical world as a language, as a metamorphosis of invisible spiritual, psychological, and ethical realms."[113] Aboriginal culture unites spirit and art with unmistakable eloquence.

Notes

1. Vasari, G. *Lives of the Artists,* p. 65.
2. "In the cultures of India, too, the shaman or medicine man was the effective possessor of the signs; he alone knew their meaning, and it is clear that the interpretation varied from individual to individual. Possession of the signs and the hidden knowledge of their meaning also guaranteed the shaman's power and influence. "In many African and Indian tribes the aim of body-painting and of the designs on warrior's shields was to make an impression on the adversary. The sign became a talisman, a weapon, a defense; the primitive fighter recognized the power of the sign (magic) and believed in its protection and its influence on the enemy." Verstockt, M. *Genesis of Form,* pp. 27–28.
3. Eliade, M. "Jade," cited in *Symbolism, the Sacred, and the Arts,* p. 141.
4. Ibid, p. 59.
5. Kutzli, R. *Creative Form Drawing,* p. 8.
6. "These marks [zigzags, ladders, circles, and spirals] are no longer seen as random accumulations but instead as a sophisticated, sequential, additive image system; no longer dismissed as idle doodlings but considered to be possibly the most complex element in Palaeolithic iconography." Bahn, P. *Images of the Ice Age,* p. 184.
7. Kutzli, R. *Creative Form Drawing,* Book 2, p. 38.
8. Rahner, H. "The Christian Mystery and the Pagan Mysteries." *The Mysteries,* Bollingen Series xxx, 2, Princeton University Press, p. 365.
9. Cited in Matanovic, M. *Light Works,* p. 13.
10. Zimmer, H. *Myth and Symbols in Indian Art and Civilization,* p. 98.
11. Ibid, p. 101.
12. Ryojun, T. Cited in Frederic, L. *Buddhism: Flammarion Iconigraphic Guides,* p. 62.
13. Zimmer, p. 140.
14. Thurman, R. *Mandala,* p. 130.
15. Ariswara, *Temples of Java,* p. 8.
16. Barrie, T. *Spiritual Path, Sacred Place: Myth, Ritual and Meaning in Architecture,* p. 125.
17. Eliade, M. "Divinities: Art and the Divine," *Symbolism, the Sacred, and the Arts,* p. 137.
18. Steiner, R. "Temple Architecture," April 27, 1924, p. 83.
19. Ibid, p. 85.
20. Govinda, A. *Psychocosmic Symbolism of the Buddhist Stupa,* p. 83.
21. Eliade, M. "Divinities: Art and the Divine," p. 121.
22. Govinda, A. *Psychocosmic Symbolism of the Buddhist Stupa,* p. 64–66.
23. Mus, P. *Borabudur,* cited in Eliade, p. 135.
24. Speiser, W. *Oriental Architecture in Color,* p. 185.
25. Barrie, T. p. 259.
26. Eliade, p. 122.
27. Steiner, R. *The Arts and Their Mission,* p. 22.
28. Govinda, A. p. 75.
29. Fisher, R. *Buddhist Art and Architecture,* pp. 79–80.
30. Leidy, D. and R. Thurman. *Mandala: The Architecture of Enlightenment,* p. 17.
31. Ibid, p. 143.
32. Bryant, B. "The Wheel of Time Sand Mandala," in *Mandala: The Architecture of Enlightenment,* p. 156.
33. Steiner, R. *The Arts and Their Mission,* p. 36.
34. Smith, B. & Weng, B. *China: A History in Art,* p. 24.
35. Steiner, R. *The Influences of Lucifer and Ahriman: Man's Responsibility for the Earth,* November 4, 1919.
36. Munsterberg, H. *Symbolism in Ancient Chinese Art,* p. 220.
37. Wang Wei, Chinese painter, 420–478 A.D.
38. Yee, C. *The Chinese Eye: An Interpretation of Chinese Painting,* p. 16.
39. Munsterberg, p. 239.
40. "The activity of perceiving the spiritual in the outer world, can . . . be called intuition, whereas the activity of making inner vision outwardly visible is imagination." Steiner, *Art As Spiritual Activity,* p. 211.
41. Pankenier, D. "Mandate of Heaven," *Archaeology,* April 1998, p. 26.
42. Graham, A.C. *Disputers of the Tao: Philosophical Argument in Ancient China.* Cited in Ryan, p. 8.
43. Eliade, M. *Shamanism,* p. 481.
44. Cited in Sullivan, W. *The Secret of the Incas,* p. 367.
45. Munsterberg, p. 40. According to esoteric tradition, the Western dragon is the unredeemed astral or emotional body. The Chinese lung is the redeemed astral body or Spirit-Self.
46. Blatchford, J. *China: Ancient Inspiration and New Directions,* p. 155.
47. Barrie, T. *Spiritual Path, Sacred Place: Myth, Ritual, and Meaning in Architecture,* p. 134.
48. From Kokin Wakashu: *The First Imperial Anthology of Japanese Poetry, with Tosa Nikki and Shinsen Waka.* Cited in B. Stephan, "Sacred Symbols: The Decorations of the New Year," *Spirit and Symbol: The Japanese New Year,* p. 52.

49. Moore, A. *Iconography of ReligIons,* p. 182.
50. Eliade, M. "Divinities: Art and the Divine," *Symbolism, the Sacred, and the Arts,* p. 61.
51. Danielou, A. *Phallus,* p. 46.
52. Ibid, p. 53.
53. Ibid, p. 27.
54. Ibid, p. 13.
55. Anderson, W. *The Face of Glory: Creativity, Consciousness, and Civilization,* p. 120.
56. Shukracharya. Cited by A.K. Coomaraswamy, *The Dance of Shiva,* p. 26.
57. Guirand, F. "Assyro-Babylonian Mythology," *New Larousse Encyclopedia of Mythology,* p. 72.
58. Mallowan, M. *Early Mesopotamia and Iran,* p. 48.
59. Eliade, M. *Symbolism, the Sacred, and the Arts,* p. 138.
60. Anderson, W. *The Face of Glory,* p. 151.
61. Mellaart, James. *Earliest Civilizations of the Near East,* p. 97–98.
62. Gibran, p. 40.
63. Wade, D., p. 238.
64. Settegast, M. p. 97. The earliest art dated so far in Africa is from a cave site in Namibia, where painted animal figures on stone slabs are believed to be twenty-five thousand years old. "The Rock Art of Tanzania and the East African Sequence." *BCSP* 23, 1986.
65. Amon was a divinity probably worshipped first in Libya before passing to Egypt in predynastic times. The ram (sheep) is believed to be the earliest domesticated animal, perhaps in late Paleolithic times. Campbell, J. *Historical Atlas of World Mythology Vol. I: The Way of the Animal Powers, Part 2: Mythologies of the Great Hunt,* p. 82.
66. Settegast, M. *Plato Prehistorian,* p. 101.
67. "The Bushman artist played an important role in this propitiation ceremony, and that by recreating visible eland upon the shelter walls, Man the Hunter was reconciled with Kaggen the Creator, thereby restoring the balance of opposing forces that was so necessary for the well-being of the Bushman psyche. Through the eland, the Bushman established and maintained communication with his god. Through the eland, the eternal cycle of sacrificing life in order to conserve and promote life, was ritually expressed." Vinnicombe, P. *People of the Eland,* p. 181. Campbell and Vinnicombe point to sympathetic magic as the major influences underlying both Paleolithic and Neolithic rock art. "There can be no doubt but that the rock paintings, whether of the Paleolithic caves or of the Kalahari Desert, served primarily a religious function relevant to the ritual lore of the hunt. The art of the caves, furthermore, was evidently of an esoteric order, hidden from general view and having to do, not only with the practice of rites to return the lives of animals slain to their source for future reappearances, but also with the initiation of youths to experiences orienting their minds to accord with the sense of these ceremonials, which from the point of view of waking consciousness would make no sense whatsoever." Campbell, J., p. xiii.
68. "The sun, for example, is also a 'fight' and a 'death thing'." Marshall, L. "The Medicine Dance of the Kung Bushmen," *Africa,* Vol. 39, No. 4, pp. 350–52.
69. Lewis-Williams, J.D. "Testing the Trance Explanation of Southern African Rock Art: Depictions of Felines," *BCSP* 22, 1985.
70. Clottes, J. and D. Lewis-Williams. The *Shamans of Prehistory.* p. 35.
71. Lewis-Williams, J.D. and T.A. Dowson, "The Signs of All Times: Entoptic Phenomena in Upper Paleolithic Art." *Current Anthropology,* vol. 29, no. 2, April 1988, p. 214.
72. Pfeiffer, J. *The Creative Explosion: An Inquiry into the Origins of Art and Religion,* p. 248.
73. Campbell, J. *Historical Atlas of World Mythology,* vol. 1, part 2, p. 166–67.
74. Joan Halifax, *Shamanic Voices: A Survey of Visionary Narratives.* Cited in Campbell, pp. 110–11.
75. Letokots Lasa, in Campbell, vol. 2, part 3, p. 381.
76. Joan Halifax, *Shamanic Voices: A Survey of Visionary Narrative.* Cited in Campbell, Historical Atlas of World Mythology, Vol. 1, Part 2, pp. 187–88.
77. John Eddy, *Medicine Wheels and Plains Indian Astronomy.* Cited in Campbell, pp. 222–223.
78. Campbell, J. Vol. I, Part 2, p. 212.
79. Hamilton, R. "Mystery of Ohio's Serpent Mound," *Ancient American,* No. 18, p. 18.
80. Schuster, C. *Patterns that Connect,* p. 136.
81. Pasztory, E. "Shamanism and North American Indian Art." Cited in *The Olmec World,* p. 31.
82. Ibid.
83. Yecuana shamans are known to have sat on carved jaguar seats during nocturnal curing rituals. Reilly, F. *The Olmec World,* p. 42.
84. Eliade, M. "Divinities: Art and the Divine," *Symbolism, the Sacred, and the Arts,* p. 58.
85. Reilly, F. "Art, Ritual, and Rulership in the Olmec World," *The Olmec World,* p. 30.
86. Ibid.
87. De La Fuente, B. Cited in R. Townsend, p. 132.
88. Schele, L. and D. Freidel, *A Forest of Kings:*

The Untold Story of the Ancient Maya, p. 68.
89. Rudolf Steiner lectured on aspects of the Mexican mystery religions. See *Inner Impulses of Evolution: The Mexican Mysteries and the Knights Templar.*
90. Campbell, J. vol. II, part 3, pp. 377–379.
91. Cobo, B. Cited in W. Sullivan, *The Secret of the Incas.* p. 237.
92. Handcock, G. *Fingerprints of the Gods,* p. 39.
93. Reiche, M. *Mystery on the Desert,* p. 70.
94. Clottes, J. and D. Lewis-Williams. T*he Shamans of Prehistory,* p. 16.
95. Ryan, R. p. 195.
96. Heyerdahl, T. 1989. *Easter Island: The Mystery Solved,* p. 149.
97. Eliade, M. *Symbolism, the Sacred, and the Arts,* p. 58.
98. Lee, G. and E. Stasack. S*pirit of Place: Petroglyphs of Hawai'i,* p. 167.
99. Furst, P. "Shamanism, Transformation, and Olmec Art," p. 72
100. Steiner, R. *Study of Man,* p. 142.
101. Schmid, *Authority and Ornament,* p. 185.
102. Morgan, W. *Prehistoric Architecture in Micronesia,* p. 109.
103. Sarfert, 1919, in Cordy, R. *The Lelu Stone Ruins, Kosrae, Mircronesia,* p. 465.
104. Archaeological evidence points to Aboriginal culture existing for at least 60,000 years. Lawlor cites findings that point to 120,000 to 150,000 years. Lawlor, R. *Voices of the First Day,* p. 9.
105. "This aerial perspective connects the storytelling to dreams or other altered states in which consciousness is projected out of the body." Lawlor, p. 286.
106. "As with a seed, the potency of an earthly location is wedded to the memory of its origin. The Aborigines called this potency the 'Dreaming' of a place, and this Dreaming constitutes the sacredness of the earth. Only in extraordinary states of consciousness can one be aware of, or attuned to, the inner dreaming of the earth." Lawlor, p. 1.
107. Lommel, A. Shamanism: *The Beginnings of Art,* p. 146.
108. McCarthy, F. *Australian Aboriginal Decorative Art,* p. 29.
109. Faulstich, P. Artistic Heritage in a Changing Pacific, "'You Read In This Country': Landscape, Self and Art in an Aboriginal Community," p. 156.
110. Lawlor, pp. 291–92. "The experience dies to itself as soon as it becomes word or image. . . . Reality and meaning escape the entombment of experience they fly through the grid trap of sign and symbol. Their fearful desertion permits the inner vision to catch only a glimpse of them fleeing. The death of experience in words [or images] can be like any other death—an initiation. Words and symbols if understood as death and initiation, allow experience to be reborn in human consciousness as fresh awareness in each generation." Lawlor, pp. 294–95.
111. Suggesting early diffusion, Campbell asserts that "there traveled not only an interest in the X-ray style of animal art, but also knowledge . . . of the shamanistic myths and rites of the great French and Spanish caves out of which that art style took its rise." Campbell, Vol. 1, Part 2, p. 133.
112. Eliade, M. *Australian Religions,* p. 119.
113. Lawlor, p. 33.

VI. PALEOLITHIC ART AND THE CAVE MYSTERIES

Paleolithic art is far more than the crude scratchings of undeveloped primitives. Rather, it bespeaks psychic traditions we must understand if we are to know not only what humans were and are but also what they can become.
—Riane Eisler

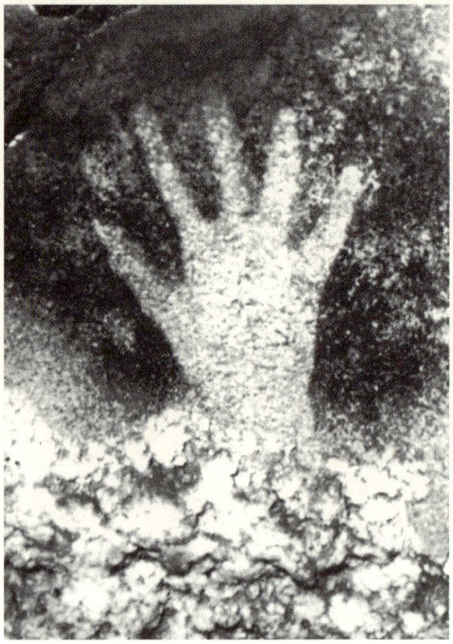

Fig. 267. The negative, stenciled handprint found in numerous Paleolithic caves is probably the result of early initiation practices of primal shaman-artists.

Imagine you have a dreamlike consciousness and your perceptions are not strictly defined but always in fluctuation. You have the experience of swimming in your constantly shifting perceptions and all is movement and metamorphosis. You do not have a strong connection to your physical body, for your awareness is that you and the world are one; there is no separation and therefore no real sense of self.

Imagine being taken as an adolescent from the security of your family, brought by a tribal elder to an isolated and unfamiliar cave, then led for perhaps hours—sometimes crawling on your belly—through dark and tortuous caverns into the womb of the earth, the lowest level of the shamanic universe. Having lived outdoors your entire life, you suffer from intense anxiety and claustrophobia because of the tight, restricted spaces of the underground passageways. You have an experience of your physical body as never before. Then, after the most constricted passage, you enter into a larger chamber where, in the dim flickering light of stone oil lamps, mysterious animal images quiver on the rough shadowy rock walls and ceiling surrounding you. You feel the living power of the animal spirits present in the chamber with you. You are instructed to chew a mineral substance—perhaps iron oxide or charcoal—mixing it with your saliva until it is a thin paste in your mouth. With one hand placed on the cave wall you are instructed to spit the liquid pigment on to the back of your hand. The pigment covers and seals your skin and a small area of the surrounding cave wall with fresh color that quickly dries. When you remove your hand a stencil image of your hand is left on the rock surface (fig. 267).

Your journey into the cave has contracted you into your physical body to the point of near-trauma, and now, as you blow the colored medium across your extended hand, the pigment suddenly defines and limits each digit of your hand. Whereas before you did not experience yourself as separate from your surroundings, now you are shocked into awareness of your hand at the end of your arm as a separate object, yet a part of you. Covered with a second skin of colored pigment and delineated by its distinct shape and size you have an intense, overpowering awareness of this thing—your hand—for the first time. In addition to the sudden awakening to your bodily limits, you see pictured before you a reflection of your hand, an afterimage of its form remaining on the rock wall, as a physical memory picture of this profound initiation into the mysteries of your physical body. The handprint on the wall of this natural sanctuary becomes an outer reminder, a pictorial recollection of this powerful event of separation—a primal experience of I and world.

In the afterglow of this revelation you remain in the cave for some time, instructed by your tribal elder, a shaman, initiated in the cave mysteries. Perhaps the large animal paintings on the subterranean walls begin to reveal secrets to you—the great sacrifice these divine-earthly creatures make in order that humanity might be free to evolve to its highest potential. Your initiation into adulthood and instruction

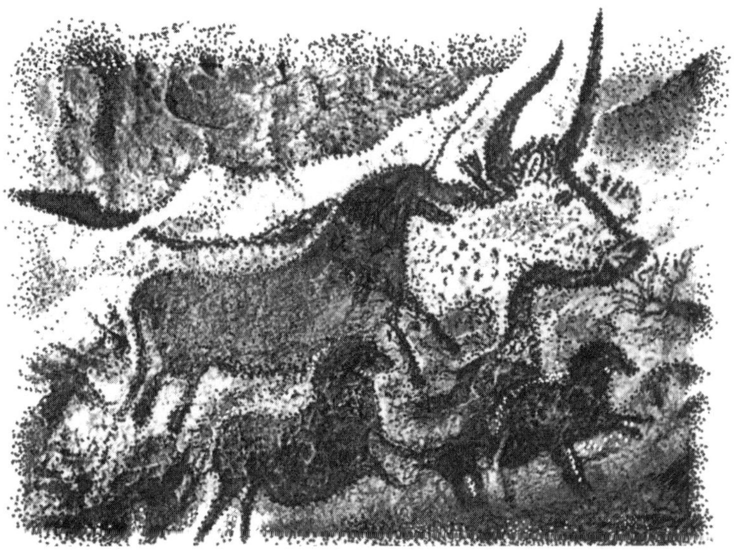

Fig. 268. A large chamber at Lascaux in France, called the Hall of the Bulls, has images of several species, but features large aurochs (extinct bovines) painted fifteen feet above the cave floor.

in the tribal codes of your people is also impressed upon you by way of these and other great pictorial images. Through visionary experience induced in part by the elder, you meet an animal totem or spirit guide. In order to capture this animal spirit as your own you draw it, lasso it with an outline of red ochre or black charcoal and place the animal that lives as an inner spirit vision outside on to the cave wall. By forming a mental picture of the vision and fixing it as an artistic rendering to the cave wall it is given its own objective reality.

Imaginatively speaking, this journey into the cave with its initiation into the experience of self as separate from the world—facilitated by an artistic, image-making activity—is analogous to entering the cave of one's skull in order to create the first mental images and rudimentary thought forms of primal cognition. Instinctive picture consciousness eventually becomes independent, critical thinking. What will become the faculty of memory is also acted out in a ritual-artistic manner by placing images in secluded cave chambers so they may be returned to and remembered over time. In this way artistic activity is a major means by which human faculties develop.

Perhaps the most striking thing about early art is the mood of mystery with which it is surrounded. If we are open to our immediate impressions and feelings concerning Paleolithic art, over and above what we think about it, we become aware of a sense of awe and wonder that arises when we are faced with such primeval images. The Paleolithic cave paintings of southern France and northern Spain (fig. 268), when viewed in the full context of their subterranean galleries, have a way of effectively bypassing our normal everyday consciousness. We begin to muse, to dream into these rock art images. In romantic terms, we could say we are taken under the spell of these pictures. Though incredibly beautiful in their primal style, these floating animal images, arresting handprints, and seemingly random abstract linear markings (fig. 3), display a world of experience far more foreign to contemporary Western consciousness than we might generally care to admit. For this reason, it is important not to lose sight of our feelings regarding the art that we observe—not our personal likes and dislikes, but our feeling-sense. It is often our feelings that inform us in a very direct manner about the character and quality, the essential nature of such work. As David Wade reminds us concerning the rich variety of cave art: "We can respond easily and directly to their beauty and to their skillful execution, whilst at the same time feeling utterly distanced from their intended purpose which was clearly far beyond anything in our ordinary experience."

It has become clear over the past century that we cannot, with any honesty, simply dismiss the greater part of prehistoric painting as primitive, unskilled work or the crude expressions of undeveloped cave dwellers. There is a need for reaching beyond our own cultural traditions and beliefs in order to understand early humanity on its own terms so that we might better approach the roots of our own spirituality. This is the first and foremost puzzle or mystery of Paleolithic art: it presents us with a genuine riddle concerning our own origins that remains unanswered to this day in spite of all the collected data and speculative interpretations available to us.

Why then, and in what context, were such paintings, engravings, and sculptures carried out? Why were so many caves cultivated as sites for mural paintings? What were the ancient artists like as human beings, and is their art connected with self-expression, survival, spiritual practices, none of these, or all of these? Can the mystery of our origins be better understood through the early artistic creations of humanity?

VI.1 Primal History, Prehistory and History

The basic character of these acts is not determined by the fact that the men who first participated in them wished to bring about some desirable objective, but the fact that they already possessed the most desirable of objectives—the immanence of deity.
—Walter Otto

In order to better approach the questions of origin and development of art, let us consider a view of human evolution in three phases: primal history, prehistory, and lastly, history as we know it.[2]

History, the third phase, is most accessible and understandable for us today because it begins principally with writing and is confirmed through physical evidence such as artifacts. History is factual, with specific dates, times, names, and places: it is detectable, measurable, quantifiable, and provable—at least to some extent.

Prehistory is not so certain or factual as history proper. The attempt is often made to force prehistory into factual history. However, it is legendary in that we know of it from oral or other "unprovable" traditions. One could say that prehistoric time is measured differently from historic, mechanical clock time. Artists and craftsmen, in fact anyone who engages in a creative activity, can slip into a comparable experience of time that defies the minute and hour hand. Grand, sweeping eras of uncertain duration, punctuated by heroic and often unbelievable occurrences, constitute the developmental phases of the prehistoric era. It has the childlike quality of being not entirely rational or logical. To our normal way of thinking prehistory is more akin to a flowing dream sequence, and, in spite of all attempts to apply the laws of measurable time to it, earlier ages of prehistory still manage to elude strict classification.

Primal history is even less fixed than prehistory, being entirely elusive to the matter-of-fact historical consciousness. It is qualitative, mythic, and entirely embryonic in nature. It is not the time of man or even of the legendary epoch of heroes, but of the mythological era of gods—the era from which all civilizations mysteriously arise. No factual records exist concerning primal history; the intellect can only speculate on the character of life in such a fantastic age. It is the time of "imminence of deity," when separation of "I" and "Thou," subject and object, concept and percept, is not yet experienced. Owen Barfield calls this situation the era of "original participation," when the self or psyche is still identified with the essential "beingness" of the universe. Primal history holds the secret of origins, birth, and the mystery of life. Imagination and intuition are windows for viewing this period, for intellect is unable to penetrate its secrets. Paleolithic cave art is a product of primal history.

Naturally, the three time divisions of primal history, prehistory, and history do not begin and end at specific dates and times. They would all be simple history if this were the case. The three phases interpenetrate each other, overlap, and flow together with no absolute boundaries. Ancient Greece is an example of all three "histories" intermingling and running together, for archaeologically confirmable sites such as Troy (history), legendary Homeric heroes, such as Odysseus (prehistory), and the mythological gods and goddesses, such as Athena (primal history), who spur on the dramatic action from the spiritual worlds, all overlap to form the full story.

Nor should we believe that factual history is all that exists today. We have our own legendary heroes in political figures and film celebrities, as well as a popular scientific mythology that often theorizes on the nature of the universe with little or no physical proof. All three types of history flow together to create our real time. Myth, legend, and fact are all a part of our understanding of reality. The human being of primal history did not yet separate the three realms of experience or give more value to the factual than to the mythical and legendary. Evidence suggests that primal humanity was only interested in the factual inasmuch as it was the condensation of meaningful mythic experience and undeniable revelation of a spiritual reality. Unfortunately, today myth has come to mean that which is not true, and the spiritual is often regarded as subjective, religious sentimentality.

However, these three ways of understanding history, and the consciousness that accompanies them, interwoven and overlapping as they are, might be summarized in the following way:

Primal History	**Prehistory**	**History**
Paleolithic	Egyptian/Greek	Post-Renaissance
myth	legend	fact
gods	heroes	humans
cosmic	cosmic-earthly	earthly
embryonic	childlike	mature
mystery images	symbolic pictures	realism/naturalism

Consider the visual arts and how they manifest themselves in each of these three phases. Realism and the depiction of material objects play an extremely important role in the art of a historic period. In prehistoric times figurative images are often superseded by symbols, while in primal history direct mystery wisdom flows through the visual sign language presented in artistic forms. Paleolithic cave paintings are perhaps the best examples of primal history in art (fig. 272, 273).

They interpret direct experience of cosmic-earthly forces and events. Most civilizations go through a primal period before reaching prehistoric and historic levels of expression. Egyptian and Greek art demonstrates the consciousness of prehistory through its depiction of symbolic heroes as representatives of the gods (fig. 96). During the Renaissance, a truly historic art begins to emerge with the development of realism. (At the beginning of the twentieth century a new mythology could be said to surface as abstract art is born.) These three types of history that in turn demonstrate three different modes of consciousness can be observed in art by way of their mythic, mystery images; their legendary, symbolic pictures; or their factual, exacting realism and naturalistic depictions (fig. 27).

After neatly packaging all of this, it is important to emphasize that just as the three types of history overlap and intermingle with each other, so do the three types of artistic expression appear simultaneously in any given period. This general outline is only a starting point for considering the evolution of consciousness and the accompanying art forms.

VI.2 The Primal Human Being

The child is father of the man.
—William Wordsworth

Cartoons, comic strips, movies, textbooks, and professional journals portray early man as an apelike cave dweller, brutish, primitive, and superstitious in his disposition to survive a harsh environment. From Alley Oop and the Flintstones to elaborate magazine and interpretive textbook renderings of Lucy and her friends, the caveman model places a modern, historic conception of man into primeval surroundings and clothes him with apelike characteristics.[3] This hairy creature with low forehead and protruding jaw—club in one hand, dragging his mate by the hair with the other hand—is so ingrained in contemporary Western consciousness that it is difficult to juxtapose it with any serious alternative. As William Anderson put it: "The prehistory of man has been summed up in a series of sad-eyed apes and hominids and this image has been imposed upon us by a series of sad-eyed biologists and palaeontologists."[4]

Yet nineteenth-century Darwinian thinking that provided the basis for this view of early humanity does not stand up under rigorous scrutiny, for there is no fossil evidence to suggest that the concept of gradually appearing species, one out of another—in particular homo sapiens out of lower primates—is justified.[5] According to scientist David Raup, "different species usually appear and disappear from the fossil record without showing the transition that Darwin postulated. New species typically appear suddenly in fossil records and persist alongside what Darwinian theory considers to be their progenitors for millions and millions of years. There is no gradual change of one to another and no replacement of one by the other."[6] As Raup points out, the fossil record reveals that new species suddenly appear and often live alongside what many erroneously consider to be their parent species. It is remarkable to realize that before 150 years ago there was no idea that early humanity was related to the ape. The prevailing picture in the West was that of Adam and Eve as the parents of humanity. This was the dominant metaphor of primal man and woman. However, this does not mean that Adam and Eve (prehistory), as recorded by oral, visual artistic, and later written tradition, is the only alternative to a Darwinian (historic) picture of humanity. (See Appendix 7.)

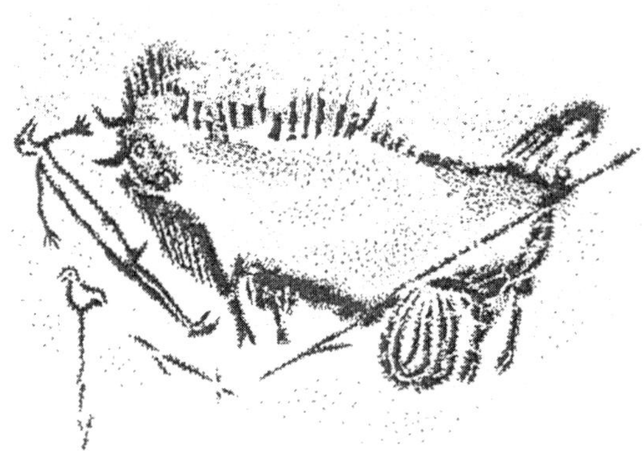

Fig. 269. Although Paleolithic artists were able to depict animals very realistically, they usually represented themselves as simple stick figures.

Imagine for a moment the primal human being, not as a brooding Neanderthal or Australopithecus, nor as the quaint Adam and Eve pictured in medieval paintings (fig. 25), but as a more delicately formed, malleable and mobile creature, like our true ancestor, the child—or more specifically the fetus at certain stages of its development. Perhaps the physical body of this primal human being is not as hardened as we are today. Perhaps the bony system is more like cartilage, unable to leave skeletal remains in the fossil record. However, the physical body of such an ancestor, no matter how wondrous in its makeup, would only be the vehicle for its more subtle nature. The soul and spiritual members of this human being would be what most characterize it in this primal condition. Living in a state of "original participation," primal humanity is unaware of the physical body as separate from the environment. The essential character of primal humanity is an unself-conscious experiencing of feelings and sensations. Unlike the person of today who identifies with his or her physical body out of a sense of self or ego, the primal human being lives in the fluctuating sensations and feelings arising out of the life of emotions, drives, passions, instincts, and formative life forces. No sense of individuality and no awareness of an independent physical body prevails in such a humanity. In fact, such primal humans are so unconscious of self and the physical body that they depict themselves as stick figures in art (fig. 269), even when the animals they paint are nearly realistic renderings, exactingly articulated.

Imagine further how such a primal being might function in the world. If a dangerous, life-threatening situation occurs, impressions and sensations of antagonistic forms and clashing colors are perceived. An exact mental representation of a corresponding object is not possible for this primal human. A visionary or clairvoyant experience might be the best way to characterize the general impressions perceived by this early humanity, with the sensations and general atmosphere of objects being more prominent than their actual physical appearance. Steiner describes this in the following way: "At our present stage of earth evolution the point to notice is that the representation or idea is a copy of the corresponding object. This is not so in the . . . [primal] consciousness. Supposing, for example, that . . . [primal] man draws near to an object which is sympathetic or advantageous to him, a color-image rises up within his soul of a clear bright quality; if something hurtful approaches him, he has an ugly, gloomy picture. The representation he sees is not a likeness, but a symbol of the object, and this symbol corresponds with the object in a quite definite way, and according to fixed laws. It follows, that a being who experiences sense-images of this kind, can direct his life accordingly."[7] Eventually over time, this form of awareness fades except in a certain few who continue to cultivate it through archaic esoteric practices. The tribal shaman and the initiate-priest are just such figures. As this form of primal awareness continues to fade, psychotropic substances and decadent cultic practices such as human sacrifice are utilized in an attempt to maintain experiences of a spiritual nature. Such practices prolong the use of atavistic clairvoyance as a means to both religious and political power.[8]

The further one goes back in time, the more the Vedic conception of maya, the illusory nature of appearance, holds sway. Early humanity places greater importance on the spiritual reality and the symbol behind the appearance than on material appearance. It is in most cases the supersensory reality that primal humanity depicts in its art forms. Primal art reveals the spirit realm, describes its terrain, and points the way in which one may enter more fully into the meaning of mystery imagery.

VI.3 Initiatory Art

Art is a help to spiritual perception.
—Paul Brunton

If we consider the primal human being to be in possession of rich psychic and spiritual capacities, then the artistic work of these people and the reasons for its creation take on greater significance than might otherwise be the case. For example, one of the recurring pictorial images created by early humanity in various regions of the world, and still created today by the Australian Aborigines, is the handprint (fig. 270). The human hand is remarkable from the standpoint of form and function (see Appendix 7). It is not limited by specialization as are horse hoofs, lion paws, and dolphin fins, for example, but it is able to make tools that serve diverse purposes. The infinite potential of the human hand plays also into its thematic meaningfulness as an image in art.

Most Paleolithic handprints are negative images shaped from the periphery as stencils. As mentioned earlier, such images are produced by chewing a mineral substance, mixing it with saliva, and then spitting or blowing the moistened

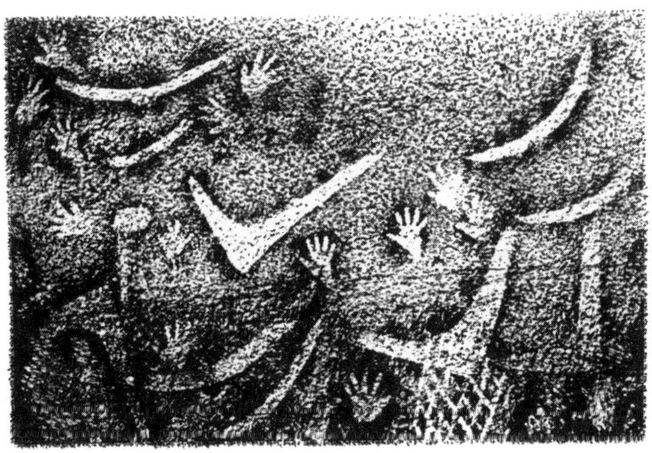

Fig. 270. The handprint appears in numerous Paleolithic and prehistoric caves. This example of Aboriginal pinting is from Carnarvon National Park, Western Queensland, Australia.

pigment over the hand, which is placed against a rock surface. The pigment would be not so much paint as a medium ritually prepared, perhaps with animal blood or fat, for the "sealing" of the hand. The result is a silhouette handprint produced in one sudden exhalation of breath or in a series of sharp, forced outbreaths. The image arises by being breathed into existence—the breath being associated with creative spirit (*pneuma*). In this way the potency-filled paint unites the person, the rock wall, and the Otherworld by way of the artistic image.

This ritualistic-artistic action painting also produces an awareness of the hand as the terminal point of one's body, thereby increasing knowledge about the physical world and initiating awareness of self through the separation of the human being from its environment. Originally ritual body painting, tattooing, scarring, and other skin art must have had a similar purpose of bringing about bodily awareness and the experience of temporary separation from nature.

Interpretations of the handprint range from that of simple childish finger painting to a sign of initiation and high spiritual authority.[9] As we have already seen, in many prehistoric settings the image of the hand carried such significance that stylized depictions of it were fashioned in precious materials and left as burial offerings for the ancestors and gods (fig. 218). Like a fingerprint, each handprint is unique and individual and such images may have served as a kind of signature or "portrait." To a culture that places emphasis on intellect and appearance, the head and face would naturally be considered the most important parts of a person. However, a culture of willful activity and doing, living in direct connection with nature, might see the hand as the most representative feature for that which is human (*homo faber*, man the doer, as opposed to *homo sapiens*, man the knower). In this sense the handprint in early art is a mystery image that, as Duane Preble suggests, serves both as "a source of art and a symbol of creativity."[10]

Artistic creations such as handprints and outline drawings lead to greater awareness of the physical body, clarifying physical discontinuity and distancing one from one's environment. Self-consciousness and the beginnings of ego awareness develop from the act of separating oneself from nature. The self cannot arise without the experience of separation. Through this experience of gradual separation, over the course of thousands of years, the human being becomes accustomed to the unfolding of an independent awareness of self and, in conjunction with it, an increased densification of the physical body takes place. Development of individuality and recognition of an objective material world are the positive side of this separation, while alienation and dislocation from nature and spirit are negative results of the same process.

Another aspect of the art of the handprint is that besides the physical, emotional, and psychic effects it has on the artist in regard to self-awareness, it also leaves a lasting image on the wall. This remaining picture is of tremendous significance because of its relation to early memory function. Steiner suggests that there are three progressive stages in the evolution of human memory: localized, rhythmic, and temporal memory.[11]

In the first stage of memory, previous experiences are called up only because of their connection with a particular place. Primal peoples erect a stone, carve a symbol, or paint an image in order to recall in vivid detail events that had taken place but are forgotten when one departs from the particular locale. Localized memory lives in the environment, not in the inner life of the person. Memory is not within oneself, but outside, where the deed took place. These memory places are marked with a feature of some kind so that when one returns to the site the memory likewise returns. Such sites are the forerunners of modern memorials that commemorate a person or event. Megalithic monuments such as standing stones can be viewed in this light (see Chapter IV).

As the human being evolves, rhythmic memory gradually replaces localized memory. Through repetition and rhythm, primal humanity is superseded by a prehistoric humanity that has powers of recollection no longer strictly bound to place. All oral traditions, all communications of knowledge, are transmitted by way of rhythmic repetition during this second stage. Chants and verses are taught and learned according to rhythm, with often thousands of lines being recalled. Words with repetitive sounds are key to this form of memory, out of which all early verse and later metrical poetry arises.[12] Images too can be repetitive, stimulating memory through recapitulation of form. (This technique is used in advertising and in the work of Andy Warhol.)

In the third phase of memory development we come to our own form of temporal memory, where neither space nor rhythm is an important factor in the power of recollection, although both may have an effect upon it. This abstract memory of ours is entirely bound up with our inner soul life—will impulses, emotions, thoughts, and mental pictures—and not with the environment. (So-called déjà vu experiences are an exception to this temporal memory.)[13]

The Paleolithic handprint, as initiatory art, is in part a likely ritual exercise in localized memory for the purpose of recalling in vivid detail one's initiation experience. In viewing Paleolithic art in this way, it becomes apparent that there is little if any decorative motivation. Primal images appear at this time largely in the service of shamanic cultus. As ritualistic art, it is created with the intention of developing faculties such as bodily awareness, physical dexterity, memory, and self-consciousness. Art of this kind is based on the principle of spiritual development, and is consequently vital to the evolution of human capacities. Such initiation art is a record of the evolution of consciousness.

VI.4 Animal Magic

The animals were not portraits but symbols; they did not reflect explicit practices but rather a complex metaphysical system or "mythogram."
—André Leroi-Gourhan

Paleolithic art has no landscapes or plants, no rivers, mountains, or clouds. There are no dwellings, trees, fires, or earth depicted in cave art. However, animal pictures densely populate the walls of primeval caves and rock shelters. Some early twentieth-century scholars believed these animal paintings were the result of strictly aesthetic interests, even though cave art rarely appears at habitation sites and is therefore not readily accessible for casual or prolonged viewing. Still, some historians maintain that cave art is exclusively artistic and only concerned with the "cult" of beauty.

Although the beauty of cave art is undeniable, other scholars point to so-called "hunting magic" as an explanation for animal themes in cave art, as numerous ethnographic parallels can be cited among present-day indigenous peoples who use animal drawings in connection with their hunting rituals. Though practices in more recent times may be substantially different from Paleolithic practices, descriptions of tribal peoples such as the Ituri Pygmies in Central Africa indicate the cultic use of pictorial images as an important part of hunting activities. Before a hunt, tribesmen clear a patch of ground and trace upon it the outline of a desired animal. At dawn, when the sun's rays strike the picture, women stand near the image and sing an enchantment while one of the hunters shoots an arrow into the animal picture. Taking up the arrow the men of the tribe set off into the bush while the women remain beside the ritual drawing. After a time, the women "know" when the men are successful and prepare a fire. The hunters return with the same animal pictured in the drawing, killed by a shot in the same part of its body as was struck in the picture. The image is then rubbed with the hair and blood of the dead beast, bringing the ritual full circle, fulfilling the "hunting magic."[14] "The underlying psychological fact is a strong identification between a living being and its image," says Jung, "which is considered to be the being's soul."[15] Paul Bahn points out that "this kind of art is intended to exert influence at a distance."[16]

In this example both the image and the imagemaking are shown to be of central importance in the procurement of food. It is noteworthy that here art links religious ritual and practical technology in the activity of tribal hunting. This unification of religion and science, through art, is characteristic of primal as well as many prehistoric cultures. However, in the case of cave paintings, few animals actually have arrows, spears, or other projectile marks associated with them. Also, the problem of accessibility is obvious in the case of most cave art. Many caves require a great expenditure of time to enter. More time would be needed to paint or etch pictures, carry out ceremonies, and then leave the cave again. For the purposes of hunting magic, this would be a very ineffective use of the hunters' time (if effective use of time were a consideration). It has been shown that hunting magic is generally carried out quickly in the open air and pictures are usually destroyed once their usefulness has been fulfilled.[17] Although hunting magic is one possible theory for cave art, it does not fully answer the question of why animal pictures are so prominent in Paleolithic caves.

"Sympathetic magic" expands on the hunting magic theory. Here pictures may be drawn in connection with the propagation of the herd in order to provide the abundance of animals that might supply meat for food and hides for clothing and shelter. Alternatively, "destructive magic" aims at ridding the hunter of animals of prey that might be dangerous to the tribe and serve as would-be competitors for food sources. Sympathetic and destructive magic may not have required as immediate a concern as hunting magic, and could have been performed at a more leisurely pace.[18]

Yet another explanation for these Paleolithic images is that they were totem animals or spirit guides. Contemporary ethnographic studies find that indigenous peoples maintain a relationship with their deceased ancestors, who may take on the form of a particular animal and in this form serve the clan or tribe as a guardian spirit. As mentioned earlier, these spirit helpers are called upon for healing, hunting, war, and other tribal concerns, often with a shaman as mediator. Such ancestral spirits can be pictured as human, animal, or anthropozoomorphic (a combination of both) and serve as messengers from the spirit world. It seems likely that many of the animal and part-animal depictions in Paleolithic caves are not created as naturalistic illustrations in order to help with the hunt or increase the herd, but as mystery images dealing with primal experiences concerning the animal's spirit nature and its relationship to the human being.

The prehistorian André Leroi-Gourhan proposed an interpretation of Paleolithic symbols and animal paintings that creates two groups of images: male and female. Male forms include the horse, stag, ibex, barbed strokes, short lines, and dots (fig. 271), while images considered female are the ox, bison, and hind, as well as triangles, ovals, and rectangles. Leroi-Gourhan also found that certain

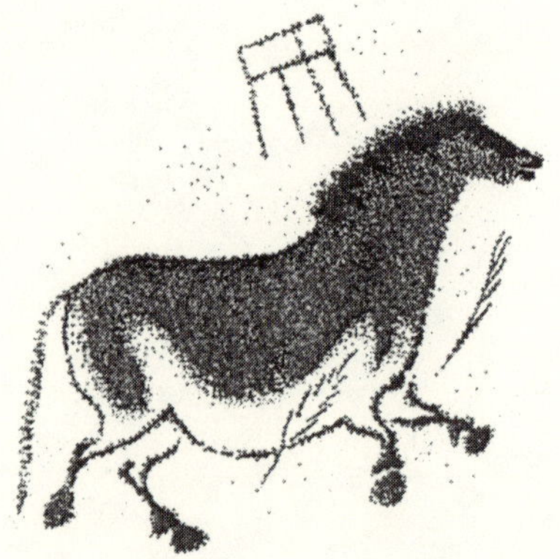

Fig. 271. It has been suggested that this horse painting from Lascaux may be an example of hunting magic because of the arrowlike figures, one of which grazes the animal's stomach. In Paleolithic art, stags, horses, barbed strokes, short lines, and dots have all been associated with masculine energy, while bison, cows, triangular forms, ovals, and rectangles are said to be feminine symbols.

animals were repeatedly pictured in each other's company too often to be random groupings. This apparent pairing of animals such as a bovine creature (female) with a horse or stag (male) gives "the impression of being . . . a system polished in the course of time—not unlike the older religions of our world, wherein there are male and female divinities whose actions do not overtly allude to sexual reproduction, but whose male and female qualities are indispensably complementary."[19]

This deliberate pairing of complementary qualities in the form of animal species can also be related to cosmic or planetary values. Traditional star wisdom links animals with the constellations as well as other celestial influences. For instance, the bovine, besides its connection with Taurus and the Chinese ox cycles, is associated with the moon. Astral qualities are conveyed through the very nature and character of each animal species, and are likewise associated with gender—moon, female; sun, male. According to many traditions the correlation of animal qualities with cosmic patterns is of more significance than their association with gender.

Bovines are traditionally considered sacred animals linked to life and fertility, and are revered as such in many parts of the world even today. In ancient Egypt there were important bull cults honoring the bovine incarnations of Ptah (the Apis) and sun-god, Re. As an ungulate, the bovine has a strongly developed metabolic system. The four-part ruminant stomach of the cow demonstrates an intensification of the digestive capacity. It is as if the entire animal is given over to the metabolic processes: nutrition, digestion, excretion, and reproduction. Moreover, the horns of the bovine are sustained by blood flowing through them. The form of the cow horn, with the crescent shape, makes it easy to see why it is a lunar symbol. It is therefore not surprising that the bison, ox, and cow are traditionally linked to feminine and lunar qualities, both having to do with regeneration and fructification. Isis, the Egyptian Mother goddess, wears cow horns as her emblem (fig. 202).

In like manner, one can speak of the stag as a creature of the sun, living attuned to the outer world with the help of a particularly acute nervous-sensory system. Lighter on its feet and less bulky than the cow, it is far more sensitive and alert to its surroundings than the bovine. Wolfgang Schad suggests that the sense-active nature of the stag is intimately connected to its antlers as "vents" for excessive metabolic activity. Whereas the horns of a cow hold back its powers of digestion, according to Schad, the deer's antlers free up and release the metabolic processes, thus allowing the animal to develop a more sensitive and graceful form.[20] An unusual thought, perhaps, but one no less convincing than the notion that horns and antlers are present solely for the purpose of butting heads.

Unlike the bovine horn, the stag antler branches out and grows a mossy, velvetlike covering sensitive to daylight. The antlers are shed annually and grow back each year with the cycle of the seasons. Schad says: "In the cow's horn the underlying bone, which grows slowly and rebuilds itself continuously, remains alive throughout the animal's life. In the hastily grown antlers, however, ossification is quick and final. . . . This mighty formative activity is followed by a complete withdrawal of life forces."[21] It might be said that in their connection with the cycle of the year and the sun's light, stag antlers act as solar sense organs. Cow horns are scarcely affected by the seasons; at most, in the female, they show rings of weakened horn formation at each pregnancy, so that the number of pregnancies can be counted on the cow's horn, like tree rings. This is another indication of the cow's sensitivity to internal generative rhythms.[22]

In summary, we might say that the cow is occupied with its inner processes, its enhanced metabolism, while the stag or deer is more active in the outer world because of its alert senses. Traditional cultures perceived these characteristics of the stag and linked it with the sun and masculine qualities. The cow, on the other hand, has from primeval times been associated with the moon and the feminine principle.

The legends of many cultures speak of the wisdom possessed by animals and how such knowledge is passed on to man. Tales often tell of how animals are the parents and teachers of humanity. Therefore spiritual beings and ancestral spirits often made their appearance through animals in order to communicate with humanity.

The wisdom of the animal is inherent in its organism, according to Hermann Poppelbaum. Whereas the human being, through inner effort of will, expenditure of thought, and moral training, needs to develop qualities such as discretion, courage, and care for posterity, the animal does not need to strive for such attributes, for it inherently possesses many of them already. In the animal such capacities are imprinted, as it were, into the physical organism and the life of instincts. Poppelbaum asserts: "Spirituality overflows out of the animal organization. . . . It is actually there, in the animal's bodily equipment . . . [and] has penetrated deeper into the animal's organism than into man's. . . . Activities, which [in man] have to be accomplished by an effort . . . in the animal are submerged in the structure of the organs. Sinking a stage deeper, beyond the inner region of the soul forces, they have imprinted themselves into the appurtenances of the body, and become visible form. The very body of the animal has become wise and provident."[23]

Steiner too suggests that the form of the various animal species depicts or makes visible the different realms of instinct. The form of each animal, with its long or short legs, extended or stubby snout, rounded or thin trunk, is a three-dimensional illustration by Nature of specific instinctual forces. In this way Nature produces living pictures of drives, passions, instincts, and urges.[24] The animal kingdom is an actual outer picture of inner instinctual conditions or soul forces. What instincts were represented in the form of the mammoth, and what desires come to expression in the lion, the stag, or the bull? According to Steiner, similar instincts, drives, and passions live in the human being, but are held in check and are not imprinted on the physical form to the same extent as they are in the animal. As late as the early nineteenth century, the practitioners of European folk medicine still believed that specific animals were associated with particular illnesses. In the animal these "illnesses" were considered to be a natural and healthy condition, but if a specific animal condition appears too strongly in the human being, creating a one-sided imbalance in the soul, then the person falls physically ill. Steiner goes so far as to suggest that the animals are living pictures of cosmic wisdom, of embodied astrality, and it is through these living pictures that we become able to grasp images and think in thought forms or mental pictures. He says, "I bear within me, although suppressed, the predispositions for the whole animal world. That I do so enables me to think 'forms,' enables me to think 'imaginations.' For the animals are fashioned in accordance with the imaginations that severally belong to them. The animals are living imaginations; they roam over the face of the earth as living imaginations. When I survey the whole world of the animals, in that moment, the imaginative world is visible to me. And the forms I see there, these same forms are also in me. I have not, however, become those forms spatially, and for this very reason they are able to be—in me—thought forms, thought pictures."[25]

According to this view, the shaman and later the temple priest are immersed in a wisdom of the animal nature as it works within the human being, and this wisdom is passed on to pupils by way of fashioning the animal gestures and forms in paint, clay, and stone, mimicking their sounds and movements in chants and dances. For primal humanity, the wisdom of the animals originates within the realm of the gods, the cosmic zodiac ("circle of animals") and is contained in primal wisdom as a visionary astronomy and living astrology. Seeing these celestial animal powers as mystery images stirs the pupil to imaginative and mental pictures that ultimately lead to concepts and thoughts about the universe. In this way, primeval humanity lays the foundations for logical thinking with the help of artistic practices.[26]

Steiner asserts the rather unorthodox view that "if we were to go back, say to the time before Thales, we would find that in the Mystery Schools there was still a clear perception of this relation of man's thinking to the animal world. 'Logic!' they would have said, 'What is it?' Nothing but zoology! Zoology is logic come alive."[27]

This is perhaps the most significant aspect of primal art: that it is a formative vehicle for shaping human capacities. To draw the outline of an animal form is to artistically rope the beast, tie it up, and tame its wild instinctual energy and vitality, capturing the nature of its particular constitution and connecting with its spirit being. "When we draw [contour lines], we really create walls of barbed wire, with which we intercept what wants to destroy or deform us from within outwards and prevent it from working too quickly. In [contour] drawing, the process is more intellectual. The old mystery teachers would always have used animal forms as an expression of what rises up out of man and must be transformed by man."[28] The paintings and engravings did not depict real animals but the spiritual potency of the animal. The creative act of drawing not only formed the artwork but effectively shaped and transformed the soul life of the individual "artist." Likewise, it affected the onlooker. Through artistic activity a significant change took place in the human being, which shaped the very nature of what it means to be human. This process continues to this day with art and technology shaping our imagination of what it means to be human. We are constantly creating ourselves.

The most recent interpretations of Paleolithic art acknowledge shamanism as a viable explanation, with one outstanding reservation. The practice of vision quests and resulting out-of-body spirit flights are often seen as hallucinatory in nature. For the most part experience of spirit worlds is viewed as illusory and unreal.

VI.5 The Shaman

Every real shaman has to feel an illumination in his body, in the inside of his head or in his brain, something that gleams like fire, that gives him the power to see with closed eyes into the darkness, into the hidden things or into the future or into the secrets of another man.
—Eskimo shaman

The term *shaman,* once used to describe the sages and medicine people of the Tungus tribes of Siberia, is now generally applied to certain people and practices found throughout the world in almost all indigenous cultures.[29]

Three essential elements are found in most shamanic traditions: (1) Shamans voluntarily enter visionary states of consciousness during which (2) they experience nonordinary realms of existence where (3) they gain knowledge and power for themselves or for their communities.[30] This journey into the supersensory, where the shaman is helped by spirit guides who appear most often in animal forms, usually leads to initiatory crisis, an experience of oneness with the fabric of the universe, and the ability to prophesy, heal, and control natural phenomena through magic. The most convincing interpretation of Paleolithic art is that it was used in connection with shamanic practices and initiation rites. That is, by way of painting the various animal species, the shaman communicates with the supersensory Otherworld and gains knowledge through this contact.

Neuropsychological research distinguishes three overlapping yet discernible stages of trance experience. They begin with the "seeing" of geometric forms, such as dots, circles, crescents, zigzags, grids, and parallel and wavy lines. These forms, called phosphenes, have a luminous, brightly colored, pulsating character that fluctuates and metamorphoses. When the subject's eyes are open, these phosphenes are seen as though projected transparently upon surfaces such as rock walls. In the second stage of trance condition, some forms are given more significance than others and are seen as images of objects: a crescent may be a bowl, a zigzag may be a snake, and a grid a ladder. The third stage is entered by way of a tunnel or vortex experience, at the end of which a bright light is seen. The geometric forms of stage one transform into the lattice structure of the vortex into which the subject is pulled. Animal, human, and anthropozoomorphic figures begin to appear. Subjects feel by this third stage they can fly and turn into animals or birds. Subjects become what they "see."

Clottes and Lewis-Williams note that "these three stages are universal and [are] wired into the human nervous system, though the meanings given to the geometrics of Stage One, the objects into which they are illusioned in Stage Two, and the hallucinations of Stage Three are all culture-specific. . . . A San shaman may see an eland antelope; an Inuit will see a polar bear or a seal. But, allowing for such cultural diversity, we can be fairly sure that the three stages of altered consciousness provide a framework for an understanding of shamanic experiences."[31] (Although some researchers acknowledge the shamanic experience, it is often viewed as hallucinatory and illusionistic in nature. This raises the question: Do such researchers see all such experiences as hallucinations, or do they believe that there are objective spiritual experiences as well?)

During the Paleolithic era, entering into a cave may have been equated with entering into deep trance by way of the tunnel experience. Images on the cave walls may have paralleled visions attained through altered states of consciousness, thereby providing a link between inner and outer experiences.

Many of the animal paintings, like the handprints, are believed to have been blown or spit rather than drawn with a brushlike tool. In this way a very different relationship to the image was made possible. Michel Lorblanchet suggests that "spitting is a way of projecting yourself onto the wall, becoming one with the horse you are painting. Thus the action melds with the myth. Perhaps a shaman did this as a way of passing into the world beyond."[32]

It is possible that many of the anthropozoomorphic figures depicted in some of the 300 known cave sites, and often called Sorcerers or Animal Masters, are indeed shamans on ritual journeys or in visionary trance states. The Sorcerer of Les Trois Frères, for example, is a 2.5-foot-long, part-animal, part-human figure, fifteen feet above the floor level of a French Pyrenees cave (fig. 272). With stag antlers and ears, alert owl eyes, and long hermit beard, bear or lion forepaws, human feet, and a short fox- or ponytail, the figure oversees numerous animal images in the subterranean chamber. It is conservatively dated at about 14,000 B.C. Throughout primal history there are many examples of these anthropozoomorphic figures with stag antlers or cow horns. The figures found at Les Trois Frères and Le Gabillou (fig. 273) are perhaps the most impressive examples of this Paleolithic figure. In later prehistory horn-or antler-crowned shamans are found represented in many places throughout the world, as we have already seen (figs. 274, 115).

In the Nordic creation myth of the *Edda,* the World Stag stands atop the World Ash Tree, Yggdrasil. From the antlers of this mythic stag, drops of water fall down, creating the twelve rivers or streams that give life to the world. Ernst Uehli suggests that the streams are a picture of the major nerves in the human head. According to him, this creation tale describes the head as an image of the cosmos,

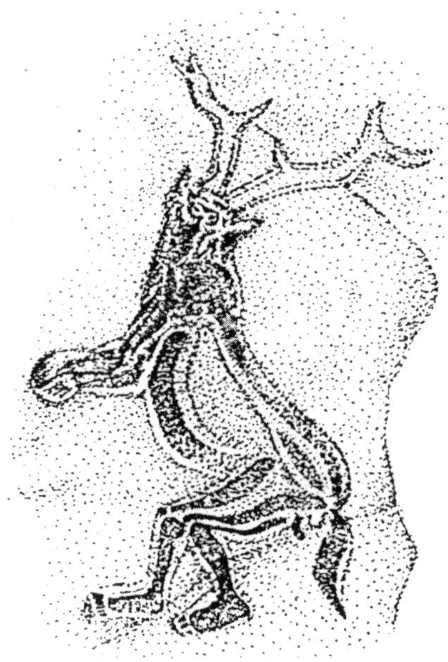

Fig. 272. The Sorcerer of Les Trois Frères, in a cave in the French Pyrenees, is an anthropozoomorphic figure with stag antlers and ears, owl eyes, a beard, bear or lion paws, a foxlike tail, and human feet. Anthropozoomorphic figures may depict shamans in ritual attire or on vision quests, or spirit beings who guide the shamans.

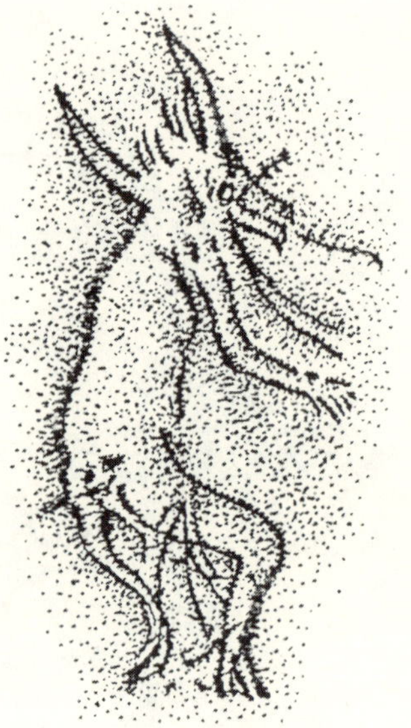

Fig. 273. Above: Figures at Le Gabillou, France, depicted with bison heads and shoulders and human legs and feet, are described as sorcerers or Animal Masters.

Fig. 274. The Siberian Tungus shaman with his antlers and ritual drum is depicted in this illustration after Nicholas Witsen's drawing of 1705 (below). A rhythmic beating of the drum helped to induce the trance state necessary for spirit flight.

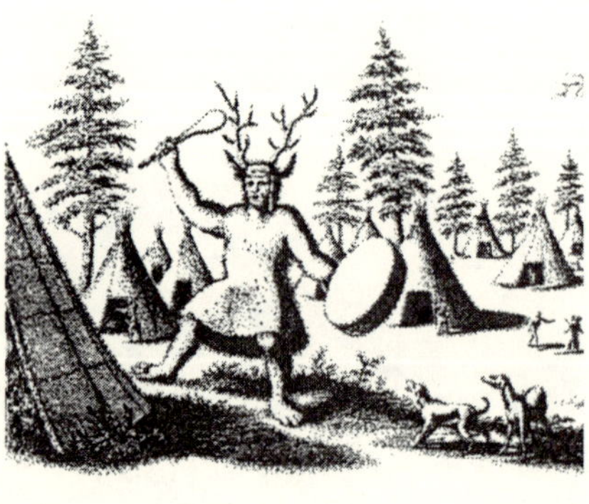

and the senses arise in order that perception of this cosmos may occur. [33] Uehli connects the stag man of Les Trois Frères to initiation practices and early mystery cults of the Paleolithic era. He sees the instruction of the candidate for these cave mysteries occurring by way of the stag metaphor in order that they may experience the forces at work in the forming of the head organization. It is through penetrating such spiritual images that primal man learns something of the significance of the senses and the nervous system, in a direct and instinctive manner.

In this way the stag antlers are linked with the human nerve-sense system, which is centered in the head and spreads throughout the rest of the organism. From this perspective, the antlers are an exact metaphor of the formative life forces connected to nerve activity, ideation, and sense perception. At the same time, the antlers may be an early artistic representation of what was perceived by primal humanity as radiating light that extends beyond, and surrounds, the head. In other words, antlers and horns may indicate primal halos or auras. The halo is well-documented in the history of art, as a spiritual emanation around the heads and bodies of buddhas, bodhisattvas, saints, and spirit beings. Antlers, horns, halos, and crowns are mystery images, imaginative pictures of extrasensory capacities that stand behind the spiritual activity of wise beings.

In the last line of the "Song of Amergin," one of the oldest remnants of Irish literature, Amergin, the Milesian bard, declares, "I can shift my shape like a god." This reference to the shamanic ability to shapeshift (the capacity to live into and identify with other objects, beings, and phenomena) can also be translated as "I am the god who creates in the head of man the fire of thought." Put simply, this line might be paraphrased: "I am the fire of imagination," or, "I burn with visions of the spirit world." Tom Cowan says about this phrase: "Shapeshifting occurs in the head and is analogous to fire, the most radically transformative of the elements."[34] All of these aspects, contained in this simple phrase by Amergin, pertain to the artistic rendering of the horned and antlered Animal Master. Life, thought, imagination, vision, fire in the head, and shapeshifting all relate to the antler-crowned shaman. So the question arises, as it did for Anne Baring and Jules Cashford, "Are these horns, then, images of extended vision, the animal here pointing the way for the shamanic flights that take place deeper inside the cave where a new vision is symbolically brought to birth?"[35] It would seem that this new vision was not just symbolically brought to birth in the Paleolithic caves, but was literally born into the world through directed ritual artistic activity, coupled with other esoteric practices.

The spiritual image of horns is mentioned in the Bible with the Hebrew prophet, Moses, who, as the visionary author of Genesis and spiritual leader of the "chosen people," is endowed with exceptional magic powers that are indicated by "horns of fire" emerging from his brow. Artists of the Renaissance depict this Old Testament figure with two rays of light or antlerlike columns of fire rising

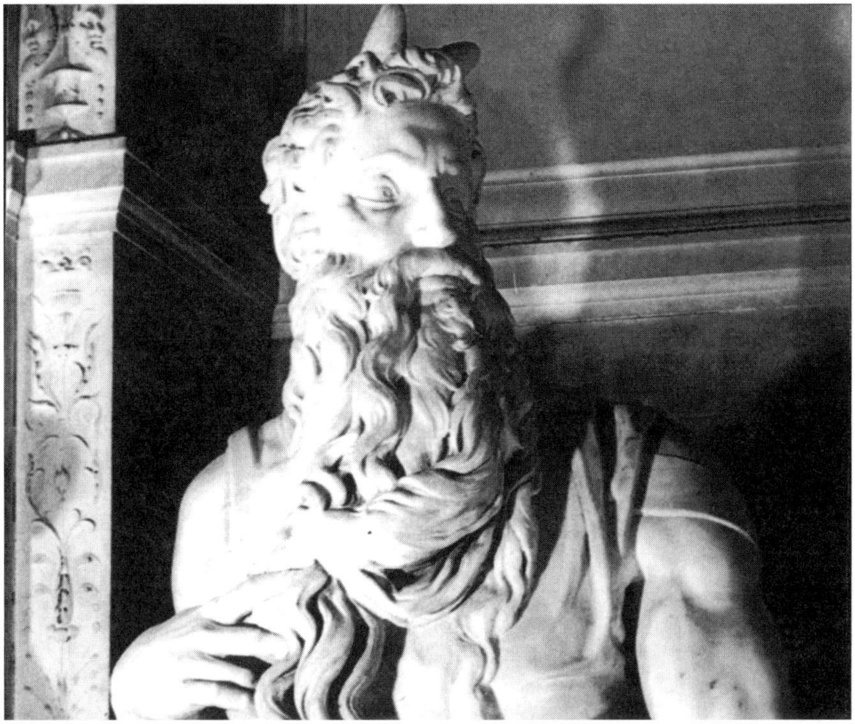

Fig. 275. Michelangelo's Moses, created for the tomb of Pope Julius II, depicts Moses in the likeness of Julius. The two horns, which are typical of Renaissance renderings of Moses, refer to his visionary capacity, and can be likened to the two-petalled brow-chakra of Indian esoteric tradition and the Shaman's horns. (Rome, Italy.)

out of his forehead. Perhaps the most powerful artistic rendering of this is the sculpture Michelangelo carved for the tomb of Pope Julius II (fig. 275). The artist clearly depicts Moses with two horns on his head. The horns are metaphors of the force, energy of vision, and prophecy possessed by Moses, as well as of the fire of creative spirit that extends beyond ordinary brain-bound thinking. Although Michelangelo would not have intended such a thing, they can also be seen as a reference to the "two-petaled" brow chakra of Indian esoteric tradition associated with the pineal gland between the eyebrows.

Images such as the Sorcerer of Les Trois Frères lead us to inquire whether such anthropozoomorphic figures represent (1) actual creatures that lived at the time, (2) fanciful beings invented by early man, (3) shamans in animal costume, (4) supersensory impressions of the shaman priests, seen through the still visionary consciousness of primal humanity, or (5) representations of spirit beings. In different cases any one of these possibilities may be true. However, it is likely that in many cases early humanity is depicting the divine animal forces, the spirit guides, as they pertain to primal, human experience. Eliade says: "There was no question of a regression into pure 'animal life'; the animal with which the shaman identified himself was already charged with a mythology, it was, in fact, a mythical animal, the ancestor or the Demiurge."[36]

Ritual masks, costumes, headdresses, crowns, capes, and other garments that may be featured in cave art, were probably donned as clairvoyant faculties began to decline. The art of costume initially had its place in cultic practices and probably approximated the actual picture formed in visionary experience.[37] This is not to say that more mundane uses were not possible for sacred objects. However, the original inspiration for sacred objects such as the table (altar), the wheel (solar symbol), the dagger (sun ray), the headdress (halo), and clothing (body aura) appears to have been ritually motivated in connection with early sacred practices. The wearing of animal skins and horns had the significance of aiding the shaman on his or her vision quest or spirit journey to find the Animal Master and spirit guide.

A powerful image found at Lascaux depicts a bird-headed human figure with erect penis positioned diagonally above a staff topped with a bird effigy, the bird features signifying the shaman's avian transformation and spirit flight (fig. 269). The figure, probably a shaman, is immediately in front of an apparently disemboweled bison crossed with a lance. Often described as a hunting accident, this picture is one of the most narrative images in Paleolithic art and may suggest an animal sacrifice. It is called the "wounded man" or "killed man" scene, and may represent an initiatory trance death rather than a hunting mishap. The animal sacrifice is made to the gods; the shaman enters into trance and is guided with the help of the animal spirit into the Otherworld. The bird staff is the magic symbol of the trance ascent for wherever it is placed it becomes the bird-topped Tree of Life at the Center of the World and the vehicle upon which the shaman rises to the Upper World. The shaman engages in a reversal of the birth experience as he enters the contracting and constricting uterine tunnels of Mother Earth to regain union with the nourishing maternal womb of creation. He is the "wounded man" in the sense that he suffers a death to his lower self in the trance condition and, aided by an animal sacrifice, soars to the top of the Staff of Life. Robert Ryan characterizes the shaman–Animal Master's relationship to the cave as a "returning to the source of creation. The ithyphallic shaman's penetration of the maternal cave of power is a return to the deep structures of the human mind, the formal source of our experience, and, at the same time, to the cosmogonic source. For the revelation of the cave art is that the two sources, human and cosmic, have concentric centers and that their shared center is inwardly encountered and experienced by opening the eye of the soul."[38] To see this scene, one must pass through the great Hall of Bulls, an open chamber covered with exquisite large animal paintings—the largest of which are bulls—and proceed down a narrower, tunnel-like corridor to a well or shaft, "apparently the most sacred place in the sanctuary, rather like the crypt of an ancient church."[39] One must descend into this shaft to view the shamanic scene.

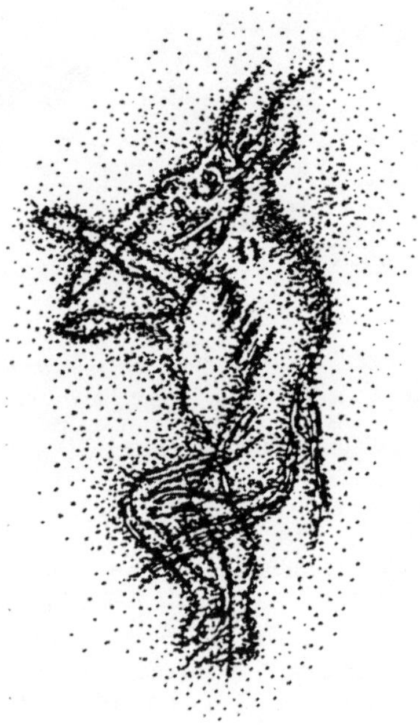

Fig. 276. Another anthropozoomorphic Animal Master at Les Trois Frères is depicted on a wall surrounded by dozens of animal images. The entire composition gives the impression of movement, perhaps even migration.

Another figure at Les Trois Frères, also ithyphallic, is portrayed with bison shoulders and head, but standing upright on human legs and feet (fig. 276). Surrounded by a herd of thirty bison, ten horses, four ibex, and a reindeer, this part- Animal Master seems to be directing the herd's movements as it plays what some believe to be a bowlike musical instrument. Others see the figure as having a bleeding nose, a typical side-effect of the shamanic trance state. The ithyphallic bison man not only possesses the full curved horns, head, shoulders, and chest of the bovine, but also boasts the uprightness of the human being. Whether this Animal Master is a visionary picture of the Paleolithic shaman with his godlike capacities or whether it is the shaman in ceremonial mask and regalia, one thing is clear—the Animal Master is an important spiritual reality for peoples from Asia to the Americas, and as such creates a powerful link between man and animal through his supernatural powers.[40]

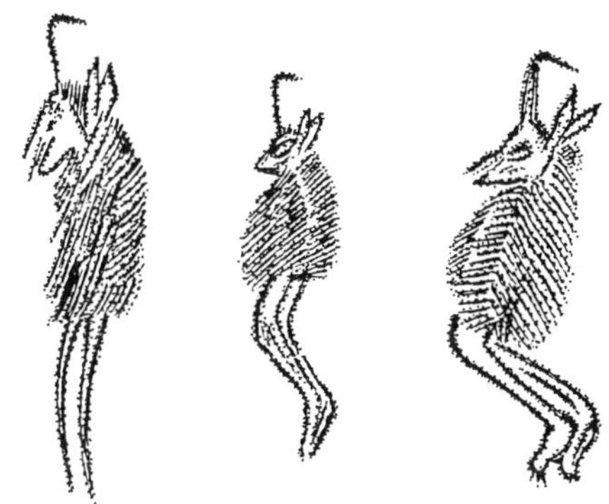

Fig. 277. These unusual anthropozoomorphic figures, reminiscent of the "flying buck" figures of South Africa and Pan of ancient Greece, are found at the Teyjat Cave in France. They suggest the shamanic Animal Master.

The Animal Master, sorcerer, or shaman is an important key to the imagery of Paleolithic art as it captures in picture form what might be called the aesthetic missing link between the animal kingdom and the human being. Perhaps our long-lost ancestor is not the lower primate we've imagined for the past century and a half, but the elusive Animal Master. Uehli suggests that the horned and hoofed Animal Master is a visionary picture or primal imagination of an earlier stage of human development (fig. 277). He also connects this figure with the Greek Pan. Gimbutas says of this latter being: "Greek Pan was a mortal god of the forest. He was a shepherd and believed to be the protector of wild animals, beekeepers, and hunters. . . . There are more than 100 recorded cult places associated with Pan's name in ancient Greece. This seems to indicate that he was popular and widely worshipped, although he was outside the pantheon of great gods and goddesses."[41] Pan is also linked to the Indian god, Shiva, and the Indus deity, Pashupati (fig. 182). Pan's satyrs were said to travel with the Greek god of viticulture, Dionysus, on his extensive wanderings. They point back to a time when humanity lived at one with nature in a "group soul" or tribal awareness. Unfortunately, Pan later serves as the image behind the medieval Christian devil with its horns and supernatural power prodding humanity on toward the assertion of independent ego with all its negative attributes.

This primal image of the Animal Master also bears a certain relationship to that other composite creature, the sphinx. As a composite being, it points to man as the hieroglyph of the universe, for wherever human-animal imagery is found, there too is a threshold to the spiritual world, the abyss of being, and the mystery of humanity and world. In historical eras such composite creatures are seen as monsters, but in primal and prehistoric times their awesome forms are like unto gods. The Animal Master imagery points to the intimate spiritual connection primal humanity shares with the animal kingdom, not merely in terms of practical needs but also in the most spiritual ways imaginable. This figure too, if not a picture of the shaman in his state of spirit transformation, is certainly an image with which the shaman is directly connected and concerned.

VI.6 The Goddess

When we look . . . at origins, at fundamental forces, we must characterize all of the creative activities of man [and woman], without distinction, as cult practices.
—Walter Otto

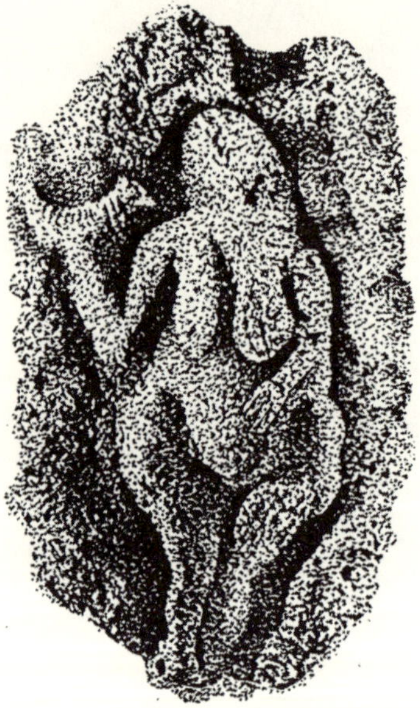

Fig. 278. The Venus of Laussel was carved in relief on a limestone wall in the south of France sometime between 25,000 and 20,000 B.C. A full-bodied female figure, she holds a cow horn in her right hand and touches her large, possibly pregnant belly with her left hand.

Besides its appearance on the head of the shaman or initiate, the horn also appears in the right hand of the so-called Venus of Laussel (fig. 278). Carved in relief on the wall of a limestone rock shelter in the south of France, this early Paleolithic image dates to 25,000–20,000 B.C., and is one of many plump or pregnant female figures that exemplify the principles of becoming, generation, and abundance. The face is not articulated, and the limbs are subsidiary to the abundant breasts, abdomen, and thighs. With one hand resting on her rounded belly and the other raised, holding a crescent-shaped horn, she has no need to wear the horn on her head as the shaman does—although she will in the Egyptian period as the goddess Isis. Fourteen sections formed by thirteen incisions on the horn may refer to the days between new and full moon. This primal image may point to the connection between cow as fertility animal and lunar rhythms at work in the female organism. The Venus of Laussel holds the horn at the level of her neck—traditionally the area of the body associated with the constellation of Taurus, the bull. Her left hand resting on her belly connects her with Virgo, the Virgin. The abdominal region, home to metabolic processes and reproduction, is the body part associated with Virgo and identifies the Venus of Laussel as a horn of plenty, an earthly cornucopia, in the form of the Great Mother and Fertility Goddess.[42] Later, in the Christian era, the Virgin Mary is depicted with the crescent moon beneath her feet and Sun-Child in her arms (fig. 279). The Venus archetype evolves over time from the Mother Goddess of the cave sanctuary, with its paintings of animals, to the Virgin Mary in the holy stable, between ox and ass. A remarkable recurring theme can be traced through the language of artistic images.[43]

Most Paleolithic Goddess images represent the life-giving motif of fecundity and abundance, as can be seen in the Venus figurines from Willensdorf (fig. 86), Lespugue, and Dolni Vestonice, with their large breasts, full buttocks, and swollen abdomens (fig. 280). It is significant that these female figurines are fashioned in the round in stone, bone, or ivory, and are not executed in painting. Male figures, and this includes the Animal Masters are almost exclusively depicted in two-dimensional paintings, drawings, and etchings—very rarely do they appear in sculpture. Their basic gesture is often that of a stick figure, angular and rigid, giving the appearance of being shaped from outside. The Venuses, of which more than 130 have been discovered, are rounded, buoyant figurines, that give an impression of inner energy and potential growth as well as a certain softness. Venus figurines are often lacking arms, hands, feet, and faces. They are only "center," formed from within, from their middle outwards. Uehli describes the nature of these figures in the following manner: "In these forms, the peripheral elements—head, arms, legs—are held back, remaining almost completely unformed, while by contrast those organs which are central, the bearers of the All-Motherly forces of life, are expressed with elemental strength. The upwelling, blossoming, fructifying motherly forces of the female organism, with its life-center in the solar plexus, the forms through which the cosmic fantasy creates bodily forms, these are the forces out of which these sculptures were created. The forming, sculpting forces well up from the center of the body and weaken as they reach the periphery of the limbs and head. So the female organism is sculpted as an archetypal gesture."[44] This suggests that hands and feet are absent not because it is more convenient to leave them out or because the artist is not skilled enough to articulate such details, but because the creative forces out of which the sculptor works demands an overall gesture of outward-welling and expansive roundness to come to expression.

Recent research has suggested that the Venus figurines, once thought to be a kind of pornographic fetish created by men, may actually have been fashioned by women. It is asserted that pregnant women may have sculpted what they saw when looking down upon their own bodies. Therefore feet, arms, and head are not depicted in any detail if at all, and breasts and belly are emphasized.

These "All-Motherly forces of life" can be seen in later Bronze Age depictions associated with the Moon Goddess Cybele, renamed Artemis by the Greeks and also known as Diana of Ephesus (fig. 85). The goddess's entire trunk is covered with egglike breasts. Originally decorated with rich color and precious metals, the first-century Roman copies of Artemis are adorned with animals sacred to the goddess, such as deer, lions, and bulls. On one life-sized Artemis statue, horned animal heads accent the lower part of her headdress, flanking and framing the goddess. Ephesus in Asia Minor, home to the Goddess, is where the Virgin Mary, mother of Jesus, in the early Christian era made her home and was declared the Mother of God.[45]

The Goddess principle is so widespread and all-encompassing in the history of art that its many different forms and attributes are often overlooked in terms of mystery symbolism. The Goddess or Great Mother stands behind the very mystery of earthly matter. The words *mother, matter, matrix, meter, measure, moon,*

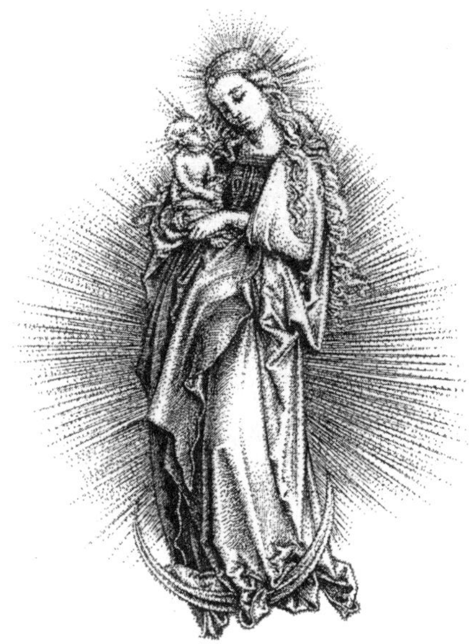

Fig. 279. Above: Mary, the Mother of God, is depicted in the Christian era carrying the Sun-Child and standing on the crescent moon. (After Dürer.)

Fig. 280. Below: The figurines of Lespugue and Dolni Vestonice all share similar features—large breasts, full buttocks, swollen abdomens—and lack faces, feet, and hands.

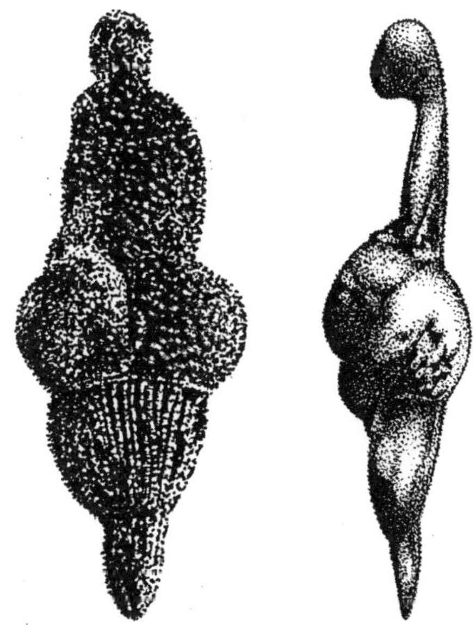

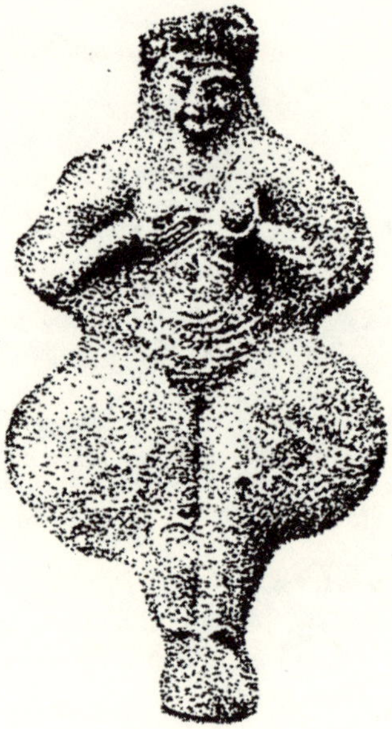

Fig. 281. The goddess of fertility, Ishtar, c. 2000 B.C., is probably an artistic descendant of the Paleolithic Venus figures.

and *month* are all derived from closely related roots. In some cultures she is the earth, in others she is the sky. She is seen as the element of water as well as the substance that binds the cosmos together. She may appear as the destroying Kali, the vengeful Ishtar (fig. 281), the gracious Isis, the beautiful Aphrodite, or the loving Virgin Mary. In all her forms she is an unmistakable revelation of the divine Sophia, the embodiment of Universal Wisdom. Vladimir Solovyov describes this Sophia being in the following words: "The eternal feminine itself strives for such realization and embodiment, for it is not a mere passive image in the divine mind but a living spiritual being possessing the fullness of powers and activities. The whole cosmic and historical process is the process of its realization and incarnation in an endless multiplicity of forms and degrees."[46]

Throughout the Paleolithic world, primal humanity practiced the mysterious pictorial language of the visual arts. Through the creation of art the world was changed, and changing the world necessarily changed humanity. Art served as a bridge between the realm of creative spiritual experience and the ever-increasing demands of developing self-awareness within a physical environment. The creative deed of artistic action confirmed the meaningfulness and marriage of spirit with matter and recorded in picture form the transformation of consciousness.

Notes

1. Wade, D. *Crystal and Dragon,* p. 194.
2. Ernst Uehli, Swiss art historian, speaks of these three kinds of history. He is author of *Atlantis und das Rätsel der Eiszeitkunst, Die Mosaiken von Ravenna, Nordisch-germanische Mythologie als Mysteriengeschichte, Die Adler-Imagination,* and *Leben und Gestaltung.*
3. African skeletal remains named Lucy, after a Beatles song, by their discoverer Donald Johanson.
4. Anderson, W. *Face of Glory,* p. 181.
5. Robert Layton describes the way in which late nineteenth-century scholars studied indigenous peoples, saying: "the religions which proved to play so great a role in many of the cultures being discovered by explorers and missionaries were generally dismissed as mere superstitions. According to the evolutionary concepts popular at the time in the West, mankind was believed to exhibit progress from irrational devotion of spirits and deities, to the rational, scientific outlook of the writers then establishing anthropology." *The Anthropology of Art,* p. 36. Streit makes a similar observation when he points out: "It was Herbert Spencer (1820–1903) in the nineteenth century who carried Darwin's theory of natural selection of the fittest as an axiom into the field of interpreting early cultures and linked this evolutionary theory to the process of evaluation. As a result the older a culture the more primitive and inferior it was considered. This is the source of contempt for the primitive psyche of early man and for archaeology contenting itself with cataloging and dating. The man behind the material aroused no interest. It was not realized that these early human beings had a rich mythic experience of the world and an intimate and close connection with nature." *Sun and Cross,* p. 11. It is just this "rich mythic experience" and "intimate and close connection with nature" that provides the backdrop for the ancient mysteries and lays the basis for early artistic production. Barfield points out that the biological picture of evolution was taken up and largely accepted by scholars who studied the human past in such a way that it made the framework into which they

fit any theory they chose to form. This framework was totally accepted, not as speculation or hypothesis, but as established fact. Thus, in their endeavors to explain the mind of early humanity, scholars placed them within a setting identical to their own and supposed the origin of human consciousness to lie in these first efforts to speculate about such phenomena. This limited approach evolved into the doctrine of animism, according to which the fancy of so-called 'primitive' humanity had imagined spirits populating nature. As Barfield explains, "in order that nature may be peopled with spirits, nature must first be devoid of spirit; but this caused the scholars no difficulty, because they never supposed the possibility of any other kind of nature." *Saving the Appearances,* p. 66.

6. Raup, D., in "Conflicts between Darwin and Paleontology," from *The Bulletin of the Field Museum of Natural History,* 50; Jan. 79, pp. 22–29. Cited in Lawlor, R. *Voices of the First Day.*

7. Steiner, R. *Lucifer Gnosis.* Steiner also states that humanity of very early times "did not have full ego-consciousness, as we do today . . . people of that period did not perceive what existed in dead nature, in the [solid] mineral nature." Steiner, *Cycle of the Year,* p. 54.

8. As direct experience of spiritual revelation faded, certain cultures employed physical aids such as drugs and blood sacrifice in order to regain immediate and partial experience of the spirit. Such practices were decadent in comparison to earlier cultus and may be considered "black magic" because of their manipulation of spiritual forces for the sake of personal power.

9. Among Native American tribes of the last few centuries the handprint was a sign of courage and prestige, often worn on the clothing of warriors. It could alert the observer to show caution or attention in a given circumstance. Pueblo and Hopi Indians marked sacred places with handprints so that supernatural beings would know who had made supplications and offerings to them.

10. Preble, D. and S. *Artforms,* frontispiece.

11. Steiner, R. *World History,* p. 16.

12. Steiner, R. *World History,* p. 17.

13. *Déjà vu* means "already seen," and is an experience of "memory" associated with a particular place, time, or situation. It is often characterized by the observation: "I have experienced this before."

14. Brodrick, A. *Prehistoric Painting,* p. 4.

15. Jung, C. *Man and His Symbols,* p. 235.

16. Bahn, P. *Images of the Ice Age,* p. 151.

17. "In true hunting magic, one can draw the animal in the sand or scratch it on an open rock surface and perform the rite of magic killing quickly." A. Marshack, *Roots of Civilization,* p. 231. This is a reasonable argument if one assumes primal peoples are interested in the economy of time and activity. The art and architecture of many prehistoric peoples actually bears witness to the fact that economy of time and effort is often of little importance.

18. Bahn, in *Images of the Ice Age,* describes the various "magico-religious" forms of art as follows: 'Sympathetic magic,' including hunting magic, operates on the same basis as pins in a wax doll: i.e., the effect resembles the cause. The depictions of animals were produced in order to control or influence the real animals in some way: any injury to the image would likewise be inflicted on its subject. Desirable effects such as ensuring that the prey would be as fine and well fed as the image were also possible. In short, this kind of art is intended to exert influence at a distance, rather like modern advertisements; it is purely functional, and directly related to the need for food." Bahn, p. 151.

19. Cited in Bahn, *Images of the Ice Age,* p. 166.

20. Schad, W. pp. 97–120.

21. Ibid., pp. 148–49.

22. Ibid., p. 149.

23. Poppelbaum, p. 89.

24. "If we were to consider the main forms of the various animals and note them down, we should be able to delineate the different realms of instinct. What instinct is as will is given as a picture in the form of the physical body of the various animals. You see, in this way meaning enters the world, if we can apply this point of view. We survey the forms of the physical animal bodies and see in them an illustration which nature herself makes of the instincts; by means of which she wishes to translate into reality what has living existence." Steiner, R. Study of Man, p. 61.

25. Steiner, *Waldorf Education for Adolescence,* Lecture 7.

26. Although intellectual thinking, reckoning, and calculation were probably not capacities of primal humanity, knowledge and understanding were nevertheless present. Paleolithic peoples fashioned outstanding works that, although not the result of critical thinking, demonstrated insight by way of instinctual awareness, dream-state awareness, and pre-analytical consciousness.

27. Steiner. *Waldorf Education for Adolescence,* Lecture 7.

28. Steiner cited in Kroth, R. *Golden Blade,* 1955, "The Art of the Caves and their Meaning."

29. "Shamanic methods are strikingly similar the world over, even for peoples whose cultures are quite different in other respects, and who have been separated by oceans and continents for tens of thousands of years." Harnes, M. *The Way of the Shaman,* p. xiii.

30. Cowan, T. *Fire in the Head: Shamanism and the Celtic Spirit,* p. 3.

31. Clottes, J. and D. Lewis-Williams, *The Shamans of Prehistory.* p. 19.

32. Lorblanchet, M. Cited in Hughes, R. "Behold the Stone Age," *Time,* Feb. 13, 1995, p. 60.

33. Uehli, p. 192.

34. Cowen, T. p. 35.

35. Baring, A., and J. Cashford. *The Myth of the Goddess,* p. 35.

36. Eliade, M. *Shamanism,* p. 460. Animal images are weightless with no ground or landscape to stand on. Size is unimportant as mammoths may be painted smaller than horses. Individual animal pictures appear, for the most part, unrelated to each other. Many of the images overlap one another; sometimes a dozen pictures are painted on top of one another. A quarter of all cave animal depictions are of the bovine family. At Lascaux as many as 2,000 paintings and engravings can be found, most of them animal pictures dating from between c. 30,000 and 10,000 B.C. At Les Trois Frères there are some 500 engravings of animals.

37. In his monumental *Historical Atlas of World Mythology,* Joseph Campbell points out: "The masks that in our demythologized time are lightly assumed for the entertainments of a costume ball or Mardi Gras—and may actually, on such occasions, release us to activities and experiences which might otherwise have been tabooed—are vestigial of an earlier magic, in which the powers to be invoked were not simply psychological, but cosmic. For the appearances of the natural order, which are separate from each other in time and space, are in fact the manifestations of energies that inform all things and can be summoned to focus at will." Vol. I, Part I, p. 93.

38. Ryan, R. *The Strong Eye of Shamanism,* p. 55.

39. Ruspoli, M. *The Cave of Lascaux:* The Final Photographs, p. 28.

40. "Among the American Indians the Master of Animals is one of the most distinctive mythic ideas. He is a supernatural ruler whose function is to exercise stewardship over the wild animals, especially the animals hunted by men." Gimbutas, M., *Language of the Goddess,* p. 175.

41. Gimbutas, *Language of the Goddess,* p. 177.

42. The crescent or chalice form represented in the bull's horns also appears as though imprinted within the female organism. As pointed out by Dorothy Cameron in *Symbols of Birth and Death in the Neolithic Era* (pp. 4–5), the female uterus and fallopian tubes bear a striking resemblance to the head and horns of a bull. In recognition of this correspondence a Neolithic fresco at Çatal Hüyük illustrates the female figure with bull's head and horns appearing on her abdomen. (See also Gimbutas, *Language of the Goddess,* pp. 265–66.) There is another organ within the human body that has this form, the larynx. With hyoid bone and thyroid cartilage, the larynx appears much like the bull's horns and head. As the organ of speech it is responsible for a birth of another kind, that of the word and language. This mystery image appears in the astrological sigil for Taurus, which is traditionally linked to the speech organs and the throat. With an upwardly open semicircle resting on top of a circle, this sigil has been interpreted as a symbol for the bull's head and horns. However, as pure graphic language the form reveals its intention and meaning. The inverted arc is open above, like a chalice moon, receiving influences that pour into it from above. Yet below is a closed and self-contained whole, a picture of unity and completeness. The two elements are like crescent moon and full moon (or sun) joined together, one resting upon the other. This, in part, accounts for how esoteric tradition links the cosmic bull forces with the formation of the larynx, as well as the power of speech (human throat) and female reproduction (the abdomen and uterus).

43. Baring, A., and J. Cashford. *Myth of the Goddess,* p. 45.

44. Uehli, E. Atlantis, p. 181.

45. *Myth of the Goddess,* p. 330.

46. Solovyov, V. "The Meaning of Love," *A Solovyov Anthology,* p. 174.

EPILOGUE

Art and the New Mysteries

Art transforms the sense-perceptual world in a "speaking" manner, creating new meaning. In this sense it is an epilogue to ancient sacred life, where everything was meaningful. And thus art is perhaps a prelude to a new epoch of mankind, where the human being is giving meaning to existence.
—Georg Kühlewind

At one time art was a sacred teaching and a spiritual practice that confirmed truths about the universe and about the human being. Owen Barfield refers to this time as one of "original participation," where a direct, instinctive relationship existed between humanity and Nature. "The essence of original participation is that there stands behind the phenomena, and on the other side of them from me, a represented, which is of the same nature as me. Whether it is called 'mana,' or by the names of many gods and demons, or God the Father, or the spirit world, it is of the same nature as the perceiving self, inasmuch as it is not mechanical or accidental, but psychic and voluntary."[1] He also speaks of "final participation," where what has been lost through self-conscious ego development—a falling away from oneness with the divine, characterized in the image of the Fall from Paradise—may be rediscovered by humanity on a new level of spiritual experience and co-creative inner initiative. "Original participation fires the heart from a source outside itself; the images enliven the heart. But in final participation . . . the heart is fired from within . . . and it is for the heart to enliven the images."[2]

Such a path of development is what Richard Tarnas calls "the deepest passion of the Western mind," that is, "to reunite with the ground of its being."[3] And what is clearly needed for this reuniting are new mysteries founded in part on an awakening to a middle path we may tread between inner and outer world, between innocence and experience, masculine and feminine, science and religion, between what the poet Schiller described as form and substance.[4] Here equanimity is required, for only in balancing these polarities is the art of freedom truly found.

Carl Jung despaired that "our Western mind, lacking all culture in this respect, has never yet devised a concept, not even a name, for the union of opposites through the middle path, that most fundamental item of inward experience which could respectably be set against the Chinese concept of Tao."[5]

However, in his discussion of aesthetics, James Joyce describes two orders of art: proper and improper. Improper art has two sides: that which excites desire for the object depicted, and that which inspires loathing or fear of it. The first form of improper art Joyce terms pornographic because it seduces one and pulls one towards it. The second kind of improper art he calls didactic, for it tries to teach one a lesson and thrusts itself upon the observer. However, proper art has nothing to do with exciting or with controlling, with pushing or pulling. As Joseph Campbell describes it: "Proper art does not move one either to desire or to loathing, either toward the object or away from it. One is held, on the contrary, in aesthetic arrest, a moment of sensational (aesthetic) contemplation, as before a recognized revelation, or in Joyce's language, an epiphany. 'The mind,' he writes, 'is arrested and raised above desire and loathing.'"[6]

Improper Art One	**Proper Art**	**Improper Art Two**
Pornographic	Freedom	Didactic
Desire	Epiphany	Loathing
Pulling towards	Aesthetic arrest	Pushing away

Similarly, Steiner describes two sources of art: that which arises as visionary inner imagination and that which is drawn out of or intuited from the outer world of experience. The one source he describes as expressionism and the other as impressionism—not to be confused with the two historical styles of art.7 These two sources must not be taken to their extremes, as can be and is done, but must be married in such a way that a middle or higher path is achieved. This middle path of "proper" art is the language of the interior nature of the universe and revelation of the spirit—not a hallucination.

Joseph Beuys declared that "everyone is an artist," and however we attempt to define it, art has the inherent characteristic of demonstrating the human condition, expressing and diagnosing what is present as the given human reality, and, just as significantly, influencing and working on that condition. Art brings healing and dispenses further motives into the inner life of the soul, whereby it works into the future forming of humanity. "The basis of artistic creation is not what is, but what might be; not the real but the possible."[8] Art is truly one of the greatest gifts of humanity, for it builds and fashions humanity. It is a moral force, for good and for ill. It is a doorway through which the spiritual gains access to, and is made visible in, the physical, material world. It creates enjoyment and pleasure, as well as catharsis and metamorphosis. Spirit and art are inseparable, just as the images we survey in the history of art are inseparable from human development. Art literally provides us with a record of our evolving consciousness, pictures of the transformation of humanity.

And thus noble humankind works mightily
For century after century on its own kind,
For what good people can accomplish
Is not accomplished in the narrow space of life.
That is why we live on after death,
No less effective there than once we were in life.
The good deed and the lovely word
Strive on immortally as we strove mortally.
Thus too, the artist lives through time unmeasured.
Enjoy your immortality!
—Goethe, "The Artist's Apotheosis"[9]

APPENDIX 1: The Spiritual in Postmodern Art

We say that the present age possesses no art—who is responsible for this? It is indeed a shame that despite all our rhapsodies about the ancients we pay so little attention to our own possibilities. . . . The past may well look with pity at the poverty of our civilization; the future will laugh at the barrenness of our art. We are destroying art in destroying the beautiful in life.
—Kakuzo Okakura

According to Hans Beilting, the "era of art" began in about A.D. 1400.[10] Before that time the concept of art was not yet a real consideration. Images were created and venerated but were not appreciated aesthetically. This coincides with what Owen Barfield calls "original participation."

In the 1960s when it became apparent that "anything can be art" and "everyone is an artist," a curious thing happened. Art ended! That is, according to philosopher and art critic Arthur Danto, the progressive narrative we know as art history ended. Since the advent of the Postmodern movement, we have crossed a threshold. At this point, Danto says, the meaning of art can no longer be found through sense experience but must be sought conceptually, through thought. Conceptual art leads to self-reflection and philosophy. This notion was already suggested by Hegel (who claimed that art, philosophy, and religion are all three occasions of Absolute Spirit) when he said, "Art invites us to intellectual consideration, and that not for the purpose of creating art again, but for knowing philosophically what art is."[11] In other words, art promotes consciousness.

Steiner too felt the "significant factor" in the further spiritual development of humanity "will be that, in the process of attempting to understand the concept of art, [we] devise an art of the conceptual, in which the work and activity of ideation will be fulfilled with images, with reality, and that what now appears as dry science will in the future come closer to art."[12]

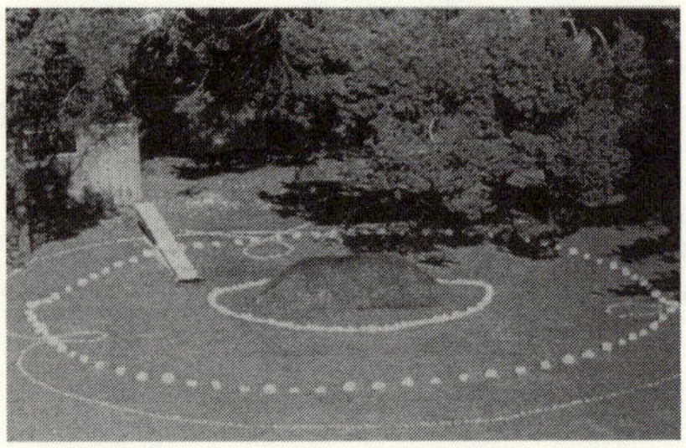

Fig. 282. In the tradition of Beuys, an international collaboration between Horst Kornberger, Tom Müller and Luke Gleeson resulted in the creation of *Kompost, 2000*, in Perth, Australia, as a "fermenting of minds" and a fertilizing of the earth.

Whether we choose to view the "era of art" as ended or whether we deepen our understanding of what art is, or both, our contemporary Postmodern setting is the fire and ash out of which the phoenix of a future spirit and art will be born. It is not possible to deal adequately with the spiritual in Postmodern art in the present volume, but a few names might be mentioned and some points made in passing.

In the realms of sculpture, installation, and performance, such artists as Michael Howard, Gertraud Goodwin, David Nash, Andy Goldsworthy, and Fern Shaffer come to mind. They and other less known practitioners (fig. 282) have found a way of meeting nature in meaningful encounters. Their works, sometimes whimsical, sometimes forceful, engage our participation with Nature in a way that earlier art forms are often unable to do. Their work is a hopeful indication that beyond the hype of the gallery and art market, a genuine pursuit of spirit is taking place—a development toward true spiritual freedom, a real transformation of human consciousness.

In the realm of painting (thought by some to be dead, like art itself) Gerard Wagner (color plate 1) needs to be mentioned.[13] Although his work is of the twentieth century, his influence on the painterly use of color as the primary stimulus for imagery will have far-reaching effects into the twenty-first century. Wagner coaxes the figurative element out of the free-flowing essential nature, from what Kandinsky called the "inner necessity," of color itself. For this reason Wagner has been called "one of the greatest Goethean [phenomenological] painters of the twentieth century." Sergei Prokofieff has said of him: "He stood on the threshold to the spiritual world [and] it became a color reality in his paintings. This contact with higher worlds while painting brought something religious into his art."[14] With his methodological approach to painting, Wagner unites science and art in such a way that a truly contemporary spiritual path is made visible. In Wagner's work, it seems that Absolute Spirit—in the sense of Hegel's trinity of art, philosophy, and religion—is manifest.

If this is the end of art, at least it is a happy ending!

APPENDIX 2: Rudolf Steiner and Anthroposophy

Through art we can know another's view of the universe.
—Marcel Proust

Rudolf Steiner was a person who, from an early age, had spiritual experiences not unlike those of the traditional shaman, in which nature spirits, souls of the dead, and other spiritual phenomena appeared before the eyes of his soul. However, not until he discovered geometry as a student was he able to find validation of his spiritual experiences. The young Steiner realized that "geometry was something that only the mind by the exercise of its own powers could grasp."[15] This was a spiritual activity that the rest of the world recognized, and it ultimately led him to his conviction that the spiritual world is accessible by means of enhanced powers of thinking. Later this would prove to be his justification for regarding the spiritual world as no less worthy of methodical research than the natural world. He received his doctorate in philosophy with a dissertation on "The Fundamental Problem of the Theory of Knowledge: The Reconciliation of the Philosophical Consciousness with Itself."

So what does a philosopher have to do with the arts? As a young man, Steiner had no training and little talent in any of the arts. However, he did have vision, "second sight." He combined this vision with scientific method to create a contemporary spiritual science that recognizes the human condition as being that of an artist standing between the inner and outer worlds of religion and science, subjectivity and objectivity. Steiner's entire worldview, called Anthroposophy ("awareness of one's humanity"), points to this creative nature of the human being within a living, creative universe.

Steiner wrote numerous books and gave thousands of lectures during his lifetime, only a fraction of them dealing directly with the arts. However, the artistic was an essential theme throughout his life's work. At the age of twenty-seven he shared his ideas on art for the first time with the Vienna Goethe Society, presenting the foundations of his theory of art that would be the starting point for all of his own artistic work. In his lecture "Goethe, the Father of a New Science of Aesthetics," Steiner suggests that art is not the bringing down of spiritual ideals and the clothing of them in physical material but the redeeming and raising of the material world, lifting it to the spiritual: "not the embodiment of the supersensible, but the transformation of the sense-perceptible."[16] Another point Steiner makes is what Kandinsky calls "inner necessity," that is, the inner lawfulness of an object and how this interior aspect is made visible through its outer form and gesture. "In the artist's work the whole exterior must express the whole inner nature," according to Steiner. "Thus the laws with which the artist goes to work are none other than the eternal laws of nature, but pure, uninfluenced by hindrances. Artistic creation rests not on what is, but on what could be; not on the actual but on the possible."[17]

Steiner had been lecturing to the Theosophical Society on spiritual themes for many years and had even become the General Secretary of the German section, though he never became a member of the Theosophical Society himself. He agreed to this arrangement on the condition that he would not be expected to adhere to any "party line" or preach theosophical doctrine, but would be free to speak out of his own spiritual vision and research. In 1907 the German section, with Steiner at its head, hosted an international conference in Munich, and he took on the decoration of a rented auditorium, arranging the program in order to include all the arts. This created a schism between those who connected themselves to an esoteric stream that sought only the pursuit of spiritual development and those wishing to link their striving to a concern for the earth. At the Munich Congress, Steiner virtually drew a line on the ground, declaring the arts to be an essential ingredient in realizing the effectiveness of a truly esoteric life integrated into daily life in the

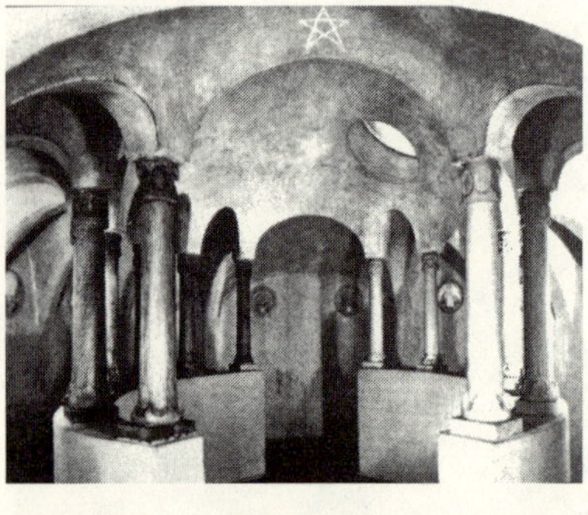

Fig. 283. The Malsch building was Steiner's first attempt at designing a structure in the sacred architectural tradition. It was inspired by a question posed by artist Karl Stockmeyer. (Copyright © Verlag am Goetheanum.)

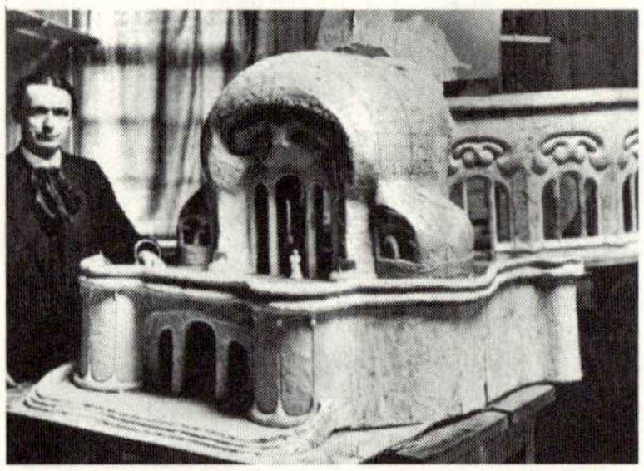

Fig. 284. The first Goetheanum was built on a hill outside of Basel, Switzerland and named for the poet-scientist Johann Wolfgang von Goethe. Work began in 1913 and the unfinished building was destroyed by fire in 1923.

modern world. This, he declared, would require the artistic transformation of one's environment: "The human being can only experience true harmony of soul where what the soul knows to be its most valuable thoughts, feelings, and impulses are mirrored for the senses in the forms, colors, and so on of one's surroundings."[18]

It is not known for certain if the Munich artists attended this milestone event, but it is likely that artists such as Kandinsky, Klee, and Jawlensky, who were familiar with Steiner's work, knew it was taking place.

It was for this conference that Steiner developed a series of seven seals intended to serve as sculpted capital reliefs on columns. Each of the motifs, though unique, was related to the next motif in the series through the principle of metamorphosis. In 1908, a twenty-one-year-old artist named Karl Stockmeyer, who had attended the Munich Congress, asked Steiner what a building would look like that had such columns. Steiner enthusiastically described an elliptical space supported by two rows of seven columns, fourteen in all. These columns were to support a triaxial ellipsoid cupola with a central axis running from west to east. Stockmeyer, with Steiner's aid, set about constructing a model of this building in his hometown of Malsch, Germany (fig. 283). Measuring on plan only about 2.5 by 3.5 meters, the model structure, which still stands today, is large enough to accommodate small gatherings of less than two dozen people. This was a first attempt by Steiner to establish an organic relationship between the longitudinal character of an axial building, such as a cathedral, and the circular character of a central-axis building. Rudolf Steiner laid the foundation stone for this building on April 5, 1909, reciting the words:

> *With the laying of this foundation stone of the Malsch building we entreat the blessings of the Masters of Wisdom and all high and highest beings of the spiritual hierarchies that are connected with earth evolution. We entreat that all of your power of spirit may stream through in harmony all that is brought, felt, willed and done here. On this building may there shine the light of the Spirits of the East; the Spirits of the West may they reflect this light; the Spirits of the North may they strengthen and the Spirits of the South warm it. So that the Spirits of the East, West, North and South may stream through this building. In pain and suffering our Mother Earth has become materialized. It is our task to once again spiritualize her, to redeem her, in that through the power of our hands we fashion a spirit-filled work of art. May this stone be a first foundation stone for the redemption and transformation of our planet Earth, and may the power of this stone work a thousandfold.*[19]

Shortly afterwards, a larger rendering of this interior space was constructed as a meeting room in the Stuttgart House of the Theosophical Society, but was later destroyed by the National Socialists in the 1930s, when Steiner's work was outlawed in Germany.

Following the construction of these two buildings, plans were being made for a large-scale theater in Munich called the Johannes Building.[20] Permission to build was denied by the city council of Munich, but the setback allowed a change of venue to a hilltop site outside of Basel, Switzerland. There the building was renamed the Goetheanum, after the German poet-scientist, and featured not an elliptical space but two interpenetrating domes of different sizes (fig. 284). It proved to be a completely new direction in architectural design in combining the principles of both central and axial space.

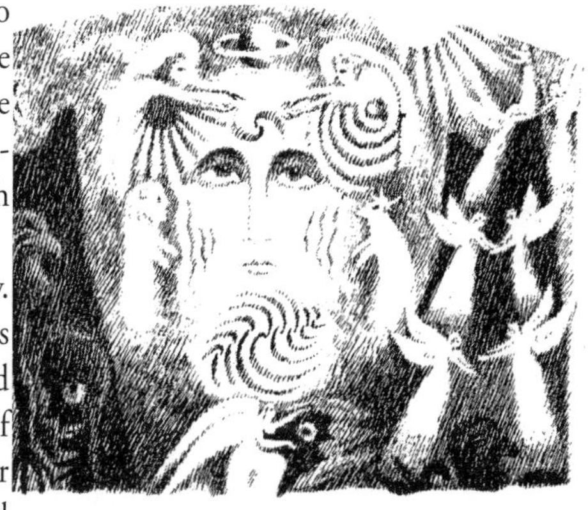

Fig. 285. The west, red window of the Goetheanum depicts cosmic and earthly influences that work upon the human being who is attempting to follow a spiritual path. (After Steiner.)

In the Goetheanum, Steiner initiated a new type of stained glass window. A dentist's drill was used to engrave thick slabs of single-colored glass to allow images of lighter color to contrast with darker. No fragmented pieces of glass were held together with dark lines of lead. Each window was a single continuous whole of etched monochrome figures and images depicting the progressive path of inner development (figs. 16, 285). This medium was used again in the second Goetheanum but with a new etching technique that Steiner had developed with the assistance of the Russian artist Assia Turgeniev. In order to avoid contour drawing, cross-hatching, pointillism, and other techniques that were felt to cut off the image from its surrounding environment or in some way make the images artistically "untrue," Steiner applied a slant-line style to the etched-glass renderings. This promoted a "breathing" between the image and its surroundings, thus establishing a more "living" relationship between object and surroundings.

Another of Steiner's artistic endeavors was as a playwright. He called his plays "mystery dramas," for they are intense, lengthy productions, like the ancient Greek dramas (regarded by Aristotle as "cathartic") and take the better part of a day to perform. *The Portal of Initiation: A Rosicrucian Mystery* was first produced in Munich in 1910 and three successive plays followed in 1911, 1912, and 1913.[21] The central figure in the dramas is a young painter named Johannes, who, together with his circle of acquaintances, goes through the trials of a modern spiritual seeker. The plays describe the characters in varied situations that give rise to supernormal encounters. Spiritual beings and elemental spirits appear as well as flashbacks dealing with karmic relationships and former incarnations. Steiner's entire worldview is cast in artistic form in these dramas and the dramas stimulated the building of the first Goetheanum.

During rehearsals for the second mystery drama, *The Soul's Probation,* before the first Goetheanum was in its building stage, the actor playing Johannes asked Steiner what the painting would look like that this character was pretending to work on during the third scene. Steiner immediately took up a brush and tempera paints from backstage and created there on the spot his first painting entitled *Light Weaving* (fig. 286). The picture represents spiritual beings—the Elohim, at the moment of creation, fashioning with streaming light. The painting is almost entirely abstract apart from some primitive faces and winglike forms in white, blue-black, and red. This was the first of many renderings—pastel sketches and watercolor paintings—through which Steiner would indicate what he called "painting out of the color." His insistence that

Fig. 286. Light Weaving is Rudolf Steiner's first painting. It was created for the character Johannes, an artist, in Steiner's first mystery drama. It shows creator beings streaming their light into the earth. (Copyright © Rudolf Steiner Nachlassverwaltung.)

color is the essential language in the art of painting is apparent from his lectures on color: "If we were to speak more deeply of painting, the significance of the connection between the inner soul-life of the universe and color would reveal itself. It would be meaningless ever to paint with colors, if colors were not something very different from what they appear to be to outer physical perception. . . . Color is the language of nature's soul, the speech of the soul of the universe." He was fifty years old when he painted his first picture and he declared it would take him forty years to become an artist.

Steiner believed significant discoveries would be made in the future through color research in painting: "We can see a time before us—if we immerse ourselves fully in the perceptions and feelings which can proceed for us out of the spiritual-scientific world conception—a time when the path to the artistic will be in many respects different than in times gone by, when it will be much more full of life. That which is the medium of artistic creativity will be experienced much more intimately by the human soul than in times past; colour and tone will be much more intimately lived through, lived through morally and spiritually; and in the creations of artists we shall confront at the same time the tracks of artist-souls in the cosmos. . . . In this respect human

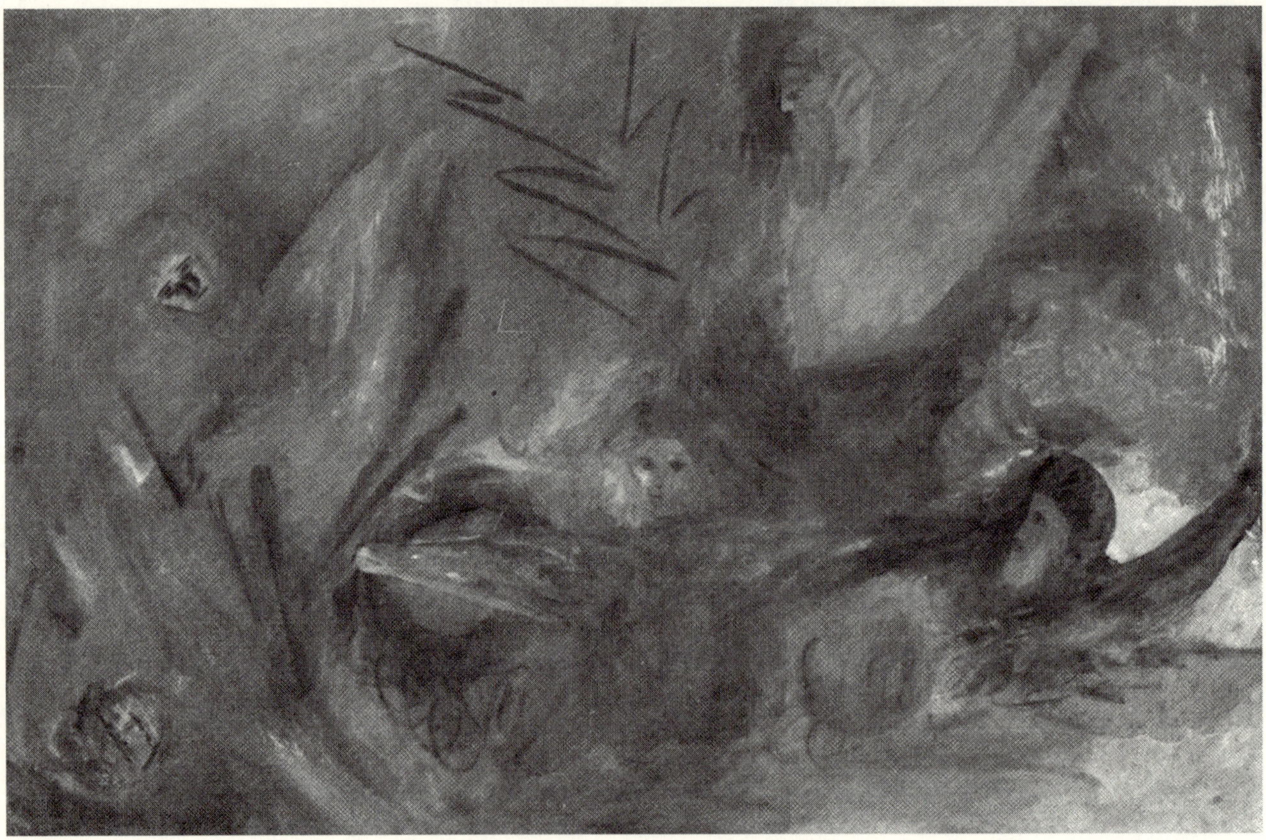

beings will make significant discoveries in the future. They will really unite their moral-spiritual being with what sense appearance presents us. An infinite deepening of the human soul can be foreseen in this domain."[22]

Steiner planned large-scale murals to be painted on the interior domes of the first Goetheanum, and developed his own plant-color pigments for this task. Made entirely from natural plant substances, these colors were intended as an alternative to synthetic pigments, which were just beginning to be mass produced. Motifs based on Steiner's sketches were painted on the ceiling by artists from America, Russia, and all over Europe who came to work on the Goetheanum. The sketches included scenes of creation, the formation of the senses, ancient India (fig. 287), Persia, Egypt, and Greece, as well as portrayals of the guiding Time Spirits who inspired more recent events. All of the flowing transparent washes of color and imagery unfolded toward the figure of Goethe's character Faust holding a child. Above the child appears the only word in the painting, "Ich," the German word for the human "I" or individuality. The images move on to culminate in the central motif of the ceiling painting, the Representative of Humanity. This figure Steiner intended to be seen in all freedom and divorced from any religious associations as the Being of Love or the Christ Being, the Logos, bearer of the universal "I."

Below this painted motif of the Representative of Humanity, at the back of the stage area, was to be placed a twenty-seven-foot-tall carved wood sculpture of the same theme, often referred to as *The Group* (fig. 18). One of the largest wood sculptures in the world, this statue is comparable to Michelangelo's *David* in its cultural significance as a spiritual imagination for its time. It depicts the human being striding between the spiritual beings that influence and tempt the free human soul in one direction or another. Below, in his subterranean cave, is Ahriman, the inspirer of cold, calculated, mechanistic intelligence. He works towards the reduction of man and universe into a complex supermachine. He is fashioned as a concave, angular, sclerotic figure, pointed and critical, exuding fear and loathing. Above the central figure's left arm is Lucifer, "the Light Bringer," who, inspiring heated passion and overflowing enthusiasm, desires that human beings become gods with no connection to earthly things. When this being's influence penetrates the physical body, fever and inflammation are the outcome. He is rendered as a fallen angel, full of himself, in rounded, convex forms. To the left of the central figure, both Lucifer and Ahriman appear again, working this time together in a concerted effort against humanity. One might see the three temptations of Christ or of Buddha in such an arrangement.

The ultimate significance of this work lies in its portrayal of human destiny. As Michelangelo's *David* (fig. 288) and Albrecht Dürer's *Knight, Death, and the Devil* (fig. 289) were for their time, *The Group* is an image of the modern human being meeting the world without and the world within, in freedom. Whatever one

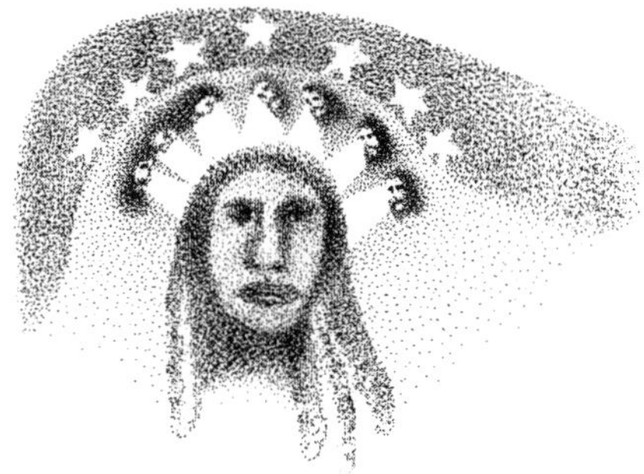

Fig. 287. The Indian Cultural Epoch (above) is one of the sketches Steiner provided for artists painting the ceiling murals of the Goetheanum. It depicts the Indian human being receiving inspiration from the planetary spheres through the Seven Holy Rishis. (After Steiner.)

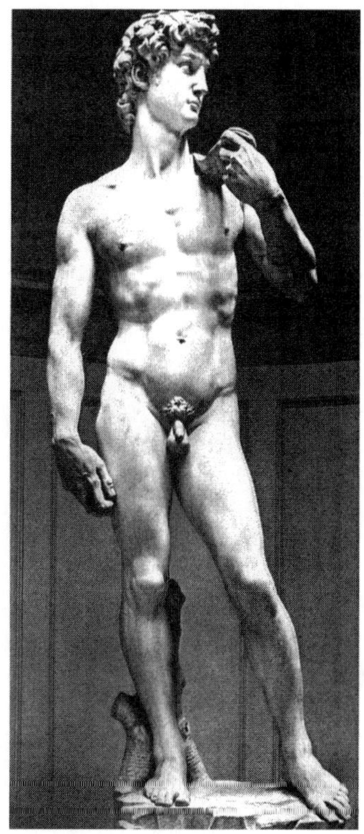

Fig. 288. In his *David* (1504), Michelangelo portrayed the human being about to encounter his adversary. (Florence, Italy.)

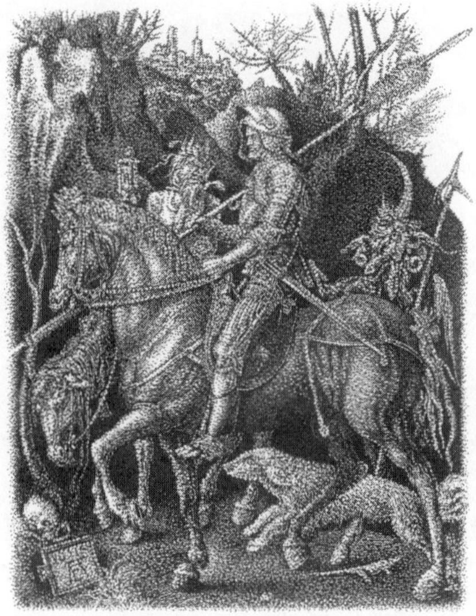

Fig. 289. Above: Albrecht Dürer depicted the human condition allegorically as a knight on a quest between death and devil. (After Dürer.)

Fig. 290. The Second Goetheanum was an inspiration to modern architects such as Le Corbusier for its use of dramatically modeled concrete. (Copyright © Thorwald Thiersch.)

thinks of Steiner's philosophy, there can be no denying that this wood sculpture is truly one of the masterpieces of twentieth-century art. The same is true of the painted cupolas, the sculptured capitals and the organic architecture of the first Goetheanum, all meant to form one integrated work of art. The second Goetheanum, entirely different from the first building, is an example of the initial building impulse metamorphosed to suit a later time, a different building material, and an expanded purpose (fig. 290).

During the planning and construction of the first and second Goetheanum buildings, Steiner also designed numerous residential dwellings, artist's studios, and utility buildings for the area. All of the smaller structures were based on the principle of outer form following the purpose and inner function of the building. Such thoughts concerning architectural forms were entertained by other architects of the day. In America, Louis Sullivan said that "each part [of a building] must so clearly express its function that the function can be read through the part."[23] Frank Lloyd Wright, a pupil of Sullivan, said: "By organic architecture I mean an architecture that develops from within outward in harmony with the conditions of its being as distinguished from one that is applied from without."[24] Steiner's utility structures strikingly demonstrate the principle of outer form arising from the function of the building. Especially in the cases of the Heating House and the Transformer House, one can see how the architectural forms have been shaped in such a way as to demonstrate the actions of boiling water and rising steam or the transfer of electricity.

Besides working nonstop as a lecturer and author, Steiner also designed his own book covers and logos, bringing a new impulse to the graphic arts. He pointed out that the printer's ink on the cover of a book suggests weight that can either restrict easy opening of a book or can offer an invitation to open the book, depending on design placement. He regularly created his and other author's book covers with a leading form, usually abstract, and inwardly expressive of the book's content, on the upper left corner so that the lower right corner would be free of imagery and would in effect create light to draw the hand to it for opening the book. "The place where we touch or take hold of an object [or book] should be made lighter than the rest of it," Steiner suggested. "It is as though the human being were

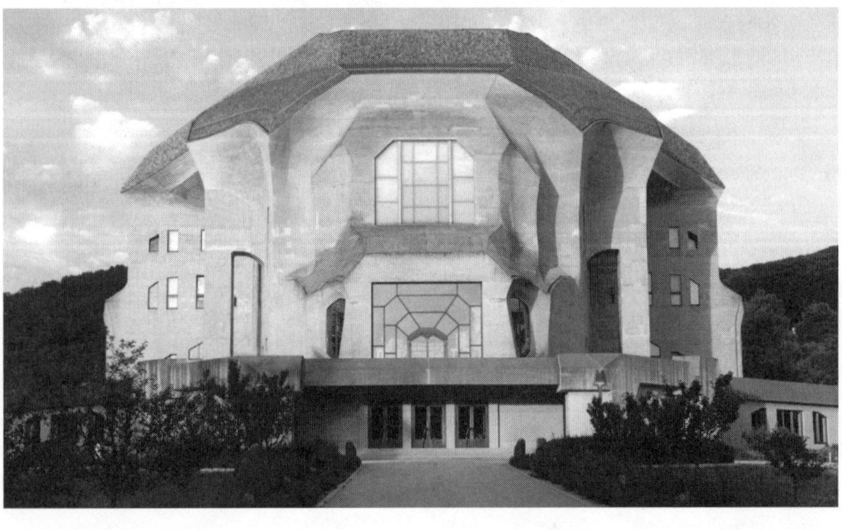

radiating light . . . books bound [and designed] in such a way that the cover does not tell one that it is supposed to be opened, are sins in the world of appearance, which is the domain of art."[25] In the same way that he used leading forms to introduce the subject of a book in purely graphic terms, he also created closing vignettes that graphically summed up and punctuated a body of text (fig. 291). One is reminded of the art nouveau and William Morris movements and their attempts to revitalize the art of book design.

Perhaps best described as an offshoot of the graphic arts, Rudolf Steiner revived the linear design work known in Latin as ars lineandi ("the making of lines"). This "form drawing" is used therapeutically, pedagogically, and artistically in medical clinics, Camphill communities, Waldorf/Steiner schools, as well as in art institutes. An example of this art form can be seen in his planetary seals and the Mystery Drama seals (fig. 299).

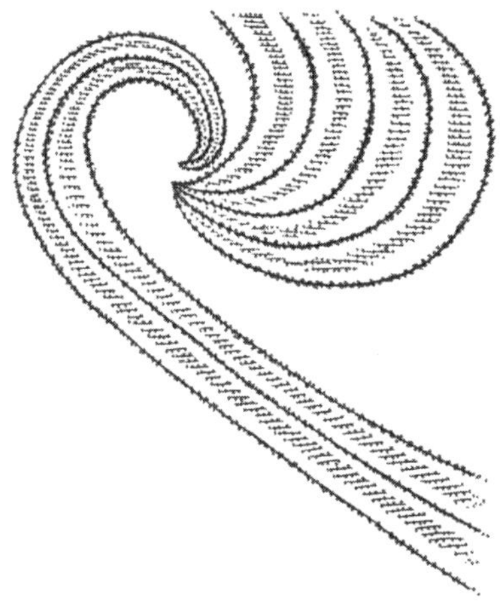

Fig. 291. Above: Rudolf Steiner created a number of closing vignettes. This one, for Steiner's article "Internationale Wirtschaft und dreigliedrigen Organismus," was published in 1919. (After Steiner.)

Fig. 292. Below: Eurythmy figures designed by Steiner indicate the colors and gestures corresponding to the different consonantal sounds. This is the figure for the sound "N." (After Steiner.)

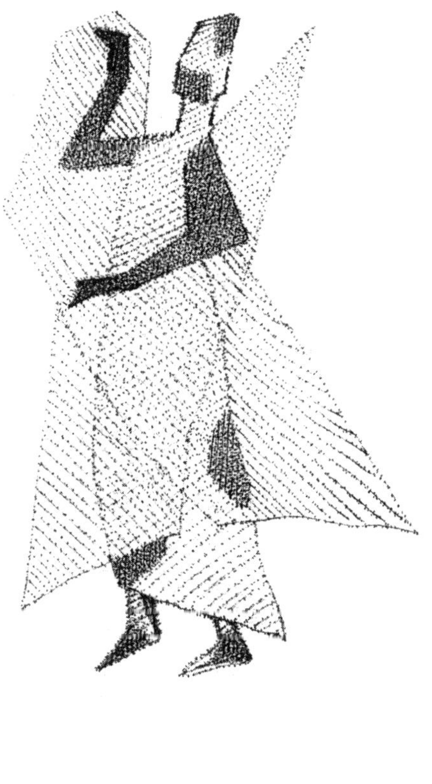

Steiner gave a speech and drama course that became the basis for numerous drama schools, stage groups, and director trainings, as in the case of Michael Chekhov's work, whose pupils included such celebrities as Gregory Peck, Marilyn Monroe, and Yul Brynner. Steiner's indications to opera singers have been developed into several schools of voice training. And when requested, he developed a form of movement he called eurythmy. In it movements make visible the sounds of speech and the tones of music by means of gesture (fig. 292). Eurythmy schools and professional eurythmy stage groups are recognized by the international dance community for their unique contributions to the performing arts. Rudolf Steiner's poetry set a standard that can only be described in terms of mantric verse. He wrote hundreds of verses. One he gave to the English sculptor Edith Maryon reads as follows:

The healing social life is found
When in the mirror of each human soul
The entire community finds its reflection,
And when in the community
The virtue of each one is living.

When we think of a "Renaissance Man," Leonardo da Vinci comes immediately to mind. If there were a twentieth-century Renaissance man, a modern master capable in all the arts and sciences, surely Rudolf Steiner would be such a one. Generally known as a philosopher, scientist, and educator, this remarkable individual has had an influence on the visual arts of our era that has yet to be fully recognized.

In his autobiography, Steiner rather matter-of-factly states: "What had been revealed to me through spiritual perception as the law of human evolution appeared in clear manifestation before my mind in the development of art."[26]

APPENDIX 3: Celtic Christianity and the Christ Mystery

But we speak the wisdom of God in a mystery.
—1 Corinthians 2:7

It is a curious fact that Christianity spread throughout Ireland virtually unopposed in the early centuries A.D. The first missionaries of the Roman church found Christianity already established on the Emerald Isle, as a fifth-century letter written by Saint Patrick attests: "In the days of old the law of God was well planted and propagated in Ireland; I do not wish to take credit for the work of my predecessors; I share the task with all those whom God has called and foreordained."[27] The sixth-century Welsh bard Taliesin confirms this when he says, "Christ, the Word from the beginning, was from the beginning our teacher, and we never lost his teachings. Christianity was in Asia a new thing; but there was never a time when the druids of Britain held not its doctrines."[28] Taliesin suggests that before the advent of historic Christianity, Christ was revered by those who were initiated into the earlier Mysteries of Hibernia.

Tradition tells of Irish druids who were aware of the death and resurrection of Christ simply through their "seeing" into the elements. One story tells of King Conchubar inquiring of his druid, Bucrach, what the signs of the full moon, darkened sun, and earthquakes on Good Friday A.D. 33 all meant. Bucrach responds, "Jesus Christ, the Son of God, is now being crucified."[29]

Legendary history and esoteric tradition state that the druid priesthood observed the manifestation of the spiritual sun forces in the changes occurring in nature.[30] For this reason, Christ the Sun Being was known in the Hibernian Mysteries as the "Lord of the Elements." According to esoteric Christianity the coming of Christ was not just for humanity but for Nature and the entire cosmos.

A kind of Christianized druid priesthood emerged in Ireland, a priesthood that established its new ritual centers upon earlier mystery sites and transformed the menhirs of old into the high crosses of the new religion.[31] The transition from pre-Christian standing stone to early Christian cross is well-documented in art (fig. 137). In Europe the ancient mysteries found their transformation in the new Christian Mysteries.

Hibernian megalithic art was founded on "the direct representation of the spiritual, and all that belongs to the spirit."[32] But the primal wisdom was gradually replaced by a knowledge that had to do with the external sense world. Early mystery images diminished as an art arose that relied more and more on realism. And although this "spiritual" art form of the megalithic cultures was eventually lost, it now awaits rediscovery.

Though megalithic monuments fell into disuse with the appearance of Christianity, many of the major churches and cathedrals throughout Europe were built on these older pre-Christian sites. Chartres Cathedral is an example, built on an altarlike promontory of granite that rises above the limestone plain of La Beauce, France. The name Chartres is derived from the Celtic word *cairn*, which means "place of the altar." This locale was sacred to the Celtic peoples of France, the Carnutes. Before the rise of Christianity a druidic cult of the black Madonna existed at Chartres. It anticipated the birth, in a grotto, of a Sun Child. A carved wooden statue of mother and child, darkened by fire, was worshipped here, and solemn processions brought the sculpture out every spring into the light of day amid celebrations of renewal and hope.[33] When the cathedral was built, the life-sized carving was taken in by the church until the time of French Revolution, when it was destroyed. Black Madonna traditions have survived elsewhere in the world, and the new religion is clearly anticipated in the old mystery.

A transformation of ancient mystery teachings appears in the philosophy of Plato, for he says of the macrocosm: "God has extended the body of the world on the soul of the world in the form of a cross."[34] This Logos was made flesh by entering into the human process of earthly incarnation and death. In this way the Logos or Christ fulfills not only the predictions of the Hebrew prophets, but also the spiritual mandates of the ancient mysteries. As Steiner says in *Christianity as Mystical Fact*, "Initiates raised themselves through initiation up into the sphere of the Logos and carried this Logos influence with them in their human life. The fundamental difference between them and Jesus was the fact that the Logos, in the course of its evolution, individualized itself into One Divine Individuality who descended into Jesus of Nazareth at the Baptism, and so the Logos manifested its whole Divine individuality through the personality of Jesus as far as it was possible to express Divinity by human means."[35] This is the unique character of the Christ Mystery, which is depicted from various sides in Christian art.

APPENDIX 4: The Southern Mysteries

In the golden age the gods, robed in air, walked among men.
— Hesiod

In ancient Egypt, the human being was imagined as being laid in the coffin of the physical body at birth. This physical body was a work of art created by the gods and therefore was not allowed to be destroyed at death. Its divine laws and harmonious proportions served as a model for constructing the temple architecture and its art. The body was necessary for further earthly as well as spiritual development, although it led on the one hand to a plunging into materialism, and on the other to a concern for the redemption of matter. Founded by Hermes Trismegistus, "the inventor of all the arts and sciences known to the Egyptians,"[36] the Egyptian Mysteries focused on the riddle of the physical body, of material death, and of spiritual resurrection. Egyptian esoteric tradition leads back through a Southern Mystery stream to the biblical Cain, son

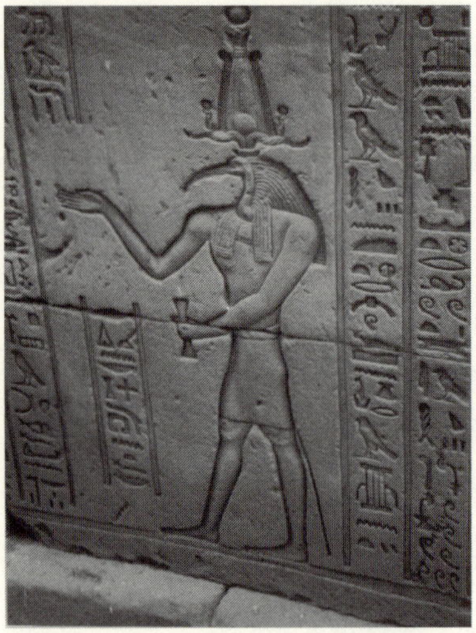

Fig. 293. Thoth, the Egyptian god of divine intelligence, was known to the Greeks as Hermes Trismegistus (Hermes the Thrice Great) and to the Hebrews as Enoch. Bas-relief from Hathor Temple, Dendera. (Copyright © Dot Mason.)

of Adam, who worked in the soil and cultivated plants in an agrarian relationship to the earth and the sun. The name Cain means "he who can" or, ironically, "he who is able." Abel, Cain's younger brother, was a nomad and a shepherd, living freely from the wild produce of nature as a hunter-gatherer. Abel lived out of the mysteries of the moon, Cain out of those of the sun. According to a Rosicrucian tradition, Cain was borne by Eve before Adam was created by Jehovah.[37] Jehovah thus refused the offerings of Cain but accepted those of Abel. In his rejection, Cain slew Abel, and according to legend, the task of Cain's descendants was to transform their impassioned willpower through the arts and crafts. This tradition speaks of three sons of Cain—Jabal, a builder; Tubal, a master of metal work; and Jubal, the creator of musical instruments. A daughter of Cain is credited with inventing spinning and weaving.[38] The great initiate, Enoch, of the Cain stream (there was also a descendent of Seth called Enoch—Seth was the younger brother of Abel and carried on Abel's lineage) is credited with building the first town. Hellenistic tradition speaks of Enoch as being Hermes Tristmegistus (the Thrice Great), founder of the Egyptian civilization. Enoch-Hermes, known also as the god Thoth to Egyptians, was seen as the embodiment of divine intelligence (fig. 293). He was the "lord of writing," "the mighty speaker," "the judge of the two combatants."[39]

Hiram, also a descendant of Cain, is likewise an inheritor of this line's talent in art and technology. He is responsible for the realization of Solomon's temple, the first permanent structure to house the sacred Ark of the Covenant. King Solomon, a descendant of the Seth line, possessed great wisdom, directly inspired by God, but detached from earthly accomplishments. Hiram, a master builder, possessed the practical skills and passionate enthusiasm to make the temple a reality. The Temple Legend, which concerns the tension between Hiram and Solomon, as well as the struggle around Hiram's three apprentices in the building of the temple, is an esoteric picture of the soul's initiation into religious piety and knowledge of the outer world. The Queen of Sheba is the soul of humanity who must, as Bernard Lievegoed puts it, choose between "detached piety, which does not concern itself with worldly conquest [Solomon], and the masterful wisdom which is achieved through the overcoming of earthly passions and desires [Hiram]."[40]

This Cainite, or Southern, stream passes from Egypt and Israel to Europe by way of the engineering skills and technical knowledge, as well as the legal and judicial practices, of Rome. This technical-legalistic development was an exoteric outcome of these Southern Mysteries that were founded on esoteric insight into the human physical body. This stream worked in turn on the growth and development of Christianity. According to Steiner, the spread of Christianity had to do with the "system of law that we call the Roman Catholic religion. There, God, with attendant gods, is essentially a Being who rules from the supersensible world according to the Roman concept of justice. There we find the ideas of debt and default established. They are legal ideas that never existed in the mysteries of the East or in the Greek philosophy of life. In this

Christianity the juridical concepts of Rome are established. It is a religious stream saturated with legalities. Everything that finds expression in life can assume a form of beauty, but we must confess that even that juridical-political scene in which the God of the World becomes the Judge of the World and winds up the whole evaluation of the earth by one legal act, even that magnificent painting of Michelangelo in the Sistine Chapel, is only a glorious expression of Christianity saturated by legalism. It is just this Christianity saturated by legalism that finds its culmination in the 'Last Judgment.'"[41]

It was this "legal" character of the Southern stream that in Central Europe led to a mechanistic interpretation of the mysteries of the human being, but it was also this stream that brought to birth the Rosicrucian movement, which took on the inner struggle against the juridical forms of the Church. Through their study of "hermetic scriptures," the Rosicrucians occupied themselves with medicine, alchemy, and the improvement of various crafts. Their search for the Philosophers' Stone was, when sincere, the treading of an esoteric Christian path and a continuation of the Southern Mystery stream carried over from ancient Egypt.

Thus this Southern Mystery stream appears in the Cain line and works through the founding of the Egyptian culture, as well as through the building of Solomon's Temple. It then appears in ancient Roman technology, and later in Middle European banking interests and business skills. Lievegoed characterizes the inner and outer aspects in the following way: "The exoteric stream, which finally led to materialism, went via Egypt and Rome to our bourgeois materialistic culture. The esoteric stream went via the Jewish people. . . to the Lazarus-John mystery and the medieval form to be found in the Rosicrucianism of the intellectual soul period. This Rosicrucianism also has to find a new form in the [present] consciousness soul age through uniting itself with the new mysteries."[42]

APPENDIX 5: World Megaliths

The diversity of cult sites confirms the ceremonial function of the monuments; the mounds covering tombs were not only places of burial but also ceremonial centers.
—Jean-Pierre Mohen

Although there is a great concentration of megalithic sites associated with the pre-Celtic peoples in Western Europe, similar sites can be found throughout the world, from Scandinavia and Africa to the Far East and North and South America. The erecting of large stone structures is clearly a worldwide practice. Western European megaliths are generally dated between c. 5000 and 1000 B.C., the same time period in which the great structures of Egypt were built.[43]

In the Caucasus Mountain region around the Black Sea an unusual megalithic style developed about the middle of the third millennium B.C. Rectangular-shaped stone slabs were placed in such a way as to form an enclosed and roofed box chamber (fig. 294). Entrance was made through a single round "porthole," large enough for a small person to slip through. Also called a "soul hole" or "oracle hole," the opening is associated with the passing of the dead and sounding forth of proclamations from the spirit world, alluding to both burial and shamanic practice. A plug-stone was used to close the chamber from outside. Richly fashioned metal and stone artifacts have been recovered from some of these monuments that were used as burial chambers for highborn persons.[44]

Chambers with porthole openings have also been found in Pakistan and India, where megalithic practices for the dead were still active into the nineteenth century. In association with burial mounds (tumuli) and dolmens for the dead, standing stones were sometimes erected in order to house ancestral spirits that would come to live in the locale.

Megalithic chambers are also found in coastal areas of the Near East, such as Palestine and Israel. These monuments are generally dated to around the fourth millennium B.C. and also have standing stones associated with them. This is the neighborhood where Jacob, while sleeping on a stone, had his dream of the "ladder" and vision of God. Upon waking, he set his bedstone upright "for a pillar" and anointed it with oil, exclaiming that the stone was "none other but the house of God, and this [stone] is the gate of heaven" (Genesis 28:11). According to legend this stone was then taken to the Temple of Jerusalem where the kings of Judah were crowned as they sat upon it. We are told that a daughter of the last

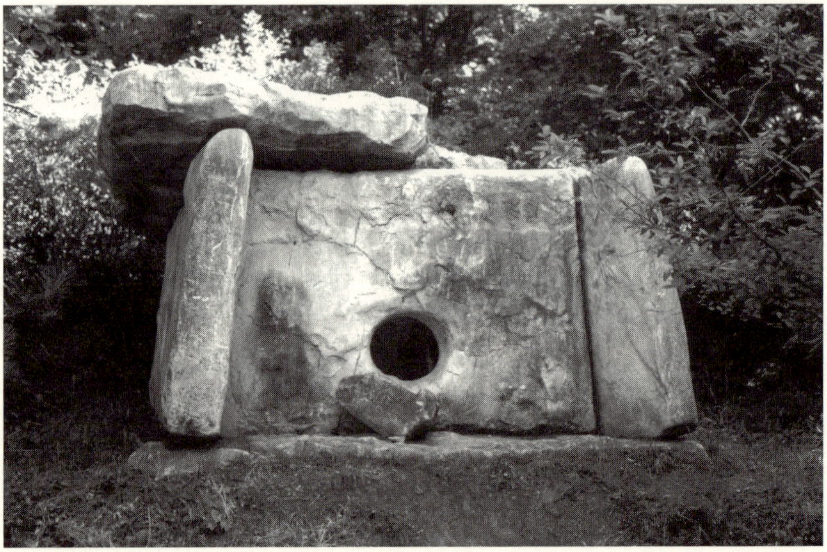

Fig. 294. A unique type of megalithic chamber made of rectangular stone slabs is found in the Caucasus Mountain region around the Black Sea. Entrance is gained through a "soul hole."

king of Judah took the stone to Ireland when she married into the royal line of Irish kings and there it was used for the crowning rituals among the Irish. Tradition says it was moved to Scone, Scotland, between A.D. 500 and A.D. 900, where it was likewise used for royal coronations. Edward I brought the Stone of Scone to London in 1297, where it was placed beneath a specially built Coronation Chair in Westminster Abbey. Today, Jacob's "gate of heaven" stone still rests in Westminster Abbey.

The Kaffir, a tribe of the Hindu Kush, say of the upright stones they honor: "This stands for God; but we know not His shape."[45] It is also of note that Hermes, "the messenger of the gods" in Greek mythology, was often honored by an upright stone supported by a pile of smaller rocks. *Hermes* (*herma*) means "stone heap," and throughout the prehistoric Mediterranean such stacked stones served as boundary markers and landmarks for wayfarers. Also, father (*pater*) and stone (*petros*) are related as mother (*mater*) is linked to matter.

Other megalithic sites are found in Malta, Algeria, Ethiopia, Nigeria, Madagascar, and Egypt. A 6500-year-old astronomical stone alignment called Nabta, in southwestern Egypt, has recently been discovered, with a stone circle twelve feet in diameter and four upright slabs aligned north-south to what would have been the summer solstice in the era of its construction. Excavations have uncovered several cow burials used in rituals and it is believed by some that the Nabta culture gave rise to the later Egyptian dynasties, which likewise consecrated elaborate tombs of megalithic proportions with the burial of bulls.

Jean-Pierre Mohen describes the building of megalithic tumuli in traditional cultures: "Once all the stones were assembled at the building-site, three oxen were killed: the fat from their bodies was used to grease the blocks, and everyone had some meat. The astrologer indicated where to dig holes to set up the columns, and the stones were finally put in place and then covered with a tumulus. . . . A nobleman who died while on a voyage or away at war, so that his body could not be brought back home, was commemorated by a standing stone set up beside the tumulus."[46]

In Tibet and China, rows of menhirs often lead up to dolmen and tumuli. Dolmen, called *che-pin* ("stone tables") in China, and *ko-in-dol* ("supported stones") in Manchuria and Korea, are often massive in size.[47] It is believed that megalithic monuments such as standing stones and dolmen spread across Japan in about the third century B.C. as a part of the Yayoi culture. During the Kofun period, from the third to the seventh centuries A.D., thousands of tumuli were built, including the colossal "keyhole" type. The largest of these barrows is the fifth-century Mausoleum of Emperor Nintoku in Osaka. The keyhole ground plan points to a consecrated place where the mystery of death is entered and unlocked (fig. 295).

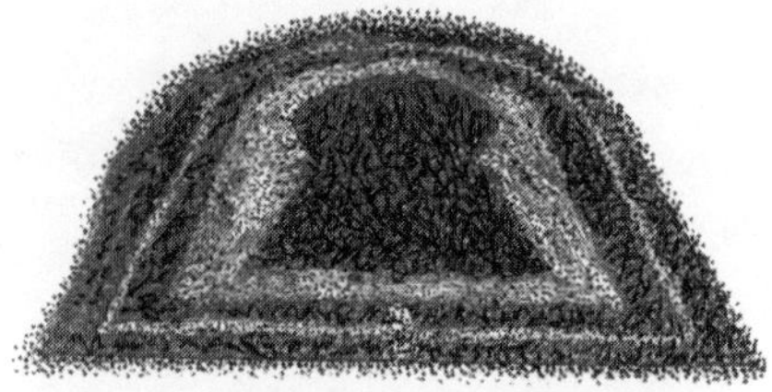

Fig. 295. This keyhole-type tumulus, rendered here as an aerial view, was built in the fifth century A.D. as the mausoleum for Emperor Nintoku in Osaka, Japan.

Most Pacific megaliths are dated to after the time of Christ, and they can be found in such places as Malekula in the New Hebrides, Tongatabu in Tonga, Nuku Hiva in the Marquesas Islands, Rapa Nui (Easter Island), and Micronesia (figs. 257–59). In Borneo, standing stones were erected to commemorate an act of courage, and a buffalo was ceremoniously sacrificed as part of the ritual observance.[48]

Megalithic sites in South America appeared before the second millennium B.C. in the upland valley of San Agustin, Magdalena, in Colombia. Built upon terraces cut into the mountainside at an altitude of 6000 feet, dolmen and tumuli can be found along with large stone sculptures. The statue-menhirs anticipate later South and Central American stone sculpture, such as those found in the Olmec civilization (fig. 233).

Over fifty dolmens survive in North America, mostly along the Northeast coastal region where granite is in abundance. The largest of these is located in North Salem, New York, an hour outside of New York City. Resting on five upright boulders, the capstone weighs an estimated ninety tons (fig. 296). An informational sign at the site explains the dolmen as the result of glacial activity. Megalithic chambers and standing stones are found at the Mystery Hill complex in North Salem, New Hampshire, and astronomical alignments have been demonstrated at this and other North American megalithic sites.

As mentioned earlier, megalithic standing stones were seen as the residence of ancestral spirits or other deities. Tumuli, dolmen and stone circles could be repositories for the dead as well as sites for sacred rituals and initiation proceedings. Megalithic monuments were constructed by many cultures that were linked only by their primal spirit and art.

Fig. 296. This dolmen is one of fifty known megaliths of its kind in North America and is located just north of New York City. An informational sign at the site explains the dolmen as the result of glacial activity during the last Ice Age. Traditional wisdom and archaeological evidence point to the dolmen as a sacred site of human construction.

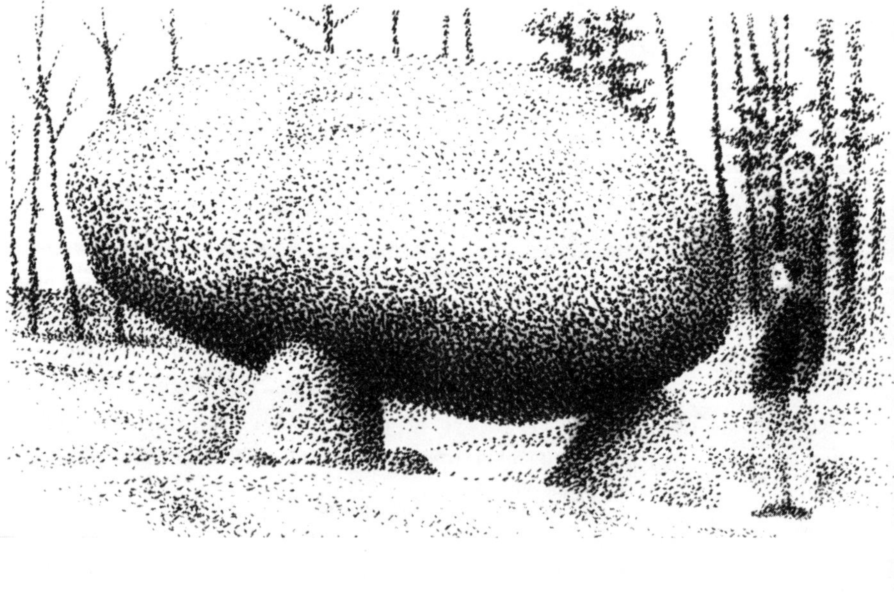

APPENDIX 6: The Serpent

The prominence of the serpent in the mythologies—whether of the primal, tribal class or of the later, historical orders—is a mystery of profound psychological and sociological import. Repeatedly shedding its skin to be born again, the serpent—like the moon that sheds its shadow in rebirth—typifies life-energy and consciousness locked within temporal space, delivering and suffering births and deaths.

—Joseph Campbell

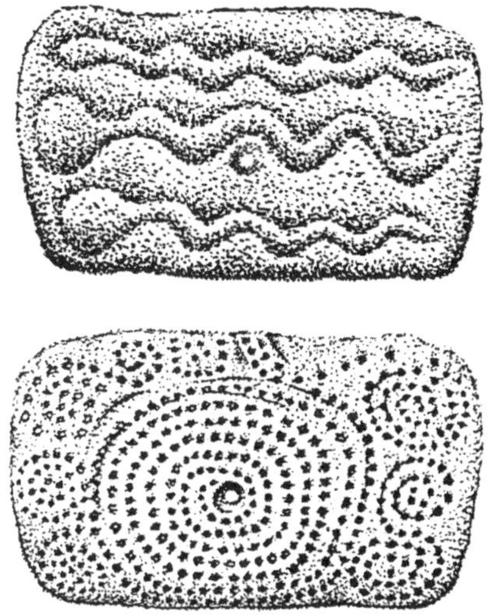

Fig. 297. Above: Spirals and serpent forces have been considered synonymous from the earliest of times, as this rendering of a mammoth ivory from Paleolithic Siberia demonstrates.

The coils, spirals, and meanders of the serpent appear in the very earliest art forms, and the serpent's energy is associated with elemental forces, not the least of which is the sun. Perhaps the oldest snake and spiral image is engraved on a Paleolithic mammoth ivory from Siberia. It features, surrounded by six smaller spirals, a large spiral of dots emanating from a central drill-hole. The opposite side of the tablet bears three undulating serpents. As a talisman, its purpose is unknown (fig. 297). Marija Gimbutas says, "The dynamism of the serpent is a very ancient and recurrent human preoccupation. The snake's energy, it was believed, was drawn from water and the sun. The archaic metaphor that pairs the magical power of the serpent with the creative force in nature must have crystallized very early from a natural intuition. This imaginative metaphor is thoroughly integrated in the art of Old Europe: snake coils as Divine Eyes appear singly or joined (a double spiral) as a design motif on ceramics, temples, and tombs."[49] Snakes were thought to have good eyesight, and so represented the all-seeing eye of the sun. For this reason they served as guardians of the temples, oracles, and treasuries.

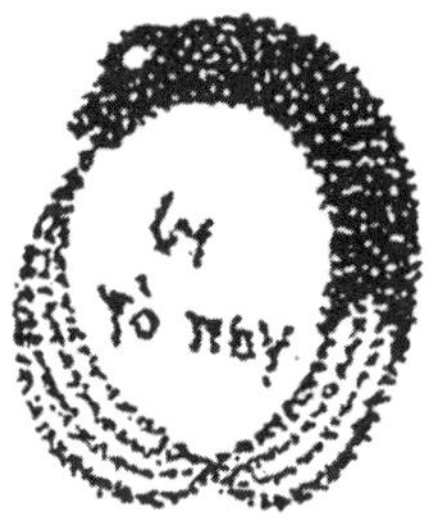

Fig. 298. Left: The *ouroboros,* the snake that bites its own tail, is a symbol of unending, cyclical time and represents the universe as in this ancient example linked to Cleopatra. The inscription reads, "The All in One."

Devouring its own tail as the *ouroboros,* the snake was a symbol of cosmic movement and eternal time (fig. 298). Compare this ancient image with Rudolf Steiner's seal design created to accompany one of his play's programs (fig. 299). The Egyptians used the sacred *uraeus,* the viper Haje coiled in a circle, as a crown on the falcon head of Horus, god of the rising sun, to represent the sun's daily cycle (fig. 300). Hieroglyphic texts in the tomb of Seti I state, "The souls of all the gods reside in the serpents."[50]

Fire, wind, life, breath, and spirit are elements associated with the snake that mark it as a creature of the Goddess. "Its vital influence was felt not only in life creation, but also in fertility and increase, and particularly in the regeneration of dying life energy"—all characteristics of Goddess worship.[51]

The snake as primal earth energy is described in many myths and legends

Fig. 299. Below: Rudolf Steiner designed his own *ouroboros* motif as a seal for his fourth mystery drama, The *Soul's Awakening,* 1913. He placed the words "I know myself" in relation to this image. (After Steiner.)

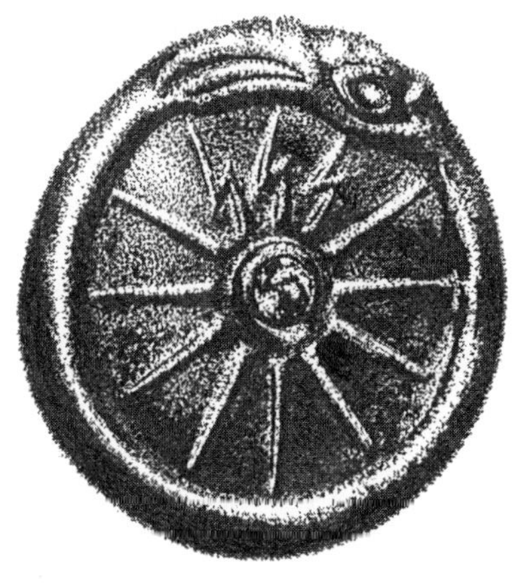

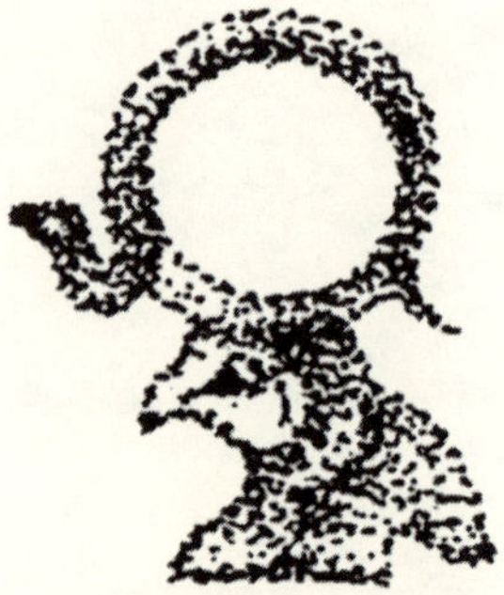

Fig. 300. Horus, the falcon-headed god (above) of the Egyptians, wears the coiled *uraeus* snake as a crown, which also suggests a halo. Its circular design indicates the cyclical nature of the sun.

Fig. 301. Below: The image of the serpent winding up the tree not only arises out of the Old Testament, but can also be found in the Americas at Chichén Itzá, Yucatan. The Serpent on the Tree is a picture of the caduceus, an upright staff entwined by one or two serpents representing the curative powers of Asclepius, god of medicine.

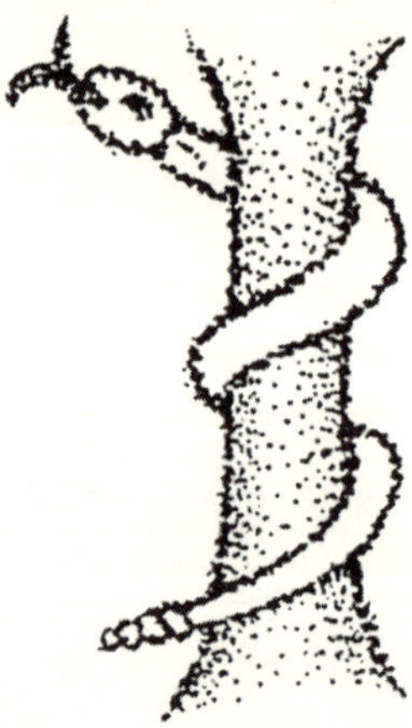

throughout the world. In heroic times the Greeks represented the rainbow by three blue serpents and, according to Homer, this symbolism appeared on Agamemnon's armor. The Australian Aborigines speak of a "Rainbow Serpent" in their Dreamtime creation saga, and in the Andes the serpent is identified with tectonic upheavals.

The practice of nature religions represented by the serpent was gradually overthrown, a defeat symbolized in the many serpent killings found in Greek legends. Zeus kills the serpent Syphon, Apollo kills the serpent Python, and Hercules kills the serpent Ladon.[52] This overcoming of the serpent forces may point to a change of old social and political orders, but it may also indicate significant changes in the spiritual make-up of the human being as well. The fading of primal consciousness with its atavistic clairvoyance, and the birth of intellectual cognition—logical, critical, analytical thinking—may be related to the shedding of the so-called reptilian brain functions of instinctive awareness. The sculpted group Laocoön, discussed in Chapter II, portrays this very theme with the twist that it is not the serpent but its human representatives that are slain (fig. 78).

The serpent ascending the Tree of Life is more than a Judeo-Christian symbol. It is an image that appears in Pre-Columbian relief sculpture at Chichén Itzá in the Yucatan (fig. 301) and in the Feathered Serpent of the Americas. The serpent in Asian tradition is a protector of the world and is adopted by Buddhism from its outset. Legend claims that the Naga serpent kings appeared at the birth of the Buddha, and one of them later disguises himself as a human king to listen to a sermon by the Buddha. One of the Nagas, named Mucilinda, is depicted sheltering the meditating Buddha during a torrential rainstorm by coiling itself around him to form a protective awning with its hood (fig. 302).

Although Judeo-Christian mythology associates the serpent with the tempter, Lucifer ("the light bringer") and the devil, it must be remembered that, according to this metaphor, along with the Fall (into sin) came freedom. This freedom from union with God was according to divine plan, although it was meant to have happened more gradually. Still, the serpent is not always negative in Western culture, for we have managed to maintain the symbolic associations of the snake with the medical profession. Traditionally the upright staff of Mercury is joined by one or two vertically winding snakes, which symbolize the ascending life forces and healing powers of nature. The healing serpents born of Demeter, the Earth Mother, climb the caduceus of Asclepius, god of medicine. (Asclepius is identified with the Egyptian pharaoh Imenhotep.)

The rod of Moses, which could change into a serpent, is a similar picture. This mystery image of the rod expresses the principle of clear thinking in its overcoming of ancient, instinctive vision, according to Emil Bock. In Indian Hatha

Yoga practices, the Kundalini serpent, residing at the base of the spine, is grasped by the tail, and, working from below upwards, is transformed into the staff of magical powers and instinctive vision. This utilization of the most unconscious forces of human nature as a starting point of a spiritual path was the opposite approach to that which Moses promoted at the dawn of self-consciousness. The serpent ruled over the human being as the staff of ancient clairvoyance in the spine and central nervous system. The staff of Moses represents control of the serpent's energy. "It takes hold of the serpent at the head; it takes its course from above to below, taking its point of departure from the clearly conscious thought element and not permitting any step through which the clear consciousness of thinking-experiences are interrupted. Thereby it is the staff of freedom and ego. When it comes more and more clearly into man's possession, it develops . . . into a spiritual frontal spine in the supersensory human form."[53] However, more and more this serpent force emerged as "temptation and doom on the tree of man's being."[54] Today humanity is the Staff of Life on which the serpent powers are sacrificed. Moses represents the first initiate to lift the lower elements of human nature and transform them on a Western spiritual path in awakened consciousness. According to legend, the staff (a brazen serpent) of Moses was kept in the Temple of Jerusalem until the time of Isaiah, when it was destroyed by King Hezekiah (II Kings 18:4). This indicates that at the time of the prophets, a further stage in the development of consciousness is necessary and "certain spiritual directions of the Moses age had to be opposed."[55] Steiner suggests, "When you gaze upon the serpent, you see a sign for your I (ego). You must vividly feel that the independent I and the serpent belong together. The right way of seeing, is at first symbolically. For example, when the human being concentrates on the spine, in this one sees the serpent."[56]

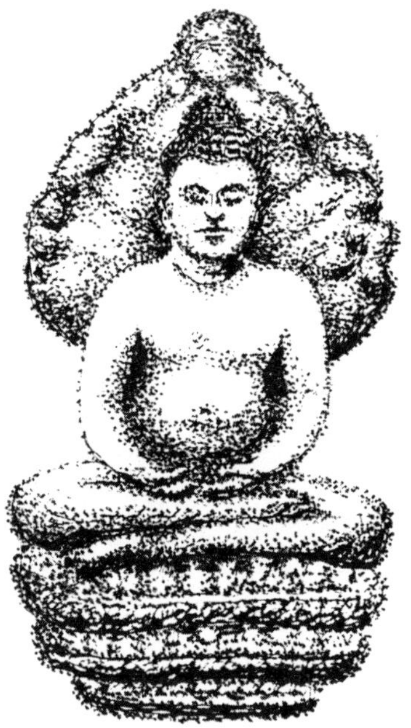

Fig. 302. Above: Mucilinda, one of the royal Naga serpents, is remembered for coiling himself around Siddartha and sheltering the future Buddha from the rain with his hood.

Although the serpent is cursed by God in Genesis 3:14–15, Jesus advises his followers to be as "wise as serpents and as harmless as doves" (Matthew 10:16). There are examples of bishop's and abbot's staffs or croziers with this symbolism clearly spelled out (fig. 303). Certain early Gnostic sects saw the serpent as a symbol of Christ. Hippolytus, describing an early Christian cult, delivers such testimony as: "No one can be saved and rise up again without the Son, who is the Serpent."[57]

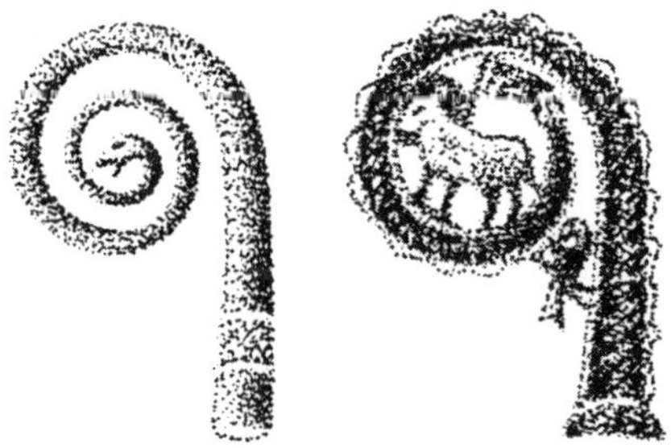

Fig. 303. Above left: Some pastoral staves, as in this rendering of a French abbot's crozier, show the serpent as a symbol of Christ.

Above right: A bishop's crozier depicts the serpent, the lamb, and the dove as a trinity in the bestiary of Christian faith. The serpent imparts wisdom, the dove embodies harmlessness, and the Lamb of God is Christ.

The image of the serpent is far-reaching and of deep spiritual significance throughout the course of history. At certain times its energy and power is regarded as good, while at others it is considered uncontrollable and evil. Whether associated with earth energy, Lucifer and the Goddess or with cosmic forces, solar divinity, and Christ, the serpent has always been a spiritual power to be reckoned with.

APPENDIX 7: Primal Humanity

It is not a question here of how we must turn, twist, limit, or curtail the phenomenon so that it can still be explained. . . but it is a question rather of the direction in which we must expand our ideas to come to terms with the phenomenon.

—Friedrich Schelling

When the physiognomy of a young chimpanzee is considered side by side with that of an adult of the same species, it becomes clear that the young chimp begins at a humanlike stage before developing toward its apelike maturity (fig. 304). It starts out with a rounded skull, high forehead, and vertical jaw. Only as it grows older does the animal become more specialized and fixed in its form with elongated skull, low forehead, and horizontal jaw. The young simian looks almost human, whereas the adult ape becomes more truly an animal. We might ask how the human being can evolve from a creature that itself develops away from what is characteristically human in appearance.

The same question arises if we look at the human hand, which, as we have seen, is an important theme in prehistoric art. The human hand is held back in its development compared to the animal paw. Whereas the various animal species have developed their limbs into highly specialized tools, the human hand has not become function-specific as have the wings of birds, the claws of bears, the hoofs of horses, or the flippers of seals. The human hand is an example of arrested development, as comparative anatomy, embryology, and paleontology demonstrate. What the human hand retains is a certain universality of form and function. Wolfgang Schad, in *Man and Mammals: Toward a Biology of Form*, says: "It is just the imperfection of man's hand that permits him a choice, a choice that no animal can make to the same extent. Man's perfection is his imperfection: he can learn to choose freely what nature has not decided for him. In most cases the animal is permanently tied to the tool; its limbs have become and thus remain dependent on a certain environment."[58]

Such observations as the retention of primary characteristics in the human form can lead to the conclusion that humanity is not necessarily at the top of the genealogical tree but in fact finds its place much further down the trunk. If popular science had not grown so accustomed to seeing *Homo sapiens* at the top of the evolutionary list, it probably would have been moved lower down long ago, at least to where the primary mammals and pouched animals are placed.[59] Though many scientists are reluctant to shift the human being's position on the ancestral tree, it becomes apparent that the human being may well provide a model for revealing the unity within the tremendous variety of the animal kingdom. For Steiner, the human being "does not provide the archetype for any single animal; [but] is instead the archetype that reveals how all the animal species, in their abundant diversity, form a coherent whole."[60]

According to such a picture the human being does not spring from the animal kingdom in the way customarily believed by evolutionists, but contains all the animals in the form of tendencies. As the plant kingdom takes on insectlike forms and characteristics, so too do the higher mammals suggest human characteristics in their features. This does not mean that man has evolved from animals any more than insects have evolved from their codependent plants. Each stands within a unique kingdom of nature, yet is intimately connected with the other.

Such a theory of evolution, radical as it may seem in placing the human being not as a finished end product of animal development but as an evolving kingdom of nature in its own right, does not contradict any existing scientific observations. It is simply a different interpretation of the data. This view finds itself between the polarized arguments of the religious creationists and the scientific evolutionists, and articulates a more artistically balanced alternative (not simply a compromise) based entirely on the developmental phenomena and the language of form visible within the living world of nature.

This approach to the question of origins suggests that our early human ancestors may have been of such a form and substance that would not have been able to leave fossil evidence in their wake. This idea is not without precedent, for it has been demonstrated that important transition stages in the development of siliceous sponges from the Cretaceous period must have been of a kind that could not fossilize. Schad points out: "All the fossil and contemporary organisms we can observe are related to one another through ancestors that actually existed. We can imagine, however, that these omnipotential forms, like the vegetative cone of the plant, which remains in an embryonic state, could not be preserved as fossils because of their tentative plasticity and lack of firm substance. Yet they must have existed, or there could not be the obvious relationships we now see among their descendants."[61] So too with the human being.

Observation of the early embryonic stages of human development reveal a being with a malleable body, composed of soft and pliable living substance. Even for some time after birth the child is not yet as solid and firm as the adult. The infant's bones remain flexible, and the skull only gradually closes at the fontanel. We might imagine the primal human being as much less dense and less hardened than the human being of today—a soft and supple creature in an atmosphere dense with moisture. Steiner suggests: "The further we go back in earth evolution, the more liquid man becomes and the more he is really a soft jellylike mass—not formed out of present-day water—but out of a substance somewhat like albumen."[62] Imagine an early humanity living in a primeval, womblike condition where the earth is only just beginning to solidify. As described by Steiner, primal humanity at this time has a high, fluid forehead and a unique cartilaginous form. If such an evolutionary scenario were the case, then primal humanity, our direct ancestors, could not be descended from the ape or leave fossil remains such as the Neanderthal with its receding brow and horizontal jaw. Many researchers now disclaim the Neanderthal as a direct ancestor of *Homo sapiens,* and see it as a parallel branch.

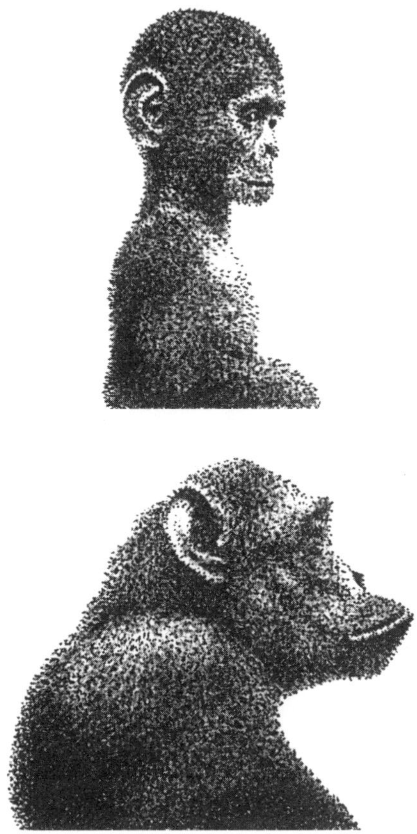

Fig. 304. The head of a young chimpanzee reveals a greater similarity to that of a human than to the head of the mature chimpanzee. According to its form, the chimpanzee appears to grow away from human resemblance rather than toward it.

According to Steiner, before the present human race with its solid bones, a more supple humanity with a high culture existed in a very different earth environment (fig. 305).[63] This primal humanity had a naive curiosity regarding organic form as the basis of "artistic" expression. "People had an especially sensitive feeling for the way water begins to freeze. This gave them the specific impulse to push it in one direction and another, so that the ice-forms appearing in the water took on certain shapes. Indeed people went so far as to keep their hands in the water while the shapes developed and their hands grew numb. In this way, when the water froze under the waves their hands cast up, it assumed the most remarkable artistic shapes, which of course again melted away."[64]

Such a picture of early humanity, although seemingly science fiction, is not incompatible with observable facts or with early art and mythology. For millennia the origins of humanity have been explained in imaginative, mythological terms with an emphasis on spiritual aspects of development. Every ancient culture has its creation myths. The theory of natural selection and the notion of humanity evolving from lower primates are a mere 150 years old. This modern myth of man as animal, evolving into a postmodern picture of man as a machine that might one day download its capacities into sophisticated computer systems, is no less science fiction than the picture of humanity proposed above. Our artistic heritage offers a valuable glimpse of primal humanity, one that challenges the pale and shallow "caveman" caricature of the modern era. The image of what a human being is must be constantly reevaluated as consciousness evolves and our worldview changes. What will we believe our origins to be in another 150 years, or in another millennium? The arts give us an insightful glimpse into the inner life of humanity as well as an overview and future vision of our universe. What is important is how we decide to understand and interpret spirit and art.

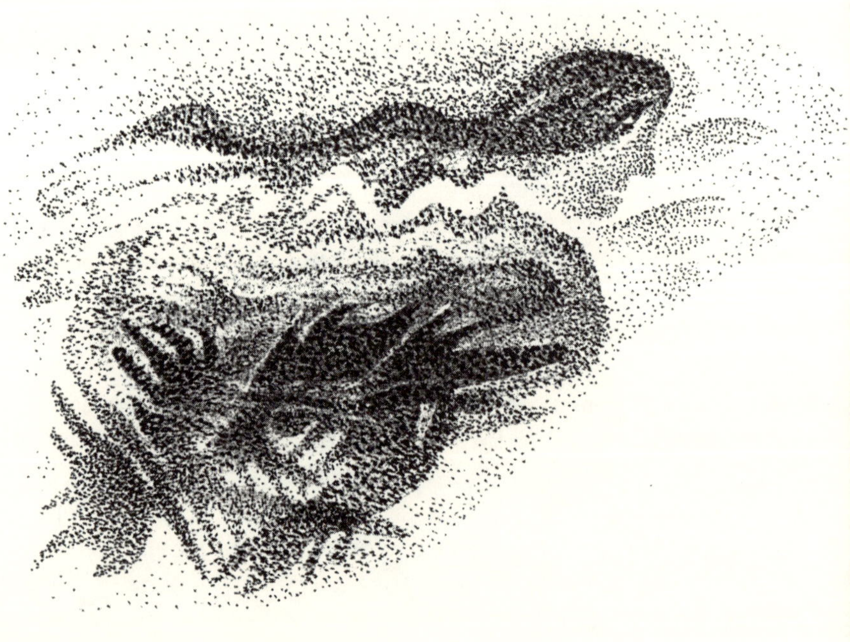

Fig. 305. Archetypal Man/Animal, 1924, a watercolor painting by Rudolf Steiner of the primal human being. (After Steiner.)

Notes

1. Barfield, O. *Saving the Appearances,* p. 42.
2. Barfield, p. 172.
3. Tarnas, R. *The Passion of the Western Mind,* p. 443.
4. Schiller, F. *Letters on the Aesthetic Education of Man,* p. 74.
5. Cited in Argüelles, p. 90.
6. Campbell, J. *World Atlas of Mythology,* p. xiii.
7. Herbert Kuhn, in his *Die Felsbilder Europas,* likewise describes two modes of artistic representation: "imaginative" and "sensory."
8. Steiner, R. "The Aesthetics of Goethe's World-view," cited in *Art as Spiritual Activity,* p. 130.
9. Goethe, J. "The Artist's Apotheosis," cited in *Art as Spiritual Activity,* p. 133.
10. Belting, H. *Likeness and Presence: A History of Image before the Era of Art.*
11. Hegel, G.W.F. *Aesthetics,* II. Cited in Danto, p. 31.
12. Steiner, R. *Das Wesen des Musicalischen. Cited in Rinder, Knowledge of Higher Worlds: Rudolf Steiner's Blackboard Drawings,* p. 32.
13. Gerard Wagner (1906–99). See Wagner, E. *Gerard Wagner: Katalog zur Ausstellung.*
14. Prokofieff, S. *Das Goetheanum: Wochenschrift für Anthroposophy,* "Nachrichten," December 19, 1999.
15. Hemleben, J. *Rudolf Steiner,* p. 16.
16. Steiner. Cited in Seddon, R. *Understanding the Human Being,* p. 155.
17. Ibid., p. 156.
18. Steiner, *Lucifer Gnosis,* No. 34, 1907.
19. Steiner, R. *Bilder okkulter Siegel und Säulen,* pp. 112–13.
20. The name *Johannes* points to the biblical figure of John, the only apostle present at the crucifixion and "the one whom Jesus loved." Steiner refers to this figure in lectures on Christology as the first Christian initiate. In his last address, a lecture given on September 29, 1924, Steiner describes a special link between John the Apostle and John the Baptist.
21. *The Soul's Probation, The Guardian of the Threshold, and The Soul's Awakening.*
22. Steiner, R. January 1, 1915. Cited in Wagner, G. and E. Koch, p. 11.
23. Sullivan. L. *Kindergarten Talks and Other Writings,* 1909.
24. Wright, F.L. *In the Cause of Architecture,* 1914.
25. Steiner. Cited in Hauck, H. *Handwork Indications,* p. 41.
26. Steiner. *The Course of My Life,* p. 347.
27. Streit, J. *Sun and Cross,* p. 68.
28. Bamford, C. *Celtic Christianity: Ecology and Holiness,* p. 11.
29. Keating, J. *The General History of Ireland.* Cited in Streit, p. 68.
30. "Over in Asia the Mystery of Golgotha took place; in Jerusalem the events came to pass that were later made known to men in the Gospels by the way of tradition. But in the moment when the tragedy of the Mystery of Golgotha was being enacted in Palestine, in that very moment it was known and beheld clairvoyantly in the Mysteries of Hibernia. No report was brought by word of mouth, no communication whatever was possible; but in the Mysteries of Hibernia the event was fulfilled in a symbol, in a picture, at the same time that it was fulfilled in actual fact in Jerusalem. Men came to know of it, not through tradition but by a spiritual path." Steiner, R. *Mystery Centers,* pp. 78–79.
31. These Celtic priests wore their hair long in druid fashion, and shaved a tonsure from ear to ear at the front of their scalp, in the style of St. John the Evangelist. The Roman monks, like St. Peter, shaved a circular tonsure on the crown of the head, and followed a distinctly Petrine missionary path. With the cross as its herald, this Southern stream of Christianity recognized only the "correct doctrine" of the Roman Church. The Celtic Johannine path was based on the spiritual experience of the individual. "You will know the truth and the truth will set you free" (John 8:32). This latter stream spread throughout Europe with the sign of the sun cross (circle and cross), as a transformation of the Hibernian or Western Mystery stream. It was eventually superseded by Southern Christianity around A.D. 900. See Streit, pp. 157–72, and Lievegoed, p. 31.
32. Steiner, R. *Mystery Centers,* p. 81.
33. Querido, R. *The Golden Age of Chartres: The Teachings of a Mystery School and the Eternal Feminine,* pp. 21–25.
34. Steiner, *Christianity as Mystical Fact,* p. 225.
35. Ibid, p. 141.
36. Budge, E. *Egyptian Book of the Dead,* p. cxviii.
37. Steiner, R. *Temple Legends,* p. 58.
38. Lievegoed, B. *Mystery Streams in Europe and the New Mysteries,* p. 55.
39. Budge, p. cxviii.
40. Steiner, *Temple Legends,* p. 58.

41. Cited in Lievegoed, pp. 49–50.
42. Lievegoed, p. 63.
43. Mohen, J.P. *The World of Megaliths,* pp. 47–48.
44. Ibid., pp. 46–47.
45. Wood-Martin. Cited in Merry, E. *The Flaming Door,* p. 185.
46. Mohen, p. 57.
47. Joussaume, R. *Dolmens for the Dead,* p. 280.
48. Zink, D. The *Ancient Stones Speak,* pp. 150–75.
49. Gimbutas, M. *Language of the Goddess,* p. 58.
50. Charbonneau-Lassay, L. *The Bestiary of Christ,* p. 154.
51. Gimbutas, M. *Language of the Goddess,* p. 121.
52. Eisler, R. *The Chalice and the Blade,* p. 87.
53. Bock, E. *Moses,* pp. 105–6.
54. Ibid., p. 109.
55. Ibid.
56. Steiner, R. Cited in Grosse, R. p. 73.
57. Hippolytus, *Elenchos,* V. Cited in Leisegang, "The Mystery of the Serpent," *The Mysteries,* pp. 230-31.
58. Schad, W. *Man and Mammals,* p. 258.
59. Poppelbaum, H. *Man and Animal: Their Essential Differences,* p. 43.
60. Steiner, R. *Evolution of Earth and Man,* p. 267. "We must say that the ape descended from man, not that man descended from the ape," p. 55.
61. Schad, pp. 258–59.
62. Steiner, *Evolution of Earth and Man,* p. 55.
63. Ibid., pp. 58–59.
64. Steiner, R. *Cycle of the Year,* p. 65.

BIBLIOGRAPHY

Alexandrian, S. 1969. *Surrealist Art.* New York: Praeger.

Amiet, P. 1980. *Art of the Near East.* New York: Abrams.

Anderson, W. 1990. *Green Man: The Archetype of Our Oneness with the Earth.* New York: HarperCollins.

________. 1996. *The Face of Glory: Creativity, Consciousness and Civilization.* London: University Press of New England.

Ariswara. 1992. *Temples of Java.* Jakarta: Intermasa.

Argüelles, J. 1975. *The Transformative Vision.* Berkeley, CA: Shambhala.

Artress, L. 1995. *Walking a Sacred Path: Rediscovering the Labyrinth as a Spiritual Tool.* New York: Riverhead Books.

Bahn, P. and J. Vertut, 1988. *Images of the Ice Age.* New York: Facts on File.

Bamford, C. 1987. *Celtic Christianity: Ecology and Holiness.* Rochester, VT: Inner Traditions/Lindisfarne.

________, et al. 1994. *Homage to Pythagoras.* Hudson, NY: Lindisfarne.

Barfield, O. 1988. *Saving the Appearances: A Study in Idolatry.* Middletown, CT: Wesleyan University Press.

Baring, A. and J. Cashford. 1991. *The Myth of the Goddess: Evolution of an Image.* New York: Viking/Penguin.

Barnes, F. 1982. *Prehistoric Rock Art.* Salt Lake City, Utah: Wasatch Publishers.

Barrie, T. 1996. *Spiritual Path, Sacred Place: Myth, Ritual, and Meaning in Architecture.* Boston: Shambhala.

Barron, S. and W.D. Dube. 1997. *German Expressionism: Art and Society.* New York: Rizzoli.

Barrow, T. 1984. *An Illustrated Guide to Maori Art.* Honolulu: University of Hawaii Press.

Barzun, J. 1975. *The Use and Abuse of Art.* Princeton, NJ: Princeton University Press.

Beal, G. 1994. *Voyages and Vessels: David Nash.* Omaha, NB: Joslyn Art Museum.

Benson, J.L. 1970. *Horse, Bird, and Man: The Origins of Greek Painting.* Amherst, MA: University of Massachusetts Press.

Biesantz, H. 1979. *The Goetheanum: Rudolf Steiner's Architectural Impulse.* London: Rudolf Steiner Press.

Blatchford, J. 1989. *China: Ancient Inspiration and New Directions.* Sacramento, CA: Rudolf Steiner College Publications.

Blattmann, G. 1985. *The Sun: The Ancient Mysteries and the New Physics.* Edinburgh: Floris.

Blavatsky, H.P. 1977. *The Secret Doctrine.* Pasadena, CA: Theosophical University Press.

Bock, E. 1986. *Moses: From the Mysteries of Egypt to the Judges of Israel.* Edinburgh: Floris.

Bovi, A. 1971. *Kandinsky.* London: Hamlyn Publications.

Brandon, R. and B. Stephan. 1994. *Spirit and Symbol: The Japanese New Year.* Honolulu Academy of Arts.

Brauen, M. 1997. *The Mandala: Sacred Circle in Tibetan Buddhism.* Boston: Shambhala.

Brennan, M. 1983. *The Stars and the Stones: Ancient Art and Astronomy in Ireland.* London: Thames & Hudson.

Brion, M. 1966. *Art of the Romantic Era: Romanticism, Classicism, Realism.* New York: Praeger.

Brodrick, A. 1948. *Prehistoric Painting.* London: Avalon Press.

Brown, J. 1996. *The Riddles of the Pacific.* Kempton, IL: Adventures Unlimited Press.

Brunton, P. 1987. *The Notebooks: Human Experience, the Arts in Culture.* Vol. 9. New York: Larson Publications.

Bryce, D. 1989. *Symbolism of the Celtic Cross.* York Beach, ME: Samuel Weiser.

Budge, E.A.W. 1967. *The Egyptian Book of the Dead: The Papyrus of Ani.* New York: Dover Publications.

Cahill, R.E. 1993. *New England's Ancient Mysteries.* Salem, MA: Old Saltbox Publishing House, Inc.

Campbell, J. 1988. *Historical Atlas of World Mythology.* Vol. I & II. New York: Harper & Row.

________. 1990. *The Mysteries: Papers from the Eranos Yearbooks.* Bollingen Series XXX, 2. Princeton, NJ: Princeton University Press.

_____ and M. Gimbutas. 1995. *Language of the Goddess.* San Francisco: Harper.

________ and B. Moyers. 1988. *The Power of Myth.* New York: Doubleday.

Camphausen, R. 1996. *The Yoni: Sacred Symbol of Female Creative Power.* Rochester, VT: Inner Traditions International.

Carmichael, A. 1977. *The Sun Dances.* Edinburgh: Floris.

Carpenter, T. 1991. *Art and Myth in Ancient Greece.* London: Thames & Hudson.

Casson, L. 1970. *Ancient Egypt.* New York: Time-Life Books.

Charbonneau-Lassay, L. 1991. *The Bestiary of Christ.* New York: Parabola Books.

Chiang, Y. 1964. *The Chinese Eye: An Interpretation of Chinese Painting.* Bloomington, IN: Indiana University Press.

Chipp, H. 1973. *Theories of Modern Art: A Sourcebook by Artists and Critics.* Berkeley, CA: University of California Press.

Choucha, N. 1992. *Surrealism and the Occult: Shamanism, Magic, Alchemy, and the Birth of an Artistic Movement.* Rochester, VT: Destiny Books.

Christie, A. 1996. *Chinese Mythology.* New York: Barnes & Noble Books.

Clark, K. 1993. *Leonardo da Vinci.* New York: Penguin.

_______. 1973. *The Romantic Rebellion: Romantic Versus Classical Art.* New York: Harper & Row.

Clottes, J. and J. Courtin. 1994. *The Cave Beneath the Sea: Palaeolithic Images at Cosquer.* New York: Abrams.

_______ and D. Lewis-Williams. 1998. *The Shamans of Prehistory.* New York: Abrams.

Coe, M., R. Dirhl, F. K. Reilly III, L. Schele, et al. 1995. *The Olmec World: Ritual and Rulership.* New York: Abrams.

______, D. Snow and E. Benson. 1986. *Atlas of Ancient America.* New York: Facts on File.

Conway, W. M. 1958. *The Writings of Albrecht Dürer.* New York: Philosophical Library.

Cooke, I. 1987. *Journey to the Stones.* Penzance, England: Men-an-tol Studio.

Coomaraswamy, A. 1934. *The Transformation of Nature in Art.* New York: Dover Publications.

Corbin, G. 1988. *Native Arts of North America, Africa, and the South Pacific: An Introduction.* New York: Harper & Row.

Cowan, J. 1991. *Letters from a Wild State: An Aboriginal Perspective.* London: Element.

Cowan, T. 1993. *Fire in the Head: Shamanism and the Celtic Spirits.* New York: HarperCollins.

Cox, J.H. with W. Davenport, 1974. *Hawaiian Sculpture.* Honolulu: University of Hawaii Press.

______, with E. Stasack. 1980. *Hawaiian Petroglyphs.* Honolulu: Bishop Museum Press.

Critchlow, K. 1982. *Time Stands Still: New Light on Megalithic Science.* New York: St. Martin's Press.

Crumlin, R. and A. Knight. 1995. *Aboriginal Art and Spirituality,* North Blackburn, Australia: Dove.

Danielou, A. 1995. *The Phallus: Sacred Symbol of Male Creative Power.* Rochester, VT: Inner Traditions.

Danto, A. 1992. *Beyond the Brillo Box: The Visual Arts in Post-Historical Perspectives.* New York: Farrar, Straus and Giroux.

________. 1997. *After the End of Art: Contemporary Art and the Pale of History.* Princeton, NJ: Princeton University Press.

Dark, P. and R. Rose. 1993. *Artistic Heritage in a Changing Pacific.* Honolulu: University of Hawaii Press.

Dempsey, C. 1992. *The Portrayal of Love: Botticelli's* Primavera *and Humanist Culture at the Time of Lorenzo the Magnificent.* Princeton, NJ: Princeton University Press.

Deneck, M. 1971. *Indian Art.* London: Hamlyn.

Devereux, P. 1990. *Places of Power—Secret Energies at Ancient Sites: A Guide to Observed or Measured Phenomena.* London: Blandford.

Dillenberger, J. 1990. *Image and Sprit in Sacred & Secular Art.* New York: Crossroads.

Doob, P. 1990. *The Idea of the Labyrinth from Classical Antiquity through the Middle Ages.* Ithaca, NY: Cornell University Press.

Eisler, R. 1988. *The Chalice and the Blade.* San Francisco: Harper & Row.

Eliade, M. 1991. *Images and Symbols: Studies in Religious Symbolism.* Princeton, NJ: Princeton University Press.

________. 1964. *Shamanism: Archaic Techniques of Ecstasy.* Princeton, NJ: Princeton University Press.

________. 1985. *Symbolism, the Sacred, and the Arts.* New York: Crossroad Publishing Co.

Emerson, R.W. 1898. *The Complete Prose Works.* London: Ward, Lock & Co.

Fagan, B, 1995. *Ancient North America: The Archaeology of a Continent.* London: Thames & Hudson.

Fant, Å., A. Klingborg, and A.J. Wilkes. 1975. *Rudolf Steiner's Sculpture in Dornach.* London: Rudolf Steiner Press.

Faulstich, P. 1993. *Artistic Heritage in a Changing Pacific.* Honolulu: University of Hawaii Press.

Feder, T. H. 1978. *Great Treasures of Pompeii and Herculaneum.* New York: Abbeville Press.

Fell, B. 1989. *America* B.C. New York: Pocket Books/Simon & Schuster.

________. 1982. *Bronze Age America.* Boston: Little, Brown and Co.

Felshin, N. 1995. *But Is It Art? The Spirit of Art as Activism.* Seattle: Bay Press.

Ferrier, R. 1989. *The Arts of Persia.* New Haven, CT: Yale University Press.

Ferrua, A. 1991. *The Unknown Catacomb: A Unique Discovery of Early Christian Art.* New Lanark, Scotland: Geddes and Grosset.

Fideler, D. 1993. *Jesus Christ, Sun of God: Ancient Cosmology and Early Christian Symbolism.* Wheaton, IL: Quest Books.

Firez-David, L. 1988. *Women's Dionysian Initiation: The Villa of the Mysteries in Pompeii.* Dallas, TX: Spring Publishing.

Fisher, R. 1993. *Buddhist Art and Architecture.* London: Thames & Hudson.

Fitzgerald, A. 1996. *An Artist's Book of Inspiration.* Hudson, NY: Lindisfarne.

Fletcher, J. 1987. *Art Inspired by Rudolf Steiner.* London: Mercury Arts Publishing.

Frederic, L. 1995. *Buddhism: Flammarion Iconographic Guides.* New York: Flammarion.

Freud, S. 1947. *Leonardo da Vinci: A Study in Psychosexuality.* New York: Random House.

Furst, P. and J. Furst. 1982. *North American Indian Art.* New York: Rizzoli.

Gablik, S. 1984. *Has Modernism Failed?* New York: Thames & Hudson.

________. 1991. *The Reenchantment of Art.* New York: Thames & Hudson.

________. 1995. *Conversations Before the End of Time.* New York: Thames & Hudson

_____. 1979 *Progress in Art.* New York: Rizzoli.

Gage, J. 1980. *Goethe on Art.* London: Scolar Press.

_____. 1969. *Color in Turner: Poetry and Truth.* New York: Paeger.

Garbini, G. 1966. *The Ancient World.* New York: McGraw-Hill.

Gerard, M. 1968. *Dali.* New York: Harry N. Abrams.

Gibran, K. 1970. *Spiritual Sayings.* New York: Bantam Books.

Giedion, S. 1964. *The Eternal Present: The Beginnings of Architecture.* New York: Pantheon.

Gillon, W. 1984. *A Short History of African Art.* New York: Facts on File.

Gimbutas, M. 1991. *The Civilization of the Goddess.* New York: HarperCollins.

________, and J. Campbell. 1995 *Language of the Goddess.* San Francisco: HarperSanFrancisco.

Godwin, J. 1981. *Mystery Religions in the Ancient World.* London: Thames & Hudson.

Goethe, J. 1883. *The Poems of Goethe.* London: Bell and Sons.

Govinda, A. 1976. *Psychocosmic Symbolism of the Buddhist Stupa.* Berkeley, CA: Dharma Press.

Greub, S. 1985. *Authority and Ornament: Art of the Sepik River.* Basel, Switzerland: Tribal Art Center.

Grey, A. 1998. *The Mission of Art.* Boston: Shambhala.

Grosse, R. 1983. *Der silberkessel von Gundestrup: Ein Zeugnis Des Lauterungs und Einweihungsweges bei den Kelten.* Dornach, Switzerland: Philosophisch-Anthroposophische Verlag am Goetheanum.

Hadingham, E. 1984. *Early Man and the Cosmos.* Norman, OK: University of Oklahoma Press.

Hale, W. 1965. *The Horizon Book of Ancient Greece.* New York: American Heritage.

Hamilton, R. 1997. "Mystery of Ohio's Serpent Mound," *Ancient American.* No. 18.

Hancock, G. 1995. *Fingerprints of the Gods.* New York: Crown.

Harner, M. 1980. *The Way of the Shaman.* New York: Bantam.

Hartmann, H. 1952. *Der Totenkult Irland.* Heidelberg: Winter Verlag.

Hauck, H. 1968. *Handwork Indications, Part I.* London: Rudolf Steiner Press.

Hawkins, G. 1965. *Stonehenge Decoded.* Garden City, NY: Delta/Dell

Heidenreich, A. 1962. *The Catacombs: Pictures from the Life of Early Christianity.* London: Christian Community Press.

Hemleben. J. 1975. *Rudolf Steiner.* East Grinstead, Sussex: Henry Goulden.

Herm, G. 1976. *The Celts.* New York: St. Martin's Press.

Heyerdahl, T. 1989. *Easter Island: The Mystery Solved.* New York: Random House.

Hiebel, F. 1949. *The Gospel of Hellas: The Mission of Ancient Greece and the Advent of Christ.* Spring Valley, NY: Anthroposophic Press.

Howard, M. 1998. *Art As Spiritual Activity.* Hudson, NY: Anthroposophic Press.

Hunter, S. and J. Jacobus. 1992. *Modern Art: Painting, Sculpture, Architecture.* New York: Harry N. Abrams.

Huntington, S. 1999. *The Art of Ancient India: Buddhist, Hindu, Jain.* New York: Weatherhill.

James, G. W. 1974. *Indian Blankets and Their Makers.* New York: Dover Publications.

James, J. 1985. *Chartes: The Masons Who Built a Legend.* Boston: Routledge and Kegan Paul.

James, V. 1991. *Ancient Sites of O'ahu: Archaeological Places of Interest in the Hawaiian Islands.* Honolulu: Bishop Museum Press.

________. 1995. *Ancient Sites of Hawai'i: Archaeological Places of Interest on the Big Island.* Honolulu: Mutual Publishing.

Johnson, B. 1994. *Lady of the Beasts: The Goddess and Her Sacred Animals.* Rochester, VT: Inner Traditions.

Joussaume, R. 1985. *Dolmens for the Dead: Megalith-Building Throughout the World.* Ithaca, NY: Cornell University Press.

Joyce, J. 1991. *Portrait of the Artist as a Young Man.* New York: Penguin.

Jung, C. 1964. *Man and his Symbols.* Garden City, NY: Doubleday.

________. 1989. *The Spirit in Man, Art and Literature.* London: Routledge.

Kagan, A. 1989. *Marc Chagall.* New York: Abbeville.

Kalweit, H. 1988. *Dreamtime and Inner Space: The World of the Shaman.* Boston: Shambhala.

Kandinsky, W. 1972. *Concerning the Spiritual in Art.* New York: George Wittenborn.

________. 1979. *Point and Line to Plane.* New York: Dover.

Kemper, C. 1966. *Der Bau.* Stuttgart: Verlag Freies Geistesleben.

Kerenyi, C. 1944. "The Mysteries of the Kabeiroi." See Campbell, J. 1955. *The Mysteries: Papers from the Eranos Yearbooks.* Bollingen Series XXX, 2. Princeton, NJ: Princeton University Press.

Koch, E. and G. Wagner. 1980. *The Individuality of Colour.* London: Rudolf Steiner Press.

Kostof, S. 1985. *A History of Architecture: Settings and Rituals.* New York: Oxford University Press.

Krauss, R. 1987. *The Originality of the Avant-Garde and Other Modernist Myths.* Cambridge, MA: MIT Press.

Krupp, E. 1983. *Echoes of the Ancient Skies: The Astronomy of Lost Civilizations.* New York: Plume Books.

________. 1979. *In Search of Ancient Astronomies.* New York: McGraw-Hill.

Kühlewind, G. 1993. *Feeling Knowing.* Fair Oaks, CA: Rudolf Steiner College Press.

Kühn, H. 1955. *On the Track of Prehistoric Man.* New York: Random House.

Kuspit, D. 1994. *The Cult of the Avant-Garde Artist.* New York: Cambridge University Press.

Kutzli, R. 1981. *Creative Form Drawing I.* Gloucester, UK: Hawthorn Press.

________. 1986. *Langobardische Kunst.* Stuttgart: Verlag Urachhaus.

Laming-Emperaire, A. 1959. *Lascaux: Paintings and Engravings.* Baltimore: Penguin.

Larsen, S. 1988. *The Shaman's Doorway: Opening Imagination to Power and Myth.* Barrytown, NY: Station Hill Press.

Lawlor, R. 1991 *Voices of the First Day: Awakening in the Aboriginal Dreamtime.* Rochester, VT: Inner Traditions.

Layton, R. 1991. *The Anthropology of Art.* New York: Cambridge University Press.

Leakey, M. 1983. *Africa's Vanishing Art: The Rock Painting of Tanzania.* New York: Doubleday.

Lee, G. and E. Stasack. 1999. *Spirit of Place: Petroglyphs of Hawai'i.* Los Osos, CA: Bearsville and Cloud Mountain Presses.

Lee, S. 1982. *A History of Far Eastern Art.* New York: Harry N. Abrams.

Leidy, D. and R. Thurman, 1997. *Mandala: The Architecture of Enlightenment.* Boston: Shambhala Publishing.

Leroi-Gourhan, A. 1967. *Treasures of Prehistoric Art.* New York: Harry N. Abrams.

Lessing, G.E. 1969. *Laocoön.* New York: Noonday.

Lewis-Williams, J.D. 1990. *Discovering South African Rock Art.* Capetown: David Philip.

Lievegoed, B. 1982. *Mystery Streams in Europe and the New Mysteries.* Hudson, NY: Anthroposophic Press.

Lindsay, K. and P. Vergo. 1982. *Kandinsky: Complete Writings on Art.* Boston: G.K. Hall.

Linrothe, R. 1999. *Ruthless Compassion: Wrathful Deities in Early Indo-Tibetan Esoteric Buddhist Art.* Boston: Shambhala.

Linton, R. and P. Wingert. 1946. *Arts of the South Seas.* New York: Simon & Schuster.

Lippard, L. R. 1983. *Overlay: Contemporary Art and the Art of Prehistory.* New York: Pantheon.

Lipsey. R. 1988. *An Art of Our Own: The Spiritual in Twentieth Century Art.* Boston: Shambhala.

Lloyd, S. 1978. *The Archaeology of Mesopotamia: From the Old Stone Age to the Persian Conquest.* London: Thames & Hudson.

Lommel, A. 1967. *Shamanism: The Beginnings of Art.* New York: McGraw-Hill Book Company.

Lorblanchet, M. 1991. "Spitting Images: Replicating the Spotted Horse of Pech Merle," *Archaeology.* Vol. 44, No. 6.

Mallowan, M. 1965. *Early Mesopotamia and Iran.* London: Thames & Hudson.

Malraux, A. 1978. *Voices of Silence.* Princeton, NJ: Princeton University Press.

Mann, A.T. 1993. *Sacred Architecture.* Rockport, MA: Element.

Marshack, A. 1972. *The Roots of Civilization: The Cognitive Beginnings of Man's First Art, Symbol and Notation.* New York: McGraw-Hill.

Matanovic, M. 1985. *Light Works: Explorations in Art, Culture, and Creativity.* Issagnah, WA: Lorian Press.

Matthews, J. 1991. *Taliesin: Shamanism and the Bardic Mysteries in Britain and Ireland.* London: Aquarian.

McCarthy, F. 1958. *Australian Aboriginal Decorative Art.* Sydney: Australian Museum.

McDermott, R. 1984. *The Essential Steiner.* San Francisco: HarperSanFrancisco.

Mellaart, J. 1965. *Earliest Civilizations of the Near East.* London: Thames & Hudson.

Merry, E. 1983. *The Flaming Door: The Mission of the Celtic Folk-Soul.* Edinburgh: Floris.

Meyer, M. 1987. *The Ancient Mysteries: A Sourcebook,* San Francisco: HarperCollins.

Michell, J. 1986. *The New View Over Atlantis.* New York: HarperCollins.

_____. 1989. *Secrets of the Stones: New Revelations of Astro-Archaeology and the Mystical Sciences of Antiquity.* Rochester, VT: Inner Traditions.

Middleton, C. 1994. *Johann Wolfgang von Goethe: Selected Poems.* Princeton, NJ: Princeton University Press.

Miller, M. 1996. *The Art of Mesoamerica: From Olmec to Aztec.* London: Thames & Hudson.

Moffitt, J. 1988. *Occultism in Avant Garde Art: The Case of Joseph Beuys.* Ann Arbor, MI: UMI Research Press.

Mohen, J.-P. 1990. *The World of Megaliths.* New York: Facts on File.

Moody, R. 1976. *Life after Life.* New York: Bantam.

Moore, A. 1977. *Iconography of Religions: An Introduction.* Philadelphia: Fortress.

Morgan, W. 1988. *Prehistoric Architecture in Micronesia.* Austin, TX: University of Texas Press.

Munsterberg, H. 1986. *Symbolism in Ancient Chinese Art.* New York: Hacker Art Books.

Oberhuber, K. 1999. *Raphael: The Paintings.* New York: Pergamon.

Okladnikov. A. 1981. *Art of the Amur: Ancient Art of the Russian Far East.* New York: Harry N. Abrams.

Orenstein, G. F. 1990. *The Reflowering of the Goddess.* New York: Pergamon.

Ortega y Gasset, J. 1972. *The Dehumanization of Art and Other Essays on Art, Culture, and Literature.* Princeton, NJ: Princeton University Press.

Otto, W. 1986. *Dionysus: Myth and Cult.* Dallas, TX: Spring Publications.

Patterson, A. 1992. *Rock Art Symbols of the Greater Southwest.* Boulder, CO: Johnson Books.

Pennick, N. 1979. *The Ancient Science of Geomancy: Living in Harmony with the Earth.* London: Thames & Hudson.

Petracos, B. 1971. *Delphi.* Athens: Esperos Editions.

Pfeiffer, J. 1982 *The Creative Explosion: An Inquiry into the Origins of Art and Religion.* New York: Harper & Row.

Piggott, S. 1975. *The Druids.* London: Thames & Hudson.

Pike, D. 1974. *Anasazi: Ancient People of the Rock.* New York: Harmony.

Pogacnik, M. 1996. *Nature Spirits and Elemental Beings: Working with the Intelligence in Nature.* Findhorn, Scotland: Findhorn Press.

Powell, T.G.E. 1987. *The Celts.* London: Thames & Hudson.

Popplebaum, H. 1960. *Man and Animal.* London: Anthroposophical Publishing Co.

Postman, N. 1985. *Amusing Ourselves to Death.* New York: Penguin.

Preble, D. and S. Preble. 1994. *Artforms.* New York: HarperCollins.

Prokofieff, S. 1993. *The Spiritual Origins of Eastern Europe and the Future Mysteries of the Holy Grail.* London: Temple Lodge.

Querido, R. 1987. *The Golden Age of Chartres.* Edinburgh: Floris.

Raab, R. et al. 1972. *Sprechender Beton: Wie Rudolf Steiner den Stahlbeton Verwendete.* Dornach: Philosophische-Anthroposophische Verlag.

Rachleff, O. 1990. *The Occult in Art.* London: Cromwell.

Raine, K. 1970. *William Blake.* London: Thames & Hudson.

Rashe. H. 1983. *The Language of Color in the First Goetheanum.* Dornach, Switzerland: Walter Keller Verlag.

Rasmussen, K. 1921. *Eskimo Folk-Tales.* London: Glydendal.

________. 1927. *Across Arctic America.* New York: G.P. Putnam's Sons.

Rawson, P. 1967. *The Art of Southeast Asia.* New York: Praeger.

Read, H. 1965. *The Origins of Form in Art.* New York: Horizon.

________. 1964. *The Meaning of Art.* Baltimore: Penguin.

Regier, K. 1987. *The Spiritual Image in Modern Art.* Wheaton, IL: Quest.

Reiche, M. 1949. *Mystery on the Desert.* Nazca, Peru: Association Maria Reiche.

Reichel-Dolmatoff, G. 1975. *The Shaman and the Jaguar: A Study of Narcotic Drugs among the Indians of Colombia.* Philadelphia: Temple University Press.

Rhie, M. and R. Thurman. 1996. *Wisdom and Compassion: The Sacred Art of Tibet.* New York: Abradale Press.

Richter, G. 1985. *Art and Human Consciousness.* Spring Valley, NY: Anthroposophic Press.

Rinder, L. 1997. *Knowledge of Higher Worlds.* Berkeley, CA: University of California, Berkeley Art Museum.

Ringborn, S. 1970. *The Sounding Cosmos: A Study in the Spiritualism of Kandinsky and the Genesis of Abstract Painting.* Helsinki, Finland: Abo Akademi.

Rinpoche, S. 1995. *Glimpse after Glimpse.* New York: HarperCollins.

Ritchie, C. 1979. *Rock Art of Africa.* Philadelphia: Art Alliance Press.

Roberts, J. 1988. *Holbein.* London: Bloomsbury.

Rodin, A. 1965. *Cathedrals of France.* New York: Country Life.

Roggenkamp, W. and H. Gerbert. 1979. *Bewegung und Form in Graphik Rudolf Steiners.* Stuttgart: Verlag Freies Geistesleben.

Rolleston, T. 1911. *Myths and Legends of the Celtic Race.* London: Harrap.

Rookmaaker, H.R. 1978. *Modern Art and the Death of Culture.* Downers Grove, IL: Inter-Varsity Press.

Rosenblum, R. 1975. *Modern Painting and the Northern Romantic Tradition: Friedrich to Rothko.* New York: Harper & Row.

Rowley, G. 1959. *Principles of Chinese Painting.* Princeton, NJ: Princeton University Press.

Ryan, R. 1999. *The Strong Eye of Shamanism: A Journey Into the Caves of Consciousness.* Rochester, VT: Inner Traditions.

Schad, W. 1977. *Man and Mammals: Toward a Biology of Form.* Garden City, NY: Waldorf Press.

Schiller, F. 1965. *Letters on the Aesthetic Education of Man.* New York: Ungar.

Schuré, E. (no date) *The Great Initiates: Sketch of the Secret History of Religions.* London: Rider & Co.

Schuster, C. and E. Carpenter. 1996. *Patterns that Connect: Social Symbolism in Ancient and Tribal Art.* New York: Harry N. Abrams.

Schütze, A. 1937. *Mithras-Mysterium und Urchristentum.* Stuttgart: Verlag Urachhaus.

Schwenk, T. 1965. *Sensitive Chaos.* London: Rudolf Steiner Press.

Seddon, R. 1993. *Understanding the Human Being: Selected Writings of Rudolf Steiner.* London: Rudolf Steiner Press.

Selz, J. 1975. *Turner.* Munich: Südwest Verlag.

Settegast, M. 1987. *Plato Prehistorian: 10,000 to 5,000* B.C. *in Myth and Archaeology.* Cambridge: Rotenberg Press.

Shmeid, C. K. 1985. "Catalogue." In S. Greub, *Authority and Ornament.* Basel, Switzerland: Tribal Art Center.

Singh, M. 1993. *The Sun: Symbol of Power and Life.* New York: Harry N. Abrams.

Slain, L. 1991. *Art and Physics: Parallel Visions in Space, Time, and Light.* New York: William Morrow.

Smith, B. and B. Weng. (no date) *China: A History in Art.* New York: Doubleday.

Snyder, J. 1989. *Medieval Art: Painting, Sculpture, Architecture, 4th–14th Century.* New York: Harry N. Abrams.

Speiser, W. 1965. *Oriental Architecture in Color.* New York: Viking.

Squire, C. 1975. *Celtic Myth and Legend.* Newcastle, England: Newcastle.

Stachelhaus, H. 1987. *Joseph Beuys.* New York: Abbeville.

Steiner, R. 1971. *Ancient Myths: Their Meaning and Connection with Evolution.* London: Rudolf Steiner Press.

________. 1999. *Architecture as a Synthesis of the Arts.* London: Rudolf Steiner Press.

________. 1964. *The Arts and Their Mission.* Hudson, NY: Anthroposophic Press.

________. 1987. *Aspects of Human Evolution.* Hudson, NY: Anthroposophic Press.

________. 1948. *Christianity As Mystical Fact.* London: Rudolf Steiner Publishing Co.

________. 1971. *Colour.* London: Rudolf Steiner Press.

_____. 1951. *The Course of My Life.* New York: Anthroposophic Press.

________. 1972. *Curative Education.* London: Rudolf Steiner Press.

________. 1984. *The Cycle of the Year.* Spring Valley, NY: Anthroposophic Press.

________. 1971. *Egyptian Myths and Mysteries.* Hudson, NY: Anthroposophic Press.

________. 1987. *The Evolution of Earth and Man and Influence of the Stars.* Hudson, NY: Anthroposophic Press.

________. 1984. *Inner Impulses of Evolution: The Mexican Mysteries, the Knights Templar.* Hudson, NY: Anthroposophic Press.

________. 1969. *Knowledge of the Higher Worlds and Its Attainment.* London: Rudolf Steiner Press.

________. 1981. *Kunstgeschichte als Abbild Innerer Geistiger Impulse: IX.* Dornach, Switzerland: Rudolf Steiner Verlag.

________. 1966. *Man in the Past, the Present and the Future: The Sun-Initiation of the Druid Priest and his Moon-Science.* London: Rudolf Steiner Press.

________. 1983. *Metamorphoses of the Soul: Paths of Experience.* London: Rudolf Steiner Press.

________. 1989. *Mystery Centers.* Blauvelt, NY: Garber.

________. 1972. *The Social Future.* Spring Valley, NY: Anthroposophic Press.

________. 1961. *Spiritual Foundations of Morality.* Vancouver, BC: Steiner Book Center.

________. 1966. *Study of Man.* London: Rudolf Steiner Press.

________. 1985. *Temple Legends.* London: Rudolf Steiner Press.

________. 1987. *Universe, Earth, and Man.* London: Rudolf Steiner Press.

________. 1996. *Waldorf Education for Adolescence.* Hudson, NY: Anthroposophic Press.

________. 1926. *Wege zu Einem Neuen Baustil.* Dornach: Philosophisch-Anthroposophischer Verlag am Goetheanum.

________. 1977. *World History in the Light of Anthroposophy.* London: Rudolf Steiner Press.

Streit, J. 1984. *Sun and Cross: The Development from Megalithic Culture to Early Christianity in Ireland.* Edinburgh: Floris.

Sullivan, L. 1979. *Kindergarten Chats and Other Writings.* New York: Dover Publishing.

Sullivan, W. 1996. *The Secret of the Incas: Myth, Astronomy, and the War Against Time.* New York: Three Rivers Press.

Tarnas, R. 1991. *The Passion of the Western Mind: Understanding the Ideas That Have Shaped Our World View.* New York: Ballantine.

Teichmann, F. *Die ägyptischen Mysterien: Quellen einer Hochkulture.* Stuttgart: Verlag Freies Geistesleben.

________. 1978. *Der Mensch und Sein Tempel: Ägypten.* Stuttgart: Urachhaus.

________. 1983. *Der Mensch und Sein Tempel: Megalithkultur in Irland, England und der Bretagne.* Stuttgart: Urachhaus.

Thomas, N. 1995. *Oceanic Art.* London: Thames & Hudson.

Tisdall, C. 1979. *Joseph Beuys.* London: Thames & Hudson.

Todd, I. 1976. *Çatal Hüyük in Perspective,* Menlo Park, CA: Cummings.

Tolstoy, L. 1981. *What Is Art?* Indianapolis: Bobbs-Merrill.

Tomberg, V. 1983. *The Four Sacrifices of Christ and the Appearance of Christ in the Etheric.* Spring Valley, NY: Candeur Manuscripts.

Tomkins, C. 1965. *The Bride and the Bachelors: Five Masters of the Avant-Garde.* New York: Viking.

Townsend, R. 1992. *The ancient Americans: Art from Sacred Landscapes.* Munich: Prestel Verlag.

Toynbee, J. 1965. *The Art of the Romans.* New York: Praeger.

Tuchman, M. 1986. *The Spiritual in Art: Abstract Painting 1890–1985.* New York: Abbeville Press.

Tucker, M. 1992. *Dreaming with Open Eyes: The Shamanic Spirit in Twentieth Century Art and Culture.* San Francisco: Aquarian/Harper.

Tzu, L. 1963. *Tao Te Ching.* Baltimore, MD: Penguin.

Ucko, P. and A. Rosenfeld, 1973. *Palaeolithic Cave Art.* New York: McGraw-Hill.

Uehli, E. 1980. *Atlantis und das Ratsel der Eiszeitkunst.* Stuttgart: J. Ch. Mellinger Verlag.

Ulansey, D. 1991. *The Origins of the Mithraic Mysteries: Cosmology and Salvation in the Ancient World.* New York: Oxford University Press.

Van der Leeuw, G. 1963. *Sacred and Profane Beauty: The Holy in Art.* New York: Abingdon Press.

Vasari, G. 1970. *Lives of the Artists.* Harmondsworth, Middlesex, UK: Penguin.

Verstockt, M. 1987. *The Genesis of Form: From Chaos to Geometry.* London: Muller, Blond and White.

Vinnicombe, P. 1976. *People of the Eland.* Pietermaritzburg, South Africa: University of Natal Press.

Wade, D. 1993. *Crystal and Dragon: The Cosmic Dance of Symmetry and Chaos in Nature, Art, and Consciousness.* Rochester, VT: Destiny Books.

Walsh, R. 1990. *The Spirit of Shamanism.* Los Angeles: Jeremy P. Tarcher.

Walters, D. 1988. *Feng Shui: The Chinese Art of Designing a Harmonious Environment.* New York: Simon & Schuster.

Walther, I. and R. Metzger. 1993. *Van Gogh: The Complete Paintings.* Cologne: Taschen.

Wardwell, A. 1994. *Island Ancestors: Oceanic Art from the Masco Collection.* Detroit, Mich.: Detroit Institute of Art/University of Washington Press.

Wasserman, J. 1993. *Art and Symbols of the Occult: Images of Power and Wisdom.* Rochester, VT: Destiny.

Watson, A. 2000. "Sounds of the Spirit World." *Scientific American: Discovering Archaeology.* (Jan./Feb.).

Welburn, A. 1991. *The Beginnings of Christianity: Essene Mystery, Gnostic Revelation, and Christian Vision.* Edinburgh: Floris.

Welsh, R. and J. M. Joosten. 1969. *Two Mondrian Sketchbooks: 1912–1914.* Amsterdam: Meulenhoff.

West, J. A. 1979. *Serpent in the Sky.* New York: Harper & Row.

Wilkinson, R. 1992. *Reading Egyptian Art.* London: Thames & Hudson.

Willet, F. 1993. *African Art.: An Introduction* London: Thames & Hudson.

Wilson, F. 1998. *The Hand.* New York: Vintage.

Wind, E. 1967. *Pagan Mysteries of the Renaissance.* Harmondsworth, Middlesex, England: Penguin.

Wolf, T. 1976. *The Painted Word.* New York: Bantam.

Wood, J. E. 1978. *Sun, Moon, and Standing Stones.* London: Oxford University Press.

Wright, F. L. 1987. *In the Cause of Architecture.* New York: McGraw-Hill.

Zimmer. H. 1972. *Myths and Symbols in Indian Art and Civilization.* Princeton, NJ: Bollingen Series VI. Princeton University Press.

_______1984. *Artistic Form and Yoga in the Sacred Images of India.* Princeton, NJ: Princeton University Press.

Zink, D.D. 1979. *The Ancient Stones Speak.* New York: Jonathan-James Book/E.P. Dutton.

Zoeteman, K. 1991. *The Wisdom of the Living Earth: Gaiasophy, An Approach to Ecology.* Hudson, N.Y.: Lindisfarne.